DATE DUE

PUBLIC ADMINISTRATION IN AMERICA

THIRD EDITION

PUBLIC ADMINISTRATION IN AMERICA

THIRD EDITION

George J. Gordon
Illinois State University

St. Martin's Press   New York

**DEDICATED
TO THE MEMORY OF
ROSCOE C. MARTIN
AND
BERYL B. GORDON**

Library of Congress Catalog Card Number: 85-61286
Copyright © 1986 by St. Martin's Press, Inc.
All Rights Reserved.
Manufactured in the United States of America.
09876
fedcb
For information, write St. Martin's Press, Inc.,
175 Fifth Avenue, New York, N.Y. 10010

cover design: Tom McKeveny

ISBN: 0-312-65391-3

ACKNOWLEDGMENTS

Figure 3-1, "Support and Opposition to American Involvement in Vietnam," The Gallup Poll as reported in John E. Mueller, "Trends in Popular Support for the Wars in Korea and Vietnam," *American Political Science Review*, LXV (1971), and Gallup Opinion Index (March 1971 and February 1973). Reprinted by permission of the American Political Science Association and the Gallup Poll, Princeton, New Jersey.

Figure 5-1, "Picket Fence Federalism: A Schematic Representation," adapted from Deil S. Wright, *Understanding Intergovernmental Relations*, 2nd ed. Copyright © 1982, 1978 by Wadsworth, Inc. Reprinted by permission of Brooks/Cole Publishing Company, Monterey, California.

Table 6-1, "Theory X and Theory Y: A Summary," from Douglas McGregor, "Theory X and Theory Y," in Robert T. Golembiewski and Michael Cohen, eds., *People in Public Service: A Reader in Public Personnel Administration* (Itasca, Ill.: F. E. Peacock, 1970), p. 380. Reproduced by permission of the publisher, F. E. Peacock Publishers, Inc., Itasca, Illinois.

Figure 6-1, "A Simplified Model of a Political System," from David Easton, *A Framework for Political Analysis*. Copyright © 1965, 1979 by David Easton. Reprinted by permission of the University of Chicago Press.

Table 6-2, "Common Characteristics of Open Systems," adapted from Daniel Katz and Robert L. Kahn, *The Social Psychology of Organizations*, 2nd ed., pp. 23–30. By permission of John Wiley & Sons, Inc.

Table 6-3, "Values and Characteristics of Theory Z," adapted from Clyde McKee, "An Analysis of 'Theory Z': How It Is Used in Japan's Public Sector," paper

Acknowledgments and copyrights continue at the back of the book on pages 622–623, which constitute an extension of the copyright page.

Contents

Preface

This book is designed as a basic, comprehensive text for use in public administration courses. It is *basic* in the sense that the reader is assumed to have some background knowledge of government and politics in the United States, but not necessarily specific information about administrative politics or managing government bureaucracies. Consequently, terms and concepts are defined and explained as they are introduced throughout the text, and key linkages among different dimensions of the subject are identified and discussed. It is *comprehensive* in that it provides coverage of subjects most public administration textbooks include—such as decision making, budgetary processes, and organization theory—and also of some areas not always discussed in other books, such as federalism and intergovernmental relations, government regulation, and administrative leadership.

The book has three principal emphases. The first is on the central importance of public administration in modern government. With literally thousands of separate public programs at all governmental levels, and hundreds of billions of dollars spent each year in managing them, the scope of administrative operations is immense. (That scope also has changed somewhat in recent years, as America's citizens consider basic questions about the appropriate place and influence of government in our lives.) The second emphasis is on the role and impact of politics in shaping public bureaucracies. Government agencies are affected by political currents and decisions, and students should be aware of the many ways in which political interests and administrative activities are intertwined. This book takes the position that it is not necessarily wrong or harmful that politics plays such a prominent role. The discussion of politics is explanatory rather than moralistic; "pros" and "cons" of issues such as government regulation are carefully examined, and the reader is encouraged to draw independent conclusions. The third emphasis is on management aspects of public administration, on concerns relating to the operation of public programs, from the perspective of the public agency manager. Among such concerns are communication and coordination, program planning, collective bargaining with public employees, and dealing with the phenomenon of "fiscal stress" which confronts more and more governments and agencies.

Much has changed in all these respects since the second edition of this text was published in 1982. I have tried to reflect the scope and possible consequences of developments in the past four years. At the same time I have sought to lay out clearly the links between the recent and more distant past, and to identify major currents and trends that will command our attention in the immediate future. Not least among these is the broad impact of changes in the role of government resulting from a host of initiatives undertaken by the Reagan administration.

I am indebted to many individuals who contributed to the preparation of this edition. Valuable research assistance was furnished by Debra Holzhauer, Justine Schlund, Victoria Soderberg, and Vikki Wulf. Staff members at Milner Library, Illinois State University, provided generous assistance in finding relevant materials; especially helpful were Marian Carroll, Garold Cole, and Joan Winters. Faculty colleagues at Illinois State University provided useful information and insights, and stimulated my own thinking. These included Thomas Eimermann, Ann Elder, Richard Hartwig, George Kiser, Gary Klass, Alan Monroe, Nancy Lind, Richard Payne, and Frederick Roberts. Hibbert Roberts, chairman of the political science department, again strongly encouraged me in this enterprise; this book bears his imprint in more ways than one.

Still others were generous with time, energy, and information in my behalf. National government officials, past and present, include Alan Campbell, director of the U.S. Office of Personnel Management (OPM) during the Carter administration; Ann Brazzier, Patrick Korten, Andrea Sheldon, and Edward Shell of OPM; Cynthia Cates Colella and Albert Richter, both formerly with the U.S. Advisory Commission on Intergovernmental Relations (ACIR); and Alan V. Stevens of the U.S. Bureau of the Census. Others deserving of acknowledgment include Irene Fraser of the American Hospital Association, Chicago; and Ellen Holroyd of the State of Illinois Library in Springfield, Illinois. The reviewers commissioned by St. Martin's Press—Walter F. Baber of the University of Nevada at Reno, Donald F. Kettl of the University of Virginia, and Douglas H. Shumavon of Miami University (Ohio)—were uniformly helpful in their critiques; Michael Weber, Peter Dougherty, Sarah Rosenthal, Anne McCoy, and Faye Zucker of St. Martin's Press also greatly facilitated my efforts. My wife Myra, and our children Daniel and Rachel, were endlessly patient and supportive, and I am grateful. These individuals richly deserve much of the credit for whatever strengths are present in the book; mine alone is the responsibility for its weaknesses.

George J. Gordon
Normal, Illinois
1986

TO THE STUDENT

This text will help you enlarge your knowledge and understanding of what public administration is all about. Several features of the book will aid you in your studies. Chapter summaries present concise restatements of key points covered in the chapters. Notes are grouped at the end of each chapter; an effort has been made to furnish extensive source references in the hope you will become familiar with the literature in this field. Suggested readings at the end of each chapter list important sources for further research and information. Finally, a glossary of terms at the end of the book will help you review key concepts, techniques, laws, and institutions pertaining to public administration.

G.J.G.

PART ONE

Introduction

This opening section explores essential facts and concepts in public administration. In chapter 1, and throughout the book, the emphasis is on the political setting of public administration and the impact of politics on administrative decisions. We first will describe the most common structural arrangements of executive branch agencies. We will discuss the growth of government generally, and public administration in particular. We will explore similarities and differences between public and private administration, taking note of some ways in which they overlap in practice. We then will examine public administration as a field of study, especially its evolution from a relatively uncomplicated field in the early 1900s to the complex and unsettled discipline it is today.

In chapter 2 we will explore the setting in which public administration operates. We will consider traditional conceptions of how public bureaucracy ought to function and then compare them with the broad realities of American governmental bureaucracy, and we will discuss why the differences are important. We also will examine the underlying values in American administrative practice. Of central importance are the tensions between *political* values—such as individual liberty, representation, and popular control—and *administrative* values—such as bureaucratic efficiency, economy, and political neutrality. In addition, we will analyze the impact of social change and controversy on our values.

1

Approaching the Study of Public Administration

Public administration in America today is a large enterprise encompassing the daily activities of literally millions of government workers, at all levels, and touching the daily life of virtually every American. The growth of government activity and public bureaucracy is one of the most significant social phenomena of recent decades. It has become the subject of considerable discussion among scholars and practitioners. At the same time, politicians of every stripe have criticized the bureaucracy—Jimmy Carter promised in 1976 to "clean up the horrible bureaucratic mess in Washington"; in 1980 Ronald Reagan promised to "get the federal government off your backs." Alabama Governor George Wallace put it more directly during the 1960s, chiding "pointy-headed bureaucrats who don't carry nothin' in those briefcases of theirs except their sack lunch!" Many other politicians have run, with some success, "against" the bureaucracy.[1] The "taxpayers' revolt," which surfaced swiftly and intensely in the late 1970s, is in part a reaction against perceived bureaucratic excesses. It has even been suggested that the language of bureaucracy (its jargon) has harmed the English language as a whole.[2] In one way or another, most of us are familiar with government bureaucracy.

Our consciousness of bureaucracy varies with the situation. We are aware of it when we fill out our income tax return (especially when we pay additional tax on April 15!), apply for a government loan to finance our college education, hear a television news story on the latest controversy in Congress over actions of the Federal Trade Commission, or deal directly with that most visible of public administrators, a police officer.

We are less conscious of the role of bureaucracy under other circumstances. Much bureaucratic decision making is obscure or just not directly meaningful to us. For an example of hidden bureaucratic decision making, consider the procedures followed by President John F. Kennedy and his advisers in resolving the Cuban missile crisis of 1962. These included covert photographic flights over Cuba and secret messengers carrying notes back and forth to Soviet diplomats. For an example of bureaucratic decisions not directly meaningful to us, consider the testing procedures used by the U.S. Food and Drug Administration for determining the purity of food additives or the effectiveness of a new drug. While such routine procedures may be important in individual instances, they generate little publicity or public attention.

Whatever our awareness of particular bureaucratic activities or decisions, the institution of bureaucracy evokes strong feelings among millions of Americans. A frequent response to any mention of "the bureaucracy" is negative; bureaucrats are unpopular with many of those they serve. Bureaucracy has become a favorite scapegoat for many of society's current ills. There are several reasons for this: government agencies are clearly influential; we don't elect our bureaucrats (in any but a handful of cases); and they are convenient, increasingly visible targets. We hear a great deal about the growing power of bureaucracy and bureaucrats, the arbitrary nature of many decisions, the lack of accountability, impersonal treatment, and cases of simple incompetence.

All in all, the public's regard for public administrators is at a low ebb, far below what it was forty or fifty years ago. First in the Great Depression of the 1930s, then during and after World War II, public administrators and their organizations enjoyed far greater public confidence than they do today. The general public, through their elected officials, looked to the administrative apparatus of government to take on increasing responsibility. Congress, state legislatures, city councils, mayors, governors, and presidents alike delegated growing amounts of discretionary power to administrative officials, in effect directing them to make the day-to-day choices involved in applying laws. No national referendum was held on the question: "Shall bureaucrats be given more responsibility?" But public acceptance of greater governmental involvement in a wider range of societal activities outweighed opposition to growth of government generally, and government bureaucracy in particular. Indeed, once bureaucratic involvement in national policy making began to increase, heightened public demand for government services ensured continuation of greater administrative activity, at least until the late 1970s and the 1980s (see Table 1-1).

Thus, the trends of growth begun during Franklin Roosevelt's New Deal and consolidated under Harry Truman and, significantly, under Dwight Eisenhower's Republican administration, rested on a foundation of popular support and legitimacy that now, clearly, has eroded. This weakening of support seems to have developed as a reaction against particular governmental behavior—enforcement of civil rights laws, the Vietnam War, the Watergate scandals—and against a government widely viewed as becoming too distant from the people in terms of accountability, too close in terms of influence over private lives, and inept and wasteful, if not self-serving and corrupt.

Table 1-1

AN ELASTIC YARDSTICK FOR MEASURING THE GROWTH OF AMERICAN GOVERNMENT

	1955[a]	1983[a]	Percent change from 1955 to 1983
Dollar Expenditures (in billions)[b]			
National	70.3	733.4	943.2
State-Local	40.4	434.1	974.5
Total	110.7	1167.5	954.7
Public Expenditures as a Percent of GNP[c]			
National	17.6	22.2	26.1
State-Local	10.1	13.1	29.7
Total	27.7	35.3	27.4
Public Sector Employees[d] (in millions)			
National	2.378	2.752	15.7
State-Local	5.054	13.099	159.2
Total	7.432	15.851	113.3
Public Sector Employees per 1,000 Population[e]			
National	14.4	12.1	−16.0
State-Local	30.6	57.8	88.9
Total	45.0	69.9	55.3

[a]Fiscal year.

[b]Excluding intergovernmental cash transfers; shown in current dollars, that is, not controlled for inflation.

[c]GNP, in current dollars, is based on calendar years 1955 and 1983.

[d]Figures for public-sector employees represent civilian workers only, both full-time and part-time.

[e]The national population figure used in calculating 1983 data is based upon 1982 U.S. Bureau of the Census estimates of 226,547,000.

Sources: Data on public expenditures in 1955 are taken from U.S. Bureau of the Census, *Historical Statistics of the United States, Colonial Times to 1970, Part 2* (Washington, D.C.: U.S. Government Printing Office, 1975), Series Y522–32, p. 1,119; Series Y590–604, p. 1,123; and Series Y671–81, p. 1,127. Data on 1983 expenditures are taken from U.S. Department of Commerce, Bureau of Economic Analysis, *Survey of Current Business,* 64 (Washington, D.C.: U.S. Government Printing Office, July 1984), pp. 44–46. Gross National Product (GNP) data for 1955 are taken from U.S. Bureau of the Census, *Statistical Abstract of the United States: 1979,* 100th edition (Washington, D.C.: U.S. Government Printing Office, 1979). GNP data for 1983 are taken from U.S. Department of Commerce, Bureau of Economic Analysis, *Survey of Current Business,* p. 22. Data on public employment for 1955 are taken from U.S. Bureau of the Census, *Historical Statistics of the United States, Part 2,* Series Y272–89, p. 1100. Data on public employment for 1983 are taken from U.S. Department of Commerce, Bureau of Economic Analysis, *Survey of Current Business,* p. 1100–10. Population figures for 1955 are taken from U.S. Bureau of the Census, *Historical Statistics of the United States, Part 2,* Series A6–8, p. 8; and for 1983, from U.S. Bureau of the Census, *Public Employment in 1982* (Washington, D.C.: U.S. Government Printing Office, 1983), Series GE82, No. 1, p. 96.

The sharp decline in bureaucracy's general public standing has coincided with both increasing complexity in the nation's problems and (ironically) much higher levels of competence among government bureaucrats. Both Jimmy Carter and Ronald Reagan, even as they undertook to reduce the size and role of bureaucracies, acknowledged the honesty, integrity,

THE MEANING OF "BUREAUCRACY"

A *bureaucracy* or a *bureaucratic organization* is characterized by an internal division of labor, specialization of work performed, a vertical hierarchy or chain of command, well-defined routines for carrying out operating tasks, reliance on precedent (previous actions) in resolving problems, and a clear set of rules regarding managerial control over organizational activities. It is assumed that most of those working in a bureaucracy are professionals in their specialties, and that their occupational loyalties rest with their organizations rather than with a political party or other external affiliation. Because much of public management in American governments occurs within bureaucratic structures, there is a tendency to use *bureaucracy* as just another term for public administration or public management; but it has a more specific meaning than either of those, particularly with regard to the form or structure of administrative agencies.

and demonstrated talents of the vast majority of administrative officials. There is surprisingly strong evidence of favorable citizen reaction to direct dealings with bureaucrats.[3] It has even been suggested by a reputable observer that public administrators *"could not be engaged in more important or more honorable work, . . .* however they may be judged by the public they serve."[4] Why, then, have these officials lost so much prestige? Part of the answer is that they may appear to constitute something of a government elite in an era where the voice of the people is being heard more forcefully. Or perhaps the very complexity of the problems currently confronting government decreases the likelihood of *complete* solutions, despite the serious efforts of more competent people. Finally, perhaps the public has come to expect too much from its government (sometimes encouraged by public officials themselves) and has made bureaucrats into scapegoats for not meeting its expectations. Whether bureaucrats are deserving of these sentiments is another matter.

Public administration scholar Charles Goodsell has suggested that government bureaucracies and administrators do not, in fact, deserve such harsh criticism.[5] The essence of his argument is that despite shortcomings inevitably found in such complex organizations, America's government bureaucracies perform quite well. This is the case whether bureaucratic performance is measured by objective standards, in comparison with that in most of the other nations of the world, or (as noted above) in terms of citizens' satisfaction in their dealings with government administrators.[6] Goodsell summarizes his position this way:

> Any large administrative apparatus, including that found in the United States, is riddled with individual instances of inefficiency, maladministration, arrogant behavior, repressive management, and abused power. My point is simply that . . . *these deficiencies are particularized rather than generalized* and that they occur within tolerable ranges of proportionate incidence. They do not

constitute a comprehensive inadequacy or overarching threat within the society or political system. Bureaucracy is, instead, a multitudinous, diverse reality in which is found a vast mix of performance and quality. Within this mix, acceptable and responsible conduct is far more common than unacceptable or irresponsible behavior. The drumbeat of antibureaucratic criticism . . . supports a *powerful myth* that wildly exaggerates shortcomings in the government's performance and invariably underestimates government's achievements.[7]

In stating his case, Goodsell focuses attention on the frequently unthinking criticisms of bureaucracy that have characterized much of our national dialogue in the recent past. Using bureaucracy as a scapegoat only makes it more difficult for us to acquire a clearer understanding of what it really is and how it really operates, in our governmental system and our society at large.

WHAT IS PUBLIC ADMINISTRATION?

Public administration may be defined as *all processes, organizations, and individuals (the latter acting in official positions and roles) associated with carrying out laws and other rules adopted or issued by legislatures, executives, and courts.* This definition should be understood to include considerable administrative involvement in formulation as well as implementation of legislation and executive orders; we will discuss this more fully later. Public administration is simultaneously a field of academic study and of professional training, from which substantial numbers of government employees currently are drawn.

Note that the first definition does not limit the participants in public administration to administrative personnel, or even to people in government. It can and does refer to a varied assortment of individuals and groups with an interest in the consequences of administrative action. That certainly includes, perhaps foremost, administrators themselves. But it also includes members of the legislature, legislative committees, and their staffs; higher executives in the administrative apparatus of government; judges; political party officials whose partisan interests overlap extensively with issues of public policy; lobbyists (that is, leaders and members of interest groups) seeking from the government various policies, regulations, and actions; mass-media personnel, particularly in their "watchdog" role over actions and decisions of public officials; and members of society at large, who can have some impact, even when not well organized, on the directions public policy follows. Furthermore, public administration involves all of those mentioned in shifting patterns of reciprocal (mutual) relationships—in state and local governments as well as Washington, and in national-state-local relations. The politics of administration involves agency interactions with those *outside* the formal structure as well as interactions among those *within* administrative agencies; we are concerned with both.

The Managerial Role

Let us consider another dimension of public administration, the *managerial* or *management* side of it. While the emphasis in this book is on the "politics of bureaucracy," as some have called it,[8] management practice has always occupied a place of major importance in the discipline of public administration. Indeed, it is increasingly important in making government programs both efficient and effective. Managerial aspects of public administration have as their primary focus the *internal* workings of government agencies, that is, all the structures, dynamics, and processes connected with operating government programs. Thus, while perhaps appearing to be interchangeable terms, *public administration* (as used in this text) describes a broader range of concerns than *public management*. Both are concerned with implementing policies and programs enacted through authoritative institutions of government. But the latter seems to imply an emphasis on how to organize for internal control and direction for maximum effectiveness, while the former is concerned with those aspects and more.

Joseph L. Bower and Charles J. Christenson, both of the Harvard Business School, have suggested some of the skills needed in a managerial role. They note that in addition to political sophistication, "plans must be developed, an organization built or altered, systems of information created to track progress, and a system of measurement and compensation developed that captures and retains the interest of those individuals needed. Beyond these somewhat architectural skills, individual relationships must be cultivated. Meetings must be called; the right people must be contacted—in the right sequence."[9] These sorts of activities, which can surely be performed with greater or lesser competence, are the indispensable foundation upon which actual programmatic operations are built and sustained. An important point for the public manager is that *action* is expected, even if not necessarily advisable or convenient. The manager must act, and be able to move the organization to act, in the face of deadlines that are well-nigh immovable and of choices that may not be ideal.[10] In a simplified form, and lacking much of the richness of the daily environment, these elements make up a large part of the public manager's existence in, and contribution to, the totality of public administration.

PRINCIPAL STRUCTURES OF THE NATIONAL EXECUTIVE BRANCH

The Constitution of the United States is silent on the subject of public administration, except to refer to the president's responsibility to "faithfully execute the laws." The structures we have are the product of congressional action, as are many of the procedures followed within administration. The national executive branch is organized primarily into five major types of agencies; there are four formal bases, or foundations, of organization and two broad categories of administrative employees. These deserve consideration because they affect both the way administrative entities function and the content of policies they help to enact.

Questions of organizational structure may not appear, at first glance, to carry many political overtones. But formal organizational arrangements do not just happen, and they are not politically neutral in their consequences.[11] The choice of organizational structure may both reflect and promote some political interests over others. The reflection of political interests stems from a particular structure being the product of decisions reached through the political process by a particular majority coalition, whether directly (as through congressional action) or indirectly (as when the president proposes executive reorganization). Those who organize or reorganize an agency in a certain way obviously have reasons for doing so, one of which is usually promotion and protection of their own political and policy interests. As one example, through the creation of the Department of Energy President Carter achieved greater control over previously scattered agencies in the energy-policy field, such as the Federal Energy Regulatory Commission (formerly the Federal Power Commission) and the Federal Energy Administration.

The principal types of agencies are (1) cabinet-level departments, (2) independent regulatory agencies, (3) government corporations, (4) various units of the Executive Office of the President, and (5) other independent agencies (see Figure 1-1). These agencies can be organized according to function (general area of policy concern), geographic area, clientele, or work process. The two broad categories of employees are specialists and generalists, although these are not the only ways to categorize administrative employees. Let us consider each of these in turn.[12]

Cabinet-level departments (or just *departments*) are the most visible (though not necessarily the largest) national executive organizations; this is also true in most states and localities. As of mid-1984, there were thirteen departments in the national executive branch—for example, the Departments of State, Defense, Commerce, the Treasury, Justice, Labor, and the Interior. During Jimmy Carter's presidency, two organizational changes were made. In 1977, a new Department of Energy was created, and in 1979, the existing Department of Health, Education, and Welfare (HEW) was divided into the Departments of Education and of Health and Human Services. Each department is headed by a secretary and a series of top-level subordinates, all of whom are appointed by the president with the approval of the Senate (such approval is rarely withheld). They serve "at the pleasure of the president," meaning that the president can dismiss them for reasons of political disloyalty without having to explain why (legally, that is—political repercussions are another matter).

Departments are composed of many smaller administrative units with a variety of titles, such as bureau, office, administration, and service. Within the Department of Transportation, for example, one finds the Ur-

Figure 1-1 Major Agencies of the United States Government

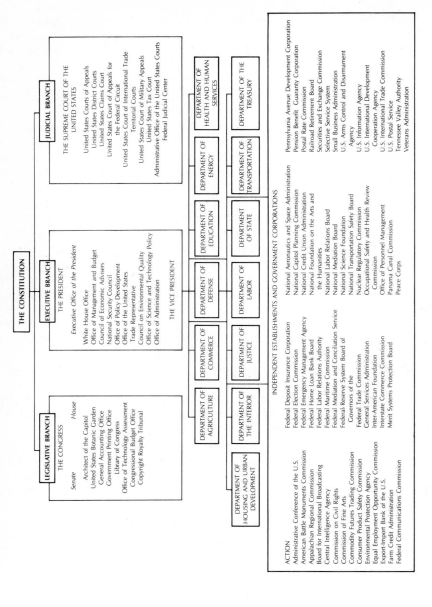

Source: Adapted from the *U.S. Government Organization Manual, 1983–1984*, p. 810.

Figure 1-2 Structure of the U.S. Department of Transportation

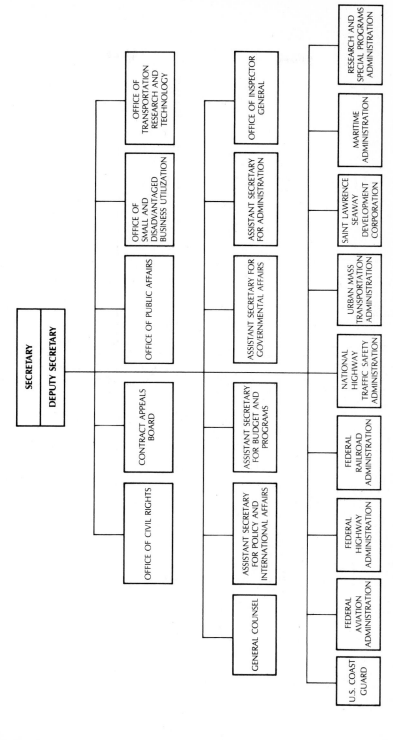

Source: U.S. Government Organization Manual, 1983–1984, p. 830.

Figure 1-3 Structure of the U.S. Department of Agriculture

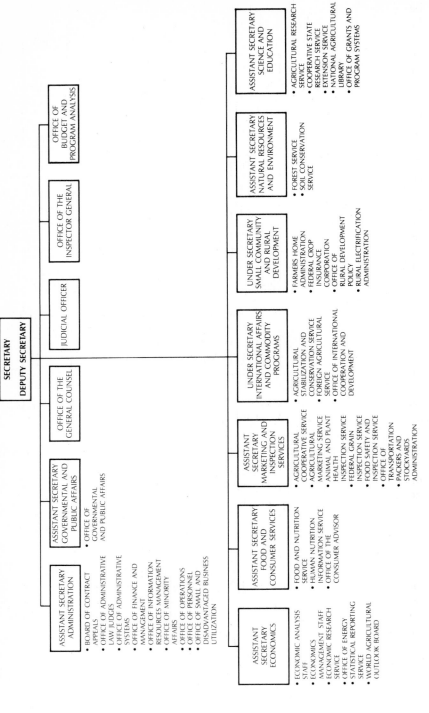

Source: U.S. Government Organization Manual, 1983–1984, p. 816.

ban Mass Transportation Administration and the Bureau of Motor Carrier Safety; within Agriculture, the Office of Rural Development Policy and the Agricultural Marketing Service (see Figures 1-2 and 1-3). The fact that these are located within the same departmental structure does not necessarily mean they work cooperatively on any one venture; in fact, conflict among agencies within the same department is not uncommon. Where they are formally "located" has little bearing on patterns of cooperation or conflict within the administrative apparatus. Finally, departments and their sub-units generally are responsible for carrying out specific operating programs enacted by Congress; they have, and attempt to maintain, fairly specific program jurisdictions (areas of programmatic responsibility) and often concrete program objectives.[13]

Independent regulatory agencies are a second major type of administrative entity, usually identified as a "commission" or "board." Among such agencies are the Federal Trade Commission (FTC), Federal Reserve Board (FRB), National Labor Relations Board (NLRB), and Interstate Commerce Commission (ICC). They differ from cabinet-level departments in a number of important ways. First, they have a different function, namely, to oversee and regulate activities of various parts of the private economic sector. Second, their leadership is plural rather than singular; that is, they are headed by a board or commission of several individuals (usually five to nine) instead of a secretary. Third, they are designed to be somewhat independent of other institutions and political forces. Members of these agencies are appointed by the president with Senate approval (as are senior department officials) but are better protected legally against dismissal by the president; in addition, they normally serve a term of office longer than that of the appointing president. In relation to Congress, these agencies are supposedly somewhat freer to do their jobs than are departments and their subunits; while this is questionable in practice, the design does have some impact.[14] Finally, these agencies are designed to regulate private-sector enterprises in a detached and objective manner, with some expectation of effectiveness in preventing abuses, corruption, and the like. Some controversy has existed, however, over just how detached and objective these agencies have been in relation to those they regulate.

Independent regulatory agencies are not the only government entities having regulative responsibilities, however. A phenomenon of considerable importance is the growth of government regulation in the past two decades through a wide variety of other administrative instruments. Examples would include the Federal Aviation Administration, state departments of transportation, and the U.S. Food and Drug Administration. These agencies have important roles to play in their respective policy areas with regard to the setting of rules and standards for those in the private sector. The increasing incidence of government regulation has spawned rising political discontent over the scope and content of regulatory activity, which some say contributed to President Reagan's impressive 1980 victory. In chapter 14, we will explore regulatory administration and politics more fully.

Government corporations are national, state, or local government agencies identical to private corporations in most of their structures and operations, but government-owned. Also, while some (such as Amtrak and local public utilities) seek to make a profit, others (such as the Federal Savings and Loan Insurance Corporation and the Lower Colorado River Authority of the state of Texas) do not.[15] These agencies are conceived as corporate entities for a number of reasons. Their legislative charters permit somewhat greater latitude in day-to-day operations than is the case with other agencies; they have power to acquire, develop, and dispose of real estate and other kinds of property, acting in their own name rather than that of the parent government; and they have power to bring suit in a court of law—and liability to be sued—also in their own name. They are headed by a board of directors, much as private corporations are, and are engaged in a wide variety of governmental activities. Three of the newest such entities are the National Rail Passenger Service Corporation (Amtrak), the Corporation for Public Broadcasting, and the U.S. Postal Service; two of the oldest, both founded in the 1930s, are the Federal Deposit Insurance Corporation (FDIC) and the Tennessee Valley Authority (TVA).[16]

The *Executive Office of the President* (EOP) is now nearing its fiftieth year. The EOP is a collection of administrative bodies physically and organizationally housed close to the office of the president and designed precisely to work for the president. Several of these entities are especially prominent and important: (1) The White House Office is located at 1600 Pennsylvania Avenue and consists of the president's key staff aides and staff directors. (2) The Office of Management and Budget (OMB) assists the president in assembling budget requests for the entire executive branch, forwarding them to Capitol Hill as the president's annual Budget Message, coordinating programs, developing high-quality executive talent, and supervising management processes throughout the executive branch. (3) The Council of Economic Advisors (CEA) is the president's principal research arm for economic policy, and it frequently influences the president's economic thinking (not surprisingly, since presidents usually appoint economists to the CEA who generally reflect their own economic philosophies).[17] (4) Agencies like the National Security Council, which we might label a broad overview forum, consist of the president and vice-president together with key cabinet secretaries and other officials. Their purpose is to assess the overall condition of broad administration policies. They become directly involved in policy making to a greater or lesser degree according to the president's inclinations. Dwight Eisenhower, for example, made far greater use of the National Security Council (NSC) than did either John F. Kennedy or Lyndon Johnson. This was due in large part to pressing cold-war policy development needs during the 1950s, combined with Eisenhower's greater inclination to rely on his executive staff. Much of the councils' routine activities are devoted to evaluating existing policy and its impact, but the potential exists for the councils to fulfill more systematic policy-making roles.

Finally, there are miscellaneous agencies that we might call *other independent agencies*—those that have no departmental "home" but fit no other category we have discussed. Among these are the Office of Personnel Management (OPM) and the Merit Systems Protection Board (MSPB), formerly combined as the U.S. Civil Service Commission, which together oversee the national government's personnel system; the General Services Administration (GSA), the government's office of property and supply; and the Environmental Protection Agency (EPA).

The foundations of organization referred to earlier were function, geographic area, clientele, and work process. The most common organizational foundation is *function*, indicating that an agency is concerned with a fairly distinct policy area but not limited to a particular geographic area. Organization according to *geography* indicates that an agency's work is in a specific region; examples include TVA, the Pacific Command of the Navy, and the Alaskan Command of the Air Force. The other two foundations of organization are less visible.

Clientele-based agencies are those that appear to address problems of a specific segment of the population, such as the Veterans' Administration (VA) or the Bureau of Indian Affairs (BIA). The label *clientele-based agency* may be misleading for two reasons. First, *every* agency has a clientele of some kind, a group or groups in the general population on whose behalf many of its programs are conducted—for example, farmers and the Department of Agriculture, skilled and semiskilled laborers and the Labor Department, and coal interests and the Bureau of Mines.

The label also may be misleading because these clienteles may not always be satisfied clienteles. The VA and the BIA are, in fact, excellent illustrations of agencies whose clienteles have gotten up-in-arms about some aspect of agency performance. In 1975, various veterans' groups and individual veterans complained vigorously about the VA's alleged shortcomings in awarding and processing veterans' benefits, to the point that a virtual sit-in took place in the office of the VA director. As for the BIA, it was, for a time, a principal target of the American Indian Movement and others who expressed dissatisfaction with government management of Indian problems on and off the reservation. In both instances, a clientele was the most dissatisfied group, which is not uncommon in bureaucratic politics.

Finally, *work process* agencies engage predominantly, if not exclusively, in data gathering and analysis for some higher-ranking official or office, and rarely if ever participate formally in policy making (though their work can have policy implications). Agencies such as the Economic Research Staff of the Department of Agriculture, the Economic Studies Division of the Federal Energy Regulatory Commission, and the Soils Research Staff of the U.S. Geological Survey fall into this category.

Individual administrators occupying the multitude of positions in the various agencies can be categorized several different ways. For example, most national government administrators are *merit employees*—those hired and presumably retained and promoted because they have the skills and training necessary to perform their jobs. Of approximately 2.9 million full-time civilian employees of the national government, about 93 percent work under a merit system of some kind. The remaining 7 percent include unionized employees not under a merit hiring procedure—for example, blue-collar workers in shipyards and weapons factories—as well as *political appointees*, some of whom can be removed by the president. In the latter group, numbering some 2,700 individuals, are the highest-ranking officials of the executive branch—cabinet secretaries and undersecretaries, regulatory agency commissioners, and EOP personnel, among others.

Another way of viewing administrative employees is as either *specialists* or *generalists*, categories that generally correspond to the merit and political designations discussed above. The term *specialist* refers to employees at lower and middle levels of the formal hierarchy whose responsibilities center on fairly specific programmatic areas. The term *generalist* is used to describe those in the higher ranks of an agency whose responsibilities cover a wider cross-section of activities within the agency, involving some degree of supervision of various specialists in the ranks below.

The national executive branch, then, is organized primarily into five major types of agencies, with four formal bases of organization (function being the most common) and with two broad categories of employees. The picture in state and local government varies somewhat, and is worth considering briefly for the same reasons we have examined the national executive branch: the structure has some impact on the way the machinery functions and on the content of policies it helps carry out.

STATE AND LOCAL EXECUTIVE STRUCTURES

In general, states and larger local governments resemble the national government in composition and organization of their executive-branch agencies. Most states now have numerous cabinet-level departments that stand in much the same relationship to the governor as do national departments to the president; states also have a wide variety of regulatory agencies, some government corporations, and miscellaneous agencies. Many governors, though not all, have fairly strong executive office staffs responsive to the governor's leadership (see chapter 4).

Some state agency structures reflect past or present influences of particular interest groups more than those in Washington do. One example is Pennsylvania's powerful Department of Mines and Mineral Industries, indicative of the role played in the state's economy by coal mine owners over the years. Another is Illinois' Department of Aging, created in the mid-1970s in response to the emergence of a growing constituency with common problems of senior citizenship. So-called special interests have ''their'' agencies in the national government, of course, but a pattern found in many states is creation of somewhat higher-level agencies in response to constituency pressures. Another distinctive feature of state executive structures is greater legislative control over some individual agencies' budgets and personnel compared to Congress's hold over national government agencies. This varies, however, from state to state.

Larger cities like New York, Chicago, Houston, Philadelphia, Boston, and Miami have bureaucratic arrangements not unlike those in state and national governments. (Figure 1-4 shows Houston's government organization.) There is a fair amount of administrative specialization, a directly elected chief executive (mayor) with a highly developed executive office staff, and similar bases of organization. There are, however, some differences. Local party politics frequently play a more prominent role in shaping municipal policy making—for example, in Chicago, Boston, and New York. Local public employee unions have a great deal of influence in many cities (see chapter 11). And government activity is more heavily oriented to providing such essential services as water, sewage disposal and sanitation, and police and fire protection, than to broader policy concerns such as long-term welfare reform or mass transit development.

In many smaller communities, as well as in most counties and townships, bureaucratic structures are not very numerous or sophisticated. This can also mean (though it does not always) that professional expertise in local government is inferior to that found in many state governments and the national government. Lack of expertise is often reflected in the limited quantity and quality of programs enacted by many local governments, a pattern visible particularly in most county governments (except the very largest), many smaller towns and villages, and most special districts.[18] Many local governments, as noted earlier, concentrate on providing basic urban services, with less emphasis placed on the sorts of operating programs and regulatory activities that characterize state and national administration. The larger the unit of local government, the more likely its bureaucracy will resemble state and national administrative agencies.

EXPLAINING THE GROWTH OF GOVERNMENT BUREAUCRACY

The growth of public administrative functions did not just happen; at the same time, it is not altogether clear exactly what accounts for it. A number of possibilities exist, each of which is worth examining for the influence it may have had on expanding the roles of public administrative agencies.

One explanation commonly cited is that technological complexity, beginning in the 1800s, gradually exceeded the capacities of legislative bodies and of political generalists to cope successfully. This view assumes that professional specialization in a host of fields—the physical and social sci-

Figure 1-4 City of Houston Organization Chart

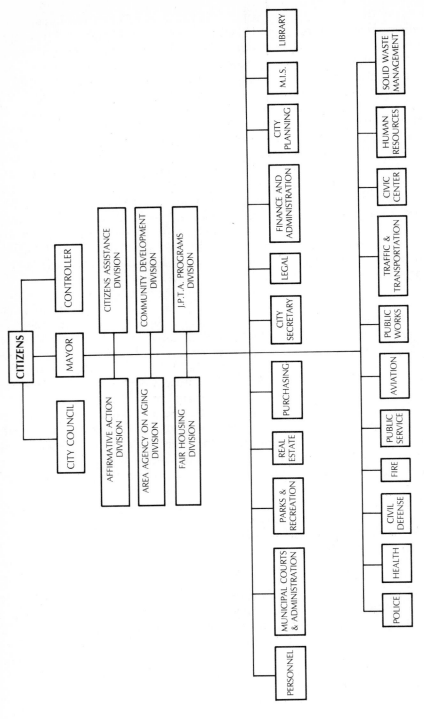

Source: Office of City Controller, Annual Financial Report of the City of Houston, Texas (1984)

ences, management itself, and professions like law—in effect invaded the public service just as it assumed far greater importance in society at large. Thus, as both the nation's problems and methods of addressing them became more complex, specialized bureaucracies were more necessary in the process of discharging government's responsibilities—or so the argument runs. To some extent, technological complexity *has* had an important effect on bureaucracy (see chapter 2), but whether it triggered bureaucratic growth, by itself, is not certain.

A second view holds that political pressures helped create a diversified bureaucracy. This was due primarily to increasingly diverse economic and social interests throughout our society and to governmental recognition of them in formal ways. Political scientist James Q. Wilson has referred to the phenomenon of *clientelism*—relationships between individual government agencies and particular economic groupings. This pattern first appeared about the time of the Civil War; Wilson cites another political scientist, Richard L. Schott, who noted that "whereas earlier . . . departments had been formed around specialized governmental functions (foreign affairs, war, finance, and the like), the new departments of this period—Agriculture, Labor, and Commerce—were devoted to the interests and aspirations of particular economic groups."[19] That trend has intensified in this century, so that it is now entirely appropriate to speak of bureaucratic clienteles or constituencies, in the same sense that legislators have constituencies. (See chapter 3 for an elaboration of this theme.) This view, then, suggests that bureaucracies have been created in response to political demand for government action in specific policy fields.

Another explanation, with its roots in the discipline of economics, holds that governmental responses to crisis situations (such as wars) cause both revenues and expenditures of government to move sharply upward. More important, after the crisis has passed, the levels do not return to their precrisis status, and new ideas of what is acceptable emerge—resulting in new "normal" levels of government activity.[20] As we shall see in chapter 12 on government budgeting, national government expenditure levels underwent precisely this sort of shift after the Civil War and again after World War II, with political acceptability of the change generally high in both cases. This explanation emphasizes indirectly society's increasing readiness to turn to government for managing society's responses to major (and, perhaps, not so major) problems; we will discuss in chapter 2 how our values concerning government action may also have helped shape bureaucratic roles, even though those values have not been constant.

One final explanation, also going back to the 1800s, overlaps all of the previous ones. As the private economy became both national in scope and industrial in nature—compared to the period before 1850—there developed an implicit base of public acceptance of greater regulation by the national government of private economic activities. Once begun, many of those regulative actions spawned new ones that, combined with the other forces at work (particularly crisis-related action), led to steady growth of public administrative entities. It would appear that all of these explanations have some merit; taken together, they paint a clearer picture of how government bureaucracy has reached the scope that it has. Among other things, considering "how we got here" may be useful in light of contemporary efforts to impose curbs or restraints on administrative agencies.

PUBLIC AND PRIVATE ADMINISTRATION: SIMILARITIES AND DIFFERENCES

Many similarities exist between administrative activities in the public and the private sectors. In fact, many elements of public administration have their roots in the private sector. There are those who assume that whatever differences exist are relatively minor, and that what will work effectively in one setting also will in the other. Thus, for example, the recurring political theme that we should "make government more businesslike," or "bring sound management methods from business into government." But the easy assumption that there are few if any important differences between public and private administrative activities is inaccurate. While some parallels do exist, there are also critical disparities between the two.

First the similarities. In both settings, managers and those to whom they are accountable have an interest in running programs and other activities that are properly designed, appropriately directed to meeting the goals stated for them, at least reasonably efficient in expenditure of organizational resources, and effective in their impacts. Public and private managers both have to be concerned with meeting their staffing needs, motivating subordinates, and financing and otherwise conducting their operations so as to promote their maximum advantage. In all this, there is some "politics," both internal to the organization and external to it. There are agreements to be reached and maintained, elements of persuasion and coercion, gains and losses to be realized, all of which must be planned for and acted on in the organization's interest. The president of Chrysler and the Secretary of Health and Human Services—as well as Chrysler's chief research engineer and the administrator at the U.S. Food and Drug Administration—have to be concerned with many of these same managerial needs.

On the other hand, important elements of the managerial environment (including the "politics") differ for public and private managers.[21] One fundamental difference is that in the private sector products or services are furnished to individuals based on their own needs or wants, in exchange for a direct (usually money) payment—a "quid pro quo" transaction. In the public sector, however, the goal of the manager is to operate programs or provide services on a collective basis rather than to individuals directly, supported in the great majority of cases by tax revenues, not quid pro quo payments for services rendered. Another key difference is the fact that private organizations set their own broad goals, while public organizations and managers are obligated to pursue goals *set for them by their legislatures.* Public managers thus have relatively little freedom to alter basic organizational goals. Also, while private managers can use an internal measure (the "bottom line" of profit or loss) to evaluate their organization's performance, public managers are subject ultimately to evaluation by outside forces (especially the legislature, the chief executive, the courts, and often the public itself), and it is those outside forces that have the critical "last word" in judging how well a public organization discharges its responsibilties. Beyond that, public managers are evaluated in somewhat more nebulous terms, for example, effectiveness in satisfying interested clienteles, and success in holding and expanding political support. Meaningful objective performance measures have been largely lacking in the public sector until very recently, even where managers have sought to use them. New emphases on efficiency, productivity, and accountability have produced fresh concern for such measures, but they are still at a very early stage of development in many governments (see chapter 13).

Other differences also exist. For one thing, many public organizations hold a monopoly on providing certain essential public services. Consequently, they have been able to survive even in the absence of highest-quality performance of their functions. Another difference is that concerns about achieving results in the public sector must compete for attention with procedural concerns. Values such as participation and public accountability, as well as political influences, make it necessary for public managers to divide their attention between substantive results and how to obtain them. It is difficult to achieve maximum economy and efficiency while keeping a wary eye on possible political repercussions—and many public managers must do just that.

In contrast to the profit-oriented concern shared by most of management in the private sector, there are often conflicting incentives among citizens, elected representatives, and administrative supervisors and leaders. If agreement is lacking on *what* is to be done and *why* (not to mention *how*, as noted above), an organization will not function with the same smoothness as it would were incentives agreed upon. Just as economic measures of performance have no counterpart in the public sector, general economic incentives have no parallel either.

Furthermore, most public organizations suffer from diffused responsibility, often resulting in absence of accountability for decisions made. Separation of powers is one factor in this, but a fragmented executive branch in most large governments (including those at the local level) is another. In contrast, centralized executive responsibility is a key feature of many profit-oriented organizations. (It should be noted, however, that there are exceptions to this generalization in both types of organization.) Also, public organizations, unlike private ones, entrust a fair amount of decision responsibility to citizen groups, courts, and boards or commissions of various types. Thus, a clear chain of command is not possible because of numerous opportunities for outside pressures to be felt.

There are still other important differences. Public-sector managers frequently must operate structures designed by other groups (in some states, these can include private interest groups as well as government entities), work with people whose careers are in many respects outside management's control, and accomplish their goals in less time than is usually allowed corporate managers. Finally, unlike many private managers, the public manager must operate in much more of a goldfish bowl of publicity, subject to scrutiny and criticism from the press and from many others outside the agency and government itself.

Among the most important of these latter concerns are the distinctly tighter time schedules that must be met in public agencies, and the goldfish bowl. It has been noted, for instance, that IBM had about ten years to establish the 360 computer series, and that it took George Romney, then president of American Motors, fourteen years to make the idea of a Detroit-made compact car acceptable both inside his company and in the marketplace.[22] (How times have changed!) Contrast that to the challenge faced by William Ruckelshaus, first administrator of the U.S. Environmental Protection Agency (EPA) in November 1970, who by law was given a total of *sixty days* to begin to change auto industry behavior in regard to auto emissions. As for the public spotlight, public managers must cope with what may be a steady stream of critical comments from outside, regardless of how well others understand agency purposes, empathize with operating difficulties, or consider political constraints on the manager. Conversely, the skilled public manager may be able to turn the press (and others) to the agency's side, and there are advantages in doing so: making recruiting new staff easier, facilitating the acquisition of more money, or perhaps preventing potential critics from gaining credibility.[23] Private managers may, at times, have to face the same kind of public criticism or have similar opportunities to generate good press. But for the most part, their activities are significantly less exposed to public view, until the final product has been arrived at.

Thus, while many administrative activities are common to both public and private sectors, major differences between them are also evident. As a result, there are obvious limits to how much the public sector can borrow advantageously from the private sector to improve the management of public affairs.

In comparing public and private sectors, two other dimensions merit consideration. In practice, the two sectors are increasingly interdependent—witness the difficulties, in the early 1980s, of the Chrysler corporation and the government actions essential to its survival. There is also a growing tendency for governments (especially local) to enter into contractual arrangements with private firms for delivery of services, such as garbage collection and fire protection. Thus, there has been a considerable blurring of what many still believe is a clear boundary between the two sectors.[24] However, even these emerging realities do not change the basic point: significant (and perhaps enduring) differences exist between public and private management.

PUBLIC ADMINISTRATION AS A FIELD OF STUDY

The principal focus of public administration as an academic field of study has changed more than once since its emergence in the late 1800s. Changing and overlapping conceptions of the subject sometimes reflected and sometimes preceded evolution in administrative practice in the ''real world'' of government, and cross-fertilization of ideas between practitioners and academics has been prominent throughout the twentieth century. Because so many public administrators were trained in formal academic programs, thus promoting the impact that academic disciplines have had on government administrative practices, it is useful to review major emphases that have characterized and helped shape the academic field.[25]

In the earliest period, from roughly 1887 to 1933, public administration was viewed as distinct and separate from politics, more akin to business and business methods than to anything political. Woodrow Wilson, in his classic essay ''The Study of Administration,'' wrote that administration ''is removed from the hurry and strife of politics. . . . Administrative questions are not political questions. Although politics sets the tasks for administration, it should not be suffered to manipulate its offices.''[26] The concept of a dichotomy between politics and administration was widely accepted during this period, based on not only the writings of Wilson but also the first textbook in the field, by Frank Goodnow, entitled (significantly) *Politics and Administration* and published in 1900. According to Goodnow, the bureaucracy was to administer—impartially and nonpolitically—the programs enacted by the legislative branch, subject only to judicial interpretation.[27] The dichotomy between politics and administration was reinforced by Leonard D. White's *Introduction to the Study of Public Administration* (1926). White captured the conventional wisdom of administrative theory: politics and administration were separate; management could be studied scientifically to discover the best methods of operation; public administration was capable of becoming a value-free science; and politically neutral administration should be focused on attainment of economy and efficiency in government, and nothing more.[28]

The next phase in development of the discipline was the movement toward discovering ''principles'' of public administration. This was an offshoot of the scientific approach to administration and was based on the belief that there existed certain permanent principles of administration which, if they could only be discovered and applied, could transform the performance of administrative tasks. Publication in 1927 of F. W. Willoughby's *Principles of Public Administration* marked the beginning of a decade in which identifying and correctly applying these principles was the predominant concern of many in and out of academic circles. Luther Gulick and Lyndall Urwick's *Papers on the Science of Administration*, published in 1937, defined seven principles that have become professional watchwords: planning, organizing, staffing, directing, coordinating, reporting, and budgeting (known by the acronym POSDCORB). Gulick and Urwick reemphasized the importance of these administrative principles, declared their applicability to almost any human organization regardless of what the organization was or why it existed, and stressed the fundamental desirability of efficiency as underlying administrative "science."[29]

Even as Gulick and Urwick wrote, however, the dominant themes of public administration were changing. The orthodoxy of the first thirty years or so of this century—that is, the willingness of most of those in public administration to "embrace, without basic skepticism, the Wilsonian dichotomy"[30] between politics and administration—was no longer as widely shared. The New Deal of Franklin D. Roosevelt, accompanied by a vastly expanded governmental role and the creation of scores of new administrative agencies in Washington, significantly changed the social and political contexts of public administration and set off a crisis for the field. There were three major developments in the period 1933–1945: (1) a "drastic expansion in the public conception of the obligations and responsibilities of government in social and economic affairs," (2) the emergence of an "enduring emphasis upon presidential leadership," and (3) the change in the nature of the federal system, with a "[shift] to the national scene [of] the responsibility for most of the important policy decisions" in the economy and society at large.[31] Roosevelt had demonstrated, in political scientist Alan Altshuler's words, "that patronage might be of great value in aiding a vigorous President to push through programs of social and economic reform."[32] Emphasis on political neutrality could have obstructed presidential leadership in achieving social reforms supported by many academics. These developments caused considerable turmoil in the study of public administration as it was cast loose from its original intellectual moorings without a clear alternative direction.

In the 1940s, with World War II commanding an even greater commitment in terms of government activity, the turmoil increased. This was due in part to an influx of academics in the field to national government agencies, during the war effort, who took back to their campuses a considerably altered perspective on what was important to teach about administration, especially in relation to the political process, and public administration's explicit role in making public policy.[33] During this same period, less than a decade after Gulick and Urwick had published their *Papers*, the principles of administration were coming under increasing fire. The theme was sounded more than once that the principles were logically inconsistent, potentially contradictory, and gave no clues concerning how to choose the one most appropriate for particular situations. For example, one principle held that for purposes of control, workers should be grouped according to *either* function, work process, clientele, or geography. There is nothing to suggest standards for using one instead of another, nor whether these are mutually exclusive categories.[34] (As we have seen, these four categories are still used in government bureaucracy.) Critiques of this sort came from many scholars in the field, but few had greater impact than Herbert Simon, in 1946 and 1947. In "The Proverbs of Administration,"[35] Simon likened the principles to contradictory proverbs, as paired opposites; for example, if "Look before you leap" is a useful proverb, so also is "He who hesitates is lost"! Both are memorable, often applicable, and *mutually exclusive*, without any hint of how to choose between them. Simon argued that the principles were much the same, that is, interesting, but of little real value in defining administrative processes. His book *Administrative Behavior* (1947) developed this line of argument further and contributed significantly to the weakening of the principles approach.

No comparable set of values replaced the POSDCORB principles, but different concerns began to emerge. Through the 1940s and into the 1950s, public administration found its relationship to political science—its parent discipline—one of growing uneasiness. Political science itself was undergoing significant change in the post–World War II period, most of it in the direction of developing more sophisticated, empirical (including statistical) methods of researching political phenomena, but always on the assumption that objectivity in research methods was of the highest importance.

The problem for public administration in this behavioral era was that many functions and processes of administration do not lend themselves to the same sorts of quantitative research as do, for example, legislative voting patterns, election data, and survey research of public opinion. As Altshuler points out, administrative decision making is frequently informal; many decisions are made in partial or total secrecy; the exact values of administrators and the alternatives they consider are difficult to identify and analyze; and traditional emphasis on efficiency (which has by no means disappeared) contrasts sharply with the core concerns of modern political science.[36] As a consequence, public administration became (again quoting Altshuler) a "rather peripheral subfield of political science," with many questioning its place in the larger discipline.

Another related development was the growth of research into administrative and organizational behavior, which sought to examine all sorts of organizations, not only, or even necessarily, *public* entities. This movement worked from the assumption that the social psychology of organizations made less important the question of precisely what kind of organization was to be studied, and sought to integrate research from not only social psychology but also sociology, business administration, and information science. This field, known currently as "organizational behavior," represents an attempt to synthesize much of what is known about organized group behavior within the boundaries of formal organizations.

Altshuler questions whether this direction—as valuable as it has been in furthering our understanding of human behavior in an increasingly organized society—has resulted in research findings that have *political* relevance, that is, relevance to the research directions of contemporary political science.[37] Public administration scholar Nicholas Henry goes further, asserting that public administration has begun to declare its intellectual and institutional independence from political science and business-administrative science, moving instead toward establishment of autonomous departments or programs. He cites data that indicate a strong trend developing in this direction, including sharp increases in both undergraduate and graduate enrollment in public administration courses and in the number of separate academic units at universities around the country that focus on public administration, urban affairs, and public policy.[38]

DILEMMAS IN THE STUDY OF PUBLIC ADMINISTRATION

Woven through a century of history of public administration are two dilemmas, one explicit throughout most of that period, the other only recently emerging in the literature. The first concerns whether public administration is peculiarly *public*, or is simply a governmental application of generic administrative concepts and practices.[39] Early views advanced by Wilson, Goodnow, and White clearly took the latter position in their advocacy of a politics-administration dichotomy. Later writers in the 1950s and 1960s, on the other hand, gave primary emphasis to the close interrelationships between the political process and administrative activity. The issue is still far from settled, especially since numerous schools of business administration in the 1960s and 1970s added public-sector *tracks* or whole programs to their curricula, suggesting once again (and from a different direction) that there is something called *administration* (or *management*) that cuts across public-private lines as well as the boundaries of a number of academic disciplines. Public administration scholar Allen Schick has observed that for almost a hundred years, "the generic approach has vied with political science for dominion over public administration," and that the contest continues on, "as the 'political' approach . . . has gravitated toward schools or programs in public affairs, policy studies, policy sciences, and similar policy approaches."[40] If this interpretation is correct, it means that the move toward disciplinary autonomy cited by Henry may be more apparent than real—that public administration as a field is still being pulled in different directions, while demonstrating considerable adaptability as to core content, essential assumptions, and basic approach.

This dilemma is related to the second, more contemporary difficulty: whether it is appropriate to call public administration a true *profession*, much as law or medicine might be called. What constitutes a profession can be debated, but it is possible to identify certain characteristics. A *profession* is "(1) a reasonably clear-cut occupational field, (2) which ordinarily requires higher education through at least the bachelor's level, and (3) which offers a lifetime career to its members."[41] A profession is characterized by members whose training is multidisciplinary in nature and by strong linkages between theory and practice in the field (as is the case, for example, in engineering and the physical sciences).[42] Public administration scholar Dwight Waldo, one of the outstanding figures in the field, has urged others to look upon public administration as a profession, both in these terms and owing to its status, disciplined approaches, and self-conscious identity. Others, however, have taken sharp issue with that characterization. Richard Schott has argued that public administration is far too diffuse, too diversified, to be a true profession. He notes, among other things, serious disagreement among practitioners and educators about what constitutes the "core knowledge" of the field, and that most middle- and upper-level officials in public service have little if any formal training in public administration or public affairs (though many of these same individuals are professionals in *other* fields, working now in responsible government posts). He also suggests that there is little sense of community among practitioners of the field, and that schools of public administration or public affairs are not subject to accreditation by a central organization as are schools of law, engineering, medicine, social work, and the like.[43] These themes have been echoed by, among others, political scientist Vincent Ostrom[44] and Allen Schick.[45]

Ironically, there has been movement among educators in the field aimed at countering some of these criticisms. Along with departments of public affairs and the like, newly created departments of public administration exist at major universities around the country, with emphasis on training for the field (or craft, or profession) of public administration. Simultaneously, the National Association of Schools of Public Affairs and Administration (NASPAA) has enacted a set of standards for the educating of would-be public administrators, raising at least the possibility of greater commonality in the training and background of those who move into the ranks of civil servants at all levels of government, and perhaps into higher management positions as well. However, these dilemmas (both of them) are real and still very much with us.

Public administration as an academic field of study, then, is not a settled discipline.[46] There are somewhat blurred boundaries between it and other fields, many loose ends in terms of what to study and how, a history of conflict with its parent discipline (political science), and growing controversy over just where public administration belongs intellectually and institutionally. It is within this volatile setting that we take up our study of public administration.

A WORD ABOUT THIS BOOK

Two brief comments are in order about what to look for in this book. First, two essential and recurring themes sounded in the pages that follow are: (1) the *control* and *accountability* of public administrative agencies within the context of the larger political system, and (2) the *effectiveness* of government agencies and programs in the "real world" of public management. An effort is made to treat these issues separately, but it is inevitable that they overlap, in both our treatment of them and the working environments of public administration.

Second, the discussion of public bureaucracy can and does go on at three different (but interrelated) levels of analysis, that is, with a focus on three distinct dimensions of the administrative process. One is the *role and function of government bureaucracy in society at large*—what differences large, complex, and influential agencies make in a nation founded on diffuse notions of popular rule (note the implicit importance of the control/accountability theme). A second dimension or level of analysis is the *management of public organizations*, broadly defined—issues and challenges confronting the individual public manager. And third is the *role of the individual*—the contribution, in whatever form, of a person working as a bureaucrat and the problems and opportunities associated with that role. *All of these are interrelated, in an ultimate sense*, and explaining why that is so is a major purpose of this book.

SUMMARY

Public administration has become a prominent and influential force in American government and society, especially in recent years. Most of us have some familiarity with bureaucracy, and many of our most pressing current political issues are related to administrative agencies and actions. There has been a noticeable decrease in public support for government bureaucracy when compared to forty or fifty years ago.

Public administration is the set of processes, organizations, and individuals associated with implementing laws and other rules enacted by legislatures, executives, and courts. This includes administrative agency involvement in the formulation of many such rules as well as their application. Public administration is simultaneously an academic field of study and an active field of training. Those who participate in public administration include administrators themselves, legislators and legislative staffs, higher executives, judges, political party officials, interest group leaders and members, mass media representatives, and the general public. Public administration and its politics involve interactions both internal and external to the formal agency structure. Public administration is also characterized by a distinctly managerial component, focusing on the internal dynamics of public organizations. Public managers need certain kinds of skills, among them facility in effective management of information, personnel, and budgeting. A successful public manager must be able to direct activities in both the short and long term and is responsible for defining and bringing about action. Most managers operate in an environment of bureaucratic organizations, shaping both formal structure and operating tendencies.

Public administration in the national government is characterized by several different types of agencies, a number of methods of agency organization, and several ways of categorizing administrative employees—each of which may affect what agencies do and how they do it. The principal agencies are cabinet-level departments, independent regulatory agencies, government corporations, divisions of the Executive Office of the President, and other miscellaneous agencies. These can be organized according to function (the most common basis of organization), geographic area, clientele served, or work process. Administrative personnel can be classified according to whether they were hired by merit procedures or through political appointment and whether they are specialists or generalists.

The organizational structure of state and local executive branches is generally comparable to that of the national government. Most states and larger localities have departmental organization and executive office staff support for the chief executive similar to that in Washington. In larger local governments, some essentials of organization are the same as at the national and state levels—for example, administrative specialization, chief executives with some degree of staff support, and similar bases of organization. But local political parties, employee unions, and the nature of government activity all represent differences on the local scene as compared with the national government. Smaller local governments differ much more sharply in their less extensive bureaucratic development and, not uncommonly, less professional expertise. The larger a local government, the more likely its bureaucracy will resemble state and national bureaucracies in structure and program.

Several explanations have been advanced for the rise of government bureaucracy. Some observers cite technological complexity; others see political pressures in an increasingly diverse society as a root cause; still others explain bureaucratic growth in terms of government responding to social and economic crises. Greater public acceptance, over the years, undoubtedly has reinforced the impact of these factors on the growth of bureaucracy.

There are similarities, and a number of more significant differences, between public and private management. Among the most important differences are that public managers must pursue broad goals set by others, and are evaluated by outside forces; neither is true of private managers. In addition, public managers generally cannot design their own organization's structures or control the careers of many subordinates; they also have far less time to accomplish their goals, and must operate in a goldfish bowl. Both public and private managers are expected to be similarly competent, effective, and efficient. There is growing overlap of the two sectors.

Public administration as a field of study has been characterized by several major and partially overlapping schools of thought: (1) the politics-administration dichotomy, (2) the objectives of economy and efficiency as the keynote of public administration, (3) the search for principles of administration, (4) a rejection of the "principles" approach, (5) a turning toward different perspectives on administrative behavior—for example, social and psychological factors in internal organizational processes, (6) a growing ferment regarding the links between public administration and its parent discipline of political science, and (7) developing trends that seem to carry the study of administration away from not only political science but also from allied fields of administrative study and toward disciplinary autonomy. Currently there are still troubling dilemmas in the study of administration, notably disagreement over viewing administration as generic or as peculiarly public, and issues surrounding the question of public administration as a true profession. This book will focus on the interrelationships between politics and public administration, with some attention to managerial aspects as well.

NOTES

1. See, for example, "Big Government: Everyone Is Running Against the Bureaucracy," *Congressional Quarterly Weekly Report*, 34 (October 23, 1976), 3036–37; and "Bureaucrats Under Fire," *National Journal*, 10 (September 30, 1978), 1540–41.
2. A number of authors have recently commented on the relationship between the proliferation of bureaucratic jargon and the deterioration of the English language, some writing in a serious vein, others in a semiserious or humorous vein. For serious commentary, see, among others, Alvin M. Weinberg, *Reflections on Big Science* (Cambridge, Mass.: M.I.T. Press, 1967), chapter 2, especially p. 54. For more jocular treatment of the subject, see James H. Boren, *When in Doubt, Mumble: A Bureaucrat's Handbook* (New York: Van Nostrand Reinhold, 1972); John Kidner, *A Guide to Creative Bureaucracy: The Kidner Report—A Satirical Look at Bureaucracy at the Paper Clip and Stapler Level* (Washington, D.C.: Acropolis Books, 1972); and Edwin Newman, *Strictly Speaking: Will America Be the Death of English?* (Indianapolis: Bobbs-Merrill, 1974), and *A Civil Tongue* (Indianapolis: Bobbs-Merrill, 1976).
3. See Charles T. Goodsell, *The Case for Bureaucracy: A Public Administration Polemic*, 2nd ed. (Chatham, N.J.: Chatham House, 1985), chapter 2.
4. Dwight Waldo, "Introduction: Trends and Issues in Education for Public Administration," in Guthrie S. Birkhead and James D. Carroll, eds., *Education for Public Service 1979* (Syracuse: Maxwell School of Citizenship and Public Affairs, Syracuse University, 1979), pp. 13–26, at pp. 25–26.
5. Goodsell, *The Case for Bureaucracy*.
6. Ibid., pp. 14–15.

7. Ibid., p. ix (emphasis added). Possible consequences of this intense criticism of bureaucracy and bureaucrats are discussed in Bernard Rosen, "Effective Continuity of U.S. Government Operations in Jeopardy," *Public Administration Review*, 43 (September/October 1983), 383–92, especially 383–86; H. Brinton Milward and Hal G. Rainey, "Don't Blame the Bureaucracy!" *Journal of Public Policy*, 3 (May 1983), 149–68; Charles F. Bingman, "Changes in Public Organization," *The Bureaucrat*, 12 (Winter 1983–84), 24–28; and Bruce Adams, "The Frustrations of Government Service," *Public Administration Review*, 44 (January/February 1984), 5–13. See also Douglas Costle, "In Defense of the Public Service," *Public Administration Times*, 3 (May 1, 1980), 3; Michael J. Wriston, "In Defense of Bureaucracy," *Public Administration Review*, 40 (March/April 1980), 179–83; and Herbert Kaufman, "Fear of Bureaucracy: A Raging Pandemic," *Public Administration Review*, 41 (January/February 1981), 1–9.
8. See, for example, Lewis C. Mainzer, *Political Bureaucracy* (Glenview, Ill.: Scott, Foresman, 1973); Kenneth J. Meier, *Politics and the Bureaucracy: Policy Making in the Fourth Branch of Government* (North Scituate, Mass.: Duxbury, 1979); and B. Guy Peters, *The Politics of Bureaucracy: A Comparative Perspective*, 2nd ed. (New York: Longman, 1984).
9. Joseph L. Bower and Charles J. Christenson, *Public Management: Text and Cases* (Homewood, Ill.: Irwin, 1978), p. 4.
10. Ibid., p. 3.
11. See Harold Seidman, *Politics, Position, and Power: The Dynamics of Federal Organization*, 3rd ed. (New York: Oxford University Press, 1980).
12. A useful introduction to this subject is James W. Davis, Jr., *The National Executive Branch* (New York: The Free Press, 1970).
13. Praeger Publishers of New York City has put out an excellent series on U.S. government departments and agencies, covering several dozen administrative entities in detail.
14. See Kenneth J. Meier, "The Impact of Regulatory Organization Structure: IRCs or DRAs?" *Southern Review of Public Administration*, 3 (March 1980), 427–43.
15. See Roscoe C. Martin et al., *River Basin Administration and the Delaware* (Syracuse, N.Y.: Syracuse University Press, 1960), pp. 244–51.
16. TVA is perhaps the most extensively studied agency in the history of our nation. A partial listing of the literature includes David E. Lilienthal's spirited book *TVA: Democracy on the March* (New York: Harper and Brothers, 1944); Philip Selznick's critical study *TVA and the Grass Roots: A Study in the Sociology of Formal Organization* (Berkeley and Los Angeles: University of California Press, 1949); Roscoe C. Martin, ed., *TVA: The First Twenty Years* (University, Ala., and Knoxville, Tenn.: University of Alabama Press and University of Tennessee Press, 1956); Preston J. Hubbard, *Origins of the TVA: The Muscle Shoals Controversy, 1920–1932* (Nashville: Vanderbilt University Press, 1961); Victor C. Hobday, *Sparks at the Grass Roots: Municipal Distribution of TVA Electricity in Tennessee* (Knoxville: University of Tennessee Press, 1969); Marguerite Owen, *The Tennessee Valley Authority* (New York: Praeger, 1973); North Callahan, *TVA: Bridge over Troubled Waters* (New York: A. S. Barnes, 1980); Michael R. Fitzgerald, Stephen J. Rechichar, Robert F. Durant, and Larry W. Thomas, *Intragovernmental Regulation and the Public Interest: Air Pollution Control in the Tennessee Valley* (Knoxville: Bureau of Public Administration, University of Tennessee, 1983); Erwin C. Hargrove and Paul K. Conkin, eds., *TVA: Fifty Years of Grass-Roots Bureaucracy* (Ur-

bana, Ill.: University of Illinois Press, 1983); Steven M. Neuse, "TVA at Age Fifty—Reflections and Retrospect," *Public Administration Review*, 43 (November/December 1983), 491–99; Stephen J. Rechichar and Michael R. Fitzgerald, *The Consequences of Administrative Decision: TVA's Economic Development Mission and Intragovernmental Regulation* (Knoxville: Bureau of Public Administration, University of Tennessee, 1983); and Michael R. Fitzgerald and Steven M. Neuse, eds., "TVA: The Second Fifty Years—A Symposium," *Public Administration Quarterly*, 8 (Summer 1984), 138–259.

17. See Edward S. Flash, Jr., *Economic Advice and Presidential Leadership: The Council of Economic Advisors* (New York: Columbia University Press, 1965).

18. John Rehfuss, *Public Administration as Political Process* (New York: Charles Scribner's Sons, 1973), pp. 64–68.

19. James Q. Wilson, "The Rise of the Bureaucratic State," *The Public Interest*, 41 (Fall 1975), 77–103, at p. 88. See also Stephen Skowronek, *Building a New American State: The Expansion of National Administrative Capacities, 1877–1920* (New York: Cambridge University Press, 1982); Paul P. Van Riper, "The American Administrative State: Wilson and the Founders—An Unorthodox View," *Public Administration Review*, 43 (November/December 1983), 477–90; and Patrick D. Larkey, Chandler Stolp, and Mark Winer, "Why Does Government Grow?" in Trudi C. Miller, ed., *Public Sector Performance: A Conceptual Turning Point* (Baltimore: The Johns Hopkins University Press, 1984).

20. For a fuller treatment of this view, see Nicholas Henry, *Public Administration and Public Affairs*, 2nd ed. (Englewood Cliffs, N.J.: Prentice-Hall, 1980), pp. 7–9.

21. This discussion draws upon Joseph L. Bower, "Effective Public Management: It Isn't the Same as Effective Business Management," *Harvard Business Review*, 55 (March/April 1977), 131–40; Brian W. Rapp, "You Can't Manage City Hall the Way You Manage General Motors," *Good Government*, 92 (Summer 1975), 12–15; and Michael A. Murray, "Comparing Public and Private Management," *Public Administration Review*, 35 (July/August 1975), 364-71. See also Robert N. Anthony and Regina Herzlinger, *Management Control in Nonprofit Organizations*, rev. ed. (Homewood, Ill.: Irwin, 1980); Frederick S. Lane, "Managing Not-for-Profit Organizations," *Public Administration Review*, 40 (September/October 1980), 526–30; and Gordon Chase and Betsy Reveal, *How to Manage in the Public Sector* (Reading, Mass.: Addison-Wesley, 1983).

22. Bower, "Effective Public Management," p. 135.

23. See the comments of Gordon Chase, former administrator of the New York City Health Service Administration, in ibid., p. 136.

24. See Hal G. Rainey, Robert W. Backoff, and Charles H. Levine, "Comparing Public and Private Organization," *Public Administration Review*, 36 (March/April 1976), 223–44; Patricia S. Florestano and Stephen B. Gordon, "Public vs. Private: Small Government Contracting with the Private Sector," *Public Administration Review*, 40 (January/February 1980), 29–34; Ira Sharkansky, "Policy Making and Service Delivery on the Margins of Government: The Case of Contractors," *Public Administration Review*, 40 (March/April 1980), 116–23; Lloyd D. Musolf and Harold Seidman, "The Blurred Boundaries of Public Administration," *Public Administration Review*, 40 (March/April 1980), 124–30; R. Scott Fosler and Renee A. Berger, eds., *Public-Private Partnership in American Cities: Seven Case Studies* (Lexington, Mass.: Lexington Books, 1982); and Salisbury M. Adams, ed., "Forum—Public/Private Partnership," *The Bureaucrat*, 12 (Spring 1983), 6–31.

25. This section relies on Alan A. Altshuler, "The Study of American Public Administration," in Alan A. Altshuler and Norman C. Thomas, eds., *The Politics of the Federal Bureaucracy*, 2nd ed. (New York: Harper & Row, 1977), pp. 2–17; Nicholas Henry, "Paradigms of Public Administration," *Public Administration Review*, 35 (July/August 1975), 378–86; Frederick C. Mosher, ed., *American Public Administration: Past, Present, Future* (University, Ala.: University of Alabama Press, 1975, under sponsorship of the Maxwell School of Citizenship and Public Affairs, Syracuse University, and the National Association of Schools of Public Affairs and Administration); Dwight Waldo, *The Study of Public Administration* (New York: Random House, 1955); Waldo, ed., *Public Administration in a Time of Turbulence* (Scranton, Pa.: Chandler, 1971); and Waldo, *The Enterprise of Public Administration* (Novato, Cal.: Chandler & Sharp Publishers, 1980).
26. Quoted by Altshuler, "The Study of American Public Administration," p. 2.
27. Henry, "Paradigms of Public Administration," p. 379.
28. Ibid.
29. Altshuler, "The Study of American Public Administration," p. 3; Henry, "Paradigms of Public Administration," pp. 379–80.
30. Rowland Egger, "The Period of Crisis: 1933 to 1945," in Frederick C. Mosher, ed., *American Public Administration: Past, Present, Future* (University, Ala.: University of Alabama Press, 1975), pp. 49–96, at p. 55.
31. Ibid., pp. 91–92.
32. Altshuler, "The Study of American Public Administration," p. 3.
33. See James W. Fesler, "Public Administration and the Social Sciences: 1946 to 1960," in Frederick C. Mosher, ed., *American Public Administration: Past, Present, Future* (University, Ala.: University of Alabama Press, 1975), pp. 97–141.
34. Henry, "Paradigms of Public Administration," p. 380; and Altshuler, "The Study of American Public Administration," p. 5.
35. Herbert A. Simon, "The Proverbs of Administration," *Public Administration Review*, 6 (Winter 1946), 53–67.
36. Altshuler, "The Study of American Public Administration," pp. 10–11.
37. Ibid., p. 13.
38. Henry, "Paradigms of Public Administration," pp. 384–85.
39. See Allen Schick, "The Trauma of Politics: Public Administration in the Sixties," in Frederick C. Mosher, ed., *American Public Administration: Past, Present, Future* (University, Ala.: University of Alabama Press, 1975), pp. 142–80, at pp. 166–67.
40. Ibid., p. 167.
41. This definition was suggested by Frederick C. Mosher in *Democracy in the Public Service*, 2nd ed. (New York: Oxford University Press, 1982), chapter 5.
42. I am indebted to Professor Don L. Bowen for suggesting these ideas.
43. Richard L. Schott, "Public Administration as a Profession: Problems and Prospects," *Public Administration Review*, 36 (May/June 1976), 253–59.
44. Vincent Ostrom, *The Intellectual Crisis in American Public Administration*, rev. ed. (University, Ala.: University of Alabama Press, 1974).
45. Schick, "The Trauma of Politics: Public Administration in the Sixties," p. 159.
46. For further information on the academic field of public administration, see Joseph A. Uveges, Jr., ed., *Public Administration: History and Theory in Contemporary Perspective* (New York: Marcel Dekker, 1982), and Keith M. Henderson, *The Study of Public Administration* (Lanham, Md.: University Press of America, 1983).

SUGGESTED READINGS

Charlesworth, James C., ed. *Theory and Practice of Public Administration: Scope, Objectives, and Methods.* Philadelphia: American Academy of Political and Social Science, 1968.

Goodsell, Charles T. *The Case for Bureaucracy: A Public Administration Polemic,* 2nd ed. Chatham, N.J.: Chatham House, 1985.

Martin, Roscoe C. "Political Science and Public Administration: A Note on the State of the Union." *American Political Science Review,* 46 (September 1952), 660–76.

Mosher, Frederick C. *Democracy and the Public Service,* 2nd ed. New York: Oxford University Press, 1982.

_____, ed. *American Public Administration: Past, Present, Future.* University, Ala.: University of Alabama Press, 1975.

Ostrom, Vincent. *The Intellectual Crisis in American Public Administration,* rev. ed. University, Ala.: University of Alabama Press, 1974.

Waldo, Dwight. *The Enterprise of Public Administration.* Novato, Cal.: Chandler & Sharp Publishers, 1980.

_____. "Public Administration." *International Encyclopedia of the Social Sciences,* 13. New York: Macmillan and The Free Press, 1968.

_____, ed. *Public Administration in a Time of Turbulence.* Scranton, Pa.: Chandler, 1971.

Wilson, James Q. "The Rise of the Bureaucratic State." *The Public Interest,* 41 (Fall 1975), 77–103.

2

The Context of Public Administration: The Political System, Values, and Social Change

PUBLIC administration does not exist in a vacuum. It is powerfully influenced by the broader governmental system of which it is a part—the constitutional allocations of political power, the ways power is exercised in practice by others in and out of government, and the overall roles assigned to administrators in governing the nation. In turn, the governmental system, like all other human institutions, has been shaped by society's values and beliefs, both past and present, about what government should do and how it should be done. A major influence is the social setting of government—the society's basic values, the extent of agreement on those values, how directly they relate to the conduct of government, and how government reflects and shapes those values. Values about other institutions in society—business, education, religion—also play a part in shaping government and public administration by creating demands and expectations that may need to be met through government action. The public demands a national-level commitment to education, for example, and expects government to conduct its affairs in a "businesslike" way, with a high degree of economy and efficiency.

Equally important to the context of public administration is social change—in (among other things) the makeup of the population, the nature of the economy, social relationships such as marriage/divorce and the "generation gap," and where people choose to live (city or suburb, "sun belt" or "snow belt"). Social change is important because as new social arrangements and patterns of behavior emerge, new problems inevitably arise with which government policy makers must contend. It is also important because as society changes, so do our values and priorities.

In recent decades public administration has been sharply affected by these varieties of change—in values concerning the role of government, in administrative concepts, in general social values and public demands. On the one hand, modern bureaucracy is the result of past evolution in theory and practice. Institutional change in general tends to be cumulative; that is, as patterns of behavior come and go, they leave behind carry-over effects, which then mingle with, and become indistinguishable from, the patterns that replace them. So it is with our administrative machinery, in which much of what we do today reflects lingering influences of the past. On the other hand, in contemporary America social values and established institutional patterns are undergoing rapid, unpredictable, and turbulent change. Today, many basic values are changing—toward marriage and family life, sex roles, the place of (and respect for) authority, material possessions, the environment, and human rights, to name only a few. For traditional institutions, including bureaucracy, to respond to such social upheaval is a large order, and much recent criticism of bureaucracy focuses on its apparent failure to do so.

THE POLITICAL SYSTEM AND GOVERNMENT BUREAUCRACY

In this section we will examine several traditional conceptions relating to bureaucratic activity, and discuss briefly how our political system has affected American bureaucracies in light of these conceptions. This is an introductory treatment only. The complexity of our politics cannot be described adequately in a few words; the same is true of the impacts of that complexity on our public administrative institutions. However, even this brief discussion will help to set the stage for exploring more fully the political values that underlie our governmental arrangements; administrative values that have helped to shape the conduct of public administration, more specifically; and the many facets of social change.

Traditional Conceptions of Bureaucracy in Government

Bureaucracy has traditionally been conceived in terms of implementing, or carrying out, directives of other institutions of government, as a servant of political forces external to it but not a political force in its own right. This notion of *bureaucratic neutrality* is central to an understanding of the way executive-branch bureaucracies have been designed to function in Western governments for nearly a century. A number of companion assumptions have also been evident in administrative practice.

First, bureaucratic behavior is assumed to follow the intent of the legislature, in the form of legislative enactments and guidelines for implementation. With legislative intent as a principal guiding force, bureaucracy's responsibility to the legislature is clearly established. It relies on the legislature for substantive policy direction and financial and political support. The legislature, in turn, looks to the bureaucracy for faithful and competent administration of the laws.

Second, there is a legitimate function of legislative oversight, or supervision, of bureaucratic behavior that logically complements legislative intent. The legislature, in other words, is expected to oversee the work of the bureaucracy to insure conformity with legislative intent. Present in both assumptions is the expectation that bureaucracy is distinctly subordinate in the political process to the will and initiative of other parts of the government. In no way did traditional conceptions of bureaucratic activity allow for significant autonomy (independence), discretion (freedom to make choices), or direct political involvement.

Third, bureaucratic behavior is assumed to be subject to direction by the chief executive of the government. The apparent contradiction between chief executive direction and legislative direction of the bureaucracy stems from the fact that these traditional assumptions were derived from parliamentary forms of government, in which the chief executive and top-level ministers were themselves members of the legislature. The chief executive (prime minister or premier) was usually leader of the majority party in the legislature (parliament), thus creating a situation in which bureaucratic responsiveness to the chief executive and to the legislature were one and the same thing. There is, however, a real contradiction—and often, a political conflict—between chief executive and legislative control of the bureaucracy in a system such as ours. Here, the chief executive and top-level executives are independent of the legislature—indeed, they are almost always constitutionally prohibited from serving in the legislature at the same time that they hold executive office.

Finally, it was traditionally assumed that the bureaucracy would be a neutral, professional, competent structure staffed by specialists in both general administrative processes and their respective specific policy areas. These notions—of a competent bureaucracy responding in a politically neutral manner to initiatives of executives and legislators external to it—seem to conform to the image of administration held by many Americans and have had a powerful influence on administrative design and practice in this country. That this image is not altogether accurate, however, is the focus of the next section. (See also chapters 3 and 13.)

Dynamics of Policy Making in the United States

In many parliamentary governments there is little question about how authority is exercised, by whom, and through what channels. In the United

States, however, such questions take on importance because there are no similarly convenient answers. Government power and authority in America are highly fragmented and scattered. This is by design, for the framers of the Constitution feared nothing so much as excessive concentrations of power. They did all they could, therefore, to see to it that power was divided among the different branches of the national government, and they gave each branch various means of checking the power of the other two. Examples include the president's power to veto an act of Congress (and Congress's power to override a presidential veto by a two-thirds majority) and the requirement that the Senate must confirm the great majority of presidential appointments to executive and judicial positions. Such a division of power within national, state, and local governments places bureaucracy in a very different position from the one it occupies in parliamentary systems.

The making of public policy in the United States and the participation of bureaucracy in that process are characterized by a number of major features. For one thing, the process lacks a centralized mechanism that "directs traffic" comprehensively. There are, rather, many centers of power scattered throughout the executive and legislative branches. This lack of centralization produces a great deal of slack in the decision-making system. That is, in the absence of tight legislative or executive control, there are many opportunities for lower-ranking executives to affect implementation of a law. This phenomenon of *administrative discretion* is widespread, arising not only from structural separation of powers but also from political conflicts that characterize executive-legislative relations, and from statutory language that often is broad, even vague.

It follows that there are many "power vacuums" randomly scattered through the decision-making process. Where power is splintered, in other words, there will be some exercise of it not clearly defined and therefore "up for grabs." This is the basis for some, but not all, of the conflict between the president and Congress, and between many governors and their legislatures. It also means that others in the decision-making process can compete for small amounts of power, increasing their influence (if they can) a little at a time. And among the most active contenders for these small quantities of power are interest groups and bureaucratic agencies, both of which seek to dominate policy making in the areas of greatest concern to them.

It is not only formal governmental power that is fragmented and scattered in American politics. So also is the ability to influence policy making in specific subject-matter areas. In other words, there is no one overarching policy process in which the same top government officials make all decisions and take responsibility for them. Rather, the policy-making process is broken into many little parts, with responsibility over each part determined by a combination of structural, functional, and political factors. In such a setting, it is not uncommon for public administrators to become significant "players" in the political game, to assume a stance that is *not* neutral, to take policy initiatives in small ways that nonetheless influence the long-term development of policies and especially specific programs under their jurisdiction—in short, to be politicians.

Thus, bureaucracy in American government differs from traditional notions of bureaucracy in important ways. First, it functions in a system in which power is far from centralized. Second, bureaucracy has at its disposal a great deal of discretionary power in making day-to-day decisions and in dealing with broader policy questions. Third, accountability is enforced through multiple channels due to the fragmentation of higher political authority.

How does all this affect behavior of public administrators? It would be impossible to answer that question entirely in a few well-chosen words, but two general observations suggest the nature of the political environment. First, political scientist Graham Allison, in his analysis of the Cuban missile crisis of 1962, noted that top executives are not in a position of *commanding* the bureaucracy to act; rather, "government leaders can substantially disturb, but not substantially control, the behavior of these organizations."[1] This clearly implies that bureaucracies have independent momentum with which political leaders must interfere if they are to influence bureaucratic activity—hardly the conditions suggested by traditional conceptions. Second, the focus of bureaucratic activity is predominantly on the respective areas of agency jurisdiction, and a bureaucracy will usually contest any significant change in the policy area over which it has jurisdiction.[2] Both of these phenomena indicate the nonneutral stance of American public bureaucracy. This is one of the most important differences between American bureaucratic practice and any ideal model of bureaucracy against which it might be measured.

POLITICAL VALUES

Our discussion of political and administrative values has three purposes: (1) to understand fundamental beliefs underlying American government and public bureaucracy, (2) to recognize the impact both sets of values have on public administration, and (3) to see the ways they conflict conceptually—and how that conflict affects conduct of public administration.

The term *political values*, as used here, refers to basic beliefs and assumptions not only about politics and the political system but also about appropriate government relationships to private activity, especially economic activity. The last falls under the heading of political values and has relevance to a discussion of public administration because of increasing governmental responsibility in regulating business and industry.

The United States has defined itself politically as a "liberal democracy,'' and economically as a capitalist system.[3] Two political concepts, popular sovereignty and limited government, are central to the notion of liberal democracy. *Popular sovereignty*—government by the ultimate consent of the governed—implies some degree of popular participation in voting and other political endeavors. While this does not necessarily mean mass or universal political involvement, America has in fact moved toward ever wider participation in voting and lately in other areas, including administrative decision making. The specific vehicle for popular rule has been representative government. Initially, Americans placed emphasis on legislative representation; the Constitution stresses that. More recently, concern has grown for political representation and demographic representativeness elsewhere in politics, notably in administrative organizations and processes. As the public grew dissatisfied with the degree of popular control over bureaucracy, greater representativeness in bureaucracy was seized upon as the solution. Political scientist Herbert Kaufman has gone so far as to suggest that ''the quest for representativeness in this generation *centers primarily* on administrative agencies.''[4]

The second central concept, *limited government*, reflects the predominant view of those who framed the Constitution that government posed a basic threat to individual liberties. In their prior experience, of course, their (British) government had in fact suppressed personal liberties; and they wanted to prevent that from happening again. Limited government was to be achieved through four devices: (1) separation of powers among executive, legislative, and judicial branches of government; (2) a system of checks and balances, whereby the exercise of even a fundamental power by one branch would require involvement of a second branch (for example, the requirement of Senate approval of treaties negotiated by the president); (3) federalism, under which certain powers were allotted to the national government while others were retained by the states (political entities to some degree independent of control by the national government); and (4) judicial review, by which courts could invalidate, on constitutional grounds, laws and actions of other government entities. In addition to this multiple fragmentation of government powers, the Bill of Rights (the first ten amendments to the Constitution) established broad areas of protection for individual liberties against encroachment by official government actions.

Two related concepts widely reflected in American society are *individualism* and *pluralism*.[5] Our emphasis on the individual is evident in the complex of civil rights and liberties protections, but individualism also implies the right to participate meaningfully in the political process. Pluralism, on the other hand, stresses the appropriateness of group organization as a means of securing protection for broad group interests in society. As political scientist Richard Page has put it:

Pluralism, as a theory and practice, assumes that groups are *good:* that citizens have the right to organize to advance their interests; that groups with differing interests will bargain and compete; and that the result of bargaining and competition among group interests is the interest of the whole community or nation—the public interest.[6]

The right of citizens to "organize to advance their interests" links individualism and pluralism, suggesting that individual freedom includes the right to become active in organized interest groups.

Directly related to individualism and pluralism is the notion of political and economic competition, primarily among groups but also among individuals. Limited government suggests that competition will be loosely regulated by government; in theory, competition itself will establish boundaries of acceptable behavior among the competitors, and allocate the fruits of victory. This fits very comfortably with capitalist theories. These economic doctrines, geared to private profit and general economic growth, emphasize maximum freedom for private entrepreneurs (individuals) and minimal government involvement in decisions and operations of the private economic sector. Two assumptions link capitalism to political values of limited government, individualism, and pluralism: (1) the individual is assumed to be both self-sufficient and capable of self-governing, therefore minimizing the need for government; and (2) the individual is thought to be better off both politically and economically if government is restricted from interfering where it is not needed.

In the past century, government's relationship to the economy has changed dramatically, and what once was minimal involvement has become much more. Have limited government and capitalism, then, been lost? Some argue that they have. A careful reading of American political history suggests, however, that government programs for economic development and social welfare are not brand-new ideas, that a "governmental obligation to ensure economic well-being and social justice is a Whig, Progressive, New Deal, and contemporary tenet [value]. But the dominant values have been liberal and capitalist, not radical and socialist."[7]

Government, in other words, has expanded upon earlier values in American politics, rather than establishing totally new directions, in pursuing modern economic and social programs. At the same time, these developments have been geared to basically capitalist themes, such as sustaining economic competition in the private sector and reconciling the entrepreneur's right to reap the benefits of free enterprise with the buying public's right to good-quality products at a fair price. While these aims may be the subject of controversy, they are a long way from socialism. Also, it is apparent that demands by powerful economic interest groups have resulted in increasing governmental protection for, rather than control of or interference with, those interests. That too represents a modification of capitalism. Finally, in the United States and other postindustrial nations, the industrial-growth economy so central to traditional capitalism has been changing to a service-oriented economy—providing services in such areas as finance, insurance, real estate, health care, education, and child care. In short, the private sector itself is changing, as well as government's relationship to it. This has had an effect on our political values, most notably by lessening our commitment to limited government. (A renewal of that commitment may now be under way, however.)

It should be noted that our values generally emphasize *how* things are accomplished more than *what* is accomplished. Our political values stress the importance of means, not ends; the end does not justify the means; rather, procedures are valued for their own sake. Fair procedure lends legitimacy to what is done. Thus our commitment to "due process of law"— though there is a gap between ideal and reality. Our ideology does not attempt to define specifically what is good or correct public policy. We leave it to the political process to formulate policy and concentrate on ensuring that the process is characterized by some degree of public access to decision making and decision makers, some degree of equity in the distribution of political and economic benefits, and a great deal of competition among diverse political interests. How *much* access (or equity or competition) exists is itself a matter requiring political resolution. These values serve as standards against which to measure reality in our politics; only rarely do realities match the rhetoric or thinking. But that does not alter the importance of these values nor their influence on what we may *try* to accomplish in our political system.

A major political value in America has been *democracy,* and increasing emphasis has been placed on democratizing the political process. What that entails has not always been clear, however. Some elements of democracy are universally supported, or nearly so, while others are the subject of controversy. Most agree, for example, that *majority rule* and *minority rights* are fundamental. The former enables the political system to make and implement decisions through popular control, while the latter permits those not in the majority freedom to voice their political views and to otherwise be politically active. Directly related to these principles is the free exchange of political ideas—the freedom to speak, write, and publish political concepts and commentaries, including those out of favor with officials and the majority of citizens. Most of us would at least pay lip service to free expression of ideas.[8] Most would also agree that democracy requires widespread participation in the election of public officials, through the right to vote and to take active part in political campaigns.

An element emphasized recently as essential to democratic government is direct participation in making and administering important decisions by those most directly affected.[9] There has been considerable resistance to this idea both in the abstract and in practice, since it would require extensive reallocation of political resources and power. Nevertheless, calls for "participatory democracy" in general and "participative management" in particular have met with some positive response. Two examples, which illustrate the challenges raised and conflict generated, are the demand for decentralization of urban government decision making to give city residents, especially the poor, more voice in running their schools,[10] in the location of public housing, in the construction of highways, and so on; and the provision for "maximum feasible participation" by the urban poor in community-action agencies, as part of the War on Poverty in the mid-1960s.[11] Direct participation, if implemented, would have the effect of expanding the number of decision makers at the same time that it altered decision-making mechanisms and almost certainly the content of some decisions. Whether representative democracy requires direct participation on a wide scale is open to debate, but merely raising the question has already had an impact on our thinking about democracy, as well as on the ways some government decisions are made.

Another idea, closely related to direct participation, is an expanded definition of what constitutes "representativeness" in our major institutions. The claim is made, with some justification, that numerous groups in the population—women, blacks, and Hispanics in particular—have been regularly excluded from decision making in government, business and industry, religious hierarchies, labor organizations, and political parties; consequently, these institutions have not been sufficiently responsive to the needs, interests, and preferences of such groups. It is argued that this systematic exclusion from power must be corrected, and increased direct representation of these groups in key decision-making positions, in proportion to their respective percentages of the total population, has been advocated as the most appropriate remedy.

There are three important underlying assumptions made by proponents of this view. One is that traditional modes of representation are inadequate, since they have operated to sustain majority representation only, rather than to articulate and respond to views and values of those who for a variety of reasons have rarely been part of a majority political coalition.[12] Another assumption is that each of these groups has distinct and identifiable group interests requiring concentrated political activity. The last assumption is that it is desirable or necessary to make more representative not only institutions of government but also economic, religious, and other social institutions, some of which historically have not viewed representativeness as a value of any great importance. Not surprisingly, considerable political tension has been generated over this issue; whether this view of representativeness will become dominant remains to be seen. Since 1972, national government guidelines for *affirmative action* have been laid down and compliance with them made a prerequisite for receiving financial aid in educational institutions, local police forces, collegiate athletics, and a host of other programs and institutions. But compliance has often been grudging at best, and has been accompanied only intermittently by fundamental change in the attitudes and values in question.

Public administration in America has been profoundly affected by the evolution of and recent upheavals in political values. It has been shaped in part by the devices for ensuring limited government (separation of powers, checks and balances, federalism, and judicial review), while also having a profound effect on those devices. In particular, government bureaucracies have both contributed to and benefited from what some have called the tilt toward the executive branch of government (and away from Congress) during much of this century, seriously altering the separation of powers and the effectiveness of checks and balances in the traditional sense.[13]

Furthermore, issues involving economic competition and regulation, public participation, and popular representativeness have tended recently to center (though not exclusively) on the role of administrative entities. A crucial issue in the 1980s (as noted in chapter 1) is the manner, scope, specificity, and implications of government (mainly administrative) regulation of the economy. And there are still other links between political values and public administration. One is the diversity of interest groups, which creates the potential for political alliances with those in positions of influence in the government (see chapter 3). Another is renewed concern for democratic values and political accountability, which poses new questions about effective control of bureaucracies. It is clear that if public administration had been shaped solely by changing political values and the interplay of political forces, it would have been altered considerably from its earliest forms and practices in the nineteenth century. However, administrative values have also figured prominently in its evolution. To these we now turn.

ADMINISTRATIVE VALUES

American public administration is grounded in certain fundamental assumptions that have dominated administrative thinking for nearly a century. Chief among them are the following.[14] First, it has been freely assumed that politics and administration are separate and distinct. Political determination of broad policy directions and administrative management of public programs have been thought to be different processes, in different hands. Professional administrators viewed their role in the early twentieth century as subordinate and responsive to prevailing political majorities in Congress and the White House. Theirs was not to initiate but to wait on initiatives from others. Administration was to be not only neutral politically but also passive. This conception of bureaucracy is not unlike that of a finely tuned machine, activated only when someone else pushes the button.

Another common assumption has been that partisan politics should not intrude upon processes of management itself, although political control of administration was considered entirely appropriate and, indeed, consistent with bureaucratic neutrality. It was also assumed in the early 1900s that administrative processes and functions could be studied scientifically, and that by such scientific examination it would be possible to identify various principles of administration to guide administrative conduct. (These were business practices first, then they were grafted onto public administration.) Finally, it was thought that the purpose of developing a *science* of administration, as well as the principal measure of administrative performance, was economy and efficiency in government, a standard also adopted from business and industrial practice. Companion values have included job-related competence (merit) instead of political loyalty tests as the primary basis for personnel decisions, faith in the work ethic and in statistical evaluations of work performance, and a basic social consensus underlying the public administrative process.[15]

These values first emerged in a period of government reform—the late 1800s and early 1900s—following some fifty to seventy-five years in which politics and administration had been deeply intertwined. Political and administrative jobs had been bartered crudely in exchange for political favors and support, and the guiding principle in public personnel administration had been ''to the victors belong the spoils of victory.'' The reform effort was based on the belief that politics of all kinds could have *only* an adverse effect on administration, thus making necessary separation of the two.

Heavily politicized administration had indeed been wasteful and inefficient, and there had been undeniably negative effects on the quality and effectiveness of what government did. Thus there arose attempts to separate politics and administration that had as their ultimate goals economy and efficiency, and a companion concern with discovering principles of administration, stemming from a desire to hasten the attainment of economy and efficiency. It should be emphasized, however, that these were not merely ''passing fancies.'' They held sway firmly in virtually all the major approaches to administration until after World War II and, significantly, among large segments of the general population even up to the present time. Some political reformers and others who seek to bring better management practices into government still cling to the doctrines of economy and efficiency almost as a matter of faith. And presidents from Teddy Roosevelt to Ronald Reagan (and other politicians as well) have found it politically advantageous to speak of improved economy and efficiency as a goal of their tenure in public office. There are, however, some problems posed by administrative values that stress separation of politics and administration while emphasizing efficiency.

First, they are not all consistent with the political values articulated by the Constitution. The framers did not seek to establish an extensive bureaucratic structure, nor (as far as we can tell) did they foresee one:

> They placed their faith in periodic elections, legislatures, and an elected chief executive rather than in a bureaucracy, however pure and efficient. There is nothing to suggest that they believed sound administration could compensate for bad political decisions. Redressing grievances and bad political decisions [was] the function of the political process, rather than of administrative machinery.[16]

Thus the dichotomy between politics and administration probably would have been seen by the framers either as undesirable, since government through the political process was central to the constitutional scheme, or as impossible.[17] It seems likely that they would have regarded with suspicion any developments that had the effect of insulating important decision makers, such as administrators, from effective control by the voters or their elected representatives. Yet the administrative values that we have discussed here suggest precisely that sort of insulation, although for reasons that many thought laudable when they were first formulated.

Second, it has become clear on the basis of a substantial body of research since World War II that public administration is not merely machinery for implementing decisions made by other government institutions. As we saw earlier, public agencies and administrators have both authority and the power of initiative to make a host of decisions—large and small—that have real impact on public policy. Protections against undue political manipulation instituted a century ago in response to unmistakable excesses have given rise to the possibility of administrative excesses, because control over policy making is more indirect and therefore more difficult for elected leaders and their immediate subordinates to exercise.

Third, there is some tension, if not outright conflict, between the major emphases of the Constitution and those of administrative values. The framers sought, perhaps above all else, to prevent unchecked exercise of political power by any institution of government or by government as a whole. While they undoubtedly would not have advocated deliberate waste or wanton corruption, they were far more concerned with preventing growth of concentrated political power, regardless of who wielded the power or with what degree of effectiveness (or efficiency). Thus they fragmented the formal powers of government so as to create a certain amount of *inevitable—and calculated—inefficiency.* Furthermore, as noted previously, the framers placed great reliance on the political process and on representative institutions (legislatures in particular) as devices for resolving political conflicts and representing the sovereign people. At the same time, however, they also sought to make the new national government effective and competent within its sphere of activity; their interest in creating limited government was tempered by fear of its not being able to act at all, thus permitting social discord and chaos to occur unchecked. In sum, the framers contemplated a political system that could both tolerate and benefit from somewhat inefficient exercise of power (the benefit being that government would have greater difficulty infringing on individual liberties), that would freely resort to the political process for making decisions and solving problems, and that would be *able* to act, when necessary.[18]

The values of administration, on the other hand, clearly point toward efficiency not merely as a desirable feature of government operation but as a key standard for evaluating government performance.[19] The reformers who first sought to increase efficiency in government associated most forms of politics with inefficiency—in many instances, rightly so—and as a result were largely "antipolitics." Their values strongly inclined toward political neutrality as a key feature of both the composition and operation of public administrative agencies, and thus as a major remedy for inefficiency. (It should be noted, however, that these reform efforts *had* political effects—in particular, narrowing channels of access to government employment for those who could not meet new criteria of merit, and building public organizations around a predominantly white, middle-class ethic.)

A recent study by political scientist Douglas Yates explores more fully the conflicts between these two sets of values (Yates treats them, with somewhat more precision, as normative *models* of "pluralist democracy" and "administrative efficiency").[20] He summarizes the main conflicts this way:

> 1. In the pluralist model, power is dispersed and divided; in the efficiency model, power is concentrated. Related to this, in the pluralist model governmental policymaking is decentralized; in the efficiency model it is centralized.
>
> 2. In the pluralist model there is a suspicion of executive power (in fact of any concentration of power); in the efficiency model, great emphasis is placed on centralizing power in the hands of the chief executive [for the sake of accountability].
>
> 3. In the pluralist model, power is given to politicians, interest groups, and citizens; in the efficiency model, much power is given to experts and professional bureaucrats.
>
> 4. In the pluralist model, political bargaining and accommodation are considered to be at the heart of the democratic process; in the efficiency model, there is a strong urge to keep politics out of administration.
>
> 5. The pluralist model emphasizes individuals' and political actors' own determination of interest . . .; the efficiency model emphasizes technical or scientific rationality (which can be better discovered by detached expert analysis than by consulting the desires of voters and politicians).[21]

It is small wonder, then, that while both sets of values have continued to influence American government, inconsistencies between them have been difficult to reconcile—a structurally fragmented government operating on broadly democratic principles makes *in*efficiency more likely than efficiency. And in a time of growing complexity, social change, and far-reaching government activity, reconciling these values becomes an even greater challenge.[22]

SOCIAL CHANGE AND PUBLIC ADMINISTRATION

The social setting of public administration, like the context of values, has both direct and indirect impact, and changes in that setting, like changes in values, carry with them potentially far-reaching implications. Several societal changes of the past half century have been of particular importance in shaping contemporary public administration.

The most obvious change is population growth, and shifts in the demographic makeup of the population. We have become a nation of nearly 240 million inhabitants, from less than half that many a century ago and less than two-thirds of that number (151 million) in 1950.[23] This striking growth in numbers has meant a parallel increase in demands for public services, demands directed more often than not at administrative agencies, especially at the state and local level—for example, police and fire protection, teachers and other educational personnel, sanitation, and health services. Complicating and intensifying this increased service demand is a second, related development: the continuing concentration of people in urban areas. In the period 1950–1970, the greatest population growth occurred in suburban rings around larger cities, mainly in the Northeast and Midwest. More recently, however, the pace of urban in-migration has slowed (the population of rural and small town counties increased 15 percent during the 1970s nationwide). Perhaps more important, there have been major shifts in both population and economic activity from the Northeast/ Midwest ("snow belt") region to the South/West ("sun belt") region.

The scope of these changes has been dramatic as well as significant. For example, more than 90 percent of the nation's population growth during the 1970s occurred outside the snow belt, and the states in that region lost more than 750,000 manufacturing jobs in the same period.[24] Such changes carry with them serious social, economic, policy, and administrative implications, for regions on *both* ends of the migration streams. Even within the sun belt, growth has been concentrated in particular areas. In Florida, the coastal population doubled between 1964 and 1984; eight million people now live in that state's Atlantic and Gulf Coast counties. Similarly, the nearly four million people living in the seventeen coastal counties of Texas represent a 64 percent increase in the period 1960–1984.

Several other important demographic shifts should also be mentioned. First, during the 1970s the proportion of blacks living in central cities declined (from 59 percent to 55 percent of all blacks)—the first time such a decline has occurred since the great influx of blacks to Northern cities during World War II. Second, almost 10 percent of our people aged five or older (twenty-three million) speak a foreign language at home; nearly half of those individuals speak Spanish. Third, after a period when the number of children under five declined, a small "echo" of the postwar baby boom has now appeared. Consequently, the school-age population, which shrank during most of the 1970s, will begin to grow again in the near future. These changes pose new and complex problems for those who administer government programs—in education, economic development, housing, and a host of others.

Technological change has also been of crucial import to public administration. We have experienced a revolution in electronic communications, both in terms of linking widely separated parts of the world virtually instantaneously via satellite, and in terms of mass communications capabilities, whereby literally millions of people can witness an event simultaneously (as well as "live and in color"). Technology, in the form of automation and other mechanical advances, has also permitted mass production and distribution of durable goods on a scale never before known. The "knowledge explosion" is a further dimension of technological change, giving rise to both the education industry and the expansion of scientific research supported by millions of dollars in government, and other, funds. Government regulation of, and participation in, increasingly complex technologies—the space program, energy research, control of environmental pollution and toxic wastes—demands far more sophisticated and specialized bureaucracies. This drastic alteration in responsibilities has had a permanent effect on the nature and course of American public administration.

The need for increased specialization is evident throughout much of both public and private administration. As tasks and skills become more complex, mastering any one of them demands more of an individual's time and attention, thus possibly hampering acquisition of broad skills. Specialization, of course, is a core value in traditional conceptions of public bureaucracy; thus movement toward greater specialization represents extension of an existing feature rather than a new one. A very important consequence for public administration has been that specialists inside and outside of government have been able to be—indeed, have had to be—in closer working contact with one another as part of the policy-making process. This reinforces the dual patterns of more informed decision making (because of the knowledge resources that can be brought to bear), and of less centrally directed decision making (due to top executives' limited ability to fully comprehend all the specialties of people in their organizations). Specialization is a major reason for fragmenting and compartmentalizing decision-making responsibility within a bureaucracy, permitting a specialized staff or organization considerable discretionary authority within its jurisdiction. To the extent that personnel systems are based on job-related competence, and competence is judged to include increasingly specialized knowledge, these tendencies are likely to be reinforced.

Political decisions to address new problems, that is, to identify certain conditions present in society as problems, have also resulted in enlarged responsibilities for administrative bodies. This is to suggest that many of today's challenges—environmental pollution, mass transit, energy sources and conservation, and population growth and stability, to name only a few major ones—have actually been with us for some time in one form or another, and "discovering" them as problems is really a result of deciding as a society that to do nothing about them would be inviting trouble. In all the cases cited, and in some others, changes in societal values about what is important or right preceded identification of the problems. Previously, they were not widely regarded as problem areas requiring public action. Although that has changed today, there is still debate over the scope and nature of particular problems and what governmental actions are appropriate to solve them. Administrative entities empowered to deal with these problems thus are drawn into controversies surrounding the nature of the problems themselves.

In sum, the combined effects on bureaucracy of population growth and geographic redistribution, vast changes in our knowledge and technological capabilities, specialization, and the rise of new, complex social problems have been profound and probably irreversible. Accompanied by changes in some of our most fundamental political and administrative values, change in American society has led to new, unforeseen, and complex pressures on our machinery of government at all levels.

THE CHANGING VALUE CONTEXT AND BUREAUCRACY UNDER PRESSURE

During the 1960s and 1970s a host of values—social, political, administrative—were subjected to scrutiny, generating social change as well as resulting from it. Value change, however, is not a new phenomenon; evolution of even fundamental values has been a continuing part of American history. One evolving value concerns limited government. Beginning in the late 1800s government came gradually to be viewed more as a positive instrument of social change than as something to be guarded against, feared, or mistrusted. Increasing international involvements have prompted growth in our military and diplomatic machinery, and a growing conception of government as a *guarantor* of rights and liberties, and even of economic well-being, has given rise to more governmental activity in a larger number of domestic policy areas. The image of government as provider and protector, rather than as threat to individual liberty, has become widely accepted—though this may now be changing. Perhaps most important, public expectations have changed, with more and more people looking to government for reasonable solutions to their problems.

The devices used to ensure limited government—separation of powers, checks and balances, federalism, and judicial review—have reflected these changes. Federalism was modified due to the national government's increasing role in domestic affairs, and due to the rise of intergovernmental relations in domestic policy making.[25] Separation of powers was affected by the expanding role of the president and executive-branch agencies relative to Congress, notably in their ability to initiate public policy proposals. (Congress itself assisted in the growth of presidential power by delegating considerable legislative authority to the White House.) Change in the relative influence of the presidency also affected the concept of checks and balances.[26] Judicial review became more important in that the U.S. Supreme Court upheld the general trend of expanded national government power, especially after the late 1930s.[27]

The scope of these changes is illustrated by enactment of a graduated income tax in 1914; by Theodore Roosevelt's early natural resource conservation efforts; by Woodrow Wilson's League of Nations venture; by Franklin Roosevelt's New Deal; and by far-reaching White House initiatives of the past two decades. Most innovative presidents have called on existing bureaucracies and/or created new ones to implement their programs; Congress has sometimes pressured bureaucracy to follow *its* directives in opposition to presidential leadership. In any case, a considerable amount of new administrative activity has grown up as a direct result of our redefining the role government should play in our lives.

Government's relationship to the private economic sector has also been modified in response to changing views about government's general domestic responsibilities. In the early 1900s regulation of business and industry centered on preventing development of monopolies (antitrust efforts) and maintaining fair trade (business) practices. But as business and industry grew into nationwide—and then international—enterprises, the scope of government regulation broadened as well, first geographically and later substantively: the quality of food and pharmaceuticals (U.S. Food and Drug Administration), pricing and other practices in the oil industry (Federal Energy Regulatory Commission), stock-market regulation (Securities and Exchange Commission), and more recently, environmental quality (Environmental Protection Agency) and consumer protection (Consumer Product Safety Commission), to name a few. This is not to say that government regulation has always been effective, consistent, or even present on all occasions,[28] but it does indicate that government policy directions have changed markedly from earlier laissez-faire (hands off) attitudes. These patterns have been largely repeated in many state governments, where one also finds environmental protection agencies, consumer agencies, and intrastate commerce regulatory bodies. The relationship of government to private enterprise has clearly changed in the past fifty years, and here too the burden has fallen principally on administrative agencies.

Democratic values emphasized in our thinking have changed also. Demands for direct participation and greater representativeness have crucial administrative implications. As bureaucratic decision makers have gained in influence, criteria for their selection (based on job-related competence) and methods used for their selection (competitive examinations) have come under increasing fire for having promoted unrepresentative and unresponsive public bureaucracies.[29] Similarly, growing emphasis on promoting economic and social equality through government action gave rise to a movement known as the New Public Administration, composed of both scholars and practitioners whose paramount concern in administering public programs is social equity, that is, a fairer distribution of the benefits available from government.[30] Considerations such as these cast administrators into advocacy roles—actively pursuing particular policy goals while seeking to uphold well-defined sets of social-political values. Whether this is appropriate is a matter of opinion, but it is clearly not in the tradition of bureaucratic neutrality. Those who subscribe to the New Public Administration argue, however, that bureaucratic neutrality has been sacrificed in the past to comfortable working arrangements with large and powerful political interests (see chapter 3). They maintain that representing the interests of those lacking substantial influence is not only politically and socially justifiable but also consistent with past bureaucratic behavior, which had favored different, stronger interests.

Administrative values have been both redefined and reordered in relative importance. Whereas we devoted considerable effort in this century to strengthening the merit system, which promoted politically neutral competence in public administration, the current emphasis seems to have shifted away from strictly merit principles and toward greater representativeness and participation. Herbert Kaufman has suggested that the values of political neutrality and representativeness pull us in different directions, that strengthening one means weakening the other. That is, emphasizing competence may produce a less-than-representative public service due to differences in opportunities to acquire and develop skills, while seeking greater representativeness means emphasizing personal characteristics not necessarily related to seemingly objective job qualifications.[31]

Kaufman has also noted that a third value—strong executive leadership—has been more popular during periods when representativeness was emphasized more than political neutrality. Historically, strong leadership was enhanced when the public expected political representativeness in government institutions and when pressures for merit reform were strongly felt.

It appears that during the period since Kaufman's observations, we have been in the midst of a historical cycle in which disenchantment with politically neutral bureaucracy has grown, pressures for reform along representative lines have been generated, and (according to some survey data) there is renewed interest in stronger executive leadership.[32] Here, as elsewhere, old values have not been totally discarded; rather, they have been modified and adapted to different needs in different times. Bureaucracies that have attempted to continue operating according to only the old values have encountered difficulty, yet it has not been possible for those seeking change to bring it about completely. This conflict of values largely explains the tension currently surrounding the administrative process.

One final source of pressure on bureaucracy is growing interest on the part of chief executives at all levels of government to reassert more effective control over the policy-making process. Presidents in this century, of both parties, have increasingly been frustrated in their attempts to gain regular support for their programs from well-entrenched administrative structures and personnel and have either induced the bureaucracies to work with them or have bypassed them, often setting up rival centers of bureaucratic influence. None of these efforts has been completely successful. Administrative agencies have demonstrated both staying power and considerable political savvy in whittling down a president's ability to coerce them or to work around them.[33] One result has been attempts by recent presidents (notably Nixon, Carter, and Reagan) to restore chief executive influence by more forcefully setting presidential priorities, increasing the number of political appointees in bureaucratic agencies (see chapter 10), proposing more agency reorganizations, and attempting to impose tighter budget controls (see chapter 12). This reflects the link noted by Kaufman between strong executive leadership and greater representativeness in government (meaning, here, representation of the political majority that elected the chief executive).

In sum, then, bureaucracy is under pressure because political insulation provided by the merit system has come to frustrate both chief executives, hampered in their efforts to set policy directions effectively, and citizens, who may have found professional bureaucrats inaccessible and/or unresponsive. The administrative values of political neutrality and professional competence have therefore been challenged increasingly, and other values offered (sometimes forcefully) as alternatives. Bureaucracy is also under pressure because, in contrast to some earlier periods when it was viewed as a source of innovation and initiative, it is now seen as a major obstacle to needed change—even though we may not agree on what changes are desirable or necessary, which only adds to the pressure. Finally, it is possible (though not conclusively demonstrated) that the rather impressive track record of government agencies in years past may have raised public expectations unduly by creating the impression (often with help from agency public relations personnel) that even in more complex and difficult times the bureaucracy can cope, if not conquer.[34] Failure to meet inflated expectations may thus be a part of today's bureaucratic dilemmas.

SUMMARY

Contemporary public administration has been shaped by the political system of which it is a part, by past and present political values and administrative values, and by social change. Traditional conceptions of bureaucracy and its role in government include: (1) political neutrality in carrying out decisions of other government institutions, (2) legislative intent as a principal guiding force for the actions of bureaucracy, (3) legislative oversight of bureaucracy as a legitimate corollary to legislative intent, (4) direction by the chief executive of administrative activities (which, in a system of separation of powers, creates the possibility of conflict over control of bureaucracy), and (5) professional competence in bureaucracy. These conceptions, while exerting a powerful hold on our beliefs, are not altogether accurate.

Because of the fragmented nature of the policy-making process in America, government administrators function in a political environment where: (1) there is no central policy coordinator with total control, (2) there is, as a result, slack in the system, allowing administrators considerable discretion, and (3) not all decision-making power or authority is clearly allocated, resulting in many small conflicts over fragments of power. In such a setting, public administrators are often active in political roles and take policy initiatives that are not neutral, thus departing from traditional views about bureaucratic roles and functions. American bureaucrats are in a position to develop semiindependence from elected leaders. Furthermore, bureaucratic activity is organized around jurisdiction over particular policy areas; bureaucracies seek to prevent changes in jurisdiction that might harm their political interests or those of their supporters.

Politically, our system is a liberal democracy; economically, a generally capitalist one. Key political values have included popular sovereignty, limited government, individualism, and pluralism. We have also emphasized individual liberty as a central objective of the political system and stressed democratic principles. Widely supported democratic principles include majority rule, minority rights, and the free exchange of political ideas. More controversial are direct participation and a broadened definition of *representativeness* in decision-making institutions. Our political values have fit comfortably, for the most part, with the economic doctrines of capitalism; and government economic policies, while increasingly regulative, have sought to sustain competition and protect the rewards of competitive success.

Major administrative values have included separation of politics and administration, scientific development of administrative principles, and attainment of economy and efficiency in government as the paramount objective of a politically neutral "science of administration." These values were the basis of administrative reform in the late nineteenth and early twentieth centuries, and were a reaction against practices of the previous fifty to seventy-five years. These values, in varying degree, have had continuing popular appeal and have been used quite effectively as part of campaign oratory by candidates for the presidency and hundreds of other offices.

However, our political and administrative values are not entirely consistent with each other. The framers of the Constitution assumed that there would be effective political control by the voters or their elected representatives over all important decision makers, while the reformers intended to insulate administration from direct partisan control. Such insulation has become cause for concern as administrators have assumed or been delegated ever greater policy-making responsibility and authority. In addition, one set of values is based on the assumption that individual liberty and the public interest are best served by keeping government restrained—and therefore unable to infringe upon our freedoms—while the other set of values is geared toward improving the ability of government agencies to operate efficiently—also in the public interest. Changes in particular values have served to intensify pressures already existing on administrative institutions, especially in recent years.

Public administration also has had to respond to rapid social change: population growth and urbanization, technological advances, increased specialization, and the emergence of new, complex social problems.

Accompanying social change have been modifications in underlying values, both political and administrative, with direct and significant impact on public administration. Government, generally, has become more active, with the chief executive and the bureaucracy spearheading the expansion of its role in society. Government's relationship to the private economic sector has increasingly taken the form of concern for product and environmental quality, consumer protection, and regulation of numerous business and industry practices. The concept of democracy has changed, with greater concern for broad, direct participation and more representativeness. This has resulted in pressures for change in administrative agencies that would de-emphasize political neutrality and job-related competence as all-important values and place greater weight on popular involvement and control. The quest for control over bureaucracy has centered on chief executives, who are seen as most likely to possess the resources necessary to exercise such control. Finally, high public expectations have affected government agencies to the extent that there is considerable dissatisfaction with many aspects of bureaucratic performance, and considerable pressure being brought to remedy the things thought to be wrong.

NOTES

1. Graham Allison, *Essence of Decision: Explaining the Cuban Missile Crisis* (Boston: Little, Brown, 1971). This quote is taken from an earlier version of the book, which appeared as "Conceptual Models and the Cuban Missile Crisis," *American Political Science Review*, 63 (September 1969), 698.
2. See Matthew Holden, " 'Imperialism' in Bureaucracy," *American Political Science Review*, 60 (December 1966), 943–51.
3. This discussion is based on the excellent treatment by Richard S. Page in "The Ideological-Philosophical Setting of American Public Administration," in Dwight Waldo, ed., *Public Administration in a Time of Turbulence* (Scranton, Pa.: Chandler, 1971), pp. 59–73. See, in the same volume, Allen Schick, "Toward the Cybernetic State," pp. 214–33. For an advocacy treatment of liberal democracy, see Harold W. Chase and Paul Dolan, *The Case for Democratic Capitalism* (New York: Crowell, 1964). See also Douglas Yates, *Bureaucratic Democracy: The Search for Democracy and Efficiency in American Government* (Cambridge, Mass.: Harvard University Press, 1982), pp. 10–13.
4. Herbert Kaufman, "Administrative Decentralization and Political Power," *Pub-*

lic Administration Review, 29 (January/February 1969), 3–15, at p. 5 (emphasis added).

5. Page, "Ideological-Philosophical Setting," p. 61.
6. There are, however, other ways to view the public interest. See Glendon Schubert, *The Public Interest* (Glencoe, Ill.: The Free Press, 1960).
7. Page, "Ideological-Philosophical Setting," pp. 61–62. See also Louis Hartz, *The Liberal Tradition in America* (New York: Harcourt, Brace and World, 1955).
8. Numerous studies of public opinion suggest, however, that many Americans are inconsistent in our willingness to allow free expression of *unpopular* ideas such as communist ideology or advocacy of elective abortion.
9. Though given renewed emphasis in recent decades, the idea of direct participation dates back to the founding of the Republic. Douglas Yates cites historian Andrew Hacker, a scholarly expert on the political thought of James Madison. Hacker suggests that Madison recognized the need for government to "regulate the activities of groups in society," but that he (Madison) also "wanted groups to have a positive role in making governmental policy." See Yates, *Bureaucratic Democracy,* pp. 10–11.
10. See, especially, Naomi Levine with Richard Cohen, *Ocean Hill-Brownsville: Schools in Crisis* (New York: Popular Library, 1969); Alan Rosenthal, ed., *Governing Education: A Reader on Politics, Power, and Public School Policy* (Garden City, N.Y.: Doubleday, 1969); and Marilyn Gittell and Alan G. Hevesi, eds., *The Politics of Urban Education* (New York: Praeger, 1969).
11. See Daniel P. Moynihan, *Maximum Feasible Misunderstanding* (New York: The Free Press, 1969). The literature on community control includes, among others, Alan A. Altshuler, *Community Control: The Black Demand for Participation in Large American Cities* (New York: Pegasus, 1970); Milton Kotler, *Neighborhood Government: The Local Foundations of Political Life* (Indianapolis: Bobbs-Merrill, 1969); Eric Nordlinger, *Decentralizing the City: A Study of Boston's Little City Halls* (Boston: Boston Urban Observatory, 1972); and Joseph Zimmerman, *The Federated City: Community Control in Large Cities* (New York: St. Martin's, 1972).
12. As noted previously, that *is* one aim of democracy as we have understood the concept. What is argued is that majority representation without full representation of the minority is no longer sufficient for a democracy.
13. See Lawrence C. Dodd and Richard L. Schott, *Congress and the Administrative State* (New York: Wiley, 1979), chapter 1, especially p. 6.
14. This discussion is taken from Dwight Waldo, "Public Administration," *The Journal of Politics,* 30 (May 1968), 443–79, at p. 448, cited by Page, "Ideological-Philosophical Setting," p. 62. Waldo's *The Administrative State: A Study of the Political Theory of American Public Administration* (New York: The Ronald Press, 1948) is a valuable examination of the evolution of our thinking regarding public administration.
15. James J. Heaphey, "Four Pillars of Public Administration: Challenge and Response," in Dwight Waldo, ed., *Public Administration in a Time of Turbulence* (Scranton, Pa.: Chandler, 1971), pp. 74–94.
16. Page, "Ideological-Philosophical Setting," p. 63.
17. It is also likely, however, that they would have objected equally to the *blatant* politicizing of administration that occurred during the mid-1800s.
18. This balanced view of power held by the framers finds an analogy in the writing a century later of Woodrow Wilson, one of the foremost administrative reformers. In his famous essay "The Study of Administration" (1887), Wilson ad-

vanced the "politics/administration dichotomy" and the notion of bureaucratic neutrality. What is not as well remembered is that Wilson also argued that administrators should exercise "large powers and unhampered discretion." The principal emphasis of his essay, then, may be reinterpreted by giving more weight to Wilson's prescription for what Jameson Doig has called "administrative energy and administrative discretion." See Doig, " 'If I See a Murderous Fellow Sharpening a Knife Cleverly . . .': The Wilsonian Dichotomy and the Public Authority Tradition," *Public Administration Review*, 43 (July/August 1983), 292–304, especially pp. 292–94. The quote cited is from p. 294.

19. Martin Landau, "Redundancy, Rationality, and the Problem of Duplication and Overlap," *Public Administration Review,* 29 (July/August 1969), 346–58.

20. It should be noted that "liberal democracy" and "pluralist democracy" are parallel—but not identical—concepts.

21. Yates, *Bureaucratic Democracy*, pp. 31–33.

22. In *Bureaucratic Democracy*, Douglas Yates offers a thoughtful and carefully crafted approach to how these values can in fact be reconciled.

23. The U.S. Bureau of the Census makes available, after each decennial (ten-year) census, many volumes of data that illuminate the changes in American society. This section relies on summary treatments of census data found in Theodore H. White's *The Making of the President 1960* (New York: Atheneum, 1961), chapter 8, "Retrospect on Yesterday's Future" and *The Making of the President 1972* (New York: Atheneum, 1973), chapter 6, "The Web of Numbers"; President's Commission for a National Agenda for the Eighties, *A National Agenda for the Eighties* (New York: New American Library, 1981), chapter 2, "The Demographic Background: Toward a Portrait of America in the Eighties"; and various reports published by the U.S. Bureau of the Census, Department of Commerce (some data reported in the Bloomington-Normal [Ill.] *Daily Pantagraph*, April 12, 1981, p. F-3; April 20, 1982, p. A-1; May 21, 1984, p. A-1; May 25, 1984, p. C-3; and June 3, 1984, p. A-5).

24. *SIAM Intergovernmental News*, 5 (July 1981), p. 7 (published by the American Society for Public Administration, Section on Intergovernmental Administration and Management [SIAM], Washington).

25. See Richard H. Leach, *American Federalism* (New York: Norton, 1970); Michael D. Reagan and John G. Sanzone, *The New Federalism*, 2nd ed. (New York: Oxford University Press, 1981); Deil S. Wright, *Understanding Intergovernmental Relations*, 2nd ed. (Monterey, Cal.: Brooks/Cole, 1982); Parris N. Glendening and Mavis Mann Reeves, *Pragmatic Federalism: An Intergovernmental View of American Government*, 2nd ed. (Pacific Palisades, Cal.: Palisades Publishers, 1984); and chapter 5 of this book.

26. See Dorothy Buckton James, *The Contemporary Presidency,* 2nd ed. (Indianapolis: Bobbs-Merrill, 1974); and Thomas E. Cronin, *The State of the Presidency,* 2nd ed. (Boston: Little, Brown, 1980).

27. See, among others, Kenneth T. Palmer, *State Politics in the United States*, 2nd ed. (New York: St. Martin's, 1977), pp. 30–31.

28. See, for example, Robert C. Fellmeth, *The Interstate Commerce Comission: Ralph Nader's Study Group Report on the Interstate Commerce Commission and Transportation* (New York: Grossman, 1970); and Louis M. Kohlmeier, Jr., *The Regulators: Watchdog Agencies and the Public Interest* (New York: Harper & Row, 1969).

29. See Kaufman, "Administrative Decentralization and Political Power."

30. See Frank Marini, ed., *Toward a New Public Administration: The Minnowbrook Per-*

spective (Scranton, Pa.: Chandler, 1971); H. George Frederickson, ed., "Social Equity and Public Administration: A Symposium," *Public Administration Review*, 34 (January/February 1974), 1–51; and H. George Frederickson, *New Public Administration* (University, Ala.: University of Alabama Press, 1980).
31. Kaufman, "Administrative Decentralization and Political Power."
32. Louis Harris, "Confidence and Concern: Citizens View American Government," a study conducted under contract with, and printed by, the Subcommittee on Intergovernmental Relations, Committee on Government Operations, U.S. Senate (Washington, D.C.: U.S. Government Printing Office, 1974), at p. 36.
33. For an example of presidential inability to coerce the cooperation of bureaucracies—even in times of crisis—see Graham Allison, *Essence of Decision: Explaining the Cuban Missile Crisis* (Boston: Little, Brown, 1971).
34. Francis E. Rourke, *Bureaucracy, Politics, and Public Policy,* 3rd ed. (Boston: Little, Brown, 1984), especially chapter 3.

SUGGESTED READINGS

Altshuler, Alan A. *Community Control: The Black Demand for Participation in Large American Cities.* New York: Pegasus, 1970.

Chase, Harold W., and Paul Dolan. *The Case for Democratic Capitalism.* New York: Crowell, 1964.

Frederickson, H. George, ed. *Politics, Public Administration, and Neighborhood Control.* San Francisco: Chandler, 1973.

Harris, Louis. "Confidence and Concern: Citizens View American Government." A study conducted under contract with, and printed by, the Subcommittee on Intergovernmental Relations, Committee on Government Operations, U.S. Senate. Washington, D.C.: U.S. Government Printing Office, 1974.

Heaphey, James J. "Four Pillars of Public Administration: Challenge and Response." In Dwight Waldo, ed., *Public Administration in a Time of Turbulence.* Scranton, Pa.: Chandler, 1971, pp. 74–94.

Kaufman, Herbert. "Administrative Decentralization and Political Power." *Public Administration Review,* 29 (January/February 1969), 3–15.

Marini, Frank, ed. *Toward a New Public Administration: The Minnowbrook Perspective.* Scranton, Pa.: Chandler, 1971.

Moynihan, Daniel P. *Maximum Feasible Misunderstanding.* New York: The Free Press, 1969.

Page, Richard S. "The Ideological-Philosophical Setting of American Public Administration." In Dwight Waldo, ed., *Public Administration in a Time of Turbulence.* Scranton, Pa.: Chandler, 1971, pp. 59–73.

Yates, Douglas. *Bureaucratic Democracy: The Search for Democracy and Efficiency in American Government.* Cambridge, Mass.: Harvard University Press, 1982.

Zimmerman, Joseph. *The Federated City: Community Control in Large Cities.* New York: St. Martin's, 1972.

PART TWO

The Political Setting of Public Administration

The next three chapters deal with various aspects of the political environment within which public administration functions. Chapter 3 discusses key elements of politics and power in bureaucracy. The discussion focuses on the dispersal of power throughout government and what that means for public administrators, the foundations of bureaucratic power, the political implications of structure, bureaucrats as political actors, and problems of accountability. Bureaucrats are seen as active participants in political interaction, with considerable variety and complexity in the manner of their involvement.

Chapter 4 examines chief executives and their leadership of bureaucracy at national, state, and local levels. Similarities and differences among them are given careful attention, particularly with regard to leadership resources. How chief executives interact with those in administrative agencies and what difference they make to bureaucratic operations are also discussed.

Chapter 5 deals with an aspect of American government of increasing importance to public administration—the changing nature of federalism and intergovernmental (national-state-local) relations. Description of the formal federal setting is followed by examination of intergovernmental relations within federalism. Particular attention is given to fiscal and administrative relations among the different levels and units of government. The changing nature of American federalism has profoundly affected the management of government programs, at all levels, and it is essential that we understand how the two are interrelated.

PART TWO

The Political Setting of Public Administration

3

Bureaucratic Politics and Bureaucratic Power

In this chapter we resume our discussion of the politics of American public administration. Here we shall deal with four principal themes. First, we will consider the political environment in which bureaucracy functions. Second, we will examine foundations of bureaucratic power, chief among which are the ability to build, retain, and mobilize political support for administrative agencies and programs and to make use of expertise in a particular field. Third, we will look at "subsystem politics," studying the way in which bureaucrats enter directly into political alliances with others in and out of government in order to pursue shared, or at least complementary, programmatic and political objectives. Fourth, we will discuss the political accountability of nonelected government officials (most bureaucrats are nonelected), identify several limitations on bureaucratic accountability, and assess the possibilities for overcoming those limitations.

THE POLITICAL CONTEXT OF BUREAUCRATIC POWER

Administrative agencies, like all other government institutions, function within a framework of widely scattered political power. Both the formal framework of governmental power and the actual competition for power reflect this lack of centralization in the political system. The formal framework refers to structural arrangements of the Constitution such as separation of powers, checks and balances, federalism, and judicial review. Competition for power includes conflicts among the branches of government and within them (especially within Congress), factional conflict within the two major political parties, and continual jockeying for position and influence among interest groups. This dispersal of power is sustained and supported by the noncentralized nature of American society, with its strong cultural emphases upon individualism and pluralism, and the accompanying acceptance of individual and group competition as appropriate mechanisms for getting ahead in politics and in other pursuits.

Wide dispersal of political power creates both constraints and opportunities for political actors (individuals, groups, institutions). The major problem facing any group or agency is that the quest for influence in a particular policy area is usually keenly competitive, with many other groups and agencies also seeking to have their preferences adopted as public policy. A current example concerns government energy policy, an area of considerable interest to the petroleum industry, manufacturers of electrical appliances, environmental groups, the utility industry, and consumer groups. Others with a stake in energy policy include coal companies, labor unions whose members are or may be employed in energy-related work, and government agencies such as the national Department of Energy, state utility commissions, and state and national resource conservation agencies, which have responsibilities affecting, and affected by, decisions on energy.

A somewhat more specific example revolves around the decision by the U.S. Food and Drug Administration (FDA) early in 1977 to ban saccharin from the market because of its suspected cancer-causing properties. Among those who sought to reverse the ban were manufacturers of saccharin and of a wide variety of low-calorie food products using saccharin, and an unexpectedly large number among the general public who needed or wanted to have saccharin available (diabetics and others on sugar-restricted diets, for example). Those supporting the ban, besides the FDA, included some members of Congress, consumer advocate Ralph Nader's public-health research organization, and others fearful of increased incidence of cancer. Though the FDA acted on congressional authority in imposing the ban, it did not have the last word on the subject because of Congress's ability to modify the FDA's powers—a situation faced by many agencies and their allies. In November 1977, after eight months of often bitter debate, Congress voted to delay the ban for eighteen months (to mid-1979), pending new studies of saccharin and of the broader issue of cancer-causing properties in food products. Congress subsequently extended the moratorium for consecutive two-year periods—in 1979, 1981, 1983, and 1985—while research on saccharin continued.[1]

Perhaps the key to why bureaucratic agencies must play political roles is the lack of cohesive political majorities within the two houses of Congress, and the resultant fuzziness in programmatic mandates enacted by Congress.[2] Political scientist Norton Long, writing more than thirty years ago, observed that "it is a commonplace that the American party system provides neither a mandate for a platform nor a mandate for leadership. . . . The mandate that the parties do not supply must be attained through public relations and the mobilization of group support."[3] Long went on to suggest that the parties fail to provide "either a clear-cut decision as to what [administrative agencies] should do or an adequately mobilized political support for a course of action."[4] He continued:

> The weakness in party structure both permits and makes necessary the present dimensions of the political activities of the administrative branch— permits because it fails to protect administration from pressures and fails to provide adequate direction and support, makes necessary because it fails to develop a consensus on a leadership and a program that makes possible administration on the basis of accepted decisional premises.[5]

COMMENTS ON THE RELATIONSHIP OF PUBLIC ADMINISTRATION TO POLITICS

"The exercise of discretionary power, the making of value choices, is a characteristic and increasing function of administrators and bureaucrats; they are thus importantly engaged in politics."

—from Wallace S. Sayre, "Premises of Public Administration: Past and Emerging," *Public Administration Review*, Spring 1958.

"Economy and efficiency are demonstrably not the prime purposes of public administration. . . . Supreme Court Justice Louis D. Brandeis emphasized that 'the doctrine of separation of powers was adopted, not to promote efficiency but to preclude the exercise of arbitrary power.' The basic issues of . . . organization and administration relate to power: who shall control it and to what ends?"

—from Harold Seidman, *Politics, Position, and Power: The Dynamics of Federal Organization*, Oxford University Press, 1980.

"Political science and public administration not only have a natural mutual affinity through interest in the same general subject matter area: they also have a mutual and reciprocal need for each other. Robbed of concern for a vigorous and vital administration, political science would become largely a thing of library and classroom, hardly worthy to treat of so buoyant a subject as government. On its part, administration cries for the intellectual stimulation which can come only from the thinker of general qualities of mind."

—from Roscoe C. Martin, "Political Science and Public Administration: A Note on the State of the Union," *American Political Science Review*, September 1952.

"A theory of public administration means in our time a theory of politics also."

—from John M. Gaus, "Trends in the Theory of Public Administration," *Public Administration Review*, Summer 1950.

Thus Congress, lacking majorities that can speak with a clear voice for a sustained period of time, is characterized instead by shifting political coalitions, the composition of which vary from one issue (and even one vote) to the next.

Another factor contributing to the lack of clarity in legislative mandates to government agencies is the inability of legislatures as institutions—and of individual legislators—to define precisely the exact steps required to put into effect a desired policy or program:

> Legislators, not being technical experts, frequently write laws embodying goals that are exemplary but which lack details. Skeletal legislation, as it is frequently called, is phrased in occasionally grand and, therefore, fuzzy terms. The implementing agency is told by the legislature [in national, state, or local government] to provide a *safe* environment for workers, to see that school children are served meals with *adequate* nutritional content, . . . to *assist* the *visually impaired*, to maintain *adequate* income levels, and so on.[6]

Most of the time—but especially when basic statutory language is ambiguous—legislators delegate to administrators the authority necessary to breathe life (and specific meaning) into such provisions of a law, and then to implement them. (Ambiguous language also can be the result of political compromises. It is always easier, for example, to agree on support for "quality education" than it is to define just what that is.) The usual pattern, then—for whatever reason—is legislative enactment of statutes that are phrased in general terms, accompanied by legislative delegation of authority (to define and implement those statutes) to administrative agencies.

Thus agencies are placed in the position of making judgments about legislative intent and decisions about program management, which carry with them significant political implications. Congress, however, does not simply leave bureaucrats to their own devices. As noted in chapter 2, *legislative oversight* is a legitimate function of Congress, one which can sometimes result in fairly strict control by a legislative committee or subcommittee of actions by administrators under its jurisdiction. Other potential controls also exist, which we will examine in the discussion of bureaucratic accountability later in this chapter.

Presidents, who might be expected to provide leadership for bureaucracy from a solid base of political support, ordinarily lack the sort of political backing that would permit them to take unequivocal policy positions. Another observation by Long, though made during the Truman presidency, still is applicable today:

> The broad alliance of conflicting groups that makes up Presidential majorities scarcely coheres [around] any definite pattern of objectives. . . . The President must in large part be, if not all things to all men, at least many things to many men. As a consequence, the contradictions in his power base invade administration.[7]

For a variety of reasons, presidents may avoid taking the lead in giving direction to administrative implementation of public policy. For administrators there is both benefit and cost in such presidential nondirection: benefit, in not having to follow every presidential dictate exactly; cost, in not being able to rely routinely on presidential power, influence, or prestige for political support. Presidents may lend their political backing to administrative agencies, but only when supporting a given program is advantageous to their political interests.

Before discussing the principal political resources of administrative agencies, some other generalizations are in order concerning the political context of bureaucratic power. First, formal definitions of agency power or responsibility are not likely to tell the complete story about actual power or influence. Second, although bureaucratic agencies generally occupy a power position somewhere between total independence from president and Congress and total domination by either or both, just how much independence they have in any specific situation also is heavily influenced by the power relationships they have with other political actors and institutions. Agencies with relatively low political standing may be dependent on the support of Congress or the president in order to function adequately, thus running the risk of allowing others to call the shots. Those with high political standing, or with strong backing from other supporters, are better able to stand on their own in relation to Capitol Hill and the White House. These generalizations also hold true in state and local politics.

Third, acquisition and exercise of bureaucratic power are frequently characterized by conflicts among agencies over program *jurisdiction*—the area of responsibility assigned to an agency by Congress or the president. One study of *bureaucratic imperialism*—the tendency for agencies to seek expansion of their program responsibilities—suggests that such expansionism arises "from the simple fact that, whatever the purposes of the administrative politician, his first necessity is to maintain sufficient power for his agency. *Power is organized around constituency and constituency around jurisdiction.*"[8] Bureaucratic agencies, in their quest for "sufficient power," will seek support from permanent and semipermanent coalitions of constituency groups, which in turn are organized to pursue policy objectives of their own. To have a chance of securing backing from such groups, administrative agencies must be responsible for managing government programs of interest to these potentially supportive constituencies. Thus, agencies always seek to obtain control over programs that have strong support from influential constituencies.

Consider, for example, what happened when President Carter issued his administration's Urban Policy in 1978. Both the Departments of Housing and Urban Development (HUD) and of Health, Education and Welfare (as it was then known) sought to capture the lion's share of the new or expanded programs that were to be a part of that policy. Both department secretaries—Harris of HUD and Califano of HEW—understood that administrative responsibility for such programs meant added, or consolidated, political support from such organized interests as the construction industry, public-employee unions, transportation employees, business and industrial groups concerned with their urban environments, and groups representing the urban poor.[9] Similarly, a state bureau of highways may attempt to centralize all highway-related programs under its jurisdiction, contesting the control of even the state secretary of transportation in the process, because of benefits to be derived from the political backing of highway engineers, auto manufacturers, trucking firms, and various labor unions.

Bureaucratic imperialism, however, is neither universal nor automatic; for example, an agency may deny (in its own political interests) that it has legal authority to exercise powers within some specified, and unpopular, area of jurisdiction. Thus in the 1940s the Federal Power Commission denied that the Natural Gas Act of 1938 conferred on it powers of regulation over the oil industry that many outside the industry desired to see the FPC exercise, but that its political allies in the industry sought to curb. The point is not that agencies are inherently imperialistic or nonimperialistic; rather, that an agency's decisions regarding program jurisdiction usually take into account potential political repercussions. Thus, conflicts over agency jurisdiction are serious contests for political power.

Finally, governmental institutions, including administrative agencies, have at least two roles to play in the exercise of power and decision-making authority—roles that overlap but are conceptually distinct and can sometimes conflict. On the one hand, they may act as unified entities, seeking to maximize their influence and their share of available political rewards and benefits. On the other hand, government institutions also serve as arenas of political competition, within which various political forces contend for dominant influence in decision-making processes. This is especially evident in Congress, where rival political coalitions are frequently in noisy dispute over well-publicized issues. When it is reported that ''Congress voted today to . . . ,'' what this really means is that a majority coalition was successfully formed on a given vote. At issue, also, every time Congress makes a decision is control of the way the question is presented, possible amendments, use of numerous tactics to speed up or delay consideration, and other tactical questions. There is far less visible conflict in the bureaucracy than in Congress, but this pattern of conflict resolution within the institution is much the same, complete with conflict over shaping the issue, moving it along or ''foot-dragging,'' and so forth. The bureaucracy, like Congress, operates within a complex web of political forces and must respond in some manner to the external (and frequently internal) pressures brought to bear on the administration of government programs.

Ordinarily, administrative agencies try to strike a manageable balance between what they *can* and *want* to do to further their own programmatic interests, and what they *must* do to ensure their survival and prosperity, however that is defined. Achieving such a balance requires a willingness to compromise, a sure instinct in deciding when to seek a larger or smaller share of the pie, and an ability to read accurately political forecasts for both the long and the short run. In addition to those internal skills, however, an agency must first have and maintain the two crucial foundations or sources of bureaucratic power mentioned earlier: political support, and expertise in the subject matter of its program responsibilities. Let us consider each of these in turn.

FOUNDATIONS OF POWER: POLITICAL SUPPORT

Political support for an administrative agency in national politics has a number of key dimensions. First and perhaps foremost, Congress is a major potential source of support which must be cultivated carefully and continuously. In most instances, an agency derives its principal backing from one part of Congress—a committee or subcommittee with authority to oversee the agency's operations—rather than from Congress as a whole. Rare indeed is the agency with anything close to universal support in Congress, though it does happen—witness the long-term high status of the Federal Bureau of Investigation (FBI) under the directorship of J. Edgar Hoover, to the point that many inside and outside Washington felt that Hoover had more effective influence in Congress than did his nominal superior in the Justice Department, the attorney general. But that is an exceptional case; most agencies are faced with the task of continually generating and holding support from committees, subcommittees, and even individual members of Congress. They attempt to do this in a number of ways. Among them are responding promptly to requests for information; effectively promoting and managing programs in which legislators are known to have an interest; cooperating administratively with legislators' political needs; and anticipating legislative preferences regarding the operations of particular programs.

A second source of political support is the executive branch, meaning both presidential support and that of other administrators and agencies lodged formally in the executive hierarchy. Presidential influence can be decisive in determining success or failure, and an agency will do what it can to win presidential favor in both the short and long run. An important corollary of presidential backing is favorable reviews of agency budget requests by the Office of Management and Budget (OMB), which molds the executive branch budget proposals submitted to Congress each year. OMB does not itself allocate funds to the agencies, but its support means that an agency can concentrate on persuading Congress—which does hold the purse strings—to back its programs financially, without having to expend a great deal of time, personnel, or political resources on first convincing

OMB of their worth. The best position for an agency to be in is one where its programmatic responsibilities occupy a high-priority place on presidential policy agendas year in and year out (the FBI fit this description for close to fifty years), but as suggested earlier, few agencies achieve this kind of enviable support. Far more common is a pattern of agencies and their programs having to compete for presidential favor and having to settle for a "win some, lose some" record. Presidential support for an agency can be earned, among other ways, by giving stronger *agency* support to programs the agency itself administers that are consistent with the president's policy priorities; by sharing (at least on the surface) presidential concerns about *how* programs are managed (as numerous agencies did by emphasizing greater managerial efficiency during the Carter administration); and by avoiding public conflict with the president over policy and program priorities.

Another means of acquiring executive branch support is by allying with another agency or agencies in quest of common objectives. Such interagency alliances tend to be limited in scope and duration. Since most agencies are very protective of their program jurisdictions (for reasons we shall soon consider more fully), and since there is an element of risk in that a cooperating agency might also be a potential rival, most agencies enter rather carefully into alliances with others, even though they may share limited objectives. An example of such bureaucratic alliance is the periodic joining of forces by the Army, the Navy, and the Air Force in support of defense appropriations, even as each is contending with the others for a share of the fiscal pie. But these are occasional alliances, brought about by specific and passing needs, which usually do not outweigh more enduring differences among agencies. In sum, although cooperation with other agencies may indeed be a means of acquiring support, it has its limitations. The agencies with which cooperation would be most logical in terms of programmatic interest are the very ones with the greatest potential for conflict over jurisdictional responsibilities.

A third major source of support, which is carefully cultivated, is constituent or clientele groups that look to the agency for satisfaction of their policy demands. Such groups come under the heading of *interest groups*, as that term is commonly used, and represent an organized expression of political opinion by a portion (usually a small portion) of the general adult population.[10] They tend to be groups affected directly by the agency's operations, and therefore they have a tangible stake in its programmatic output and impact. The political relationship which usually develops between an agency and such a group is one of reciprocity, where each has some political commodity from which the other can benefit. The agency's greatest strength is its expertise and the control it exercises over particular government programs that are of interest to the group. The group in turn has political resources that it makes available to the agency in return for agency attention to its needs and desires. The group may provide channels of communication to other influential individuals and groups in the political process, help the agency sell its program to Congress and the president, or aid the agency in anticipating changes in the political environment that would present problems or provide opportunities. Examples of such agency-clientele group relationships include, among many others, the Pentagon and defense contractors, various entities in the Department of Agriculture and the tobacco industry, the Maritime Administration and the shipping industry, state commerce commissions and private business associations, and both state and national Departments of Labor and the labor movement.

Administrative agencies often have more than one constituent group, creating both advantages and disadvantages. A principal advantage is that with multiple sources of support, an agency can operate more effectively in the political process without having to rely too heavily on any one source of assistance. A corresponding disadvantage stems from the fact that various clientele groups often have differing sets of interests, which move them to demand different things from an agency or to demand the same things but not in the same order of priority. Not infrequently, an agency faces a situation where satisfying one preference or set of preferences will inhibit or prevent its satisfying other preferences.

An agency must also deal with Congress or a specific committee as though it were a clientele group, with demands and expectations that must be satisfied. An agency is well advised to consider congressional clientele groups as being among its most important, especially when confronted with conflicting sets of demands. It is unwise, in other words, to regularly disregard demands coming from Congress, even if this means making other (private) clientele groups unhappy with a given decision. As we shall see later in this chapter, however, agencies have some means at their disposal to avoid being caught, most of the time, in a squeeze between their congressional and private clientele groups.

In state politics, agencies are frequently tied even more closely to private interest groups. Where the governor has somewhat limited formal powers or informal influence, or where the state legislature is relatively passive or weak, support from interest groups is often the greatest source of strength for an administrative agency, and sometimes the only source. Even where the governor and the legislature are strong (as in New York, California, Illinois, and Michigan), the support of key interest groups can benefit an agency significantly. For example, the Illinois Agricultural Association (the state component of the American Farm Bureau Federation) is a vital source of political strength for the state Department of Agriculture, and in California, farm organizations help sustain both the Department of Agriculture and the Department of Water Resources. In return, of course, the agencies are expected to advocate and defend the interests of their supporters (for example, water for California's farmers), and these relationships often become at least semipermanent.

One other aspect of agency-clientele relationships is quite important. As noted earlier, administrative organizations cherish their control over particular government programs and try to maintain effective direction of them. Sometimes, however, an agency may have to yield some control over its programs to outside influences—legislators, a private clientele group, or some other group—in return for continuing political support. If this yielding of control is temporary, an agency loses little and may gain a great deal in the long run. If, however, the yielding of control proves to be permanent, the agency is said to have undergone *cooptation*, a process whereby a set of outside interests acquires the ability to influence the agency's long-term policies. Cooptation can mean that *all* of the agency's substantive policies are subject to influence, not just those of most direct concern to the outside group or groups.

Numerous examples of cooptation may be cited. One of the best-known academic studies of this process is sociologist Philip Selznick's *TVA and the Grass Roots*,[11] which asserts that the Tennessee Valley Authority allowed the making of its agricultural development policies to be taken over by a coalition of entrenched, politically conservative interest groups already dominant in agricultural politics in the TVA region.[12] Another example concerns the relationship that developed between some urban community-action groups and municipal administrations—"city hall"—in the late 1960s.[13] City government leaders occasionally succeeded in coopting a group's leadership by giving them some of what they wanted, plus greater political visibility, in exchange for moderating other demands. This occurred especially in communities with well-entrenched local political organizations, such as Chicago, where community-action groups chose to settle for "half a loaf" rather than risk forfeiting all chance to have some impact on the way decisions were made and resources allocated in the city government system. As these examples demonstrate, cooptation can work both ways. TVA illustrates a government agency's being coopted by stronger nongovernmental groups, while the fate of the community-action groups shows how powerful government structures are capable of coopting nongovernmental groups. Either way, cooptation involves a surrender by a weaker entity to a stronger one of some power to shape the course of the weaker entity's long-term activities.

A fourth source of political support for an administrative agency is the general public. The potential weight of the unorganized public is great; if mobilized and concentrated on a particular issue, public opinion can tilt the political balance of power decisively. The problem for any political actor is to mobilize the public successfully—no easy task. Most Americans ordinarily pay scant attention to public issues until and unless the issues develop considerable salience or controversy.[14]

Yet the public's attention can be directed and its feelings made manifest with regard to a pending major policy decision. The public can, in some instances, force a decision to be made—for example, the withdrawal of American troops from Vietnam (see Figure 3-1), government decisions to

Figure 3-1 Support for and Opposition to American Involvement in Vietnam

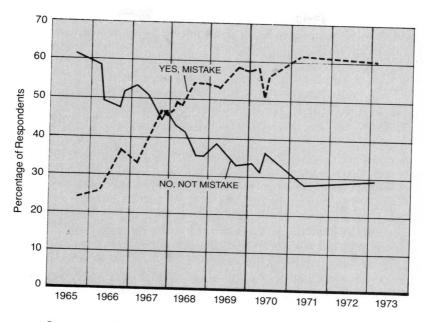

Question: "In view of the developments since we entered Vietnam, do you think the U.S. made a mistake in sending troops to fight in Vietnam?"

Source: Gallup Poll as reported in John E. Mueller, "Trends in Popular Support for the Wars in Korea and Vietnam," American Political Science Review, 65 (1971), and Gallup Opinion Index (March 1971, and February 1973).

mount a far more concerted effort than previously to combat environmental pollution, the multitude of reforms in the wake of Watergate, and reducing government spending. Without broad public demand and backing, these policy directions, which represented significant changes from earlier policies, could not have been proposed or sustained through the political process. The general public, in short, can provide a valuable political foundation to strengthen the hand of those in government who feel that a given policy should be adopted or scrapped. As numerous studies of public opinion have suggested, when the general public has strong feelings on a matter of importance to large numbers of people, the governmental response is usually not inconsistent with those feelings.[15] An agency supported by broad public opinion can generate political support for itself and its programs if it takes advantage of the opportunity.

An agency's overall task, in political terms, can best be understood as maintaining control of its programmatic responsibilities while simultaneously maintaining adequate support for its operations, without making any of its clientele groups overly unhappy with the way it is performing its functions. This is far from easy, and it is the exception rather than the rule when an agency succeeds on all fronts. More frequent is the pattern of agency adaptation and accommodation to particularly strong interests, from which political backing can be obtained in sufficient quantity to outweigh any costs incurred, in terms of diminished program control or dissatisfaction among weaker clientele groups.

FOUNDATIONS OF POWER: BUREAUCRATIC EXPERTISE

The other major foundation of bureaucratic power is the substantive expertise an agency can bring to bear on programs for which it is responsible. As society has become more complex and interdependent and technological advances have followed one another with astounding speed, people with know-how—the experts—have acquired increasing influence because of their specialized knowledge. Government is obviously subject to the same forces (particularly of technological change) as the rest of society, with the result that government experts now play a large and central role in numerous public policy decisions.

Political scientist Francis Rourke has suggested that the influence of experts rests on five major components.[16] The five principal components are (1) full-time attention by experts to a problem or subject-matter area, giving rise to both demand and opportunity for professionalism in public service; (2) specialization in the subject; (3) a monopoly on information in the subject area, which, if successfully maintained by only one staff of experts, makes them indispensable in any decision making involving ''their'' subject; (4) a pattern of increasing reliance on bureaucratic experts for technical advice; and (5) increasing control by experts of bureaucratic discretion.

The last three of these components deserve discussion. While a monopoly of information is desirable from a particular agency's point of view, it is rarely achieved in everyday practice. This is partly because no agency controls all governmental sources of information on any given subject, partly because government itself does not control all information sources in society, and partly because information—itself a source of power and influence—is the subject of intense interagency competition. Thus, where an expert staff has a monopoly on information relevant to making a given decision, its influence is greater. Conversely, influence can be more effectively contested where there is greater diversity of information sources.[17]

Reliance on expert advice, while on the increase, is not without limits; the influence of experts, therefore, is similarly constrained. Not every decision of an agency revolves around technical criteria or data. And even when an issue involves technical data, top-level administrators, for political or other reasons, may prefer a decision that is not the best according to technical criteria.[18] Thus expert advisers play a role in many agencies which, while important and influential, has its limitations.

There are two aspects worth noting about increasing control of bureaucratic discretion by experts. First, by exercising discretion, an expert maximizes the ability to decide just how vigorously or casually to implement public policies over which the agency has jurisdiction. Second, bureaucratic discretion enables agency experts to influence policy decisions by defining the decisional alternatives from which higher-level officials choose the course to be followed. To the extent that responsible policy makers permit bureaucratic experts to define available alternatives, they strengthen the experts' influence, through what the experts choose to include and not include among the alternatives they present.[19]

Experts possess one more resource that has been useful in presenting a positive public image—their ability to employ the language of their respective trades, speaking in terms and concepts unfamiliar to most of us. This use of specialized language (some might say, jargon) has become a common phenomenon among experts in and out of government, posing problems for the layman who seeks to understand complex developments and issues. By using jargon, bureaucratic experts make it very difficult for others to challenge them on their own territory, so to speak; if we cannot fathom what it is they have proposed, how can we argue against it? This resource, moreover, has been greatly enhanced by the fact that, in countless cases, proposals put forward by experts have yielded very positive and beneficial results. As Rourke has noted, this combination of obscurity of means and clarity of results has helped consolidate the position, prestige, and influence of experts in government agencies.[20]

In recent years, however, the obscurity of means that previously was a source of strength for experts has contributed to growing public disenchantment with ''big government,'' bureaucracy, and experts in general. With the increasing desire for broader public involvement in decision making (see chapter 2) has come greater unwillingness to take the experts' word for it, and a more insistent demand that experts make clear to the general public just what it is they are doing, proposing, and advocating. In the long run, public reactions and attitudes may have more effect on the influence and power of government experts than any characteristic or action of the experts themselves.

THE POLITICS OF ORGANIZATIONAL STRUCTURE

Another dimension of the political setting is the particular form of administrative organization. As noted in chapter 1, structural arrangements can have political implications for administrative agencies. Here we shall take a closer look at the political meaning of structural arrangements, using as an illustration the U.S. Department of Education (DOE), established in 1977 by the Carter administration.

Organizational form can signify a number of things. First, a particular structure demonstrates commitment to one set of policy objectives instead of another. It also can foreshadow adoption of a distinct policy *direction*, either in an individual policy area or in broader policy terms. The Carter decision to reorganize existing education agencies—bringing most of them into DOE from the Department of Health, Education and Welfare (HEW)—signaled an increased emphasis on dealing with broad educational problems and issues. Previous organizational arrangements seemed to suggest that education, while important, was *no more* important than matters of health or welfare policy. Also, as a practical matter, education concerns frequently had to compete with health and welfare issues for the attention of the Secretary of HEW and of other top political leaders.

Another example of organizational structure reflecting policy direction was President Nixon's reorganizing the Bureau of the Budget as the Office of Management and Budget (OMB) in 1970. That action reflected Nixon's intention to strengthen executive branch management processes, with OMB bearing primary responsibility for directing that effort. Stronger presidential management of national government programs had been one of Nixon's concerns in the 1968 presidential campaign, and this was organizational evidence that his concern had been genuine.

Second, a particular structure helps to order political priorities, promoting some programs over others. Jimmy Carter's merger of existing education agencies into the DOE changed both symbolism and reality in the administrative politics of education. As implied earlier, the relatively higher priority of education was highlighted by creation of a Cabinet department to deal with it; such a status carries with it increased prestige (not to mention visibility) that is very useful to an agency. Furthermore, that sort of political commitment from the chief executive, combined with more prominent organizational status, often leads to increased influence in the legislature.

Finally, a particular structure can provide greater access for some, and less for others, to key government decision makers. This perhaps is the most vivid lesson of the DOE. The campaign for its creation was led by the National Education Association (NEA), which represents hundreds of thousands of teachers across the country. Presidential candidate Jimmy Carter was known to be sympathetic to many of the NEA's policy positions, and pledged early in the 1976 campaign to create a new education department. In turn the NEA was one of Carter's staunchest supporters for the presidency. Obviously, creation of the department for which so many teachers had campaigned increased substantially the degree of access to educational policy makers enjoyed by the NEA in particular, and by teachers generally. The importance of access, generally, cannot be overestimated. NEA's strong negative reaction to Ronald Reagan's proposed elimination of DOE in 1981 testifies to that.

In this connection, we should recall comments made earlier about agency jurisdiction and how it relates to access and agency structure. Structure and jurisdiction are at least indirectly related, and while changes in jurisdiction may not necessarily be accompanied by a change in structure, any reformation of structure will almost inevitably mean some reallocation of program jurisdiction. Access and jurisdiction are also related. Clientele groups have meaningful access, at best, only to those administrators responsible for "their" programs. Changes in jurisdiction mean, at a minimum, that clienteles will need to reestablish lines of access, and such changes could well cause greater difficulties for these groups. Furthermore, clienteles normally much prefer to have all related programs clustered under one administrative roof, since that facilitates their having impact on the full range of programs. It is likely, also, that such an arrangement will be managed by administrators sympathetic to programs for which they are responsible, whereas scattering the same programs among different agencies and administrators may result in more hostile treatment of both programs and clienteles.

Our discussion has centered until now on the executive branch of the national government. However, these generalizations apply with equal force to other governments' executive branches, and to some other specific circumstances and issues in the politics of organization. Probably the clearest example that illustrates the same concepts in a different setting is the recurring struggle in cities and towns across the country over the form of local government structure to be adopted. This controversy has its roots in the late nineteenth and early twentieth centuries, when growing concentrations of European immigrants appeared in America's larger cities, as well as some smaller ones, accompanied by more—and more powerful—political-party organizations and their "bosses."

The effort to reform American municipal government, according to rhetoric of the time, was designed to bring about "economy and efficiency" in government, "to take the politics out of local government," and to promote government "in the interest of the whole community." Municipal reform usually involved (and still involves) one or more of the following structural arrangements: (1) the method of selecting the chief executive—whether to have a popularly elected mayor or a city manager chosen by and responsible to the city council; (2) the extent of the chief executive's powers, though this usually meant whether the mayor in particular was formally strong or weak;[21] (3) whether municipal elections were to have candidates selected by political parties or on a nonpartisan basis; and (4) whether members of the city council were to be selected to represent specific areas of the city (that is, by wards) or selected at-large.[22]

Political rhetoric aside, decisions about these fundamental arrangements carried with them major implications for the distribution of local political power. Citywide minorities, for example, had little chance of winning representation in at-large council elections, but a better chance in ward elections (provided ward boundaries were drawn up to reflect, rather than fragment, their population concentrations). Similarly, there were numerous instances where a chief executive elected under the strong-mayor form was almost certain to be more favorable to ethnic or minority concerns in local politics than one chosen under a weak-mayor or city-manager form, because ethnic voters constituted the political majority in many such cities.

Leading proponents of structural reform in the late 1800s were almost entirely middle class and above, while the most vocal opponents were lower middle class and below. Historian Melvin Holli has described the urban structural reform movement as ''built upon a narrow middle and patrician class base and a business concept of social responsibility,'' and characterized by ''zeal for efficiency and economy.'' The structural reformers also, according to Holli, ''blamed the immigrant for the city's shortcomings,'' and devoted considerable effort to ''exterminating lower-class vices, which they saw as the underlying causes of municipal problems.''[23] Given this socioeconomic polarization, it seems clear that respective group preferences for or against structural reform did not happen by mere chance, but arose out of perceived group self-interest.

In sum, there are gainers and losers in this facet of politics as in all others. Organizational arrangements in many different settings reflect ''values, conflicts, and competing forces. . . .''[24] They are, therefore, anything but neutral.

BUREAUCRATS AS POLITICIANS: SUBSYSTEM POLITICS IN AMERICA

We turn now to how bureaucrats manage their political alliances, with regular collaboration often leading to establishment of semipermanent ties. These political roles are relevant to agency efforts to secure needed political support from interested clientele groups and various committees, subcommittees, and individual members of Congress.

One place to begin is by considering certain important parallels between the national government bureaucracy and Congress. They have three features in common that are important in this context. First, within both institutions there is a well-established pattern of division of labor, that is, dividing the work to be done among numerous smaller, specialized units. In Congress this means the committees and subcommittees of each chamber; in the bureaucracy it refers to the multitude of bureaus, staffs, branches, and divisions that comprise larger executive agencies. Second, the divisions within both Congress and the bureaucracy are organized primarily according to function, dealing with a general area of policy concern such as housing, education, or defense. Third, in both institutions the *specialized nature* of these smaller units is the principal source of their influence in the policy-making process.

It is a pervasive rule of Washington political life that, all other things being equal, larger institutions defer to (that is, respect and follow) the judgments of their smaller, more specialized units. This pattern of regularized deference to smaller units means that in the great majority of cases these units tend to be focal points of important decision making. In Congress, though action by the full House and Senate is required for enactment of legislation, the proposals reported out of committees usually form the core of bills that eventually reach passage. Amendment of committee proposals is possible, but the initial form of legislation carries some weight, and key committee and subcommittee members are often influential throughout the entire process of deliberation in the full chamber.[25] In the bureaucracy, specialized personnel (the experts described earlier) wield considerable influence in the formulation of proposals that make their way up the formal hierarchical ladder (and make their way to Congress as well), and in daily processes of program implementation.

In short, it is misleading to assume that influence is concentrated at the top of formal organizational structures in either Congress or the bureaucracy. The fine details of lawmaking, as well as of legislative oversight of administration, are the responsibility of subject-matter committees and subcommittees of Congress, each assigned jurisdiction over particular administrative agencies and their programs. Only infrequently do such matters engage the attention of the full House or Senate. Similarly, the ''nuts and bolts'' of administration normally are concentrated in the lower levels of organizations, not at, or even very near, the top. Thus, in the broad picture of policy making in Washington, there is a high degree of fragmentation, with many small centers of influence operating in their respective areas of expertise.

We have seen previously that bureaucratic expertise is a source of bureaucratic power. Members of Congress also seek to become specialized, for two reasons. First, they are encouraged to do so on the grounds that this is the best route to influence in Congress, and second, they quickly recognize that by becoming influential they can do more for their voters back home. For sound political reasons, most seek to join congressional committees that have jurisdiction over areas of public policy affecting their electoral constituencies. A representative from rural Kansas, for example, is likely to apply for membership on the House Agriculture Committee, hoping also to be on its subcomittee dealing with subsidies for wheat farmers, wheat export policies, and so on. A representative from a black and poor section of a large city would be likely to seek assignment to the Banking, Finance, and Urban Affairs Committee or perhaps to the Education and Labor Committee—bodies that deal directly with problems of urban constituents. A senator from a state with a major coastal or inland port or a rail transportation center would cherish a position on the Interstate and Foreign Commerce Committee. And so it goes, all through Congress.

Members of Congress do not always get their first choice of assignment, obviously. But in pursuit of their own electoral fortunes and policy objectives, legislators are attracted to those committees in which they can have the most impact in policy areas of interest to them personally, and where they can maximize their political influence in support of constituency interests that could be decisive in their reelection bids.[26] This leads naturally to their having increasing contact with others interested in the same policy areas: administrators in agencies with jurisdiction over relevant programs; interest groups that, even more than legislators or bureaucrats, have specialized interests as the focal point of their existence and activities; and other members of Congess with an interest in the same area(s) of public policy.

What results from this complex of shared specialized interests, or what we might call *specialization in common*, is the potential for pooling political resources by individuals and small groups in different parts of the policy-making process in order to achieve common purposes. Hundreds of quiet, informal alliances have grown up in this manner,[27] with the term "policy subsystem"—or simply, "subsystem"—being used to describe them.

What is a *subsystem?* In general usage, the term refers to "a structure dependent upon a larger political entity but one that functions with a high degree of autonomy."[28] We define it here as any political alliance uniting some members of an administrative agency, a congressional committee or subcommittee, and an interest group with shared values and preferences in the same substantive area of public policy making. Subsystems are informal alliances or coalitions that link individuals in different parts of the formal policy structure. Their members usually have some influence in the policy-making process, due in part to their formal or official positions—bureau chief, committee or subcommittee chairman, or member. The essential strength of a subsystem, however, is its ability to combine the benefits of bureaucratic expertise, congressional leverage, and interest group capabilities in organizing and communicating the opinions of those most concerned with a particular public issue. All subsystems have that potential; some, of course, are far more powerful than others.

One example of a very influential subsystem is the so-called military-industrial complex, composed of civilian and military personnel in the Pentagon, key members of the House and Senate Armed Services Committees and each chamber's Appropriations subcommittee on armed services, and major government contractors for military hardware. The presence in this subsystem of large industries supplying military equipment significantly expands the number of affiliated legislators. By being located in New York state, for example, Grumman Aircraft can influence the votes of New York's congressional delegation, especially its two senators and the representatives from the congressional districts in which Grumman's plants are located; so also with Boeing in Washington state, McDonnell-Douglas in Missouri, and Lockheed in Georgia. Thus, members of key congressional committees are not the only legislators who might belong to a subsystem; others may also belong due to their constituency interests.

Another good example of a subsystem is the "highway lobby." Members of the House Public Works and Transportation Committee (among others), officials of the Bureau of Public Roads, and powerful interest groups such as auto manufacturers, auto workers' unions, tire companies and their unions, road contractors and their unions, and oil companies and their unions (plus members of Congress from their states) have a common interest in maintaining and expanding highway usage. States represented include, among others, Michigan, Missouri, California, Texas, and Oklahoma; some key legislators come from those states. Little wonder that Congress has given ground so reluctantly on expansion of mass transit funding, or that it has defended using the Highway Trust Fund to pay only for new roads.

Still another example is the tobacco subsystem, which for years resisted all efforts to limit or regulate the sale of cigarettes and other tobacco products. They were successful mainly because tobacco is largely a southern crop, and congressional committee chairmen (including, notably, the chairman of the House Agriculture Committee) tended to be disproportionately from the South because of the seniority system. Supporting them were bureaucrats in the Agriculture and Commerce Departments. It was politically risky, if not foolish, for a member of Congress to challenge the united front of southern committee chairmen in what was, until the mid-1960s, a losing fight against tobacco. Significantly, when the Congress-based tobacco subsystem *was* successfully challenged, it was by another subsystem with its principal strength elsewhere—in the U.S. Public Health Service and the Federal Trade Commission.[29]

Subsystem activity tends to remain behind the scenes. Policy decisions are reached in a spirit of friendly, quiet cooperation among various interested and influential people; many of their decisions turn out to be the key ones. Bureaucrats derive considerable benefit from this arrangement because they can usually count on adequate political support from both within government (Congress) and without (interest groups). The three-sided relationship allows any one component of the subsystem to activate their joint effort toward common objectives with the full cooperation of the others. Unless challenged from outside—by other subsystems, adverse publicity, or perhaps the president—a subsystem may well be able largely to dominate a policy-making area. Admittedly, even a strong subsystem cannot ignore the possibility of rivals emerging. For example, in the controversy during the 1960s over requiring a health warning on cigarette packages, the powerful tobacco lobby lost out; similarly, automobile-exhaust-emission controls were imposed over the objections of auto manufacturers. Under routine circumstances, however, subsystems—including their administrative participants—can enjoy decisive influence in the policy-making process. Indeed, in the examples just cited the two subsystems have succeeded in diluting the impact of seemingly adverse policy decisions, by weakening enforcement or lobbying successfully for other, more favorable legislation.

The influence of similar alliances is often less extensive in state and local policy making than in national politics. There are several reasons for this. First, in many state legislatures individual committees do not have the same kind of independent standing or jurisdictional control over policy areas that congressional committees possess. Policy making is more centralized in the hands of legislative leaders, making less productive any interest group relationship with an individual committee. Second, in many states and localities the policy-making process is dominated by less diverse groups than is the case nationally, and as a consequence the process lacks the intense competitiveness over access and influence characteristic of Washington politics. The necessity to develop close working relations with an individual committee or agency is therefore not as great. Third, especially in local government, the policy process is much more informal than at the national level. For many interest groups, particularly stronger ones, there is fairly regular opportunity for consultation on policy preferences, and their influence is often felt throughout local government, not in just one part of it. Thus, though some elements of subsystem politics also can be found in state and local governments, the general patterns identifiable in the national policy process do not operate to the same extent elsewhere.

"Issue Networks" and Subsystems: Similarities and Differences

Subsystem politics has been the subject of informed discussion since the late 1950s. Within the past decade, however, several observers have taken note of another pattern of interaction developing in the policy process. This is the phenomenon of so-called "issue networks" which, like subsystems, involve a variety of political actors attempting jointly to influence the course of public policy.[30] Unlike subsystems, however, issue networks are more open and fluid groupings of individuals, in and out of government. In political scientist Hugh Heclo's words, an issue network is "a *shared-knowledge* group having to do with some aspect [or problem] of public policy"[31]—but without the degree of permanence characteristic of subsystem alliances. Such a network may exist only when a policy question emerges that activates a wide range of interests; members of the "network" may not deal with one another regularly, outside of their network contacts; and, significantly, they may not agree on the nature of the policy problem, or possible solutions to it. In all these respects, issue networks differ from subsystems.

Examples of issue networks include the various groups and public officials involved in health policy (insurance companies, medical associations, hospitals and hospital organizations, U.S. Public Health Service personnel, and nutrition specialists, among others); and energy policy (oil companies, consumer groups, Department of Energy program managers, the nuclear power industry, tax reformers, and civil rights groups interested in more jobs—again, among others).[32] In these examples, the participants did not reach even general agreement on policy directions merely by activating the network. Rather, once a policy question was perceived as affecting a broad range of interests, groups and individuals advocating those interests jumped into the fray over policy development, thus *creating* the network as part of addressing the policy issues at hand. (This was especially true of energy policy under Jimmy Carter. Small wonder that energy policy was not clearly defined under such circumstances.)

The foundation of shared knowledge that unites network participants often does not lead to creation of a "shared-action" *coalition*, or of a "shared-belief" (conventional interest) group.[33] Such networks function with relative autonomy, like subsystems, but "rarely in any controlled, well-organized way"[34] (or even with agreement on policy content among the principals involved)—very much *un*like subsystems. Thus, issue networks contribute further to the fragmentation present in national policy making, and in somewhat new ways.

BUREAUCRATIC POWER AND POLITICAL ACCOUNTABILITY: MORE QUESTIONS THAN ANSWERS

Having discussed the political context of bureaucratic power, key sources of that power, and the informal alliances through which much of that power is exercised, let us now consider to what extent bureaucracy is or can be made accountable for what it does or fails to do. It was suggested in chapter 2 that political accountability of the bureaucracy is enforced through multiple channels, both legislative and executive. As we have seen, political interests in the legislature and in the executive branch are frequently in conflict with one another, making it difficult to enforce accountability with consistency or effectiveness. The question is made more complex by the fact that most bureaucracies operate under authority delegated by both the chief executive and the legislative branch, and with considerable discretion to make independent choices. The difficulty is further compounded by the hybrid systems of personnel management found in different parts of the executive hierarchy in the national government and in many states and localities. Frequently, top-echelon executives owe their positions to appointment through political channels, but the bulk of their subordinates are hired and usually retained through job-competence-related merit procedures, which some say have produced more job security for public employees than is healthy for the public service. In state and local government the mix of "political" and "merit" employees in a bureaucracy varies widely, and the presence of public employee unions raises other issues of bureaucratic accountability.

Another factor, referred to earlier, is the inability of top executives to command absolute responsiveness to their leadership from administrative subordinates. A substantial portion of the work of top executives is devoted to overseeing and monitoring activities of their underlings in an effort to bring about as much congruence as possible between executive directives and work actually done.[35] However, the president in particular operates under severe handicaps in this effort. Due to restraints on his time, the necessity of concentrating on a limited number of general policy priorities, and the complexity of administrative operations, a considerable proportion of bureaucratic activity escapes critical examination by the White House. Furthermore, as noted by journalist David Broder, subsystems represent "powerful centrifugal forces" in the nation's capital. He writes: "The interest groups that benefit from specific programs, the agency bureaucracies that run those programs and the congressional subcommittee members and staffs who create, finance, and oversee those programs are *tenaciously resistant to directives from the president.*"[36] Thus, the task of holding bureaucracy accountable for what it does assumes formidable proportions.

The term *accountability* itself poses some problems. It can mean different things to different people. At a minimum, it suggests that bureaucracy, or any governmental entity, functions as part of a larger political system, not independent of it, and as a result must be subject to some controls that cause it to give a general accounting of and for its actions. The most it might mean is that there should be an accounting of each and every action taken by an administrator, with authoritative approval given or withheld, and adjustments in future behavior made accordingly. The latter, as an ideal type, seems to be what some mean by accountability, but, as a practical matter, how much accountability we can realistically expect and strive for is far from a settled question.

Accountability implies several things. First, it implies that a political entity (in this case, the bureaucracy) is not beyond control of other entities in a checks-and-balances system or, ultimately, beyond reach of the consent of the governed. Also, it implies that to the extent such an entity exercises delegated authority and discretion in decision making, as our bureaucracy certainly does, it also has some responsibility to adhere to the broad will of the governed, however that will has been expressed. This also assumes it is possible to define the public will,[37] and to define the point at which accountability has been achieved and maintained. While in theory it may be possible to define these concepts and circumstances, in practice it is difficult to do so with certainty or finality. One approach is to interpret election results as representing the will of the majority, and to define bureaucratic accountability as accountability to the chief executive (president, governor, mayor), who is dominant in setting policy directions and standards by which subsequent administrative behavior will be judged. Opponents of a given chief executive or of executive power in general would resist such definition, however, looking instead to legislatures and sometimes to the judiciary to lay out broad guidelines for measuring bureaucratic accountability. Political conflict over criteria of accountability ensures less than complete adherence to whatever standards one may have.

In sum, it is not simply a matter of bureaucracy being or not being "accountable." Rather, bureaucracy and all other institutions of government can only be accountable *to* officials or institutions outside themselves. Furthermore, the question of accountable *for what* must also be answered in meaningful ways (see chapter 13 for a discussion of program evaluation). Also, "the bureaucracy" cannot be viewed whole; its many subparts have institutional bases, lives, and priorities of their own. All these factors act as constraints on the political accountability of bureaucratic power.

Is it impossible, then, to speak in practical terms of accountability? No, it is not. Allowing for limitations such as those just outlined, it is possible not only to prescribe in theory but to describe in fact some forms and aspects of accountability that characterize political relationships between bureaucracy and other parts of the American polity—though these too have their limitations.

First, both the president and Congress have some instruments of control at their disposal (governors, local executives, and state and local legislatures generally have less extensive powers over their bureaucracies). The president's arsenal includes (1) powers of appointment and dismissal that, although restricted to the very top positions, give him the ability to staff key leadership posts in the executive branch; (2) considerable initiative in lawmaking, which helps shape the legislative environment surrounding bureaucratic implementation of congressional enactments (this includes congressional delegation of authority to the president to formulate rules and regulations under which the bureaucracy functions); (3) the Executive Office of the President (EOP), through which the president can make known his preferences and intentions to the bureaucracy, directly and indirectly; (4) specific entities of EOP, notably the White House Office and the Office of Management and Budget, which carry the full prestige of the presidency when they interact with the bureaucracy and, in the case of OMB, can exert financial leverage that can be persuasive; (5) access to the mass media, through which the president can generate favorable or unfavorable publicity; and (6) power to initiate bureaucratic restructuring, a course of action extremely unwelcome to most agencies,[38] though in the past it has been used sparingly. A shrewd president can make use of these instruments to bring about considerable responsiveness to his leadership, though the process requires a considerable expenditure of his political capital.

Congress also has some tools at its disposal with which to conduct legislative oversight of administration.[39] They include (1) appropriations power—the classic "power of the purse"—and the implied (sometimes real) threat that can represent to an agency's fiscal well-being; (2) power to conduct legislative postaudits of agency spending through the General Accounting Office (GAO) headed by the comptroller-general, which operates

under the direction of Congress; (3) hearings before congressional committees in which bureaucrats may have to answer very specifically for their
actions (most notably during budget hearings before appropriations committees and subcommittees); and (4) occasional devices such as senatorial
confirmation of presidential appointees and special investigating committees. These are not perfect instruments, but they do afford Congress many
opportunities to look into bureaucratic activities and to maintain a degree
of control over the administrative apparatus.

Bureaucrats and bureaucracies are also held to account by the clientele
groups they serve, perhaps more effectively than by either the president or
Congress. An administrative agency is politically obligated to its allies in a
subsystem, resulting in a pattern of mutually reinforcing accountability.
But this is a highly noncentralized arrangement; the fact that an agency is
held to account within its own subsystem is no guarantee that either the
agency or the subsystem is accountable in any meaningful way to anyone
outside of it. In fact, some observers believe that this form of accountability
is one of the least effective from the standpoint of the political system at
large.[40] They hold that this pattern of exercising power is self-perpetuating
to the point that political costs would be excessive for anyone, including the
president, who sought to lessen subsystem influence on policy making. In
this view, accountability to any but the most narrow constituencies is unlikely, thus fostering a growing alienation from the governmental process
on the part of all those not adequately represented through subsystem (or
issue network) politics. To the extent this view is accurate, it suggests a limited form of accountability based on previous political commitments, and
exercise of power through very narrow political channels.

Partly because of bureau-clientele ties, a number of recent studies
have questioned whether legislative oversight as presently conducted is
even minimally effective as a means of holding bureaucracies to account to
the political system at large. The core concern of those raising this possibility is that *changes within Congress itself* have produced a markedly reduced
capacity for congressional supervision of administrative activities. These
changes include an emphasis on wider participation by members of Congress in policy-making processes, a resultant dispersion of power within
Congress from its standing committees to much more numerous (and more
autonomous) subcommittees, and a tendency for members of Congress to
devote more of their time to constituent services in pursuit of their own reelection. There also has emerged a generalized pattern of behavior
whereby legislators regularly call upon administrative agencies (and their
clientele groups) to facilitate the rendering of services to the public. Formal
responsibility for legislative oversight also has passed to subcommittees
rather than full committees; but while more hearings have been held and
more pages filled with testimony, the net effect has been one of *less effective
oversight.* This is attributable to members of Congress simultaneously becoming (1) more dependent upon agencies and interest groups, as they call

on them for increased constituent service, and (2) less inclined to "challenge the existing relationships between agencies and interest groups," and thus "less likely to investigate agencies' implementation of policy unless that implementation flies in the face of these major interest groups."[41]

If congressional oversight through subcommittees is indeed less reliable now than in the past, bureaucratic autonomy may be greater than is ideally desirable. We might describe this pattern, and others like it, as a case of the "micro-institutions" (committees and subcommittees) within Congress being unable or unwilling to hold agencies to account for their actions. But it appears that Congress—as a "macro-institution"—also is rather limited in its oversight capabilities. This is principally because legislators often lack incentive to use available oversight instruments (and frequently have incentive *not* to use them), and because the instruments themselves have proved to be fairly "weak reeds" of congressional control.

In June 1983 Congress lost one oversight instrument it had employed, on occasion, for over fifty years—the legislative veto—when the Supreme Court declared it unconstitutional in a 7-2 ruling.[42] This veto, included in more than 200 statutes enacted since 1932, "require[d] the executive branch (1) to inform Congress or committees within Congress of the actions that the executive branch plan[ned] to take in implementing that law or portions of it; and (2) to receive from Congress explicit or implicit approval of the actions before actually carrying them out."[43] Within a fixed time period, usually sixty to ninety days, one or both chambers of Congress had the option to vote down, by simple majority, a proposed administrative action; after World War II, congressional committees also exercised that option. But the veto was increasingly criticized, mainly on the grounds that it unconstitutionally intruded on the president's authority to direct executive branch agencies. This belief persisted in spite of growing feeling on Capitol Hill (and elsewhere) that the legislative veto was an effective means of controlling allegedly burdensome government regulations issued by administrative agencies (see chapter 14). After the high Court's ruling, Congress began "exploring new ways of reining in executive branch . . . discretion."[44] But in the next year, Congress also enacted thirty provisions *allowing* legislative vetoes of agency decisions (most called for committee review of proposed agency actions).[45] Congressional efforts in this regard thus have been somewhat mixed since the veto was struck down, but congressional interest in controlling the exercise of administrative discretion is still very much in evidence.

In sum, though there may be telling weaknesses in legislative oversight of government bureaucracies, they are not beyond remedy, and there may be alternative means of supervising administrative agencies. (In chapter 15, we will discuss some other instruments of accountability which facilitate *public* scrutiny of bureaucratic actions.) This discussion highlights one aspect of the situation that merits explicit emphasis: if we are not content with administrative agencies' behavior, we might do well to pressure Congress to make the desired changes. As political scientist Morris Fiorina notes, "United States congressmen gave us the Washington establishment. Ultimately, only they can take it away."[46]

Some other mechanisms of accountability also exist. Bureaucracies are legally accountable to the courts for their observance of individual rights and liberties, whether in their investigative capacities (particularly pertinent in the case of regulatory agencies) or in the course of routine activities. In this respect they differ hardly at all from the president and Congress, in that the courts have the ultimate say in defining acceptable legal boundaries of governmental behavior. It is symptomatic of the growth in the bureaucracy and in its impact on our national life that the most rapidly expanding area of court litigation has been in administrative law—cases arising out of administrative rules and regulations and their application to individuals, groups, and public and private enterprises.

The courts have taken on a more activist role in recent years, not only maintaining traditional guarantees, but also, in some instances, taking over supervision of administrative entities.[47] In the words of one observer: "Judicial review has passed from matters of procedure to matters of both procedure and substance. . . . Courts have not merely sat in judgment on administrative action but on inaction as well; they have required agencies to do things the agencies themselves had declined to do."[48] Three examples illustrate this trend.[49] One is the case of U.S. District Court Judge Frank Johnson, who took over supervision of Alabama state prisons, mental hospitals, highway patrol, and other institutions in order to remedy violations of constitutional rights of prisoners, mental patients, and other citizens that had occurred as part of routine administrative processes under Alabama's jurisdiction. Another example is a judge presiding in a class-action suit, who "not only appointed expert witnesses, suggested areas of inquiry, and took over from the parties a substantial degree of the management of the case, but also went so far as to order that $250,000 from an award required of the defendants be paid for social science research on the effectiveness of the decree."[50] Still another example is the U.S. District Court judge who ordered New York City to close an ancient and badly overcrowded city jail known as the Tombs, and to transfer the prisoners held there to a facility on Riker's Island. Whether such activism on the part of the courts is desirable from all standpoints has been questioned.

Bureaucratic agencies are also held to account by competing interest groups, the mass media, and the major political parties. Interest groups competing with agencies for political advantage, either individually or as part of rival subsystems, seek to monitor actions of bureaus and bureaucrats for reasons of self-interest, but in doing so they make it harder (but by no means impossible) for activities and programs to be conducted out of public view. The news media's interest in bureaucratic activity is founded on a powerful ethic of American journalism: that the press, acting in an adversary relationship to public officials, serves as a watchdog over what the government does. In particular, the investigatory potential of the news media makes bureaucracies wary. Part of an agency's political strength is good public relations, and adverse publicity resulting from a media investigation—even if unwarranted and even if successfully counteracted—can damage an agency's political standing. Thus the mere possibility of such an inquiry is enough to prompt most agencies to exercise some caution.

As in the case of bureaucracy-legislature interactions, relationships between administrators and press personnel are often two-sided. This creates the possibility that the press, far from maintaining a critical and objective perspective on administrators, may become involved in continuing relationships, the principal product of which is an ability to publicize agency programs. Under such circumstances, it is still possible for a reporter, editor, or even publisher to investigate or critique agency performance. But if an agency official continually provides good copy for a reporter and also provides inside tips or leads on stories that the reporter can take credit for "breaking," it is less likely that an agency will be subjected to the feared "spotlight of publicity." This is politics on an intensely interpersonal level, but it can matter a great deal in determining how much information, and of what kinds, will come to public attention about a given agency.[51]

As for political parties, their organizational interest in winning elections overlaps numerous policy areas and brings them into contact with agencies responsible for administering those areas. Since agency actions can have a direct impact on the interests of the parties' various constituent groups, party officials have their own stake in trying to secure policies favorable to those groups. The impact of party leaders seems to be greater at state and local levels than at the national level, partly because state and local bureaucratic decision making is often more openly politicized and thus more susceptible to frankly partisan pressures, and partly because state and local party organizations are stronger than national party committees. Thus, while political parties are not a major constraint on bureaucratic activity or a key means of insuring accountability, they do play their part.

Finally, there is some measure of bureaucratic accountability to the public. Although the general populace rarely has direct access to, or control over, a given bureaucratic entity, a widespread public outcry over bureaucrats' actions can have an effect. This ordinarily requires public pressure on other organs of government to get them to tighten the reins on an agency. Such pressure must be sustained over a sufficient period and with sufficient intensity to overcome political resistance from the agency and its supporters, but it can be done.

Administrative Discretion and Political Accountability: An Alternative Perspective

In discussions of how we might hold bureaucrats and their agencies accountable, there often is an implicit assumption made that accountability is needed in order to keep these officials "in line"—that their natural tendency is to "go astray" unless they are closely watched. There is no question, of course, that in our political system of checks and balances, every government entity *ultimately* must be held to account. In recent decades, however, that principle—as applied to administrative agencies—seems to have acquired an additional dimension that is not necessarily accurate. Many people seem to assume (wrongly) that administrative discretion can only be abused, at the expense of the public interest, and can serve no useful or constructive purpose. Many also bemoan the fact that neither Congress nor the president is able to control administrative actions fully or effectively—as if to say that elected officials can act *only* beneficially, while administrators can be expected to act *only* in narrowly focused, inefficient, destructive, and otherwise irresponsible fashion (recall Charles Goodsell's remarks about perceived bureaucratic shortcomings, compared to the realities, quoted in chapter 1). Yet there is reason to wonder if this view of discretion is valid.

For one thing, administrative discretion was an important (though often overlooked) element in the thinking and writing of administrative reformers of a century ago. Woodrow Wilson, one of the foremost reformers, argued in his classic essay "The Study of Administration" (1887) that administrators should be granted "large powers and unhampered discretion"—both "administrative energy and administrative discretion"[52]—as essential elements of their functioning in accordance with the notion of "political" neutrality. His expectation was that given the opportunity, administrators would exercise competent professional judgment as they carried out their assigned duties. This would serve the public interest (because sound public policy would result) and in turn the political interests of elected officials, of either political party (who could then take the credit for effective governance). In sum, he saw discretion as necessary for administrative *effectiveness* as well as neutrality.

Furthermore, one contemporary observer has suggested that administrative discretion has a very positive side to it, in that administrators frequently are *better* situated than are legislators to make decisions on the basis of the broader public interest[53]—and (according to this view) most administrators do so, most of the time. For Congress to interfere with that pattern of activity, by imposing various restraints and controls, actually brings about the kind of narrow responsiveness to private interests such controls seem designed to prevent. There are two reasons for this: (1) very often, "[i]nterest groups usurp public power *through congressional committees*,"[54] exercising considerable influence through both subsystems and issue networks; and (2) as noted previously, legislators are strongly inclined to look after their own policy priorities and constituency interests, and in the process *they pressure administrators* to conform to their wishes. Thus it is possible that if oversight of administration is left to legislators acting primarily in their *committee* roles, actions taken by administrators may be more narrowly conceived and implemented than would be the case if those same administrators were left to their own devices to a greater degree. (A similar result could be achieved if more oversight responsibilities rested with Congress as a whole, as opposed to committee oversight.[55])

This is not, by any means, a call for complete autonomy for administrators. There is ample reason to be as concerned about abuses of power, or fraud, or corruption among public administrators as among any other government officials. It *is* to say, however, that we might do well to place greater implicit faith in administrators than we now do, if we want them to *be able* to act responsibly. In this view, it would still be possible to hold them ultimately accountable, consistent with our scheme of government and with public expectations for accountability—and at least as effectively as we do at the present time.[56]

SUMMARY

Bureaucratic power is exercised in the context of widely dispersed political power. Neither the legislature nor the chief executive has a power base that is sufficiently unified to permit decisive control over the bureaucracy. Administrative agencies are keenly interested in building political power bases of their own, and they seek to acquire program jurisdictions that bring with them constituency support for their activities. Also, these agencies frequently are centers of political conflict and must seek to maintain themselves through adaptation to pressures that are placed on them. How well they succeed can be important in determining their long-term well-being.

Bureaucratic agencies have two major foundations of power: (1) adequate political support, and (2) expertise in the programs they administer. Sources of political support include key legislative committees and subcommittees, chief executives and their staffs, other executive agencies (especially those directly under the chief executive), clientele groups who follow agency affairs because of their own interest in the same program areas, and the general public, which can occasionally be mobilized on behalf of particular agency objectives. The political impact of bureaucratic expertise stems from full-time attention to a specialized subject matter area, a monopoly or near-monopoly on relevant information, a pattern of reliance on experts for technical advice, and experts' growing control of bureaucratic discretion. The experts' prestige has also helped consolidate the influence they wield in the government.

Organizational structure has political significance in a number of respects: (1) it demonstrates commitment, whether symbolic or substantive, to particular policy objectives; (2) it can signal adoption of specific policy directions; (3) it serves to order political priorities by emphasizing some programs over others; and (4) it can provide different degrees of access to decision makers—greater for some groups and interests than for others.

The DOE experience demonstrates the importance of organizational structure, including limitations on that importance. The politics of organization is also significant in settings other than executive branch arrangements. A leading example is recurring conflict over the form of local government structures, a political struggle that has gone on intermittently in many cities and towns since the late nineteenth century.

Subsystem politics in America is built around coalitions that bring together interest group representatives and government officials with a common interest and shared preferences in a policy area. A subsystem ordinarily includes a congressional committee or subcommittee member, a representative of an interest group, and a bureaucrat from the responsible administrative agency; more than one of each (and others as well) may be a part of the subsystem. Because both Congress and the bureaucracy generally divide work among subunits, whose expertise they respect, quiet, informal alliances of specialists (subsystems) often dominate their respective policy areas. Bureaucrats contribute expertise to their subsystems and receive in return an opportunity to share control of a policy area. Similar patterns of political collaboration exist in state and local politics, but usually not in precisely this form nor to the same extent. "Issue networks" also are different from subsystems, but add to the fragmentation in national policy making.

Promoting political accountability of bureaucratic power is not an easy task. Because the bureaucracy operates under delegated executive and legislative authority, tight controls from either are difficult to impose, and tight controls from both would be likely to conflict. "Accountability" suggests that bureaucracy is or should be answerable to other institutions and to the public for what it does, though this is difficult to put into practice because of the noncentralized nature of both government and bureaucracy. The president and Congress (and their state and local counterparts) each have methods of influencing bureaucratic behavior that, while somewhat effective, require continuing effort and vigilance. Bureaucracies also are accountable to their clientele groups, although it has been argued that this actually reduces accountability to the larger political system. In recent years, some have questioned whether Congress is still able to exercise meaningful oversight of administration, in terms of maintaining accountability to the political system at large. Other interest groups, the news media, and political party organizations—each for its own reasons—also seek to hold bureaucratic agencies accountable by monitoring agency activities. The news media, in particular, have the ability to uncover and publicize information adverse to agency political interests, though they do not always do so. In addition, bureaucratic agencies have some accountability to the courts, in that their actions are limited (and sometimes mandated) by legal guidelines laid down in judicial decisions. Finally, the general public can be mobilized either in support of or in opposition to actions taken in the administrative process. All these instruments of accountability have some impact on bureaucratic behavior, but none is perfect. It also is possible that more, not less, administrative discretion would serve the political system well, providing for pursuit of both the broader public interest and administrative accountability in an ultimate sense.

NOTES

1. An excellent summary of the saccharin controversy can be found in *Congressional Quarterly (CQ) Almanac*, vol. 33: 95th Congress, First Session, 1977 (Washington, D.C.: Congressional Quarterly, Inc., 1977), pp. 495–99; *CQ Almanac*, vol. 35: 96th Congress, First Session, 1979 (Washington, D.C.: Congressional Quarterly, Inc., 1979), pp. 534–35; *CQ Weekly Report*, 38 (June 14, 1980), 1648; *CQ Weekly Report*, 39 (June 20, 1981), 1091; *CQ Weekly Report*, 39 (September 19, 1981), 1791–93; *CQ Almanac*, vol. 39; 98th Congress, First Session, 1983 (Washington, D.C.: Congressional Quarterly, Inc., 1983), pp. 401–2; and *CQ Weekly Report*, 43 (May 18, 1985), 967.
2. See Allan W. Lerner and John Wanat, "Fuzziness and Bureaucracy," *Public Administration Review*, 43 (November/December 1983), 500–9.
3. Norton E. Long, "Power and Administration," *Public Administration Review*, 9 (Autumn 1949), 257–64, at p. 258.
4. Ibid., pp. 258–59.
5. Ibid., p. 259.
6. Lerner and Wanat, "Fuzziness and Bureaucracy," p. 502.
7. Long, "Power and Administration," p. 259.
8. Matthew Holden, " 'Imperialism' in Bureaucracy," *American Political Science Review*, 60 (December 1966), 943–51, at p. 951 (emphasis added).
9. See Richard E. Morgan, John C. Donovan, and Christian P. Potholm, *American Politics: Directions of Change, Dynamics of Choice* (Reading, Mass.: Addison-Wesley, 1979), pp. 10–11.
10. For an introduction to the theoretical roles and political activities of interest groups in American politics, see David B. Truman, *The Governmental Process* (New York: Knopf, 1951); V. O. Key, Jr., *Politics, Parties, and Pressure Groups*, 5th ed. (New York: Crowell, 1964), especially chapters 2 through 6; Lester W. Milbrath, *The Washington Lobbyists* (Chicago: Rand McNally, 1963; reprint ed., Westport, Conn.: Greenwood Press, 1976); L. Harmon Zeigler and G. Wayne Peak, *Interest Groups in American Society*, 2nd ed. (Englewood Cliffs, N.J.: Prentice-Hall, 1972); Allan J. Cigler and Burdett A. Loomis, *Interest Group Politics* (Washington, D.C.: CQ Press, 1983); and Jeffrey M. Berry, *The Interest Group Society* (Boston: Little, Brown, 1984).
11. Berkeley and Los Angeles: University of California Press, 1949.
12. Selznick's study concentrated, in the words of the subtitle, on the "sociology of formal organization." He has been criticized in at least one later study for ignoring considerations of politics. See O. Ruth McQuown, "From National Agency to Regional Institution: A Study of TVA in the Political Process" (unpublished Ph.D. dissertation, University of Florida, Gainesville, 1961).
13. See James L. Sundquist, with the collaboration of David W. Davis, *Making Federalism Work: A Study of Program Coordination at the Community Level* (Washington, D.C.: Brookings, 1969).
14. See, among others, V. O. Key, Jr., *Public Opinion and American Democracy* (New

York: Knopf, 1961); and Alan D. Monroe, *Public Opinion in America* (New York: Harper & Row, 1975).

15. See, for example, Warren Miller and Donald E. Stokes, "Constituency Influence in Congress," *American Political Science Review*, 57 (1963), 45–56; and Monroe, *Public Opinion in America*.

16. Francis E. Rourke, *Bureaucracy, Politics, and Public Policy*, 3rd ed. (Boston: Little, Brown, 1984).

17. See Anthony Downs, *Inside Bureaucracy* (Boston: Little, Brown, 1967), chapter 10, especially pp. 118–27; and Martin Landau, "Redundancy, Rationality, and the Problem of Duplication and Overlap," *Public Administration Review*, 29 (July/August 1969), 346–58.

18. See chapter 8 for elaboration of this point.

19. Graham Allison, in *Essence of Decision: Explaining the Cuban Missile Crisis* (Boston: Little, Brown, 1971), describes in detail John F. Kennedy's reliance on the Air Force and the Central Intelligence Agency (CIA) for intelligence information necessary in deciding how to respond to the presence of Soviet offensive missiles in Cuba in late 1962.

20. Rourke, *Bureaucracy, Politics, and Public Policy*, p. 94.

21. It is sometimes difficult to assess a mayor's strengths. For example, to judge strictly by a reading of *formal* powers, one of the weaker mayors among America's big-city chief executives was Richard J. Daley of Chicago—in reality one of the most powerful mayors for over twenty years—locally, in the state of Illinois, and nationally—until his death in late 1976.

22. Robert L. Lineberry and Ira Sharkansky, *Urban Politics and Public Policy*, 3rd ed. (New York: Harper & Row, 1978), pp. 161–66.

23. Melvin G. Holli, "Varieties of Urban Reform," in Alexander B. Callow, Jr., ed., *American Urban History*, 2nd ed. (New York: Oxford University Press, 1973), at pp. 253–54. The selection appeared originally in Holli's *Reform in Detroit: Hazen S. Pingree and Urban Politics* (New York: Oxford University Press, 1969).

24. Harold Seidman, *Politics, Position, and Power: The Dynamics of Federal Organization*, 3rd ed. (New York: Oxford University Press, 1980), p. 14.

25. The influence of committees and their members in the full chamber varies considerably, depending in large part on certain factors within the committees themselves. Richard Fenno describes and analyzes one powerful committee in "The House Appropriations Committee as a Political System: The Problem of Integration," *American Political Science Review*, 56 (June 1962), 310–24. An expanded study of the same committee is Fenno's *The Power of the Purse: Appropriations Politics in Congress* (Boston: Little, Brown, 1966). See also his *Congressmen in Committees* (Boston: Little, Brown, 1973).

26. Note that this implies *selective* attention to constituency interests, often focusing on objectives and preferences of influential friends and allies before—or at the expense of—objectives and preferences of others less powerful who live in the same constituency.

27. See Douglas Cater, *Power in Washington* (New York: Random House, 1964).

28. A. Lee Fritschler, *Smoking and Politics: Policy Making and the Federal Bureaucracy*, 3rd ed. (Englewood Cliffs, N.J.: Prentice-Hall, 1983), p. 6. The literature on subsystem politics, in addition to Fritschler's book, includes Ernest S. Griffith, *The Impasse of Democracy* (New York: Harrison-Hilton Books, 1939), and *Congress: Its Contemporary Role* (New York: New York University Press, 1961); Ar-

thur Maass, *Muddy Waters: The Army Engineers and the Nation's Rivers* (Cambridge: Harvard University Press, 1951); J. Leiper Freeman, *The Political Process* (New York: Random House, 1965); and Emmette S. Redford, "A Case Analysis of Congressional Activity: Civil Aviation, 1957–58," *The Journal of Politics*, 22 (May 1960), 228–58, and *Democracy in the Administrative State* (New York: Oxford University Press, 1969), especially chapter 4.

29. Fritschler, *Smoking and Politics*, is an excellent case study of subsystem politics involving the cigarette-health controversy.
30. See Hugh Heclo, "Issue Networks and the Executive Establishment," in Anthony King, ed., *The New American Political System* (Washington, D.C.: American Enterprise Institute for Public Policy Research, 1978), at pp. 102–5.
31. Ibid., p. 103.
32. Ibid., pp. 104–5. For a careful assessment of the congressional politics surrounding enactment of President Carter's National Energy Plan, see Michael J. Malbin, "Rhetoric and Leadership: A Look Backward at the Carter National Energy Plan," in Anthony King, ed., *Both Ends of the Avenue: The Presidency, the Executive Branch, and Congress in the 1980s* (Washington, D.C.: American Enterprise Institute for Public Policy Research, 1983), pp. 212–45.
33. Heclo, "Issue Networks and the Executive Establishment," p. 104.
34. Ibid.
35. See Herbert Kaufman, with the collaboration of Michael Couzens, *Administrative Feedback: Monitoring Subordinates' Behavior* (Washington, D.C.: Brookings, 1973).
36. Bloomington-Normal (Ill.) *Daily Pantagraph*, July 2, 1980, p. A-4 (emphasis added).
37. See Glendon Schubert, *The Public Interest* (Glencoe, Ill.: The Free Press, 1960).
38. See the comments earlier in this chapter regarding structure, jurisdiction, and clientele politics.
39. See, among others, Joseph P. Harris, *Congressional Control of Administration* (Washington, D.C.: Brookings, 1964), and Allen Schick, "Politics through Law: Congressional Limitations on Executive Discretion," in Anthony King, ed., *Both Ends of the Avenue: The Presidency, the Executive Branch, and Congress in the 1980s* (Washington, D.C.: American Enterprise Institute for Public Policy Research, 1983), pp. 154–84, especially pp. 170–79.
40. For an articulate statement of the view that interest groups and their allies dominate politics and policy making to the detriment of the larger political process, see Theodore J. Lowi, *The End of Liberalism: The Second Republic of the United States*, 2nd ed. (New York: Norton, 1979).
41. Lawrence C. Dodd and Richard L. Schott, *Congress and the Administrative State* (New York: Wiley, 1979), p. 183. This book (especially chapters 5 and 6) is one of the best studies of change within Congress and its relationship to changes in legislative oversight. In this regard, see also Morris P. Fiorina, *Congress: Keystone of the Washington Establishment* (New Haven: Yale University Press, 1977), especially chapters 5 and 7. More generally, see Morris S. Ogul, *Congress Oversees the Bureaucracy: Studies in Legislative Supervision* (Pittsburgh: University of Pittsburgh Press, 1977); Randall B. Ripley and Grace A. Franklin, *Congress, the Bureaucracy, and Public Policy*, 3rd ed. (Homewood, Ill.: Dorsey, 1984); Douglas Arnold, *Congress and the Bureaucracy* (New Haven: Yale University Press, 1980); and David Mayhew, *Congress: The Electoral Connection* (New Haven: Yale Univer-

sity Press, 1974). For a case study of legislative oversight, see John P. Bradley, "Shaping Administrative Policy with the Aid of Congressional Oversight: The Senate Finance Committee and Medicare," *Western Political Quarterly*, 33 (December 1980), 492–501. The development of both the constituent-service emphasis and internal congressional decentralization (and the attendant increase in congressional staff) are examined in Samuel C. Patterson, "The Semi-Sovereign Congress," in Anthony King, ed., *The New American Political System* (Washington, D.C.: American Enterprise Institute for Public Policy Research, 1978), pp. 125–77, especially pp. 149–53 and 160–67; Harrison W. Fox, Jr., and Susan Webb Hammond, *Congressional Staffs: The Invisible Force in American Lawmaking* (New York: The Free Press, 1979); and John R. Johannes, *To Serve the People: Congress and Constituency Service* (Lincoln, Neb.: University of Nebraska Press, 1984).

42. *Immigration and Naturalization Service v. Chadha*, 103 S. Ct. 2764 (1983).

43. Dodd and Schott, *Congress and the Administrative State*, p. 229

44. *CQ Almanac*, vol. 39: 98th Congress, First Session, 1983 (Washington, D.C.: Congressional Quarterly, Inc., 1983), p. 565.

45. *CQ Weekly Report*, 42 (July 21, 1984), 1797. For an incisive analysis of the legislative veto, see Barbara Hinkson Craig, *The Legislative Veto: Congressional Control of Regulation* (Boulder, Colo.: Westview, 1983).

46. Fiorina, *Congress: Keystone of the Washington Establishment*, p. 86. See also James Q. Wilson, "The Rise of the Bureaucratic State," *The Public Interest*, 41 (Fall 1975), 77–103, at p. 103. For a study of legislative influence on the activities of public administrators in two state governments, see Richard C. Elling, "State Legislative Influence in the Administrative Process: Consequences and Constraints," *Public Administration Quarterly*, 7 (Winter 1984), 457–81.

47. See, for example, Martin Shapiro, *The Supreme Court and Administrative Agencies* (New York: The Free Press, 1968); Kenneth Culp Davis, *Administrative Law Treatise*, 2nd ed. (Rochester, N.Y.: Lawyers Co-Operative Publishing Company, 1977); Roger C. Cramton, "Judicial Lawmaking and Administration in the Leviathan State," *Public Administration Review*, 36 (September/October 1976), 551–55; David Bazelon, "The Impact of the Courts on Public Administration," *Indiana Law Journal*, 52 (1976), 101–10; Donald L. Horowitz, "The Courts as Guardians of the Public Interest," *Public Administration Review*, 37 (March/April 1977), 148–54; and Linda Harriman and Jeffrey D. Straussman, "Do Judges Determine Budget Decisions? Federal Court Decisions in Prison Reform and State Spending for Corrections," *Public Administration Review*, 43 (March/April 1983), 343–51.

48. Horowitz, "The Courts as Guardians of the Public Interest," p. 150.

49. Cramton, "Judicial Lawmaking and Administration in the Leviathan State," p. 553.

50. Ibid.

51. For insightful discussions of relations between government officials and the press, see Delmer D. Dunn, *Public Officials and the Press* (Reading, Mass.: Addison-Wesley, 1969), especially chapter 7; William J. Small, *Political Power and the Press* (New York: Norton, 1972); Leon V. Sigal, *Reporters and Officials* (Lexington, Mass.: D. C. Heath, 1973), especially chapter 7; and Stephen Hess, *The Government-Press Connection* (Washington, D.C.: Brookings, 1984).

52. See Jameson Doig, "'If I See a Murderous Fellow Sharpening a Knife Cleverly . . .': The Wilsonian Dichotomy and the Public Authority Tradition," *Public*

Administration Review, 43 (July/August 1983), 292–304, especially pp. 292–94.
53. H. Kenneth Hibbeln, "Confronting the Pathology of Administrative Discretion," paper delivered at the annual meeting of the American Society for Public Administration; Denver, Colorado; April 8–11, 1984.
54. Ibid., p. 15 (emphasis added).
55. Ibid., p. 17.
56. See, among others, Bernard Rosen, *Holding Government Bureaucracies Accountable* (New York: Praeger, 1982); and Richard C. Elling, "Bureaucratic Accountability: Problems and Paradoxes; Panaceas and (Occasionally) Palliatives," *Public Administration Review*, 43 (January/February 1983), 82–89.

SUGGESTED READINGS

Berry, Jeffrey M. *The Interest Group Society*. Boston: Little, Brown, 1984.

Cater, Douglass. *Power in Washington*. New York: Random House, 1964.

Dodd, Lawrence C., and Richard L. Schott. *Congress and the Administrative State*. New York: Wiley, 1979.

Fiorina, Morris P. *Congress: Keystone of the Washington Establishment*. New Haven: Yale University Press, 1977.

Fox, Harrison W., Jr., and Susan Webb Hammond. *Congressional Staffs: The Invisible Force in American Lawmaking*. New York: The Free Press, 1979.

Holden, Matthew. "'Imperialism' in Bureaucracy." *American Political Science Review*, 60 (December 1966), 943–51.

Johannes, John R. *To Serve the People: Congress and Constituency Service*. Lincoln, Neb.: University of Nebraska Press, 1984.

Kaufman, Herbert, with the collaboration of Michael Couzens. *Administrative Feedback: Monitoring Subordinates' Behavior*. Washington, D.C.: Brookings, 1973.

Long, Norton E. "Power and Administration." *Public Administration Review*, 9 (Autumn 1949), 257–64.

Miller, Warren, and Donald E. Stokes. "Constituency Influence in Congress." *American Political Science Review*, 57 (1963), 45–56.

Pfeffer, Jeffrey. *Power in Organizations*. Marshfield, Mass.: Pitman, 1981.

Rosen, Bernard. *Holding Government Bureaucracies Accountable*. New York: Praeger, 1982.

Seidman, Harold. *Politics, Position, and Power: The Dynamics of Federal Organization*, 3rd ed. New York: Oxford University Press, 1980.

Truman, David B. *The Governmental Process*. New York: Knopf, 1951.

4

Chief Executives and Bureaucratic Leadership

AMERICAN chief executives—presidents, governors, mayors, city managers, county administrators, and county executives—stand apart from the executive branch agencies they are said to lead. Unlike most modern bureaucrats, these leaders and their immediate subordinates obtain their positions through elections (presidents, governors, mayors, and county executives) or are answerable to elected officials (cabinet secretaries and undersecretaries, other high-level political appointees, county administrators, and city managers). These officials are responsible in the eyes of most of the public for the operations of the bureaucracies that make up their respective executive branches, and historically they have taken much of the "heat" for bureaucratic failure. At the same time, however, they are not really a part of their bureaucratic structures, which are highly fragmented according to function and operate with a good deal of autonomy (see chapter 3) and which depend on chief executives for only part of their political support.

Yet chief executives clearly are expected to set general policy directions for the bureaucracy and to provide the necessary leadership for management of government agencies and programs. If they are to fulfill those expectations, they need some measure of effective influence, if not control, over bureaucratic agencies not primarily interested in the executive's political success or failure. Chief executives require deliberate strategies, and various forms of leverage, in dealing with administrative agencies, if they are to succeed in directing administrative behavior toward fulfillment of their (executives') policy objectives.

Certainly in the *formulation* of broad policy directions executive leadership has been evident, especially in the past two decades; presidential, gubernatorial, and local executive initiatives have been commonplace and have come to be regarded as marking the opening round of policy deliberations on many issues. The ability of chief executives to influence their bureaucracies significantly, however, cannot be taken for granted. Where the chief executive controls most of the key mechanisms of governmental and political party power—such as party nominations for office, patronage in government hiring, and awarding of government contracts—we can expect to find relatively responsive bureaucracies. Examples of such chief executives are Governor Huey Long of Louisiana during the 1930s, and the late Mayor Richard J. Daley of Chicago.[1] The degree of chief executive control over the bureaucracy may vary with the extent of such powers—comparisons among state governors are revealing in this respect[2]—but there are other factors involved as well.

Chief executives' control over the bureaucracy is frequently challenged by the legislative branch and others (such as opposition party spokesmen) who seek a voice in agency decisions. More importantly, in most instances *their control is effectively challenged from within by bureaucrats themselves.* For, as discussed in chapter 3, presidents (and most governors and many mayors) have diverse and frequently disunited coalitions of political support, which do not enable them to operate with a free hand or to speak with a consistent voice. Bureaucracies, on the other hand, have a limited range of policy interests due to the need for specialization. By concentrating its efforts in one policy area, an agency can develop its expertise and turn it into a political resource, and nurture the support of those in the legislature and the public who seek favorable agency treatment of their interests. Thus agency responses to executive directives are usually calculated in terms of their effect on agency interests rather than on the interests of the chief executive. Since in most cases an agency is not beholden to the chief executive for its political survival, and since the chief executive is unlikely to risk either political resources or political defeat every time an agency fails to follow orders from above, executive leadership is much more *the product of political persuasion* than of any clearly defined command authority.[3]

To persuade public bureaucracies to follow their lead, chief executives must convince agency personnel that there will be reasonable political and fiscal support for their specialized program interests, as long as those programs are integrated acceptably within the executives' broad policy directions. In some cases that can be accomplished easily—for example, agencies dealing with antipoverty programs under a poverty-conscious Lyndon Johnson, and the Pentagon overseeing a substantial defense buildup under Ronald Reagan. A variation of the same approach involves the chief executive singling out one favored program within an agency for support, keeping agency hopes alive that other programs will be similarly favored by the executive later. In other cases, where agency programs clearly occupy a low priority on a chief executive's policy agenda, the agency may adapt *procedurally* to executive priorities—such as trying to economize under an executive (at any level) emphasizing spending reductions. Even if policy differences continue to exist, both agency and chief executive advance their interests by such a tactic—indicative of the agency's fear of greater retribution from an unfriendly chief executive. Direct conflict, of course, is another possibility, though usually a last resort for both sides.

Two elements of chief executive-bureaucracy relationships shape how the former operates to influence the latter's activities. One is the general nature of linkages between the two; the other is specific instruments a chief executive can employ in the quest for control over bureaucratic behavior. Control is rarely complete, but the quest goes on.

CHIEF EXECUTIVE–BUREAUCRATIC LINKAGES

Interactions between chief executives and their administrative bureaucracies take various forms, but all have some impact both on the executive's political and policy fortunes and on bureaucratic behavior. Public administration scholar Douglas Fox, in his study of city and state bureaucracy,[4] spoke of *policy development* and *policy implementation* as distinct phases of gubernatorial and local executive involvement with their respective bureaucracies. We shall use that approach in discussing these linkages, at those levels of government and in Washington.

Development of policy in broad outline is probably what chief executives do best in their capacity as leaders of bureaucracy. Yet even executives with extensive formal and political power, such as the president and some governors, still must depend on professionals in the bureaucracy for program advice, and indeed for proposing new programs. The chief executive's dependence on experts varies among different policy areas. ''The more technically complex the work of a bureau and the more structurally autonomous it is, the less impact he has on its policy development.''[5] Policy areas such as energy conservation, public health, or transportation require more technical expertise than most chief executives possess. Another factor affecting executive dependence on bureaucracy for policy development is the diversity of information sources within the chief executives' staffs, and among those that can be called upon outside government as well (for example, issue networks). Political considerations can often reduce dependence on experts; for example, economists' recommendations on tax policy may be offset by judgments about public reaction. There may also be some choice as to *which* bureaucracy a chief executive relies on. But without question, *some* bureau or agency helps direct the course of policy development, in formative stages and often beyond.[6]

Policy implementation makes chief executives even more dependent on bureaucracies. Influence over implementation is generally limited to fairly broad-gauged actions (such as budget cuts and personnel measures) and related also to existing institutional resources. At the national level, for example, OMB has placed greater emphasis in recent years on program management, including introducing specific techniques into the bureaucracy and more management analysis by OMB personnel of what the bureaucracy is actually doing. This creates at least the potential for more effective presidential control over implementation. Similar developments have taken place at the state level, with management instruments such as departments of administration, new budget systems, and centralized planning increasingly available for gubernatorial use.

Local chief executives must rely on formal authority and perhaps party leadership to influence implementation, and even then the examples of successful mayors are few. Richard Daley in Chicago and Richard Lee in New Haven gained effective control of their city councils, boards of zoning appeals, and finance committees through adroit use of nomination to fill vacancies and through party patronage; Daley, in particular, was also successful in dealing with the city's public employee unions. But most mayors do not succeed in achieving this kind of control over major portions of their cities' policies. Lee himself wrestled with New Haven's police, education, and health bureaucracies, much as any other mayor would have, due to their professionalism and structural autonomy.[7]

Thus, most chief executives, including presidents, must contend with a dual difficulty. They must rely on bureaucratic expertise for much of the content of policy—especially in highly technical areas—at the same time that they must seek agency compliance in implementing policy as they desire.[8] A rising emphasis on program management, including strengthening the tools available to chief executives for coordinating and analyzing policy implementation, may bring some change, but for now most chief executives must induce cooperation from bureaucracy as they always have, rather than being able to count on it as a matter of course. This poses a continuing challenge, one that should not be underestimated for its complexity or for the sophistication needed to grapple with it.

Making the overall task of bureaucratic leadership more complex—but also possibly strengthening the chief executive as bureaucratic leader—is the fact that chief executives, generally, exercise leadership in three distinguishable, but overlapping, "arenas." One, the broadest of the three, is the *public* arena, in which the chief executive commonly seeks to "set the agenda" of public discussion of policy issues and concerns. John F. Kennedy, on the eve of his election in 1960, expressed the sense of this kind of leadership when he said that the task of the president is to "set before the American people the unfinished public business of our country." A second arena is the *legislative* one, where a chief executive plays a major role in proposing legislation and influencing the course of legislative deliberations. Much of Congress's business is shaped significantly by "the President's program," sent to Capitol Hill from the White House; an analogous situation often exists in many state legislatures and city councils. Finally, as already noted, chief executives must confront the "administrative" or *bureaucratic* arena, attempting to move administrators to manage programs and policies as the chief executive wants them implemented.

Because of the political dynamics linking these three arenas, the actions of executives in one arena may have impact in at least one other. For example, a series of major legislative successes may create political "fallout," whereby the chief executive encounters somewhat less bureaucratic resistance to his initiatives; this happened a number of times in 1981, Ronald Reagan's first year in the White House. Though our focus is on *bureaucratic* leadership, we also will take note of significant features of each of the other two arenas as we proceed.[9]

PRESIDENTIAL LEADERSHIP: STRENGTHS AND WEAKNESSES

The strengths of a president vary in relation to the particular arena or constituency with which he deals, and some things that enhance his leadership in one set of circumstances may add little to or even detract from his leadership at other times. A commonly noted source of strength, for example, is the character, personality, and style a president brings to the job, as well as his enjoyment of power, his ability to cope with the demands and pressures of his office, and his aspiring to what some call the "moral leadership of the nation"—a function we seem to expect of presidents.

A second source of strength, with potential impact in every aspect of leadership, is the president's ability to initiate a wide variety of ideas, proposals, and actions to which others must then respond. This power to initiate, in executive politics as elsewhere, provides an important advantage because the way in which a question or proposal is first put forward can significantly affect the outcome of the decision process.

Another source of strength is the capability of chief executives to respond to crisis situations, and that capacity is reinforced by public expectations that the chief executive will coordinate and direct governmental actions in the wake of floods, blizzards, droughts, outbreaks of violence, and other crises. When much of Alaska was devastated by an earthquake in 1964, Lyndon Johnson directed the effort to rebuild water and sewer systems, transportation networks, homes, and businesses. This required a particularly urgent effort due to the short construction season, but it was accomplished in large part because "the continuing strong interest of the president was made known in a convincing fashion to both the bureaucracy and the Alaskans."[10] The harsh winters of 1976-1979 provided numerous instances in which both the president and state governors in the East and Midwest declared fuel and other weather-related emergencies, while governors of several western and mountain states were declaring drought emergencies. The eruptions of Mt. St. Helens in the state of Washington triggered a massive governmental response involving literally thousands of public officials, but their efforts were coordinated principally by state and local chief executives, aided by disaster-relief agencies. And when Hurricane Dianna caused millions of dollars worth of damage in Florida and North Carolina in the fall of 1984, it was the governors of those states, together with hundreds of local executives, who directed cleanup efforts while ensuring that food and shelter—and moral support—were made available as necessary to affected residents.

Presidential power has been called upon regularly in times of economic and military crisis—for example, Franklin Roosevelt's economic leadership during the Great Depression of the 1930s, Richard Nixon's invoking of wage and price controls (in an effort to control inflation) in 1970, and the 444-day crisis involving Iran's seizure of American hostages during 1979–1981. As a rule, powers created or invoked to meet specific crises do not disappear entirely after the crisis has passed. Hence, each time the president is called upon to deal with a crisis, presidential powers are further enhanced. A vivid demonstration of that generalization came in 1978, when a law took effect (passed in 1976 at Gerald Ford's initiative) that ended a continuous state of national emergency dating from *1933!* Presidential powers during that time had included, among others, power to seize property, to organize and control the means of production, to declare martial law, and to restrict travel.[11] It is significant that such emergency powers lasted so long past the end of particular crises, our acceptance of presidential authority apparently being that great. Vietnam and Watergate, however, may have changed that (at least for a while).

Political Appointees and the Bureaucracy

While not unrelated to these sources of strength, a president's ability to direct the bureaucracy effectively has depended more heavily on a different complex of factors within the governmental apparatus. One set of controls used by many presidents in the nineteenth century—extensive discretionary powers over appointment and dismissal of administrative employees—has been largely unavailable to twentieth-century presidents due to merit reform.[12] The president has the power to appoint some 2,700 executive branch employees out of a total of some 2.9 million civilian employees. (Establishment of the Senior Executive Service, under the Civil Service Reform Act of 1978, increased both presidential appointment authority and the potential for presidential influence over high-ranking career bureaucrats. See chapter 10.) As a practical matter, the president's power to appoint is more significant in the long-range composition of public policy than is his power to dismiss,[13] since not all appointees are removable and those who are seldom find themselves actually fired. Often, but not always, the president has been able to guide the activities of these appointees, but his ability to control their respective bureaucracies through them usually has been more limited.

Limitations on presidential influence over political appointees, and on the influence of presidents and appointees alike over the bureaucracy, are complex and deserving of examination. An essential element, already implied, of presidential-bureaucratic interactions is that they are not direct—there are important layers of both political and career personnel between the White House and the bureaus. Another factor, noted by political scientist Harold Seidman, is that Cabinet officers are not merely "extensions of the presidency [with] no competing loyalties."[14] The president cannot automatically assume perfect obedience (or anywhere near that) from even a high-ranking political appointee who "has to spend some of his political currency heeding the qualms and wishes of the bureaucracy,"[15] in order to be reasonably effective in departmental leadership. Cabinet secretaries often are pulled in opposite directions by competing political forces—the president and their own departments—due to the more focused policy interests of the latter. Secretaries of cabinet-level departments cannot be expected to act strictly as "the president's men"; as a result, a unified cabinet is unlikely. But at the same time, a president "should . . . safeguard the powers and prestige of his department heads as those of his own office. To the extent that the status and authority of any department head are downgraded, he is *less able to resist* the pressures brought upon him by his constituencies, congressional committees, and the bureaucracy."[16]

Political appointees, in turn, have had their own difficulties in direct-

---

RONALD REAGAN ON "CABINET GOVERNMENT"

Cabinet members usually become advocates for their departments to the administration. We turned it around in California and said the cabinet officer is an advocate to those departments of the policies of the administration. We're going to try very hard to direct this new cabinet I've appointed so it will reflect the policy of my administration. . . . I think a lot of presidents delegated to a "second cabinet." By that I mean they appointed a cabinet and then they found they had to have staff members around them in the White House. And then, of course, you had turf battles and friction. You had situations where cabinet officers had no communication with the president. . . .

Source: U.S. News and World Report, January 19, 1981, p. 26.

Crucial to my strategy of spending control will be the appointment to top government positions of men and women who share my economic philosophy. We will have an administration in which the word from the top isn't lost or hidden in the bureaucracy. . . . [We will bring about] a new structuring of the presidential cabinet that will make cabinet officers the managers of the national administration—not captives of the bureaucracy or special interests they are supposed to direct.

Source: Richard P. Nathan, The Administrative Presidency (New York: Wiley, 1983), p. 72.

ing the activities of their respective bureaucracies. One way to explain this is that these appointees comprise a "government of strangers"—certainly to their departments, often to each other and to White House staff members, sometimes even to the president who appointed them.[17] It is more than simply a case of bureaucrats being in government longer than most appointees (though that is part of it). Rather, newly appointed executives have to spend part of their limited time in office (two years or less for many secretaries, undersecretaries, and assistant secretaries[18]) learning both formal and informal rules of the game in their departments. Thus, implementation of presidential policy initiatives is delayed for significant periods of time within cabinet departments—and in politics, delay can signify ultimate defeat for a policy or program.

Once having become acclimated, political appointees (and new presidents) are often rudely confronted with other operating realities of bureaucratic politics. One major reality is that there are important differences between political leaders and career officials in their respective modes of operation. The former seek to accomplish many things in a short time, with what they hope is overt political appeal; they are thus interested in quick, dramatic actions, especially upon first taking office. Bureaucrats, on the other hand, are usually inclined toward behaviors that have been described as *gradualism, indirection, political caution*, and a concern for *maintaining relationships*.[19] Gradualism—moving slowly—has the advantage of "reducing the agonies of change."[20] Indirection, or avoiding direct confrontations, is aimed at minimizing the potential number of sources of opposition to a program, personnel action, or implementation strategy. Political caution is designed to prevent unintentional or unwarranted identification of a career official with particular political appointees; this could easily compromise an official's career status (informally if not formally) and reputation. Finally, maintaining relationships is especially crucial for career employees, whose professional existence and effectiveness depend centrally upon "agency career ladders, cross-agency networks, and various pockets of career development . . ."[21] through which the employee's activities can continually be carried out.

Inevitable tensions are generated as a result of interactions among officials with these divergent approaches to discharging their public responsibilities. In particular, criticisms of the bureaucracy or of bureaucrats—across the board—are voiced frequently by political leaders anxious to see movement in key policy areas and frustrated by a bureaucratic environment many do not understand. Some of the kinder terms used to describe bureaucrats and their agencies are "unresponsive," "slow moving," and "disloyal" (to the president).[22] But there is a lesson here to be learned—namely, that what are regarded as inherent deficiencies of bureaucracy "are often its strengths. Effective functioning [of government] requires a high degree of stability, uniformity, and awareness of the impact of new policies, regulations, and procedures on the affected public."[23] Bureaucrats are usually in a better position to assess such impacts than are Washing-

CHIEF EXECUTIVES' ATTITUDES TOWARD GOVERNMENTAL ADMINISTRATION

President Eisenhower, in a letter to Henry Luce, the publisher of Time *magazine, who had called the presidency insufficiently aggressive, August 1960:*
. . . the government of the United States has become too big, too complex, and too pervasive in its influence on all our lives for one individual to pretend to direct the details of its important and critical programming. Competent assistants are mandatory; without them the Executive Branch would bog down. To command the loyalties and dedication and best efforts of capable and outstanding individuals requires patience, understanding, a readiness to delegate, and an acceptance of responsibility for any honest errors—real or apparent—those associates and subordinates might make. Such loyalty from such people cannot be won by shifting responsibility, whining, scolding or demagoguery. Principal subordinates must have confidence that they and their positions are widely respected, and the chief must do his part in assuring that this is so.

Source: Joseph Bower, "Effective Public Management," *Harvard Business Review* (March/April 1977).

Jimmy Carter, then Governor of Georgia, to the National Governors Conference, June 1974:
On the campaign trail, a lot of promises are made by candidates for public office to improve economy and efficiency in government if they are elected. This pledge has a natural appeal to the financially overburdened taxpayer. But when the winning candidates take office, they too often find that it's easier to talk about economy and efficiency in government than to accomplish it. Entrenched bureaucracy is hard to move from its existing patterns.. . .
     As a citizen interested in government and as a former legislator, I had long believed that too many governmental programs are botched because they are started in haste without adequate planning or establishment of goals. Too often they never really attack the targeted problems. . . .

Source: Carter Presidential Campaign office, Atlanta, Georgia.

Ronald Reagan, then president-elect, early in 1981:
The time has come where there has to be a change of direction in this country, and it's going to begin with reducing government spending. . . . You can cut layers and layers without hitting muscle fiber. Keep trying. That's what we were sent here for.

Source: U.S. News and World Report, February 9, 1981, p. 19.

ton's executive "strangers." Furthermore, as one observer has put it, ". . . civil servants can provide some of their most valuable service by resisting what political appointees [and, by implication, presidents] want." Bureaucratic resistance based on expertise and on concern for program effectiveness—as opposed to simply obstructionism—is the only viable alternative to letting things go wrong, and then saying "I told you so."[24]

Hugh Heclo, a long-time observer of administrative politics, sums up these tendencies this way:

> It is not simply a question of civil servants resisting any confrontations or change but of preferences for fights that do not lead to too much unnecessary antagonism and uproar—changes that do not extend uncertainty in too many directions at once. . . . [These sorts of behavior] go beyond conventional images of bureaucratic inertia. Such tendencies can find a *good deal of justification* in an environment of complex and uncertain political leadership on the one hand and long agency tenures and individualistic job protections on the other.[25]

One thing that apparently surprised some recent presidents was the inability of their highest-level departmental political appointees to overcome these patterns of bureaucratic behavior. Because departmental appointees work more closely than do presidents or White House staff with their bureaucracies, there is a tendency for them to take on the perspectives of their department; this is often at the expense of what might be called "presidentialist" perspectives.[26] In the words of one recent commentary: "A new President typically sends his Cabinet members forth to the departments to carry out his will—and presently discovers that they have . . . 'married the natives.' "[27] This can lead to a very frustrating situation for the president, who may have expected the sort of control over his appointees that others do, and who finds instead that his Cabinet members serve more as emissaries *from* the departments than *to* them. One consequence can be conflict between not only departments, but the secretaries themselves, over program jurisdiction (see box). Another more serious result is a drain on the president's time and resources, if he chooses to mediate a succession of conflicts. More likely, he will delegate responsibility for mediation to others on the White House staff, or he will resign himself to having to work around such conflicts. None of these choices is especially attractive.

In the days when Ehrlichman was Nixon's chief flak catcher, a bureaucratic cold war for control of overseas narcotics investigations turned hot when rival Treasury and Justice department raiding parties converged on a heroin factory in France and started shooting—at each other. One side blew the whistle—"whoever had the most wounded," says Ehrlichman—and he had to hale Attorney General John Mitchell and Treasury Secretary David Kennedy to the White House to make peace. "But they'd both been briefed to the nines by their bureaucracies," he recalls, "and they niggled and they piggled and they argued on and on for an entire Saturday. You would hope that at that lofty level they'd be able to say, 'We're the President's men and who cares what our underlings say?' But that's not the way it happens at all. The only unusual thing in that case was the gunfire."

Source: Newsweek, January 26, 1981, p. 42.

Under the Reagan administration, especially in its first two years, there were developments in Washington executive politics which may represent the start of a long-term shift in some of the patterns discussed above. Ronald Reagan, more than any other recent president, came into office not only with a firm determination to change the operations of the national government bureaucracy, but also with an *explicit management strategy* for doing so.[28] Political scientist Richard Nathan, writing in 1983, described the principal elements of this strategy:

> The key ingredient has been the appointment of loyal and committed policy officials. But this is only one dimension. The internal organization and operation of the White House staff is another. Loyal "Reaganites" have been placed in key White House policy-making positions, with experienced Washington hands assigned to parallel posts to promote the administration's policies in the legislative process and in the media. Tensions between the White House staff and cabinet officers have been minimized through the use of cabinet councils in which cabinet members have an important policy-making role. *Appointed policy officials in agency posts have penetrated administrative operations by grabbing hold of spending, regulatory, and personnel decisions.* From the beginning, these and other administrative tactics have been used aggressively by the Reagan administration.[29]

Furthermore, President Reagan differed from other recent presidents (Johnson, Nixon, and Carter) in that his initial strategy appeared to avoid particular problems that had beset them—Johnson's overly ambitious management design founded on economic principles, Nixon's political heavy-handedness, or Carter's excessive personal attention to detail. The strategy that emerged in the early weeks and months of 1981, and continued throughout much of President Reagan's first term, consisted of the following elements: (1) selecting Cabinet secretaries whose views were closely in line with those of the president (this had been done before, but not as systematically); (2) selecting *sub*cabinet officials (that is, undersecretaries, assistant secretaries, and other deputies among the ranks of the political appointees referred to earlier) who also shared the president's values and objectives; (3) motivating Cabinet and subcabinet officials to give attention to agency operations and administrative processes; (4) using the budget process as the central organizing framework for public policy making; and (5) avoiding overreliance on centralized White House clearance and control systems.[30]

There are several important points to be made here. First, actions taken by Reagan staff and policy officials regarding career personnel demonstrated that one need not rely on the ultimate instrument of dismissal to make significant changes in the behavior of career officials. Many positions were eliminated in the career ranks, and those filling them reassigned (though there were *some* layoffs). These "reductions in force" (RIFs) sent a signal throughout the bureaucracy that, unlike some presidents, Reagan was absolutely serious about making cuts in the size (and, by implication, the scope) of government. It also indicated that what many saw as the relative security of the career civil service could and would be breached, if it contributed to advancing the policy goals—especially in domestic policy—of the Reagan administration. (Another way this point was made was by deliberately reassigning responsible career officials to new jobs in which their responsibilities were routine or menial.) Second, a number of Reagan's subcabinet officials remained in their positions for well over two years, reducing the impact of their being "strangers" in the executive branch. Third, the combination of budgetary and operating strategies (which we will discuss more fully below and in chapter 12) has had the effect of disrupting some of the behavior patterns associated with senior careerists. It is much more difficult to practice gradualism or indirection, for example, when executive branch political leadership is clearly intent upon *accelerating* change, and *creating* confrontation, in administrative operations. Thus, "[r]egardless of what the Reagan administration will face in the future [and, perhaps, regardless of who succeeds him], it has already left a distinct imprint on the federal establishment."[31]

Presidential Budgetary Role

As implied above, a far more potent instrument of presidential control is his role in the formulation of executive branch budget proposals that go to Congress each year. The president's programmatic and budgetary priorities form the guidelines by which the Office of Management and Budget—working directly with and for the president—evaluates each agency's request for funds, so that it is possible for the president to influence substantially how much money is included in his Budget Message to Congress for every agency in the executive branch. Congress, of course, is not bound by presidential recommendations for agency budgetary allocations. But it ordinarily appropriates to each agency a dollar amount not appreciably different from, although usually lower than, that requested by the president and OMB.[32] In the early 1970s, another pattern developed where a Democrat-controlled Congress clashed with two Republican presidents over spending priorities and amounts, with the Senate especially inclined to vote larger sums than the president had asked. Under Richard Nixon this precipitated bitter conflicts over presidential vetoes and over Nixon's impounding (withholding authority to spend) appropriated funds (see chapter 12). Jimmy Carter, a Democrat with a Democratic Congress, generated less friction on budget matters than Nixon had, although some of his proposals were treated unfavorably. And Ronald Reagan, with a Republican Senate and apparent public backing in his efforts to control spending, has nevertheless encountered congressional resistance to his initiatives. In sum, the president has considerable influence over the amounts of money received by executive agencies, but his influence—and even his legal authority—cannot be said to be absolute. There is continual competition for control of agency funding, with the president having a major coordinating role.

A second function related to budgetary coordination emerged for OMB in the 1970s, chiefly at the instigation of President Nixon. When the old Bureau of the Budget (BOB), which had existed in the Executive Office of the President since 1939, was transformed into OMB in 1970, the change in title was not merely cosmetic. (Figure 4-1 shows the OMB organization chart.) It signaled Nixon's intent to gain greater mastery over operations and management practices of the sprawling bureaucracy. Even though Nixon's effort suffered from lack of an explicit strategy, as noted earlier, he did succeed to some degree in modifying management practices and in presidential monitoring of them.

Another function of OMB relating to bureaucratic agencies should be noted. When administrators seek to propose legislation for consideration by Congress, *central clearance* with OMB is required as a formality. This gives the president an opportunity to review possible proposals with an eye to their consistency with his legislative program. Agencies and their administrators may deal informally with Congress, but as a matter of routine most agencies seek clearance and do not openly defy the president and OMB if clearance is denied.

Starting in the last part of the Carter administration and continuing under President Reagan, OMB became involved in numerous efforts to control agency activities more fully. One device is budgeting the paperwork requirements agencies impose on other governments and the private sector. With passage of the Paperwork Reduction Act in late 1980, a new Office of Information and Regulatory Affairs within OMB was established, charged with reviewing all requests for information from the public made by government agencies.[33] Other steps primarily affected regulatory agencies—a focus of central concern under Ronald Reagan. Early in his term of office, the president put heavy emphasis on central clearance of proposed regulations, and issued several directives that enhanced the position of presidential leadership (and control) in this regard. Other proposals put forward—some adopted in whole or in part—included requiring cost-benefit analysis of proposed regulations, as well as so-called "inflation-impact" statements. The role of OMB as presidential staff coordinator of regulatory clearance became more clearly defined as the president pursued his policy of scaling down the national government's role in economic regulation (see Chapter 14).

One other point should be made. During the first months of his administration, Ronald Reagan demonstrated just how great an impact a president can have on bureaucratic agencies, through his successful efforts—supported by a more conservative Congress—to make deep cuts in national government spending. The president's fierce determination to alter significantly the nature and scope of national government activity was reflected in

Figure 4-1 Office of Management and Budget*

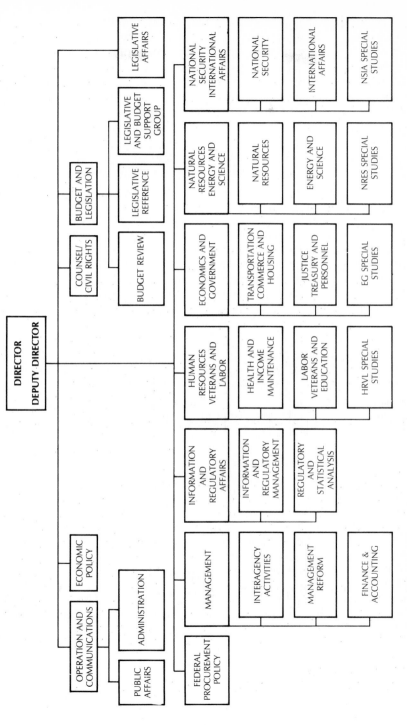

*Part of the Executive Office of the President.
Source: Office of Management and Budget, Office of Public Affairs, October 1984.

the billions of dollars cut from executive budget submissions and projections for fiscal years 1982, 1983, and beyond. The impact of these cuts, combined with fundamental changes in philosophy and program emphasis issuing from the White House, put the entire bureaucracy on notice that it could no longer expect to conduct "business as usual." Clearly, influence over the budget gave this president tremendous leverage over the fortunes of individual agencies. Indeed, the uses Reagan made of presidential authority in this regard exceeded what many observers had thought was possible. Congressional support, strong personal leadership, and a shrewd grasp of political realities combined with formal authority to constitute a formidable new force in budget making, as in the political arena at large.

Executive Branch Reorganization

A third instrument of chief executive control is periodic reorganization of administrative agencies. Like budgetary coordination, reorganization authority is a legacy of reform movements in the early 1900s. Traditionally, reorganization was aimed at increasing economy and efficiency, clear chains of command, and the like. And with few exceptions, presidents (and governors) who possess generous reorganization authority have approached their efforts apparently with those kinds of ideas in mind.

Proponents of reorganization often seem to regard it as a panacea, a cure-all, for correcting bureaucratic ills; they see the chief executive being able to "purify the bureaucratic blood and . . . prevent stagnation."[34] Reorganizations at various times have been touted as a means of eliminating waste and saving billions of dollars, restoring to economic health a chronically ailing maritime industry, reducing airport noise, and controlling crime in the streets.[35] Yet there is reason to think that such rationales have been oversold, that reorganizations—while useful—have higher political costs and fewer benefits for a chief executive than many imagine.

This is so because the "standard reorganization strategies for rationalizing and simplifying the executive branch often clash with one another."[36] Political scientist Herbert Kaufman lists seven basic prescriptions for reorganization: (1) limiting the number of program subordinates under a given executive, (2) grouping related functions under a common command (as happened in the creation of both the Defense Department and the Department of Housing and Urban Development), (3) increasing the number of executive staff positions, (4) granting extensive reorganization powers to elected or appointed executives, (5) insulating career public servants against political pressures, (6) decentralizing administration, and (7) expanding opportunities for public participation in the administrative process.[37] In the name of economy, efficiency, and responsiveness, these have been tried repeatedly in one form or another.

However, one must be selective as to which prescription to use, depending on circumstances and on the objectives of individual(s) pursuing reorganization. The first four prescriptions tend toward *centralization* of authority; the last three tend to promote *dispersal* of authority.[38] More important, these prescriptions in combination involve trade-offs of advantages and disadvantages. It is impossible to reap only benefits from reorganizing without also having to cope with attendant disadvantages, and hard choices must be made about which disadvantages will be accepted in order to gain other benefits. For example, grouping related functions under a common command is at odds with protecting an agency from political pressures; similarly, increasing decentralization and public participation clashes with limiting the number of subordinates effectively involved in program administration. Adding staff positions goes against decentralization; insulating administrators against political pressures interferes with executive reorganization authority; decentralization coupled with protection from political pressures can severely weaken command capabilities of the chief executive.[39] Reorganizations matter most in terms of the distribution of influence, the flows of communication, and the course of policy—*not* in terms of economy and efficiency! Therein lies the appeal of this device for the sophisticated executive; and "the genius of the reorganizer is to know which trade-off to make at a given time."[40] It is no easy job.

Information Resources

Control over information represents a fourth broad approach to maintaining presidential influence over bureaucratic agencies, as well as general influence in the policy-making process. It is said that knowledge constitutes power, and in an era of intensive specialization, that holds true as never before. The president, of course, must deal with a highly specialized and expert bureaucracy (increasingly, inside as well as outside the presidential establishment itself).[41] How then is the president to gather facts and figures necessary to informed decision making without being dominated by, or becoming excessively dependent upon, his sources of information?

To a large extent the president is dependent upon specialized bureaucratic agencies. There is reliance also on information supplied by the network of presidential advisory groups, both those within the Executive Office of the President (EOP) and those having independent status.[42] The president's ability to keep his information network functioning adequately while avoiding dependence on any one source of information is crucial to his retention of political leadership and policy initiative. Franklin Roosevelt was perhaps the master of the art. He assured himself of a constant stream of facts, ideas, suggestions, and countersuggestions by (1) centralizing decision-making responsibility in the Oval Office, (2) delegating responsibility for proposing policy alternatives rather widely so as to involve large numbers of administrators in the process of "brain-storming" for ideas, (3) actively encouraging open debate and discussion among members of his administration, and (4) leaving just about everyone somewhat uncertain of whose ideas might be acted upon in any given situation. He also took care to follow suggestions from a variety of sources, thus demonstrating his intention to take useful ideas and follow them up irrespective of the source.[43]

Roosevelt's technique had the effect of generating more ideas than he could use, but it was to his advantage as a political leader to have that volume of information combined with the ability (which he carefully cultivated) to make the final choices himself. Presidents since FDR have had a far more difficult task in this regard due to the growth of virtually every major institution in the executive branch. There is more information than any one person can absorb and utilize; there are more competitors, both institutional and personal, for access to and control of information; and the greatly increased quantities of information generated by others for their own use and political advantage pose an obstacle to presidential policy direction that is difficult to surmount.

Recent presidents have tried to deal with their growing information needs by (1) increasing the information capabilities of EOP; (2) enlarging the presidential establishment by making existing staffs bigger and by creating new ones, with corresponding increases in the political and programmatic responsibilities entrusted to them; and (3) delegating greater operating authority to EOP personnel. These changes have improved the president's information base for assessing alternatives and making choices, thereby creating something of a counterforce to the information generated in other parts of the bureaucracy and elsewhere. Furthermore, the proliferation of presidential staffs has permitted more specialization within EOP, thus strengthening the president's policy-making effectiveness vis-a-vis the expertise of the bureaucracy. Finally, by broadening the authority of assistants and staffs to speak and act in his name, the president has enhanced his ability both to transmit and to acquire information through his immediate subordinates. This is important because presidents (and other chief executives) frequently encounter difficulty in transmitting and receiving accurate information through the bureaucratic hierarchy.

A major obstacle in transmitting information from one level in a hierarchy to the next is the tendency for a portion of the information to be screened out by those who receive it and in turn send it on. This may be deliberate, aimed at frustrating the will of the official sending the information, or it may be done without any particular motive—perhaps even unconsciously. Depending on how many levels there are in the structure, a great deal of information—as much as 98 percent under certain circumstances— can be distorted and even lost in this manner.[44] A chief executive, or any other top-level official, cannot casually assume that his or her communications—including instructions, statements of policy, or major program directives—travel down the hierarchy simply on the strength of their having been issued. There must be follow-up (sometimes repeated checks) to ensure that communications have been received and accurately understood by those for whom they were intended.

Obtaining reliable information that gives a clear, complete picture of what is going on in the bureaucracy is the other side of the coin. A truism of administrative practice is that unless there is some disruption in the normal routines of administration, the chief executive does not have to be informed about administrative activities. Such an assumption is justified on the grounds that the chief executive's responsibilities are broader than the activities of a single bureaucratic agency and that his or her attention should be directed to individual entities only if there is some special reason for doing so. In traditional administrative thinking, this assumption is called the *exception principle,* suggesting that only exceptions to routine operations merit involvement of the chief executive. But the exception principle does not always work well in practice. For one thing, there is a strong, if natural, reluctance to communicate bad news—such as the existence of a problem that the agency finds hard to handle on its own—through the hierarchy, and least of all from an immediate subordinate to a superior official or agency. Also, for its own reasons, an agency may prefer not to call attention to activities that are likely to be unpopular with its nominal superior. Therefore, for the president (or other chief executive) to have accurate, comprehensive information requires a successful effort to overcome built-in resistance to a free upward flow of communication.

The president can facilitate the transmission of information from EOP to the rest of the bureaucracy by maintaining regular follow-up checks for compliance and by requiring regular feedback from the agencies, though the *formality* of feedback is easier to establish than is useful substantive content.[45] Administrative agencies resist supplying feedback in the same way— and for many of the same reasons—that they resist other types of upward communication. Consequently, presidential (and other) monitoring of bureaucratic activity requires deliberate, concentrated action in order to have any chance of keeping some semblance of control from the top.

Among the ways of coping with problems in acquiring information are (1) making use of external sources of information (newspapers and other media, interest groups, and so on); (2) creating overlapping substantive areas of responsibility within or among bureaus, resulting in a measure of duplication of information sources and presumably more reliable information; (3) using informal channels to supplement formal ones; and (4) deliberately bypassing formal structures and intermediate layers of bureaucracy to contact directly the person or persons with the information being sought.[46] Franklin Roosevelt and John Kennedy, in particular, frequently telephoned lower-echelon bureaucrats to get from them information that was moving too slowly, or not at all, through formal hierarchical channels. Such a practice has two effects, both desirable from the president's point of view: it gets the particular information into his hands more quickly, and it signals to the rest of the bureaucracy that the president is prepared to bypass the usual channels when he deems it necessary. The latter is likely to reduce the time required to transmit communications through channels;

the threat of being bypassed can motivate those responsible for forwarding information to the president to do so with a minimum of delay, outweighing any contrary motivations to obstruct or distort.

Let us consider one other issue concerning presidents and the control of information. A president, by simply withholding all or some information, can decisively influence the shape of internal deliberations, press reports, public debate, and even global confrontations. Three examples illustrate this point: (1) the Cuban missile crisis of 1962, when tight secrecy was essential for successfully negotiating the removal of Soviet missiles from Cuba, (2) the American buildup in Vietnam in the mid-1960s, when any information unfavorable to Lyndon Johnson's Vietnam policies was systematically withheld from the mass media and the public, and (3) the Nixon administration's secret (and illegal) domestic surveillance of anti-Vietnam War activists and civil rights organizers.

This device, however, has its limits, and failure to control information can also have major policy implications. A classic illustration involved President Kennedy's explanations of just what was promised to anti-Castro Cubans who wanted to invade Cuba at the Bay of Pigs in 1961. The invasion became a fiasco for the United States because, first, air cover promised for the landing on the beaches never materialized, and second, Kennedy's spokesmen—particularly a Pentagon press officer with years of experience on the job—denied any American involvement in either the planning or the execution of the abortive invasion. These spokesmen followed up their denials, once they were known to be false, with claims that the national interest had both required and justified their giving out false information! The documented falsehoods of the Nixon White House in regard to the Watergate affair also demonstrate the power of the president to influence the course of public discussion, as well as the dramatic consequences of not maintaining complete information control. The essential points are these: (1) presidents, through their control of information, can substantially affect debate and decision in and out of government, not to mention how others perceive public issues or the president's order of priorities; and (2) conflicts over access to, and use of, information involve crucial questions of political influence, with high stakes for the president and others in politics.

A president, on the other hand, can find himself forced to react to a situation in which *he* lacks information vital to an impending decision. Perhaps surprisingly, one such case was the Cuban missile crisis. President Kennedy needed to establish beyond doubt that Soviet missiles had been installed in Cuba before deciding what actions to take. But despite the great urgency, he had difficulty obtaining the necessary (photographic) evidence, due to the time consumed by bureaucratic processing of the information and at least one interagency squabble—over whose pilots (Air Force or CIA) would fly whose planes over the western end of Cuba, where the missiles were ultimately spotted.[47] If presidents are not able to acquire information readily in the most extraordinary circumstances, even in a potential nuclear crisis, then they clearly cannot depend on routine flows of information.

Just how effective, then, is information control in the total picture of presidential leadership? The answer is mixed. In terms of public and congressional leadership by the president, control of information can be a crucial instrument. But with respect to the bureaucracy, the president's leadership is subject to greater constraints, if for no other reason than that his control of information is less secure. The bureaucracy has more to do with shaping the available alternatives for presidential decisions—through provision of information—than any other institution or person.

In summary, presidential leadership rests on a base with the following components: (1) great public visibility and considerable fundamental respect for the presidency, though the latter has declined noticeably in recent years; (2) the president's own desire to provide leadership and the individual style of leadership he employs; (3) the power to initiate proposals, debates, and actions to which others must then respond; (4) the ability to coordinate governmental responses to crisis, whether foreign or domestic; (5) the ability to make appointments to positions in the executive branch, though the actual functioning of political appointees is highly complex and rife with pitfalls for the chief executive; (6) the authority to coordinate executive budget requests and to oversee implementation and management practices of executive agencies; (7) reorganization authority, though this too poses many problems for the chief executive; and (8) control of information, though the president's position of considerable institutional strength carries with it important liabilities as well. Vital, of course, is the way in which a president makes use of each of these potential sources of strength, as well as how he copes with the weaknesses in his leadership base.[48]

THE OFFICE OF GOVERNOR: CONTINUITY AND CHANGE

The patterns of leadership found among American governors are predictably varied; while the fifty states do not display fifty different types of governor, there are important distinctions among the offices as well as their occupants. Some governors, notably in the larger urban-industrial states of the Northeast and Midwest, rather closely resemble the president in their public visibility, their formal powers, the scope of their responsibilities, their institutional and staff resources, and the size and complexity of the bureaucracies with which they must contend. They are a minority, however. Many governors, especially those in states with more homogeneous economies, societies, and traditions, tend to have more limited grants of effective administrative authority and consequently a less active role in directing the implementation of state government policies. This is true even though most governors have acquired numerous additional powers (especially budgetary) under recent revisions in state constitutions and, in most instances, have exercised considerable influence in the proposing and development of state policy. Also true, however, is the comment of one observer that, taken as a group, governors are not nearly as strong at the state level as the president is at the national level.[49]

A major part of the variation among governors, in formal powers as well as in actual leadership behavior, is traceable to differences in socioeconomic characteristics and political systems of their respective states. For example, states with large and diverse populations and economic activities seem to have, as a result of that diversity, a greater variety of problems, requiring a strong chief executive to direct the state government's responses to those problems. Political scientist Kenneth Palmer has noted that as states more closely resemble the nation in their social heterogeneity, they must also "approximate the [national] executive in their assignment of administrative authority to their governors."[50]

Another factor associated with strong governors is a competitive two-party system, as opposed to a situation in which one party is dominant in most state elections. In many cases governors are acknowledged leaders of their parties, thereby strengthening the political leverage available in the exercise of policy leadership. Smaller states and states with one party dominant in their politics—groupings which may overlap—tend toward weaker formal powers in their governors' offices, although there are exceptions to that rule. Also, weak formal powers do not necessarily imply weakness in practice; informal bargaining, personal charm, wealth, and public relations can go a long way toward overcoming deficiencies in gubernatorial authority.[51]

Many governors, however, find their positions defined—and often restricted—by legal and political factors that are formal in nature. The most important of these are of state constitutional origin, reflective of an earlier age in which many constitutions were drafted, and in which there were powerful societal values favoring sharp restrictions on gubernatorial powers. One observer has commented that "the American governorship was conceived in mistrust and born in a strait jacket. . . ."[52] In many instances, state government power was tightly constrained "across the board," with all branches and entities given only such authority as could be rigidly defined. But it is fair to say that the office of governor was the most frequent target of those seeking to limit power. Until the early 1960s, most governors still suffered from the legacy of constitutional restrictiveness; between 1921 and 1962 only five states adopted new constitutions that reflected contemporary political and administrative needs in the governor's office.[53]

Since 1964, however, there has been considerable change in state constitutions, most of it favorable to the exercise of stronger gubernatorial leadership—including leadership of state bureaucracies. Between 1964 and 1976, ten states comprehensively revised their constitutions; between 1966 and 1976, a total of twenty-seven states "streamlined the amendment process, making it easier to adjust the constitutional framework as the needs of state government required."[54] As amending the constitution was made easier, efforts increased to update provisions bearing on the exercise of governors' powers; these included strengthening the office of lieutenant governor, facilitating executive reorganization, and loosening restrictions on borrowing and taxing.[55] Though many constitutional constraints still exist on gubernatorial (and other officials') power, the situation is very different when compared to only twenty years ago.

Another feature of many state constitutions is the separate election of top-level executive officials, such as state attorney general, treasurer, and secretary of state. Forty-eight states elect at least one of these officials separately from the governor; a few even choose their lieutenant governors independently.[56] Thus the potential exists for a governor's having to compete with other officials for effective control and direction of state programs, budgets, and bureaucracies. However, one observer has noted that most governors surveyed on this question had had few serious difficulties in securing cooperation from other key elected executive officials.[57] Some difficulties, though, still exist.

Even among governors with few competing elective officials, there are frequently limitations on powers of appointment and dismissal for subordinate executive branch positions. While not even the president has unlimited authority in this respect, the authority of state governors seems to be considerably less extensive in comparison. In many states, for example, there are boards and commissions created by the legislature to which the governor cannot name members. In other instances, appointees cannot be removed by the governor, except under the most extraordinary circumstances, once they have taken office. And most governors face the political necessity of at least tolerating appointees sponsored by political party or interest group supporters. In fact, in some rural states, a bureau or department head might be selected by a committee made up entirely or in part of persons the agency serves; a common example of this is found in selection of many state agriculture department directors. Such committees are constituted independently of the governor and the private interests represented exercise at least a veto—and sometimes considerably more power than that—over appointments that appear to be under gubernatorial control.[58] The net effect is to reduce the leverage that a governor has over subordinates, thus very likely frustrating efforts to develop and implement consistent policies.

A third constitutional feature still found in many states is the specific mandating of programs and/or allocation of funds—requirements that reduce the ability of the governor (and everyone else) to make policy choices based on the best estimates of current societal and programmatic needs.

Specified in the constitutions of some states, for example, are very detailed budgetary allocations that would require a constitutional amendment to change. As recently as the late 1960s, Alabama's constitution effectively earmarked (reserved for specified uses) nearly 90 percent of its annual budget before the governor and legislature even began considering state priorities and spending.[59] Although constitutional provisions elsewhere may not be as restrictive, they nevertheless limit gubernatorial freedom of action beyond the usual constitutional and political checks and balances.

Another constraint on some governors' leadership resources is the fact that they serve a two-year term or a single four-year term without possibility of immediate reelection. As of 1984, however, forty-six states had four-year gubernatorial terms, permitted their governors to serve successive terms, or both.[60] Some states (for example, New York, California, and Illinois) permit *unlimited* reelection. Others (for example, Pennsylvania) constitutionally limit their governors to no more than two consecutive terms. This may seem a minor restriction compared to others, but there is evidence that in the last year of a term where reelection is not possible, a governor has fewer policy options available and less effective control of political resources, because more attention is being paid to who the new governor might be than to the incumbent's program leadership.

Governors, of course, are affected to some extent by the nature of their states' bureaucratic structures and operations. Here too state constitutions play some part to the extent that they mandate the existence of specific agencies, commissions, and boards (in sharp contrast to the national Constitution's broad provisions). But more important than the constitutional framework are the dynamics of the relationships involving the chief executive and the bureaucracy. How extensive, for example, are the governor's powers of appointment and dismissal? We have already noted that these are often limited. What of the governor's role in budget making and planning? As part of the general strengthening of authority during the 1960s and 1970s, this role is now of major importance. As of 1984, executive budgets existed—with direct involvement of the governor—in forty-four of the fifty states.[61] With regard to planning, gubernatorial power is extensive in virtually all fifty states, though in only twenty-eight is the planning function formally assigned to the governor's office.[62] How effective is the state legislature as a political and policy counterweight to gubernatorial initiative? (Note that this question did not arise concerning Congress and the president.) In many states—even after legislative reapportionment and efforts to modernize operations—legislatures are still characterized by high rates of turnover in membership, part-time sessions, and deficiencies in staffing and committee resources. Under these circumstances, it might be assumed that the governor has even more influence in the absence of effective legislative opposition and/or consultation; but in reality what frequently results is a legislature just effective enough to oppose and frustrate but incapable of coming up with its own serious policy alternatives.

The strength of the governor's own staff and executive office resources, including information capabilities, must also be assessed. In these
areas many states have made considerable progress in recent decades, with
a consequent increase in gubernatorial effectiveness. Over two-thirds of the
states have created a department of administration to assist the governor in
directing the bureaucracy's operations,[63] and in a number of others the governor's personal staff has been expanded to include qualified subject matter specialists, who strengthen the reservoir of expertise available in the executive office itself.

Two other formal powers that can augment the governor's position are
the veto power over legislation and executive-branch reorganization authority. All but one of the governors have at least the same sort of veto power
the president has (the exception being North Carolina's), and about half of
the governors also have an *item veto*, which permits the governor to disapprove specific provisions of a bill while signing the remainder into law, a
power the president lacks. In Illinois the governor has in addition an *amend-
atory veto*, empowering him not only to disapprove a provision but also to
propose alternative language to the legislature; this could mean rewriting
the content and even the intent of the legislation, if the legislature goes
along. As for executive reorganization, there is a difference between being
able to propose a "package" plan, subject only to legislative veto by one or
both houses, and having to submit reorganization plans as part of the usual
legislative process. Having to allow the legislature to amend, revise, and
otherwise tinker with the proposals, even to the point of completely rewriting them, is a form—and a sign—of gubernatorial weakness compared to
the package approach. (This is in addition to the concerns discussed earlier
with reference to the president.) Many governors now have the option of
proposing reorganization packages.

It is clear that variations in a governor's powers make some difference
in the exercise of gubernatorial leadership over state government generally,
and state bureaucracies in particular. Yet there is some question about just
how actively—and for what general purposes—governors *seek to use* the
powers available to them; variations in this dimension of leadership, to the
extent they exist, complicate our assessment of governors' influence over
their bureaucracies. In one recent study, focusing on the different roles governors might play in exercising administrative leadership, political scientists Glenn Abney and Thomas Lauth suggested that most governors seem
"more inclined to seek to be *managers* rather than policy leaders [—] not because they lack formal powers over administration, but because they are apparently personally incapable or disinclined to use those powers which
they do possess."[64] In other words, based on Abney and Lauth's findings,
governors perceive their roles in a more limited way than a reading of their
formal powers might suggest. In many instances, these powers are used
primarily in support of existing administrative activity without attempting
to lead the machinery of government in new policy directions. This is so

even though formal gubernatorial authority is readily available to a chief executive actively seeking to provide policy direction. One result of governors *not* supplying policy leadership may be, in Abney and Lauth's words, that "our states are now better run [managed] than they are governed [led]"— or, worse, that they are "neither well governed nor well run."[65] This is ironic, since many of those who sought to strengthen the office of governor were motivated originally by a desire that governors provide precisely this kind of activist policy leadership—for the bureaucracy as well as others in state government.[66]

From the governor's standpoint, a formula for greater effectiveness would appear to combine the following: (1) extensive personnel controls; (2) a central role in budget making and planning for state executive branch agencies; (3) considerable political strength in the legislature; (4) a competent and responsive executive office establishment with ample information resources; (5) at least minimal cooperation from independently elected executives; (6) some authority to reorganize the executive branch, subject only to legislative veto; (7) more extensive veto power; and (8) a four-year rather than a two-year term and the ability to seek reelection. With state governors emerging in the 1960s and 1970s as important national political figures (for example, Ronald Reagan, Jimmy Carter, and the late Nelson Rockefeller all served as governors), and with public reawakening to the potential importance of the states themselves, the strength or weakness of governors is a matter of growing political importance as well as of central relevance to the making and implementing of public policy.

MAYORS, CITY MANAGERS, AND COUNTY EXECUTIVES: VARIATIONS ON RECURRING THEMES

If it is difficult to generalize among fifty state governors, it is next to impossible to do so among the chief executives of American local governments. There are about 82,000 units of local government, of which fewer than half have chief executives separate from their legislative arms. There is considerable variation in the modes of election of these chief executives, as well as in the formal powers they exercise.

First, a word is in order about different types of local governments. Approximately 39,000 local governments are "general" or multiple-purpose governments, with responsibility and authority for providing local services such as police and fire protection, water supply, utilities, streets and roads, and sewage and sanitation facilities. Municipalities (cities, boroughs, some villages, and other municipal corporations), counties, and townships fall into this category. It is here that separate chief executives are found, such as mayors, city managers, and county executives, though not all general local governments are headed by a single chief executive (for example, townships and New England towns).

The other 43,000 local governments are single-purpose governments, responsible for providing one governmental service (parks, schools, libraries, fire protection, water, airport service, and so on) to the public. These "special districts" are characterized almost without exception by a fusion of legislative, executive, and administrative functions under the direction of a board or commission, which appoints a professional administrator to manage the district's daily affairs. A common example is the local school district with its elected school board and appointed superintendent; about 34 percent of all special districts, in fact, are school districts.[67] Other prominent examples of special districts are the Port Authority of New York and New Jersey, with responsibility for a major portion of the transportation complex in and around metropolitan New York, including all three airports; the Chicago Park District; and a growing number of mass transportation districts in other major urban centers. Our discussion of local chief executives, however, will not include administrators of single-purpose districts; we will focus entirely on elected (mayors and county executives) and appointed (city managers and county administrators) officials in municipal and county government.

Of these four types of local chief executive, the mayor is by far the most prominent. Yet mayors vary widely in their formal and practical strength in office; indeed, the terms "strong mayor" and "weak mayor" are commonly used to distinguish between different sets of mayoral powers. A *strong* mayor is one who (1) is the sole chief executive exercising substantive policy responsibilities, as opposed to a ceremonial mayor working in the shadow of a city manager's administrative role; (2) serves a four-year (rather than a two-year) term in office, allowing for fuller development of executive policies; (3) has a central role in formation of the local government budget, usually with the assistance of a full-time city finance director and a finance department; (4) is influential in local politics, especially in party politics where local elections are partisan; (5) has both appointment and dismissal powers over other executive officials—the more extensive such powers, the greater the mayor's control; (6) has veto power over legislation; (7) has no limit on seeking reelection; and (8) can call upon an expert bureaucracy inclined to follow the mayor's policy leadership. The more fully this description applies to a particular mayor, the stronger that mayor will be in local politics and policy making.

A *weak* mayor, by contrast, lacks some if not most of these powers, and is often found alongside a city manager who is the actual chief administrator of the community. One survey found that in 151 cities of 50,000 population with a formal mayor-council structure, only 39 had a strong mayor.[68] It has been estimated that two-thirds of all mayors lack a veto power. And while a majority now serves a four-year term of office, a substantial minority still serves for only two years. It can happen, of course, that a mayor lacking some powers can compensate by making skillful use of those that are available. For example, the city of Chicago—on paper—has a relatively weak mayor form of government, but the late Mayor Richard Daley's personnel control and his leadership in the Cook County Democratic party more than made up for any weaknesses in formal powers. Other resources that can help overcome formal weakness include personal and political skills in relation to the local media and the electorate and the political connections necessary to acquire significant sums of money from state and national government aid programs.

City managers, in contrast to mayors, are not directly elected by local voters for a fixed term of office. They are chosen by the city council and serve for as long as the council members approve of their performance. The original design of the city manager's position included the notion that the manager would be "nonpolitical," administering policies agreed upon by the city council but taking no part in policy formulation.[69] In practice, however, city managers frequently exercise considerable leadership in city government, proposing a variety of actions to the council for approval or disapproval and in general playing an initiator's role. One contributing factor is the manager's expertise and the legitimacy this provides; another is the fact that managers are full-time professionals and in many instances the mayor (ceremonial) and city council members are part-time. Also, the manager's staff resources ordinarily exceed those of either mayor or council.[70] Numerous studies have indicated not only that city managers are policy initiators and political actors in reality but also that their fulfilling a policy-making role is quite consistent with the expectations held by others in local politics about the manager's job.[71]

In the area of policy implementation, most mayors face problems not unlike those of many governors, in that city bureaucracies are frequently highly professionalized and quite autonomous in structure or in operation (or both). It requires a considerable investment of executive resources—assuming the mayor *has* such resources—to direct the implementation of programs under the mayor's leadership. A weak mayor cannot do it; a strong one may be able to, but also may not. City managers may have some advantage here, in that many city charters specifically establish them as chief administrators endowed with the authority necessary to take charge of ongoing administrative responsibilities, subject always to the ultimate approval of the city council. Formal administrative powers seem to matter most to the city manager's exercise of leadership, if for no other reason than that the manager, by deliberate design, is not assumed to have access to party or other political resources, as many mayors do.

The office of county executive (or, as it is sometimes known, president of the county board) is a relatively new office of local government. County government historically has been a fairly passive, non-policy-oriented governmental unit, concentrating on administration of programs enacted at the state level (primarily agricultural and rural-related) and on maintaining a very few local services. Recently, however, there has been something of an awakening in county government as many counties have become steadily more urbanized, so that now county government is seen by some as representing another potential governmental resource to be utilized in solving social, economic, and service-provision problems.

As was the case in other governments that grew more active, counties that have taken on more responsibilities have strengthened their policy-making capabilities, and some have placed central responsibility for policy formulation in the hands of a chief executive, separately elected by all the voters of the county. There are now some 250 elected-executive counties located in eighteen states, and another eighteen elected executives in jurisdictions resulting from city-county consolidations or separations (the latter including, among others, New York City, Philadelphia, San Francisco, Denver, Indianapolis, and Nashville).[72] The largest county with an elected executive (excluding consolidated or separated jurisdictions) is Cook County, Illinois (Chicago), with a population of well over five million people; others with more than one million inhabitants each are Nassau and Suffolk counties on Long Island (outside New York City); Erie County, New York (Buffalo); King County, Washington (Seattle); and Milwaukee County, Wisconsin. Most, however (about 200), have less than 100,000 inhabitants each. And, though the evidence is limited, it appears that a substantial and growing number of county executives are strong executives in the same sense as strong mayors, with considerable formal authority.[73] Most counties, however, still do not have a popularly elected executive, and most county governments are operated primarily by county boards, whose functions are legislative and whose powers are not well developed. The strong county executive is the exception, not the rule, among America's 3,000 counties.

Recently, the position of administrator—an appointed post—has emerged in county government. County administrators usually exercise authority delegated by the county board, with much the same kind of relationship to the board that city managers have with their city councils. Currently, there is considerable interest on the part of county board members around the nation in establishing this position. However, it seems unlikely that these officials will be potent ''chief administrators,'' because most counties (unlike most cities) have one or more separately elected administrative officials (for example, coroner, auditor, and sheriff) who commonly have a history of independence in their own operations. It is not clear whether that will change, as county administrators become more numerous and better established.

COMMONALITIES AND DIFFERENCES IN LEADERSHIP RESOURCES

The institutional, legal, and personal factors that facilitate strong executive leadership seem to operate at all levels of government, though somewhat less clearly and predictably for city managers and county executives. Strong chief executives draw much of their strength from the following common features.

First, the power to initiate policy proposals and to follow them up politically is a key element of executive leadership. Legislatures at all levels ordinarily lack central policy formulation capabilities so that a chief executive who wishes to influence the "public agenda" of issues that occupy government attention can do so in most cases. This assumes, of course, an executive leader who seeks to lead actively—an assumption that is usually, but not always, valid.

Second, a central role in executive budget making strengthens the overall influence of the chief executive. If budgetary "central clearance" exists, executive agencies must pay heed to the preferences of the elected executive, at least during key stages of the budget cycle.

Third, a crucial resource is control over executive branch personnel decisions. The more extensive the authority to decide appointments and dismissals, the greater the political hold over actions of those whose tenure in office depends on pleasing their "patron" (hence the term "patronage"). Few chief executives, at any level, currently enjoy that kind of personnel domination; thus personnel control is not a major contributor to the effective strength of most chief executives.

Fourth, chief executive staff resources constitute a source of potential strength. This depends on institutional arrangements, where provision is made for adequate staff, and on the individuals who comprise the staff. A related factor is the information capability the staff creates. Here too there are institutional and personal factors involved, as well as considerations of information availability, transmission, and control.

Fifth, the ability to propose agency reorganizations enhances the chief executive's power, particularly if the legislature must accept or reject the proposals as a package. This power, however, is effective more as an implied or occasional threat, because reorganization is a major step. A chief executive who attempted more than one reorganization within a short time span would encounter either the likely defeat of the proposals and/or reduced credibility with the legislature. Reorganization authority is thus a political leadership resource of rather limited potential. Still, it is better to have it in reserve than to lack it entirely or to have to subject any reorganization proposal to the normal legislative mill.

Sixth, veto power is a useful tool, and executives who can exercise it have greater *potential* leverage over the legislature. The stronger the veto authority, the greater the leverage. Yet, as with reorganization, it should not be used indiscriminately. Veto power, in short, is not usually a "frontline" tool of positive executive leadership.

Seventh, a chief executive's political strength in the legislature, and as leader of a political party or faction, adds substantially to leadership capability in office. Research in congressional voting behavior, and to a lesser extent in state legislatures, suggests that there is considerable responsiveness on the part of many legislators to the initiative of the chief executive, particularly when party loyalty is invoked. While other considerations (such as policy preferences, constituency interests, and individual conscience) also play an important part in legislative decision making, many votes are cast strictly along party lines. If a governor is strongly supported by legislators of the same party—for example, Nelson Rockefeller in New York throughout the 1960s,[74] and Ronald Reagan in California from 1967 to 1975—it adds measurably to gubernatorial effectiveness. If, on the other hand, a governor must constantly labor to gain the support of his or her own partisans in the legislature, then leadership capability is a good deal more constrained.[75] The same principle holds true with equal import for mayors and presidents. It is important to note, also, that strength in the legislature is usually tied to the amount of popular support for the chief executive.

Some chief executives have particular advantages and disadvantages that should be noted. The president, for all his difficulties with semiautonomous bureaucracies, is better off than many governors and mayors by having fewer constitutional restrictions placed on his leadership. Many governors have a more flexible veto power (the item veto) than does the president, while many mayors lack veto power altogether. Both the president and the majority of governors are their party's acknowledged leaders, a situation many mayors can envy. Finally, most governors and city executives are limited in a broad sense by the fact that their governments' fiscal and administrative capabilities generally lag behind those of the national government, requiring them to depend in greater or lesser degree on national government grants, for some proportion of their revenues. While this is an indirect impediment on executive leadership, in some ways it can have the most adverse effects on gubernatorial or mayoral policy initiatives and on the ability to build for the long term, institutionally, at the state and local levels.

SUMMARY

American chief executives are highly visible to the public and are perceived as being able to provide political leadership and policy initiative; they are also usually considered responsible for the operations of executive branch bureaucracies. Most chief executives lack the specialization characteristic of bureaucracies and must rely on persuasion rather than on command authority when dealing with them.

Linkages between chief executives and bureaucracies come into play in policy development and policy implementation. In policy development, chief executives must depend on professionals in the bureaucracy for both general program advice and specific proposals. Executive dependency increases with program complexity and bureaucratic autonomy. In policy implementation, bureaucracies play an even greater role. For coordinating and analyzing implementation by the bureaucracy, chief executives must rely on broad-gauged actions (such as budget cuts and personnel measures) and on institutional capability in their executive offices.

The strengths of a president start with his own leadership style and personality, and his ability to take the initiative in many matters of public policy. More substantial power lies in emergency powers, which enable him to direct governmental responses to crisis (this is also a strength of governors). Over time, residual powers originating in crisis situations tend to become part of the president's leadership resources.

The president's ability to assume policy leadership successfully depends on more tangible factors, such as personnel controls, a central role in executive budget making, and (under Ronald Reagan) exercising tighter control over agency management processes. All of these involve complex interactions with the bureaucracy, especially channels of influence through political appointees. Reorganization, an oft-tried device, usually fails to live up to its advance billing. A major factor is control over, and the uses of, information. Presidents have the ability to control the release of information in such a way as to affect significantly the course of public (and governmental) perceptions, debates, and decisions about public issues; but they can also be less than fully informed themselves.

Chief executive leadership at the state level is varied due to the diversity of state government bureaucratic structures. The position of governor in most states is stronger today than previously, but there are still numerous governors with limited formal ability to dominate the policy process in their state capitals. Stronger governors seem to be found in states that are socially and economically heterogeneous and two-party competitive. In terms of government structure and political factors, gubernatorial power is enhanced by personnel controls, budgetary influence, political strength in the legislature, strong staff resources, cooperation from other elected executives, power to reorganize the executive branch, veto power, and a longer term of office. Many governors have some of these resources, but few have them all. Also, not all governors aspire to policy leadership.

Executive leadership at the local level is most prominent in general local governments—municipalities and counties (excluding townships)—and much less so in special districts. Strong mayors usually are the sole, substantive chief executive, serve for four years, direct budgetary decisions, play a significant role in local party politics, exercise control over personnel decisions, exercise a veto power, have no limit on reelection, and wield effective influence over the local bureaucracy. Weak mayors lack many or most of these formal powers and political resources. It is possible, however, for a few powers, skillfully utilized, to offset the absence of other powers. City managers are chief administrators with a tradition of remaining outside the role of political chief executive. Yet many are active initiators of policy proposals and directors of city administration. County executives are still relatively new and not very numerous. It appears that county executive leadership is dependent on many of the same factors that determine the extent of mayoral leadership. County administrators, while becoming more numerous, are not yet (and may not become) major centers of executive power in county government.

Features facilitating strong executive leadership at all levels include policy initiative, a strong budget role, personnel controls, staff resources, reorganization power, veto power, and strength in the legislature and/or a political party. Each type of chief executive has some advantages and disadvantages that the others lack, besides the variations in leadership qualities that occur from individual to individual.

NOTES

1. For an enlightening study of the Long years, see T. Harry Williams, *Huey Long* (New York: Knopf, 1969). Three useful, and contrasting, studies of Chicago's Mayor Daley are Mike Royko, *Boss: Richard J. Daley of Chicago* (New York: Dutton, 1971); Len O'Connor, *Clout: Mayor Daley and His City* (Chicago: Henry Regnery Company, 1975); and Milton Rakove, *Don't Make No Waves . . . Don't Back No Losers: An Insider's Analysis of the Daley Machine* (Bloomington: Indiana University Press, 1975). Political developments in Chicago since Daley's death in 1976 are examined in Samuel K. Gove and Louis H. Masotti, eds., *After Daley: Chicago Politics in Transition* (Urbana, Ill.: University of Illinois Press, 1982).
2. See Thad L. Beyle and J. Oliver Williams, eds., *The American Governor in Behavioral Perspective* (New York: Harper & Row, 1972); Thad L. Beyle, "Governors," in Virginia Gray, Herbert Jacob, and Kenneth N. Vines, eds., *Politics in the American States: A Comparative Analysis*, 4th ed. (Boston: Little, Brown, 1983), pp. 180–221; and Larry Sabato, *Goodbye to Good-Time Charlie: The American Governorship Transformed*, 2nd ed. (Washington, D.C.: CQ Press, 1983).
3. See Richard E. Neustadt, *Presidential Power: The Politics of Leadership from FDR to Carter* (New York: Wiley, 1980).
4. Douglas Fox, *The Politics of City and State Bureaucracy* (Pacific Palisades, Calif.: Goodyear Publishing, 1974), chapter 2.
5. Ibid., p. 25.
6. Ibid., pp. 24–25.
7. Ibid., pp. 29–31 and 35.
8. For an illuminating study of one governor's interactions with four state agencies, see Martha Wagner Weinberg, *Managing the State* (Cambridge, Mass.: M.I.T. Press, 1977).
9. Recent studies of presidential leadership, in particular, which deal with the interrelationships among these arenas include Frank Kessler, *The Dilemmas of Presidential Leadership: Of Caretakers and Kings* (Englewood Cliffs, N.J.: Prentice-Hall, 1982), and Bert A. Rockman, *The Leadership Question: The Presidency and the American System* (New York: Praeger, 1984).
10. Dwight A. Ink, "The President as Manager," *Public Administration Review*, 36 (September/October 1976), 508–15, at p. 515.

11. This account is taken from an Associated Press story that appeared in the Bloomington-Normal (Ill.) *Daily Pantagraph*, September 15, 1978, p. A-5.

12. Frank J. Sorauf has pointed out that there are political costs involved in exercising this legal authority to appoint and dismiss political supporters, because favorable treatment for some means disappointment for others. See *Party Politics in America*, 5th ed. (Boston: Little, Brown, 1984). See also the comments of former Pennsylvania Governor William Scranton, quoted in Sabato, *Goodbye to Good-Time Charlie*, p. 68.

13. See, among others, G. Calvin Mackenzie, *The Politics of Presidential Appointments* (New York: The Free Press, 1981), and John W. Macy, Bruce Adams, and J. Jackson Walter, *America's Unelected Government: Appointing the President's Team* (Cambridge, Mass.: Ballinger, 1983).

14. Harold Seidman, *Politics, Position, and Power: The Dynamics of Federal Organization*, 3rd ed. (New York: Oxford University Press, 1980), p. 116.

15. Thomas E. Cronin, *The State of the Presidency*, 2nd ed. (Boston: Little, Brown, 1980), p. 237. See also Mark R. Yessian, "The Generalist Perspective in the HEW Bureaucracy: An Account from the Field," *Public Administration Review*, 40 (March/April 1980), 138–49.

16. Seidman, *Politics, Position, and Power*, p. 96 (emphasis added). See also Cronin, *The State of the Presidency*, p. 228.

17. See Hugh Heclo, *A Government of Strangers: Executive Politics in Washington* (Washington, D.C.: Brookings, 1977).

18. This generalization held true for the period 1960–1972; see ibid., pp. 103–4.

19. Ibid., pp. 143–48.

20. Ibid., p. 143.

21. Ibid., p. 146.

22. Seidman, *Politics, Position, and Power*, p. 88.

23. Ibid.

24. Heclo, *A Government of Strangers*, pp. 176–77.

25. Ibid., pp. 144 and 148 (emphasis added).

26. See Cronin, *The State of the Presidency*, chapter 7.

27. *Newsweek*, January 26, 1981, p. 42.

28. The following treatment of President Reagan's management strategy is taken from Richard P. Nathan, *The Administrative Presidency* (New York: Wiley, 1983), chapters 6 and 7.

29. Ibid., p. 69 (emphasis added).

30. Ibid., p. 88.

31. Ibid., p. 81. Further discussion of the Reagan administration's management of the national bureaucracy can be found in Hugh Heclo, "One Executive Branch or Many?" In Anthony King, ed., *Both Ends of the Avenue: The Presidency, the Executive Branch, and Congress in the 1980s* (Washington, D.C.: American Enterprise Institute for Public Policy Research, 1983), pp. 26–58, at pp. 42–49, Chester Newland, "A Mid-Term Appraisal—The Reagan Presidency: Limited Government and Political Administration," *Public Administration Review*, 43 (January/February 1983), 1–21; and Fred I. Greenstein, ed., *The Reagan Presidency: An Early Assessment* (Baltimore: The Johns Hopkins University Press, 1983). Other sources dealing with presidential-bureaucratic relations include I. M. Destler, *Presidents, Bureaucrats, and Foreign Policy*, 2nd ed. (Princeton, N.J.: Princeton University Press, 1975), and "National Security Management: What

Presidents Have Wrought,'' *Political Science Quarterly*, 95 (Winter 1980–81), 573–88; Donald P. Warwick, *A Theory of Public Bureaucracy* (Cambridge, Mass.: Harvard University Press, 1975); Thomas P. Murphy, Donald E. Nuechterlein, and Ronald J. Stupak, *Inside the Bureaucracy: The View from the Assistant Secretary's Desk* (Boulder, Colo.: Westview, 1978); and Francis E. Rourke, ''Grappling with the Bureaucracy,'' in Arnold J. Meltsner, ed., *Politics and the Oval Office* (San Francisco: Institute for Contemporary Studies, 1981).

32. See Richard Fenno, *The Power of the Purse: Appropriations Politics in Congress* (Boston: Little, Brown, 1966); Lance T. LeLoup, *Budgetary Politics*, 2nd ed. (Brunswick, Ohio: King's Court, 1980); Robert D. Lee, Jr., and Ronald W. Johnson, *Public Budgeting Systems*, 3rd ed. (Baltimore: University Park Press, 1982); and Aaron Wildavsky, *The Politics of the Budgetary Process*, 4th ed. (Boston: Little, Brown, 1984).

33. See *Congressional Quarterly Weekly Report*, 38 (November 29, 1980), 3456–58; and *Congressional Quarterly Weekly Report*, 38 (December 6, 1980), 3520.

34. Seidman, *Politics, Position, and Power*, p. 3.

35. Ibid., p. 4.

36. Herbert Kaufman, ''Reflections on Administrative Reorganization,'' in Joseph A. Pechman, ed., *Setting National Priorities: The 1978 Budget* (Washington, D.C.: Brookings, 1977), pp. 391–418, at p. 392. This discussion relies extensively on Kaufman's treatment.

37. Ibid., pp. 392–94.

38. Ibid., p. 399.

39. Ibid., pp. 400–2.

40. Ibid., p. 402. For further discussion of executive reorganization, see David S. Brown, '' 'Reforming' the Bureaucracy: Some Suggestions for the New President,'' *Public Administration Review*, 37 (March/April 1977), 163–70, at pp. 165–66; Peter Szanton, ed., *Federal Reorganization: What Have We Learned?* (Chatham, N.J.: Chatham House, 1981), especially Lester M. Salamon, ''The Question of Goals''; I. M. Destler, ''Reorganization: When and How?''; and, also by Destler, ''Implementing Reorganization'' (pp. 58–84, 114–30, and 155–70, respectively); and Walter F. Baber, ''Reform for Principle and Profit,'' *The Bureaucrat*, 13 (Summer 1984), 33–37.

41. John C. Donovan, ''The Domestic Council and the Politics of Presidential Leadership,'' paper presented to the American Society for Public Administration, New York, March 23, 1972, at p. 5. See also Donovan's *The Policy Makers* (New York: Pegasus, 1970), p. 48; Margaret Jane Wyszomirski, ''The De-Institutionalization of Presidential Staff Agencies,'' *Public Administration Review*, 42 (September/October 1982), 448–58; and John Hart, *The Presidential Branch* (Elmsford, N.Y.: Pergamon, forthcoming).

42. See Thomas E. Cronin and Sanford D. Greenberg, *The Presidential Advisory System* (New York: Harper & Row, 1969).

43. Arthur Schlesinger, Jr., *The Coming of the New Deal* (Boston: Houghton Mifflin, 1958), especially pp. 521–29 and 533–37. Those portions are reprinted in Francis E. Rourke, ed., *Bureaucratic Power in National Politics*, 3rd ed. (Boston: Little, Brown, 1978), pp. 257–69.

44. See Anthony Downs, *Inside Bureaucracy* (Boston: Little, Brown, 1967), pp. 116–18.

45. See Herbert Kaufman, with the collaboration of Michael Couzens, *Administra-*

tive Feedback: Monitoring Subordinates' Behavior (Washington, D.C.: Brookings, 1973).

46. Downs, *Inside Bureaucracy*, pp. 118–26.

47. Graham Allison, *Essence of Decision: Explaining the Cuban Missile Crisis* (Boston: Little, Brown, 1971), pp. 122–23.

48. See Kessler, *The Dilemmas of Presidential Leadership;* Rockman, *The Leadership Question;* and Harold M. Barger, *The Impossible Presidency: Illusions and Realities of Executive Power* (Glenview, Ill.: Scott, Foresman, 1984). For cross-national perspectives on chief executives and their bureaucracies, see Joel D. Aberbach, Robert D. Putnam, and Bert A. Rockman, *Bureaucrats and Politicians in Western Democracies* (Cambridge, Mass.: Harvard University Press, 1981); and Colin Campbell, *Governments under Stress: Political Executives and Key Bureaucrats in Washington, London, and Ottawa* (Buffalo, N.Y.: University of Toronto Press, 1983).

49. Duane Lockard, ed., "A Mini-Symposium: The Strong Governorship: Status and Problems," *Public Administration Review,* 36 (January/February 1976), 90–98, at p. 96.

50. Kenneth T. Palmer, *State Politics in the United States,* 2nd ed. (New York: St. Martin's, 1977), p. 101.

51. Ibid., pp. 101–2. See also E. Lee Bernick, "Gubernatorial Tools: Formal vs. Informal," *Journal of Politics,* 41 (May 1979), 656–64, at p. 657; Beyle, "Governors," in Gray, Jacob, and Vines, *Politics in the American States,* p. 193; and Sabato, *Goodbye to Good-Time Charlie,* p. 89.

52. Terry Sanford, *Storm Over the States* (New York: McGraw-Hill, 1967), p. 30.

53. Sabato, *Goodbye to Good-Time Charlie,* p. 59.

54. Ibid.

55. Ibid., pp. 59–60.

56. *Book of the States 1980–1981* (Lexington, Ky.: Council of State Governments, 1981), pp. 182–83. This is a biennial publication of the Council of State Governments. For more information on these and other elected state executives, see Ann H. Elder and George C. Kiser, *Governing American States and Communities: Constraints and Opportunities* (Glenview, Ill.: Scott, Foresman, 1983), pp. 175–78. Sabato focuses specifically on the office of lieutenant governor in *Goodbye to Good-Time Charlie,* pp. 69–74.

57. Sabato, *Goodbye to Good-Time Charlie,* p. 65.

58. Palmer, *State Politics in the United States,* p. 77.

59. Ira Sharkansky, *The Politics of Taxing and Spending* (Indianapolis: Bobbs-Merrill, 1969), p. 89.

60. Carl W. Stenberg, "States Under the Spotlight: An Intergovernmental View," *Public Administration Review,* 45 (March/April 1985), 319–26, at p. 321.

61. Ibid.

62. Sabato, *Goodbye to Good-Time Charlie,* pp. 83–84.

63. Fox, *The Politics of City and State Bureaucracy,* p. 29.

64. Glenn Abney and Thomas P. Lauth, "The Governor as Chief Administrator," *Public Administration Review,* 43 (January/February 1983), 40–49, at p. 48.

65. Ibid.

66. Among other useful sources dealing with gubernatorial leadership in state administration, see Thomas P. Lauth, "Impact of the Method of Agency Head Selection on Gubernatorial Influence Over State Agency Appropriations," and

Diane Kincaid Blair, "Gubernatorial Appointments and Legislative Influence," in Dale Krane and Donato J. Pugliese, eds., "Symposium: State and Local Government Administration," in *Public Administration Quarterly*, 7 (Winter 1984), pp. 396–409 and 429–40, respectively.

67. U.S. Bureau of the Census, *1982 Census of Governments: Volume I, Governmental Organization* (Washington, D.C.: U.S. Government Printing Office, 1982), Table A, p. VI.

68. Russell M. Ross and Kenneth F. Millsap, *The Relative Power Position of Mayors in Mayor-Council Cities* (Iowa City: Laboratory for Political Research, University of Iowa, 1971), cited in Fox, *The Politics of City and State Bureaucracy*, p. 31.

69. This is a reference to the concept of separating "policy" and "politics" from "administration," which was quite prominent in the drive for municipal reform in the late 1800s and early 1900s. See chapter 2. See also Martin J. Schiesl, *The Politics of Efficiency: Municipal Administration and Reform in America, 1880–1920* (Berkeley, Calif.: University of California Press, 1977).

70. Fox, *The Politics of City and State Bureaucracy*, p. 34.

71. Ibid. See also J. David Woodard, "Ethics and the City Manager," in *The Bureaucrat*, 13 (Spring 1984), 53–57.

72. *Governmental Facts*, Bulletin Number 371-H of the Governmental Research Institute, Cleveland, April 18, 1980. I am indebted to Professor Thomas D. Wilson of Illinois State University for directing me to this data source.

73. Ibid.

74. For an interesting account of Rockefeller's tenure as governor of New York, see Robert H. Connery and Gerald Benjamin, *Rockefeller of New York: Executive Power in the Statehouse* (Ithaca, N. Y.: Cornell University Press, 1979).

75. See Sarah McCally Morehouse, "The State Political Party and the Policymaking Process," *American Political Science Review*, 67 (March 1973), 55–72, and *State Politics, Parties and Policy* (New York: Holt, Rinehart and Winston, 1981).

SUGGESTED READINGS

Beyle, Thad L. "Governors," in Gray, Virginia, Herbert Jacob, and Kenneth N. Vines, eds. *Politics in the American States: A Comparative Analysis*, 4th ed. Boston: Little, Brown, 1983.

Beyle, Thad L., and J. Oliver Williams, eds. *The American Governor in Behavioral Perspective*. New York: Harper & Row, 1972.

Cronin, Thomas E. *The State of the Presidency*, 2nd ed. Boston: Little, Brown, 1980.

Fox, Douglas M. *The Politics of City and State Bureaucracy*. Pacific Palisades, Calif.: Goodyear Publishing, 1974.

Greer, Ann L. *The Mayor's Mandate: Municipal Statecraft and Political Trust*. Cambridge, Mass.: Schenkman, 1974.

Heclo, Hugh. *A Government of Strangers: Executive Politics in Washington*. Washington, D. C.: Brookings, 1977.

Kessler, Frank. *The Dilemmas of Presidential Leadership: Of Caretakers and Kings*. Englewood Cliffs, N.J.: Prentice-Hall, 1982.

Koenig, Louis W. *The Chief Executive*, 4th ed. New York: Harcourt Brace Jovanovich, 1981.

Nathan, Richard P. *The Administrative Presidency*. New York: Wiley, 1983.

Neustadt, Richard. *Presidential Power: The Politics of Leadership from FDR to Carter*. New York: Wiley, 1980.

Palmer, Kenneth T. *State Politics in the United States*, 2nd ed. New York: St. Martin's, 1977.

Rakove, Milton. *Don't Make No Waves . . . Don't Back No Losers: An Insider's Analysis of the Daley Machine*. Bloomington: Indiana University Press, 1975.

Rockman, Bert A. *The Leadership Question: The Presidency and the American System*. New York: Praeger, 1984.

Sabato, Larry. *Goodbye to Good-Time Charlie: The American Governorship Transformed*, 2nd ed. Washington, D.C.: CQ Press, 1983.

Seidman, Harold. *Politics, Position, and Power: The Dynamics of Federal Organization*, 3rd ed. New York: Oxford University Press, 1980.

Weinberg, Martha Wagner. *Managing the State*. Cambridge, Mass.: M.I.T. Press, 1977.

5

Federalism and Intergovernmental Relations

A widely recognized feature of American government and politics is the federal system. Federalism provides for national and state governments existing independently of each other in the same territory and commanding the loyalties of the same individuals as citizens of both state and nation. The powers of both governmental levels are drawn from the same fundamental source—the sovereign people—and are exercised concurrently. The original rationale for establishing a federal system in the United States was to prevent concentration of power in a strong national government, with the states viewed as counterweights and protectors of individual liberties against a central power. Yet the nature and operation of federalism have not always been agreed upon, and are not today. Indeed, this nation was torn by a civil war over the twin issues of slavery and the extent of the states' authority in opposition to the national government. Since the New Deal, and with rising emphasis in the last few years, many Americans (including public officials of both major political parties) have expressed concern about the wide-ranging authority of the national government, focusing among other things on how it has affected state and local government powers. Ronald Reagan, for one, has stressed his belief that there needs to be a redistribution of authority *back* to states and localities from Washington, and his administration has undertaken comprehensive efforts to bring that about. The 1980 election may turn out to have signaled the end of an era of national government activism, just as the 1932 election of Franklin Roosevelt marked its beginning. But that question aside, it is likely that controversy over the balance among various levels of government will continue, as it has throughout much of this century.

133

Public administration is at the heart of many of the questions and controversies that have characterized contemporary federalism. The two have had a reciprocal effect on one another. The administration of national government programs has required recognition of and accommodation to the existence, prerogatives, and preferences of states and localities that have their own decision-making apparatus and political majorities. At the same time, the growth of bureaucracy at all levels of government has helped reshape the federal system.

In this chapter our concerns will include (1) the definition of federalism and a brief historical review of its evolution; (2) the rise of intergovernmental relations (IGR)—the multitude of formal and informal contacts among governmental entities throughout the federal system, and how these have modified federalism as a formal concept; (3) the tremendous expansion since 1960 of financial assistance from the national government to states and localities and accompanying shifts in the leverage exerted by the former over the latter; (4) administrative and political consequences of increased intergovernmental aid, especially administrative complexity and bureaucratic controls accompanying national government grants, and the political conflicts generated as a result; (5) growing concern about managing IGR and the grants system, with an eye to simplifying the process of obtaining aid; and (6) questions about the future course of IGR, including the impacts of diminished national government fiscal support for many of its own activities, as well as those at state and local levels.

Before we begin, a comment is in order about one key term in this discussion, namely, *federal*. Technically, *federal* refers to the nature of the formal relationships among different levels of government and of various qualities or characteristics of those relationships. In a more colloquial sense, however, many people use the term when referring to the national government (''the federal government''). Such usage, which has roots in debates over ratification of the Constitution in the 1780s, can lead to confusion when thinking about federalism and IGR. In this chapter and elsewhere, when reference is made to *the national government*, that is the phrase employed; *federal* is used in its more technical sense, for the sake of clarity.

THE NATURE OF FEDERALISM: THE FORMAL SETTING

The most elementary definition of federalism suggests that it is a *constitutional* division of governmental power between a central or national government and a set of regional units (such as the American states, Canadian provinces, Swiss cantons, Soviet federated republics, and so on); that under a federal arrangement both the national and the regional governments have some independent as well as some shared powers over their citizens;

that neither government owes its legal existence to the other (as local governments in the United States do to the states); and that as a matter of law neither may dictate to the other(s) in matters of structural organization, fiscal policies, or definition of essential functions. This definition clearly implies that the regional governments have substantial independence from the national government, but that both may exercise powers of government directly over their citizens. It leaves open, however, some pertinent questions about how authority is to be exercised *simultaneously* by different units of government sharing jurisdiction over the same territory and citizenry.

Federalism also is an explicitly *political* arrangement. This relates in important ways to how power in a governmental system is distributed, structured, and exercised. A federal arrangement is designed to restrain and counteract centralized power through "a multiple structuring of political decision-making centers that act in different geographical regions. . . ."[1] Such a system makes it less likely that a central government could achieve an excessive concentration of power—which might endanger the freedoms of the people—because of the presence of separate, legitimate, and authoritative governmental units operating individually within the same overall territory. Finally, federalism has an increasingly important *fiscal/administrative* dimension. This pertains both to the operations of government programs that have impact on at least one other level or unit of government, and to the growing interrelatedness and complexity of programs created, funded, and managed by different governments. We will treat the phenomenon of intergovernmental relations in considerably more detail, later in this chapter.

In the early 1800s, the U.S. Supreme Court defined some essential boundaries in national-state relations, with long-term implications. The fundamental issue was the scope of national authority, particularly when it overlapped and conflicted with state powers. Specific questions included whether states could tax national government agencies (they cannot,[2] and later rulings established mutual intergovernmental tax immunity); whether the national power to regulate interstate commerce superseded state regulatory actions setting up conflicting rules (it does, with some exceptions); and whether the states could interfere in any way with national enforcement of national laws (they cannot). Some other issues were resolved in Congress and by presidential action. The question of slavery, however, proved insoluble through the political system. This failure, coupled with irreconcilable differences (related to slavery) over national versus state sovereignty, resulted in secession and in the creation of a confederation of eleven states. The Civil War followed, culminating in a Union victory that was both military and political: slavery was ended, the Union preserved, and a federal, not confederate (state-centered), system reaffirmed.

The next half-century was a time of transition in American federalism. Many basic decisions affecting the legal structuring of federalism were behind us, and as government generally became more active in dealing with problems of society, it became more common to find some form of joint or overlapping governmental activities. A number of new national programs combined participation by (especially) state governments with use of the first cash grants-in-aid from the national government to the states; examples include the Agricultural Extension Act of 1914, the Federal Aid Highway Act of 1916, and the Vocational Education Act of 1917.[3] Fundamental legal questions were receding in importance, but modern intergovernmental relations had not yet come into full bloom.

INTERGOVERNMENTAL RELATIONS: THE NEW FACE OF FEDERALISM

Intergovernmental relations is a relatively new term, which has come into common usage only in the past fifty years. It has been said to designate "an important body of activities or interactions occurring between governmental units of all types and levels within the [United States] federal system."[4] Intergovernmental relations embrace, in political scientist Deil Wright's words, "all the permutations and combinations of relations among the units of government in our system."[5] These include national-state and interstate relations—the areas traditionally emphasized in the study of federalism—but also national-local, state-local, interlocal, and national-state-local relations. In addition, there are a number of other key features of IGR worth noting.

One is the fact that they are virtually invisible to many citizens, a "hidden dimension of government," in the words of Edmund Muskie, then chairman of the Senate Subcommittee on Intergovernmental Relations. Speaking at the first hearings of the newly formed subcommittee in 1962, Muskie observed: "Performing as almost a fourth branch of government in meeting the needs of our people, it nonetheless has no direct electorate, operates from no set perspective, is under no special control, and moves in no particular direction. . . . Programs in this field make an unpredictable impact on our society and our economy. The world of intergovernmental relations is represented by no policy-making body—there is no executive, no legislative, and no judiciary."[6] This is so in spite of the fact (or perhaps in part because of it) that most Americans have not been aware of the extent to which IGR has become a part of American governance.

Another feature of IGR is that although we speak of inter*governmental* relations, "[i]t is human beings clothed with office who are the real determiners of what the relations between units of government will be. Consequently, the concept of intergovernmental relations necessarily has to be formulated largely in terms of human relations and human behavior. . . ."[7] In Wright's words, "The individual actions and attitudes of public officials are at the core of IGR."[8] Who the officials are, the roles they play in the governmental process, their policy views, and the interests they seek to promote all have a bearing on the conduct of IGR.

Third, the term IGR does not refer to one-time contacts, occasional interactions, or formal agreements. Rather, it is the "continuous, day-to-day patterns of contact and exchanges of information and views"[9] among government officials, in informal, practical, and problem-oriented ways. Virtually all policy areas have an intergovernmental dimension, and some are almost totally the product of shared policy formulation, implementation, or financing. Examples of such policy areas include public housing, agriculture, transportation, and education. However, the fact that policy is fashioned through intergovernmental processes does not mean that government officials agree with one another on all or even most major aspects of a program; IGR can be cooperative or competitive/conflicting, or some combination, and still be IGR.

Another key feature of IGR is the involvement of public officials at all levels of government. Clearly involved are chief executives and legislators in Washington, the state capital, the county seat, and city hall, since theirs is the principal responsibility for enactment of programs that become a part of IGR. In the past twenty-five years, another set of public officials—appointed administrators—has warranted increasing attention in IGR. Administrative agencies at all levels of government have assumed greater responsibility, and as IGR has generally become more pervasive, intergovernmental *administrative* relations have taken on ever greater significance. (An issue of some importance in IGR, discussed later in this chapter, concerns the degree to which influence has become concentrated in the administrative arm of government at all levels without effective means of control by elected officials.)

THE "POLITICS" OF IGR: AN OVERVIEW

The structure of intergovernmental relations is . . . a federal one in which the powers and responsibilities of government in general are shared among specific governments. However, *the sharing of power and responsibility is not equal, nor is it unalterable.* As a result, the structure of authority [in IGR] tends to be rather loose, and it invites frequent clashes between governments over the right to make certain kinds of decisions. *Conflict often arises in the course of day-to-day interactions between governments* as they seek to define and redefine their relationships with one another in order to satisfy the demands of their respective citizenries.

Source: Russell L. Hanson, "The Intergovernmental Setting of State Politics," in Virginia Gray, Herbert Jacob, and Kenneth N. Vines, eds., *Politics in the American States: A Comparative Analysis,* 4th ed. (Boston: Little, Brown, 1983), p. 28 (emphasis added).

Political scientist Richard Leach has pointed out two other important aspects of modern IGR. First, "action in the American federal state is not confined to governments alone."[10] Although we speak of inter*governmental* relations, many public purposes are accomplished through nongovernmental institutions and organizations. Thus IGR, properly understood, also includes the public functions of organizations not formally part of any government (voluntary action groups, civic organizations, and so on).

Leach's second point is that action in the federal system is taken on parts of a general problem rather than on the total problem area—action is fragmented rather than comprehensive. Governments are prone to act in response to relatively specific pressures for narrow objectives, and find it difficult and politically unprofitable to do otherwise. Thus, government policies exist in such areas as water quality and noise pollution, but no *one* policy governs the nation's approach to environmental quality. Similarly, there are policies concerning urban mass transit and public housing, but there is no *one* overall urban policy. A major reason for this is the ability of literally hundreds of governmental agencies at all levels to act independently of one another, so that a policy emerges only in incomplete form and, in the majority of cases, lacking a centrally coordinated direction.[11] Contributing to this, of course, is the fact—discussed previously—that the national government itself is far from a monolithic entity. A wide spectrum of political opinions and issue preferences is reflected in the multitude of national government activities. It is thus impossible to speak of what *the* national government desires, intends to do, or is actually doing, as if there were only one preference, intention, or action. The same may be said, though perhaps to a lesser extent, of many state and local governments as well. Thus, when different governments *do* try to integrate their efforts through cooperative activity, their joint undertakings may well be built on a foundation of programs that are not consistent in intent, design, or execution. IGR is characterized both by this lack of central direction and by mounting efforts in recent years to overcome it.

The Courts and Intergovernmental Relations

Does the rise to prominence of IGR mean that the legal side of federalism is no longer of any consequence? No, quite the contrary. Both national and state judiciaries have been called upon increasingly in recent years to resolve federalism-related disputes. Indeed, the U.S. Supreme Court has handed down a number of significant rulings—in areas such as municipal immunity from national government antitrust laws, state and local personnel management practices, and local regulation of handguns—with a direct bearing on the particular powers that may be exercised by different governments in the federal system.

One far-reaching decision came in March 1985, when the Supreme

Court resolved a continuing dispute concerning the liability of municipal officials to be sued for alleged violations of national government antitrust laws. In *Town of Hallie v. City of Eau Claire*, the Court ruled that municipal governments are immune from antitrust suits even if their anticompetitive activities are not required by state law or actively supervised by state governments.[12] At issue was a dispute between the city of Eau Claire, Wisconsin, which owns and operates a sewage treatment plant, and several nearby towns (including Hallie) seeking provision of sewage treatment service to their residents.[13] Eau Claire officials had refused to provide such service unless the residents agreed to have their property annexed to the city, on the grounds that Wisconsin state law permitted them to define the geographic area to be served. Town officials, on the other hand, claimed that the city's refusal to provide access to the sewage treatment facility constituted an illegal monopolization of the service, in violation of the Sherman Act. Previous Supreme Court decisions related to this issue had required municipalities to demonstrate that anticompetitive activities had been approved by their respective state governments, and had made municipal antitrust immunity dependent upon specific, case-by-case grants of immunity by the states (especially regarding regulation of commercial activities).[14] Those previous rulings had ''left municipal governments and their officials exposed to triple damages from companies or other private parties claiming denial of a franchise on services ranging from cable television and mass transit to sewage treatment and ambulance transportation.''[15] In October 1984, Congress passed a statute protecting local governments from monetary damage awards in such antitrust suits. However, the statute also provided that the courts still could grant injunctions against cities and counties ordering them to cease ''anti-competitive'' practices.[16] Informed observers believe, however, that the *Town of Hallie* decision effectively wipes out most areas of municipal antitrust liability.

The high court has become extensively involved in a wide variety of other cases as well. In 1982 the Court ruled, for example, that New York state could not apply its own labor relations laws to prohibit strikes on the Long Island Railroad. The Court said that national railroad legislation governing labor relations must apply, even though the Long Island line was taken over by the state twenty years ago, receives an annual subsidy of $200 million, and operates exclusively within the state; in addition, the railroad workers are state employees.[17] The following year the Court ruled that under provisions of the national Age Discrimination in Employment Act, the state of Wyoming could not require its game wardens to retire at age 55. The Court thus sustained Congress' use of the commerce clause in the U.S. Constitution as a basis for limiting the powers of the states in personnel matters.[18] Also in 1983 the Court left standing an appellate court decision which upheld the right of a municipal government (in this case Morton Grove, Illinois) to ban the possession of handguns within city limits.[19] And in February 1985 the Court, in a 5–4 decision, ruled that state and local governments are subject to the minimum-wage and overtime requirements of the national government's Fair Labor Standards Act, in setting terms and conditions of employment for their employees. The Court's opinion held, among other things, that there is nothing in the wage and overtime requirements that is ''destructive of state sovereignty or violative of any constitutional provision''—a forthright assertion of national government authority in an area some regard as central to state and local government management.[20] (Congress later acted to dilute the effects of this decision.)

It is not only the Supreme Court, or national government courts alone, that have had an impact on IGR. For example, a U.S. District Court ruled in 1981 that the state of Indiana was responsible for paying the transportation (busing) costs of the Indianapolis school system, which had been sued successfully by local minority groups for racial discrimination. The court ruled that the discrimination in question was a result of the state's role in creating UNIGOV, the metropolitan government of greater Indianapolis. As a result, the state was liable for the costs of busing to overcome the effects of the segregation that had resulted from the creation of UNIGOV.[21] Also, the California Court of Appeal ruled in 1983 that a San Francisco handgun ordinance similar to the one passed in Morton Grove conflicted with state laws allowing firearms to be kept in businesses and private homes without a license.[22]

It also should be noted that early in 1984, the U.S. Supreme Court handed down another significant federalism-related decision. The Court, by a 5–4 margin, sharply limited the power of other national government courts, ruling that the lower courts have no authority to order *state* officials to obey state laws. The decision greatly expanded the scope of the Eleventh Amendment, the relatively obscure provision giving state governments immunity from being sued in U.S. courts without their consent; previously, the Court had held repeatedly that the amendment did not apply to suits charging individual state officials with violating the law.[23] This decision strengthened the ability of state officials to operate independently within the federal framework—unlike some of the cases mentioned earlier, and indeed contrary to many pervasive trends in American law for at least a generation. (The implications for administration of civil rights statutes alone are considerable. The overall role of the courts, referred to in chapter 3, also is likely to be reduced.)

The courts, then, have been a highly significant force in shaping the organization and operation of the federal system. The continuing expansion of IGR has served only to increase the reach of judicial decision making, since more governments and their actions are potentially affected by any given ruling. That is testimony to the increased complexity within American federalism, and it is that subject to which we now turn our attention.

CONTEMPORARY INTERGOVERNMENTAL RELATIONS: THE RISE OF COMPLEXITY

It was under Franklin Roosevelt, a Democrat, in the 1930s and 1940s that national government activity underwent a quantum leap in terms of scope and diversity, and IGR became more closely interwoven with general (and more centralized) governmental undertakings. Rarely with any fanfare, but steadily nonetheless, intergovernmental aid and joint efforts became more important components of public policy making. Thus, for example, national government grants for rural highway construction and maintenance (begun in 1916) became more numerous; grants for urban renewal became more widely used; direct aid to urban governments for airport construction and other transportation purposes also appeared on the scene.[24] In the 1950s, under a Republican president, the pace of national government expansion slackened, but it did not stop completely. Significantly, it was just after Dwight Eisenhower took office in 1953 that the Department of Health, Education and Welfare was created, paving the way for later expansion of grants and other provisions relating to social services. Throughout this thirty-year period, increased national government activity and rising importance of IGR paralleled one another—and indeed, often coincided. With the advent of the 1960s, however, IGR experienced its own quantum leap, into new forms and new impacts.

In the last two decades, "the texture of our intergovernmental relations has been transformed . . ."[25]—by the rapid proliferation of financial transactions among different levels of government, by development of a multitude of new and often permanent linkages among program administrators at all levels, by establishment of new forms of government—such as economic development districts and health planning agencies—and by issuance of literally thousands of rules, guidelines, and regulations (often accompanying fiscal aid packages) to hundreds of governmental units. All this has sparked political controversy of various kinds. It has also posed immense new challenges to those responsible for effectively administering government programs in a constantly changing environment. The fact that these developments have been largely interrelated has made it all the more difficult to cope with them.

In the discussion that follows, several principal themes stand out. One is the importance, in this context as well as in broader administrative terms, of government purposes organized according to *function*. Functional alliances, in fact, have tended to dominate contemporary IGR and have become centers of ongoing controversy as a result. Another theme, closely linked to the first, is the growing political and managerial struggle between elected public officials and administrative/functional specialists (and their respective political allies) for control of major IGR programmatic directions. A third, broader theme focuses on the tensions between forces promoting greater *centralization* in the general governmental system and those resisting it. Nowhere is that issue more crucial than in the federalism/IGR realm, since a prime purpose of federalism is to prevent excessive centralization of public authority. Self-conscious efforts both to centralize and to *de*centralize government programs have been numerous in the last two decades, and no end to either is in sight. Within all of these themes there are fiscal, administrative, and political dimensions.

INTERGOVERNMENTAL FISCAL RELATIONS

Intergovernmental fiscal relations, or *fiscal federalism*, is central to contemporary IGR. While there have been some forms of financial aid from one governmental level to another throughout American history, the scope of such transactions in various forms has expanded rapidly and dramatically in the past forty years. This applies to national government aid to states and localities and, to a lesser extent, state aid to local governments.

Intergovernmental aid has taken on greater importance for a relatively simple reason. State and local governments have weaker economic bases and less productive systems of taxation than the national government possesses (with some exceptions, such as Texas and Alaska), yet the former provide the great bulk of public services in health, education, welfare, housing, highway construction, police protection, parks and recreation, conservation, and agricultural services. The national government, with far stronger fiscal resources, delivers *directly* only a few public services, such as Social Security benefits, veterans' payments, and farmers' subsidies.[26] In essence, the national government, with the greatest tax resources, delivers the fewest services directly; local governments, with the narrowest and weakest tax bases, are frequently the most heavily laden with costly service obligations (police, fire, streets and roads, sewage and sanitation, water, and utilities); the states fall between them.

There are two basic reasons for the revenue-raising disparity among different governmental levels. First, local and state governments have limited geographic areas—often dependent on one or two products or resources—from which to extract revenues (for instance, coal in West Virginia). A more diversified economy is a more stable and productive source of government income, and only the national government has access to the nation's full range of economic resources.

Second, different types of taxes yield different amounts of revenue from the same income base. The most responsive, or elastic, tax—showing the greatest increase in revenue for a given rise in taxable income—is the *graduated income tax* (*graduated* meaning that the tax rate rises as income increases). Somewhat less elastic is the *sales tax*, where a flat percentage rate is levied on the amount of purchase; some sales taxes are general, with few exemptions, while others are selective, applying to certain items only. Least elastic is the *personal property tax*, levied on real estate and other personal belongings. The national government is the principal user of the graduated income tax; states rely on sales and other excise taxes; and local governments, including special districts, depend most heavily on personal property taxes (though sales and wage taxes have come into increasing use by state and local governments).[27]

Thus, the government with the broadest tax base (the national government) also uses the best generator of revenue, while the governments with the narrowest and least diversified tax base (local governments) employ the least elastic tax (with the states again falling between the two). The result is a "fiscal mismatch," not only between the service needs and fiscal capacities of different levels of government, but also among different governments at the same level in terms of their varying abilities to pay for needed public services (for example, rich versus poor school districts). Rising service demands on government at all levels have placed a particular strain on those governments least able to expand their tax revenues rapidly (that is, local units). The consequence of all this has been increasing demand for aid from higher levels of government to help pay for proliferating government services.

Grants-in-Aid

The growing needs of state and local government coincided with rising interest in Congress and the executive branch in expanding and upgrading available public services, regardless of the specific government providing them. The stage was set, by the 1960s, for the national government (and some states) to utilize financial assistance on a much larger scale than before, as a means of providing expanded public services. The principal device adopted to bring all this about was the grant-in-aid—an established mechanism for thirty years, now to be given a substantially enlarged role.

Grants-in-aid may be defined as "money payments furnished by a higher to a lower level of government to be used for specified purposes and subject to conditions spelled out in law or administrative regulation."[28] This form of cash transfer is used most widely by the national government, although states also make some use of it. At the time of John F. Kennedy's inauguration in 1961, some forty-five separate grant authorizations (statutes) existed. (Under each authorization, multiple allocations of funds can be made.) But in the period 1965–1966, when Lyndon B. Johnson commanded decisive Democratic majorities in both chambers of Congress, he took advantage of the opportunity to legislate a host of new grant programs as he pursued his vision of the "Great Society." By the time Richard Nixon entered the White House (only eight years after Kennedy had), the number of grants had mushroomed to about 400—and, using the criterion of separate authorizations, the U.S. Advisory Commission on Intergovernmental

Relations (ACIR) estimated that almost 500 grant programs existed in fiscal year (FY) 1978, and some 540 grants in FY 1981. (Under the Reagan administration, however, the number of grants has dropped to about 400, as of fiscal year 1985—with significant adverse implications for state and local delivery of many public services, and for the fiscal well-being of many state and local jurisdictions.) Grants have financed state and local programs in virtually every major domestic policy area—urban renewal, highways, mass transit, education, recreation, public health, and so on. Equally dramatic is the increase in dollar amounts appropriated under national grant programs. In FY 1960 the figure was about $7 billion; by 1970 it had risen to $24 billion; five years later, it was almost $50 billion and by FY 1981, it was just under $95 billion.[29] The Reagan administration, however, has succeeded in its efforts to slow the rate of growth in spending for grants, actually reducing the FY 1982 level by 7 percent (to $88.2 billion), and attempting since then to ''hold the line'' against the kind of dramatic annual increases that characterized the late 1960s and the 1970s (see Table 5-1).

National grants-in-aid have been enacted to achieve certain broad purposes.[30] These include (1) establishing minimum nationwide standards for programs operating in all parts of the country, (2) equalizing resources among the states by allocating proportionately more money to poorer states (the ''Robin Hood principle'' of taking from the rich and giving to the poor), (3) improving state and local program adequacy, (4) concentrating research resources on a problem that crosses government boundary lines or that attracts interest from numerous governments (such as air pollution), and (5) increasing public services without enlarging the structure of the national government or its apparent role in domestic politics. Other purposes have included improvements in the structure and operation of state and local agencies (such as merit personnel practices or better planning), demonstration and experimentation in national policy, encouragement of general social objectives such as nondiscrimination in hiring, and provision of services to otherwise underserviced portions of the population. The importance of grants-in-aid in the total picture of domestic programs and administration is suggested by the fact that throughout the 1970s they provided approximately *one-fourth* of state-local revenues each fiscal year, although that proportion began to decline after 1978. The decline became even more dramatic in the early 1980s, following Ronald Reagan's election to the presidency (see Table 5-1).

National grant programs were used in the 1960s to foster state and local planning activities where none had existed previously or where they were not systematic or well developed. Beginning with the Housing Act of 1954, funding had been made available specifically to assist state and local planners in preparing proposals related to housing program grants; this pattern was repeated in the host of new programs enacted in the years following. As national goals came to be stressed, Congress and the bureaucracy took this one step further, setting requirements for planning as a pre-

Table 5-1

NATIONAL GOVERNMENT GRANTS-IN-AID: NUMBER OF GRANT PROGRAMS, CURRENT DOLLARS AND CONSTANT (1972) DOLLARS, AND AS A PROPORTION OF STATE/LOCAL RECEIPTS AND EXPENDITURES (DOLLAR AMOUNTS IN BILLIONS)

Fiscal Year	Number of Grant Programs[1]	Amount (Current $)	Annual Percentage Increase or Decrease (−)	Amount (1972 $)	Annual Percentage Increase or Decrease (−)	Percent of State/Local Receipts from Own Source	Percent of State/Local Expenditures
1955	n.a.	$ 3.2	—	$ 5.6	—	11.8%	10.1%
1960	132	7.0	—	10.8	—	16.8	14.7
1965	379[2]	10.9	—	15.5	—	17.7	15.3
1970	n.a.	24.0	—	27.0	—	22.9	19.2
1975	442	49.8	—	39.2	—	29.1	23.0
1976	n.a.	59.1	18.7	43.5	11.0	31.1	24.2
1977	n.a.	68.4	15.7	46.7	7.4	31.0	25.9
1978	492	77.9	13.9	49.4	5.8	31.7	26.8
1979	n.a.	82.9	6.4	48.1	− 2.6	31.3	26.3
1980	n.a.	91.5	10.4	48.2	0.2	31.7	26.3
1981	539	94.8	3.6	46.1	− 4.4	30.1	25.2
1982	441	88.2	− 7.0	40.4	−12.4	25.6	21.9
1983	n.a.	92.5	4.9	40.7	0.7	24.7	21.6
1984	405	97.6	5.5	41.3	1.5	23.7	21.2
1985 est.	n.a.	107.0	9.7	43.5	5.3	24.3	n.a.
1986 est.	n.a.	100.7	− 5.9	39.3	− 9.7	21.4	n.a.

n.a. = not available.

1. This figure includes categorical grants, block grants, and revenue sharing. In FY 1984 there were 392 categorical grants, 12 block grants, and the revenue sharing program, for a total of 405 grant programs.

2. The number of grants in 1965 was not available; the figure shown is for FY 1967.

Sources: Adapted from U.S. Advisory Commission on Intergovernmental Relations, *Significant Features of Fiscal Federalism,* 1984 edition, Table 8 (Washington, D.C.: U.S. Government Printing Office, March 1985), p. 21; and U.S. Office of Management and Budget, *Special Analyses: Budget of the United States Government, Fiscal Year 1986* (Washington, D.C.: U.S. Government Printing Office, 1985), Table H-7, p. H-19.

condition for grant assistance. The Demonstration Cities and Metropolitan Development Act of 1966 (the Model Cities Act) stipulated, in addition, that grant applications from local governments in metropolitan areas must first have been screened by an areawide comprehensive planning agency as to the project's relationship to overall area development, with the screening agency's comments (if any) accompanying the project application. Regional planning commissions (RPCs) and councils of government (COGs) were designated as the screening agencies for metropolitan areas; similar entities were formed for nonmetropolitan areas when the requirements were subsequently extended. Planning became a prominent emphasis within the grant system, and fulfillment of national guidelines became a criterion for aid—and, not surprisingly, an occasional point of dispute between aid applicants and grantors. Significantly, most decisions in this area were in the hands of professional bureaucrats and bureaucracies, with less direct involvement of either elected executives or legislators at any level of government.

The advantages of grants-in-aid are numerous. First, the national government affords a single focal point for bringing about a greater degree of concerted action on a policy problem (bearing in mind, of course, the diversity within the national government). Second, political minorities in states and localities have an opportunity to seek some measure of national support for their policy demands, as blacks and other social-political minorities did in the 1960s. Third, grants-in-aid are an appropriate means of dealing with problems of nationwide scope; many policy questions are also interrelated in terms of their impact, such as questions linking highways, urban transportation, and air pollution, or education, unemployment, poverty, and welfare. While a fully coordinated attack on such sets of problems has yet to be mounted (and is not likely to be), a greater degree of consistency is possible at the national level than among fifty separate states and 82,000 local governments.

Finally, and perhaps most important as a rationale, it has been suggested that national funds assist states and localities with programs and projects that benefit citizens outside the borders of the recipient government. These ripple effects—or, more formally, *externalities*—justify national monetary support for state or local efforts because of the wider benefits realized. Three examples illustrate the point: (1) a state job training center, whose graduates may find employment in other states, (2) a state park system (such as Kentucky's, one of the best), which attracts tourists and vacationers from a much wider geographic area, and (3) local education systems, which, in a mobile society such as ours, are undoubtedly investing in the future productivity and contributions of persons who will reap the benefits of their education elsewhere. Since the nation as a whole gains from such investments of state and local funds, there is good reason to add grant funding from the national treasury.

Grants-in-aid have taken several forms. One way to distinguish among the various types is to ask how specifically the purposes or uses of the money are spelled out in the legislation or administrative regulations under which it is allocated. Another way is to determine whether the grant allocations are made by a common formula or by national agency approval of specific project applications. Let us look at each of these in turn.

Categorical and *block* grants differ in that the former have narrowly defined purposes and the latter's purposes are much more broadly specified—in both cases, by the grantors. The principal difference is that the agency responsible for administering a categorical grant also has a great deal to say about the precise uses of the money, "leaving very little discretionary room on the part of a recipient government."[31] Block grants, while also given out for use in a specific policy area (such as community development or public health), leave much more discretion and flexibility as to use of such funds in the hands of recipient governments. The extreme specificity of categorical grants has been described as "hardening of the categories," which

> . . . created such proliferation of minutely targeted grants that by the late 1960s a local government wishing to improve its recreational amenities had to make separate applications to several different agencies if its total program included buying land for park purposes; building a swimming pool on it; operating an activity center for senior citizens; putting in trees and shrubbery; and purchasing sports equipment. In the area of urban transportation . . . there are [or have been] separate categorical grant programs covering car pool demonstration projects; urban transportation planning; urban area traffic operations improvement; urban mass transportation basic grants (based on a formula for fund distribution); and mass transit grants (on a project application basis).[32]

With as many as 540 such grants operative in the early 1980s (though, as noted, there are fewer now), the categorical grant business has been more than a little complicated (see Table 5-2 for a comparison of the scope of categorical grant assistance before 1960 and in FY 1984).

The second way to distinguish grant-in-aid types is whether they are allocated according to a formula or in response to individual government applications. Of the nearly 400 categoricals in existence in 1984, approximately two-thirds were *project grants*, available by application; the remaining one-third were *formula grants*, for purposes such as aid to the blind—an ongoing need and one common to many government jurisdictions. On the other hand, although individual project grants outnumber formula grants, the dollar amounts available under the latter exceed those of the former by about the same two-to-one ratio.[33] The five block grant programs in operation at the end of the 1970s were all formula grants, with less direct bureaucratic control than under categorical grants. The same is true of the new block grants introduced under the Reagan administration (we will discuss more fully the recent expansion of block grants, and the reduction in the number of categoricals, later in this chapter).

Table 5-2
THE SCOPE OF NATIONAL AID HAS INCREASED DRAMATICALLY

Prior to 1960—Few and Far Between	*1984—Categorical Grants for Everything (But for Less Than Before)* **Budget Subfunction**	**Number of Programs**
1787 Education Land Grants	Department of Defense	7
1862 Agricultural Education (land grant colleges)	General Science and Basic Research	1
1914 Agricultural Extension	Energy	12
• 50–50 matching	Water Resources	4
• state plan approved	Conservation and Land Management	12
• first modern conditional money grant	Recreational Resources	9
1916 Federal Aid Highways	Pollution Control and Abatement	28
1917 Vocational Education	Other Natural Resources	5
1921 Public Health Assistance	Agricultural Research and Services	9
1935 Social Security	Mortgage Credit and Thrift Insurance	2
1935 Public Assistance	Other Advancement and Regulation of Commerce	5
1937 Housing	Ground Transportation	31
1946 Airport Aid	Water Transportation	1
1946 Hospital and Medical Facilities	Air Transportation	1
1948 Water Pollution Control	Other Transportation	1
1949 Urban Renewal	Community Development	7
1950 Federal Impact School Aid	Area and Regional Development	24
1954 State and Local Planning Assistance	Disaster Relief and Insurance	12
1954 Small Watershed Protection	Elementary, Secondary, and Vocational Education	53
1955 Air Pollution Control	Higher Education	8
1956 Library Aid	Research and General Education Aids	12
1958 College Student Aid	Training and Employment	13
	Other Labor Services	2
	Social Services	56
	Health	40
	Public Assistance and Other Income Supplements	24
	Veterans Benefits and Services	5
	Administration of Justice	7
	General Property and Records Management	1
	Total	392

Sources: ACIR, In Brief: The Federal Role in the Federal System: The Dynamics of Growth (Washington, D.C.: ACIR, December 1980), pp 2–3; ACIR, A Catalog of Federal Grant-In-Aid Programs to State and Local Governments: Grants Funded, FY 1984 (Washington, D.C.: ACIR, December 1984), Table 2.

With grants-in-aid of all types, the proportion of total expenditure paid by the national government varies considerably. Congress defines some grants as representing important national initiatives and sets the national government share at 100 percent. Other grants require dollar-for-dollar matching funds by the recipient government, which still doubles the total amount of money available to the recipient. Some other grant allocations require recipients to share the burden to some extent, but not fifty-fifty (sometimes as little as 1 percent of the total). The national share, then, is at least one-half, and can cover the total.

Several other observations should be made with reference to Tables 5-1 and 5-2. First, only two dozen categorical grant programs account for *almost 90 percent* of total spending for categoricals. These include the Medicaid program, child nutrition grants, wastewater treatment plant construction, Aid to Families with Dependent Children (AFDC), training and employment programs, low-rent public housing, and community development programs. Second, while spending for intergovernmental aid has risen at the rate of about 5 percent annually since 1982, grant spending reached its peak in *constant* dollars—that is, adjusted for inflation—in FY 1978–1980. A sharp aid reduction then occurred between FY 1981 and 1982, before spending levels began edging upward again. Also, national government assistance as a proportion of both state/local revenues and state/local expenditures began to decline after FY 1980, but that proportionate decline has *continued* even though grant spending (in both current and constant dollars) increased.[34]

The expansion of grants-in-aid during the 1960s was accompanied by qualitative and administrative changes. First, project grants became far more numerous (the rapid growth in grants of the mid-1960s was primarily in this form). Second, there was an increased variety of matching-grant formulas. Third, it became possible to apply for multiple-function instead of single-function grants, though the number of these was small. Fourth, Congress broadened the eligibility of grant recipients and increased joint-recipient possibilities. Fifth, under President Johnson, aid was concentrated in large urban areas and directed to the urban poor in numerous new ventures. Sixth, there was increased national aid not only to governments but also to private institutions, including corporations, universities, and nonprofit organizations. Finally, the national government made funding available specifically to assist state and local jurisdictions in improving both their planning capabilities and their actual planning activities.[35] All of these changes grew out of an expanding emphasis on achieving *national* goals under the direction of the national government.[36]

The year 1960 marked something of a turning point. Prior to that time, aid had been used primarily to *supplement* policy actions of states and localities, but under Kennedy and Johnson, presidential and congressional initiatives were couched more in terms of national purposes. Given this emphasis, it was deemed entirely appropriate to write into grant legislation substantive and procedural requirements that would promote those purposes.[37] *Administration* of these programs remained predominantly in the hands of state and local governments, but the national role in defining the uses of grant funds was clearly becoming decisive in determining general policy directions and many specific state and local program activities.

Categorical Grants and Administrative Complexity

We have noted already a number of administrative dimensions in the preceding discussion of grants-in-aid. These include the objectives of providing more and better public services (with growing emphasis recently on efficiency and effectiveness—both squarely in our administrative traditions), establishing minimum uniform programmatic standards nationwide, enhancing both the procedure and the substance of state and local programs, and strengthening the planning function. *How* all this was to be done, however, was and is a serious question. The use of categorical grants, rather than some other instrument of assistance, contributed directly to the rise of administrative complexity. This is so because of historical patterns in grants management that are worth reviewing.

Most grants, it should be noted, went to state governments before 1960; even today, states receive more than two-thirds of all formula grants and act as a conduit for the majority of project grants to local governments.[38] As Congress deliberated over enactment of successive aid programs, a principal concern was "to assure that the national purposes of programs authorized . . . were not obscured or lost by dividing up administrative responsibility among the host of state agencies which could advance jurisdictional claims" within state governments.[39] One way to prevent such jurisdictional jostling would have been through assertion of strong gubernatorial prerogatives, whereby the appropriate state agency would have been designated to receive given grant funds and to administer program activities under congressional authorization. As we saw in chapter 4, however, the office of governor—especially in the early years of grant activity—was ill equipped to serve that function. State executive branch operations were often under no unified direction, leading to considerable administrative chaos. "With the proliferation of grant-in-aid programs . . . the organizational and administrative disarray within most state governments no longer could be safely ignored" by the Congress.[40]

One response from the national level was the "single state agency" requirement, whereby only one agency was designated to administer national grants and to establish direct relationships with its counterpart in the national government bureaucracy. Such provisions first appeared in the 1916 Highway Act, and were duplicated the next year in the Vocational Education Act. Currently applicable laws either name a specific state agency or call for designation of one in policy areas such as child welfare, library services, urban planning, water-pollution control, civil defense, and law-enforcement assistance.[41] Thus, before and during the 1960s, administration of grant funds was largely in the hands of professional administrative personnel in individual agencies.

As the aid system grew more specialized, agency personnel at the national level came to work even more closely with their state and local counterparts. Partly as a result of national grants policy, the latter were now much more professionalized than previously, operating under state merit systems that had created a contingent of administrators whose backgrounds, interests, and professional competencies were similar to those of national government administrators. "With each new category and subcategory of aid, a new crop of specialists and subspecialists popped up at all levels of government to administer the wide variety of programs. . . ."[42] Thus, aid administrators in the national Department of Housing and Urban Development (HUD) developed ongoing working and fiscal ties with housing administrators in state and local governments; officials of the Bureau of Public Roads, with state and local highway department personnel; national educational administrators, with their counterparts in state departments of education and officials in myriad local school districts; and Agriculture Department staffs, with state and (especially) county agricultural officials.

This process of strengthening intergovernmental administrative linkages had led to a situation largely invisible to the general public, but fraught with consequences for the governmental process. Political scientist Harold Seidman, among others, has suggested that what we have in a number of important functional areas are "largely self-governing professional guilds"[43] comprised of bureaucrats at all levels with common programmatic concerns. The ACIR, describing the same phenomenon, coined the term "vertical functional autocracies"[44]—the "autocracy" label signifying not only operating autonomy from chief executives and legislators but also the extent of control over essential program decisions.

The development of intergovernmental administrative ties gave rise to a new label for the federal system. Whereas *dual federalism* was likened to a layer cake, with different levels of government clearly distinguished from one another, and whereas growing cooperation was likened to a marble cake, in which functions of different levels of government were intermingled, the new vertical administrative patterns gave rise to the term *picket-fence federalism*, illustrated in Figure 5-1. Former North Carolina Governor Terry Sanford, writing in 1967, provided this definition:

> The lines of authority, the concerns and interests, the flow of money, and the direction of programs run straight down like a number of pickets stuck into the ground. There is, as in a picket fence, a connecting cross slat, but that does little to support anything. In this metaphor it stands for the gov-

Figure 5-1 Picket-Fence* Federalism: A Schematic Representation

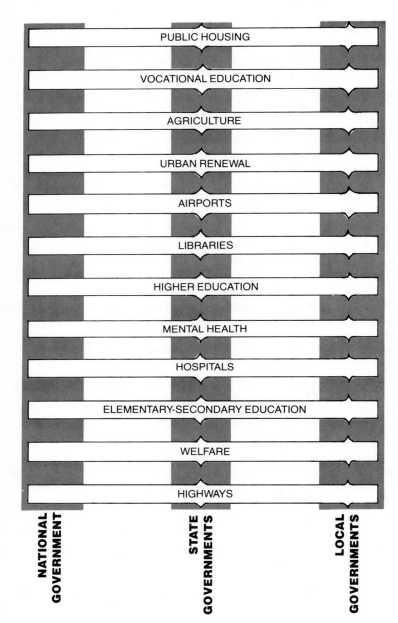

PUBLIC HOUSING

VOCATIONAL EDUCATION

AGRICULTURE

URBAN RENEWAL

AIRPORTS

LIBRARIES

HIGHER EDUCATION

MENTAL HEALTH

HOSPITALS

ELEMENTARY-SECONDARY EDUCATION

WELFARE

HIGHWAYS

NATIONAL GOVERNMENT

STATE GOVERNMENTS

LOCAL GOVERNMENTS

*Each picket represents the political and administrative ties among specialists in each policy area at all three levels of government.

Source: Adapted from Deil S. Wright, *Understanding Intergovernmental Relations,* 2nd ed. (Monterey, Calif.: Brooks/Coles, 1982), p. 63.

ernments. It holds the pickets in line; it does not bring them together. The picket-like programs are not connected at the bottom.[45]

The bureaucratic officials within each of these "pickets," together with their clientele groups at all levels, do not always agree, of course, on the substance and procedures of programs they administer. But the responsibility for formulating many basic policies and for resolving many of the conflicts that arise rests largely—and often exclusively—within the discretion of these functional groupings. How that situation can be reconciled with democratic values of public accountability and control is an important question, and one not easily answered. One hopeful sign, however, has been noted: the "pickets" may have already been somewhat altered. In 1977, only ten years after Sanford used the label for the first time, David B. Walker of ACIR suggested a variation, namely, *bamboo-fence federalism*. Walker asserted that this new label more accurately "captures the vertical functionalism, continuing professionalism, [and] *greater flexibility and realism*" of contemporary public administrators, even though most still give primary emphasis to their functional concerns (including protection of programmatic interests as a high priority).[46]

Categorical Grants: Growing Dissatisfaction

The tremendous proliferation of grants, the rise of "vertical functional autocracies," picket- or bamboo-fence federalism, and particularly the duplicative and overlapping nature of so many available grants, soon led to a growing chorus of concern about management of grants and about the impacts they were having on recipient governments. (For a summary of the most frequent criticisms, see box.)

These criticisms suggest several dimensions of the "politics of grants."[47] One is provision of essential public services, and equality or inequality among (and sometimes within) jurisdictions in the levels of those services. Another is the tensions that exist among different levels and units of government over setting program priorities, and program management itself. A third dimension is the procedural pitfalls which can hamper applicant governments in their efforts to obtain grant assistance. Many state and local officials tell numerous "horror stories" about applications rejected on seemingly narrow technical grounds, having to resubmit applications because a relatively minor section was improperly filled out, and the like. Underlying all such concerns, however, is a common theme: considerable conflict between elected state and local officials ("generalists"), on the one hand, and the specialists of their *own* bureaucracies as well as those in the national government's administrative agencies (see Figure 5-1). Much of the criticism came from state/local chief executives and legislators, and was directed explicitly toward the increasing control that bureaucrats at *all* levels

CATEGORICAL GRANTS: THE MOST COMMON CRITICISMS*

1. The proliferation of project grants has conflicted with equalizing governmental resources; applying successfully for such grants has required professional skills (the "art of *grantsmanship*") most likely to be found in already affluent states and communities.
2. Restricting categorical aid uses has distorted state and local policy priorities. (Some have argued, however, that even if true, categorical grants were *designed* to induce states and localities to become active in policy areas where they had not moved on their own.)
3. State and local leaders might gradually yield policy *initiative* to aid grantors in Congress and the bureaucracy, increasingly waiting for "Washington" to make the first move in establishing new policies.
4. The national government did (and does) not aid all public services; thus, greater *in*equality of available services often has resulted.
5. States and localities required to put up matching funds to receive aid have had a harder time meeting their other (unaided) service obligations. This has been especially important for financially pressed cities, which spend considerable sums on public services that Congress has not supported through grant funding to any great degree (e.g., fire protection and sidewalk maintenance). In contrast, suburbs often have devoted much of their budgets to strongly aided functions, e.g., education, parks, and public health.
6. Many state and local officials have objected to the paperwork, uncertainty, and delays associated with applying for categorical aid. Application forms often are complex and difficult to fill out. Worse, aid sometimes has been approved after expenditures dependent upon that aid already have been made. Worse still, a grant occasionally has been *dis*approved after state or local funds were spent.
7. Coordination of hundreds of grants, spread across scores of agencies, has been a persistent problem (see text).

*The fact that these criticisms often are expressed does not necessarily mean that they are accurate.

were coming to have over government aid programs. As the criticisms grew more intense (and as they became more of a partisan issue dividing Democrats and Republicans), the critics gained more of a hearing in Congress and, significantly, at the White House. Concern grew steadily under Presidents Nixon, Ford, Carter, and Reagan about the ability of state and local elected leaders to direct their own governments' programs effectively.

Increasing attention also was given to the immense problem of grant *coordination*, which emerged due to the sheer number of grants and the variety of sources within the national bureaucracy. The example of urban transportation grants given earlier illustrates the availability of grants from different national agencies for similar, often overlapping purposes, making it difficult to select the most appropriate grant program. Also, many general development projects in states and communities had component parts funded independently by separate national agencies. As a result, a grant applicant was faced with applying separately for each part of the overall project, thereby running the risk of applications being approved for some portions of the project but not for others. Furthermore, most national aid-granting agencies did not have much (if any) knowledge of which other programs were being funded by other agencies; and at the other end of the aid pipeline, most recipient governments knew or cared little about what other governments were receiving, or even applying for. Thus a chaotic situation prevailed. Grant applications were being reviewed and approved or rejected by national agencies with no central instrument for keeping track of which states and localities were asking for or receiving how much aid for what purposes. Nor was there provision for monitoring in any systematic way which agencies were responsible for programs with similar purposes or for determining the actual effects of grant funds. State and local officials, meanwhile, were chafing under what many considered unreasonable guidelines for spending grant money, in addition to the problems they encountered in obtaining funding in the first place.

The problems of coordination have been compounded at the recipient ends of the aid pipelines by growing intergovernmental administrative linkages in horizontal as well as vertical dimensions. "Councils of governments, contracting arrangements, consortia, cooperative agreements, regional interagency councils, commissions, multi-jurisdiction functional agencies, ad hoc planning groups, temporary clearing houses, and a multitude of other intergovernmental structures have multiplied from one end of the country to the other."[48] Interstate compacts, such as the New York Port Authority, have come into greater prominence; other regional bodies crossing state lines, created by either state or national governments, have been established.[49] Also, there has been a vast increase in the phenomenon of *substate regionalism*. Special districts of all kinds (excepting school districts) have proliferated in recent years—many in response to national government encouragement—for a variety of purposes (planning, review of grant applications, economic development, public health, and provision of care for the aging, among many others). Here again the picket-fence analogy is evident because national, state, and local administrative officials all have active roles in substate regional functions. Indeed, one observer suggests that national government agencies "have established *their own independent* local government systems,"[50] referring among others to Health Systems Agencies (HSAs), Areawide Agencies on Aging ("triple-As"), and Economic Development Districts (EDDs). By one account, over 1,800 special-purpose local agencies emerged in the 1960s and 1970s.[51] The administrative difficulties this poses are considerable, since special districts are free to compete for grant monies available to all other types of local government—and many do, successfully. Thus they also are woven into the pattern of functionally organized administrative relationships. At the same time, they are among the most invisible of all forms of government.[52]

GRANT REFORM: MULTIPLE EFFORTS, MORE COMPLEXITY

By the late 1960s, pressures were mounting for changes in the sprawling grant-in-aid system, particularly in grants management. With Richard Nixon's election in 1968 signaling the end of the "Great Society" era, if not all its trappings, the time seemed ripe for steps to be taken to reduce the growing chaos of the grant system as it was. While various concepts and options had been explored from time to time during the 1960s, few actions had been taken. The changes that followed, and that have continued up to the present, have taken two forms: reform of the manner in which national funds were made available to states and localities (fiscal reform), and efforts to reduce the programmatic influence of the national government (administrative reform). We will consider these, and their major components, in turn.

Fiscal Reform: General Revenue Sharing

A concentrated political reaction had set in during the late 1960s to the "strings" (conditions and specifications) attached to grant-in-aid funding. Increasingly, state and local elected officials sought financial assistance that would permit them greater discretion in spending decisions. The Nixon proposal for general revenue-sharing (GRS) appeared to meet such demands.

The principle behind revenue sharing is a simple one: a portion of tax revenues would be returned to states and to general-purpose local governments in accordance with a prescribed formula defined by Congress and automatically followed each fiscal year. There would be, as proponents put it, "no strings attached" to revenue-sharing funds; recipient governments could use the money for almost any purpose. There would also be no need for a state or local government to apply for the funds; once the formula was determined, the money would be forthcoming with no uncertainty and no delay. Such an arrangement seems to respond directly to the sharpest criticisms of the grant-in-aid system. It was not until Richard Nixon entered the White House, however, that serious effort was made to enact revenue-sharing legislation with full presidential backing.

What made revenue sharing so appealing to Nixon was that it allowed him to satisfy a number of political constituencies simultaneously at a relatively low cost (starting at $5.3 billion per year and rising to some $6 billion annually). As an alternative to grants, it held great appeal to disgruntled state and local officials, including a fair number of Democrats. These officials also welcomed the additional revenue that would supplement existing grants-in-aid. But revenue sharing permitted Nixon to pay a political debt as well to the electoral coalition that had put him in the White House. He had campaigned in 1968 for the votes of the "forgotten Americans," the "silent majority" comprising (in the words of some observers at the time) "the un-young, the un-poor, and the un-black." Much of Johnson's Great Society program had been addressed to the plight of the poor, especially in large central cities, and the ghetto violence of the mid- and late 1960s had led many to resent expenditures on programs aimed at aiding the urban poor, whom they blamed for the violence. Whether these public perceptions and attitudes were justified—and considerable evidence suggests they were not—is not the point. The heart of the matter was that Nixon was proposing a way whereby local political majorities—through their elected officials—could reassert their priorities in local and state spending, and not be bound to grant programs with which they disagreed more and more strongly on policy as well as on procedural grounds.

In the original legislation, recipient governments (states, municipalities, counties, and townships) could use the money largely as their executives and legislatures saw fit. States were permitted to apply their share to any program, with no restrictions; because special districts (including school districts) were excluded from receiving GRS money, many states used the bulk of their funding as aid to education. Local governments were largely unrestricted as well. Both states and localities were obligated to observe certain procedural guidelines, such as complying with civil rights requirements, reporting revenue-sharing uses, and not using GRS money as matching funds for other national grants.

When Congress approved an extension of general revenue sharing in the fall of 1976, a number of requirements were changed; the annual appropriation was increased; and using GRS money as matching funds was permitted. The 1980 extension carried forward many existing provisions (allocation formulas, auditing requirements, nondiscriminatory standards, provisions for citizen participation in decisions about use), and it provided for a mandatory allocation of $4.6 billion each year for local governments in fiscal 1981–1983. However, due to the improving fiscal condition of numerous states, an effort was made by President Carter and others to cut the states out of the program. After a prolonged and intense debate, a compromise was adopted whereby the states were barred from participation in fiscal 1981 but could receive $2.3 billion annually in the next two years (subject to appropriations by Congress each year). Also, if a state received GRS funds in 1982 or 1983, it was obligated to "decline or refund categorical grants in an amount equal to its . . . payment."[53] When Congress enacted the 1983 extension, it terminated the state share entirely as of October 1 of that year. Also, the amount allocated annually to eligible local governments was frozen at $4.6 billion, thus representing a reduction in the total appropriations for the program.

General revenue sharing has had the effect of reducing the concern for national goals, standards, and policies; substituting state and local political will for national perspectives; defining state/local rather than national majorities as the key electoral decision makers about program spending; and building greater discretion for state and local elected officials into the inter-governmental fiscal system. But it seems fair to say that GRS never lived up to its advance billing, despite the fact that it attracted quite a following among state and local officials. Even when it was most strongly supported at the White House, it represented only a small proportion of total spending for intergovernmental aid. Early in Ronald Reagan's second term, however, the president proposed the total elimination of revenue sharing, and preliminary FY 1986 budget resolutions in Congress included a provision for ending the program by FY 1987.[54] It appears that the Reagan administration's willingness to allow general revenue sharing to lapse can be traced to two policy preferences: (1) a strong and continuing interest in reducing national government spending; and (2) a basic commitment to another alternative to categoricals, namely, block grants.

Fiscal Reform: Block Grants

If general revenue sharing represented, in principle, a bold departure from existing categorical aid and its attendant problems, block grants were a more modest attempt (at least initially) to "decategorize" aid to states and localities. Five such programs were operating when Ronald Reagan took office in 1981, with varying degrees of faithfulness to the original design; two actually were products of the 1960s (the Partnership for Health Act of 1966 and the Omnibus Crime Control and Safe Streets Act of 1968). The other three were Title I of the Comprehensive Employment and Training Act (CETA) of 1973, a manpower training program; the Community Development Block Grant program (CDBG), enacted in 1974; and the Title XX (Social Services) amendments to the Social Security Act, also enacted in 1974.[55]

Block grants represent a "middle way" between the restrictiveness alleged by critics of categorical grants, and the elimination of *all* national-level influence and responsibility in intergovernmental aid. Generally, block grants have the following features: (1) recipient jurisdictions have fairly wide discretion within the designated program area, (2) administration, reporting, planning, and other program features are designed to minimize grantor supervision and control, (3) most allocation provisions are based on a formula, which is also intended to limit grantor discretion as well as to decrease fiscal uncertainty for the grantees, (4) eligibility provisions are fairly precise, tending to favor general local governments as opposed to special districts, and generalist officials over program specialists, (5) the grantor retains a degree of administrative discretion in managing the programs, and (6) matching fund requirements tend to be relatively low.[56] The original block grant concept retained the notion that national goals were to be pursued in a program area through expenditure of allocated funds; ACIR noted in 1977 that block grants "do not imply a hands-off [national] role, nor one confined to purely procedural matters."[57] These observations clearly were descriptive of the block grants of the 1960s and 1970s; whether they apply equally to those established under Ronald Reagan is less certain.

The Reagan block grants differ in important respects from the earlier ones.[58] One obvious difference is the increase from four such grants in FY 1981 to twelve in FY 1984, with others being considered. More important is the explicit linkage between establishment of block grants and elimination of categoricals. Creation of block grants was accompanied by a reduction in the number of categorical programs from 534 in FY 1981 to 392 in FY 1984— a decrease of 142, or about 27 percent.[59] In 1981–1982 alone, 77 categoricals were consolidated into nine new or revised block grants, and another 60 categorical programs were terminated outright.[60] In subsequent actions, Congress (at the president's urging) replaced the CETA block grant with the Job Training Partnership Act (while creating six new categoricals in lieu of the fifteen that existed under CETA), and added a new one (Urban Mass Transportation Capital and Operating Assistance).[61]

A third difference is the fact that recent block grants have been accompanied by a decline not only in the number of categoricals, but also in total spending for intergovernmental assistance. The Reagan administration consistently has sought to slow the growth of national government spending, if not reduce it (see chapter 12). Many of the early spending cuts came in intergovernmental aid, though that aid has increased slowly since the first wave of reductions (see Table 5–1). Moreover, there is evidence that President Reagan *used the block-grant strategy implicitly to cut spending*, and not simply to alter the degree of program control exercised by government administrators through categorical grants.

A fourth difference lies in the contractual nature of the new block grants, involving contracts between national and state governments. In the view of Senator Orrin Hatch (R.-Utah), of the Senate Labor and Human Resources Committee, "This contractual relationship allows certain program protections, while removing the [national] bureaucracy from interference with state operations."[62] Finally, the use of state-national contracts (among other things) reflects the administration's emphasis on increasing the states' role, within the president's broader vision of a "revitalized" (and considerably revamped) federal system. This emphasis suggests yet another difference between "old" and "new" block grants: the implicit subordination of national purposes to those of the states.

Fiscal Reform: Impacts of Change

Both general revenue sharing and block grants were introduced on the national political scene amid considerable fanfare; both were advanced as important solutions to major problems—confusion, overlapping, "red tape," inequities, rigidity—associated with the existing grants system. With more than a decade of experience behind us, including a number of evaluations of both programs, it is useful to assess the pros and cons in more substantive terms, to see just how close the rhetoric came to the realities. It is also useful to consider some consequences that few observers forecast.

Various studies of GRS suggested the following patterns of use: (1) funding was allocated more to existing operating programs than to new ones, (2) the single largest category of use in smaller communities was capital expenditures—for new municipal buildings, water works, even public golf courses, (3) keeping tax rates stable in inflationary times became a principal concern of many local decision makers in deliberations over use of GRS monies, (4) local political majorities became, if anything, stronger and more entrenched, (5) alleviation of poverty in larger cities (a major aim of many categoricals in the 1960s) was not a primary purpose of GRS use in the 1970s or 1980s, and (6) there was little structural change in the local governments receiving GRS funds, contrary to some expectations. A major consequence of the shift to this form of aid was a decline in public policy concern for needy minorities—many concentrated in the poorest central cities. The distinction between local political majorities and minorities as primary beneficiaries of GRS and categorical grants, respectively, was a significant one, and the effects on each are a crucial corollary to debates over forms of national government assistance. The politics of fiscal federalism laps over into such policy fields as urban policy and civil rights. To stress ''increasing the flexibility of state and local governments'' (meaning their elected officials) is to deemphasize the policy concerns, prevalent in the 1960s more than now, with problems of urban minority groups, and with problems of poverty more generally.[63]

Thus, the same things may be said about block grants, both old and new.[64] In addition, neither ''generation'' of block grants has operated precisely as their strongest advocates foresaw. Soon after being enacted, the early block grants showed signs of what some called ''creeping categorization''—a pattern of various abuses being discovered in the course of grant implementation, followed by gradual reassertion of national agency control in order to prevent further abuse. In more recent years, both old and new block grant programs have taken unexpected turns. One observer summarized some of the impressions (and frustrations) of block grant operations, as viewed from the local level:

> Seemingly secure entitlement block grants can quickly crumble, as CETA and LEAA [Law Enforcement Assistance Administration] recently have. Seemingly simple programs can become more [complex and] categorical, as CETA, LEAA, and to a lesser extent CDBG have. Promises of ''local'' autonomy can vanish into thin air as state grant and contracting procedures—and [national] statutes, regulations, and administrative discretion—intervene. . . . In reality, *the most significant issue of the Reagan block grants from a local perspective is not grant consolidation, state control, or loosened mandates. Rather it is* [the issue of] *funding level.*[65]

If the last contention is true, then the current debates over federalism and IGR—at least with respect to intergovernmental aid—will fall increasingly within the orbit of decisions about government budgeting and spending reductions. In turn, that may rob us of an opportunity that arises only infrequently—namely, to make decisions consciously (and, one hopes, thoughtfully) *on the merits* about possible changes of direction in American federalism.

Both general revenue sharing and block grants have achieved, at least in part, what their proponents intended for them: to loosen the strings on aid from Washington. However, powerful forces continue to support categorical aid—a fact reflected in the perpetuation of nearly 400 such programs. The debate is likely to continue for some time over the direction of intergovernmental aid, with further significant change a distinct possibility. How far such change will go, and with what specific policy consequences, is at the heart of the choices we may be asked to make through the remainder of the 1980s.

Administrative Reform: "Decentralization"

Other efforts begun in the 1960s to reduce national government influence have taken two directions. The first of these, chronologically, was the movement for "citizen participation" in administrative decision making, especially decisions on expenditure of grant funds. By incorporating such requirements in a large number of grant authorizations, Congress was responding to substantial pressures from previously underrepresented constituencies, notably poorer urban minority groups (see chapter 2). The underlying assumption was that government officials had been insensitive to needs of aid recipients in the past, and that as aid categories multiplied it would be necessary to have a measure of clientele representation. Thus, in many grants as well as GRS, provision was made for public hearings—and sometimes for more formalized participation—at crucial points in the decision-making process. As we shall see in more detail in chapter 15, the promise of citizen participation may well have been greater than actual performance, not least because some administrators may have succeeded in coopting potential adversaries from citizen groups.

Administrative Reform: "Managing" Fiscal Federalism

Another approach to bringing the grants system (and functional specialists) under better control centered on achieving better coordination among proliferating aid programs. We have already referred to aspects of the coordination problem; the solutions proposed in the late 1960s and early 1970s deserve mention, as do more recent developments.

The earliest efforts focused on coordination among aid applicants and stressed region-wide coordinative mechanisms. Several specific legislative steps were taken by Congress. Section 204 of the Model Cities Act of 1966, discussed earlier, stipulated that applications from local governments in metropolitan areas must first have been screened by an areawide comprehensive planning agency. Then, in 1968, Congress passed the Intergovernmental Cooperation Act, which contained three important provisions. Title IV of the act directed that more regularized evaluation-and-review procedures be set up for grant requests. Section 401(b) directed that the planning process take into consideration as fully as possible all national, state, regional, and local viewpoints that might be pertinent to the policy under consideration. And Section 401(c) made it national policy to seek maximum congruence (matching) between national program objectives and the objectives of state, regional, and local planning. These were lofty if somewhat ambiguous goals but deemed necessary in the face of widespread local (and state) unwillingness to consider effects of their own programs and planning on those of neighboring jurisdictions. Though interlocal cooperation was on the rise, there was still a good deal of hostility and competition, which made prior consultation about grant applications unsystematic at best. The 1966 and 1968 legislative acts were geared to forcing such consultation where it was not occurring voluntarily. In 1969, as part of the new emphasis on OMB's managerial function, Richard Nixon assigned the agency primary responsibility for overseeing implementation of these coordinative provisions. The thrust of OMB's efforts in this regard was threefold: to strengthen general-purpose units of state and local government (and their political executives), to rationalize grants, and to improve organizational arrangements by which services are delivered.[66]

The tactics OMB employed were aimed at increasing consultation with states and localities and at providing "governors and mayors with the information and management tools necessary to achieve some degree of control over *their* functional bureaucracies."[67] A number of specific tools were adopted. *Circular A-85* was designed to give state/local associations, as gubernatorial and mayoral representatives, an opportunity to consult with national officials in developing and implementing national government (grant) programs. *Circular A-95* established a Project Notification and Review System under which "clearinghouses" at state, regional, and metropolitan levels were to receive notification by governments in their jurisdiction that intended to apply for national aid, *before* they did so. The clearinghouses performed two functions subsequent to such notification—they transmitted this information to other governmental entities in the affected area and solicited comments, and they assessed the applications for conformity with established state, regional, and local planning. Other parts of A-95 required national government agencies engaging in direct development projects similarly to consult in advance with state and local officials (generalists), and provided governors with an opportunity to review state plans required by some national aid programs before those plans were submitted to the funding agency. *Circular A-98* required national agencies to provide information to state clearinghouses on the amount, location, and purpose of grants once approval had been given to a project. A-98 and A-95, taken together, ideally should have provided better information about grant funding—both actual and prospective. Both circulars were intended to make program officials (specialists) ''more responsive to the views of central political executives, and to *promote communication and coordination* among different levels of government.''[68] Indeed, improving coordination *through* better communication was a consistent theme in the IGR arena (see chapter 7 for a general discussion of both topics).

One other entity reflecting the same theme was the Federal Regional Council, composed of the regional directors of major agencies in each of ten administrative regions established by President Nixon. These bodies served a coordinative role, seeking to integrate programs managed by the different agencies within their regions. This represented an attempt to foster coordination at an intermediate level between agency headquarters in the nation's capital and state and local levels, supplementing other efforts to improve overall coordination of government activities.

Emphasis also has been placed recently on more information and training. Information resources currently available to grant seekers include the ''bible'' of grantsmanship, the Catalog of Federal Domestic Assistance (CFDA), put out by the national government; a computerized information system based largely on the CFDA, known as the Federal Awards Assistance Data System (FAADS); and publications of the Grants Management Advisory Service in Washington and the Grantsmanship Center in Los Angeles. Training is receiving more attention from government bodies at all levels, as well as from nongovernmental organizations such as the National Assistance Management Association.

Administrative Reform: Change and Continuity

Despite the design of the instruments for reforming grants management, their effectiveness was questioned seriously by numerous observers. For example, it was found that national agency officials often simply ignored both A-85 and A-95 requirements. Also, many state and local chief executives did not avail themselves of much of the information that OMB believed would enhance their managerial capacities (even though, as noted in chapter 4, many governors apparently seek out a role as manager rather than as a more activist policy leader). Furthermore, many aid applicants clearly misunderstood or were not even aware of the purposes of Circular A-95. Activities under A-85 reached the point that, in 1978, President Carter rescinded that circular; virtually all participants in A-85 consultation procedures apparently exhibited only halfhearted commitment to the objectives that A-85 was designed to accomplish.[69]

During his first term President Reagan ordered changes in two of the other management instruments discussed above. In July 1982 he rescinded Circular A-95 and replaced it with an executive order (EO 12372) which placed in the hands of state governments primary responsibility for coordinating consultation among grant applicants. According to administration spokesmen, this was done in order to end an A-95 process that in their view had become "highly bureaucratic and burdensome," "paperbound," and emphasized "procedures over substance"[70] (though that was by no means a universal view). The other presidential action came in February 1983, also through an executive order, when Federal Regional Councils were abolished.[71] Both changes were entirely consistent with the president's goal (referred to earlier) of strengthening the role and influence of state governments in the overall operations of the federal system. States were perceived to be in the best position to take over FRC activities, and were specifically placed in charge of intergovernmental consultation processes with regard to applications for grants from Washington. The net effect of these changes, coupled with the more visible (and politically more sensitive) reductions in grant funding, is far from clear. What *is* clear, however, is that Ronald Reagan has succeeded in redirecting many intergovernmental activities "away from Washington" and toward state governments. Without question, President Reagan has had more of an impact on American federalism than any president since Lyndon Johnson. What makes this more significant is that the Reagan changes have been designed almost entirely to *undo* many of the initiatives of the Johnson years.

PROSPECTS AND ISSUES IN IGR: A LOOK AHEAD

Any attempt to forecast even the near future in IGR admittedly must be a speculative venture. But certain indications already exist. One issue that has been addressed both by academics and politicians is the extent to which *intergovernmental regulation* has become part of IGR.[72] These regulations, which have become far more numerous since the 1960s, have been enacted as part of national government bureaucracies' efforts to direct implementation of categorical grant assistance programs. In most instances the regulations are designed to implement *other* national government legislation aimed at achieving wide-ranging social and economic objectives (see Table 5–3).

Political scientist Donald Kettl explains the rise of this phenomenon: "The [national] government cannot constitutionally order state and local governments to examine the environmental impact of projects they propose or to keep their financial records in specified ways. The . . . government can, however, set those standards as conditions for [both categorical and block] grants."[73]

Literally hundreds of such regulations now exist (though these too have been the subject of study by the Reagan administration). A small sampling may help to convey the scope of this regulation.[74] Under statutory au-

Table 5-3
SELECTED NATIONAL GOVERNMENT STATUTES WITH REGULATORY IMPACT ON STATE AND LOCAL GOVERNMENTS

Title	Objective
Age Discrimination in Employment Act (1974)	Prevent discrimination on the basis of age in state and local government employment
Civil Rights Act of 1964 (Title VI)	Prevent discrimination on the basis of race, color, or national origin in nationally assisted programs
Clean Air Act Amendments of 1970	Establish nationwide air quality and emissions standards
Davis-Bacon Act (1931)	Assure that locally prevailing wages are paid to construction workers employed under national government contracts and financial assistance programs
Equal Employment Opportunity Act of 1972	Prevent discrimination on the basis of race, color, religion, sex, or national origin in state and local government employment
Federal Water Pollution Control Act Amendments of 1972	Establish national government effluent limitations to control the discharge of pollutants
Hatch Act (1940)	Prohibit public employees from engaging in certain political activities
National Environmental Policy Act of 1969	Assure consideration of the environmental impact of major national government actions
Resource Conservation and Recovery Act of 1976	Establish standards for the control of hazardous wastes
Water Quality Act (1965)	Establish national government water quality standards for interstate waters

Source: Adapted from U.S. Advisory Commission on Intergovernmental Relations, *Regulatory Federalism: Policy, Process, Impact and Reform*, Report Number A-95 (Washington, D.C.: U.S. Government Printing Office, February 1984), pp. 19–21.

thority from Congress, the Environmental Protection Agency may prescribe the treatment local governments must give their drinking water, as well as the inspections some states must conduct on automobile emission controls. Health-care regulations govern the operation of Medicaid programs run by state governments with funding by the national government. National mine-safety regulations set standards for operation of state and local gravel pits. One reason for the creation of new special-purpose local ''quasi-governments'' (such as regional health planning organizations) was a regulatory requirement imposed by agency officials who distrusted—and therefore wanted to bypass—traditional local political institutions.[75] Professor Kettl summarizes the consequences:

> In all of these areas, the [national] government has spun out elaborate re-
> quirements about who can make decisions, who must be consulted, and even
> how records of performance must be filed. Rules stipulate who must benefit
> from [nationally] aided programs, and how state and local governments must
> administer those benefits. These regulations have created a wide channel of
> [national] influence over the most intimate details of state and local opera-
> tions. They have also made state and local governments front-line administra-
> tors for numerous national programs.[76]

(The point has been made, however, that such regulations often have positive substantive aspects as well; the experience of numerous states has "indicated how important—and useful—[national] requirements [turn] out to
be."[77])

Two varieties of regulations have developed: (1) so-called crosscutting
rules, which apply across-the-board to many national aid programs; and (2)
program-based rules applying to individual programs. Some rules govern
administrative and fiscal policy, e.g., the 1931 Davis-Bacon Act and the 1940
Hatch Act; other rules govern social and economic policy, e.g., the 1964
Civil Rights Act and the 1969 National Environmental Policy Act[78] (see Table 5-3). It is perhaps significant that even Ronald Reagan—with his firm
commitment to reducing national government influence—endorsed intergovernmental regulation when, in the summer of 1984, Congress passed
legislation (supported by the president) providing for withholding a portion of national government highway funds from states that do not enact a
minimum drinking age of 21.[79] This, in spite of a comprehensive review being conducted by OMB of all federalism-related regulations, with an eye to
reducing both their scope and their impact.

Two particular aspects of regulatory federalism deserve mention. One
is the concern that many mandated activities are costly—for example, paying prevailing wages (determined by the U.S. Labor Department) on construction projects receiving national government funds or providing physical access for the handicapped—and governments requiring others to fulfill
such mandates have not been supplying necessary funding. This has
placed numerous local governments in increasingly difficult financial positions, since the programmatic assistance is not sufficient to pay for mandated activities. Also, the costs of meeting specific requirements imposed
by, among others, the Environmental Protection Agency and the Department of Housing and Urban Development have become more difficult to
bear. The other aspect of the mandating question is the impression, widely
shared, that national government mandates have been the hardest to bear.
No clear generalizations are as yet possible, but in at least one instance that
fear was unfounded. In early 1981, Shirley Hufstedler, outgoing Secretary
of Education in the Carter administration, noted that the legislature in the
state of Washington investigated what it saw as "burdensome" national

regulations in the education field, and "found to its chagrin that four-fifths of the burden was imposed by state rather than [national] law."[80] This is not to downgrade the significance of the mandating issue in general; however, it *is* to suggest that grouping "national and state" mandates together may foster false impressions about which governments have caused the lion's share of the problem. This is already under scrutiny and will bear watching in the next few years.

A second issue that has recently surfaced is the tension between states in the "snow belt" and the "sun belt" over distributional effects of aid formulas going to each region of the country.[81] Because many grants are based in part on consideration of need, the snow belt states have been able to assert a claim to a proportionately larger share of national grant funding since they are presently faced with economic and political decline. The 1980 census figures indicate clearly that states in the West and South—California, Florida, Texas, and Arizona, among others—gained large numbers of new inhabitants during the 1970s, bringing with them greater political strength in Congress and the Electoral College, and enhancing their clout in the grants process. That is so because population is also a key factor in existing grants formulas. Thus a confrontation between population (sun belt) and need (snow belt) factors in current grant arrangements has developed, and promises to remain with us. Indeed, a report by President Reagan's transition team early in 1981 suggested that it become national policy *not* to resist and compensate for the movement of population to the sun belt, but rather to encourage the Northeast and Midwest to adjust to their diminished roles. The outcry from many in the snow belt that greeted that recommendation is indicative of what we can perhaps expect as this debate intensifies.

A third issue, articulated in Ronald Reagan's 1982 State of the Union message, was the president's proposal for a "New Federalism."[82] This was a call for a "dramatic shift of some forty social, transportation, and community development programs (and revenues to help pay for them in the early phase) to states. Reagan also proposed a 'swap' of the three principal welfare programs for the poor. The [national] government would assume the full costs of the Medicaid health program, while states took over food stamps and Aid to Families with Dependent Children [AFDC]."[83] Despite considerable fanfare associated with the proposal, nothing came of it during President Reagan's first four years in the White House. However, continued efforts to reduce national government spending might lead again to this sort of proposal, as might more systematic efforts, by the president and others, to "sort out" governmental functions by level of government.

A fourth issue raised in recent years is whether we may be entering a new era of "contentious federalism," referring to the recent increase in the number and frequency of policy conflicts between national and state governments. In the past ten years, for example, such conflict has centered on national government management of radioactive wastes, and of public lands in the western part of the country—the "Sagebrush rebellion" of 1979–1981.[84] The latter was a classic example of regional governments in a federal system confronting the central government over particular policies of the latter. The "rebellion" grew out of frustration with grazing cutbacks and environmental protection measures that the Interior Department's Bureau of Land Management had imposed on public rangelands during the 1970s. Real estate developers, loggers, miners, and other commercial interests joined forces to protest the Carter administration's attempts to revise longstanding arrangements over the use of national government lands and water.

The rebellion took the form of legislative demands—passed by the legislatures of Arizona, Nevada, New Mexico, Utah, and Wyoming—that national lands within their respective states should be turned over to the state government. Subsequently, legislative proposals were drawn up by western senators in Congress that would have produced the same result. However, with the prodevelopment stance adopted by Interior Secretary James Watt, the frustrations eased and the rebellion ran its course. (Interestingly, most western governors did not join the rebels, with some distinctly critical of the rebellion and the seeming motivations—commercial development primarily—that lay behind it.)

In looking to the future of IGR, other areas of importance also exist. For example, we need a continuing examination of our assumptions and possible misconceptions about the workings of the federal system as we set about trying to "reform" it. One illustration of that principle is the easy assumption that improved coordination is possible through strengthened central management. At least one observer has suggested that local jurisdictions—even neighborhoods within cities—can "be allowed the flexibility to coordinate and integrate resources to meet specific needs in their communities without diminishing the intent of the individual grant programs"—to "coordinate grants from below." She goes on to say that "when grant forms facilitate local ingenuity, national intentions are likely to be enhanced since national program goals will be implemented through mechanisms that fit the diverse capabilities of service providers in the local communities where programs have to be carried out."[85] Another possibly erroneous assumption is the belief that recipient governments can be lured by money into pursuing whatever objectives the national government has set. Though tempting, this assumption has been questioned; one study suggests that grants achieve only an opportunity for the national government to *bargain* over policy purposes with the recipient government rather than "buying compliance."[86] Such considerations must be kept in mind, lest we put into effect reforms intended as solutions that instead become part of the problem, or at best fail to solve the perceived shortcomings of the status quo.

IGR AND PUBLIC ADMINISTRATION

The diffuse nature of federalism (perhaps not as diffuse now as in the past) has combined with growing intergovernmental ties in all directions to create a situation that is complex indeed. Public administration has been altered, perhaps permanently, by rapid change in intergovernmental relations.

It is clear, for example, that the patterns of political influence termed *subsystem politics* in the national government (see chapter 3) have been extended into intergovernmental politics. Despite recent efforts to gain greater control of their bureaucracies, most chief executives have failed to stem the growth of vertical functional bureaucratic linkages—the "autocracies" referred to by ACIR. One reason for the inability of a president or governor to overcome the institutional strength of bureaucracies is precisely that the latter can call on political support from at least one other level or unit of government much more easily than a chief executive can. Intergovernmental administrative relations, in other words, have served to strengthen existing bureaucratic autonomy at *every* level of government.

A second area of serious concern for public administration resulting from the workings of the federal system is fiscal relations, and especially continuing financial difficulties of some American governments. Problems like those experienced in New York City in the mid-1970s may come to hound political leaders, administrators, and citizens in other communities, large and small, struggling to avoid fiscal chaos because of declining property-tax bases and escalating service costs. Intergovernmental aid can do much to bail out a city here and a suburb there, but a real question exists whether costs imposed by inflation, rising service needs, and growing public employee union militancy can in fact be met over the long term by infusions of aid. The core of the problem is that recipient governments can easily develop a continuing dependency on such aid, whether national or state, and it is possible that needed aid will not always be there. Programs funded through intergovernmental aid, in whole or in part, could face more sharp cuts or even curtailment if funding declines or ceases. Program cuts, efficiency, and priority setting are relatively new concerns in public administration—in degree, if not in substance—arising out of the very real fiscal crunch enveloping this country and all of its governments.

A third area of concern is control over grants-in-aid and other funding. A stark reality of intergovernmental relations is bureaucratic—and "interbureaucratic"—controls on much of the money flowing from one level to another, raising questions about public accountability and about the ability of chief executives to coordinate spending effectively. Public administrators have a great deal of discretionary authority over public spending, and the age-old issue of fiscal responsibility and accountability has taken a new form as a result. A related concern is that some government institutions, such as state legislatures, have lacked until recently any real access to key decision makers or any impact on decisions regarding intergovernmental funding.[87] For the most part, bureaucrats are in the driver's seat when it comes to categorical grant funding, still by far the largest part of intergovernmental aid. Whether that is all to the good is an important question. Whether it will remain that way is another.

Of course, future actions of the Reagan presidency, in several key respects, will be of crucial importance to IGR and the federal system. Continued emphasis on spending cuts in intergovernmental aid will have significant long-term consequences for state and local governments, not to mention the national government's major domestic agencies. Similarly, efforts to transfer to state governments large areas of new responsibility will have important implications for all concerned—not least, those served by the programs in question. Also, the president's proposal in the late spring of 1985 to eliminate the individual income tax deduction for state and local taxes paid raised the prospect of a substantially altered political environment in which state and local officials might find it much more difficult to persuade their constituents to accept higher taxes. Indeed, one effect of that tax reform (to whatever extent it is adopted) might be to *interfere* with the president's professed desire to see state and local governments shoulder a greater share of the responsibility for governance in the federal system. In sum, our discussion of contemporary federalism has made clear the importance of the Reagan presidency for the federal system. The remainder of the 1980s may well see further efforts to alter past courses of action with regard to IGR. How successful those attempts are may have an important bearing on the shape of American federalism for decades to come.

Finally, scholars in the field of federalism will continue, in all likelihood, their efforts to bring some intellectual order out of the seeming chaos that has occurred in IGR just since 1960. There have been spirited debates, for example, about the appropriate degree of centralization as a remedy for bureaucratic control of categorical grants; so, also, with the question of just how functional or dysfunctional contemporary IGR has come to be.[88] It is no exaggeration to suggest that few areas of governance in this country are as complex or as challenging as this one has proved to be.

SUMMARY

Federalism, in its original meaning, defined an arrangement of governments in which a central government and regional units each have some independent standing in the governmental system. Federalism has important constitutional, political, and fiscal/administrative dimensions. Our federal system has evolved through a variety of choices and changes, with intergovernmental relations predominant on the contemporary federal scene.

IGR involves virtually all governments and public officials, though largely out of public view; it is highly informal and very dependent on human interactions; and it involves the private sector. The role of the courts (particularly the U.S. Supreme Court) in shaping federalism has become more prominent, with a number of key decisions handed down in the 1980s.

Contemporary IGR has become highly complex in the past two decades. Contributing to the complexity are the present grants system, functional alliances among program administrators, and continuing tensions between political executives and functional specialists (and their respective clienteles). Bureaucratic activity at all levels is central to IGR and to *fiscal federalism*.

Categorical grants are the most widely used form of fiscal assistance, numbering almost 400 in the mid-1980s. Besides being used to achieve a wide range of programmatic purposes, grants also have served to encourage a number of changes in the behavior of recipient governments (upgrading personnel systems, fostering planning, promoting nondiscrimination). For a period of some twenty years between the early 1960s and early 1980s, categorical grants, of both project and formula types, increasingly were used to promote explicitly "national" purposes.

That has led to considerable administrative complexity. Political and administrative choices made early in the history of cash grants set a precedent for "single state agency" relationships with national agencies in charge of a given grant program. A sequence of events was thus set in motion that has led to the creation of "self-governing guilds" (also called "vertical functional autocracies"), and picket- or bamboo-fence federalism. These allied interests gradually consolidated control over grant programs, giving rise to a political reaction that sparked a search for ways to control those guilds or autocracies. That search continues. However, coordination is increasingly difficult to achieve, given proliferation of politically potent units of government and of both horizontal and vertical linkages among them.

Grant reform has occurred in several ways. Fiscal reforms have included general revenue sharing and block grants, though neither (even now) approaches categorical grants in scope or funding. Under Ronald Reagan, block grants assumed new political importance. Administrative reforms have taken the form of either decentralization—in particular, citizen participation—or efforts to improve coordination and management of the grants system. Much of this has occurred under direction of the president and OMB, and it appears that this pattern will continue. Improved information and communication also have been stressed recently.

Issues to be dealt with in the immediate future include intergovernmental regulation; emerging conflict between snow belt and sun belt states and between national and state governments; changes in the extent of bu-

reaucratic autonomy at all levels of government; continuing fiscal constraints facing government across the board; the policy directions of the
Reagan administration that affect IGR; and the challenge of maintaining
governmental accountability in the federal system. Continued complexity
in IGR is all but certain.

NOTES

1. Miguel Acosta Romero, "Mexican Federalism: Conception and Reality," *Public Administration Review*, 42 (September/October 1982), 399–404, at p. 400.
2. *McCulloch v. Maryland*, 4 Wheaton 316 (1819).
3. W. Brooke Graves, *American Intergovernmental Relations* (New York: Scribner's, 1964), pp. 516–26.
4. William Anderson, *Intergovernmental Relations in Review* (Minneapolis: University of Minnesota Press, 1960), p. 3, cited by Deil S. Wright, *Understanding Intergovernmental Relations*, 2nd ed. (Monterey, Calif.: Brooks/Cole, 1982), p. 6.
5. Wright, *Understanding Intergovernmental Relations*, p. 9.
6. Quoted in ibid., p. 6.
7. Anderson, *Intergovernmental Relations in Review*, p. 4.
8. Wright, *Understanding Intergovernmental Relations*, p. 11.
9. Ibid., p. 16.
10. Richard H. Leach, *American Federalism* (New York: Norton, 1970), p. 59.
11. Ibid., pp. 61–63. See also chapters 3 and 13.
12. 105 S. Ct. 1713 (1985).
13. This account is taken from "Court Increases Local Antitrust Immunity," *Public Administration Times*, 8 (April 15, 1985), 3 (published by the American Society for Public Administration; Washington, D.C.).
14. The latter ruling was made in the case of *Community Communications Co. v. City of Boulder*, 456 U.S. 1001 (1982). The facts of the case are discussed in Neal R. Peirce, "Courts vs. 'New Federalism,'" Bloomington-Normal (Ill.) *Daily Pantagraph*, May 2, 1982, p. A-11. See also Rochelle L. Stanfield, "Cities and Counties Ask Congress: 'Save Us from the Antitrust Laws,'" *National Journal*, 15 (March 12, 1983), 558–61.
15. "Court Increases Local Antitrust Immunity."
16. *Congressional Quarterly (CQ) Weekly Report*, 42 (October 13, 1984), 2624. See also *SIAM Intergovernmental News*, 8 (Autumn 1984), 1 (published by the American Society for Public Administration, Section on Intergovernmental Administration and Management, Washington, D.C.).
17. *United Transportation Union v. Long Island Railroad Company*, 455 U.S. 678 (1982); cited by Peirce, "Courts vs. 'New Federalism.'"
18. *Equal Employment Opportunity Commission (EEOC) v. Wyoming*, 460 U.S. 226 (1983). Maxine Kurtz discusses the background of the case, and the ruling, in "Court Strikes Down State Retirement Law," *Public Administration Times*, 6 (April 1, 1983), 3.
19. *Quilici v. Village of Morton Grove*, 104 S. Ct. 194 (1983).
20. *Garcia v. San Antonio Metropolitan Transit Authority*, 105 S. Ct. 1005 (1985). The passage quoted appears on page 25 of the decision.
21. Russell L. Hanson, "The Intergovernmental Setting of State Politics," in Vir-

ginia Gray, Herbert Jacob, and Kenneth N. Vines, eds., *Politics in the American States: A Comparative Analysis*, 4th ed. (Boston: Little, Brown, 1983), p. 35.

22. Associated Press wire service report, which appeared in the Bloomington-Normal (Ill.) *Daily Pantagraph*, October 4, 1983, p. A-1.

23. *Pennhurst State School & Hospital v. Halderman*, 104 S. Ct. 900 (1984). See also Gary L. McDowell, "Were the Anti-Federalists Right? Judicial Activism and the Problem of Consolidated Government," *Publius: The Journal of Federalism* 12 (Summer 1982), 99–108.

24. For a comprehensive overview of national government aid to cities prior to the 1960s, see Roscoe C. Martin, *The Cities and the Federal System* (New York: Atherton, 1965).

25. Catherine Lovell, "Where We Are in IGR and Some of the Implications," *Southern Review of Public Administration*, 3 (June 1979), 6–20, at p. 6.

26. Michael D. Reagan and John G. Sanzone, *The New Federalism*, 2nd ed. (New York: Oxford University Press, 1981), p. 33.

27. Ibid., pp. 37–43. See also Parris N. Glendening and Mavis Mann Reeves, *Pragmatic Federalism: An Intergovernmental View of American Government*, 2nd ed. (Pacific Palisades, Calif.: Palisades Publishers, 1984), pp. 253–56. For a fuller treatment of government revenue systems, see George F. Break, *Financing Government in a Federal System* (Washington, D.C.: Brookings, 1980), and David B. Walker, *Toward a Functioning Federalism* (Cambridge, Mass.: Winthrop, 1981), especially chapter 6.

28. Reagan and Sanzone, *The New Federalism*, p. 54.

29. U.S. Office of Management and Budget, *Special Analyses: Budget of the United States Government, Fiscal Year 1982* (Washington, D.C.: U.S. Government Printing Office, 1981), p. 255.

30. The following description relies on Reagan and Sanzone, *The New Federalism*, chapter 3. See also George E. Hale and Marian Lief Palley, *The Politics of Federal Grants* (Washington, D.C.: Congressional Quarterly Press, 1981), pp. 18–21.

31. Reagan and Sanzone, *The New Federalism*, p. 57.

32. Ibid., pp. 125–26.

33. See U.S. Advisory Commission on Intergovernmental Relations, *Categorical Grants: Their Role and Design*, Report Number A-52 (Washington, D.C.: U.S. Government Printing Office, 1978).

34. For further information on developments in grant funding, see, among others, Richard P. Nathan and Fred C. Doolittle, "Federal Grants: Giving and Taking Away," *Political Science Quarterly*, 100 (Spring 1985), 53–74; and "Grant Funds Decline For States, Localities" *Public Administration Times*, 8 (February 15, 1985), 3.

35. See Daniel J. Elazar, *American Federalism: A View from the States*, 3rd ed. (New York: Harper & Row, 1984), pp. 85–91.

36. Ironically, it was under Eisenhower—a Republican president—that a systematic effort had been made to define broad national goals in the late 1950s. See President's Commission on National Goals, *Goals for Americans* (Englewood Cliffs, N.J.: Prentice-Hall, 1960). Almost three decades later, this report still makes interesting reading.

37. See James L. Sundquist, with the collaboration of David W. Davis, *Making Federalism Work: A Study of Program Coordination at the Community Level* (Washington, D.C.: Brookings, 1969), pp. 3–6.

38. U.S. Advisory Commission on Intergovernmental Relations, *Categorical Grants: Their Role and Design*. See also Raymond A. Shapek, *Managing Federalism: Evolution and Development of the Grant-in-Aid System* (Charlottesville, Va.: Community Collaborators, 1981), chapter 1.
39. Harold Seidman, *Politics, Position, and Power: The Dynamics of Federal Organization*, 3rd ed. (New York: Oxford University Press, 1980), p. 179.
40. Ibid.
41. Ibid., pp. 179–81.
42. U.S. Advisory Commission on Intergovernmental Relations, *Improving Urban America: A Challenge to Federalism* (Washington, D.C.: Advisory Commission on Intergovernmental Relations, 1976), p. 5.
43. Seidman, *Politics, Position, and Power*, p. 176.
44. See U.S. Advisory Commission on Intergovernmental Relations, *Urban America and the Federal System* (Washington, D.C.: Advisory Commission on Intergovernmental Relations, October 1969), p. 5.
45. Terry Sanford, *Storm Over the States* (New York: McGraw-Hill, 1967), p. 80.
46. David B. Walker, "Federal Aid Administrators and the Federal System," *Intergovernmental Perspective*, 3 (Fall 1977), 10–17, at p. 17 (emphasis added).
47. See Hale and Palley, *The Politics of Federal Grants*. See also Lawrence D. Brown, James W. Fossett, and Kenneth T. Palmer, *The Changing Politics of Federal Grants* (Washington, D.C.: Brookings, 1984).
48. Lovell, "Where We Are in IGR and Some of the Implications," p. 8.
49. See Richard H. Leach and Redding S. Sugg, Jr., *The Administration of Interstate Compacts* (Baton Rouge: Louisiana State University Press, 1959); Weldon V. Barton, *Interstate Compacts in the Political Process* (Chapel Hill: University of North Carolina Press, 1967); Martha Derthick, with Gary Bombardier, *Between State and Nation: Regional Organizations of the United States* (Washington, D.C.: Brookings, 1974); J. Norman Reid, "Regional Councils in Metropolitan and Nonmetropolitan Areas: Some Characteristics," Economic Development Division Working Paper No. 8002, U.S. Department of Agriculture, March 1980 (photocopied); and Nelson Wikstrom, "Studying Regional Councils: The Quest for a Developmental Theory," *Southern Review of Public Administration*, 4 (June 1980), 81–98, and *Councils of Governments: A Study of Political Incrementalism* (Chicago: Nelson-Hall, 1977).
50. Seidman, *Politics, Position, and Power*, p. 176 (emphasis added).
51. David B. Walker, "A New Intergovernmental System in 1977," *Publius: The Journal of Federalism*, 8 (Winter 1978), 101–16, at p. 106.
52. See U.S. Advisory Commission on Intergovernmental Relations, *Substate Regionalism and the Federal System*, 5 vols. (Washington, D.C.: Advisory Commission on Intergovernmental Relations, 1973 and 1974); Charlie B. Tyler, ed., "Developments in Substate Regionalism: A Mini-Symposium," *Southern Review of Public Administration*, 2 (June 1978), 77–121; J. Norman Reid, Jerome M. Stam, and Beth W. Honadle, "Federal Programs Supporting Substate Regionalism: 1977–1979," Economic Development Division Working Paper No. 8005, U.S. Department of Agriculture, April 1980 (photocopied); and J. Norman Reid, "Characteristics of Federal Programs Supporting Substate Regionalism," Economic Development Division Working Paper No. 8006, U.S. Department of Agriculture, May 1980 (photocopied).
53. *CQ Weekly Report*, 38 (December 20, 1980), 3628–29.

54. The potential fiscal impacts of eliminating GRS are explored in Tom Iverson, "General Revenue Sharing Dependency In Kentucky: A Fiscal Strait Jacket," *Public Administration Quarterly*, 7 (Fall 1983), 262–73; and "Taxes Could Rise 45% if Revenue Sharing Ends," Associated Press wire service report of a National League of Cities survey, appearing in the Bloomington-Normal (Ill.) *Daily Pantagraph*, November 24, 1982, p. A-5.

55. This portion of the block grants discussion rests on the treatment of Reagan and Sanzone, *The New Federalism*, chapter 5. See also U.S. Advisory Commission on Intergovernmental Relations, *Block Grants: A Comparative Analysis*, Report Number A-60 (Washington, D.C.: U.S. Government Printing Office, 1977), and a series of individual ACIR reports on the major block grant programs in operation during the mid-1970s. General treatment of these earlier block grants can be found in Reagan and Sanzone, *The New Federalism*, pp. 131–46; Hale and Palley, *The Politics of Federal Grants*, pp. 107–11; and Shapek, *Managing Federalism*, chapter 6. For treatment of the CDBG program, see Paul R. Dommel, Richard P. Nathan, Sarah F. Liebschutz, Margaret T. Wrightson, and associates, *Decentralizing Community Development* (Washington, D.C.: Brookings, 1978); Raymond A. Rosenfeld, "Local Implementation Decisions for Community Development Block Grants," *Public Administration Review*, 39 (September/October 1979), 448–57; Paul Terrell, "Beyond the Categories: Human Service Managers View the New Federal Aid," *Public Administration Review*, 40 (January/February 1980), 47–54; Donald F. Kettl, *Managing Community Development in the New Federalism* (New York: Praeger, 1980); Paul G. Farnham, "The Targeting of Federal Aid: Continued Ambivalence," *Public Policy* 29 (Winter 1981), 75–92; and Ruth Ross, ed., "The Community Development Block Grant Program," *Publius: The Journal of Federalism*, 13 (Summer 1983), 1–95.

56. Wright, *Understanding Intergovernmental Relations*, p. 97.

57. U.S. Advisory Commission on Intergovernmental Relations, *Block Grants: A Comparative Analysis*, p. 39.

58. This discussion of the Reagan block grants relies principally on U.S. Advisory Commission on Intergovernmental Relations, *A Catalog of Federal Grant-in-Aid Programs to State and Local Governments: Grants Funded, FY 1984*, Report Number M-139 (Washington, D.C.: U.S. Government Printing Office, December 1984). The author is indebted to Cynthia Cates Colella and Albert Richter for their assistance.

59. Ibid., p. 2.

60. Bruce D. McDowell, "Intergovernmental Consultation Changes Provide Opportunities," *U.S. Advisory Commission on Intergovernmental Relations Bulletin No. 82-3*, December 1982, p. 24.

61. U.S. Advisory Commission on Intergovernmental Relations, *A Catalog of Federal Grant-in-Aid Programs to State and Local Governments*, p. 1.

62. Quoted in *Congressional Quarterly (CQ) Almanac*, vol. 37: 97th Congress, First Session, 1981 (Washington, D.C.: Congressional Quarterly, Inc., 1981), pp. 464–65.

63. Among other sources on GRS, see David A. Caputo and Richard L. Cole, "General Revenue Sharing Expenditure Decisions in Cities Over 50,000," *Public Administration Review*, 35 (March/April 1975), 136–42; Richard P. Nathan, Allen D. Manvel, Susannah E. Calkins, and associates, *Monitoring Revenue Sharing* (Washington, D.C.: Brookings, 1975); Richard P. Nathan, Charles F. Adams, Jr.,

and associates, *Revenue Sharing: The Second Round* (Washington, D.C.: Brookings, 1977); Shapek, *Managing Federalism*, chapter 5; and David A. Caputo and Richard L. Cole, "City Officials and General Revenue Sharing," *Publius: The Journal of Federalism*, 13 (Winter 1983), 41–54.

64. For further information on the more recent block grants, see, among others, *Early Observations On Block Grant Implementation*, A Report to the Congress of the United States by the Comptroller General, General Accounting Office Report No. GGD–82–79 (Washington, D.C.: U.S. Government Printing Office, August 24, 1982); David Swain, "Block Grants Make Little Or No Difference: A Local Perspective," *Public Administration Quarterly*, 7 (Spring 1983), 4–21; *Community Services Block Grant: New State Role Brings Program and Administrative Changes*, A Report to the Congress of the United States by the Comptroller General, General Accounting Office Report No. HRD–84–76 (Washington, D.C.: U.S. Government Printing Office, September 28, 1984); and David R. Morgan and Robert E. England, "The Small Cities Block Grant Program: An Assessment of Programmatic Change Under State Control," *Public Administration Review*, 44 (November/December 1984), 477–82.

65. Swain, "Block Grants Make Little Or No Difference," pp. 15–17 (emphasis added). See also Robert W. Burchell, James H. Carr, Richard L. Florida, and James Nemeth, *The New Reality of Municipal Finance: The Rise and Fall of the Intergovernmental City* (New Brunswick, N.J.: Rutgers University, Center for Urban Policy Research, 1984).

66. Gary Bombardier, "The Managerial Function of OMB: Intergovernmental Relations as a Test Case," *Public Policy*, 23 (1975), 317–54, at p. 326.

67. Ibid., p. 328 (emphasis added).

68. Ibid., pp. 329–30 (emphasis added).

69. Ibid., pp. 328–32. Research on Circular A-95 includes *Office of Management and Budget Circular A-95: An Assessment* (Washington, D.C.: Intergovernmental Affairs Division, Office of Management and Budget, 1978); George J. Gordon, "Office of Management and Budget Circular A-95: Perspectives and Implications," *Publius: The Journal of Federalism*, 4 (Winter 1974), 45–68, and "OMB Circular A-95: An Overview," paper delivered at the 1978 annual conference of the American Society for Public Administration; Michael Steinman, "The A-95 Review Process: Suggestions for a New Perspective," *State and Local Government Review*, 14 (January 1982), 32–36; Philip A. Russo, Jr., "In Search of Intergovernmental Coordination: The A-95 Project Notification and Review System," *Publius: The Journal of Federalism*, 12 (Spring 1982), 49–62; and Irene Fraser Rothenberg, "National Support for Regional Review: Federal Compliance and the Future of Intergovernmental Coordination," *Publius: The Journal of Federalism*, 13 (Fall 1983), 43–58.

70. Statement of Joseph R. Wright, Jr., Deputy Director of the Office of Management and Budget, before the Senate Subcommittee on Intergovernmental Relations, Committee on Governmental Affairs, on Proposed State and Local Review Policies, April 26, 1982. The transition from A-95 to the new executive order, and preliminary findings about operations of the new system, are discussed in Irene Fraser Rothenberg and George J. Gordon, " 'Out with the Old, In with the New': The New Federalism, Intergovernmental Coordination, and Executive Order 12372," *Pubilus: The Journal of Federalism*, 14 (Summer 1984),

31–48; Irene Fraser Rothenberg, "Regional Coordination of Federal Programs: Has the Difficult Grown Impossible?" *Journal of Policy Analysis and Management*, 4 (Fall 1984), 1–16; and George J. Gordon and Irene Fraser Rothenberg, "Regional Coordination of Federal Categorical Grants: Change and Continuity Under the New Federalism," *Journal of the American Planning Association*, 51 (Spring 1985), 200–8.

71. Executive Order 12407, "Federal Regional Councils," *Federal Register*, 48 (February 1983), 7717. For an examination of the contributions these organizations made, see Robert W. Gage, "Federal Regional Councils: Networking Organizations for Policy Management in the Intergovernmental System," *Public Administration Review*, 44 (March/April 1984), 134–45.

72. See, among others, U.S. Advisory Commission on Intergovernmental Relations, *State Mandating of Local Expenditures* (Washington, D.C.: ACIR, 1978); Catherine H. Lovell, et al., *Federal and State Mandating on Local Government—Issues and Impacts*, Report to the National Science Foundation, June 1979; Marcia Whicker Taylor and Charlie B. Tyer, "State Mandated Local Government Expenditures: An Analysis and Evaluation," *Southern Review of Public Administration*, 4 (June 1980), 5–25; Catherine H. Lovell and Charles Tobin, "The Mandate Issue," *Public Administration Review*, 41 (May/June 1981), 318–31; Donald F. Kettl, "Regulating the Cities," *Publius: The Journal of Federalism*, 11 (Spring 1981), 111–25; Catherine Lovell, "Mandating: Operationalizing Domination," *Publius: The Journal of Federalism*, 11 (Spring 1981), 59–78; David R. Beam, "Washington's Regulation of States and Localities: Origins and Issues," and Timothy J. Conlan and Steven L. Abrams, "Federal Intergovernmental Regulation: Symbolic Politics In The New Congress," *Intergovernmental Perspective*, 7 (Summer 1981), 8–18 and 19–26, respectively; Max Neiman and Catherine Lovell, "Federal and State Mandating: A First Look at the Mandate Terrain," *Administration and Society*, 14 (November 1982), 343–72; Donald F. Kettl, *The Regulation of American Federalism* (Baton Rouge: Louisiana State University Press, 1983); Jerry L. Mashaw and Susan Rose-Ackerman, "Federalism and Regulation," in George C. Eads and Michael Fix, *The Reagan Regulatory Strategy: An Assessment* (Washington, D.C.: Urban Institute Press, 1984), pp. 111–45; and Jane Massey and Jeffrey D. Straussman, "Another Look at the Mandate Issue: Are Conditions-of-Aid Really So Burdensome?" *Public Administration Review*, 45 (March/April 1985), 292–300.

73. Kettl, *The Regulation of American Federalism*, pp. 3–4.

74. Ibid., pp. 4–5.

75. Walker, "A New Intergovernmental System in 1977," p. 106.

76. Kettl, *The Regulation of American Federalism*, p. 4.

77. C. Gregory Buntz and Beryl A. Radin, "Managing Intergovernmental Conflict: The Case of Human Services," *Public Administration Review*, 43 (September/October 1983), 403–10, at p. 406.

78. Kettl, *The Regulation of American Federalism*, pp. 5–6.

79. *CQ Weekly Report*, 42 (July 7, 1984), 1614.

80. Shirley Hufstedler, in a special report to the Los Angeles *Times*, reprinted in the Bloomington-Normal (Ill.) *Daily Pantagraph*, January 18, 1981, p. A-11.

81. See Robert Jay Dilger, *The Sunbelt/Snowbelt Controversy* (Irvington, N.Y.: Columbia University Press, 1982). Not unexpectedly, there is evidence of "sun belt"

gains in national government aid during the early 1980s. See, among others, "Grant Funds Decline For States, Localities," *Public Administration Times*, 8 (February 15, 1985), 3.

82. See *CQ Almanac*, vol. 38: 97th Congress, Second Session, 1982 (Washington, D.C.: Congressional Quarterly, Inc., 1982), pp. 536–39; and Neal Peirce, "Reagan's 'New Federalism': 'Single bold stroke' was lost," Bloomington-Normal (Ill.) *Daily Pantagraph*, January 22, 1984, p. A-15.

83. *CQ Almanac*, vol. 38, p. 536.

84. See Richard C. Kearney and Robert B. Garey, "American Federalism and the Management of Radioactive Wastes," *Public Administration Review*, 42 (January/February 1982), 14–24; the phrase "contentious federalism" is theirs. This description of the Sagebrush rebellion relies on the account of Tom Arrandale of Editorial Research Reports, reprinted in *Today*, 5 (April 8, 1983), 7 (published by King's Court Communications; Brunswick, Ohio).

85. Catherine H. Lovell, "Coordinating Federal Grants from Below," *Public Administration Review*, 39 (September/October 1979), 432–39, at p. 438.

86. See Helen Ingram, "Policy Implementation Through Bargaining: The Case of Federal Grants-in-Aid," *Public Policy*, 25 (Fall 1977), 499–526.

87. See James E. Skok, "Federal Funds and State Legislatures: Executive-Legislative Conflict in State Government," *Public Administration Review*, 40 (November/December 1980), 561–67; and *Federal Assistance System Should Be Changed to Permit Greater Involvement by State Legislatures*, A Report to the Congress of the United States by the Comptroller General, General Accounting Office Report No. GGD-81-3 (Washington, D.C.: U.S. Government Printing Office, December 15, 1980).

88. See, for example, Catherine H. Lovell, "Some Thoughts on Hyperintergovernmentalization," in Richard H. Leach, ed., *Intergovernmental Relations in the 1980s* (New York: Marcel Dekker, 1983), pp. 87–97. The realities of managing in the context of contemporary IGR are examined in Arnold Howitt, *Managing Federalism: Studies in Intergovernmental Relations* (Washington, D.C.: Congressional Quarterly Press, 1984). A useful focus on state governments is provided in Jack M. Treadway, *Public Policy Making in the American States* (New York: Praeger, 1985). Other sources bearing on the future course of IGR include Thomas J. Anton, "Intergovernmental Change in the United States," and John Leslie King and Kenneth L. Kraemer, "Information Systems and Intergovernmental Relations," both found in Trudi C. Miller, ed., *Public Sector Performance: A Conceptual Turning Point* (Baltimore: The Johns Hopkins University Press, 1984).

SUGGESTED READINGS

Bombardier, Gary. "The Managerial Function of OMB: Intergovernmental Relations as a Test Case." *Public Policy*, 23 (1975), 317–54.

Brown, Lawrence D., James W. Fossett, and Kenneth T. Palmer. *The Changing Politics of Federal Grants*. Washington, D.C.: Brookings, 1984.

Derthick, Martha, with Gary Bombardier. *Between State and Nation: Regional Organizations of the United States*. Washington, D.C.: Brookings, 1974.

Elazar, Daniel J. *American Federalism: A View from the States,* 3rd ed. New York: Harper & Row, 1984.

Glendening, Parris N., and Mavis Mann Reeves. *Pragmatic Federalism: An Intergovernmental View of American Government,* 2nd ed. Pacific Palisades, Calif.: Palisades Publishers, 1984.

Hale, George E., and Marian Lief Palley. *The Politics of Federal Grants.* Washington, D.C.: Congressional Quarterly Press, 1981.

Hawkins, Robert B., Jr., ed. *American Federalism.* San Francisco: Institute for Contemporary Studies, 1982.

House, Peter W., and Wilbur A. Steger. *Modern Federalism: An Analytic Approach.* Lexington, Mass.: Lexington Books, 1982.

Howitt, Arnold M. *Managing Federalism: Studies in Intergovernmental Relations.* Washington, D.C.: Congressional Quarterly Press, 1984.

Kettl, Donald F. *The Regulation of American Federalism.* Baton Rouge: Louisiana State University Press, 1983.

Leach, Richard H., ed. *Intergovernmental Relations in the 1980s.* New York: Marcel Dekker, 1983.

Lovell, Catherine H. "Where We Are in IGR and Some of the Implications." *Southern Review of Public Administration,* 3 (June 1979), 6–20.

Lovell, Catherine H., et al. *Federal and State Mandating on Local Governments—Issues and Impacts.* Report to the National Science Foundation, June 1979.

Publius: The Journal of Federalism. Philadelphia: Center for the Study of Federalism, Temple University.

Reagan, Michael D., and John G. Sanzone. *The New Federalism,* 2nd ed. New York: Oxford University Press, 1981.

Shapek, Raymond A. *Managing Federalism: Evolution and Development of the Grant-in-Aid System.* Charlottesville, Va.: Community Collaborators, 1981.

Walker, David B. *Toward a Functioning Federalism.* Cambridge, Mass.: Winthrop, 1981.

Wright, Deil S. *Understanding Intergovernmental Relations,* 2nd ed. Monterey, Calif.: Brooks/Cole, 1982.

Wright, Deil S., and Harvey L. White, eds. *Federalism and Intergovernmental Relations.* Washington, D.C.: American Society for Public Administration, 1984.

PART THREE

Organizations: Theory and Behavior

This section addresses the subjects of organization theory, internal dynamics of organization, decision making, and administrative leadership. Chapter 6 reviews the evolution of organization theory, beginning with late nineteenth-century writings and following developments in theory up to the present time. Organization theory has moved from a formalistic, relatively machinelike view of organizations to more diverse and comprehensive concepts, reflecting growing complexity in approaches to organization and in organizations themselves.

Chapter 7 discusses some of the most important dynamics of organization, including communication, coordination, centralization and decentralization, "line" and "staff" functions, "tall" and "flat" hierarchies, and alternative forms of organization structure.

Chapter 8 examines administrative decision making—considerations that enter into decision processes and how decision makers deal with them. The meaning of "rationality" in decision making, alternatives to the rational approach, the impact of personal and organizational goals, and influences in the decisional environment are treated.

Chapter 9 deals with administrative leadership and its "tasks" within organizations. After a review of principal approaches to leadership, six tasks are discussed and leader roles examined carefully. While it is far from clear just what makes a good leader, certain characteristics and behaviors, as well as situational factors, appear to contribute to effective leadership.

6

Organization Theory

ORGANIZATION theory deals with the formal structure, internal workings, and external environment of complex human organizations. It has focused on prescribing how work and workers *ought* to be organized and on attempting to explain actual consequences of organizational behavior (including individual behavior) on work being done and on the organization itself. The study of organizations—which spans business administration, sociology, political science, economic theory, and psychology as well as public administration—has evolved over a period of nearly a century. It has had to contend with changing assumptions about men and women as workers in an organizational setting; with numerous and often contradictory hypotheses and research findings about what motivates workers and how motivation is affected by different types of tasks, employees, and situations; and with a variety of views, both past and present, regarding the reciprocal impacts of organizations and the environments in which they operate. Some of the discussion will be familiar to anyone who has worked in an organization—which in our society means most of us.

Categorizing the major organization theories is no easy task. On one level, they can be distinguished according to whether they concentrate on needs, objectives, methods, and problems of management; on personal and social needs of workers within organizations; or on attempts by organizations to control their social, political, or economic environment. On another level, it is possible to identify numerous specific theories, each with its own principal assumptions and emphases. Some of these theories overlap to an extent, sharing certain values and viewpoints while differing significantly in other respects. We shall examine four major areas of organization theory: (1) formal theories, (2) the human relations school, (3) the organizational humanism approach, and (4) modern organization theory.

FORMAL THEORIES OF ORGANIZATION

While formal organization theory as we think of it originated in the late nineteenth century, some formative thinking on the subject dates back many centuries. Such concepts of organization, in fact, were largely derived from the highly structured arrangements of most military forces throughout history and from relatively rigidly structured ecclesiastical organizations. Most notably, the idea of a *vertical hierarchy* (chain of command)—found in the great majority of contemporary organizations—springs from military and religious roots. Some other features of formal theory, such as the need for defining certain set procedures, also originated in very early organizations. However, the most prominent model of bureaucracy as an explicit form of social organization was formulated by German sociologist Max Weber late in the nineteenth century (though it was not translated into English until the 1940s).[1]

Max Weber and the Bureaucratic Model

The model set forth by Weber was intended to identify systematically the necessary components in a well-structured government bureaucracy. Weber prescribed the following key elements:

1. *Division of labor and functional specialization*—the work divided according to type and purpose, with clear areas of jurisdiction marked out for each working unit and an emphasis on eliminating overlapping and duplication of functions
2. *Hierarchy*—a clear vertical "chain of command" in which each unit is subordinate to the one above it and superior to the one below it
3. *Formal framework of rules and procedures*—designed to ensure stability, predictability, and impersonality in bureaucratic operations, and thus equal treatment for all who deal with the organization, as well as reliability of performance
4. *Maintenance of files and other records*—to ensure that actions taken are both appropriate to the situation and consistent with past actions in similar circumstances
5. *Professionalization*—employees who are (a) appointed (not elected) on the basis of their job-related skills, (b) full-time and career oriented, and (c) paid a regular salary and provided with a retirement pension.[2]

In addition to these explicit elements, two others should be mentioned. Weber obviously intended a government bureaucracy of the type outlined to be endowed with sufficient *legal* and *political* authority to function adequately. His model of bureaucracy, in fact, is based on both legal and rational authority[3] derived from a fixed central point in the political process, and is assumed to function under that authority.

This model of bureaucracy represented an effort by Weber to both *pre-*

scribe and *de*scribe what he saw as the ideal-type form of organization, as it was then emerging in European experience. It is clearly a formalistic model, one that lacks such dimensions as informal lines of authority and communication or concern for the individual worker in the bureaucracy. Also, Weber himself indicated that the model was not meant to apply to all conceivable organizational situations, and that it represented only a broad framework rather than an all-encompassing model complete in every detail. However, despite these limitations, the Weber model was the first effort to define systematically the dimensions of this new form of social organization and to prescribe or explain its operations in abstract and theoretical terms.

One of the central purposes served by the Weber model, as he conceived of it, was making possible an optimum degree of *control* in an organization. The quest for control lay at the heart of virtually every element of the model mentioned earlier. In particular, the *formalism* suggested by rules, procedures, and files, and the exercise of authority through a *hierarchy*, point to Weber's overriding concern for organizations that would be both smoothly functioning and effectively *managed*. Thus, in this formal theory (and in others), to the extent that management concerns are emphasized, what is ultimately sought is control "from the top down" over all organizational activities and needs. Consequently, there is a tendency toward *encouraging uniformity* rather than permitting diversity—in values as well as behavior—within the organization, in order to facilitate control. This important generalization has *political* as well as managerial applications and implications.

A comparison of the Weber model to contemporary American public administration illustrates the attractiveness of the model as a yardstick against which to measure actual administrative arrangements and the limitations on its applicability to very different times and circumstances. American public bureaucracies operate within a formal framework of vertical hierarchy; extensive division of labor and specialization; specific rules, procedures, and routines; and a high degree of professionalization complete with extensive merit systems, career emphases, and salary and fringe benefits. Yet strong as these similarities with Weber's model are, there are equally prominent differences.

First, while there is a vertical hierarchy comprising the formal bureaucratic structure, those within that hierarchy respond to commands, inducements, and decisions that arise from outside it. Thus the vertical hierarchy is often (sometimes at best) only one of the "chains of command" active in the bureaucracy (a reflection of our political diversity).

Second, Weber's division of labor and specialization were designed to reduce functional overlap among bureaucratic units, so that functions performed by a given entity were the responsibility of *only* that entity. This, in Weber's view, was in the best interests of efficient operation. By contrast, American bureaucracy, though specialized, is shot through with functional overlap, reflecting among other things overlapping societal interests. As an example, a vocational training program could logically be placed under the jurisdiction either of the Labor Department (since the program is vocationally focused) or of Education (DOE) (since it emphasizes training, a DOE responsibility in programs not related to labor). Furthermore, functional overlap is practically guaranteed in a federal system where separate governments organize their bureaucracies independently.

Third, the kind of professionalization foreseen by Weber has been achieved only partially in American bureaucracy. This is in one sense a matter of definition. Weber's ''professionals'' were so defined because they were making the bureaucracy their careers, were competent to perform the tasks for which they were hired, and were paid in the manner that other professionals were paid. American bureaucracy differs from this ideal in two respects. First, there is a wide variety of personnel systems, from the fully developed merit system in which job-related competence is the most important qualification for employment, to the most open, deliberate patronage system where political loyalty and connections are major criteria in personnel decisions. The U.S. Civil Service; such states as Minnesota, California, and Wisconsin; and many city-manager cities make personnel decisions largely or entirely on a merit basis. Patronage is found in many other states as well as in numerous urban and rural governments throughout the country—sometimes even where a merit system appears to operate.

The second departure from the Weber ideal of professionalism is that more and more professions in the private sector—law, medicine, engineering, social and physical sciences, or management—are represented among government employees. Whereas Weber seemed to be seeking a ''professional bureaucrat,'' American experience has yielded ''bureaucratic professionals,'' persons trained in various private-sector professions who find careers in the public service. Weber's conception appears to be narrower than the American reality with regard to the scope and diversity of skills of his bureaucrats, as well as the variety of their professional loyalties (recall, in this regard, the debate mentioned in chapter 1 over whether public administration in this country is truly a profession).

A further implication of professionalization is that employees of a Weberian bureaucracy would be judged by their *continuing* competence in their jobs. In this regard, American merit systems also diverge from Weber's model. In the majority of cases, those who secure a merit position need only to serve a probationary period (usually six to eighteen months) before earning job security. How rapidly one rises through the ranks or how easily one can transfer to a new position may well be affected by periodic evaluations of competence, but it is the exception rather than the rule to find an employee dismissed from the public service solely for incompetence on the job.

Finally, Weber placed considerable emphasis on career employment, but it is only since 1955 that the national government and some states and localities have attempted to structure their personnel systems so as to foster a career emphasis as an integral part of public-sector employment.

In summary, the Weber model's applicability to American public administration is limited in important respects, even though we have emulated much of this model. The fundamental importance lies in its defining and describing bureaucracy as a structure of social organization, as a means of promoting hierarchical control, and in paving the way for further theory, explanation, and prescription regarding large and complex organizations.

Frederick Taylor and "Scientific Management"

Frederick Taylor's theory of "scientific management"[4] marked the beginning of the managerial tradition in organization theory, and was designed to assist private-sector management in adapting production practices to the needs of an emerging industrial economy in the early 1900s. Prior to Taylor there was little systematic organization of work in private industry, and his writings became the principal source of ideas on the subject. Taylor differed from Weber in his focus (private industry) and in prescribing a "science" of management incorporating specific steps and procedures for implementation (Weber's more abstract model of bureaucracy did not specify actual operations). Both men, however, were formal theorists in that they gave major emphasis to formal structure and rules, dealt hardly at all with the employees' working environment, and directly or indirectly equated the control needs of those at the top of the hierarchy with the needs of the organization as a whole.

The theory of scientific management rested on four underlying values. First was *efficiency* in production—obtaining the maximum possible from a given investment of resources. Second was *rationality* in work procedures—the arrangement of work in the most direct relationship to objectives sought. Third was *productivity*—maintaining the highest levels possible. Fourth was *profit*, which Taylor conceived of as the ultimate objective of everyone within the organization. These values formed the framework within which the remainder of his theory was worked out.

Taylor made several other critical assumptions. He viewed authority within the organization as highly centralized at top management levels. He assumed a vertical hierarchy through which top management conveyed orders to those below. And he thought that at each level of the organization responsibility and authority were fixed at a central point. Taylor also believed that there was "one best way" to do any particular task,[5] that through scientific research the one best way could be discovered and applied, that the ideal method could be taught to workers responsible for the particular task, and that scientific selection of workers for their capabilities in performing the task(s) would be the most rational way to achieve the organization's overall objectives.[6]

What management needed to do to increase productivity, and thus profits, was threefold. First, the most efficient tools and procedures had to be developed. In this connection Taylor relied on so-called "time and motion" studies, which concentrated on identifying the most economical set of physical movements associated with each step of a work process. Taylor was a pioneer in such studies, although he was only one of a number of researchers in this area.[7] Second, in teaching the new techniques to workers, emphasis was to be placed on standardizing the procedures to enable workers to discharge their responsibilities routinely yet efficiently. Third, there was need to develop and apply criteria for selecting workers that emphasized task-related capabilities. Note, again, that management was to be entirely responsible for implementing this "science" of management.

As with any model or theory, there were shortcomings alleged in scientific management, particularly as it came to be applied in industry and, later, government. A theoretical difficulty which received considerable attention from later scholars was that the worker under scientific management was seen as merely a cog in the industrial machine, with motives and incentives that were purely financial and no other needs on or off the job worthy of incorporation in the theory. (Taylor viewed management, too, in rather one-dimensional terms, but critiques of his theory concentrated on the consequences of viewing workers so narrowly. Weber's model was criticized on much the same grounds.)

Taylor's theory ran into real trouble when American industry tried to put it into practice. Taylor had assumed that management and labor would share the same objectives and that there would be no conflict over organizing to achieve them. Management would naturally seek efficiency, rationality, and productivity in order to maximize profits, and Taylor thought labor would support and work toward those same goals because, at the time, laborers were paid "by the piece" (that is, so much per item produced), and the greater the number turned out, the more money earned. Thus Taylor projected a united labor-management interest in his science of management. The problem was that this unity of interest was assumed without accounting for how it might be affected by the law of supply and demand. In the simplest terms, Taylor projected that demand for a product would always keep pace with supply, and thus that maximum productivity would always be a goal of both management and workers. In practice, however, production levels sometimes came to exceed public demand for a product. When this occurred, management laid off some workers, retaining only the number needed on the job for each to maintain maximum productivity without causing total output to exceed demand. This touched off vigorous opposition by workers who were laid off and their labor unions (then in their infancy). Most industrial managers had enough power to withstand labor's reaction, but Taylor's theory came under increasing fire.

Nevertheless, Taylor inaugurated a new direction in organization theory. Scientific management took hold not only in the private sector but also in public administration. For a time the values of efficiency, rationality, and productivity were virtually official doctrine in the national bureaucracy, and an important body of theory in public administration evolved largely from Taylor's work. Scientific management has had lasting influence on organization theory—directly, as it has shaped values and structures in numerous private and public enterprises; indirectly, as other theories either followed from it or developed in reaction to it. In particular, scientific management is generally regarded as having had tangible impact on the principles approach to public administration.

The "Principles" and Other Early Writings

Leonard D. White, in his pioneering *Introduction to the Study of Public Administration* (1926), clearly borrowed from Taylor in asserting that management procedures could be studied scientifically to discover the best method of operation. This was not only White's view—it was commonly held by most students of public administration of that period. Together with the politics-administration dichotomy, the quest for economy and efficiency, and the notion of public administration as a value-free science, the scientific study of management practices was at the core of public administration theory.

Other elements of Taylorism appeared in the ''principles of administration'' approach, which became prominent in the 1930s. The very effort to discover principles was itself derived from the scientific approach to management, and individual principles reflected Taylor's continuing influence on the study of organizations, both public and private. The writings of Henri Fayol, F. W. Willoughby, and the team of Luther Gulick and Lyndall Urwick[8] set forth the essential themes of the principles approach.

In chapter 1 we referred to the set of seven principles known by the acronym POSDCORB—planning, organizing, staffing, directing, coordinating, reporting, and budgeting; these were formulated by Gulick and Urwick in 1937,[9] following from the writings of Fayol. But there were other important principles besides POSDCORB, resembling in most instances some aspects of the thinking of Weber and Taylor. The major ones were:

1. *Unity of command*—direction by a single individual at each level of an organization and at the top of the structure
2. *Hierarchy*—the vertical ordering of superior-subordinate relations in an organization, with a clear chain of command implied
3. *Functional specialization*—division of labor and subject matter specialization as a main contributor to work efficiency
4. *Narrow span of control*—each supervisor having responsibility for the activities of a limited number of subordinates, again in the interests of efficient and effective operation
5. *Authority parallel with responsibility*—each responsible official endowed with the authority necessary to direct operations in the particular organizational unit

6. *Rational organizational arrangement*—according to function or purpose, geographic area, process performed, or people served (clientele)—the particular type (or combination) being selected with an eye to maximizing efficiency and effectiveness of performance.[10]

As we also saw in chapter 1, the principles were increasingly criticized for inconsistency and inapplicability. Developments in both theory and practice overtook the principles, developments not limited only to public administration; in particular, new approaches in psychology and sociology focused attention on those who made up the work force of an organization. The human relations approach constituted the next major phase in the evolution of organization theory and signaled the advent of the informal tradition. Those who embraced this approach did so because they were increasingly dissatisfied with one or more dimensions of scientific management. In the process they triggered an intense controversy over the nature of organizations, and over what aspects of organization were most appropriate as "building blocks" for successful management. In a sense, that controversy (begun in the late 1920s and early 1930s) continues to the present day.

THE HUMAN RELATIONS SCHOOL

The informal tradition differs from the formal in both major assumptions and principal research directions. Whereas formal theories assumed that workers were rational in their actions and motivations, seeking to maximize their gains in economic terms, informal theories looked beyond economic motivations and viewed workers as having *non*economic needs on the job and being motivated (at least potentially) through satisfaction of those needs. Thus researchers in the informal school sought to determine which noneconomic factors in the work situation, broadly defined, might have impact—and what kinds of impact—on workers and their performance.

The Hawthorne Studies

The first major study in the human relations approach to organization was conducted at the Western Electric plant in Hawthorne, Illinois, in the late 1920s and early 1930s.[11] Elton Mayo and his associates at the Harvard Business School began the study in order to measure the effects of worker fatigue on production. But it was expanded over a period of five years, resulting in a set of findings about productivity and job-related factors other than economic reward. Specifically, the study centered on how workers reacted to actions of management, how variations in physical working conditions affected output, and how social interactions among workers affected their work. It is significant that Mayo did not initially intend to examine all these relationships; it became necessary to investigate some of them after early results did not turn out as expected.

In one experiment, male workers making parts of telephone switches were paid by the piece and, according to the Taylor theory, were expected as a result to try to maximize their production output. To the surprise of both Mayo and the management of Western Electric, production stabilized well below the expected level, primarily due to the workers' reluctance to increase it beyond a certain point. This appeared to be a result of their fear of layoffs, and nothing management did or said could change their attitude— or their level of productivity. This was totally unexpected and not explained by anything in the theory of scientific management.

Another experiment involved varying the physical surroundings of a group of female workers assembling telephone relays, and observing changes in output. It was assumed that improvements in working conditions would lead to greater output, and that changes for the worse would cause a drop in productivity. This same experiment also was run for the men making switches. The results, however, did not conform to expectations, on two accounts. First, production levels of the women went up after each change in working conditions, regardless of whether conditions had been improved (better lighting, bigger working area, more frequent rest breaks) or worsened. It appeared that the women were responding in part to being subjects of an experiment. (Such a reaction has become known as the "Hawthorne effect.") More to the point, to the extent that management was paying consistent attention to them and their work, they seemed ready to produce at steadily higher levels. The second result that ran counter to expectations was that members of the male work group reacted entirely differently from the women. No matter what changes were made in working conditions, the men seemed to lag behind their previous level of productivity. Other findings also ran counter to the concepts of scientific management, suggesting that a new theory was needed.

Mayo and his associates concluded that within the formal organizational framework there was an *informal social structure* operating that tangibly influenced the behavior and motivations of the workers. Among the men, for example, there was pressure not to produce too much or too little and not get too closely tied to management.[12] There was also, quite clearly, pressure to conform to the group's production target level, in preference to any set by management. And among both men and women there was pressure to regard oneself as a group member and to react to management in those terms, rather than reacting strictly as an individual. This was very important in light of contrary assumptions made about workers by Taylor and other formal theorists. The work of the Mayo team also revealed the importance of noneconomic incentives and motivations on the job, in contrast to the "rational economic" assumptions of formal theorists.[13]

In sum, the Hawthorne studies opened the way to investigation of factors other than formal organizational structure and operations, and they established the importance of social structure and worker interaction. They became the basis for the human relations school of organization theory, which stressed the social and psychological dimensions of organizations, particularly the satisfactions workers derived from the work situation and effective motivating forces on the job.

Leadership in Organizations

A major emphasis in the human relations school during the 1930s was the study of organizational leadership, and how—if at all—leadership affected workers' behavior and the organization's general performance. Two of the most important scholars in the area were Chester Barnard and Kurt Lewin. Barnard examined the nature of authority within organizations, concentrating on leader-follower interaction, while Lewin studied different leadership styles and the effects they had on subordinates.

Chester Barnard spent his professional life in executive positions in the private sector (e.g., as president of the New Jersey Bell Telephone Company). Writing on the basis of that experience, he theorized that leadership could not be exercised by those at the top of a hierarchy solely at their discretion. Rather, leadership depended for its effectiveness largely upon the willingness of others (followers) to accept and respond to it. Barnard maintained that workers in an organization had a social-psychological "zone of acceptance" (sometimes referred to as "zone of indifference"), meaning the extent to which a follower is willing to be led, to obey commands or directives from a leader.[14] Barnard was, of course, assuming noncoercive commands not accompanied by the application of brute force. His main point was that those being led have a great deal to do with the nature and effectiveness of leadership over them. Whatever legal, political, or organizational authority leaders possess, followers must grant leaders authority over themselves.

Barnard's view of leadership also included the idea that leaders and followers each had something the other sought and could in effect exchange these commodities to their mutual advantage. Organization leaders could offer appropriate incentives to workers, and workers could contribute to the welfare of the organization through improved job performance. This early version of what has come to be known as *exchange theory*[15] reflected Barnard's position that coercive leadership relying on negative incentives (punishments or wage reductions, for example) was less effective than supportive leadership offering positive inducements. In other words, Barnard thought that the carrot was more effective than the stick as a motivator.

Kurt Lewin, founder of the Group Dynamics School at the University of Iowa earlier in the 1930s, conducted a series of experiments aimed at testing the effects of different types of leaders on the work output and group atmosphere of ten-year-old boys.[16] Lewin and his associates trained adult leaders in three leadership styles, then rotated different leaders among groups of boys making masks. The leadership styles were (1) author-itarian—a threatening, intimidating, coercive leader who permitted "no nonsense" in the work group (thus suppressing the natural high-spirited-ness of young boys), who specialized in finding fault with individual workers, and who resorted to scapegoating when things went wrong; (2) laissez-faire ("hands off")—a distant, nonthreatening leader who gave no direction, said nothing concerning cooperation among the workers or the need to keep on working, and gave no encouragement to the boys; and (3) democratic—a leader who stressed the job "we" have to do, maintained a relaxed and informal atmosphere, kept a loose hold on the reins in terms of exercising leadership authority, was very positive and supportive, encour-aged the boys to do their best, lavished praise for work well done, and en-couraged those who were becoming proficient at mask making to assist those still having some difficulty.

The principal findings in the Iowa experiments were revealing, insofar as it is possible to draw firm conclusions from a study in which ten-year-old boys were the subjects. First, productivity was greatest under the authori-tarian leader, with the democratic leader second, and the laissez-faire leader third. The only exception to this pattern was during "leader-out" periods, when the leader left the group on its own. Groups under demo-cratic leadership maintained highest production in those periods, with authoritarian-led groups falling off sharply without the presence and coer-cive motivation of the authoritarian leader. Second, interaction among group members varied dramatically according to the style of leadership, as did levels of group satisfaction with the work experience. Democratic lead-ership was clearly most conducive to interpersonal cooperation and group integration, as well as worker satisfaction. Authoritarian leadership led to considerable hostility among some group members and apathy on the part of others, with tensions running very high. Laissez-faire leadership had the least impact on worker behavior and attitudes.

There are limitations on the findings of the Iowa experiments, as on all such research. The major one is the extent to which we can apply these findings to other, more complex situations. Many tasks in business, indus-try, and government are more complicated than making masks; adult work-ers' personal and psychological needs may be different from those of ten-year-old boys'; hierarchical organizations with multiple layers of "leaders" and "followers" present different problems of group motivation; and a work force that is socially, economically, ethnically, and professionally di-verse is infinitely more difficult to deal with than a homogeneous group of boys.

Yet the findings of this experiment and the conceptions suggested by Barnard both pointed to the possible importance of leadership as another variable in getting the most and the best out of workers. Like the concern for working conditions and social interaction, this represented a fertile new field of inquiry, with some reason to think that "better leadership" might well help to make a better organization. The fact that the Iowa results may not be universally applicable does not offset, by any means, their significance in the study of organizations.

Critiques of the Human Relations School

More recent scholars have devoted some attention to shortcomings in the human relations school of organization theory. The principal criticisms have revolved around three points. First and most commonly noted is failure to take account of the potential for conflict between workers and managers.[17] Critics have pointed out that "good human relations" seemed to be advanced as the remedy for just about any difficulty between employers and employees; yet where basic conflicts exist over such things as long-range goals, work methods, and specific task assignments, it is not enough simply to make the worker feel important. In this respect, human relations proponents were guilty of the same oversight that had been made by formal theorists. That is, neither approach to organizations seemed to acknowledge that conflict was a real possibility, and one that had to be dealt with conceptually as well as in daily practice.

Second, the human relations school seemed to discount almost entirely the effects of formal structure on those in the organization. Also, the "rational-economic" incentives so much in favor with formal theorists were given little if any emphasis in these later formulations. This is not surprising in light of the fact that it was formal theory with which the human relations school was in sharpest conceptual disagreement, and it was, after all, the first body of theory to take issue with the Weber-Taylor-Fayol-Gulick approach. Even so, there is some accuracy in such criticisms.

A study conducted by William F. Whyte in the 1950s found that whether a company had a "flat" or "tall" hierarchy (that is, few or many levels within the formal structure) *did* seem to make some difference in the amount of conflict and tension that existed between labor and management.[18] Whyte also found, in another study, that for some production workers (a relatively small percentage) economic incentive plans served as more effective motivators than did noneconomic incentives, contrary to Mayo's contentions.[19] Other research has pointed to similar conclusions concerning monetary incentives, though apparently depending in part on how large a wage or salary differential is offered.[20]

Third, it has been contended that the kind and complexity of technologies employed in an organization matter considerably more in shaping informal social structure and human interaction than do the factors that Mayo, Lewin, and others regarded as pivotal. Robert Blauner in particular has made this point persuasively, stressing impersonal factors (that is, technology) as crucial.[21] It is possible, however, that this is not really a contradiction of the human relations findings, since Blauner, writing in the 1960s, was observing an organizational environment in which technology played a much bigger part than it had during the 1930s, when human relations emphases first emerged. Still, this does suggest that as factors in the work situation change, theories previously useful in analyzing organizations may have less applicability.

These are not the first critiques of the human relations approach, however. Another body of research begun in the 1940s and 1950s contributed a different perspective on the worker's place in the organization, and on what satisfactions and motivations existed in the work situation. This approach, known as *organizational* or *industrial humanism*, was concerned with what factors in the overall organizational picture contributed to the psychological and psychosocial health of the worker. In particular, it defined the worker's relationship to the *work itself* as an important variable in maintaining motivation and job satisfaction, something quite different from worker-supervisor or worker-worker interactions. Organizational humanism marked a turning point, serving as something of a bridge between the human relations approach and what we refer to as modern organization theory.

ORGANIZATIONAL HUMANISM

Organizational humanism was based on several assumptions that differed perceptibly from those of both formal organization theory and the human relations school. First, work held some intrinsic interest, which would itself serve to motivate the worker to perform it well. Second, individuals worked not only to satisfy off-the-job needs and desires, but some on the job as well. This suggested, in effect, that workers sought satisfactions *in the work*, and that achieving those satisfactions was a separate and distinct objective related to the most fundamental reasons for working. Third, work was a central life interest to the worker, not merely something to be tolerated or endured.

A fourth assumption, following directly from the notion of the centrality of work and of on-the-job satisfactions, proved to be a harbinger of things to come in contemporary organization theory. It was that management was better advised to promote positive motivation—through delegating responsibility, permitting discretion and creativity on the job, and involving the worker in important policy decisions affecting the work environment—than to assume that workers were inherently disinterested in the work and would avoid doing it if possible. The latter view of workers was an implicit part of formal theories of organization, and even human relations scholars seemed to share it to some extent. Organizational humanists, however, assumed the opposite. They did so in light of their research

Table 6-1
THEORY X AND THEORY Y: A SUMMARY

Underlying Belief System: Theory X

1. Most work is distasteful for most people.
2. Most people prefer close and continuous direction.
3. Most people can exercise little or no creativity in solving organizational problems.
4. Motivation occurs mostly or only as a response to "bread-and-butter" issues—threat or punishment—and is strictly an individual matter.

Underlying Belief System: Theory Y

1. Most people can find work as natural as play, if conditions permit.
2. Most people prefer and can provide self-control in achieving organizational objectives.
3. Most people can exercise significant creativity in solving organizational problems.
4. Motivation often occurs in response to ego and social rewards, particularly under conditions of full employment, and motivation is often dependent upon groups.

Source: Douglas McGregor, "Theory X and Theory Y," in Robert T. Golembiewski and Michael Cohen, *People in Public Service: A Reader in Public Personnel Administration* (Itasca, Ill.: F.E. Peacock, 1970), p. 380.

findings, which showed that authoritarian management practices designed to control lazy, irresponsible employees were resulting in unhappy and frustrated workers and poor work performance.

Douglas McGregor was among the pioneers of organizational humanism, arguing that workers could be self-motivating due to their own interest in the work and their own inclination to perform it.[22] McGregor's Theory Y was in sharp contrast to what he called Theory X—the earlier view that workers were lazy, wanted to avoid doing the work, and needed to be forced to do it (see Table 6-1 for summaries of Theories X and Y). Another major figure among organizational humanists was social psychologist Chris Argyris, whose view of work as a central life interest was fundamental to this approach.[23] Argyris also pointed out the need of workers to identify with their work, a further source of motivation to perform it well.

The writings of Rensis Likert emphasized employee participation in as many phases of management as possible, directed by a leader or leaders in the democratic mold (consistent with Kurt Lewin's findings). And Frederick Herzberg, in a study of over 200 accountants and engineers and some nonprofessional employees in a Pittsburgh firm, found that motivators such as salary, fringe benefits, good lighting, and adequate facilities served only to meet workers' minimum expectations, without producing real satisfaction on the job. What *did* yield personal satisfaction were such things as recognition for good job performance, opportunity to take initiative and exhibit creativity, and responsibility entrusted to individual workers and groups of workers. These intangibles, according to Herzberg's study, proved to be far better motivators than such tangible features as salary or fringe benefits, because they were the most satisfying aspects of the jobs.[24]

Among the most important research in organizational humanism was the work of Abraham Maslow, who wrote of "self-actualizing" workers achieving the highest degree of self-fulfillment on the job through maximum use of their creative capacities and individual independence.[25] Maslow viewed the worker as having a "hierarchy of needs," each level of which had to be satisfied before the individual could go on to the next one. The first level of the hierarchy was *physiological needs*—food, shelter, the basic means of survival. Next was *minimum job security*—a reasonable assurance (but not necessarily a guarantee) of continued employment. After these essentials came *social needs*—group acceptance on and off the job and interpersonal relationships that are positive and supportive. *Ego satisfaction* and *independence needs* represented the fourth step in Maslow's hierarchy, derived from accomplishments in one's work and public recognition of them. (A management practice of some importance in this regard is "public praise, private criticism" for an employee.) Finally, Maslow's highest level was *self-actualization*—feelings of personal fulfillment resulting from independent, creative, and responsible job performance.

As the worker satisfied the needs of one level, he or she was seen as being further motivated to work toward satisfying the needs of the next higher level. Thus Maslow placed his emphasis on interactions among the essential needs of the employee on and off the job, the work being done, the attitude of both management and employee toward work performance, and the relationship among employees in the work situation. In a sense, Maslow incorporated those aspects of the human relations approach centering on interpersonal interactions among workers into a larger and more complex scheme. The "hierarchy of needs," like other formulations in organizational humanism, assumed that worker satisfactions could be affected by many factors in the organization, both close to the work situation itself and more distant from it.

Organizational humanism is not without its critics, however. Robert Dubin found, for example, that fewer than 10 percent of the workers he studied in an industrial work group preferred the informality, job-centeredness, and independence on the job so highly valued in organizational humanism.[26] He suggested that different workers have widely varying needs, and that no *one* approach could successfully meet all of them. Some workers needed strong direction from a leader, not independence; lack of direction caused them to be anxious and frustrated in their work. Some really did work for the money. Some simply did not get along with their coworkers, and to emphasize group interaction would cause additional problems instead of solving existing ones. Some were not especially interested in participation in organizational decision making. Some were content to achieve certain needs in Maslow's hierarchy without continuing to strive for higher-level satisfactions, thus posing motivation problems for managers relying on Maslow's formulations. Dubin, in sum, suggested that placing too much faith in organizational humanism should be avoided. The varied needs of employees in an organization had to be taken into account.

A more recent critique of organizational humanism came from two sociologists who questioned some assumptions about the need for workers to self-actualize in their jobs and to participate in organizational decision making. H. Roy Kaplan and Curt Tausky maintained that various assumptions of organizational humanism seem to have been grounded more in ideological beliefs than in empirical data, and that there is mounting evidence that they do not stand up to empirical research and testing.[27] According to Kaplan and Tausky, many organizational humanists mistakenly viewed employee motivations and satisfactions in a one-dimensional manner, failing to take account of those for whom work was *not* intrinsically interesting and fulfilling, for whom creativity and independence were not valued features of their work, and for whom monetary and other tangible benefits were of the first order of importance. Theirs is a wide-ranging challenge, echoing to some degree Dubin's earlier critique.

Citing their own research and that of numerous other scholars in the 1950s, 1960s, and 1970s, Kaplan and Tausky made the following central points:

1. Professionals (such as scientists in basic research, academics, managers in government and private industry, and research-and-development engineers) are most likely to be intrinsically dedicated to their work, yet they also work in many cases because of extrinsic rewards, such as salary or fringe benefits.[28]
2. Most manual laborers and lower-level salaried workers derive satisfaction off their jobs rather than on the job, a finding made in a 1975 study by Dubin and two associates.[29]
3. The assumption that "participation increases satisfaction and satisfaction is reflected in increased work effort" is "tenuous," since numerous studies fail to reflect expected connections among greater worker participation, job satisfaction, and more (and more cheerful) work.[30]
4. There is a widespread commitment to work in this country that would appear *not* to depend upon work being intrinsically interesting.
5. People from blue-collar origins often seek different things in and from their work than do middle- and upper-class individuals, being more likely to place their emphasis on extrinsic rewards and, to some extent, on supervision on the job. This is consistent with a good deal of sociological literature emphasizing social class as an important determinant of individual attitudes and orientations toward work, and it is inconsistent with more generalized assumptions of the organizational humanists that self-actualization is a primary need—even a natural instinct—of all or most human beings in a work situation.

In sum, Kaplan and Tausky brought together substantial evidence suggesting that organizational humanism may be more limited in its applicability than its proponents have believed. By attempting to define where those limits lie, they have helped illuminate both particular difficulties with this theory of organization and the more fundamental necessity to avoid overgeneralizing about ways in which employees react to their work and respond to different motivational approaches.

One further criticism of organizational humanism should be mentioned, though it is implicit in Kaplan and Tausky's commentary. The *kind* of work being done—routine or nonroutine, individualized or small-group or assembly-line—may have a great deal to do with the possibilities for motivating and satisfying workers on the basis of intrinsic job interest. It often appears that the more routine the task, the greater the possibility for worker dissatisfaction, or at least for frustration and boredom. That phenomenon alone limits the applicability of organizational humanism.

On the other hand, there may be some ways to combat this problem. One approach is to make more systematic the recognition for employees doing routinized tasks; the "employee of the month" award at various fast-food restaurants, complete with the individual's photograph hung over the counter, is a familiar example. Another device is to alter the routine work situation, such as an auto assembly line, and give workers the opportunity to form their own work groups, which proceed to assemble a single automobile (or other product) "from the ground up." This may have the effect of reducing boredom and frustration on the job while increasing the sense of participation in and identity with the product being turned out—in the best tradition of organizational humanism. Such programs in auto factories are in wider use in parts of western Europe than in the United States; whether they could be put into practice successfully on this side of the Atlantic is not clear. In any event, the nature of particular tasks, taken separately from the kind of supervision or the backgrounds of the workers, appears to have some relevance in explaining the success or failure of organizational humanism in different work situations.

MODERN ORGANIZATION THEORY

Modern organization theory differs from all previous approaches in four key respects. First, there is a deliberate effort to separate facts from values (assuming that is possible) and to study organization behavior empirically. Proponents of earlier approaches made quite a few assumptions grounded in the predominant economic or social values of the time, the perceived needs of management or labor, or just plain common sense. In contrast, modern organization theorists make every effort to minimize the impact of their own values on the phenomena under study.

Second, modern organization theorists make extensive use of empirical research methods unavailable even twenty years ago—including statistics, computer simulations, and quantitative techniques—which permit more sophisticated insights into the operation of organizations.

Third, modern organization theory is constructed on an interdisciplinary basis—drawing on the varied approaches of sociology, organizational psychology, public administration, business, and information science. This greatly broadens the perspectives that can be developed concerning organizational behavior and the management of large, complex enterprises.

Fourth, modern organization theory attempts to generalize about organizations in terms sufficiently broad to be applicable to many different kinds of enterprises—private business corporations, hospitals, universities, interest groups of all kinds, labor unions, voluntary agencies, and community-based organizations, for example. To do this it is necessary to deal in abstract formulations accounting for common characteristics among dissimilar organizations. Thus, such features as information and its transmission, informal group processes, power relationships, environmental stability or turbulence, and decision making become the currency, so to speak, of generalized organization theory. We will examine briefly some of the major approaches that have been developed.

A pioneering study that ushered in the modern period of organization theory was done by John Pfiffner and Frank Sherwood.[31] They described organizations as characterized by a series of overlays or networks superimposed on the formal structure, and they discussed, among other features, formal and informal communications systems, group dynamics, relative power of different parts of the organization, and decision processes. Theirs was the first comprehensive effort to integrate a variety of approaches, and it set the stage for a tremendous expansion of information about organizations and of specific approaches to studying them.

A general approach shared by virtually all modern theories is the systems approach, or *systems theory*. A *system*, in the context of modern social science, refers to "any organized collection of parts united by prescribed interactions and designed [at least ideally] for the accomplishment of a specific goal or general purpose."[32] Such a definition would be equally applicable to an automobile engine, a hospital, the Department of Interior, or a major industrial firm; the last three, of course, are *social* systems, subject to sociological, political, and psychological analysis as to function and effectiveness. The systems approach, generally, assumes the existence—for any biological, mechanical, or social entity—of *inputs*, some *means of responding* to those inputs, *outputs, feedback* from the environment in response to system outputs, and *further inputs* into the system stemming from feedback (see Figure 6-1 for an application of this approach to politics). For an organization, inputs might consist of demands for some action, resources with which to pursue organizational objectives, underlying values of those outside the organization (and within it), and support for, or at least passive acceptance of, its essential structure and goals. The means of responding to inputs would include all formal and informal decision mechanisms, judgments about how or even whether to respond to particular inputs, past history of the organization in similar circumstances and the inclination or lack of it to follow precedent, and availability of necessary resources. Outputs could refer to the rendering of services by the organization, production or processing of goods, symbolic steps taken to maintain favorable images of the organization, rules and regulations for which it has proper authority, and adjustments to demands for change or to reallocations of resources (by a legislature, for example).[33]

A crucial distinction that has been drawn regarding the application of systems theory to complex organizations is that between *closed* and *open* systems.[34] Closed systems are essentially simple systems—having very few internal variables and relationships among them, and little or no vulnerability to forces in the external environment. A primary objective of those managing a closed system is the elimination of uncertainty, which in turn "results in everything being functional—making a positive, indeed an optimum, contribution to the overall result. All resources are appropriate resources, and their allocation fits a master plan. All action is appropriate action, and *its outcomes are predictable.*"[35] Organization theorist James Thompson has noted that much of the literature in what we have called the formal theories "centers on the concepts of *planning* or *controlling*,"[36] reinforcing our earlier observation about Weber (and, implicitly, Taylor and those who came after him). Control, stability, predictability—these were the cornerstones of formal (closed system) theories of organization.

Open systems theory proceeds from very different logical premises, which many scholars argue are more appropriate to the study of contempo-

Figure 6-1   A Simplified Model of a Political System

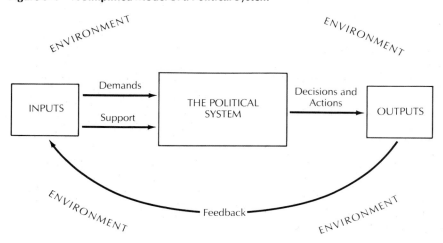

Source: David Easton, *A Framework for Political Analysis* (Englewood Cliffs, N.J.: Prentice-Hall, 1965), p. 112.

rary organizations (including public administrative agencies). Open systems are seen as highly complex and characterized by an *expectation of uncertainty*, internally and externally. This stems from the fact that, in Thompson's words, "a system contains more variables than we can comprehend at one time, or that some of the variables are subject to influences we cannot control or predict. . . ."[37] As a result, the elimination of uncertainty is not considered a viable organizational objective, and the very nature of an organization is vastly different. Again, quoting Thompson:

> Approached as a natural [open] system, the complex organization is a set of interdependent parts which together make up a whole because each contributes something and receives something from the whole, which in turn is interdependent with some larger environment. . . . Central to the natural-system approach is the concept of homeostasis, or self-stabilization, which spontaneously, or naturally, governs the necessary relationships among parts and activities and thereby keeps the system viable in the face of disturbances stemming from the environment.[38]

An obvious difference between closed and open systems is the way in which external environments impinge upon the organization. Open systems theory, together with some other modern theories, assumes considerable interdependence between organizations and their environments, with changes in the latter triggering adaptive responses within the organizations. Thus, a private firm will alter its marketing priorities in response to changing consumer preferences; a government agency can turn public criticism in its favor by providing for enlarged areas of citizen participation in decision making. In such instances, the formal "boundaries" of the organization do not serve to exclude others not formally members of it; indeed, those "inside" are willing to tailor their activities to meet externally imposed needs or wants. Also, because open systems continuously interact with their environments, there is a *need* to seek homeostasis, or equilibrium, balancing pressures and responses, demands and resources, worker incentives and contributions (to use Barnard's formulation). All this is in the long-term interest of organizational stability, which permits continued functioning in the manner expected by leaders, workers, and external clienteles. In sum, open systems theory—in sharp contrast to Weber's self-contained, "closed" bureaucracy—defines organizations as a great deal more than just formal structures, or interpersonal relations, or worker involvement in the job. It treats organizations as whole beings, complex in their makeup, and constant in their interaction with the surrounding environment.[39]

Other approaches that use the systems framework as a basis deal with organizations in a similarly broad-gauged fashion. *Information theory* is based on the view that organizations require information to prevent their evolving to a state of chaos or randomness in their operations. *Game theory* addresses itself to competition among members of an organization for gains and losses, in terms of resources and access to resources; game theory is distinctly mathematical in orientation and methods. The concept of the self-regulating organization is advanced in *cybernetics,* emphasizing feedback which triggers appropriate adaptive responses throughout the organizational system;[40] a thermostat operates on the same principle (see Table 6-2).

Mention should be made of some other approaches as well. *Organizational change* concentrates on the characteristics within organizations that promote or retard change in response to, or in anticipation of, change in demands from the external environment, particularly with regard to needs and desires for the products (however defined) of the organization.[41] *Organization development* focuses on analysis of organizational problems and formulation of possible solutions.[42] It is geared to increasing the capacity of an organization to identify, analyze, and solve internal problems as a regular function within its ongoing routines, using a social-psychological approach reminiscent to some extent of human relations approaches. *Management according to task* conceives of organizations that do not follow a single structure or format, top to bottom.[43] Rather, depending upon the set of tasks in a particular unit of the organization, that unit will be shaped structurally, socially, and technologically in the most appropriate manner. Thus, in a large and complex organization, there is likely to be considerable diversity in the arrangements of different units.

Another approach raising basic questions related to organization theory is the *New Public Administration.*[44] This contemporary movement (dating from 1970) focuses on how outputs of public organizations are distributed in society at large, and is keenly concerned with *social equity* as a guiding principle. To the extent that social equity requires change in present patterns of resource distribution, New Public Administrationists are willing to confront the political tension likely to occur. New Public Administration is also concerned with modifying established authority hierarchies because of their negative effects on subordinates and on the work of the organization, seeking instead different ways of integrating and coordinating organizational tasks (through group decision making, decentralization of responsibilities, and so on).

New Public Administration also foresees more direct involvement in public organizations of their disadvantaged-minority clienteles, in the interest of social equity (see the discussion of representativeness in chapter 2), and seeks to change (perhaps dramatically) the "socioemotional" processes that shape internal workings in many organizations. In regard to the latter, emphasis is placed on reducing an individual's reliance on the hierarchy, increasing tolerance for conflict and uncertainty, and making the prospect of taking risks a less formidable one. In sum, the New Public Administration makes social equity a central concern—public administration expert George Frederickson has called it the "supreme objective"[45]—and encourages organizations to adapt themselves as necessary in order to pursue it.

Table 6-2
COMMON CHARACTERISTICS OF OPEN SYSTEMS

Characteristic	Examples
1. Open systems import some form of energy from the external environment.	1. Cells receive oxygen from the blood stream; the body takes in oxygen from the external world; organizations must draw renewed supplies of energy from other institutions, or people, or the material environment.
2. Open systems transform the energy available to them.	2. The body converts starch and sugar into heat and action; organizations create a new product, or process materials, or train people, or provide a service.
3. Open systems "export" some product into the environment.	3. Biological organisms "export" carbon monoxide; the engineering firm constructs a bridge.
4. The pattern of activities of the energy exchange has a cyclical character; the product exported furnishes the source of energy for the repetition of the cycle of activities.	4. Industry utilizes raw materials and human labor to turn out a product that is marketed, and the profit is used to obtain more raw materials and labor to perpetuate the cycle of activities; the voluntary organization provides satisfactions to its members, who are further motivated to continue their activites.
5. To survive, open systems must arrest the process of inevitable degeneration (*entropy*), by acquiring more energy from the external environment than they expend.	5. Prisoners on a starvation diet will husband their energy to stretch their limited intake of food; organizations will attempt to acquire a comfortable margin, or reserve, in their needed resources.
6. Open systems receive information and negative feedback from their environments and must simplify all such data by coding it into a limited number of recognizable categories.	6. Individuals receive instructions, warning signals, pleasurable feelings, and the like; a thermostat regulates room temperature by a feedback mechanism; an automated power plant supplies and distributes electricity also through feedback.
7. Open systems maintain some constancy in energy exchange, and in relations among their respective parts, so that the essential character of the system is preserved (even if it expands).	7. Body temperature remains the same, despite varying external conditions; human physiological functions are maintained evenly by endocrine glands.
8. Open systems tend toward differentiation and elaboration.	8. The human body evolves from very simple cells; organizations move

Table 6-2 (continued)
COMMON CHARACTERISTICS OF OPEN SYSTEMS

Characteristic	Examples
	toward greater specialization of functions (e.g., medicine).
9. As differentiation proceeds, it is offset by two processes that bring the system together for unified functioning: *integration* and *coordination*.	9. In small groups, integration is achieved through shared norms and values; in large organizations, coordination occurs through fixed controls, e.g., setting priorities, establishing routines, scheduling activities.
10. Open systems can reach a final state from differing initial conditions and by a variety of paths.	10. Some biological organisms can develop from a variety of initial forms.

Source: Adapted, with minor modifications, from Daniel Katz and Robert L. Kahn, *The Social Psychology of Organizations*, 2nd ed. (New York: Wiley, 1978), pp. 23–30.

More recently, three other emphases have emerged in modern organization theory. One bears the label of *Theory Z*, referring to patterns of organization and operation characteristic of many contemporary Japanese corporations (and some local governments).[46] "Central to Theory Z is the assumption that productivity is a problem of social organization or . . . managerial organization, rather than technological change. Next is the idea that productivity can be improved by greater involvement of workers rather than increased supervision, threats, or increased economic rewards, all components of . . . Theory X. Once philosophical commitment is made to real involvement of employees in the processes and decisions . . ., then the key ingredients become trust, subtlety, and intimacy."[47] The key values and characteristics of Theory Z are summarized in Table 6-3.

Theory Z is suggestive of some beliefs present in our earlier thinking—and is decidedly different from others. For example, the involvement of workers is reminiscent of organizational humanism, and the positive consequences of workers having confidence in their managers echoes the human relations approach. On the other hand, our theories give little or no emphasis to managers knowing the private lives of employees (the so-called "holistic" or all-encompassing approach); generalist career paths; or collective accountability. In any event, the perceived successes of Japanese business have called attention to Theory Z, and its potential for application in our public-sector organizations is being examined increasingly.[48]

A second recent emphasis is *quality circles*, another product of Japanese management practice.[49] Not surprisingly, they reflect some of the same assumptions evident in Theory Z. Quality circles are "small groups of workers who meet on a regular basis to identify, analyze, and solve prob-

Table 6-3
VALUES AND CHARACTERISTICS OF THEORY Z

Values	Characteristics
1. Emphasis on trust, subtlety, and intimacy	1. Permanent rather than short-term employment
2. Increased involvement of workers leads to increased productivity	2. Slow rather than rapid promotions
3. If workers have confidence in their managers and believe their organizations are just and equitable, they will function well in uncertain environments, take risks for their organizations, and make personal sacrifices	3. General rather than specialized career paths
	4. Collective decision making
	5. Collective accountability
	6. Decision making is "bottom up"
	7. Decisions are made slowly at each level, but final plans are rapidly implemented
4. Good managers know the private lives of their employees	

Source: Adapted from Clyde McKee, "An Analysis of 'Theory Z': How It Is Used in Japan's Public Sector," paper delivered at the 1983 annual meeting of the American Political Science Association, Chicago; September 1983.

lems they experience in their jobs."[50] Most range in size from three to fifteen, from the same work area; thus the members are familiar with the problem identified by the group. "Through quality circles, workers serve as 'in-house' consultants on how to improve conditions and results. . . . The objectives for the circles are to: (1) enhance the quality of goods and services produced by [their] members; (2) solve work-place problems; (3) develop a closer identification with the goals of the organization; and (4) improve communication between supervisors and workers."[51] In quality circles, as in Theory Z, there are manifestations of our own earlier organization theories (for example, improving relationships between supervisors and workers).

The third emphasis of recent origin is on *public organization* theory.[52] As we discussed in chapter 1, distinctions between public and private management have received greater attention lately, and theories of organization have undergone corresponding scrutiny. In both theory and practice, however, there is as yet no clear consensus about the nature of "publicness" in organizations. Scholars are divided as to the import of an organization's *being* a public agency as opposed to a private one. Similarly, those concerned with public organizations have had to contend with the reality of increasing overlap between public and private sectors, and of so-called "intermediate" or "third-sector" organizations displaying characteristics of both public and private entities. Nevertheless, a growing body of scholarly opinion holds that public organizations *are* distinctive in important respects, and that we need to develop broader conceptual understanding of their design and behavior. (The discussion in chapter 1 about public and private managers—and similarities and differences in their management environments—is suggestive of this emphasis.) We are still in the early stages of theory building about public organizations, but the need for doing so is becoming more widely recognized and accepted across a wide variety of academic disciplines.

ORGANIZATION THEORY IN PERSPECTIVE

The subject of organization theory, for all its intellectual diversity, has been characterized by a unifying theme: the attempt to identify the elements in an organization's existence that are most important to its successfully reaching organizational goals. What those elements are, what the goals are, and indeed what comprises the organization itself, have not been agreed upon. The overlapping series of schools or approaches has given us a wide range of ideas from which to choose. The evolution of organization theory, furthermore, has reflected changing emphases in a host of academic disciplines, in business and industry, and in society at large concerning what is important in organizational life and how to go about achieving it.

Several general comments are in order. First, the various approaches have clearly overlapped chronologically and, more to the point, intellectually. The human relations school, while departing significantly from Weber and Taylor, assumed the existence of the same formal, hierarchical structure. Organizational humanism borrowed from the human relations approach. The New Public Administration and Theory Z have incorporated some elements of organizational humanism, and so on. Thus various strands of theoretical development have often been woven together as parts of different fabrics, so to speak. Each theory is not self-contained.

Second, although various approaches may fall out of favor among organization theorists of a particular period, that is not to say that their influence disappears. On the contrary, the influence of organization theories generally is cumulative, so that at any given time one may find in existing organizations some offshoots of earlier belief and practice. For example, while Weber's and Taylor's ideas of formal theory are no longer predominant among contemporary scholars, they have had a powerful influence in shaping many public and private institutions and, significantly, are still influential (however indirectly) in the thinking of many people. The same may be said for principles of administration and the human relations approach, both of which still carry some weight in theory and practice.

Furthermore, what James Thompson calls a newer tradition has emerged in the study of organizations, one that "evades the closed- versus open-system dilemma."[53] Advanced through the work of Richard Cyert, James March, and Herbert Simon,[54] this tradition views the organization as a "problem-facing and problem-solving phenomenon. The focus is on organizational processes related to choice of courses of action in an environ-

ment *which does not fully disclose* the alternatives available or the consequences of those alternatives.''[55] Thus, in this formulation, organizations
are neither fully closed nor fully open systems. In an increasingly interdependent world, the former is impractical, if not impossible. The latter,
while still possible, would produce a situation in which any organization
would be overwhelmed by the inflows of energy and information, rendering it ineffectual at best. In this mixed view of organizations, then, external
environments are regarded as very important; at the same time, organizations are seen as attempting internally to cope with enormous (and growing) uncertainty as they try to attain whatever objectives they hold.

Finally, the evolution of organization theory has included a marked
shift in assumptions about leaders and followers in an organization—from a
formal hierarchical relationship in which orders were transmitted and
obeyed to much more diverse and diffuse arrangements in which more participation is accepted as a matter of course. The control emphasis has had to
yield, at least partially, to other values, further complicating our understanding of how organizations can be effectively operated and posing new
challenges to managers themselves.

Organization theory has grown more complex over the years, paralleling what was occurring in real-life organizations throughout modern society. As more knowledge has been brought to bear, it is not surprising that
we are presently confronted by both greater diversity of approaches and
less certainty about the nature of large-scale organizations and the people
within them. That trend is likely to continue.

SUMMARY

Organization theory is a body of knowledge focusing on the formal and informal structures, internal dynamics, and surrounding social environments
of complex human organizations. Spanning several academic disciplines, it
has emphasized at different times the needs of management, the needs and
motivations of workers, and the relationship between organizations and
the stability or turbulence of their environments. Four major areas of organization theory are (1) formal theory, (2) human relations, (3) organizational humanism, and (4) modern organization theory.

Weber's model of bureaucracy incorporated the concepts of vertical hierarchy, division of labor and functional specialization, a formal framework
of rules and procedures, maintenance of files, professionalization, and adequate legal and political authority. *Control* was a central purpose of this
model. American public administration, patterned in some ways after the
Weber model, differs from it due to commands from outside the formal hierarchy, the extent of functional overlap among agencies, less than complete operation of merit personnel systems, diversity of substantive profes-

sional expertise, looseness of requirements for continuing competence, and late development of career emphases.

Taylor's theory of scientific management was geared to the needs of expanding private industry in the early 1900s. The values of efficiency, rationality, productivity, and profit were the foundation of his theory. Authority within the organization was to be concentrated in management's hands, and management was to direct discovery and implementation of the "one best way" to perform each task. In both theory and practice, scientific management encountered some difficulties, though it gained wide acceptance in both private and public organizations.

The principles approach so vital to the early development of public administration was strongly influenced by scientific management. Developing a science of management—the effort to discover principles of administration, concepts such as unity of command and functional specialization, and a formal, even mechanistic view of the organization—was highly reminiscent of Taylor's writings.

The human relations school, first of the "informal" theories, was launched with the Hawthorne studies in the late 1920s and early 1930s. Mayo and his associates found that an informal social structure, rather than pure economic motivation, greatly affected work patterns. Production target figures were set more effectively by informal agreement within the group than by what management dictated. Also, workers often reacted in the context of the group, as group members, rather than strictly in terms of individual self-interest.

Another major emphasis of the human relations school was how leadership affected worker performance and social interaction. According to Barnard, a worker's "zone of acceptance" defined leadership effectiveness far more than did formal leadership position or hierarchical arrangement. Barnard also viewed the leadership function as one of offering positive incentives to workers in exchange for their contributions to the organization and its work. Lewin studied varying effects of different leadership styles on groups of young boys doing simple tasks and found that work quality and group interaction were generally highest under democratic leadership. Though this study has its limitations, the findings are regarded as significant, and some other evidence exists to support them.

Critical appraisals of the human relations approach have maintained that (1) there was inadequate treatment of the potential for conflict within organizations; (2) the effects of formal structure and of "rational-economic" incentives should not have been discounted to the extent that they were; and (3) the technology utilized in the work situation is important in defining the informal social structure, yet was completely overlooked.

Organizational humanism was founded on four central assumptions: (1) work was, or could be made, intrinsically interesting to the worker; (2) workers sought satisfactions in their jobs; (3) work was a central life interest to the worker, not merely a means to other ends; and (4) greater involvement of the workers by management—through delegation of responsibility, opportunities for creativity and independence, and inclusion in important policy decisions—could promote positive motivation and improve worker performance and satisfaction. McGregor (Theory X and Theory Y), Argyris, Likert, and Herzberg were foremost among organizational humanists in developing these themes. Maslow analyzed the "hierarchy of needs" of workers, suggesting that as basic needs (food, shelter, job security) were met, individuals strove for social acceptance, ego satisfaction, and ultimately self-actualization through personal fulfillment in one's work.

Critiques of organizational humanism have suggested that not all workers respond to participation, independence, creativity, or motivation in Maslow's terms; some work for money, need decisive direction from supervisors, and do not get along with coworkers. Also, socioeconomic background and the routine or nonroutine nature of work may influence the effectiveness of an organizational humanist approach.

Modern organization theory is characterized by an effort to separate facts from values, utilization of empirical research methods (including statistical data and computers), incorporation of information from diverse sources, and much more complexity in the formulation and application of theory. Contributions to modern theory have come from the concept of "overlays," open systems theory, information theory, cybernetics, organization development, the New Public Administration, Theory Z, and public organization theory, among others.

Organization theory has sought to identify the elements that are crucial to organizational success. There has been both chronological and intellectual overlap from one body of theory to the next. Most theories have left their imprint upon society even after passing from prominence among theorists. The complexity of modern organization theory parallels real-life organizational complexity, and that is likely to continue to be the case.

NOTES

1. My thanks to Professor Donald Kettl of the University of Virginia for this observation.
2. H. H. Gerth and C. Wright Mills, *From Max Weber: Essays in Sociology* (New York: Oxford University Press, 1946), pp. 196–203.
3. Julien Freund, *The Sociology of Max Weber* (New York: Vintage Books, 1969), pp. 142–48.
4. Frederick W. Taylor, *The Principles of Scientific Management* (New York: Norton, 1967). The work was first published in 1911.
5. Ibid., p. 25.
6. Ibid., pp. 43–47.
7. For a humorous, first-person account of life with two other "time and motion" experts, Frank and Lillian Gilbreth, see Frank B. Gilbreth and Ernestine Gilbreth Carey, *Cheaper by the Dozen*, rev. ed. (New York: Crowell, 1963).

8. See Luther Gulick and Lyndall Urwick, eds., *Papers on the Science of Administration* (New York: Institute of Public Administration, 1937).
9. Ibid., p. 13.
10. Ibid., pp. 1–46. A contemporary analysis of the foundations of these and other principles can be found in Robert E. Goodin and Peter Wilenski, "Beyond Efficiency: The Logical Underpinnings of Administrative Principles," *Public Administration Review*, 44 (November/December 1984), 512–17.
11. The best source on the Hawthorne experiments is F. J. Roethlisberger and William J. Dickson, *Management and the Worker* (Cambridge, Mass.: Harvard University Press, 1939). See also Elton Mayo, *The Human Problems of an Industrial Civilization* (Boston: Harvard Business School, 1933), for a statement of Mayo's general approach to his research.
12. Roethlisberger and Dickson, *Management and the Worker*, p. 522.
13. See the summary of findings in Amitai Etzioni, *Modern Organizations* (Englewood Cliffs, N.J.: Prentice-Hall, 1964), at pp. 34–35.
14. See Chester Barnard, *The Functions of the Executive* (Cambridge, Mass.: Harvard University Press, 1938), especially pp. 92–94. See also William G. Scott, "Barnard on the Nature of Elitist Responsibility," *Public Administration Review*, 42 (May/June 1982), 197–201.
15. Warren G. Bennis, "Organizational Developments and the Fate of Bureaucracy," in Fred A. Kramer, ed., *Perspectives on Public Bureaucracy*, 3rd ed. (Cambridge, Mass.: Winthrop, 1981), pp. 5–25, at pp. 11–12. See also James G. March and Herbert A. Simon, *Organizations* (New York: Wiley, 1958), pp. 83–88.
16. The following is taken from Ralph White and Ronald Lippitt, "Leader Behavior and Member Reaction in Three 'Social Climates,'" in Dorwin Cartwright and Alvin Zander, eds., *Group Dynamics, Research and Theory*, 3rd ed. (New York: Harper & Row, 1968), pp. 527–53. Other studies of leadership include Philip Selznick, *Leadership in Administration* (New York: Harper & Row, 1957); Robert Guest, *Organizational Change: The Effects of Successful Leadership* (Homewood, Ill.: Dorsey and Irwin, 1962); Fred E. Fiedler, *A Theory of Leadership Effectiveness* (New York: McGraw-Hill, 1967); and Fred E. Fiedler and Martin Chemers, *Leadership and Effective Management* (Glenview, Ill.: Scott, Foresman, 1974). See also chapter 9.
17. See, for example, Etzioni, *Modern Organizations*, p. 44.
18. William F. Whyte, "Human Relations—A Progress Report," in Amitai Etzioni, ed., *Complex Organizations: A Sociological Reader* (New York: Holt, Rinehart and Winston, 1961), at p. 112.
19. William F. Whyte, *Money and Motivation: An Analysis of Incentives in Industry* (New York: Harper and Brothers, 1955), as summarized in Edgar Schein, *Organizational Psychology*, 2nd ed. (Englewood Cliffs, N.J.: Prentice-Hall, 1970), at pp. 35–37.
20. See C. R. Walker and R. H. Guest, *The Man on the Assembly Line* (Cambridge, Mass.: Harvard University Press, 1952), p. 91; cited by Etzioni in *Modern Organizations*, at p. 49.
21. Robert Blauner, *Alienation and Freedom: The Factory Worker and His Industry* (Chicago: University of Chicago Press, 1964).
22. Douglas McGregor, *The Human Side of Enterprise* (New York: McGraw-Hill, 1960); and *The Professional Manager* (New York: McGraw-Hill, 1967).
23. Chris Argyris, *Personality and Organization* (New York: Harper & Row, 1957), and *Integrating the Individual and the Organization* (New York: Wiley, 1964).

24. Frederick Herzberg, Bernard Mausner, and Barbara Synderman, *The Motivation to Work* (New York: Wiley, 1959), and Herzberg, *Work and the Nature of Man* (Cleveland: World, 1966).

25. See Abraham H. Maslow, *Motivation and Personality*, 2nd ed. (New York: Harper & Row, 1970), pp. 35–58.

26. Robert Dubin, "Industrial Worker Worlds: A Study of the 'Central Life Interests' of Industrial Workers," *Social Problems*, 4 (May 1956), 136–40. See also Dubin's "Persons and Organization," in Robert Dubin, ed., *Human Relations in Administration, with Readings*, 4th ed. (Englewood Cliffs, N.J.: Prentice-Hall, 1974).

27. H. Roy Kaplan and Curt Tausky, "Humanism in Organizations: A Critical Appraisal," *Public Administration Review*, 37 (March/April 1977), 171–80.

28. Ibid., p. 176.

29. Ibid. The study referred to is Robert Dubin, Joseph E. Champoux, and Lyman W. Porter, "Central Life Interests and Organizational Commitment of Blue-Collar and Clerical Workers," *Administrative Science Quarterly*, 20 (September 1975), 411–21.

30. Ibid., p. 172, et seq.

31. John M. Pfiffner and Frank P. Sherwood, *Administrative Organization* (Englewood Cliffs, N.J.: Prentice-Hall, 1960).

32. Jay M. Shafritz and Philip H. Whitbeck, eds., *Classics of Organization Theory* (Oak Park, Ill.: Moore Publishing, 1978), Introduction to Part III, "The Systems Perspective," p. 119.

33. A basic source applying systems theory to the political process is David Easton, *A Framework for Political Analysis* (Englewood Cliffs, N.J.: Prentice-Hall, 1965).

34. This discussion draws on James D. Thompson, *Organizations in Action* (New York: McGraw-Hill, 1967), pp. 3–24.

35. Ibid., p. 6 (emphasis added).

36. Ibid.

37. Ibid.

38. Ibid., pp. 6–7.

39. Two other excellent sources in this area are Walter Buckley, *Sociology and Modern Systems Theory* (Englewood Cliffs, N.J.: Prentice-Hall, 1967); and Daniel Katz and Robert L. Kahn, *The Social Psychology of Organizations*, 2nd ed. (New York: Wiley, 1978). A recent study applying these contrasting approaches is Robert M. O'Brien, Michael Clarke, and Sheldon Kamieniecki, "Open and Closed Systems of Decision Making: The Case of Toxic Waste Management," *Public Administration Review*, 44 (July/August 1984), 334–40.

40. See Stafford Beer, *Cybernetics and Management* (New York: Wiley, 1959); Karl Duetsch, *The Nerves of Government* (New York: The Free Press, 1963); and Katz and Kahn, *The Social Psychology of Organizations*.

41. See, among others, Jerald Hage and Michael Aiken, *Social Change in Complex Organizations* (New York: Random House, 1970).

42. See Larry Kirkhart and Neely Gardner, eds., "Symposium on Organization Development," *Public Administration Review*, 34 (March/April 1974), 97–140; Paul R. Lawrence and Jay W. Lorsch, *Developing Organizations: Diagnosis and Action* (Reading, Mass.: Addison-Wesley, 1969); and Gerald Zaltman, Robert Duncan, and Jonny Holbeck, *Innovations and Organizations* (New York: Wiley, 1973).

43. See Harold J. Leavitt, "Unhuman Organizations," and Harold J. Leavitt and

Thomas L. Whisler, "Management in the 1980s," in Harold J. Leavitt and Louis R. Pondy, eds., *Readings in Managerial Psychology* (Chicago: University of Chicago Press, 1964); cited by Warren G. Bennis, "Organizational Developments and the Fate of Bureaucracy," in Fred A. Kramer, ed., *Perspectives on Public Bureaucracy*, pp. 14–15.

44. See Frank Marini, ed., *Toward a New Public Administration: The Minnowbrook Perspective* (Scranton, Pa.: Chandler, 1971); H. George Frederickson, *New Public Administration* (University, Ala.: University of Alabama Press, 1980); and Carl Bellone, *Organization Theory and the New Public Administration* (Boston: Allyn and Bacon, 1980).

45. See Frederickson, *New Public Administration*.

46. This discussion of Theory Z relies on Clyde McKee, "An Analysis of 'Theory Z': How It Is Used in Japan's Public Sector," paper delivered at the 1983 annual meeting of the American Political Science Association, Chicago; September 1983. McKee draws extensively from the pioneering work of William G. Ouchi, *Theory Z—How American Business Can Meet the Japanese Challenge* (New York: Avon Books, 1982).

47. McKee, "An Analysis of 'Theory Z,' " p. 5.

48. See, for example, Ronald Contino and Robert M. Lorusso, "The Theory Z Turnaround of a Public Agency," *Public Administration Review*, 42 (January/February 1982), 66–72.

49. See, for example, Stephen Bryant and Joseph Kearns, " 'Workers' Brains as Well as Their Bodies': Quality Circles in a Federal Facility," *Public Administration Review*, 42 (March/April 1982), 144–50.

50. Ibid., p. 144.

51. Ibid.

52. See, among others, Donald P. Warwick, *A Theory of Public Bureaucracy: Politics, Personality, and Organization in the State Department* (Cambridge, Mass.: Harvard University Press, 1975); Michael A. Murray, "Comparing Public and Private Management," *Public Administration Review*, 35 (July/August 1975), 364–71; Hal G. Rainey, Robert W. Backoff, and Charles H. Levine, "Comparing Public and Private Organization," *Public Administration Review*, 36 (March/April 1976), 223–44; Joseph L. Bower, "Effective Public Management: It Isn't the Same as Effective Business Management," *Harvard Business Review*, 55 (March/April 1977), 131–40; Hal G. Rainey, "Public Organization Theory: The Rising Challenge," *Public Administration Review*, 43 (March/April 1983), 176–82; James L. Perry and Kenneth L. Kraemer, eds., *Public Management: Public and Private Perspectives* (Palo Alto, Calif.: Mayfield, 1983); Barry Bozeman, "Dimensions of 'Publicness': An Approach to Public Organization Theory," in Barry Bozeman and Jeffrey Straussman, eds., *New Directions in Public Administration* (Monterey, Calif.: Brooks/Cole, 1984), pp. 46–62; and Robert B. Denhardt, *Theories of Public Organizations* (Monterey, Calif.: Brooks/Cole, 1984).

53. Thompson, *Organizations in Action*, p. 8.

54. See March and Simon, *Organizations*; Richard M. Cyert and James G. March, *A Behavioral Theory of the Firm* (Englewood Cliffs, N.J.: Prentice- Hall, 1963); and Herbert A. Simon, *Administrative Behavior*, 3rd ed. (New York: The Free Press, 1976).

55. Thompson, *Organizations in Action*, p. 9 (emphasis added).

SUGGESTED READINGS

Argyris, Chris. *Integrating the Individual and the Organization.* New York: Wiley, 1964.

Barnard, Chester. *The Functions of the Executive.* Cambridge, Mass.: Harvard University Press, 1938.

Bennis, Warren G., and Philip E. Slater. *The Temporary Society.* New York: Harper & Row, 1968.

Denhardt, Robert B. *Theories of Public Organizations.* Monterey, Calif.: Brooks/Cole, 1984.

Dubin, Robert, ed. *Human Relations in Administration, with Readings,* 4th ed. Englewood Cliffs, N.J.: Prentice-Hall, 1974.

Etzioni, Amitai. *Modern Organizations.* Englewood Cliffs, N.J.: Prentice-Hall, 1964.

Frederickson, H. George. *New Public Administration.* University, Ala.: University of Alabama Press, 1980.

Gulick, Luther, and Lyndall Urwick, eds. *Papers on the Science of Administration.* New York: Institute of Public Administration, 1937.

Katz, Daniel, and Robert L. Kahn. *The Social Psychology of Organizations,* 2nd ed. New York: Wiley, 1978.

March, James G., and Herbert A. Simon. *Organizations.* New York: Wiley, 1958.

Maslow, Abraham H. *Motivation and Personality,* 2nd ed. New York: Harper & Row, 1970.

Perrow, Charles. *Complex Organizations: A Critical Essay.* Glenview, Ill.: Scott, Foresman, 1972.

Thompson, James D. *Organizations in Action.* New York: McGraw-Hill, 1967.

7

The Dynamics of Organization

ORGANIZATION theories, as useful as they are in explaining many aspects of human organizations, do not encompass explicitly all the dimensions of actual operations in large and complex enterprises. They do suggest, however, a wide range of variables relating to organization design and behavior. In the course of daily activities, many possibilities exist for assigning work, for deciding how managerial objectives are transmitted to others in the organization, for delegating responsibility, and for many similar choices. Some of these concerns are evident in the various theories discussed in chapter 6. For example, the way subordinates are regarded by managers affects the modes of communication used in conveying directives (that is, whether managers issue ''marching orders'' or set out program objectives with flexibility in evaluating performance). To take another case, application of Theory X or Theory Y would dictate the operating responsibility management chooses to delegate to others.

These concerns are part of the dynamics of organization, and we will treat them in this chapter both individually and in relation to one another. Two topics can be classified as *process* issues: (1) *communication*, a vital function in organizational life; and (2) *coordination* of activities, internally or across organizational lines. Both are central not only to effective operations in practice but also to traditional thinking about organizations. For example, the concept known as POSDCORB, discussed in chapters 1 and 6, incorporated communication and coordination as essential elements of managerial responsibility.[1] Four other topics to be discussed in this chapter are appropriately labeled *design* issues, relevant to the formal structuring of organizations. They are: (1) the functions known as *line* (substantive or policy-focused) and *staff* (support or advisory) activities, and how they are related—and differentiated—in practical terms; (2) *centralization* and *decentralization* in assigning responsibility and in overseeing operations; (3) the implications of a *tall* versus a *flat hierarchy* for managing a work force, that is, the practical differences between organizations having few structural layers and those having many; and (4) the possibilities of *alternative forms* of organization.

COMMUNICATION

In recent decades, no topic has received so much attention in both academic literature and practitioner manuals as has communication. (In this discussion, "communication" refers to the *field* and *process* of communication; "communications" refers to individual *messages* sent or received.) In the contexts of large and small groups, interpersonal relations, communication theory, the general political realm, and even relations between nations, communication has been the focus of intensive research as well as practical application.[2] This attention is not unprecedented, however, particularly in the context of organizations. Every major theory of organizations has included, explicitly or implicitly, assumptions about the nature, roles, and processes of communication in a given organizational setting.

Traditionally, observers of organizations approached the subject of communication by attempting to define various kinds and "flows" of communication. More recently, as the study of both communication and organizations has become more sophisticated, the scope and substance of the field have been altered to include more attention to social and psychological dimensions aiding or retarding effective communication.

Formal Versus Informal Communication

There are many types of communications within organizations. One of the most important ways to distinguish among different kinds is whether they are "formal" or "informal." *Formal* communications (1) originate in the authority of an official in the organization who attempts to influence some element of collective activity, (2) are directed to a particular audience within the organization, (3) follow proper organizational channels to the audience, and (4) constitute a "building block" in the continuing effort to officially state organizational purposes, strategies, and tactics. Formal communications are usually written, so that they become part of a permanent record of activity. They range from broad policy statements to specific operating memoranda.

Informal communications, on the other hand, take many forms: (1) they may come from many sources, not necessarily individuals acting in an official capacity; (2) while directed toward a selected audience, others may also become aware of the message; (3) they may follow official channels of communication, but often those who send them deliberately avoid those channels; and (4) like formal communications, they are concerned with or-ganizational life and activity, but they reflect a wider range of thinking and actions on the part of members of the organization.

There are more informal than formal communications; friends talk over lunch about agency projects or the last staff meeting much more often than officials issue formal policy directives. Informal communications sup-plement official messages and can even become a more reliable guide to what organizations actually do. Formal memoranda are the skeletal frame-work of organizational intent and activity. Less structured contacts—such as those among friends and coworkers, or through the ''grapevine''[3]— facilitate the multitude of actual operations built around the policy direc-tions set in formal communications.

In a bureaucracy with a vertical chain of command, established com-munication routes traditionally follow the hierarchy. That is, formal com-munications are more closely associated with the arrangements and struc-tures on the ''organization chart'' than are informal communications. However, it should be noted that formal communications are not confined to vertical organizational channels. A common and increasing phenome-non is *lateral* communications, cutting across the vertical hierarchy, yet still conducted relatively formally. Thus, even as the chiefs of different (and po-tentially competing) divisions within an agency pursue their respective programmatic objectives, finding that they have a common objective can prompt them to stay in touch, both formally and informally, in an effort to promote their mutual interests.

Communications do not merely travel ''top to bottom'' in an organi-zation, given the presence of both formal and informal lateral communica-tions possibilities. Still more important, however, is *upward* communica-tion—going against the grain of formal channels—but ever more crucial to the effective functioning of organizations large and small. This has a num-ber of important dimensions.

First, every organization has (or needs) *feedback* mechanisms—some means of transmitting information from those who originally received mes-sages to those who first sent them. Virtually every communication system provides for feedback, at least in theory; these can be highly formalized and sophisticated or reliant mainly on informal feedback. The problem for the top-level manager, and others, is to ensure that they will be able to learn via feedback what effects their own communications have had. Feed-back mechanisms can range from suggestion boxes, individual conversa-tions, and an open-door policy by supervisors, to regularized consultations between management and subordinates, surveys of employee opinion, and (where applicable) surveys of citizens regarding quality of the services pro-vided by a public organization.

A second factor, complicating the feedback process, is the strong tend-ency for good news to travel freely up the line, but for bad news to be sup-pressed, rerouted, or rewritten. The desire of lower-level units and personnel to present a favorable image to those higher up accounts for this phenomenon. But higher-level managers, in the interest of their own effectiveness, ordinarily need to know both good *and* bad news—to have a clear understanding of all that is going on in their organization, so that they can correct existing problems, anticipate future difficulties, and iron out internal conflicts that may hamper organizational activity.

To overcome the natural reluctance to report bad news to superiors, managers can initiate something resembling a no-fault information policy, within limits. This would encourage employees to bring problems not manageable at lower levels to the attention of higher management, but without retribution or fault finding as a penalty. To be successful, such feedback would have to develop in the context of positive, supportive interactions between superiors and subordinates; as suggested in chapter 6, the democratic leadership style is more conducive to this sort of communication than other styles (see chapter 9, also). That kind of feedback is often lacking precisely because general organizational relationships that would facilitate it have not been developed and maintained. Top management must take deliberate steps to make such feedback possible.

Overall, especially in this era of more democratic management in public and private sectors, and with subordinates increasingly demanding fuller participation in a wide range of organizational affairs, upward flows of communication have begun to approach other directions in importance. Whether formal or informal (many are the former), such messages can contribute measurably to the effective functioning of an organization.

Dimensions of Communication

Although achieving better communication is a goal to which many subscribe almost on faith, it may be useful to consider various aspects of the process; from such consideration, a fuller understanding of the potential and the pitfalls might emerge. We will briefly examine, in order, the prerequisites, purposes, obstacles (and their remedies), and consequences associated with better communication.

There are, first of all, several kinds of *prerequisites*. Structural or mechanical prerequisites include a transmitter of a message, the message itself, the medium through which it is sent, and a receiver mechanism of some sort.[4] Considerable research has been done on how the medium and the receiver, in particular, influence understanding of messages sent; the late Marshall McLuhan's work is a leading example of this kind of research on mechanistic communication models.[5] Other kinds of prerequisites, however, can be just as important—for example, the individual desire to communicate clearly; a *shared* interest in achieving common understanding, among those in communication with one another; and organizational arrangements facilitating message transmittal. In short, simply wanting to improve communication, while necessary, is not enough. This is especially true where those involved lack common definitions of the terms employed, or of the concepts and assumptions underlying the information transmitted. (That problem, for example, is important in the college classroom, where professors and students sometimes have difficulty communicating.)

Purposes of communication may seem obvious, yet they can be as varied as the people communicating. Many may use communications for purposes less constructive than achieving human understanding, organizational effectiveness, or the public interest. For example, the use of "gobbledygook" (a semirespectable term for misleading jargon or meaningless terms) is often noted as a major impediment to clear communication in organizations. While some gobbledygook just seems to happen, at other times its use may be carefully calculated by those employing it; the more they confuse potential opposition, the more they may be able to *de*fuse it. Similarly, the use of professional jargon, or of what has been labeled "bureaucratese," might be accidental or quite the opposite. Gobbledygook may be one method of fending off criticism; as noted in chapter 3, if listeners cannot fathom what is said, they cannot take issue with it.[6] For whatever reasons, a considerable amount of gobbledygook exists in government communications. Since the late 1970s, numerous efforts have been made (during both the Carter and Reagan presidencies) to reduce the incidence of "bureaucratese"—but seemingly with little permanent effect.

On the other hand, the crisp memo is a weapon of considerable po-

---

EXAMPLES OF GOBBLEDYGOOK

A developing bureaucrat might write, "On the basis of the documented report of the committee, I recommend the proposal be rejected." An accomplished bureaucrat would express himself with qualifying definition: "While the initial study committee has made a skillful and in-depth analysis of the alternative resource mixes as they relate to the proposal in question, the optimal functions as reflected by the committee's thematic projections would suggest a nonaffirmative response if the executive office were forced to make an immediate decision."

* * *

Assume, for example, that a bureaucrat wishes to state, "I doubt that it will work." By using . . . word-phrase substitution, he could write, "It is my present view that there are serious doubts about the implementation of the plan." An additional touch might translate the sentence into: "Given my present vantage point, it would appear that there are questionable, or at best, undemonstrable elements that might negatively affect the ultimate implementation of the integrated program."

Source: Adapted from James H. Boren, *When in Doubt, Mumble: A Bureaucrat's Handbook* (New York: Van Nostrand Reinhold, 1972), pp. 7–8.

tency in bureaucratic politics. It is widely acknowledged in large organizations, both public and private, that one can be influential through carefully conceived, well-written, and *brief* memoranda to key decision makers when a decision of some importance is pending. In many respects, memo writing and its potential represent everything gobbledygook does not: clarity of expression, sharpening understanding of available options, and the deliberate shaping of opinions. How clear the meaning of a communication is, then, depends heavily on how clear the sender intended it to be—and why!

Obstacles to effective communication can be found among both senders and receivers of messages. One obstacle, already noted, is lack of clarity on the part of the sender—poor word choices, failure to explain purposes of the communication, inadequate explanation of actions to be taken, and the like. Another problem is failure to have a message relayed accurately or in its entirety; the more layers in an organization structure, the more likely this is to occur (see chapter 4). A third difficulty is failure of the receiver to listen or to read; yet another is reluctance to accept the contents of the message, if it goes against the receiver's opinions on the subject of the message. Still another problem is failure of the receiver to act appropriately on the message, if he or she fails to comprehend fully its importance. Compounding all of these is the possibility (very real in large, complex organizations) that great distance will separate sender from receiver(s), making it difficult to determine the effectiveness of messages sent.

Several examples will illustrate these problems. One is the case of the radio operator on the ill-fated passenger liner *Titanic*, which hit an iceberg and sank on its maiden voyage to the United States in 1912. Afterward it became known that numerous messages warning of icebergs on its course had been received by the ship's radio man—who had failed to notify the bridge because he did not take the warnings seriously! A similar case involved a general in the Confederate armies during the Civil War who, when ordered to advance on a Union army during a critical battle, delayed for some four hours because he had misunderstood the directive; that delay ultimately cost his forces the victory. A somewhat different illustration involves experiments with a quasi-game called "rumor clinic," which have demonstrated how information can be lost while being transmitted through a series of separate relays—even when all the players are *trying* to be as accurate as they can! In the game, individuals are positioned around a room, at some distance from one another, and a report about some incident is whispered to the first player, who then repeats it (in a whisper) to the next player, and so on. Each individual is to repeat it to the next one exactly as he or she heard it. When the last player has heard the report, he or she then repeats it aloud, according to what was passed on by the next-to-last player. In the overwhelming majority of controlled cases where rumor clinic was played, the version reported by the last player differed in major respects— and often quite humorously—from that given to the initial player. Clearly, whether under controlled conditions or not, individuals do not always relay information precisely as they received it, even when they intend to do so. Partly this is a matter of listening, partly a matter of retention; but it may also demonstrate human limitations related to our screening out information, in spite of our best efforts. That is how rumors get started—and also how information can be sidetracked as it makes its way through the communication channels of an organization.

Numerous *remedies* are available to the communication-conscious manager, but they must be chosen with care, and none can be counted on to overcome the obstacles to communication completely. One is deliberate training in communication skills, for all employees. Another is more specifically targeted training for higher-level managers, designed to make them sensitive to the need for continual monitoring of messages passing through their divisions; this might be coupled with a program of incentives for improvement in communication flows. A third device, which can be used by top management personnel, is spot checking activities at lower levels of the organization to be sure that directives have been received and are being acted upon. If such monitoring from the top occurs through normal channels, it may suffer from the same problem posed for regular communications, namely, imperfect relaying; it may therefore be better for top managers to go *outside* the usual channels in following up on their directives.[7] All of these can be used in combination or individually. But perhaps the most important factor in improving communication is a clear perception on the part of employees that top management is committed to maintaining effective flows of communication, and that the process is explicitly valued for the contributions it can make to organizational operations.

The *consequences* of communication, like its purposes, cannot simply be assumed. Although many people think that better communication is a panacea for solving problems and conflicts, that is not necessarily the case. It can be, of course, that improving communication produces beneficial results in an organization, in the respects already discussed. On the other hand, communicating more clearly can complicate matters as well. The particular circumstances of communication strongly influence which kinds of results actually occur.

For example, if interpersonal hostilities exist between two individuals, and the hostile feelings are relatively temporary, it may be wiser *not* to express those feelings. After some time has passed and both people have had a chance to cool off, talking things out might then help resolve the problem, but without things being said that both parties might later regret. Take, as another possibility, two people who have a running feud; while not getting at the root of their difficulties, failure to communicate might be one short-term measure that makes it possible for the two feuding employees simply to continue functioning in a somewhat normal fashion. Also, part of organizational politics is knowing when not to speak openly about some problem, if doing so only has the effect of heating up the situation. It is perhaps better—even in the long run—not to try solving the problem if the attempt is unlikely to succeed, and if making the effort has the effect of bringing to the fore some interpersonal or substantive disagreements that are better left in the background.

Most relevant to the public administrator, the communication process in public bureaucracies generally occurs within the context of what some have labeled the *bargaining* or *political* model of communication. This model assumes the presence in an organization of considerable sustained conflict, strong tendencies toward secrecy, and motives of expediency on the part of most individuals. To the extent that public administration is viewed as a distinctively political process, this model of communication would seem to apply. Administrators would (and do) seek monopolies on key information; they would (and do) conduct their communication activities with an eye to maximum political gain; and so on. The communication process, according to this conception, becomes another weapon in the administrator's political arsenal, and clear communication of ideas, actions, or intentions could easily conflict with attaining one's political objectives.

On the other hand, an alternative model of communication, equally relevant to public administration, merits attention. While the political model is widely applicable, a *consensual* (consensus-building) model may be useful at some points in the administrative process. The underlying assumption of this model is that instead of a process founded on power struggles and political trade-offs, administrators may seek to reach agreement with potential adversaries as a means of furthering mutual aims. Under such circumstances, it is useful to communicate openly about differences that may exist, as well as areas of agreement. Communications, in this setting, should be open, with a clear inclination to share rather than guard information, even if doing so leads to recognition of disagreement. The key to successful use of this model is the common will to understand and overcome differences. There may be political risks in employing this approach, but a judgment must be made whether those risks are worth taking.

A manager choosing between these communication models must take several things into consideration. Among them are the relative probabilities of achieving organization goals with one or the other approach, the chances of reaching consensus with another agency (or agencies), and the sensitivity of information that would be shared under the consensus-building model. Other concerns could include the longer-range needs of the organization for political support from others, the agency's credibility in the administrative-political process, and the reliability of potential allies as working partners. Stronger agencies might rely on their power; weaker ones may seek consensus (all other things being equal).

What, then, is the importance of communication? Clearly, the basic processes serve to facilitate management of large enterprises in a number of ways. These include defining and fulfilling objectives, determining division and assignment of responsibilities across the full range of functions in the organization, identifying problems and opportunities in ongoing programs, anticipating long-term and short-term options (ideally with their attendant costs and benefits—see chapter 8), pinpointing problems in employee morale, soliciting ideas from individuals throughout the organization, and resolving conflicts as (or before) they occur. As with many other human activities, the particular styles and mechanisms of communication may influence just what is communicated, to what ends, the degree of effectiveness, and the consequences for the organization as a whole.[8]

COORDINATION

The concept of coordination, like communication, has almost universal appeal in the abstract. Obviously, a large and complex organization must achieve a minimally adequate degree of coordination in its multiple activities if there is to be any chance of consistency in the impacts of those activities. Put more informally, if the right hand is ever to know what the left hand is doing, their activities need some coordination at various points in the process. Coordination problems become more serious as organizations undergo growth, increasing complexity, and differentiation of functions internally. Organizational communication can be important here, it should be noted. And coordination can occur in different ways.

Just what is *coordination*? Various definitions have been advanced, most emphasizing notions such as common goals and interests, compatible objectives, and harmonious collaboration among different groups or organizations.[9] In its essentials, however, coordination is the *process of bringing together divided labor*. It is the opposite of division of labor, and the organizational cure for it where it is necessary to integrate the activities of different entities—whether separate agencies of the same government, agencies of different governments (or governments themselves), or elements of the public and private sectors. Having compatible objectives, or achieving harmony in joint efforts, may help facilitate the coordinative process, but the basic task can still be carried out even under less favorable conditions (conflict, hostility, apathy, and the like).

If we consider coordination in light of prerequisites, purposes, obstacles, remedies, and consequences—as we did with communication—some similarities are evident between the two phenomena, but also some differences. At the risk of oversimplification, it may be said that the prerequisites are virtually the same—channels and mechanisms for coordination must be deliberately established and maintained, just as for communication. The difficulty of accomplishing this varies with the degree of organizational autonomy possessed by the entities being coordinated. Regarding purposes, there is probably less variety in the objectives of those desiring coordination than we noted with respect to communication. Whereas communication can serve to mislead or confuse as well as to clarify, coordination is almost always designed to clear away difficulties in organizational activity. Since purposes are somewhat more predictable, the consequences are also, assuming a rational link between the two.

It should be noted, however, that many individuals and groups might resist efforts to clear away difficulties perceived by would-be coordinators. For their own reasons and priorities, some in and out of organizations may well prefer to engage in their assigned activities without bending their purposes to some larger, better coordinated undertaking. Such behaviors demonstrate the validity of the observation that "coordination is rarely neutral. To the extent that it results in mutual agreement or a decision on some policy, course of action, or inaction, inevitably it advances some interests at the expense of others or more than others."[10] Thus, those who seek better coordination must deal with those who would plant obstacles in that path. The obstacles to coordination merit attention, as do the remedies.

One obstacle is differing perceptions of program goals, leading perhaps inevitably to varied degrees of commitment to a coordination process that assumes substantial goal consensus among major participants. Other obstacles are divergent preferences on major or minor aspects of implementation (see chapter 13); conflicting priorities, even where substantive agreement on the total program exists; unequal fiscal capabilities; conflicting political pressures on program agencies; poor organization; breakdowns in communication; and inept leadership.[11] In addition, legal autonomy—as in the case of separate local government jurisdictions in a metropolitan area—can lead to a situation in which some or all of the obstacles mentioned might be present, but little can be done to cause the relevant officials to "coordinate their efforts." Coordinating across organizational (including governmental) boundaries, in other words, is more difficult than intraorganizational coordination.

Overcoming these obstacles is not easy, but a number of remedies do exist. One is improved communication; that can be an implicit reason for focusing on communication problems. In the abstract, there is every reason to hope that better communication—on objectives, tactics, perceived problems, or opportunities—can indeed lead to better meshing of the gears among agencies and their activities. But whether better communication actually facilitates coordination depends to a large extent on the amount of *conflict* (real and potential) present in the entities' relationships. Limited areas of conflict would permit use of the consensus-building model of communication and would tend toward improving coordination. Significant conflict, however, would probably lead to use of the political model of communication, and in that event the impulse to hoard information would work against the effort to coordinate more fully. Even in the absence of conflict, however, the will to improve coordination must be present among key personnel in the affected organizations or units.

Another principal remedy is the exercise of leadership, in two respects. First, responsible managers can devote leadership resources and exert their influence in support of coordination, demonstrating clearly their concern for improving it. Relevant managerial functions include, among others, goal setting and building consensus supportive of common goals; conflict management, aimed at containing and resolving internal disputes before they reach a level of intensity harmful to organizational effectiveness; and information management. Second, managers of different organizations or agencies, on an interpersonal level, can initiate efforts to coordinate activities of their respective entities, thus setting the context for a more formalized coordinative process. Their success ultimately would depend on their ability to go back to their organizations and build support there for coordination, in the manner described above. But their personal commitment to the endeavor would itself have some impact (see also chapter 9).

Particular organizational arrangements for strengthening coordination fall into two principal categories. One is *central coordination*, in which decisions are rendered by a coordinative entity or an individual having the power to do so. The other is *mutual adjustment* (sometimes termed *lateral coordination*), in which there exists ''consultation, sharing of information, and negotiation among equals. . . .''[12] (Note the presumption of the consensus-building model of communication.) A third possibility also exists, namely, ''a combination of these—a process in which lateral coordination is expedited, facilitated, and even coerced by leadership and pressure from an independent or higher-level coordinator.''[13]

Illustrative of these patterns—and of the relationship between divisions of labor and the rising need for coordination—are two aspects of American experience in intergovernmental relations (IGR) in the last twenty-five years. First, as more and more independent local governments were established in major metropolitan areas (a division of labor regarding provision of urban services and general governance), interest gradually grew in the possibility of mutual adjustment/lateral coordination, on a voluntary basis. Pioneering efforts were begun in the 1950s to create metropolitan area councils of government (COGs), consisting of one member from each local government in the region, to serve as a forum for airing problems and exploring avenues for possible collaboration. Hundreds of COGs now exist.

The other area of IGR pertinent to this discussion is national grants-in-aid, another example of division of labor, though not necessarily perceived that way. As grants proliferated in number, especially in the 1960s, calls for more coordination of state and local activities they funded became steadily more insistent. (Much of this interest was expressed by state and local officials.) An early response from the Johnson administration was to designate the secretary of Housing and Urban Development (HUD) as a ''convenor'' of program administrators from different departments who were working in related grant programs. Informal gatherings of these individuals were to serve as a regularized arena for consultation, from which improved program coordination presumably would result. This was not, strictly speaking, a voluntary effort, in the manner of COGs; HUD's role, and the gatherings themselves, were ordered by the president (a central coordinator). However, practical results depended on lateral coordination. In later testimony before Congress, some witnesses said that in this case, coordination, to be truly effective, would have had to be the functional equivalent of coercion from above.[14] While the president had initiated this forum, there may not have been *enough* ''central coordination''!

There is a clearer example of lateral coordination fostered by a higher-level coordinator, one that also demonstrates the links said to exist between coordination and communication. That is OMB's activity in the late 1960s and early 1970s, discussed in chapter 5, which was designed to provide tools for better coordination of grant programs by both national and state chief executives. Under Circular A-95, in particular, OMB mandated certain procedural guidelines aimed specifically at fostering lateral coordination among local governments and among state executive agencies, during the grants application process. This represented a significant innovation in national government practice, and in OMB's role. Public administration scholar James Sundquist has noted that prior to that time, Washington had chosen ''to rely almost wholly upon systems of mutual adjustment rather than of central direction, upon what could be attained through negotiation among equals rather than through the exercise of hierarchical authority.''[15] As noted in chapter 5, this version of coordination-as-process has persisted, though what the future holds in this regard is not at all clear.

Overall, then, coordination—like communication—is often highly prized, yet difficult to achieve, and not without some conceptual and operational difficulties. The more complex the organization, the greater the challenge to those who would achieve coordination of activity among its various parts. Truly smooth coordination is, at best, a sometime thing in most large enterprises.[16]

LINE AND STAFF FUNCTIONS

The notions of *line* and *staff* functions in an organization can be traced back to very traditional treatments of formal organization. *Line* activities, units, and officers are those involved primarily with substantive operations of an agency, dealing with programs or policies having direct impact on outside clienteles, and ultimately accountable to a superior in the performance of substantive responsibilities. This definition has been widely accepted in the public administration field, ever since it first emerged among the principles of public administration during the 1930s.[17] *Staff* functions were originally defined, in the same period, as consisting of support and advisory activities undergirding the ability of line personnel to carry out their duties. These could be, for example, budget making, personnel administration, planning, purchasing, and legal counsel. More recently, however, the notion of staff activities has undergone some revision (not accepted, it should be noted, by all observers, including some experts in the field). Starting in 1948 with Leonard D. White, an outstanding public administration scholar, *staff* came to mean the planning, research, and advisory activities so essential to the long-term well-being of the organization.[18] A new term—*auxiliary*—was coined for the remaining activities, which all units would need performed (budgeting, personnel, purchasing, and the like). The interrelationships among *line, staff,* and *auxiliary*—especially between the first two—have continued to be an important concern in public administration.

Several areas are important. First, the activities of such diverse units in an organization require some degree of coordination. The likelihood of conflict is greater between line personnel and staff (in this sense, research and planning) personnel; the most obvious point of potential clash is in their very different time perspectives and their order of priorities. Line personnel are usually concerned with the immediate, the concrete, the ''here and now,'' the substantive aspects of activity, while those engaged in research or planning concern themselves with where the agency may be going five or ten years hence. Thus, top management must at least integrate their activities, if not directly attempt to link them in an operational sense.

Second, there is the virtual *necessity* of some kinds of conflicts between them. An agency budget officer, charged with the responsibility of keeping budget requests in line with departmental policy, may have to cut funds from bureau estimates, and complaints may fly in both directions. The bureau chief feels that top management, personified by the budget officer, is not sufficiently aware of, or sensitive to, the importance of the bureau's work; the budget officer comes to regard the bureau as a callous spender of departmental dollars. Other examples abound: emphasis on affirmative action in hiring gives rise to a personnel office's insistence on hiring one individual over another preferred by an agency head; or a reform-minded city manager attempts to centralize the purchasing function, only to find that this infuriates department directors who have their own arrangements with suppliers and resent giving up their authority and discretion.

Finally, these traditional distinctions are increasingly coming to be seen as *less* distinct, in an era of rapid change inside and outside the organization. In particular, as long-range planning has taken on greater legitimacy—and, more to the point, has become a more significant part of the thinking of top-level line managers—the planning function has become more closely integrated with daily operations. Reciprocal understanding is growing, blurring old distinctions between line and staff. Many political leaders, in their demands for more and better program analysis before policy commitments are made, have further enhanced the position of staff personnel vis-a-vis their line counterparts. Thus, as societal demands and management techniques have changed, the old gaps have narrowed.[19]

CENTRALIZATION AND DECENTRALIZATION

The degree of centralization in an organization affects all other aspects of organizational life. Traditional management approaches, as we saw in chapter 6, have stressed how top managers would exercise the powers concentrated in their hands, in the interest of economy, efficiency, or effectiveness. The easy assumption of this traditional thinking was (and is) that it is entirely appropriate to centralize authority in an organization. Especially in recent years, however, much has been said, and written and accomplished, in support of the value of decentralization in administration. It is useful to understand what each concept means before going on to discuss why decentralization seems so much more popular lately.

Centralized management, in its extreme form, means that all essential decision making and implementation are the concentrated responsibility of those at the top. Communication becomes a one-way street, from the top down (except for structured feedback). Coordination is to be accomplished through central coordination. Meaningful participation in determining organizational direction in the long run is limited to personnel only at the highest levels. An analogy from physics would be *centripetal force*—that is, a gravitational force that pulls all objects toward the center. Nothing of any consequence goes on that is not under the direct control of top management. Some entities still function in this way, but many others at all levels of government, and in the private sector, do not.

As the scope and complexity of many organizations has increased, it has become necessary to delegate considerable amounts of operating authority to line managers (and occasionally to others), whose position in the organization is some distance from top management. An example is the restructuring of a number of national government Cabinet-level departments. The Department of Housing and Urban Development, for example, now has *regional* offices in ten major cities around the country, *district* offices within each region, and *field* offices within a district. The district office director needs—and possesses—substantial discretion in deciding how HUD policies are implemented within the geographic jurisdiction.

Employees are becoming interested in having a larger voice in organizational affairs, and decentralizing decision authority is an effective response—without top management relinquishing either oversight capacity or ultimate authority. Even if employees of a public entity do not press for internal decentralization, the national government in the last twenty-five years has used decentralization to respond to demands of *external* clienteles, especially in cases involving the poor (see chapters 5 and 15). The concepts of citizen participation and community activism trace their origins in part to decisions by Congress to broaden opportunities for citizens to take part in making decisions directly affecting their welfare. The Great Society of Lyndon Johnson, and the War on Poverty especially, carried decentralization forward.

Decentralization means greater internal complexity, generally. Ultimate policy and administrative responsibility remain with top managers, but many day-to-day operating decisions are left to others. Depending on the degree of decentralization, some or all of the programmatic activities are supervised by a multitude of middle-level managers operating under discretionary authority. Communication becomes a multichannel affair, with all manner of messages, directives, and informal contacts. Coordination, while still partly a central responsibility—and perhaps more so, in light of the dispersal of authority—is also likely to involve lateral coordination to a significant degree. It is also probable that top management will show greater willingness to include a wider range of employees in mapping out long-term strategies. If centralization is analogous to centripetal forces, decentralization has as its analog the *centrifugal* aspects of physics—wherein the major thrust of the system is *away* from the center. In practice, a decentralized system or organization is one with both centripetal and centrifugal forces at work. (It might be noted that these sorts of issues were—and still are—central to the continuing debate over American federalism, as well as specific forms of administrative organization. Much of what is said in the following section about the significance of centralization and decentralization also applies to the foundation and operation of the federal system.)

Significance of Centralization Versus Decentralization

There can be little doubt that the degree of centralization in an organization (or, for that matter, a political system) can make a difference in how things are done. But what *is* that difference? What purposes and values are served by greater or lesser centralization?

Clearly, effective control and internal program consistency are enhanced by centralization; so, also, is accountability for organization actions. If authority is highly centralized, there can be little question as to whose values and assumptions shape organizational goals, and less likelihood that management prerogatives will be challenged directly from below. Orderly operations within the organization similarly are facilitated where management responsibility is centralized.

On the other hand, centralization—even as it may facilitate control—often carries with it a certain lack of flexibility and adaptability, especially in large enterprises. One of the advantages of decentralization, according to many observers, is that it enables middle-level managers in the field to act as organizational *sensors*—able to detect new problems or opportunities, in a position to respond, on the spot, to particular policy needs, and so on. Particularly in an age of turbulence and change, organizational adaptiveness may depend in large measure on the speed with which changes in the environment are detected and brought to the attention of top management, and subsequent adjustments provided for. In many instances—large national government bureaucracies, private corporations dependent on changing markets, local government service delivery mechanisms faced with changing citizen demands—the need for this sort of adaptive capability is so great that it clearly demands some sacrifice in central control. In short, the larger need is the organization's survival amidst uncertainty and change.

Another function served by decentralization pertains to more of a political-philosophical question: to what degree are the members of an organization, or other system, meaningful participants in affairs of governance? Political systems, both ancient and modern, have confronted this question and have responded many different ways. In democratic systems (as defined in chapter 2), suspicion of centralist control runs very deep, prompting many to equate decentralization in government with popular rule in one form or another. In our society, that doctrine has lately been joined to organizational life, leading to considerable emphasis on greater participation, through decentralization, by many previously not a part of organizational decision making. Thus, for example, the community control emphasis referred to in chapter 2; thus, also, the trend on many college campuses in the 1970s to decentralize administrative decision making so as to include much larger numbers of students and student groups in important forums and councils of the university (a trend now being reversed). In the process, it is thought that democratic participation enhances the quality of decisions reached and increases the probability that affected clienteles will accept those decisions. Whether those expectations are realistic or well founded may be another question.

Here again, however, there is another side to the coin. For just as top management might have to choose between control and flexibility/adaptiveness, those who preach the virtues of decentralization must be alert to the possibility that it will be more difficult to hold accountable those who actually make decisions. The astute leader may find it possible to put through desired policy but avoid accountability by pointing to the decentralized nature of the decision process in which so many others also took part! There is the further prospect that cooptation will occur—reducing criticism or opposition by giving critics or opponents a stake in the decision process. Their being coopted would have important political consequences, in any setting, for the maintenance of meaningful opposition and the existence of informed, critical debate over proposed policy directions. Thus, decentralization (like anything else) is far from an unmixed blessing and should not be viewed as a panacea that will solve all ills of an organization.

Note in this connection the conceptual links between our discussion of centralization and decentralization, and our treatment in chapter 2 of the "administrative efficiency" and "pluralist democracy" models.[20] Advocates of centralization seek to apply the administrative efficiency model, whether consciously or not; arguments in favor of one are virtually identical to arguments for the other. Similarly, those committed to decentralization implicitly favor the "democracy" model, together with its underlying assumptions and rationales. Equally important is the fact that the centralization-decentralization debate cuts across such a wide spectrum. It is as appropriate to questions of large-scale political arrangements (for example, democratic governance or federal systems) as it is to smaller-scale organizational concerns, including the extent to which practices like "democratic" or "participative" management are encouraged within an organization.

One other area deserves mention. As long as we are referring to *decentralization*, the caveat of the late Paul Appleby (former assistant to the Secretary of Agriculture and a leading scholar in public administration) is well worth noting. He wrote, in the mid-1940s, that nothing can be decentralized until it has first been centralized.[21] That suggests—or *should* suggest—that a central authority capable of *de*centralizing is also theoretically capable of *re*centralizing! Thus, decentralization can occur only in the context of previous centralization—not the most comforting thought for those who place their faith in decentralization as the appropriate remedy for abuse of centralized power. In many instances, the "center" can assume responsibilities that had been delegated elsewhere, if decentralized operations are interfering with other values or objectives that those at the center deem important. It is one of the pitfalls affecting the whole concept of decentralization in organizations.

The feeling is still widespread, however, that decentralization has sufficient advantages to warrant taking the attendant risks. It is perhaps significant that many top-level managers share that opinion.

"TALL" VERSUS "FLAT" HIERARCHIES

When we think of bureaucracy, we tend to think of a distinct chain of command. Through it a number of essential operations can be conducted effectively. Among these are exerting managerial control, eliciting feedback from those below, providing for division of labor, and sending and receiving communications. Judging from much of the literature, we can assume that such a bureaucratic structure implicitly embraces many layers of organization in a "tall" hierarchy. Only in more recent decades has much attention been given to "flat" hierarchical arrangements, with few layers, and to some of the differences between flat and tall organizations.

Tall hierarchies evolved out of a combination of circumstances and organizational factors present in many early bureaucracies. Among the most important was, first, the diversity of tasks being performed within the same organization (for example, large industry), therefore requiring significant differentiation of each division or unit from all others, horizontally and vertically. Second, the principle that came to be known as "narrow span of control'' combined with task diversity and interdependence of activities to foster tall hierarchies.[22] Suggesting that each supervisor have only a limited number of subordinates to oversee, this notion led to "stretching" the chain of command in order to accommodate the needed ratio between supervisors and subordinates at each level, in the interest of overall coordination.[23] Third, the fact that higher-level employees in many early organizations were regarded as more professionalized than those at lower echelons gave impetus to the tendency to differentiate clearly in the organization structure between top and bottom. Finally, spurred by growing complexity of both internal tasks and technologies and of external environments, more modern organizations tended to exhibit intensified patterns along the lines just mentioned.

But flat hierarchies were not unknown even in the early 1900s, and have become more common. A flat hierarchy is one in which either top management is conducted in a collegial, "board of directors" fashion, or all subordinate units below the highest level of the organization are regarded as hierarchical equals, or both. An early example was the commission system in some local governments, in which each commissioner was the organizational equal of all the others, and responsibility for municipal leadership and management was shared coequally. A more contemporary organizational example is that of the scientific research team, in which there may well be division of labor among team members, as well as a coordinator of team efforts, but there is no one "leader" officially designated or informally acknowledged by team members, and decision making is a shared function, on the basis of mutual respect for one another's expertise (echoing to some extent organizational humanism and quality circles). Still another example is the small professional staff in a social service agency (such as a local Girl Scout office), which depends on the active participation of dedicated volunteers in the community. Other examples are found in state and national advisory commissions, "blue ribbon" citizens' panels, and the like (see Figure 7-1).

Significance of Tall Versus Flat Hierarchies

Among the most important differences between these two types of structures, communication problems in a tall hierarchy stand out. It has been noted by more than one observer that the more layers in an organization, the more difficult it is likely to be for messages to get through undistorted.[24] For lower-level employees, the problem of access to those at higher ranks is closely related. Obviously, the problem will be greater in taller hierarchies, creating the very real possibility of alienation from organization leadership among many employees (depending, of course, on how top managers conduct employee relations). Furthermore, as already suggested, problems of coordination are usually greater where organizational complexity is pres-

Figure 7-1   Tall and Flat Hierarchies

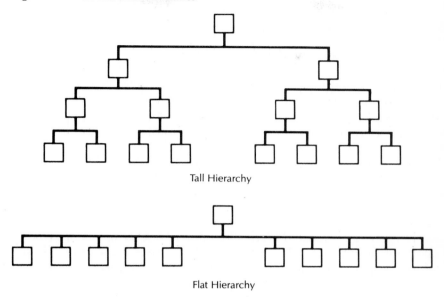

Tall Hierarchy

Flat Hierarchy

ent, and a tall hierarchy can contribute to that. Finally, issues of centralization and decentralization are more pressing in tall hierarchies.

But flat hierarchies are not without their drawbacks. For one, if organizational tasks become more diverse, there may not be enough "elbow room" in the structure to permit that diversity to be reflected; that could cause operating problems among individuals and staffs crowded too closely together organizationally. A second possible disadvantage lies in the existence of interpersonal hostilities on the same operating level of a flat hierarchy; again, there may not be enough distance to shield effectively against the adverse consequences of such feelings. That, obviously, can disrupt the substantive functioning of the organization as a whole. Finally, flat hierarchies—particularly in smaller organizational settings that have some sort of a chain of command—could facilitate the phenomenon of "too many chiefs and not enough Indians." It is not unknown for individuals operating on roughly equal footing to attempt to take charge, inappropriately, of a portion of the agency's overall tasks, in the process demonstrating that no other individual possesses either the formal or personal authority to counteract the attempt effectively. In a tall hierarchy, such a development can be dealt with "through channels"—and with potentially greater impact—partly because there *are* channels designed to handle that sort of eventuality. Thus, we find first that neither choice of structure is without its problems, and second, that the choice that is made carries with it some predictable impacts on the life of the organization.

ALTERNATIVE FORMS OF ORGANIZATION

As discussed in chapter 6, traditional formulations about bureaucratic organization assumed, among other things, division of labor, specialization, and an absence of functional overlap among various units within the organization. Apart from the question of whether these assumptions are always followed, another set of issues has now emerged that challenges the most basic assumptions about the appropriateness of bureaucracy as an organizing principle. Specifically, three developments have taken place that have encouraged informed thinking about various alternatives to bureaucracy as an organizational type.

First, the rise of new technologies has significantly altered (and expanded) the substantive tasks of public and private organizations alike. Scientific and other professional research and expertise, in a host of fields, have affected so much of public policy making that it is difficult to imagine transportation, conservation, agriculture, urban planning, housing, or national defense (to name but a few) without them. The technologies involved in operating an organization—such as electronic data processing, psychological profiles and testing, and other quantitative aids—have themselves spawned a number of new specialties in the art of management alone. The upshot of all this has been proliferation of new and different units in many organizations, devoted to functions unknown half a century ago in most organizations. Examples of this kind of change include a medical rehabilitation unit within a large insurance company, concentrating on support services for vocationally disabled individuals insured by the company; an office of planning and analysis in almost any large state government department, whose job it is, as a ''staff'' entity, to look past immediate challenges and anticipate the future; and a paralegal unit within the legal counsel's office in a large corporation, assisting in research and administrative services essential to providing high-quality legal work.

Second, as complex knowledge has grown, it has been characterized by increasing interdependence of *fields* of knowledge; the same is true of the staffs of specialists in those various fields. Thus, in the university setting, interdisciplinary plans of study, as well as research efforts, are ever more common. So, also, are interdependent teams of experts acting as consultants to industry or government organizations. Under such circumstances, hierarchical channels of authority would be highly dysfunctional, tending to interfere with the accomplishment of stated objectives. Other organizational forms have had to be developed.

Third, the rise of professionalism in many occupations has triggered a far greater emphasis on professionalism itself in organizational activities. This has had the consequence of strengthening the tendencies toward diversity in organizations and creating the need for a different avenue of management among diverse professionals. Professionalism, by itself, might have made bureaucratic hierarchy somewhat inappropriate as a principle of organization, but in combination with the factors mentioned above, many claim it has made it all the more so.

What, then, might some of the alternative forms of organization be? Several directions have been suggested, if not specific structures. One is the call for ''an end to hierarchy and competition'';[25] this is a clarion call for sweeping change in the ways we approach both structure and incentive systems within modern organizations. A second approach has been suggested by public administration scholar Warren Bennis, who has argued that Weber-style bureaucratic structure may have been entirely adequate and appropriate for dealing with generally routine and predictable tasks in a stable environment (such as during the early 1900s), but that the unpredictable nature of contemporary organizational life, coupled with a far more turbulent social environment, makes necessary new forms of organization.[26]

Bennis sees an *end to hierarchical leadership* because no one leader is capable of mastering the complex and diverse technologies present in so many organizations. Also due to technological needs, managers will increasingly become coordinators, or ''linking pins,''[27] among teams of experts operating within an almost horizontal chain of command rather than a traditional, vertical one. According to Bennis, this clearly suggests a participative style of management;[28] if the chain of command runs horizontally, it virtually requires a view of organization members as equals, not superiors and subordinates. The ''series of teams'' idea already operates in many aerospace industries, in the sorts of blue-ribbon commissions mentioned previously in connection with flat hierarchies, and in numerous professional consulting firms with considerable influence on the policy-making process.

The ''project team'' notion, a close relative of task forces, gives rise to a more formalized term describing the appropriate kind of organization. So-called *matrix* organizations, which are distinctly nonhierarchical, represent the full integration of what would otherwise be separate units of organization (line, staff, and the like). Matrix organizations are built on an essential premise of democratic decision making and assume authority that is both delegated explicitly to the members of such an organization and founded upon respect for *expertise in the particular project* (rather than upon formal rank) for which the matrix was constructed.[29] A leading example of such a structure is the experience within the National Aeronautics and Space Administration (NASA), which devised matrix organizations for the ventures to the moon and beyond (see Figure 7-2). Another application that has been suggested as being appropriate for matrix structures is in headquarters (central) units of national or state programs. In this view, it is particularly important for central program managers to be able to direct and integrate the myriad activities of their (decentralized) organizations, and a matrix arrangement facilitates this task.[30] Perhaps in part for this reason, matrix organizations are becoming somewhat more common in government agencies.

DYNAMICS OF ORGANIZATION: RETROSPECT AND PROSPECT

In this area, perhaps more so than others, the only sure thing in the immediate future is that few things are certain! Theories of organization and their actual arrangements are both in a state of flux. We have seen a bevy of proposals for doing things one way or another, none of which answers all the problems that existed before or is free of shortcomings. Yet the most interesting thing is that we seem never to cease trying—trying to devise the communication channel that is one step better, to bring about coordination of programs and projects that will be truly effective (one can hear the skeptic adding the phrase "for a change"), to establish the nonbureaucratic structure that will not suffer from *lack* of formal direction and leadership. It may well be that our biggest single problem, in the midst of such variety and richness in the possibilities available, is learning how to select the proper devices, forms, and tools to fit particular organizational and functional needs. That would require broadening management education in directions that are not now clearly perceived; it also has implications for our choices on larger questions of power, authority, and self-governance. As we discussed in chapter 2, choices made that pertain directly to administration will be made in the larger "force field" of values surrounding all our institutions. It is evident that both general and specific values are in an evolutionary process.

SUMMARY

The *dynamics* of organization help shape how daily activities are carried on within organizations. These dynamics include: (1) communication, (2) coordination, (3) line and staff functions, (4) centralization and decentralization, (5) tall and flat hierarchies, and (6) alternative forms of organization.

Communication, a crucial process in any organization for all of its members, has been studied closely in recent years. A distinction has emerged between relatively mechanistic approaches to the subject and those that emphasize the nature of the sender, medium, message, and receiver as key elements of communication. Also important are the prerequisites, purposes, obstacles, and consequences relating to the communication function.

Figure 7-2   Matrix Organizations: The NASA Example

Support personnel drawn from:	Vanguard (unmanned satellites)	Mercury (manned orbital)	Apollo (moon landings)	Mariner and Viking (Mars, Venus, etc.)
Astronautical science				
Budget and finance				
Computer services				
Engineering				
Facilities management				
Legal services				
Medical services				
Personnel				
Public relations				
Purchasing				

Organizations are characterized by both formal and informal communications; the former carry with them more of the formal authority of top-level managers, while the latter may include almost anything other than communications "through channels." Lateral communications can be either formal or informal; so, also, with upward communications, though feedback mechanisms from lower levels to higher ones are often encouraged by top management to facilitate keeping in touch with what is actually occurring throughout the organization.

Prerequisites of communication include appropriate media, a shared interest in clear communication, and common usage of terms by both sender and receiver. Purposes can include everything from promoting harmony, understanding, and cooperation, to defensiveness and self-interest. Obstacles include deliberate or inadvertent confusion on the part of the sender (for example, ''gobbledygook''), failure to relay messages, and a failure on the part of the receiver to listen or retain. Remedies include communication training and management spot checking on communication impacts. Consequences can range from solving problems to complicating their resolution, from easing tensions to increasing them, depending on the applicable communication model (political or consensus-building).

Coordination is another important function, one that brings together divided labor in an organization. Coordination, like communication, has its prerequisites, purposes, obstacles and remedies, and consequences; most attention has been paid to obstacles and remedies. Communication and leadership are often utilized in efforts to achieve better coordination. Organizational arrangements include central coordination, mutual adjustment/lateral coordination, and a mix of the two. Intergovernmental relations furnishes several examples.

Line and staff functions are among the most traditional of conceptions in the study of organizatins. Line activities have been defined almost universally as pertaining to the policy responsibilities of the organization. Staff activities originally meant support and advisory operations (budgeting, personnel, planning, purchasing), though more recently a further distinction has been drawn by some between planning or research activities (terming these ''staff'') and all other support functions (''auxiliary''). Each type of activity needs to be organized deliberately and any conflicts between them resolved (or at least made manageable); some conflict is virtually inevitable. Some have noted, lately, that the distinctions among these types of functions have become less clear.

Centralization and *decentralization* represent a virtually permanent tension between *centripetal* and *centrifugal* forces within most organizations. The former incline toward lodging in top management the authority to make most major (and many minor) decisions; the latter tend to resist that kind of centralization. Many organizations in years past exhibited a high degree of centralization; more recently the trend has been toward decentralizing agency activities. This has been due, in part, to growing complexity within the same organization, geographic and structural distance between top managers and many others in the hierarchy, and the growing pressure for more subordinate influence in organizational affairs. Centralization has the advantage of enhancing effective control and consistency of activities; it has the disadvantage of lacking flexibility and adaptiveness. Decentralization exhibits the converse characteristics (intermittent control, some lack of consistency, but also greater flexibility); it also affords greater opportunities for meaningful participation by more people in the organization. An accompanying difficulty, however, is holding accountable those who made decisions; with more participation, that is not as easy. Decentralization, moreover, can only follow centralization, and is potentially subject to *recentralization* by those at the top.

Tall hierarchies have been assumed to exist, for the most part, in bureaucracy; the possibility of a *flat* hierarchy is gaining in both recognition and actual use. Tall hierarchies evolved due to task diversity and the need for internal differentiation, combined with the principle of ''narrow span of control'' and the emphasis on professionalization at higher echelons. Flat hierarchies—emphasizing collegial organization—were not unknown in the past, and have become more common. Tall hierarchies are often associated with communication and coordination difficulties (though these are not inevitable) and with issues revolving around centralization/decentralization. Flat hierarchies, though not posing those same problems, have different ones, among them limiting organizational structuring of diverse units, and potential problems of interpersonal hostility and inappropriate exercise of power in organizations.

Alternatives to the bureaucratic form of organization have been suggested more frequently in recent years, on the grounds that bureaucracy is no longer an appropriate way to structure organizatons. Reasons cited range from the rise of new technologies and organizational functions to the development of professionalization and, consequently, a growing interdependence of specialties and specialists in many settings. An underlying theme (made explicit by some) is the turbulence and unpredictability of much of the contemporary organizational environment, and of many substantive responsibilities internal to organizations. Alternatives suggested include a task force or project-team arrangement, and a somewhat more permanent *matrix* organization.

NOTES

1. See Luther Gulick and Lyndall Urwick, eds., *Papers on the Science of Administration* (New York: Institute of Public Administration, 1937).
2. Communication in the small group is treated in John F. Cragan and David W. Wright, *Communication in Small Group Discussion: An Integrative Approach*, 2nd ed. (St. Paul: West, 1986). Sources on communication theory include, among others, David K. Berlo, *The Process of Communication* (New York: Holt, Rinehart and Winston, 1960), and Daniel Katz and Robert L. Kahn, *The Social Psychology of Organizations*, 2nd ed. (New York: Wiley, 1978). Sources on communication in organizations include Gerald M. Goldhaber, *Organizational Communication*, 3rd ed. (Dubuque, Iowa: William C. Brown, 1983), and H. Wayland Cummings, Larry W. Long, and Michael L. Lewis, *Managing Communication in Organizations: An Introduction* (Dubuque, Iowa: Gorsuch Scarisbrick, 1983).
3. An excellent analysis of how informal communication is studied, particularly the grapevine, can be found in Keith Davis, ''Methods for Studying Informal Communication,'' *Journal of Communication*, 28 (Winter 1978), 112–16.

4. Berlo, *The Process of Communication,* develops these themes extensively.
5. See, among his other works, Marshall McLuhan, *Understanding Media: The Extensions of Man* (New York: McGraw-Hill, 1964).
6. An amusing treatment of gobbledygook can be found in James H. Boren, *When in Doubt, Mumble: A Bureaucrat's Handbook* (New York: Van Nostrand Reinhold, 1972), chapter 2. See also Robert W. King, "Communicate Good Like a Bureaucrat Should," *The Bureaucrat,* 13 (Spring 1984), 20.
7. Examples of communication devices and tactics of this type can be found in Anthony Downs, *Inside Bureaucracy* (Boston: Little, Brown, 1967), chapter 10, especially pp. 124–26.
8. For further treatment of communication in administrative contexts, see Herbert A. Simon, *Administrative Behavior,* 3rd ed. (New York: The Free Press, 1976), chapter 8; and Hindy Lauer Schachter, *Public Agency Communication: Theory and Practice* (Chicago: Nelson-Hall, 1983).
9. See, for example, Harold Seidman, *Politics, Position, and Power: The Dynamics of Federal Organization,* 3rd ed. (New York: Oxford University Press, 1980), chapter 8, especially p. 204; and J. D. Williams, *Public Administration: The People's Business* (Boston: Little, Brown, 1980), p. 226.
10. Seidman, *Politics, Position, and Power,* p. 204.
11. Williams, *Public Administration: The People's Business,* chapter 10, develops these themes more fully.
12. See James L. Sundquist (with the collaboration of David W. Davis), *Making Federalism Work: A Study of Program Coordination at the Community Level* (Washington, D.C.: Brookings, 1969), p. 17. The original categorization was suggested by political economist Charles Lindblom. See also Herbert Kaufman, "Organization Theory and Political Theory," *American Political Science Review,* 58 (March 1964), 5–14, at p. 7.
13. Sundquist, *Making Federalism Work,* p. 18.
14. See George J. Gordon, "Office of Management and Budget Circular A-95: Perspectives and Implications," *Publius: The Journal of Federalism,* 4 (Winter 1974), 45–68, at p. 54.
15. Sundquist, *Making Federalism Work,* p. 19.
16. For other perspectives on this topic, see Howard E. McCurdy, "Coordination," in Thomas D. Lynch, ed., *Organization Theory and Management* (New York: Marcel Dekker, 1983), pp. 111–36, and Allen Schick, "The Coordination Option," in Peter Szanton, ed., *Federal Reorganization: What Have We Learned?* (Chatham, N.J.: Chatham House, 1981), pp. 85–113.
17. See Gulick and Urwick, eds., *Papers on the Science of Administration,* pp. 49–88.
18. Leonard D. White, *Introduction to the Study of Public Administration,* 3rd ed. (New York: Macmillan, 1948), p. 30; cited by Williams, *Public Administration: The People's Business,* p. 72.
19. This assessment may be understated. See Gerald G. Fisch, "Line-Staff Is Obsolete," *Harvard Business Review,* 39 (September–October 1961), 67–79. For a thoughtful treatment of the traditional line/staff dichotomy, and further suggestions for revising our conceptions about that dichotomy, see Jeremy F. Plant, "Line and Staff," in Thomas D. Lynch, ed., *Organization Theory and Management* (New York: Marcel Dekker, 1983), pp. 191–216.
20. See Douglas Yates, *Bureaucratic Democracy: The Search for Democracy and Efficiency in American Government* (Cambridge, Mass.: Harvard University Press, 1982), especially pp. 31–33.

21. Paul Appleby, *Big Democracy* (New York: Knopf, 1945), p. 104.
22. Downs, *Inside Bureaucracy*, p. 57.
23. Ibid.
24. Ibid., pp. 116–18. See also Peter Blau and W. Richard Scott, *Formal Organizations* (San Francisco: Chandler, 1962), pp. 121–28; and James G. March and Herbert A. Simon, *Organizations* (New York: Wiley, 1958), p. 165.
25. See Frederick C. Thayer, *An End to Hierarchy and Competition: Administration in the Post-Affluent World*, 2nd. ed. (New York: Franklin Watts/New Viewpoints, 1980).
26. Warren G. Bennis and Philip E. Slater, *The Temporary Society* (New York: Harper & Row, 1968), p. 56.
27. See Rensis Likert, *New Patterns of Management* (New York: McGraw-Hill, 1961).
28. Bennis and Slater, *The Temporary Society*, p. 6.
29. See, among others, Joan Woodward, *Industrial Organization: Theory and Practice* (New York: Oxford University Press, 1965); Joan Woodward, ed., *Industrial Organization: Behaviour and Control* (London: Oxford University Press, 1970); Stanley M. Davis, et al., *Matrix* (Reading, Mass.: Addison-Wesley, 1977); and Walter F. Baber, *Organizing the Future: Matrix Models for the Post Industrial Polity* (University, Ala.: University of Alabama Press, 1983).
30. See Mark Lincoln Chadwin, "Managing Program Headquarters Units: The Importance of Matrixing," *Public Administration Review*, 43 (July/August 1983), 305–14. See also Walter F. Baber, "Reform for Principle and Profit," *The Bureaucrat*, 13 (Summer 1984), 33–37, especially pp. 36–37.

SUGGESTED READINGS

Baber, Walter F. *Organizing the Future: Matrix Models for the Post Industrial Polity*. University, Ala.: University of Alabama Press, 1983.

Bennis, Warren G., and Philip E. Slater. *The Temporary Society*. New York: Harper & Row, 1968.

Cummings, H. Wayland, Larry W. Long, and Michael L. Lewis. *Managing Communication in Organizations: An Introduction*. Dubuque, Iowa: Gorsuch Scarisbrick, 1983.

Downs, Anthony. *Inside Bureaucracy*. Boston: Little, Brown, 1967.

Goldhaber, Gerald M. *Organizational Communication*, 3rd ed. Dubuque, Iowa: William C. Brown, 1983.

Likert, Rensis. *New Patterns of Management*. New York: McGraw-Hill, 1961.

Lynch, Thomas D., ed. *Organization Theory and Management*. New York: Marcel Dekker, 1983.

March, James G., and Herbert A. Simon. *Organizations*. New York: Wiley, 1958.

Simon, Herbert A. *Administrative Behavior*, 3rd ed. New York: The Free Press, 1976, chapter 8.

Sundquist, James L. (with the collaboration of David W. Davis). *Making Federalism Work: A Study of Program Coordination at the Community Level*. Washington, D.C.: Brookings, 1969.

Decision Making in Administration

THE making of decisions is at the heart of public administration, as it is at the heart of all organized human behavior. How decisions are made in a bureaucracy, by whom, by what standards, at what cost, and for whose benefit are questions of continuing interest as well as occasional controversy. Current quests for influence over decisions, access to decision makers, and accountability of decision makers all attest to the importance attached to the process.

The procedures by which decisions are made and applied, as well as their substance, leave a lasting imprint on administrative politics. We shall discuss the general nature of bureaucratic decisions; principal approaches to decision making; the role and impact of different kinds of goals; major features of the surrounding environment that ordinarily enter into the process; and the role politics plays in affecting the way many administrative decisions are made.

THE NATURE OF DECISIONS

Decision making in an organization involves making a choice to alter some existing condition,[1] choosing one course of action in preference to other possible courses of action, expending some amount of organizational or individual resources to implement the decision, and acting with the expectation of gaining something desirable. This definition suggests that a decision is not a single, self-contained event; rather, it is "the product of a complex social process generally extending over a considerable period of time. . . . [D]ecision making includes attention-directing or intelligence processes that determine the occasions of decision, processes for discovering and designing possible courses of action and processes for evaluating alternatives and choosing them."[2] Thus "a decision" entails a series of other choices, which may rightly be regarded as part of it.

It is assumed that a decision maker selects the course of action most appropriate to achieving a desired objective or objectives, although deciding what is most appropriate is often difficult. There is some uncertainty regarding the eventual outcome of a decision, and consequently there is a degree of risk (however small) involved in taking actions decided upon. Concerns central to the decision-making process, therefore, include increasing potential gains, monitoring the ongoing decisional process, and reducing the resource expenditure, uncertainty, and risk involved in achieving whatever gains are made.[3]

In this discussion, we will be speaking of decisions on relatively important, even fundamental, matters in organizational life. But it should be noted that the great majority of all decisions are more or less routine matters, based on previously adopted policy or programmatic premises. Routine decisions have the advantage of requiring little time or mental energy to make; they can be made according to regular schedules (shall we hire our usual extra summer help?) or where clear need exists (shall we send out the snowplows?) without having to "start fresh" each time. The central risk involved in routine decision making is that decision makers may fail to perceive a need to reconsider existing policy or program assumptions on which routine decisions are based.

For example, in an agency dependent on extra help to meet seasonal demand (such as the U. S. National Park Service), the amount of extra help needed should not *automatically* be assumed on the basis of accumulated prior experience. If, say, the price of gasoline should rise to three or four dollars per gallon, the Park Service personnel director might reasonably assume that fewer staff aides would have to be hired, since the flow of visitors would be very likely to diminish. Similarly, sending out the snowplows as a routine response to a storm in a midwestern city might have to be reexamined if the city is confronted with a "fiscal crunch" (as many now are). Work crew layoffs, reduced gasoline allocations, fewer streets plowed, fewer plows in operation—all these options might have to be explored, under nonroutine circumstances. Thus, maintaining routines that are inappropriate to changing conditions may only complicate the problems to which they were first addressed, and may help create new problems.

APPROACHES TO DECISION MAKING: CONCEPTS AND CONTROVERSIES

Few questions have occupied so much space in the literature of public administration, or generated so great a debate, as *how* to actually make decisions. Arguments have raged over such issues as the importance and relevance of goal setting, decision makers' capacities for absorbing information and objectively using it, the scope and types of data that decision makers ought to use in order to make good decisions, and the consequences of employing one or another approach to decision making. Models said to be applicable to administrative organizations have been derived from a variety of disciplines, notably economics and political science. Some have stressed ''scientific'' techniques, utilizing quantitative data and value-free measures of decision alternatives. Others, alleged by their advocates to be both more realistic and more effective, suggest that decisions can and should be made without first having to define every last goal that might be served by a given action; these models also suggest more informal measures of decision choices. Still other models have been advanced that attempt to integrate strong points of the previous models into other perspectives and approaches regarding decision making.

This is an area of intense feeling—and intense disagreement. It is also far from a settled issue, and new contributions to the literature continue to appear. Other issues also affect decision making (for example, the impacts of past decisions on a current choice), which further complicates matters. The complexity and importance of the subject makes it imperative that the student of public administration understand the nature of the controversies surrounding decision making, as well as key aspects of the process itself. We will explore the principal approaches referred to above as well as the criticisms of each, consider other dimensions of the process, and conclude by examining a consciously political approach to decision making.

"Rationality" in Decision Making: The Classical/Economic Model

The *rational* approach is derived from economic models of decision making. According to this classical outlook, decision makers are *consciously rational*— ordering their behavior so that it is ''reasonably directed toward the achievement of conscious goals.''[4] Another crucial dimension of economic rationality is the concept of *efficiency*—''maximizing output for a given input [of scarce resources], or minimizing input for a given output.''[5] In the words of political economist Anthony Downs:

> Economic analysis thus consists of two major steps: discovery of *the ends a decision maker is pursuing* and analysis of which means of attaining them are most reasonable, i. e., require the least input of scarce resources. . . . Thus, whenever economists refer to a ''rational man'' they are not designating a man whose thought processes consist exclusively of logical propositions, or a man without prejudices, or a man whose emotions are inoperative. In normal usage all of these could be considered rational men. But the economic definition refers solely to a man who moves toward his goals in a way which, to the

best of his knowledge, *uses the least possible input of scarce resources per unit of valued output.*[6]

In terms of actual behavior, a rational man (or woman): (1) can always make a decision when presented with a range of alternatives, (2) knows probable consequences of choosing each alternative, (3) ranks all alternatives in an order of preference, so that each is preferred, equal, or inferior to other options included in the ranking, (4) always chooses the highest-ranked alternative, and (5) always makes the same decision each time the same alternatives are available.[7] Such an individual normally would try to clearly separate ends (goals) from means (methods), concentrating on one or a few primary goals; pursuing too many goals simultaneously would frustrate efforts to attain them and to measure the efficiency and rationality of the process. Also, the rational decision maker would seek to gather all possible data pertaining to the range of alternatives and objectively weigh alternative solutions before selecting the best one possible (maximizing). The analysis, at every turn, would be designed to be comprehensive, taking every important relevant factor into account.[8] And the methodology at least implied would incorporate "explicitness of evaluation, quantification of values, and mathematical analysis."[9]

The economic concept of maximizing utility, and the pursuit of self-interest objectives, are central to the rational-comprehensive model of decision making.[10] So, also, are the relationships assumed to exist between means and ends—so that the decision maker is able continually to choose the most rational means for achieving the specified end—and the relationships between *costs* and *benefits* involved, in the interest of efficiency. *Cost-benefit analysis* and specification of cost-benefit ratios for each alternative presume the ability to assign a quantitative value to each alternative in a ranking, and to distinguish clearly among the values assigned. This makes it possible, in theory, to determine the optimum (best) ratio of benefits to costs, thus enabling the decision maker to make the final "best" choice.

In its essentials, this model stresses rationality of the *process* of making decisions, without reference to whether one's *goals* are also "rational." The test of a "good" decision is that "it can be shown to be the most appropriate means to [achieving] desired ends,"[11] judging in long-term perspectives. It is *procedural* criteria that must be satisfied in order to assess decision making as being rational; the decision *outcome* is a distinctly secondary consideration.

The rational model has had a powerful influence on decision theory, and on the art and craft of practical decision making, for several decades. It was not until the late 1950s that questions and criticisms began to be raised about the model, and alternative approaches to decision making suggested. Two principal themes were sounded: first, that the rational model *lacks practical applicability* outside the realm of economic theory, and second, that it is *less desirable* than other possible models as a mode of operation, especially in public administrative organizations.

Critiques of the Rational Model

The practicality of the rational model has been questioned on numerous grounds,[12] all leading to the proposition that it is not possible—and never has been—to construct a purely rational process of decision for any but the simplest, lowest-level decisions. Among the impediments on rationality suggested by critics of the model are the impossibility of distinguishing facts from values, and of analytically separating out ends and means; the impossibility of obtaining agreement among decision makers on predetermined goals; the *changing and ambiguous* nature of many political and administrative goals (we will examine this more fully, later in this chapter); pressures of time, to make a decision when it is needed; and the ability of decision makers to handle only a limited amount of information at any one time. Other problems include an inability to give one's undivided attention to a single problem or decision; costs of information acquisition; failure to secure all possible data, for reasons such as time constraints, excessive cost, or oversight; defects in communication processes or arrangements; and inability to predict all consequences of a given choice, resulting in ''some ineradicable uncertainty''[13] during and after the decision process.

Still other handicaps can be cited. These include competition among decision makers and their organizations for resources, preventing any *one* from achieving maximum utility; the need to deal with different aspects of the same problem—for example, both supply and location of new public housing,[14] or capital and operating budgets for a mass transit system; lack of precision in measuring various costs, benefits, and side effects; and unpredictable changes in the sociopolitical environment that affect substantive problems and the availability of both alternatives and resources.[15]

The other major criticism of the rational model was that the activities and calculations it required—even if they were possible—*were not desirable* as a method of making decisions. The first, and principal, spokesman for this view was political economist Charles Lindblom, who first articulated his position in 1959.[16] Lindblom argued that decision makers do not have to seek prior goal consensus in order to make sound decisions for the short run; furthermore, because goals rarely can be agreed upon in advance, *trying* to achieve consensus makes the pursuit of reasonable decisions just that much more difficult. Lindblom also claimed that means-ends analysis called for in the rational model is inappropriate if means and ends are confused (as he suggested they inevitably are). Also, public administrators cannot look to the general public to set and articulate meaningful policy goals (see chapter 13), since public opinion is highly ambiguous and diverse; even if identifiable goals do exist, they do not serve as clear guides to administrative decision. Finally, many broad goals have potential for conflict with one another. An example is the 1981 infestation of the Mediterranean fruit fly (medfly) in a portion of California's fruit and vegetable crops. Aerial spraying of the pesticide malathion, necessary to kill the fly and its larvae (a public health as well as economic concern), was said by some to pose a direct threat to the public health of the residents in areas infested by the medfly. Application of the rational model in that case would have been frustrated by, among other things, difficulty in assigning relative quantifiable values to two different public health objectives, and strong disagreement about data indicating malathion-related health hazards. Some scientists felt strongly that such hazards existed; others were equally convinced of exactly the opposite.

"Incrementalism" and "Mixed Scanning": Response and Counterresponse

As we have seen, major criticisms of the rational model centered on several of its basic assumptions: the quest for maximizing utility, emphasis on long-term consequences at the expense of concern for short-term changes, the need to formulate explicit goals, and a heavy bias in favor of economic conceptualizations of costs, benefits, and their relationships. A number of scholars and theorists have expanded upon these criticisms and argued that individual decisions, and change in general, come about through an "incremental" process. *Incrementalism*, in contrast to rationality, stresses decision making through a series of *limited successive comparisons*, with a relatively narrow range of alternatives rather than a comprehensive one, and uses the status quo, not abstract goals, as the key point of reference for decisions. Incrementalism focuses primary attention on short-term rather than long-term effects, on the most crucial consequences of an action rather than all those conceivable, and on less formalized methods of measuring costs and benefits.

Differences between rationalists and incrementalists are very sharp. First, where the rationalist attempts to maximize benefits in all phases of decision making, the incrementalist tries to "satisfice," to use economist Herbert Simon's term.[17] To satisfice is to reach a decision that is *satisfactory*, yielding benefits that suf*fice* to meet the situational needs of the decision maker. Put another way, the decision maker who satisfices is one who is willing to "settle for good-enough answers in despair at finding best answers. . . ."[18] The incremental decision maker accepts the fact that it may not be possible to get everything out of a given decision, and that settling for "half a loaf" is not unreasonable. Furthermore, the incrementalist maintains that it may well be *irrational* to "shoot for the moon" every time a decision is made, because the risks—and consequences—of failure are far greater, because resources could be expended too rapidly, and because "rationality" itself would not be cost-effective (assuming, again, it were *possible*).

Second, incrementalism, while not dismissing the importance of long-term consequences, emphasizes meeting short-term needs and solving short-term problems. Incrementalists are comfortable as "trouble-shooters," responding to immediate pressures and seeking to alleviate the worst of them. Lindblom, perhaps the leading spokesman for this school of thought, speaks of serial analyses—that is, repeated and ongoing analyses—rather than one comprehensive analysis, such as that called for in the rationalist view. Lindblom maintains that continual incremental adjustments in both the definition of a problem and the formulation of solutions is a reasonable and effective method of solving problems and making decisions.

Third, Lindblom and others suggest that the emphasis in the rational model on comprehensive evaluation of how a given decision would affect all other decisions is unrealistic. They contend that it is simply not possible to account in advance for all the ways that a particular course of action will affect other decisional processes and their outcomes.

Incrementalism also may have a practical advantage for public administrators, as they try to deal with legislative mandates that often are ambiguous. Making decisions incrementally may make it possible for administrators to satisfy the minimal expectations of legislators while gaining time to determine more specifically what those mandates are to mean in practice. Under conditions of uncertainty, of all kinds, it is difficult to pursue a classical/economic "rational" course. The frequent fuzziness of programmatic mandates enacted by legislatures[19] makes this sort of uncertainty part of most public administrators' everyday working environment.

Most important, those who have advanced the incremental approach reject the notion that economic models of decision making are the only ones that have legitimacy. They argue, at least indirectly, that noneconomic models and modes of decision making have intrinsic value, and that in some circumstances using economic models might well be inappropriate, not rational. Furthermore, the incremental model allows for measures of costs, benefits, and side effects of decisions that are not economic, or even necessarily quantitative. Incrementalists acknowledge that this approach permits subjective values to influence decisions, but they find ample justification in the fact that subjectivity plays some role in any case; they maintain that it is better to openly incorporate sound subjective judgment than to self-consciously attempt to exclude on principle all traces of subjectivity. At the same time, incrementalists are quick to endorse the need for adequate information and good-quality data, to voice concern for choosing sound courses of action, and so on. The difference is that they are prepared to make decisions even where the ideal conditions called for by the rationalists do not exist, which they say happens in an overwhelming majority of decision-making situations.

The incremental approach itself has come under fire. Two critics, in particular, stand out—one for identifying a serious shortcoming, the other for elaborating on the criticism of the first and outlining a third approach to decision making. Yehezkel Dror, in a pointed response to Lindblom, emphasized that marginal changes acceptable to incrementalists may *not* suffice to meet real and growing policy demands—that as policy needs change, decision makers may have to develop innovations bolder than those apparently contemplated by the incremental approach.[20] Dror's message was that if the incrementalist focuses solely or even primarily on small-scale changes designed to meet disjointed and short-run needs, larger needs and demands are likely to be overlooked and the decision-making process rendered impotent or, worse, irrelevant.

Dror also criticized incrementalism for making more acceptable the forces in human organizations that tend toward inertia and maintenance of the status quo. His comments suggest that one could find in incrementalism justification for the behavior of Downs' ''conserver''—the bureaucrat chiefly interested in maintaining power, prestige, and income, who takes a cautious, low-risk approach to decision making. Dror clearly leaned to a view of bureaucratic behavior that encourages both responsiveness to larger-scale needs and innovativeness in seeking solutions; he found incrementalism wanting in both respects.

Amitai Etzioni expanded on Dror's criticisms of the incremental model and offered an alternative approach, which he labeled ''mixed scanning.''[21] Etzioni's chief criticism of the incremental approach was its apparent failure to distinguish between fundamental and nonfundamental decisions. He suggested that for nonfundamental decision making the incremental approach was entirely valid and appropriate, but that in making fundamental decisions a decision maker needed to have wider perceptual horizons in order to appreciate the scope and significance of the choice to be made. More important, he felt that incrementalists tended to decide only nonfundamental matters—stemming from their emphasis on the trouble-shooter approach to solving problems—and, as a result, promoted a general aimlessness in overall policy.[22] Etzioni suggested a twofold or mixed approach to decision making that incorporates some elements of both the rational-comprehensive and incremental approaches.

Etzioni's mixed-scanning model can best be understood by using his analogy of a high-altitude weather satellite in orbit around the earth.[23] On board the satellite are two cameras—one equipped with a wide-angle lens that can scan a large area and record major weather patterns, the other equipped with a narrow-angle lens capable of zeroing in on turbulence and examining it in much finer detail. Examination by the narrow-lens camera is contingent upon the wide-lens camera first discovering large systems of turbulent weather. Conversely, the wide-lens camera is incapable of detailed analysis of storm centers and other phenomena. In sum, either camera without the other would supply some useful information, but much more can be obtained when they are used in combination. Further, the analysis provided by the narrow-lens camera is more intelligible when meteorologists have some idea of the size, location, and boundaries of the total weather system, that is, when they have a meaningful context for the detailed data. So it is also with decision making:

> Fundamental decisions are made by exploring the main alternatives the actor sees in view of his conception of his goals, but—unlike what rationalism would indicate—details and specifications are omitted so that an overview is feasible. *Incremental decisions are made but within the context set by fundamental decisions (and fundamental reviews)*. Thus, each of the two elements in mixed-scanning helps to reduce the effects of the particular shortcomings of the other; incrementalism reduces the unrealistic aspects of rationalism by limiting the details required in fundamental decisions, and . . . rationalism helps to overcome the conservative slant of incrementalism by exploring longer-run alternatives.[24]

This prescription for decision making, in turn, has been critiqued in at least two ways. First, a municipal official skeptical of both incrementalism and mixed scanning suggested that it is difficult to identify "a big or little decision. Appearances are deceiving."[25] One might infer from that statement that while fundamental decisions may be relatively easy to recognize, problems can develop when a seemingly minor choice turns out, with hindsight, to have led to unexpectedly significant outcomes. The same observer felt, not surprisingly, that perhaps too much emphasis has been placed on differences between fundamental and incremental decisions[26]—a position that implicitly undercuts the mixed-scanning model.

The other response to mixed scanning came from Lindblom himself. Writing in 1979,[27] he first noted that incrementalism as a *political* pattern— "political change by small steps (regardless of method of analysis)"[28]— varies in the *size* of step, which "can be arranged on a continuum from small to large."[29] As an example:

> Raising or lowering the discount rate from time to time is extremely incremental. Making the original decision to use the discount rate as a method of monetary control is still modestly though not extremely incremental. Reorganizing the banking system by introducing the Federal Reserve System is still incremental, though less so. Eliminating the use of money . . . is not incremental.[30]

Thus, contrary to the interpretation given it by many observers, incrementalism is not, by definition, concerned with change only in *small* steps, nor biased against large-scale alterations in the status quo. Change by increments, according to this view, is a matter of degree as well as substance.

Second, Lindblom acknowledged criticisms that suggest that "doing better usually means turning away from incrementalism."[31] In contrast, incrementalists "believe that for complex problem solving it usually means *practicing incrementalism more skillfully* and turning away from it only rarely."[32] Lindblom argued again that, contrary to the assumptions of the rational model, no one can hope to analyze a complex problem *completely*, and that calculated analytic strategies designed to *simplify* complex problems hold more promise of success than do attempts at comprehensive "scientific" analysis.[33] Also, incremental analysis can and should focus profitably on "ills to be remedied" instead of on "positive goals to be sought."[34] It is that line of reasoning that challenges the mixed-scanning model. Incrementalists feel that to the extent that a decision-making approach continues to rely on assumptions of rationality, those using that approach are destined to "fall into worse patterns of analysis and decision than those, who with their eyes open, entertain the guiding ideal of strategic analysis."[35] In sum, Lindblom would fault mixed scanning for its failure to reject the rational model completely, while defending incrementalism as a viable approach to decisions of either large or small consequence.[36]

We will have occasion to refer again to these models later in this chapter. Now we turn to other dimensions of decision making that also merit discussion.

THE PROBLEM OF GOALS

One does not have to subscribe to the rational model of decision making to acknowledge that, in one form or another, programs are managed, agencies receive and spend public funds, individuals engage in myriad activities, and administrative routines are carried on in order to fulfill some kind of purpose or purposes. In this sense, *goals* range from the most concrete to the most ambiguous formulations; they may be substantive or symbolic, individual or organizational or suborganizational, held by those inside the organization or imposed by others outside. Agency personnel may consciously select particular objectives, or others outside the agency may come to regard it as pursuing certain goals because of its programmatic choices (incrementalists argue that the latter occurs quite frequently). Formally, of course, the goals pursued by a public agency are defined in the first instance by legislatures (as noted previously). Similarly, measures of success or failure in achieving formal agency goals are devised and applied by at least some outside the agency itself.

The point of all this is to suggest that there is great variety in the types of goals that can be pursued by agency personnel acting collectively or by individuals seeking their own ends through administrative action (or inaction). We will seek to give some order to this subject by examining organizational goals, broadly defined, and then considering impacts of personal goals in public agencies.

Organizational Goals

Many casual observers of government organizations seem to believe that they exist to achieve only certain kinds of goals, such as substantive programmatic objectives (for example, adequate health care or safe, reasonably priced air travel), and that they act out of a desire to satisfy a broad public interest. Other observers assume, in contrast, that government bureaucracies are interested only in their own survival and enhancement, taking a most limited view of the public interest. Neither view is totally wrong, but both fail to take account of the complexity of goals within government agencies.

Survival and maintenance are indeed principal goals of virtually all organizations, governmental or otherwise. (An analogy to individual human behavior can be drawn here, in that survival is a fundamental instinct without being the sole purpose of our existence.) Administrative agencies, like other organizations, have as one of their goals maintenance of their own position. Such inward-oriented goals have been termed ''reflexive''[37]; they are supported by those aspects of an organization's behavior and programs that have primary impact internally rather than externally. Agencies pursue such goals by attempting to persuade a significant constituency that their functions are essential either to society at large or to an important segment of society.

Administrative agencies are also concerned with substantive goals. All government organizations work toward accomplishment of programmatic objectives, whether popular or unpopular, visible or obscure, major or minor. Programmatic objectives appear to be the *raison d'etre* of administrative agencies, and in many cases they constitute a powerful argument for an agency's existence. This type of goal has been labeled ''transitive,'' in that there is an intended programmatic impact on the environment beyond the organization itself.[38] In advancing its cause through the political process, an agency will emphasize substantive goals—their importance to particular clienteles and to the whole society, and the agency's performance in pursuit of them.

Pursuit of program goals is not without its subtleties or pitfalls, however. In the first place, an agency may have substantive goals and others that are largely symbolic.[39] Symbolic (and some substantive) goals are valuable because of the political support they can attract; in effect, the agency adopts the goals of persons outside it. Frequently an agency goal can be described as both substantive and symbolic, with merit in objective terms as well as beneficial political consequences. Finally, it is common to find agencies suggesting that they are attempting to accomplish a worthwhile but unreachable goal—for example, total eradication of poverty in the United States—yet continued pursuit of that objective yields benefits to both the agency and society. Many citizens and public officials are in favor of trying to wipe out poverty and are willing to appropriate government funds to agencies with jurisdiction to carry on the struggle, which benefits at least some of America's poor.

Another dimension of substantive goals is the tricky question of goal attainment. How do we know when a goal has been met and what happens to the agency in charge of a program when its goal has been reached? Achievement of organizational goals can be detrimental to an agency's continued operation. If an agency accomplishes its purposes, some might question the further need for it. On the other hand, if in order to avoid that embarrassing dilemma an agency does not act vigorously to "solve the problem," it risks the wrath of supporters in the legislative and executive branches, as well as clientele groups. Fortunately for most agencies the dilemma is not insoluble, because of the breadth of many goals and the different dimensions of goal-attainment situations.

First, many goals are not objectively attainable. It is possible to view a goal conceptually as "a value to be sought after, not an object to be achieved."[40] In this sense, "goals" are sets of broad directions in which organization members seek to move without necessarily expecting to accomplish them, while "objectives" are more limited purposes—related to the larger goals—which are achievable. "Adequate health care," for example, is an abstract goal; "attracting more doctors" and "building another hospital" are concrete objectives that move the organization (a community or state or nation) closer to the goal. Using this example, is it possible to reach the goal of "adequate health care" so that efforts to achieve it may cease? Not really, for two reasons. One is that definitions of what constitutes "adequacy" have to be agreed upon through the political process. There may well be continuing disagreement about what is adequate, and consequently about whether the goal has in fact been achieved. The other reason is that even if it can be agreed that "health care is now adequate," ongoing programs will be required to *keep* it that way. As a result, relevant programs continue to be necessary. (Note that the latter observation implicitly undercuts the rational model.)

Also, there may be political advantage in deliberately stating agency goals in general terms. The goal of "educational quality in our schools" is far less likely to cause problems for a Department of Education than is a goal of assuring that high school graduates are equipped with specific reading and writing skills and are qualified for entry into colleges and universities according to a prescribed entrance-test score. Also, the more generalized a goal statement, the more widely supported it is likely to be, with less chance of concerted political opposition.

Furthermore, legislative language establishing agency goals can be imprecise, due to uncertainty about specific meanings and the frequent need for compromise. For example, a health program in the Department of Health and Human Services could have as its overall goal "minimizing heart disease and related ailments among adult Americans." This is a laudable goal; no one would quarrel with it. But who is to say that the "minimum" has been reached, and by what measures? As with "adequate health care," such language is quite common in legislation and administrative regulations. Under these circumstances, all an agency with such responsibilities needs to show is that it has had *some* success in putting across its message (get more exercise, have regular checkups, etc.), with *some* resultant reduction in heart disease and related ailments, and it is likely to be able to sustain itself and its programs.

Most agencies start with a combination of interrelated goals, and many branch out into new but related areas. For example, the Tennessee Valley Authority began its existence with a primary emphasis on flood control through construction of major dams on the Tennessee River and its principal tributaries, and a secondary emphasis on generating electric power. The latter became a major emphasis during World War II because of a decision, made elsewhere, to locate a nuclear research center (the "Manhattan Project") at Oak Ridge, Tennessee, just twenty miles from TVA headquarters at Knoxville. The Oak Ridge facility required vast quantities of electricity, and the availability of low-cost TVA power was clearly a key factor influencing the location decision. TVA, naturally, responded to the demand. When the war ended, TVA had a far larger power system than it had had before the war. As a result, the relative standing of the electric power program within TVA's overall framework was dramatically altered.[41] As this example demonstrates, overall agency goals may undergo substantial and permanent modification at the instigation of decision makers *outside* the agency.

The National Aeronautics and Space Administration (NASA) provides perhaps the best example of what can happen to an agency with explicit goals that have clearly been accomplished. Charged with directing the effort to land a man on the moon before the end of the 1960s, NASA set about its business and did exactly that. After a series of Mercury, Gemini, and Apollo flights, Neil Armstrong took that "giant leap for mankind" in mid-1969. Mission accomplished—spectacularly! But what then? NASA found itself faced with growing public disenchantment over the billions of dollars spent for space exploration when its primary mission of the decade was fulfilled. Its role consequently diminished, as controversy enveloped discussion of future enterprises. NASA's attempt to generate new programs was less than wholly successful. Plans for a space shuttle, for example, did not move forward initially with the same dispatch—or political support. Note that the potential scientific value of NASA's space exploration did not have decisive impact on its fortunes, much to the chagrin and frustration of NASA personnel. Other (political) considerations had much more to do with the agency's fortunes than did its own substantive goals.

One other major point should be made about organizational goals. When public bureaucracies are repeatedly criticized for "failure to reach their goals," they may develop a tendency to articulate publicly goals that they know they can reach. Bureaucracies also know that they may suffer politically from excessive attachment to goals that turn out to be unpopular. In short, politics may influence the choice of official or unofficial organizational goals. Quoting political scientist Aaron Wildavsky:

> What we call goals or objectives may, in large part, be operationally determined by the *policies we can agree upon*. The mixture of values found in complex

policies may have to be taken in packages, so that *policies may determine goals at least as much as general objectives determine policies.*[42]

An agency, in short, may adopt as official goals only those objectives that, in the judgment of its leaders, will produce the requisite political support for its operations. This does not happen universally, but the fact that it *can* be the case should serve as a warning not to view goals as abstract, permanent, or sacred statements above politics or somehow separate from the agencies themselves.

Personal Goals

In addition to organizational goals, there are the personal goals of employees to be considered, since these also play a role in an institution's performance. Most individuals have goals of their own that working within the organization helps fulfill. These might be basic drives for earning a decent living and job security. They might relate to opportunities for professional advancement. Or they could be strong personal feelings about public policy directions that the individual believes the organization should be pursuing. Personal goals such as these could affect organizational goals in two ways: individuals might devote more time and energy to pursuing their own goals than those of the organization, and they might come into conflict with others in the organization over such things as advancement through the ranks or policy-related organization activities. Conflict among individuals diverts attention and resources from the effort to attain organizational objectives.

Anthony Downs has suggested five types of bureaucratic employees, each characterized by a particular combination of goals.[43] Two types, "climbers" and "conservers," act purely out of self-interest. Climbers are interested in increasing their power, income, and prestige, while conservers seek to maximize their job security and maintain the power, income, and prestige that they already have.[44] The three other types are, in Downs' phrase, "mixed-motive officials, [who] . . . combine self-interest and altruistic loyalty to larger values. The main difference among the three types of mixed-motive officials is the breadth of the larger values to which they are loyal."[45] The three types are "zealots," "advocates," and "statesmen," who focus their energies respectively on relatively narrow policies or concepts, on a set of somewhat wider functions or on a wider organization, and on the general welfare or public interest, broadly defined.

Although Downs' formulation is admittedly hypothetical and ideal-type, he nonetheless focuses on major motivations that relate to actual bureaucratic behavior. The essential point here is that the greater the variety of bureaucratic types and motives, the more difficult it is to attain official organizational objectives, since so many other unofficial objectives are present. Also, potential for internal conflict is increased where there is a variety of bureaucratic types, and a higher level of conflict will inhibit attainment of both official and unofficial goals.

From the standpoint of an organization's being able to fulfill its official objectives and to manage its programs effectively, the ideal situation is one in which there is a high degree of *goal congruence* among all organization members. Where leaders, themselves agreed on objectives and priorities, can count on unified support from employees in attaining shared objectives, an organization's chances of success are obviously enhanced. Such congruence, however, is the exception rather than the rule, even within the leadership. Also, within the framework of the organization at large there are likely to be numerous small groups, each with its own particularistic goals, which may be given greater weight than those of the wider organization. The importance of small-group goals has been emphasized by the findings of Elton Mayo and his associates in the Hawthorne experiments, and by John Pfiffner and Frank Sherwood in their studies a quarter of a century later (see chapter 6).[46] All this makes it even less likely that substantial goal congruence will exist. (Moreover, goal congruence can even become "too much of a good thing," by discouraging fresh thinking about organization directions and actions. It also can stifle the sort of open dialogue that often gives rise to creative and useful new ideas.[47] See the discussion of "groupthink," later in this chapter.)

DECISIONS IN THE BALANCE: THE ENVIRONMENT OF CHOICE

In addition to questions concerning goals, a number of other considerations are involved in reaching decisions. First (and often first in importance) is the matter of the resources necessary to implement a decision. The decision maker must consider both what kinds and what quantity of resources will be expended by pursuing a particular course of action. A decision to take some organizational action may require expenditures of time, personnel resources, money, and what we might call political capital (influence, prestige, and so on). The responsible official must have a reasonably clear idea—the clearer, the better—of just "how much it will cost" in terms of *all* these resources.

Decision makers are also faced with establishing whether or not potential benefits are worth probable costs. This requires answering such questions as these: Do we have sufficient time to devote to this enterprise, given our other responsibilities? Will our political supporters go along with us, or will we encounter pressure to do it differently, or perhaps not at all? Are we sufficiently certain about the probable benefits we can derive? At times, decision makers may have to choose between two mutually exclusive benefits (either this gain or that one, but not both), to decide whether to seek something now or later (entailing the risk that it might be difficult now, but impossible later), and (especially in government) to weigh the impact of values that are not central to the specific decisional equation (setting a bad political precedent, damaging democratic traditions, and so on).

A corollary concern is how to measure both costs and benefits, or even whether meaningful measures are available. One of the most tangible measures is in dollar terms, particularly regarding costs. However, there has been considerable debate in recent years, both in the academic community and in government, over different ways to measure costs and benefits, separately and in relation to each other, and over the political implications of using different sets of measures.

Finally, decision makers may base their decisions on different grounds, singly or in combination. Three such grounds are most prominent. One is substantive grounds—decisions are made "on the merits" of the question. For example, a decision using efficiency criteria, concerning the design of a highway linking two major cities, would focus on the "shortest distance between two points" in terms of mileage, travel time, and construction costs and time. A second basis is political grounds—that is, net gain or loss measured by changes in political support, resources, or pressures. Using the example of the highway, the decision as to specific route might be affected by the discovery that following a straight line between the cities would take it across some valuable farmland owned by an influential politician or a contributor to the election campaigns of incumbent officeholders. In this instance, the "shortest distance" might well include a generous curve around the perimeter of the farm property, even if this meant that total dollar costs, mileage, and construction time would increase. Also relevant to political grounds for decision making are values such as popular representation and accountability. It might be deemed necessary to adjust a highway route to accommodate active citizen groups as well as influential public officials (though that will depend in part on the extent to which such groups can become meaningfully involved in the decision-making process).[48] A third ground for decision is organizational in nature. For example, if the government's highway engineers felt strongly that a detour around the farm property would detract from economy, efficiency, sensible roadway design, and scenic value, the responsible decision maker would have to weigh the possible effect on the engineers' morale of deciding to build the curve anyway.

Note that different decisional considerations produce the need for a prior decision—namely, which factor(s) should be given predominant weight in the final decision. In the highway example, the question would be: Can the organization better afford to have on its hands an angry politician, demoralized professional employees, or displeased consumers (the highway users)? There is no easy or automatic solution to such a dilemma. Other factors would have to be taken into account, such as who else would be pleased or displeased with a particular decision. In hundreds of admin-

istrative decisions—some routine, some not—the same sorts of considerations apply. The less routine a decision is, the more carefully such considerations must be weighed.[49]

A comment is in order about the types of decision makers who are
likely to be concerned with the different grounds for decisions. Ordinarily,
the experts in an organization (the engineers in the highway example) have
as their highest priority the substance of a decision or issue rather than concerns of politics or of the organization as a whole. This is in keeping with
the main task of substantive specialists—to concentrate on the subject matter area of their expertise. Those more highly placed in an organization,
however, whether higher-ranking specialists or so-called ''political generalists,'' ordinarily have a different order of priorities, giving greater weight to
political and organizational aspects of decision making. This is not to say
that top-level officials are ignorant of, or oblivious to, the merits of a question, as we have used that term, or that specialists care little for politics. It is
to say, however, that generalists are often inclined toward more of a balancing process, weighing and choosing from among a greater number of decisional criteria.

Many generalists are appointed directly through political channels or
are otherwise politically connected to a greater extent than are the bulk of
the experts; consequently, they are under more constraint to act with sensitivity toward their political mentors (and adversaries). At the same time,
their concern for the organization as a whole prompts them to be watchful
of the morale of specialists who are likely to be dissatisfied with political
decision making that runs counter to their expert opinion and preference.
Some pressures and tensions within a bureaucracy are due to these variations in approaches to decision making in different parts of the organization's hierarchy, though such variations are not always present.[50]

In addition to the considerations already discussed, there is normally
a time factor in decision making. Time is a key resource in both making and
implementing a decision; accordingly, it is necessary to allow for sufficient
time at every stage of deliberation and action. There are, furthermore, two
other time considerations. First, the amount of time in which to reach a decision is not unlimited. Time constraints—especially during an emergency
or crisis—can profoundly affect the ability of decision makers to gather and
analyze information, and to project and compare consequences of different
alternatives, ultimately affecting the course of action selected. Second, decisions can have long-term and short-term consequences that may have to
be dealt with. For instance, anticipated benefits from a decision frequently
are long-term, while costs are short-term; thus in the immediate future
costs will outweigh benefits. A case in point is job training for the unem-
ployed; it takes time for them to become fully productive workers (as it does
for any new worker on the job), and per-capita costs of training can run
very high. How quickly and with how much certainty benefits will be derived would have to be considered. Politically, a decision that yields some

A MANAGER WITH AN EARLY DEADLINE TO MEET (AND OTHER CHALLENGES)

William Ruckelshaus, appointed the first head of the U.S. Environmental Protection Agency (EPA) in November 1970, began his administration by talking to a great many people and trying to get a sense of direction. He found many of the operations inappropriately focused. In an interview, he spoke sharply of the importance of his time horizon:

> The automobile emission problem was obviously something we were going to have to deal with. There was going to come a time—if you read the Clean Air Act, this was in January 1971, right after it passed—that [the auto companies] were going to come ask me for some more time [to comply with the emission standards]. I was going to have to decide whether or not they had made a 'good faith' effort. If this whole situation wasn't going to be completely farcical, the first thing I had to do was convince the automobile industry that we were serious about enforcement. That was immediately clear to me. Otherwise, there would be no way, two years hence or whenever they asked for an extension of time, that I could conceivably make a judgment that they had made this good faith effort. So, we had to figure out how we were going to convince them that we were serious. Every thirty days we had deadlines to meet involving very complicated matters on the Clean Air Act.

In other words, *sixty days* after taking office, Ruckelshaus had to take steps that would influence the behavior of the entire U.S. auto industry. And there would be further decisions *every thirty days*. Ruckelshaus pointed out that his goals were complicated by legislative and other acts:

> The agenda was, in the first place, spelled out in terms of the inheritance in the reorganization plan, in terms of the agencies we inherited. Secondly, we inherited, along with those agencies, a lot of implementing legislation that, like the Clean Air Act, just rapidly came on and didn't give us a lot of leeway in terms of setting not only the goals but also the method by which they were to be achieved.
> The Council on Environmental Quality had been in existence since January of that year and had in its first report laid out a very extensive environmental agenda for the administration. There had been a lot of work done on that. The president, in his message of Feburary 1970, had also laid out thirty-seven separate goals that he wanted to achieve in the next year and to translate into legislation.

Goals were also set by pressure groups and elected superiors. Ruckelshaus had to concern himself with the Sierra Club, the Audubon Society, and the Earth Day movement, not to mention General Motors, Ford, Chrysler, and (if jobs were threatened), the AFL-CIO.

Source: Adapted from Joseph L. Bower, "Effective Public Management: It Isn't the Same as Effective Business Management," *Harvard Business Review*, 55 (March/April 1977), 131–40, at pp. 135–36 (footnotes omitted).

gain right away and carries with it the promise of better things still to come is the most defensible. The essential point is that time is a relevant consideration in assessing a given course of action's costs and benefits.

Central to all of these decision-making elements is the quantity and quality of information available. All decision makers need enough information to serve as a basis for making reasoned choices, and most try to gather as much information as possible prior to making a final decision. The ideal situation (the rational-model setting) would be one in which an official had total access to all data (which could be verified for accuracy) directly related to the decisional alternatives under consideration, including comprehensive projections of all possible consequences resulting from each proposed course of action. In practice, decision makers must consciously settle for less than complete information, usually because a decision is needed promptly. Or they may try to postpone a decision, pending the acquisition of more information that will reduce the risk of making mistakes.[51] Even officials or agencies enjoying strong political support seek to accumulate hard data to back their decisions; a recurring pattern of faulty or inadequate data could endanger that support. Information, in sum, is needed to make decisions that are supportable, both objectively and politically.

The uses to which information is put are important, also. The role of *decision analysis* has assumed great prominence in the last forty years, relying on a wide variety of new techniques. Writing in 1965, Herbert Simon noted advances through which "many classes of administrative decisions have been formalized, mathematics has been applied to determine the characteristics of the 'best' or 'good' decisions, and myriads of arithmetic calculations are carried out routinely . . . to reach the actual decisions from day to day."[52] Simon and others have noted two significant developments that have facilitated use of such techniques: the improvement and wider use of sample survey techniques (to gather empirically defensible information on the nature of public policy problems), and the rapid increase in the data processing capacity of electronic computers (which seem to go through new "generations" every three or four years).[53] In addition, much greater use has been made of the experimental method in investigations of decision making.[54] In short, the *need* for information, while growing rapidly, has been joined to burgeoning *technologies* of decision making. This has resulted in vastly expanded information capability.

It may also have created an illusion of greater capabilities than we actually have. Such an illusion may exist from two standpoints. One is the problem of malfunctions that can and do occur in the myriad technological systems that underpin decision making. When these happen, data necessary to an informed decision can be inaccurate, with the predictable consequence that (at a minimum) the decision reached will be inappropriate to the problem (since the problem will have been incorrectly defined and presented). In some cases, such a malfunction could have grave consequences.

In June 1980, a computerized radar "early warning" defense system of the North American Air Defense Command—designed to indicate incoming ballistic missiles from an enemy power—gave off two different "false alarms" three days apart. After each one, U.S. military forces were briefly put into a higher state of alert. Fortunately, other (routine) decision processes were put into effect, designed to verify the initial warning—and each time, it became clear within three minutes that these were malfunctions, not nuclear attacks.[55] This example illustrates the proposition that electronic computers, while very useful, should not be totally relied upon for decision information—especially since it became known in 1981 that the first false alarm was due to *human* error and the second to a faulty computer chip! A similar illustration of the fallibility of computers came to light in September of 1984. It was revealed that the Pentagon may have purchased, in the course of a decade, as many as *fifteen million* defective microchips for installation in numerous weapons systems containing sophisticated electronic parts—including the on-board computers of B-52 bombers, regarded as the heart of America's nuclear bomber force.[56]

The other illusory aspect of computer capabilities is the simple reality that human judgment is still quite valuable in making decisions and that computers are not a substitute. Experience, while not always the best teacher, can contribute to one's judgmental capacity; so, also, can breadth of training, perceptiveness, sensitivity, and capacity for continued learning. It is the interactions between individual competencies and computer technology that normally shape the most appropriate uses of the latter—and, not infrequently, the "wisest" decisions.

There are several other significant limitations on the acquisition and use of information. Perhaps most important is the fact that we live in a world of imperfect information. It is futile to mount a search for literally *all* the information that might be obtained on a subject, and most decision makers have somewhat more modest ambitions. Compounding that problem is the fact that communication of information is often less than clear, subject to human error both at the point of origin and at the receiving end, even when both parties desire full mutual understanding[57] (see chapter 7).

Another crucial limitation on information resources is the cost entailed in obtaining information. Information costs include the personnel and time that must be devoted to its acquisition, organization, and presentation. Acquisition costs in particular can become prohibitive. The greatest value of the computer as an information storage and retrieval system is the enormous saving in time and money it makes possible in obtaining a given quantity of data, compared to the investment necessary to gather the same amount of data by traditional methods. (This, incidentally, is a clear example of long-term benefit making worthwhile a high short-term cost—in this case, the cost of installing computerized information systems.)

The last major limitation stems from the conscious and (especially) unconscious biases of those who send, relay, and receive information. We tend to attach high importance to "objective" information, yet there is great difficulty in interpreting information with complete objectivity. Even the most fair-minded individuals have subjective values that color their perceptions of data, images, or phenomena. Existing preferences can shape responses, or even receptiveness, to particular information. Thus, pure objectivity in data interpretation is an impossibility and, consequently, absolutely objective information is beyond our grasp.

Finally, there is the problem of deliberate distortion of information. Information is a source of political power, and it is often in the best interests of an agency or official to provide only that information that will have a positive political effect. We may debate the utility and wisdom of political interference with objectivity in information, but it is undeniably a significant constraint. With enough effort, deliberate distortions can be discovered and corrected, but that effort can require large investments of resources, and consequently is made only irregularly. Self-interest motives, in sum, can seriously impair objective use of data.

Decision makers also face other kinds of problems. For one thing, decision making is strongly influenced by previous decisions and policies already in effect. In other words, some decision alternatives are not available because of past decision making. Instead of working with a clean slate, decision makers must work within the confines allowed by past choices. An example would be a decision to implement an affirmative action plan in local government hiring, which might effectively foreclose any contrary options five or ten years later. The same would be true of a local decision to sell bonds for a capital construction project or for the army to change its basic emphasis on the weaponry it needs for ground warfare. Another problem is unanticipated consequences, in spite of efforts to foresee all the outcomes of each decision. Sometimes the projected outcome fails to materialize; sometimes there are unintended side effects that develop together with the projected outcome; sometimes there are only the side effects. If these unanticipated results turn out to be serious, they can cause intense problems and political repercussions.

Yet another potential pitfall in decision-making processes is the phenomenon of "groupthink," defined by social psychologist Irving Janis as "a mode of thinking that people engage in when they are deeply involved in a cohesive in-group, when members striving for unanimity override their motivation to realistically appraise alternative courses of action."[58] This phenomenon is most likely to be evident in small groups of decision makers:

> . . . when we are trying to understand how certain avoidable policy errors happen to be made, we should look into the behavior of the small group of decision makers, because all the well-known errors stemming from limitations of

an individual and of a large organization can be greatly augmented by *group processes that produce shared miscalculations.*[59]

The two basic elements in most potential "groupthink" situations are group cohesiveness and a tendency toward unanimity, or at least toward making any dissident member feel conspicuous and uncomfortable. Two other factors are the degree to which a cohesive group of decision makers becomes insulated from other influences in the decision-making process and the extent to which a cohesive group's leader promotes one preferred solution (even when that leader genuinely does not want group members to be "yes-men" and the members try to resist that). In essence, a cohesive "in-group" of individuals who generally think along similar lines can be a breeding ground for "groupthink"; recent presidents (Kennedy, Johnson, Nixon, Carter, and Reagan, in particular) have obviously surrounded themselves with advisers fitting this description. While familiarity with one's high-level advisers can facilitate the advisory process, another result can be repressing of critical analysis—the thoughtful dissenting voice that can cause those in the majority to reexamine their assumptions and commitments—with consequent errors in decisional outcomes.[60]

Finally, decision making involves *sunk costs*—certain irrecoverable costs resulting from commitment of resources. The term "sunk costs" has

---

ONE WAY TO COMBAT "GROUPTHINK": LESSONS FROM THE STATE DEPARTMENT

An institutionalized practice for the encouragement and preservation of dissent has been in effect since 1972 at the State Department. Known as the "Dissent Channel," it provides that employees here or abroad who dissent from policy recommendations of their superiors can invoke a special channel for memoranda or messages. This channel ensures: (a) that top-level officers in the Secretary's office will know about the dissent; (b) that the dissenter gets an acknowledgment within a week; and (c) that the dissenter gets a substantive response after senior decision makers (often including the Secretary, who gets a copy of each such message) have reviewed the dissenter's views and reasons. The strongest admonitions are made to Departmental superiors never to penalize dissenters for taking advantage of this channel. Ten to fourteen messages per year are sent through this channel, and it clearly has enriched the State Department's policy process.

Source: Adapted from testimony of Charles Bingman, Member, Special Panel on the Senior Executive Service, American Society for Public Administration, February 28, 1984; *The Senior Executive Service*, Hearings before the Subcommittee on Civil Service, Committee on Post Office and Civil Service, U.S. House of Representatives, 98th Congress, 2nd Session (Washington, D.C.: U.S. Government Printing Office, 1984), pp. 284–85.

two meanings. First, a given resource or commodity, once spent, cannot be spent again. For example, a piece of land committed to use as an approach ramp to a superhighway obviously cannot also be used as a hospital site. The realities of sunk costs raise the stakes in decision making. Second, sunk costs suggest that once a decision has been made to proceed in a particular policy direction, certain costs would be incurred if that direction were to be reversed later. An analogy would be a motorist at a fork in the road, pondering which one leads to his destination. If he makes the wrong choice, it will take extra time, gasoline, and wear-and-tear on the car to return to the junction and resume the trip, this time in the right direction. In administration, too, investment of extra resources, and some political risk, are required to reverse a policy direction. It is often easier to maintain a given policy course than to change it; to a degree, this explains why administrative agencies resist having to modify what they are doing.[61] If, however, the costs of *not* changing direction approach or exceed the costs of changing, the agency would be far more likely to adapt itself.[62] In any event, sunk costs represent an additional factor to be taken into account in the course of making and implementing decisions.

Implications of the Decision Environment

Given the variable nature of goals, and of elements in the decision environment such as resource availability, competing grounds for decision, information constraints, and sunk costs, it would appear that the requisite conditions for the rational-decision model are found rarely, if at all. However, though rationality as *process* is unlikely to be found in administrative decision making, reasonable, sensible, and productive decisions are not only possible, they occur frequently. Decision makers face difficult problems, particularly in a social and political environment filled with uncertainty and change. They can and must try to reduce the effects of that uncertainty, so that decisions are useful and appropriate in solving the problems at hand and in anticipating longer-term needs. Multiple methodologies might be useful to their efforts. But the rational model, as a whole process, is likely to be applicable only in very limited instances.

DECISION MAKING: LINKS TO ORGANIZATION THEORY

In chapter 6 the dilemma of "closed" versus "open" systems was treated, and the suggestion was made that a newer tradition had emerged in the study of organizations that evades that dilemma. Treating organizations as entities trying to cope with uncertainty thrust upon them by the external environment, this school of thought advances the possiblity that, in theorist James Thompson's words, "the organization must develop processes for *searching* and *learning*, as well as for *deciding*. . . . [I]t must set limits to its definitions of situations; it must make decisions in *bounded rationality*."[63] This notion of bounded (limited) rationality, so crucial to the recent reshaping of organization theory, overlaps the incrementalist and mixed-scanning approaches to decision making, with acceptance of satisficing rather than maximizing very much at the heart of it.[64] Thus, developments in the art of making decisions have been paralleled—indeed, caused in part—by evolving conceptions of complex organizations.

"POLITICAL RATIONALITY": A CONTRADICTION IN TERMS?

We have been speaking, for the most part, of decision makers in the abstract, and of models of decision making applied to theoretical situations. We now take up a question central to our overall concern in this book: whether or not it is possible to achieve any sort or degree of rationality in a public administrative system permeated by political influences and pressures. Can administrators who act at least partially in response to political stimuli be said to be acting rationally, in any sense, when they make decisions? Can "politics" and "rational decision making" be made to coexist, or at least not to be totally contradictory?

Much of the literature on rational decision making in economics and political science would seem to suggest that the answer to these questions is an unequivocal "No." Politics is frequently represented as interfering with rational processes, outweighing more objective considerations, and overriding "neutral" or "nonpolitical" measurements and data. When political considerations predominate in decision making, as they frequently do, the stigma of irrationality is attached to the process and the outcomes. To dispute this characterization of politicized decision making requires a significant modification of the meaning of rationality. In particular, what must be changed is the "currency" of rationality, the criteria by which rationality is defined and measured.

Plainly stated, rationality has traditionally been an economic measure and the currency implicitly or explicitly quantitative. Most economists—and many in other disciplines—have assumed for many years that economic-quantitative rationality is sufficient as an overall definition of the concept. Recently, however, the possibility has been raised that there may be other, equally valid, forms of rationality, specifically *political rationality*.[65] This is to say that political and economic choices are often conceived in different terms and directed toward fulfilling different kinds of objectives, and should therefore be evaluated according to different criteria.

Wildavsky has suggested that in a political setting a decision maker's need for support assumes central importance, and that political costs and benefits of decisions are crucial.[66] Political benefits that might accrue to a decision maker are self-evident: obtaining short-term policy rewards, enhanced power over future decisions, added access to, and earlier inclusion in, the decision-making process (given that both access and involvement are meaningful), and so on. Political costs, however, are less obvious and need explicit categorization, which Wildavsky provides:

> *Exchange costs* are incurred by a political leader when he needs the support of other people to get a policy adopted. He has to pay for this assistance by using up resources in the form of favors (patronage, logrolling) or coercive moves (threats or acts to veto or remove from office). By supporting a policy and influencing others to do the same, a politician antagonizes some people and may suffer their retaliation. If these *hostility costs* mount they may turn into *reelection costs*—actions that decrease his chances (or those of his friends) of being elected or reelected to office. Election costs, in turn, may become *policy costs* through inability to command the necessary formal powers to accomplish the desired policy objectives. . . . [We] may also talk about *reputation costs*, i.e., not only loss of popularity with segments of the electorate but also loss of esteem and effectiveness with other participants in the political system and loss of ability to secure policies other than the one immediately under consideration.[67]

It is apparent that, as stated here, political benefits are rarely measurable in quantifiable terms. The one set of political costs that might be measurable numerically is reelection costs, but it is difficult to determine from voting data how particular actions by politicians affect the ballot choices of thousands of voters. Their lack of easy measurability, however, does not diminish the impact political costs have on the behavior of governmental decision makers, including those in bureaucracy.

It is possible to argue, in fact, that bureaucratic decision makers tend to behave more and more like Downs' "conservers,"[68] at least partly for political reasons. Cautious behavior that minimizes risk, whether individual or institutional, is inherently political (see chapter 4). Self-interest motives, which Downs ascribes to "climbers" as well as to "conservers,"[69] are themselves political. "Mixed" motives of self-interest and altruism are also partly political. Only Downs' primarily altruistic "statesman" seems to have the general good and not politics in view, but, as Downs suggests, by his not contesting for organizational resources, the statesman's functions "will probably receive an underallocation of resources."[70] Without being so labeled, that is an argument on behalf of political rationality.

The point of all this is that there is a widespread tendency, even among some political scientists, scornfully to dismiss or downgrade as "irrational" any behavior or decision not clearly directed toward achieving the "best" results. But if criteria of political rationality were to be used—that is, establishing cost-benefit ratios in political terms—such behavior and decisional outcomes might be perfectly "rational." Perhaps most important, decisions made and measured even by the most objective economic-quantitative criteria have political implications; for example, an economically rational tax reform law will benefit some more than others. The mistake all too frequently made, in and out of government, is ignoring or denigrating those implications because they somehow "pollute" the "truly objective" decisions based on only the most "neutral" of considerations.[71] In every instance, *the choice of criteria* by which to measure decisional outcomes has political significance because of the ever-present possibility that adherence to a particular set of criteria (including quantitative data) will ultimately favor the political interests of one group over those of other groups.

Another observer who makes a similar point from a different perspective is Martin Landau.[72] He questions the traditional inclination to minimize organizational duplication and overlap in the name of efficiency, and he points out that such practices, contrary to being rational, may prove to be quite irrational. He suggests, first, that duplication of organizational features may make overall performance more reliable, in the event that any one part breaks down. As an example, he cites an automobile with dual braking systems; the secondary system may seem to be just so much extra baggage, so uneconomical, so wasteful—until the primary braking system fails![73] Within human organizations, training more than one individual or staff in essentially the same tasks fits the same description of "rational duplication"; the alternative is increased risk of organizational breakdown should any one part fail. Second, Landau asserts that overlapping parts may improve performance by allowing for greater adaptability within the organization as a whole. His examples of "rational overlapping" include, among others, biological organisms that can adapt and survive in the face of a failing part, and, significantly, the U.S. Constitution.

Why the latter as an example of "rational overlap"? Because our framework of government was calculated, from the outset, to be overlapping (and, for that matter, duplicative) in the interest of preventing political tyranny, that most efficient of governmental methods. Separation of powers and checks and balances were both designed to prevent any one branch of government from becoming predominant. And what are checks and balances except *deliberately designed overlap* in the execution of essential government functions? Similarly, our structure of federalism is clearly duplicative, yet the purpose is the same: to prevent undue concentration of power. From Landau we can infer that in working toward the accomplishment of clearly delineated political goals (in this example, preventing concentration of power), some structural and behavioral arrangements may be politically rational and defensible, even though they might appear quite irrational in economic or other "value-neutral" terms. Above all, both Landau and Wildavsky challenge the application of economic criteria to the measurement of political phenomena, as well as the assumption that economic rationality is, by definition, superior to political rationality.

In sum, then, political rationality is not at all a contradiction in terms. One can accept the propositions that politics is legitimately concerned with enabling the decision processes of government to function adequately, that basing decisions on political grounds is as valid as basing them on other grounds, and that rationality according to the currency of politics is as defensible as rationality in economic terms. Political rationality, when appropriately conceived and applied, can be a useful tool for evaluating both the processes and the outcomes of organizational decision making.

SUMMARY

Decision making involves seeking to bring about a change in order to achieve some gain, by means of a particular course of action involving expenditure of a certain amount of resources. There is some unavoidable uncertainty, and therefore some risk involved, and most decision makers seek to minimize both. Most decisions are of a relatively routine nature, though care should be taken not to allow routines to dominate.

A significant debate, still ongoing, surrounds how to actually make decisions. The "rational" model, derived from classical economics, assumes that decision makers consciously pursue known goals and seek to achieve them in the most efficient manner possible. "Rational" behavior would include quantifying and ranking alternatives, separating ends from means, comprehensively analyzing data, and seeking to maximize utility. Rationality, in this model, refers to the process of making decisions, not to goals or outcomes.

Critiques of the rational model have centered on its lack of practical applicability and its undesirability as a method of administrative decision making. Impediments on rationality are said to include, among others, distinguishing facts from values, the ambiguous nature of goals, time pressures, costs of information acquisition, and "some ineradicable uncertainty." Another critique holds that rationality is not desirable because goals cannot be, and should not have to be, agreed upon in advance of decisions.

Two major alternatives to the rational model have been suggested. Incrementalism emphasizes decision making through limited successive comparisons, aiming to "satisfice" rather than to "maximize"; incrementalists focus on meeting short-term needs and maintaining flexibility in responding to problems. In particular, incrementalists reject the necessity of self-conscious goal definition as a prerequisite to decision making. Advocates of mixed scanning, on the other hand, allege that incrementalism is not sufficiently innovative, that it is too supportive of the status quo, and that it is inadequate as an approach to fundamental decisions. Defenders of incrementalism respond that their approach is viable in dealing with both changes and problems, large and small.

Organizational goals, though often ambiguous, can influence administrative behavior and can in turn be affected by political considerations. Key goals may include agency survival and maintenance ("reflexive" goals), accomplishment of substantive program objectives ("transitive" goals), and symbolic goals. Agencies seek to articulate their goals in relatively general fashion and may be deliberately unclear about some of them to preserve their political support. Efforts to achieve certain kinds of goals may have to be ongoing, due to the nature of the problem. The personal goals of agency employees usually vary considerably, thus making goal congruence between individual and organizational goals difficult to bring about. Finally, some goals may be determined by the extent to which political support can be generated for them.

The major considerations in the decisional process are (1) the goals being sought, (2) the resources necessary, (3) projected benefits, (4) the cost-benefit ratio, (5) substantive, political, and organizational grounds for decisions, (6) the time element, (7) the quality and quantity of information available, (8) the role of decision analysis and its supporting technologies, (9) past decisions and policies, (10) the prospect of unanticipated consequences and efforts to avoid them, (11) the need to avoid "groupthink," and (12) "sunk costs"—resources expended in having made and implemented a decisional commitment and resources that would be necessary to alter it. On balance, these considerations seem to point toward a decision process where the rational model *cannot* prevail. The debate over appropriate models of decision making is part of the larger evolution of contemporary organization theory.

Another critique of rationality is founded on the premise that economic-quantitative measures may not always be appropriate in determining what is rational. By using a set of explicitly political measures, "political rationality" is possible. What is politically rational may not be economically rational, and vice versa, and applying economic concepts of rationality to political phenomena might be misleading.

NOTES

1. Some decisions are made to leave things as they are rather than to change them, but theoretically the mere fact that a decision was called for *not* to change something alters the overall situation.
2. Herbert A. Simon, "Administrative Decision Making," *Public Administration Review*, 25 (March 1965), 31–37, at pp. 35–36.
3. An extensive literature has grown up in the area of decision making, including Stephen K. Archer, "The Structure of Management Decision Theory," in Robert Golembiewski et al., eds., *Public Administration* (Chicago: Rand McNally, 1966); David Braybrooke and Charles E. Lindblom, *A Strategy of Decision* (London: Collier-Macmillan, 1963); William R. Dill, "Administrative Decision Making," in Sidney Mailick and Edward H. Van Ness, eds., *Concepts and Issues in*

Administrative Behavior (Englewood Cliffs, N.J.: Prentice-Hall, 1962); William J. Gore, *Administrative Decision Making: A Heuristic Model* (New York: Wiley, 1964); William J. Gore and J. W. Dyson, *The Making of Decisions* (New York: The Free Press, 1964); Charles E. Lindblom, "The Science of 'Muddling Through,'" *Public Administration Review*, 19 (Spring 1959), 79–88; Martin Shubik, "Studies and Theories of Decision Making," *Administrative Science Quarterly*, 3 (December 1958), 289–306; Herbert A. Simon, *Administrative Behavior*, 3rd ed. (New York: The Free Press, 1976); Allan W. Lerner, *The Politics of Decision Making: Strategy, Cooperation, and Conflict* (Beverly Hills, Calif.: Sage, 1976); and Wallace Swan, "Decision Making," in Thomas D. Lynch, ed., *Organization Theory and Management* (New York: Marcel Dekker, 1983).

4. Anthony Downs, *An Economic Theory of Democracy* (New York: Harper & Row, 1957), p. 4.
5. Ibid., p. 5.
6. Ibid., pp. 4–5 (emphasis added).
7. Ibid., pp. 6 and 208.
8. John M. Pfiffner, "Administrative Rationality," *Public Administration Review*, 20 (Summer 1960), 125–32, at p. 126; and Lindblom, "The Science of 'Muddling Through,'" p. 81.
9. Camille Cates, "Beyond Muddling: Creativity," *Public Administration Review*, 39 (November/December 1979), 527–32, at p. 528.
10. Downs, *An Economic Theory of Democracy*, p. 4.
11. Lindblom, "The Science of 'Muddling Through,'" p. 81.
12. This discussion relies on Lindblom, "The Science of 'Muddling Through'"; Pfiffner, "Administrative Rationality"; Downs, *Inside Bureaucracy* (Boston: Little, Brown, 1967); and Aaron Wildavsky, *The Politics of the Budgetary Process*, 4th ed. (Boston: Little, Brown, 1984).
13. Downs, *Inside Bureaucracy*, p. 75.
14. See Martin Meyerson and Edward C. Banfield, *Politics, Planning, and the Public Interest* (New York: The Free Press, 1955).
15. See Louis C. Gawthrop, *Administrative Politics and Social Change* (New York: St. Martin's, 1971); and Dwight Waldo, ed., *Public Administration in a Time of Turbulence* (Scranton, Pa.: Chandler, 1971).
16. The reference is to "The Science of 'Muddling Through.'" See also, by Lindblom, *The Intelligence of Democracy* (New York: The Free Press, 1965); *The Policy-Making Process* (Englewood Cliffs, N.J.: Prentice-Hall, 1968); *Politics and Markets* (New York: Basic Books, 1977); and "Still Muddling, Not Yet Through," *Public Administration Review*, 39 (November/December 1979), 517–26.
17. Simon, *Administrative Behavior*, p. xxviii.
18. Simon, "Administrative Decision Making," p. 33.
19. See Allan W. Lerner and John Wanat, "Fuzziness and Bureaucracy," *Public Administration Review*, 43 (November/December 1983), 500–9.
20. Yehezkel Dror, "Muddling Through—'Science' or Inertia," in "Governmental Decision Making" (a symposium), *Public Administration Review*, 24 (September 1964), 153–57.
21. Amitai Etzioni, "Mixed Scanning: A 'Third' Approach to Decision Making," *Public Administration Review*, 27 (December 1967), 385–92.
22. Ibid., p. 388.
23. Ibid., p. 389.

24. Ibid., pp. 389–90 (emphasis added).
25. Cates, "Beyond Muddling: Creativity," p. 529.
26. Ibid.
27. Lindblom, "Still Muddling, Not Yet Through."
28. Ibid., p. 517.
29. Ibid.
30. Ibid.
31. Ibid.
32. Ibid. (emphasis added).
33. Ibid., p. 518.
34. Ibid., p. 517.
35. Ibid., p. 518.
36. For a thoughtful statement in defense of incrementalism in the planning process, see Sam Pearsall, "Multi-Agency Planning for Natural Areas in Tennessee," *Public Administration Review*, 44 (January/February 1984), 43–48.
37. Lawrence B. Mohr, "The Concept of Organizational Goal," *American Political Science Review*, 67 (June 1973), 470–81, at p. 475.
38. Ibid., pp. 475–76.
39. See Murray Edelman, *The Symbolic Uses of Politics* (Urbana: University of Illinois Press, 1964), and *Politics as Symbolic Action* (Chicago: Markham, 1971).
40. Robert C. Young, "Goals and Goal-Setting," *Journal of the American Institute of Planners*, 32 (March 1966), 76–85, at p. 78.
41. Thirty years ago the power program was described as one in which ". . . a secondary activity, the production and sale of surplus power, has come to overshadow other program goals, some say to the considerable disadvantage of the whole." See Roscoe C. Martin, ed., *TVA: The First Twenty Years* (University, Ala., and Knoxville, Tenn.: University of Alabama Press and University of Tennessee Press, 1956), p. 267.
42. Wildavsky, *The Politics of the Budgetary Process*, 2nd ed. (Boston: Little, Brown, 1974), pp. 191–92 (emphasis added).
43. See Downs, *Inside Bureaucracy*, chapter 8.
44. Ibid., p. 88.
45. Ibid.
46. F. J. Roethlisberger and William J. Dickson, *Management and the Worker* (Cambridge, Mass.: Harvard University Press, 1939); John M. Pfiffner and Frank P. Sherwood, *Administrative Organization* (Englewood Cliffs, N.J.: Prentice-Hall, 1960).
47. See, for example, Alexander George, "The Case for Multiple Advocacy in Making Foreign Policy," *American Political Science Review*, 66 (December 1972), 751–95.
48. See Douglas Yates, *Bureaucratic Democracy: The Search for Efficiency and Democracy in American Government* (Cambridge, Mass.: Harvard University Press, 1982), p. 33; and Robert M. O'Brien, Michael Clarke, and Sheldon Kamieniecki, "Open and Closed Systems of Decision Making: The Case of Toxic Waste Management," *Public Administration Review*, 44 (July/August 1984), 334–40.
49. Some decisions are made, of course, specifically with organizational impacts in mind, provided that substantive objectives still are attained. See, for example, the discussion of how altered work schedules might affect police morale, in J. Barton Cunningham, "Compressed Shift Schedules: Altering the Relation-

ship Between Work and Non-Work,'' *Public Administration Review*, 42 (September/October 1982), 438–47.

50. It has been suggested that variations in personal goals also may be related, if indirectly, to hierarchical location. See Downs, *Inside Bureaucracy*, chapter 8, especially p. 89.
51. See Shubik, ''Studies and Theories of Decision Making,'' for an elaboration of ''probable risk'' and its minimization.
52. Simon, ''Administrative Decision Making,'' p. 31.
53. See, for example, Alice M. Rivlin, *Brookings Research Report No. 112: Making Federal Programs Work Better* (Washington, D.C.: Brookings, 1971). Recent studies of computers and their expanding role include Kenneth L. Kraemer and James N. Danziger, ''Computers and Control in the Work Environment,'' *Public Administration Review*, 44 (January/February 1984), 32–42; and James N. Danziger, William H. Dutton, Rob Kling, and Kenneth L. Kraemer, *Computers and Politics: High Technology in American Local Governments* (New York: Columbia University Press, 1982).
54. Simon, ''Administrative Decision Making,'' p. 33.
55. New York *Times*, June 6, 1980, p. A-14; and June 10, 1980, p. A-16.
56. ''Millions of Pentagon Chips May Be Defective,'' an Associated Press news story appearing in the Bloomington-Normal (Ill.) *Daily Pantagraph*, September 12, 1984, p. A-1.
57. An outstanding analysis of the problem of obtaining reliability in organizational communications can be found in Martin Landau's ''Redundancy, Rationality, and the Problem of Duplication and Overlap,'' in *Public Administration Review*, 29 (July/August 1969), 346–58. The argument that multiple channels of communication can increase the accuracy of messages going to the same receiver has been made by Downs, *Inside Bureaucracy*, chapter 10. Arthur Schlesinger and Richard Neustadt have described persuasively how various American presidents have made use of multiple channels. See Schlesinger's ''Roosevelt as Chief Administrator,'' in Francis E. Rourke, ed., *Bureaucratic Power in National Politics*, 3rd ed. (Boston: Little, Brown, 1978), pp. 257–69, especially pp. 259–63; and Neustadt's *Presidential Power: The Politics of Leadership from FDR to Carter* (New York: Wiley, 1980), chapter 7.
58. Irving L. Janis, *Victims of Groupthink: A Psychological Study of Foreign Policy Decisions and Fiascoes* (Boston: Houghton Mifflin, 1972), p. 9. I am indebted to Scott L. Brown, a former graduate student at Illinois State University, for his assistance on the topic of ''groupthink.''
59. Ibid., p. 7 (emphasis added).
60. Ibid., p. 197. Public managers at all levels, in grappling with similar problems of ''in-group'' advice, frequently solicit the opinions of outside advisors. While this course of action often is useful, it has its own pitfalls. See Howell S. Baum, ''The Advisor as Invited Intruder,'' *Public Administration Review*, 42 (November/December 1982), 546–52.
61. See Downs, *Inside Bureaucracy*, chapter 14.
62. Ibid., p. 195.
63. James D. Thompson, *Organizations in Action* (New York: McGraw-Hill, 1967), p. 9.
64. Ibid. See also John Forester, ''Bounded Rationality and the Politics of Muddling Through,'' *Public Administration Review*, 44 (January/February 1984), 23–31.

65. Aaron Wildavsky outlines concisely the nature of political rationality in *The Politics of the Budgetary Process*, 2nd ed., pp. 189–94. This discussion relies heavily on his writing there and on his critical appraisals of Planning-Programming-Budgeting (PPB) that have appeared in *Public Administration Review*.
66. Wildavsky, *The Politics of the Budgetary Process*, 2nd ed., p. 192.
67. Ibid. (emphasis added).
68. Downs, *Inside Bureaucracy*, p. 99.
69. Ibid., p. 88.
70. Ibid., p. 111.
71. Wildavsky, *The Politics of the Budgetary Process*, 2nd ed., p. 190, makes a similar point with regard to advocates of budgetary reform in the national government.
72. Landau, "Redundancy, Rationality, and the Problem of Duplication and Overlap," pp. 346–58, especially pp. 350–53.
73. Ibid., pp. 349–50. For a more recent appraisal of the potential benefits of redundancy in public organizations, see Jonathan B. Bendor, *Parallel Systems: Redundancy in Government* (Berkeley, Calif.: University of California Press, 1985).

SUGGESTED READINGS

Braybrooke, David, and Charles E. Lindblom. *A Strategy of Decision*. London: Collier-Macmillan, 1963.

Downs, Anthony. *Inside Bureaucracy*. Boston: Little, Brown, 1967, chapter 8.

Etzioni, Amitai. "Mixed Scanning: A 'Third' Approach to Decision Making." *Public Administration Review*, 27 (December 1967), 385–92.

Gore, William J., and J. W. Dyson. *The Making of Decisions*. New York: The Free Press, 1964.

"Governmental Decision Making" (a symposium). *Public Administration Review*, 24 (September 1964), 153–65.

Janis, Irving L. *Victims of Groupthink*. Boston: Houghton Mifflin, 1972.

Lindblom, Charles E. "The Science of 'Muddling Through.'" *Public Administration Review*, 19 (Spring 1959), 79–88.

———. "Still Muddling, Not Yet Through." *Public Administration Review*, 39 (November/December 1979), 517–26.

Mohr, Lawrence B. "The Concept of Organizational Goal." *American Political Science Review*, 67 (June 1973), 470–81.

Pfiffner, John M. "Administrative Rationality." *Public Administration Review*, 20 (Summer 1960), 125–32.

Simon, Herbert A. *Administrative Behavior*, 3rd ed. New York: The Free Press, 1976.

Swan, Wallace. "Decision Making." In Thomas D. Lynch, ed., *Organization Theory and Management* (New York: Marcel Dekker, 1983).

Wildavsky, Aaron. *The Politics of the Budgetary Process*, 2nd ed. Boston: Little, Brown, 1974, pp. 189–94.

9

The Tasks of Administrative Leadership

LEADERSHIP functions have attracted great interest in both ancient and modern times from scholars, generals, politicians, and more casual observers. Virtually every social order, from the most primitive society to the most complex industrial and postindustrial nations, has operated within some sort of framework in which leadership functions are differentiated, identified, and exercised by some and not others. Styles of leadership have been studied and restudied; prescriptions for leadership have been written and revised; exercise of leadership has been carefully analyzed and often sharply criticized. Despite all this attention, the question of what it takes to be an effective leader is still far from settled. More research has been done in this century, paralleling the expansion of knowledge in related fields such as social psychology, sociology, organization theory, and political science. The subject has taken on a particular urgency in the past two decades, however, as popular discontent has grown regarding existing social institutions.

Administrative leadership is exercised within specific organizational settings as well as in the context of the larger environment; both can significantly influence the style and substance of leader behavior. We will first consider briefly the impact of organizational settings, move next to traditional approaches to the study of leadership and some of the findings, and finally examine a number of roles and tasks that are, or can be, a part of the leadership function.

To focus our consideration on the exercise of leadership, we make several assumptions. First, it is assumed that the leader attains his or her position through legitimate means and remains the leader through the acquiescence of the "followership." Management psychologist Ralph Stogdill

274

suggests that groups tend to accept more readily leaders whose characteristics and abilities facilitate accomplishment of the group's specific tasks— for example, the captain of a swimming team is likely to be both a good swimmer and a good motivator.[1] It is also assumed, however, that the leader's *legitimacy* is not automatically continued, that the leader's actions contribute to or detract from the legitimacy the group accords him or her.

Second, our principal interest is in leaders within administrative hierarchies where advancement through the ranks or appointments from outside the organization by top-level superiors constitute the main methods of filling leadership slots. Third, we assume that organization members have at least a minimal interest in carrying out both the organization's overall responsibilities and their own particular responsibilities. Furthermore, we assume that the members' job performance can be affected by the ways in which top leaders and immediate supervisors conduct themselves in the course of discharging *their* responsibilities. There is ample evidence supporting the view that the interaction of leaders and followers, as well as followers' personal feelings about leaders and the way they lead, can have major consequences for work performance and the general work atmosphere.[2]

Finally, the leadership roles and tasks we will be discussing center on leaders who are in a strong position—official or unofficial—to influence significantly what happens within an organization. This is mentioned explicitly because it frequently is *not* the case; that is, some leaders are in a relatively weak position due to group structure and the nature of the work to be done.[3] One example of such leadership would be found in a research team of equally competent and well-known scientists where one member informally assumes overall direction of team tasks. As "first among equals," this leader would have to guide the others through persuasion and participative decision making. Our concern, however, is with leaders who are significantly involved with the totality of the group or organization's existence, activities, and sense of identity, and whose leadership is accepted and acknowledged by group members.

THE ORGANIZATIONAL SETTING OF LEADERSHIP

In administrative hierarchies, leadership is a multidimensional function, due to multiple levels of organization, wide variation in specific tasks and general functions, and numerous situations requiring leadership of some kind. The job of a leader within the administrative framework, therefore, is not constant, in the sense that the particular combinations of needs (organizational, personal, task-oriented, political) within groups being led are rarely the same from one set of circumstances to the next.

A useful conceptual approach to the organizational setting is sociologist Talcott Parsons' suggestion that "organizations exhibit three distinct levels of responsibility and control—*technical, managerial,* and *institutional*"[4] (moving from the narrowest to the broadest scope). These are partially analogous to the distinctions drawn previously between the types of decisions made by different kinds of bureaucrats (specialists or generalists), and among the varying grounds for reaching decisions (substantive, organizational, or political, respectively). Leadership in complex organizations is greatly affected by the variations in responsibility and control identified by Parsons, and to understand fully why that is, we will elaborate on what each level signifies.

The technical level, or suborganization, deals with problems "focused around effective performance of the technical function"—for example, teachers conducting their classes, a transit authority employee operating a bus on the prescribed route and running on time, or a government tax office processing income tax returns.[5] Major concerns at this level are the nature of the technical task (such as processing materials) and "the kinds of cooperation of different people required to get the job done effectively."[6]

The second, or managerial, level performs two functions for the technical suborganization: (1) mediating between the lower level and those who use its products, and (2) acquiring the resources necessary for carrying out technical functions. At the managerial level, decisions are made about matters such as the "broad technical task which is to be performed, the scale of operations, employment and purchasing policy, and so on."[7] In these senses, the managers control, or administer, the technical suborganization—though such control is not strictly a one-way street.

The institutional level of the organization renders the "higher-level support which makes . . . implementation of the organization's goals possible."[8] A significant point made by Parsons, pertaining to the relationships between this level and the others, bears on our discussion in chapter 4 of the relationships between chief executives and bureaucracies:

> In terms of "formal" controls, an organization may be relatively independent; but in terms of the meaning of the functions performed by the organization and hence of its "rights" to command resources and to subject its customers to discipline, it is never wholly independent.[9]

The significance of this observation is that in *operating* terms, suborganizations at the technical and managerial levels may possess considerable autonomy, but with ultimate responsibility—and accountability—vested at higher levels. (Note the further parallel between this observation and those made in chapter 2 about the existence of considerable discretion in the making of public policy in our system.)

How is administrative leadership affected by all this? One part of the answer is Parsons' observation that at each of the points dividing the levels of organization (institutional from managerial and managerial from technical), "there is a qualitative break in the simple continuity of 'line' authority because *the functions at each level are qualitatively different. Those . . . at the second level are not simply lower-order spellings-out of the top-level functions.*"[10] In other words, one of the principal challenges of leadership is to oversee a process of defining, organizing, supporting, and monitoring multiple functions, at multiple levels of organization, which by their nature tend to defy *uniform* methods of supervision. Responsibilities at each level must be clear enough—and flexible enough—to ensure that basic functions appropriate to that level or unit are in fact carried out (issues of centralization and decentralization, discussed in chapter 7, are relevant here). Particularly for elected or appointed chief executives, but for virtually any "top" official, these challenges must be of paramount concern.

These conceptions of organization help clarify another problem relevant to leadership, one discussed by Mary Parker Follett, an early student of leadership, sixty years ago.[11] The problem is one of *distance* within organizations, of difficulties encountered when directives must traverse a "tall" hierarchy (see chapter 7). According to Follett, "One might say that the strength of favourable response to [an] order is in inverse ratio to the distance the order travels."[12] Follett was speaking not only of physical or geographical distance but also of the need for collaborative effort between superiors and subordinates. She maintained that this could best be accomplished through face-to-face interaction, lessening both the physical distance and the tensions involved in giving orders. Such an observation, made during the heyday of scientific management, takes on greater significance in light of more varied organizational functions that now exist, and in light of Parsons' analysis of organization levels. While today it may be equally desirable, if not more so, to bridge the distances within complex organizations, it is also much more difficult to do so.

Thus, if leadership is to be effective, a deliberate effort must be made to overcome inevitable barriers inside organizations. Bear in mind, also, that the individual who may be a follower relative to higher-level officials may be a leader to others occupying subordinate positions. Multiple sets of leaders operating at different levels in complex organizations only complicate the tasks that each set, and each leader, must carry out.[13]

TRADITIONAL APPROACHES TO THE STUDY OF LEADERSHIP

The earliest efforts to analyze leadership employed two principal approaches, centering on the individual leader and on the leadership situation. The *traits* approach sought to explain leadership in terms of personality characteristics such as intelligence, ambition, ego drives, and interpersonal skills. Considerable emphasis was placed on leadership traits during the early years of the twentieth century, but in numerous studies since then the traits approach has been found to explain little. Furthermore, contrary to the most basic assumption of this approach, leaders were not found to possess common characteristics. The traits approach was discarded by most scholarly observers (though not necessarily in the conventional wisdom about leaders) by the 1950s. Attention shifted to a seemingly more promising avenue of exploration—namely, analysis of leadership situations and how situational factors were related to what was required in a leader in a particular set of circumstances (interestingly, Follett in the 1920s had noted situational factors).

The *situational* approach has become the general framework of analysis in most subsequent leadership studies. Rather than trying to explain leadership success or failure, particular styles of leadership, or why one person becomes a leader while another does not in terms of variations in personal skills and character, the situational approach emphasizes leader-follower interactions, the needs of the group or organization in the time period under study, the kind of work being done, general group values and ethics, and the like. From this, it follows that leaders in one situation may not be cut out to be leaders in other situations.[14] Some years ago a city manager in a midwestern city was asked to serve as president of a university in a neighboring state on the basis of the popularity and respect he had come to have. He took the position, but shortly thereafter the university governing board realized it had made a mistake—the successful city manager was an abject failure as a university president. Not only were the specific duties different; so also were the types of people, their expectations, and his interactions with university personnel as opposed to government officials. To cite another example, it has been suggested that generals do not make the best civilian political leaders because many features of military life and leadership conflict with the needs, values, and expectations of civilian (especially democratic) politics.

The point is, variations in the times, in circumstances, and in group characteristics help determine the most appropriate kinds of leadership and, to an important degree, who shall lead. Personality, skills, ambition, and the rest do make some difference, but only in the context of the social environment, setting of leadership, and demands arising from the group. "Personal traits within the situation," with emphasis on the latter, now best describes the most common approach in studying leadership.[15]

Fred Fiedler and his associates at the University of Illinois Group-Effectiveness Research Laboratory developed a three-part classification of group situations, indicating variations in leader effectiveness.[16] They suggested that group situations vary according to (1) "position power" of the leader, defined as the authority vested in the leader's official position; (2) task structure of the group—the degree to which assignments can be programmed and specified in a step-by-step fashion; and (3) leader-member personal relationships, based on affection, admiration, and trust of group members for the leader. Their general conclusion was that "the leader who is liked by his group and has a clear-cut task and high position power . . . has everything in his favor. The leader who has poor relationships with his group members, an unstructured task, and weak position power likely will be unable to exert much influence over the group."[17]

But how to choose the particular leadership style most appropriate to a given situation? Fiedler's research suggests that leadership effectiveness is related to a *combination* of interpersonal and group-situational factors. For example, if tasks are clear-cut, relations between leader and members are positive, and official position power is considerable, then a leader is best advised to be strongly directive rather than democratic and nondirective. An All-American quarterback at Notre Dame does not call the plays by taking votes in the huddle! By the same token, the chairman of a voluntary committee "cannot ask with impunity that the group members vote or act according to his instructions."[18]

This theory of leadership is important for what it suggests about what can be changed to improve leadership effectiveness—rank, task structure, concern for followers—as well as what cannot be changed—leader personality, work situation, organizational characteristics. Fiedler's research reinforces the view that both traits (within limits) and situational dynamics dictate the most effective leadership style. This must be determined almost on a case-by-case basis; it is anything but preordained.

Another general dimension of leadership is how specific styles of managerial decision making affect the power, influence, and freedom of action of leaders and followers in an organization. Figure 9-1 illustrates a continuum of leadership behavior, suggesting the range of possibilities open to leaders in choosing management techniques. Such choices, like leadership effectiveness, are conditioned to a considerable extent by the nature of the organization and the work to be done.

We turn now to tasks of leadership in an effort to describe the many facets of the leader's role. The intention here is not to make a definitive appraisal of the leader's job but rather to suggest the scope of leadership functions in a way applicable to many different organizational settings. We will consider six such tasks and attempt to suggest very broadly what makes a good leader in terms of these tasks.

LEADER AS DIRECTOR: RECONCILING PERSONAL AND ORGANIZATIONAL GOALS

An essential function of leadership is to bring some coherence to the multitude of activities within an organization. This is facilitated by persuading those in charge of various activities to emphasize the aspects of their work directed toward common organizational objectives. And this in turn re-

Figure 9-1   The Continuum of Leadership Behavior: Relations Between Managers and Nonmanagers

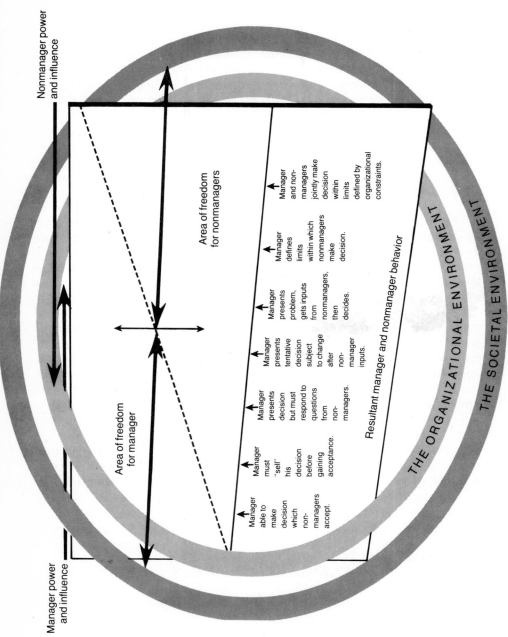

Source: Robert Tannenbaum and Warren H. Schmidt, ''How to Choose a Leadership Pattern,'' *Harvard Business Review*, 51 (May/June 1973), 167.

quires reconciling personal and organizational goals, which (as discussed in the preceding chapter) can diverge and even conflict.

The key to a leader's efforts to reconcile personal and organizational goals is to create as much psychological overlap as possible between the two. If a leader is able to induce organization members to internalize (accept as their own) general objectives of the whole, then most of this task will have been accomplished. This might be done by direct and indirect persuasion, by example, or by developing members' understanding of rationales for pursuing particular objectives or adopting specific tactics. To the extent that there is conflict over goals, of course, this task will remain an ongoing one, with considerable potential for difficulty. The optimum situation is one in which members see pursuit of organizational goals as consistent with and supportive of achieving their personal goals.

Goal articulation is a function of leadership, and how this is done may trigger positive or negative reactions among members. If negative—owing to substantive disagreement, lack of consideration for their views, or inadequate preparation—gaining members' support will be that much more difficult. Leaders often have to devote a significant amount of time, energy, and resources to winning member support for group goals, and they do not always succeed. Very often, they must settle for grudging or reluctant cooperation, which is a far cry from genuine support.

Another difficulty lies in the possibility that members' personal goals may be more important to them than the business of the organization. The types of bureaucrats Anthony Downs labeled *climbers* and *conservers*[19]—those interested respectively in achieving and preserving power, prestige, and income—attest to the fact that highly personalized goals may predominate among some organization members. The larger the proportion of total membership that falls into the climber or conserver mold, the more difficult the task of directing the organization's activities toward larger goals. A related problem is determining the true state of affairs in this regard—knowing what members' goals really are.

Besides these problems, there is the possibility that leaders' personal goals might interfere with organizational performance and attainment of group objectives, though leaders tend to be somewhat more committed to group goals than are their followers. (Commitment to achieving organizational goals seems to depend in part on the degree of responsibility for attaining them.[20]) Enlightened leadership requires a clear commitment to organizational goals that outweighs any personal objectives—and that is perceived as such by followers.

To this point we have discussed organizational goals as separate from personal goals and from feelings, values, and preferences of an organization's members. From this perspective, goals seem to exist independently of organization members—as something determined by persons outside the organization, as self-defining in the course of organization activities, or as the product of articulation by the leadership.

Political scientist Lawrence Mohr has suggested an alternative conception of organizational goals, which narrows and sharpens what is meant by the term. In Mohr's view, we may accurately label as "organizational goals" only those on which there is widespread "consensus of intent" (agreement as to purpose) among a large majority of organization members, and that relate to "mainstreams" of organizational behavior.[21] Mohr maintains that these goals must be identified on the basis of empirical investigation rather than a superficial reading of "official" pronouncements, informal discussion with leaders or members, or intuitive judgments. He raises the possibility of *being able* to identify such organizational goals empirically and precisely, and stresses the necessity of doing so. Without identifying goals in this manner, Mohr says, the results of any inquiry into the goals of an organization are likely to be misleading, or at best incomplete. The implication of this conception of goals is this: if organizational goals are formulated by achieving a "consensus of intent," then by definition there is substantial overlap between personal and organizational goals. Were this the commonly accepted and applied definition of organizational goals, the leader's task in this regard would be virtually nonexistent.

Research in the human relations school of organization theory, as well as later studies, suggests that where there are differences between an organization's official and actual goals, it is group norms among members that account for those differences and designate *actual* goals. Where leaders rely heavily on member preferences as part of goal definition, chances are greater that personal and organizational goals can be reconciled at least to some degree. This is because the followership can be expected to respond favorably to a leadership willing to "include them in" on so basic a question as the goals of *their* organization. Leaders are therefore well advised to focus on the task of goal definition. If the results here are positive, other leadership tasks will be more readily accomplished.

LEADER AS MOTIVATOR: THE CARROT OR THE STICK?

We have already discussed motivation within organizations at some length (see chapter 6). Our purpose here is to review the major themes outlined earlier and put them into perspective as part of the tasks of leaders who seek to motivate their followers in the most positive fashion.

First, if we use the analogy of the carrot or the stick to describe one kind of choice to be made in motivating members of an organization, the stick is distinctly second choice. A substantial body of research clearly suggests that coercive measures aimed at motivating employees are not effective in the long run, though they may have short-term impacts.[22] Far more likely to succeed is a combination of incentives and conditions appropriate to the interests of those doing the work. On the basis of research conducted over several decades, there is reason to believe that emphasis should be given to such things as offering attractive salaries, fringe benefits, and working conditions; creating positive social interaction among groups of workers; and making the work as interesting as possible. The problem is that different things work for different people, and leaders face a continuing challenge of tailoring these motivators as closely as they can to the needs, preferences, and attitudes of organization members or member groups. This is important not only for accomplishing immediate goals, but also for building cohesiveness in the organization through member satisfaction. It may not be possible, however, to satisfy fully each and every individual.

A 1975 study by the Society for the Advancement of Management sought to discover what workers in private companies felt was the single most positive feature in the behavior of their immediate supervisors. The most common response was that the supervisor had been "encouraging" to the employee in work performance. Since there is other evidence suggesting that the interaction between employees and their first-line supervisors is of crucial importance to the group's performance, morale, and individual job satisfaction,[23] a positive, supportive attitude toward employees on the part of the supervisor takes on added importance. It would seem, therefore, that an organization's leaders should take great care in appointing supervisors.[24] More generally, leaders should be concerned about the quality of face-to-face supervision, as well as tangible benefits or intrinsic work interest.

Motivation continues to be a complex task of leadership. There appears to be a pattern of member responsiveness to leadership that is clearly defined, and at the same time self-confident, persuasive, fair, and supportive.[25] But no rule is universally applicable; exceptions are frequent, and leaders have to remain alert if they expect to cope with the motivational problems that could arise in their organizations.

LEADER AS COORDINATOR/INTEGRATOR: MESHING THE GEARS

A function of rising importance for leaders in complex organizations has been coordinating and integrating varied functions and tasks of increasingly specialized members. Leaders, themselves usually not as knowledgeable about the specialties found in their organizations as are individual specialists, must rely on subordinates' competence at the same time that they attempt to organize their efforts into a coherent whole. If the tasks of directing and motivating members have been carried out effectively, coordinating and integrating their efforts should follow naturally—but conceptually there are a number of factors to be considered.

Most important is the tendency for individuals concentrating on their own particular work to develop "tunnel vision," through which they see the worth of their own tasks, but fail to appreciate the importance of other aspects of the organization's activity. For example, a leader attempting to change the operations of a division, staff, or branch for the purpose of strengthening (in his or her view) the organization's overall capacities and/or performance may encounter resistance from members in that subsection who believe their procedures and output are adequate for their purposes. Their frame of reference, so to speak, is *their* work, defined as work of the subsection, whereas the leadership's responsibilities encompass the work of the entire organization, with a frame of reference to match.

For a leader to overcome member resistance successfully in such a case requires the ability to convey a sense of the larger issues, needs, and contexts that gave rise to the leader's desire for change. In essence, this means broadening the horizons of these members to include a fuller picture of the organization in operation. Robert Guest, in a landmark study in the early 1960s, concluded that "for a leader to induce others to act requires that he establish for himself and for others mechanisms that allow both to be continually [accumulating] . . . facts and ideas that have had broad circulation before they are acted upon."[26] That is, by institutionalizing "idea-collecting mechanisms,"[27] a leader can better ensure wider exchange of information among members. The result, ideally, would be that when actions were proposed affecting specific work units, members of those units—by understanding larger organizational purposes—would be more inclined to accept, and even to take an active part in, what the leadership intended to do.

Mechanisms for collecting ideas are such things as newsletters, suggestion boxes, question-and-answer sessions, and advance communication of proposed actions to members. This amounts to "regularized brainstorming" for ideas, a process that, by involving members, is likely to make ultimate decisions more palatable to more people in the organization. Circulating information about actions already taken can also be beneficial. Not circulating information widely can result in built-up resentments, which can linger and affect subsequent organizational affairs.

Even in the best of circumstances, leaders will have to manage diverse operations on a smoothly coordinated time schedule. Personnel, materials, financial resources, services to consumers of the organization's output (however defined), and so on, all have to be integrated as part of the organization's ongoing activities. In this respect, advance planning is a key leadership function, in ensuring that the necessary components are on hand as needed. Every organization in existence faces that common need, and the leadership is expected to take responsibility for meeting it.

Another dimension of coordination and integration of organizational activities is the need to mesh the leadership's own tasks with those of the remainder of the organization. The need here is to avoid working at cross-purposes, making certain that leaders and followers generally share the same understanding of what the organization is about and what the intended end-products are. This ties in with the leader-as-director task in the effort to create psychological overlap among several different sets of goals. It is also linked to leader as motivator in the creation of inducements designed to move members in particular directions.

In sum, organizations comprising diverse specialties and functions require efforts at the top, as well as throughout the ranks, to bring about satisfactory coordination and integration. Organization members need some sense that their different functions somehow fit into a larger context. And leaders must take responsibility for instilling that view.

LEADER AS CATALYST/INNOVATOR: POINTING THE WAY

The conception of a leader as a spark plug, as the ''one who makes it happen,'' which is widespread in the conventional wisdom about groups and organizations (especially sports teams), appears to have some validity. But the particular conditions prevailing in the group situation may strongly affect a leader's opportunities to stimulate group action. Fred Fiedler suggests that the best opportunities occur when the leader has influence in the group, informal support, and a relatively well-structured task at hand—when ''the group is ready to be directed, and the members expect to be told what to do.''[28] As an example, Fiedler cites the captain of an airliner in its final approach before landing, when his decision, instructions, and actions are crucial, and no one would realistically want him to discuss or evaluate his options with the flight crew. Other examples of well-structured tasks where a leader is the catalyst for group action include rescue operations after a disaster, and a football team's last-minute drive for the winning touchdown. In these examples, the tasks to be performed are short term; those responsible will succeed or fail within a limited time period.

Many tasks, however, are less structured and more time-consuming. Here, too, a leader may be a successful catalyst, provided that members understand and support organizational objectives and that the leader has made clear how individual activities help promote those objectives. For example, an academic department chairman concerned about financial support for the department from the university administration may encourage faculty members to pursue research interests as well as excellence in teaching. Published articles, books, and research papers enhance a department's prestige outside the university, providing a strong argument for continued support internally. Even though such activities are conducted largely on an individual basis, a chairman can relate them to departmental well-being and thus attempt to motivate faculty members in those terms.

The process of *innovation* is tied to the role of catalyst because in many instances an organization's routine operations do not require very substantial leader participation. When normal procedures are all that is required, the leader is ordinarily in the background—in fact, is best advised to remain there so as to permit members to function with some measure of independence. However, changes in routines must usually be initiated outside the group or subgroup, since the routines may serve a stabilizing function inside the group and have the support of its members (see the earlier discussion in this chapter of "tunnel vision," and in chapter 8 regarding routine decision making). Furthermore, routines frequently evolve in a way that reflects values and preferences of the group, regarding not only the mechanics but also the very purposes of group activities. Thus group members may interpret a proposed change in routine as a comment on their purposes as well as their procedures (which may be true). The challenge to the leader, then, is to justify adequately to group members any proposed change he or she deems necessary in the context of the larger organization.[29] Clearly, the catalyst role is important if innovation is to be brought about.

LEADER AS EXTERNAL SPOKESMAN—AND "GLADIATOR"

One of the most crucial tasks for a leader is to act as representative of the organization's views and interests in the external environment. This involves articulating formal organizational positions to those outside. It also ordinarily includes an advocacy role when the organization seeks to secure additional resources or to maintain the resources it has. This "spokesman" task has become more important as organizations have become more complex, particularly so for leaders of the suborganizational units within larger hierarchical structures. The branch chief within a government bureaucracy, the plant manager in a large manufacturing conglomerate, and the academic department chairman within a college structure headed by a dean share a periodic need to "go to bat" for their organizations.

The most common setting for this role is budgetary decision making, where favorable portrayal of the organization can be decisive in influencing those who make budget recommendations for the next fiscal year. This, however, is only the most visible kind of occasion. In fact the "gladiator" task is ongoing—standing up for the organization and its members when there is a complaint about its operation, anticipating and preparing for changes in the external environment that might adversely affect the organization, or simply keeping abreast of developments in the larger organization as they relate to the values, work, and well-being of the unit.

There is evidence to suggest that few things are better for group morale than a leader who willingly and effectively defends the group's welfare.[30] Aside from the practical benefits such advocacy can produce, a leader actively supporting and defending the organization represents in a concrete form the faith placed in the members and their work. The leader, in acting as gladiator, is demonstrating that he or she is a part of the organization, rather than standing aloof. In addition, the leader as gladiator is in effect carrying out one of the cardinal principles of good management: bestow praise publicly! Defense or advocacy on behalf of the organization constitutes collective rather than individual praise, it is true, but indicates positive feedback in a strategically important fashion, and that is usually not lost on members of an organization.

LEADER AS MANAGER OF CRISIS IN THE ORGANIZATION

As we noted in chapter 4, chief executives have gained added political strength when called upon to direct governmental responses to crises of various kinds—military, economic, or natural disasters. Leaders in organizations at *all* levels are usually responsible for dealing with the occasional serious problem or difficulty that arises in their units, or that affects one of their clienteles. Examples would include the managers of a transit district in a midwestern community faced with repeated breakdowns of district buses during a harsh winter; and a city manager confronted with deadlock in efforts to end a municipal employee strike. Such problems, while not minor, generally are limited to particular suborganizations or governments, and at least have a definable end point.

A recently emergent dimension of leadership, however, goes beyond this sort of problem. This has to do with the growing fiscal pressures on many public entities, particularly in state and local administration. Linked to all of the other five roles, the leader as crisis manager must cope with an unpleasant new reality—that economic and other resources are not without limits. Also, it is clear that many citizens are unwilling to pay higher taxes in order to meet rising costs of government. These are fundamental challenges, cutting across the full range of governmental activity. And because it appears that resource scarcity will be with us for some time, these problems lack the kind of end-point characteristic of more immediate difficulties. In recent years, a variety of responses has been developed and entrusted to administrative leaders to implement. One is the growing practice of "cutback management" (the label is self-explanatory), which poses special difficulties for the leader responsible for conducting it.[31]

We will treat the problem of general resource scarcity as it relates to governmental resources in chapter 12. The problems for administrative leaders stemming from tight resources, however, are relevant here. A basic problem is that "almost all our public management strategies are predicated on assumptions of the *continuing enlargement* of public revenues and expenditures''[32]—assumptions that are now seriously questioned. This creates the necessity for managers to ''maintain organizational capacity by devising new managerial arrangements within prevailing structures that were designed under assumptions of growth.''[33] *Without* growth, and perhaps with significant contractions, the leader must deal with a very different situation, requiring new strategies and methods for rendering them acceptable to organization subordinates.

Various tactics exist for cutback management, addressed to the political and economic/technical needs of the organization, both internally and externally. Tactics designed to *resist* organizational decline include mobilizing dependent clienteles, diversifying programs, targeting high-prestige programs for elimination (to make it politically costly for those making the decision), adopting user charges for services where possible, retaining internal esprit de corps and morale by developing a siege mentality, and improving productivity. Tactics designed to *make decline smoother* include cutting programs of low prestige, or those providing services to politically weak clienteles, or those run by weak subunits. It is also possible to change leadership at each stage in the decline process, to ask employees to voluntarily sacrifice by deferring raises or by taking early retirement, and to shift programs to other agencies, thus reducing overall cost levels.[34] How effective any or all of these are, of course, is another question.

The other leader roles are profoundly affected by changes brought about by decline and the need for cutbacks. For one thing, members of an organization may all experience a shift in personal goals, tending toward the ''conserver'' mentality that is bent on ''holding on if we can.'' While to some extent that can be useful, it can also easily get out of hand, and a leader must try to channel that motivation in useful and productive directions. The ''motivator'' role is obviously affected, for in the face of deteriorating employee morale, the leader must be able to ''rally the troops'' in order to continue essential activities at an acceptable level of performance. The ''coordinator'' role must be fulfilled even more effectively—with the resource base of the organization shrinking, ever more careful coordination of human and material resources is necessary. The role of ''catalyst/innovator'' likewise is a more sensitive one, because it falls to the leader to stimulate and direct changes that must be made. Ideally, this should include the leader's having *previously anticipated* problems of decline, so that resource reserves have been acquired as ''organizational insurance.'' In this respect, foresight and keen judgment are valuable leadership assets. Concern for innovation must also be manifested in another way. Because of the possible tendency toward conserver behavior referred to earlier, organization leaders must resist pressures toward conducting only ''business as usual'' at the very time when complex and interdependent problems in the organization's environment cry out for innovative efforts at solving them. Leaders, and their organizations, are truly on the horns of a dilemma in this regard: declining resources evoke pressures for retrenchment and "holding our ground," but social and economic complexities underlying resource decline demand vigorous and innovative response. No easy solutions exist to this basic dilemma, but efforts to develop answers are essential in the immediate future. Finally, and perhaps most important, the gladiator role calls for a leader's best efforts, in order to reduce as much as possible adverse consequences of organizational decline for the administrative unit.

WHAT MAKES A GOOD LEADER?

We come back, then, to the persistent question that is at the core of most inquiries into the subject of leadership. Without claiming to have found the answers, let us suggest a number of general considerations relevant to achieving effective leadership (see Figure 9-2).

First, it appears that a leader is wise to convey to organization members that they are regarded as competent in their work. Many *are*, of course, quite competent; but the point here is that competent workers will appreciate the fact that management has taken note of their worth, and a less competent worker might work harder to live up to the leadership's expectations. The expectation of competence, in fact, may be a key factor in developing motivations to *be* competent.[35]

Second, there is strong evidence that if members of an organization perceive the leadership as receptive to ideas, feedback, comments, even complaints, from "below," then they will be far more willing to respond to leaders' directives.[36] For one thing, communications from members give leaders the clearest picture of the things important to members, as well as their general attitudes and aspirations. This cannot help but make it easier for the leaders to communicate meaningfully. More important, the leaders'

Figure 9-2   Effective Leadership

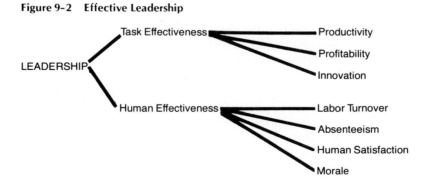

WHAT DOES IT MEAN TO BE AN "EFFECTIVE" LEADER?

My perception of research in the field is that effectiveness is typically conceptualized as "performance of the subordinate group"—usually some kind of output measure—or perhaps as compliance or adherence to the leader's directives. In any case, the effectiveness concept and measure is invariably a behavioral one. The "good" leader is one who can get his subordinates to *do* something. What happens if we force ourselves away from this marriage to behavioral concepts? What kind of insights can we get if we say that the effectiveness of a leader lies in his ability to make activity meaningful for those in his role set—not to change behavior but to give others a sense of understanding what they are doing, and especially to articulate it so they can communicate about the meaning of their behavior.

Source: From Louis Pondy, *Leadership, Where Else Can We Go?* edited by Morgan W. McCall, Jr., and Michael M. Lombardo (Durham, N.C.: Duke University Press, 1978), p. 94. Reprinted in *Harvard Business Review*, 58 (July/August 1980), 113–20, at p. 120.

---

willingness to hear and act upon useful ideas from the ranks builds a sense of cohesiveness among the members that is likely to increase each member's commitment to the organization's well-being.

Third, several studies suggest that the democratic leader is more effective in the broad view than is any other type.[37] Member satisfaction was clearly higher in democratically led groups, and interaction among group members was distinctly more relaxed and mutually supportive. At the same time, the democratic leaders in these studies did not abdicate leadership functions, but managed them in an open, participative, and supportive way. There is some reason to believe that such a style works more effectively with some types of followers than with others (for example, professionals and some in "flat" hierarchies with less formal structures), and perhaps better for some types of personalities than for others. Yet the pattern seems to be one of fairly successful leadership direction under democratic conditions.

Fourth, a 1958 study of a work group in private industry suggests indirectly some of the leadership features to which employees may respond favorably. The study indicated that the more highly employees rated supervisors on a number of key attributes, the less employees expressed a desire for unionization.[38] The attributes mentioned were fairness, authority, the ability to handle people, giving credit, readiness to discuss problems, and keeping employees informed. This combination suggests the scope of ability demanded in many leadership situations.

At the risk of oversimplification, it is worth pointing out several other important qualities of a good leader. (1) Ideally, a leader should be clear, reasonable, and consistent concerning expectations and standards of judgment for member performance. (2) A leader is well advised to deal openly, fairly, and equitably with all members, making distinctions among members only on work-related criteria. (3) A leader should maintain a fairly firm hold on the reins of leadership, while at the same time fostering a genuinely constructive two-way flow of communication by explaining rationales for proposed courses of action and by acting on worthwhile suggestions from members. (4) A leader should move carefully and democratically to secure consensus—more than merely a majority vote—on significant actions. One tactic is to strive for consensus by means of an extensive consultative process, which requires formal votes only infrequently. (5) The wise leader will try to prevent "empire-building" and other divisive tendencies within the ranks. The goal is to prevent disunity as one step toward building cohesion within the group. (6) Cronyism and favoritism should be absolutely avoided. And (7), perhaps hardest of all, a leader can greatly influence the whole course of events in the organization by setting the tone of interactions with the members. While "tone" is admittedly a vague term, the leader sets some behavioral standards that often are imitated, consciously or unconsciously, by other members of the group. Clearly, this will not happen in all instances. However, where a leader has in general acted constructively, the chances are greatly improved that members will respond in kind, both in their attitudes and behaviors toward the leader and in their general demeanor toward one another. These generalizations have their exceptions, but as standards for positive and enlightened leadership, they appear to have much to recommend them.[39]

Of course, there are some obstacles to effective leadership. For one thing, the situational potential for leadership may vary according to the organizational level of a particular group leader. It may also vary according to the flexibility that higher-level leaders permit within the rest of the organization. The tighter the rein held on subordinates by superiors, the less chance subordinates will have to exercise leadership within their own organizational bailiwicks. In addition, if an organization is highly structured—some would say bureaucratized—then the possibilities of leadership in the manner we have described are more limited. This is so because more of the decisions concerning management of organizational affairs are already settled questions, and thus are not ordinarily subject to being reopened. In this sense, bureaucracy is not conducive to leadership.

Second, individual goals may simply remain beyond the reach of the leaders' influence, though cooperation could more easily be induced from less secure members than from those with seniority, tenure, and the like. The leadership will probably have to accept some disparities between what it seeks and what individual members seek.

Third, fighting tunnel vision (among both members and leaders) may turn out to be a frustrating job.

Fourth, innovation in highly structured organizations is difficult to manage, and a body of professional opinions holds that traditional management values—of the scientific management school and its conceptual descendants—hamper development of conditions conducive to innovation.[40] Additionally, values and preferences of organization members may prove to be quite enduring, making innovation necessarily a matter of coercion. In the face of stiff resistance, a leader would have to weigh the costs of coercion against the calculated benefits of innovations.

Fifth, a gladiator will not always succeed in the external environment; depending on the mix of failure and success, this could work to the leader's disadvantage both inside and outside the organization. Part of a leader's skill should lie in knowing when to fight and when not to.

Finally, leadership is conditioned by the particular combination of people, tasks, and organizational dynamics that exists in each case. Despite what we do know about leadership, it is still not possible to construct an all-inclusive set of leadership guidelines.

LEADERSHIP AND PERSONALITY: A RETURN TO THE "TRAITS" APPROACH?

In the late 1970s and early 1980s, research findings appeared that, ironically, gave renewed emphasis to the importance of personality characteristics in potential and actual leaders.[41] This is suggestive of the "traits" approach, which has been out of favor among most students of leadership for some time, but there are important differences. One is the far greater sophistication and understanding we now possess of individual and group psychology. Another is the explicit link assumed in the recent research between personality and leader *behavior*, making assessment of personalities more meaningful. And, as indicated in the variables presented in Table 9-1 on pages 293–95, there has been a systematic effort to identify different dimensions of leader personality in much greater detail.

Leadership in contemporary organizations clearly operates under greater restraints from several standpoints—diminished legitimacy, declining resources, rising turbulence internally and externally, to name only a few. Yet many still aspire to positions of leadership, and there is evidence that leaders may be very important individuals, if we are to succeed in coping with rapid change. Despite many things that are very different from the past, there is continuing—and justifiable—interest in leadership roles.

SUMMARY

Leadership has aroused interest for many centuries. In the past few decades, however, studies of leadership have become more numerous and have cut across a wider span of human knowledge. Our discussion of leadership makes the following assumptions: that leadership is acquired and

Table 9-1
DIMENSIONS OF LEADERS' PERSONALITIES

Thinking

1. Capacity to abstract, to conceptualize, to organize, and to integrate different data into a coherent frame of reference.	Thinks concretely, item by item, fact by fact.	Can organize facts into patterns and sequences, but doesn't relate sequences to arrive at concepts.	Can relate theory to management problems, but doesn't search out concepts and ideas.	Can criticize theory and use it for long-range thinking about business.	Encyclopedic synthesist, able to organize and integrate creatively principles, values, concepts, and information from full range of arts and sciences.
2. Tolerance for ambiguity, can stand confusion until things become clear.	Needs to keep focus on one defined project at a time.	Can handle several projects but with stress.	Can handle vague project guidelines, but must always be anchored to concrete structure or method.	Can work with unspecified goals and uncertainty as long as can return to concrete orienting point occasionally.	Can tolerate ambiguity for years, doesn't get anxious waiting for long-term plans to come to fruition.
3. Intelligence, has the capacity not only to abstract, but also to be practical.	Educated, but doesn't learn much from experience.	Educated, but not very imaginative or creative.	Bright, makes good use of experience. Sometimes might seem like a hustler.	Very intelligent, draws well on reservoir of experience.	Exceptionally bright, draws on a fountain of experience. Good street smarts.
4. Judgment, knows when to act.	Rushes to judgment, without thinking things through.	Sporadic, has made some terrible bloopers along the way.	Thoughtful, but never quite sees the whole picture or implications.	Good judgment, usually sees whole picture, but has blind spots in some areas.	Excellent judgment, very few mistakes over the years.

Feelings and interrelationships

5. Authority, has the feeling that he or she belongs in boss's role.	Bends over backward to please, can't give direction or control.	Can take charge when chips are down and become boss, but doesn't like to.	Doesn't apologize for being boss, but feels arrived at position by luck and is thus tentative.	Feels deserves to be boss, earned it, but also feels many others could do as well.	A "natural" in position. Takes full charge. Reasonably certain will do it well and probably better than most.
6. Activity, takes a vigorous orientation to problems and needs of the organization.	Reactive, moves when prodded. Often does not want to know information.	On occasion takes steps, but most often after having procrastinated and frustrated subordinates.	Attacks problems in fairly secure arenas, but takes little risk. Subordinates feel "not going any place."	Attacks problems tactically from new positions and consolidates forces. Subordinates willing to follow.	Attacks problems strategically with well-defined targets. Plans long-term, step-by-step, inexorable advance ahead of competition.
7. Achievement, oriented toward organization's success rather than personal aggrandizement.	Wants to achieve, but passions don't match competence.	Great desire, but not willing to put out full effort for maximum achievement.	Intense wish to achieve that overflows into full effort, but competes too harshly and abrasively. May be ruthless. Strong need to control others.	Very motivated to achieve. Needs much external recognition, perquisites; feels defeated if not chosen. Doesn't need to over-control. Achievements are seen as personal, not organization's.	Very motivated to move upward as recognition of competence. May be disappointed if not chosen but not hungry for applause. Organization's achievements are seen as personal achievements.

Table 9-1 (continued)

8. Sensitivity, able to perceive subtleties of others' feelings.	Obtuse, can't read people's faces or their feelings between the lines of what they say.	Slow on the uptake. Dimly perceives feelings, but most often after the fact.	Picks up feelings and reads body movements, but sometimes too glibly, which may result in seeing feelings as superficial and manipulatable.	Anticipates responses and picks up group feelings. Aware more than most of the subtle cues, but second-guesses own responses to them.	Master at sensing feelings, anticipating them, and taking them seriously.
9. Involvement, sees oneself as a participating member of an organization.	Never leaves desk, won't go into the field	Occasionally will appear in the field for ceremonial occasions.	Gets out sporadically, reluctantly, and perfunctorily, and doesn't learn much.	Goes into field regularly but not easily. Sees and touches, but is felt to be distant by employees. Has difficulty drawing people out.	Allocates serious, continuing time to field visits. Mixes with employees, seeking information on their problems. Summarizes findings for employees and managers. Has finger on the pulse of the organization.
10. Maturity, has good relationships with authority figures.	Still an adolescent, always challenging bosses and resisting authority.	Armed truce with bosses, speaks up in hostile fashion under guise of honesty or tries to manipulate bosses.	Hard to predict. Sometimes has easy relationships, sometimes uncomfortable, depending on kind of boss.	Usually does well with bosses unless defensiveness is exacerbated by criticism or rivalry.	Works well with authority figures. Uniformly praised by all bosses for smoothness of working relationships with them.
11. Interdependence, accepts appropriate dependency needs of others as well as of him or herself.	Needs continuous direction and well-defined structure.	Can stand alone for a while, but needs to know higher authority is there to fall back on.	Insists on standing alone and denies need for others.	Cooperative, participative but doesn't move ahead of group. Can stand alone but not comfortable doing so.	Stands on own but invites information, criticism, and cooperation from others. Can yield temporarily to lead of more competent, specialized person without feeling loss of leadership role.
12. Articulateness, makes a good impression.	Clearly upset even when presenting reports in small meetings.	Can present reports but doesn't inspire excitement or confidence. Often displays nervous behavior.	Can make a decent presentation but it's hard work. Doesn't read audience well, seems somehow removed	Handles him or herself well in public, but has difficulty dealing with hostile questions and unfriendly audiences.	Extremely presentable, has a wide-ranging vocabulary. Inspires audience confidence, senses audience moods. Respected by peers for verbalizing and presenting their problems.
13. Stamina, has physical as well as mental energy.	Low level of involvement and enthusiasm, so runs down fast.	Often starts projects energetically but doesn't maintain interest.	Can work through a significant problem at good energy level.	High level of energy. Requires normal battery recharging.	Consistent high energy level. Always at the ready. Doesn't seem to run out of steam, paces him or herself well.
14. Adaptability, manages stress well.	Doesn't tolerate stress well. Many physical, personal, and family symptoms.	Can take stress if supported by others. Worries a lot about what might happen.	Does reasonably well under bursts of stress but not long, sustained pressures. Worries in a healthy way about solutions to problems.	Can take sustained pressure with normal symptoms. Has effective coping devices, such as consultation with others and taking time off.	Takes whatever comes down the pike and seems to thrive on it.

15. Sense of humor, doesn't take self too seriously.	Can't laugh at anything. Somber, forbidding, cold.	Can crack a smile once in a while. Humor limited to a few dimensions of behavior.	Laughs too easily at everything. Sometimes laughs inappropriately to ease own tension. Immature raconteur.	Occasional sparkle of wit. Not easily spontaneous but can laugh heartily at times. Has to work at telling a humorous story but is pleasant company.	Warm affectionate humor. Stories appropriate to place and position. Eases tensions naturally. Is welcome company.

Outward behavior characteristics

16. Vision, is clear about progression of his or her own life and career, as well as where the organization should go.	Takes no interest in career, content to move along in the managerial current.	Has poorly defined, almost unrecognized, personal goals.	Broad goals, not clearly delineated, not necessarily related to organizational goals.	Well-defined goals, but behavior suggests that the personal agenda, for which organization is a device, is paramount.	Well defined goals, consistent with organization's needs and values, constantly pursued.
17. Perseverance, able to stick to a task and see it through regardless of the difficulties encountered.	Loses interest fast.	Loses interest when encounters resistance or frustration.	Sustains interest as long as novelty or stimulation continues.	Sustains interest in face of discouragement, but gradually loses zest and optimism.	Keeps looking for ways around obstacles. Maintains optimism out of confidence a solution will be found.
18. Personal organizaton, has good sense of time.	Poorly organized; doesn't recognize priorities or keep track of information.	Organization and priorities erratic. Sometimes on top of things but easily thrown off.	Reasonably well-organized. Priorities sometimes questionable. Allows intrusion which eats time. Can answer questions but takes time to dig out information.	Well-organized. Can readily get information but doesn't have massive recall. Priorities appropriate. Governs own time.	Meticulously organized. Makes every minute count. Retrieves information readily, both from own head and organization.
19. Integrity, has a well-established value system, which has been tested in various ways in the past.	Chameleon. Can't really be trusted. Others' opinions have more weight than his or her own.	Variable. Usually responsible, but may give in under bottom-line pressure.	Ethical, but sometimes rationalizes decisions in favor of bottom line.	High standards. Struggles with ethical gray areas. Usually comes down on prudent side, doesn't shade decisions.	Beyond reproach, sometimes almost to point of rigidity.
20. Social responsibility, appreciates the need to assume leadership with respect to that responsibility.	No recognition of executive's public role or wish to fill it.	Recognizes public role but shys away from it. May veto ideas that might lead to taking it.	Recognizes role and wants to fill it out of obligation, but has no significant personal interest in it.	Recognizes executive responsibility and contributes, but in secondary roles.	Recognizes responsibility and relishes it as opportunity. Displays active leadership.

Source: Harry Levinson, "Criteria for Choosing Chief Executives," *Harvard Business Review,* 58 (July/August 1980), 114–16.

maintained legitimately; that leaders obtain their positions by some means in which the voice of the membership is not predominant; that members are at least minimally interested in carrying out their responsibilities and that leader-follower interactions can influence their behavior; and that leaders are significant participants in the totality of organizational life.

In complex organizations, leadership is multidimensional, embracing technical, managerial, and institutional levels. Leaders in such settings must direct multiple functions at each level. They must also make an effort to overcome various kinds of "distance" within the organization.

Traditionally, leadership has been studied through two approaches. The traits approach emphasized the personality and aptitudes of individuals who were leaders, in an effort to isolate "leader" characteristics. This conception was followed by the situational approach, which views all organizational circumstances—structural, interpersonal, task-related, value-related, and so on—as crucial to the kind of leadership that comes to exist. Currently a combination of the two approaches, with emphasis on the situational, is most common in studies of leadership.

Variations in group situations may significantly affect leader effectiveness. Factors in the group situation important in this regard are position power of the leader, task structure of the group, and leader-member personal relationships. Leadership appears to be most effective where a well-liked, well-respected leader occupies a high position in a group with clearly structured tasks. Under such circumstances, leaders are best advised to be directive, giving clear instructions, rather than democratic and nondirective. Where position power is weak, tasks not clearly defined, and personal relationships not as positive, leaders should be less directive and more democratic. To be effective, leadership must vary with circumstances in the group and the work situation.

The purpose of examining the tasks of leadership is to illuminate the many facets of a leader's role. "Leader as director" refers to the challenge of bringing some unity of purpose to the organization's members. "Leader as motivator" is a key task, centering on devices such as tangible benefits, positive social interaction, work interest, encouragement by job supervisors, and leadership that is self-confident, persuasive, fair, and supportive. "Leader as coordinator and integrator" involves bringing some order to the multitude of functions within a complex organization. "Leader as catalyst and innovator" is a formalized conception of the "spark plug" role in a group setting. As part of the catalyst role, a leader is also expected to introduce innovations into an organization. There are numerous difficulties that limit the leadership's ability to innovate successfully internally. "Leader as gladiator" requires engaging in advocacy for, and defense of, the organization in the external environment. "Leader as manager of crisis" involves coping with both immediate and longer-term difficulties, more serious than routine managerial challenges. Current fiscal pressures on public organizations have spawned the need for "cutback management" in many places, forcing leaders to use a variety of new tactics. Simultaneously they must strive to maintain organizational morale and performance levels, while holding to a minimum the negative effects of organizational decline.

What makes a good leader? Among other things, an effort to convey the leader's respect for members; a willingness to hear and respond to feelings and opinions of members; a democratic style and relationship to members; attributes such as fairness, giving credit, readiness to discuss problems, and keeping members informed; consistency and equity in defining standards and judging work performance; and avoidance of such pitfalls as empire-building (by either leaders or followers) and cronyism.

Virtually all of these tasks face obstacles to their full accomplishment—in the organization's dynamics, the mix of members, and the nature of the external environment. It is not possible to construct leadership guidelines that will cover every leadership situation. Recent research has reemphasized the importance of personality, particularly as it relates to leader behavior. While leadership operates within many contemporary constraints, it still occupies a place of considerable importance in organizations.

NOTES

1. Ralph M. Stogdill, *Handbook of Leadership: A Survey of Theory and Research* (New York: The Free Press, 1974), pp. 167–69.
2. See chapter 6 for a summary of several important studies concerning the nature of leadership and its significance. See also Philip Selznick, *Leadership in Administration* (New York: Harper & Row, 1957); Fred E. Fiedler, *Leader Attitudes and Group Effectiveness* (Urbana, Ill.: University of Illinois Press, 1958); Robert H. Guest, *Organizational Change: The Effects of Successful Leadership* (Homewood, Ill.: Dorsey and Irwin, 1962); Stephen R. Graubard and Gerald Holton, eds., *Excellence and Leadership in a Democracy* (New York: Columbia University Press, 1962); Fred E. Fiedler, *A Theory of Leadership Effectiveness* (New York: McGraw-Hill, 1967); Fred E. Fiedler and Martin Chemers, *Leadership and Effective Management* (Glenview, Ill.: Scott, Foresman, 1974); and Stogdill, *Handbook of Leadership*.
3. Fiedler, in *A Theory of Leadership Effectiveness*, discusses varieties of work situations as they relate to leadership. See especially his chapter 7.
4. James D. Thompson, *Organizations in Action* (New York: McGraw-Hill, 1967), p. 10. This discussion relies on Thompson's treatment of the Parsons formulation; see also Talcott Parsons, *Structure and Process in Modern Societies* (New York: The Free Press, 1960).
5. Thompson, *Organizations in Action*, p. 10.
6. Ibid.
7. Ibid., p. 11.
8. Ibid.
9. Ibid.
10. Ibid. (emphasis added).

11. Mary Parker Follett, ''The Giving of Orders,'' in Jay M. Shafritz and Philip H. Whitbeck, eds., *Classics of Organization Theory* (Oak Park, Ill.: Moore Publishing, 1978), pp. 43–51; reprinted from Henry C. Metcalf, ed., *Scientific Foundations of Business Administration* (Baltimore: Williams & Wilkins, 1926).

12. Ibid., p. 44.

13. For more extensive treatment of leadership in organizations, see Martin M. Chemers, ''The Social, Organizational, and Cultural Context of Effective Leadership,'' and James G. Hunt, ''Organizational Leadership: The Contingency Paradigm and Its Challenges,'' in Barbara Kellerman, ed., *Leadership: Multidisciplinary Perspectives* (Englewood Cliffs, N.J.: Prentice-Hall, 1984), pp. 91–112 and 113–38, respectively. See also James G. Hunt, Dian-Marie Hosking, Chester A. Schriesheim, and Rosemary Stuart, eds., *Leaders and Managers: International Perspectives on Managerial Behavior and Leadership* (Elmsford, N.Y.: Pergamon, 1984).

14. Stogdill, *Handbook of Leadership*, p. 64.

15. See Fiedler, *A Theory of Leadership Effectiveness*, p. 247.

16. Fred E. Fiedler, ''Style or Circumstance: The Leadership Enigma,'' *Psychology Today*, 2 (March 1969), 39–43.

17. Ibid., p. 41.

18. Ibid., p. 42.

19. See Anthony Downs, *Inside Bureaucracy* (Boston: Little, Brown, 1967), p. 88.

20. Stogdill, *Handbook of Leadership*, pp. 270–71.

21. Lawrence B. Mohr, ''The Concept of Organizational Goal,'' *American Political Science Review*, 67 (June 1973), 470–81, at p. 474.

22. See, for example, Stogdill, *Handbook of Leadership*; and the discussion of authoritarian leadership style in the Iowa experiment, in Ralph White and Ronald Lippitt, ''Leader Behavior and Member Reaction in Three 'Social Climates,' '' in Dorwin Cartwright and Alvin Zander, eds., *Group Dynamics: Research and Theory*, 3rd ed. (New York: Harper & Row, 1968), pp. 527–53.

23. Fiedler, *A Theory of Leadership Effectiveness*, p. 236.

24. Stogdill, *Handbook of Leadership*, p. 327.

25. Ibid., pp. 327–30.

26. Guest, *Organizational Change*, p. 131.

27. Ibid., p. 130.

28. Fiedler, *A Theory of Leadership Effectiveness*, p. 147. See the discussion, above, of situational factors.

29. For a case study of the importance of bureaucratic routines, see Graham Allison, *Essence of Decision: Explaining the Cuban Missile Crisis* (Boston: Little, Brown, 1971). Consideration is given to problems of innovation in, among others, Warren G. Bennis, ed., *American Bureaucracy* (New Brunswick, N.J.: Transaction Books, 1970), pp. 111–87, especially pp. 135–64; and Guest, *Organizational Change*. It should be noted that leadership can just as easily resist innovation desired by members as the other way around. Under the circumstance of leaders resisting innovation sought by followers, the task of ''leader as director'' will be considerably frustrated as leadership and followership goals grow further apart.

30. Anthony Downs cites the work of Georg Simmel and Lewis Coser in this regard. See *Inside Bureaucracy*, p. 105.

31. For an excellent overview of the roots and nature of fiscal stress in American government (especially local governments), see Charles H. Levine, ed., *Managing Fiscal Stress: The Crisis in the Public Sector* (Chatham, N.J.: Chatham House, 1980). This discussion relies on Levine, "Organizational Decline and Cutback Management," pp. 13–30 of that volume. Other useful sources in the growing literature on cutback management include Robert D. Behn, "How to Terminate a Public Policy: A Dozen Hints for the Would-Be Policy Terminator," *Policy Analysis*, 4 (Summer 1978), 393–413; John J. McTighe, "Management Strategies to Deal with Shrinking Resources," *Public Administration Review*, 39 (January/February 1979), 86–90; Charles H. Levine, "More on Cutback Management: Hard Questions for Hard Times," *Public Administration Review*, 39 (March/April 1979), 179–83; and Carol W. Lewis and Anthony T. Logalbo, "Cutback Principles and Practices: A Checklist for Managers," *Public Administration Review*, 40 (March/April 1980), 184–88. See also chapter 13.
32. Levine, "Organizational Decline and Cutback Management," in Levine, ed., *Managing Fiscal Stress*, p. 13 (emphasis added).
33. Ibid., p. 14.
34. Ibid., pp. 20–21.
35. For a discussion of how teacher expectations may shape student performance, see William Ryan, *Blaming the Victim*, rev. ed. (New York: Random House, 1976), chapter 2.
36. See, among others, Peter F. Drucker, *Management: Tasks, Responsibilities, Practices* (New York: Harper & Row, 1974), chapter 38.
37. See Stogdill, *Handbook of Leadership*, pp. 365–70.
38. Ibid., p. 379.
39. For more on leadership effectiveness, see Paul Hersey and John E. Stinson, eds., *Perspectives in Effectiveness* (Athens, Ohio: Center for Leadership Studies, Ohio University, and Ohio University Press, 1980); and Harry Levinson, *Executive* (Cambridge, Mass.: Harvard University Press, 1981).
40. Victor A. Thompson, "How Scientific Management Thwarts Innovation," in Warren G. Bennis, ed., *American Bureaucracy*, pp. 121–33, especially pp. 123–24. See also Thompson's *Bureaucracy and Innovation* (University, Ala.: University of Alabama Press, 1969).
41. See, for example, Harry Levinson, "Criteria for Choosing Chief Executives," *Harvard Business Review*, 58 (July/August 1980), 113–20.

SUGGESTED READINGS

Drucker, Peter F. *Management: Tasks, Responsibilities, Practices*. New York: Harper & Row, 1974, chapter 38.

Fiedler, Fred E. *Leader Attitudes and Group Effectiveness*. Urbana, Ill.: University of Illinois Press, 1958.

———. "Style or Circumstance: The Leadership Enigma." *Psychology Today*, 2 (March 1969), 39–43.

———. *A Theory of Leadership Effectiveness*. New York: McGraw-Hill, 1967.

_____, and Martin Chemers. *Leadership and Effective Management*. Glenview, Ill.: Scott, Foresman, 1974.

Graubard, Stephen R., and Gerald Holton, eds. *Excellence and Leadership in a Democracy*. New York: Columbia University Press, 1962.

Guest, Robert H. *Organizational Change: The Effects of Successful Leadership*. Homewood, Ill.: Dorsey and Irwin, 1962.

Kellerman, Barbara, ed. *Leadership: Multidisciplinary Perspectives*. Englewood Cliffs, N.J.: Prentice-Hall, 1984.

Selznick, Philip. *Leadership in Administration*. New York: Harper & Row, 1957.

Stogdill, Ralph M. *Handbook of Leadership: A Survey of Theory and Research*. New York: The Free Press, 1974.

White, Ralph, and Ronald Lippitt. "Leader Behavior and Member Reaction in Three 'Social Climates.'" In Dorwin Cartwright and Alvin Zander, eds. *Group Dynamics: Research and Theory*, 3rd ed. New York: Harper & Row, 1968, pp. 527–53.

PART FOUR

Administrative Processes

This section covers five functions central to the conduct of public administration. These are (1) public personnel administration, (2) collective bargaining in the public sector, (3) the budgetary process, (4) managing public policies and programs, and (5) the regulatory process. Each of these represents a fundamentally important set of activities in administrative practice.

The personnel function, treated in chapter 10, concerns, among other things, criteria and methods for hiring individuals into the public service in national, state, and local government; for promoting and transferring them within the ranks; and, on occasion, for dismissing them from their jobs. Politically charged issues such as veterans' preference, patronage, and affirmative action pose questions that must be answered within the domain of public personnel administration.

Collective bargaining in the public sector (chapter 11) has emerged in the past quarter-century as a new and prominent emphasis in managing public organizations. At all levels of government, but especially in state and local agencies, public employee unionization and bargaining occupy a place of importance in politics and government generally, as well as in personnel administration. Issues pertaining to effective management, employee rights, productivity, compensation, and political accountability have been generated by these developments.

The budgetary process, discussed in chapter 12, is obviously important because of rising costs of government and political conflict over allocation of government funds. It is important also because control over major aspects of budgeting represents crucial political power. In the past half-century the political stakes in the budgetary game have risen steadily.

Chapter 13 explores management of public policies and programs. This function has always been important, but in recent years growing emphasis has been placed on particular managerial activities and concerns. These include planning, program analysis, implementation, program evaluation, productivity, and (most recently) cutback management in an era of fiscal stress. This area reflects more sophisticated and systematic approaches to management, but policy problems have also become far more complex.

The regulatory process (chapter 14) has become one of the most pervasive, complex, and controversial aspects of governmental activity in recent years. At the heart of the process in the national government are the formally designated independent regulatory agencies, with legal responsibility for setting and enforcing rules and regulations that govern the operations of thousands of private industries and businesses. However, government regulation is now carried on by a host of other agencies as well, with impact on virtually every aspect of American economic and social life.

10

Public Personnel Administration

FROM the time the first executive branch agency opened its doors, even before ratification of the Constitution, the personnel function has been a vital part of American public administration. It has evolved from a relatively obscure, often routine function of government to a prominent, frequently controversial area of administrative practice. Since the early 1800s there has been considerable variation in the rules and regulations governing personnel policies and practices.

Changes have come in response to shifts in the values and assumptions of society pertaining to proper methods of filling government positions. Three values predominant in our approach to government have had strong, but shifting, impact on personnel practices. They are: (1) the quest for strong executive leadership, (2) the desire for a politically neutral, competent public service, and (3) the belief that the composition of the public service should mirror the demographic composition of American society.[1] Strong executive leadership and greater demographic representativeness have often occurred together. For example, when a strong mayor practices patronage in hiring, drawing political supporters into local bureaucracies from an ethnically diverse majority coalition, it has the effect of increasing political loyalty to the mayor in the ranks while enhancing representativeness. In such a case, both *representativeness* of social groupings and *representation* of the political majority are served through administrative appointments (see chapter 15 for more on these concepts).

On the other hand, the quest for politically neutral competence—involving formal disregard of political *party* ties in filling administrative posts—has usually been carried on in opposition to leadership-and-representativeness advocates. For example, supporters of civil service (merit) reform in the late 1800s and early 1900s harshly attacked both political ''bosses'' and the patronage systems that enabled them to dominate many states and cities. Significantly, most merit reformers also feared the potential influence of ethnic immigrants in many boss-run cities; part of their fervor was based on a strong desire to exclude the immigrants from a share of political power. In short, the reformers opposed representativeness for emerging potential rivals on the political (and social) horizon.

A more positive case for politically neutral competence rests on the assumption that public managers should be hired and promoted on the basis of their job-related skills and knowledge. Advocates of this approach contend that public programs are better administered (and public funds better spent) if those in charge possess demonstrated competence in the particular program area, management expertise, and "institutional memory"— the ability to profitably apply the lessons of past experience to current tasks. Those holding this view believe that considerations such as party loyalty—especially in hiring decisions—inevitably interfere with the quest for true managerial competence.

In response, patronage advocates stress the importance of a chief executive's being able to rely on the loyalty of his or her subordinates throughout the executive branch. While not dismissing the importance of competence, those favoring political loyalty as a key factor in making personnel decisions argue that reliance on neutral competence creates public bureaucracies largely immune to control by elected political leaders. This issue has been a part of the politics of public administration virtually since 1789, though debated more intensely at some times than at others. Since the mid-1970s, during the Carter and Reagan administrations, the debate has intensified once again. (We will explore this topic more fully, later in the chapter.)

Public personnel administration can be defined briefly as "the organizations, policies, and processes used to match the needs of governmental agencies and the people who staff those agencies."[2] Personnel administration in the public sector differs from that in business and industry in important respects, most prominently the necessity of conducting the personnel function within constraints set by other formal political institutions, by agency clienteles, professional associations of employees and other interest groups, and by political parties and the mass media.[3] Public personnel administration is no longer regarded (as it once was) as separate from the general processes of public policy making, for two reasons. First, decisions made in the personnel process have a direct bearing on who makes and implements government policies. Second, personnel decisions have themselves become policy matters, reflecting demands for employee rights, affirmative action in minority hiring, and traditional merit reforms, among others. Political scientist Joseph Cayer has noted that "personnel policies and practices are, in part, an expression of political values,"[4] and the political dimension of the field has taken on increasing importance in recent years.

Finally, the sheer size and scope of contemporary government make personnel concerns more important than ever before. Although the issue of big government is not directly tied to personnel policies, political pressures for reducing or controlling bureaucratic size affect personnel administrators and some of their decisions. A Gallup poll in the late 1970s found that 67 percent of those surveyed felt that the national government employs too many people; an earlier survey had found that 53 percent of the respondents favored reducing the number of national government employees by 5 percent per year over a three-year period.[5]

The image of a bloated national bureaucracy, however, is not completely accurate. First, in the period 1951–1983 civilian employment in the national government remained relatively stable, while state and local government employment increased dramatically (see Table 10-1). Total state-local employment more than tripled, increasing from about 4 million to just over 13 million, both full-time and part-time. The figure for "full-time equivalent" employees—all actual full-time personnel, plus the number of people who would have been needed (full time) to work the hours put in by part-time employees—was just under 11 million (see Table 10-2). During the same period, the number of national government civilian employees fluctuated, ranging from 2.35 million in the late 1950s to just under 3 million a decade later (full-time equivalent: about 2.6 million). Second, the number of national civilian employees per 1,000 population also fluctuated considerably in that same period. From a high of 16.3 in 1952, it dipped to 12.8 in the mid-1960s, then rose sharply in the late 1960s before beginning another decline that brought the ratio down to 12.4 in 1980—and it has gone still lower in the wake of concerted efforts by the Reagan administration to reduce the national government's size and scope. Thus, increases in national government civilian employment clearly have not kept pace with population growth.

These figures, however, do not truly reflect all that has happened in the past thirty-five years, in terms of the scope of national government activity, or of the numbers of public employees working under funding, mandates, or contracts of the national government. In 1978, Joseph Califano, then Secretary of HEW, observed that while his department employed some 144,000 people, it indirectly paid the salaries of about 980,000 more in state and local governments, through myriad grant-in-aid programs. Furthermore, it has been estimated that if one were to add together all personnel dependent on national government funds—state and local personnel, those in the private sector employed and paid through national government contracts, consultants, and the like—the total payroll would include about *8 million* people.[6] If one considers the scope and impact of national government employees in this light, combined with grant programs and expanded national regulatory responsibilities, then public concern about the size of government bureaucracy is not entirely groundless; it may even be

Table 10-1
GOVERNMENT CIVILIAN EMPLOYMENT AND POPULATION, 1951–1983 (FISCAL YEAR)

Fiscal Year	Government civilian employment				Population	
	National executive branch (thousands)	State and local governments (thousands)	All governmental units (thousands)	National as percent of all governmental units	Total United States (thousands)	National employment per 1,000 population
1951	2,456	4,031	6,487	37.9	154,878	15.9
1952	2,574	4,134	6,708	38.4	157,553	16.3
1953	2,532	4,282	6,814	37.2	160,184	15.8
1954	2,382	4,552	6,934	34.4	163,026	14.6
1955	2,371	4,728	7,099	33.4	165,931	14.3
1956	2,372	5,064	7,436	31.9	168,903	14.0
1957	2,391	5,380	7,771	30.8	171,984	13.9
1958	2,355	5,630	7,985	29.5	174,882	13.5
1959	2,355	5,806	8,161	28.8	177,830	13.2
1960	2,371	6,073	8,444	28.1	180,671	13.1
1961	2,407	6,295	8,702	27.7	183,691	13.1
1962	2,485	6,533	9,018	27.6	186,538	13.3
1963	2,490	6,834	9,324	26.7	189,242	13.2
1964	2,469	7,236	9,705	25.4	191,889	12.9
1965	2,496	7,683	10,179	24.5	194,303	12.8
1966	2,664	8,259	10,923	24.4	196,560	13.6
1967	2,877	8,730	11,607	24.8	198,712	14.5
1968	2,951	9,141	12,092	24.4	200,706	14.7
1969	2,980	9,496	12,476	23.9	202,677	14.7
1970	2,944	9,869	12,813	23.0	205,052	14.4
1971	2,883	10,372	13,255	21.8	207,661	13.9

Year						
1972	2,823	10,896	20.6	13,719	209,896	13.4
1973	2,775	11,286	19.7	14,061	211,909	13.1
1974	2,847	11,713	19.6	14,560	213,854	13.3
1975	2,848	12,114	19.0	14,962	215,973	13.2
1976	2,832	12,282	18.7	15,114	218,035	13.0
1977	2,789	12,704	18.0	15,493	220,904	12.6
1978	2,820	13,050	17.8	15,870	223,278	12.6
1979	2,823	13,359	17.4	16,182	225,779	12.5
1980	2,821	13,542	17.2	16,363	228,361	12.4
1981	2,806	13,274	17.5	16,080	230,523	12.2
1982	2,768	13,142	17.4	15,910	232,702	11.9
1983	2,819	13,115	17.7	15,934	234,875	12.0

Sources: Adapted from U.S. Office of Management and Budget, *Special Analyses: Budget of the United States Government, Fiscal Year 1981* (Washington, D.C.: U.S. Government Printing Office, 1980), p. 288; *Special Analyses: Budget of the United States Government, Fiscal Year 1982* (Washington, D.C.: U.S. Government Printing Office, 1981), p. 288; and *Special Analyses: Budget of the United States Government, Fiscal Year 1985* (Washington, D.C.: U.S. Government Printing Office, 1984), p. I-12 (footnotes omitted). Population data for 1980–1983 were the latest available from the U.S. Bureau of the Census as of early 1985.

Table 10-2
STATE AND LOCAL GOVERNMENT EMPLOYMENT*

| | Full-time Equivalent Employment | |
Function	Number	Percentage
TOTAL	10,885,000	100.0
Education	5,304,000	48.7
Local schools	3,971,000	36.5
Institutions of higher education	1,160,000	10.7
Other education (including libraries)	173,000	1.6
Hospitals	1,059,000	9.7
Police protection	606,000	5.6
Highways	505,000	4.6
General control	416,000	3.8
Public welfare	376,000	3.5
Correction	297,000	2.7
Financial administration	275,000	2.5
Local utilities other than water supply	258,000	2.4
Health	230,000	2.1
Local fire protection	230,000	2.1
Transit	177,000	1.6
Parks and recreation	170,000	1.6
Natural resources	168,000	1.5
Water supply	128,000	1.2
Sanitation other than sewerage	107,000	1.0
Social insurance administration	102,000	0.9
Sewerage	98,000	0.9
Housing and community development	90,000	0.8
All other	289,000	2.7

*As of October 1983.

Source: U.S. Bureau of the Census, *Public Employment in 1983* (Washington, D.C.: U.S. Government Printing Office, 1984), Series GE83, No. 1, p. 3

somewhat misplaced, in that government *roles* have changed more substantially. But concern about sheer size persists, as reflected in Gallup polls of the late 1970s and by popular support for President Reagan's efforts early in his term to limit, then reduce, the size of the "Washington bureaucracy." All this clearly can affect personnel management.

In state and local governments, the personnel picture is a bit more complicated because of substantial numbers of employees in public education. In 1983, nearly half of all state and local government "full-time equivalent" employees were working in primary, secondary, or higher education.[7] State employees (noneducation) accounted for another 19 percent, and the remaining one-third were noneducation employees in city, county, and other local governments[8] (see Table 10-2). Expansion of public employment at the state-local level between 1951 and 1983 was due in large part to a sharp rise in educational employment during the 1960s, but other state-local functional areas have now begun to catch up.

Another changing feature of public personnel administration, not reflected in numerical counts of government employees, is the rapidly shifting nature of the work force.[9] Particularly in the national government, increasing numbers of bureaucrats are more specialized, better educated, and better paid than many of their predecessors. For example, the 1960s and 1970s saw an increase of more than 50 percent in the number of engineers in the national bureaucracy, to 98,931; the number of computer specialists rose 600 percent from 1960 to 1980, to 46,361; attorneys number 15,532, almost twice the number of two decades ago; and the number of social scientists, psychologists, and welfare workers has risen more than 230 percent, to 58,166. As a consequence, the national executive branch is "less and less an army of up-through-the-ranks paper pushers and clerks. Its fundamental mission has changed; the balance has shifted toward well-credentialed and highly paid professionals and technocrats."[10]

The national government's role—and its relationship to states, localities, and private consultants and contractors—has been fundamentally affected as well. It has been suggested that state and local governments, and private entities contracting with the national government, are "increasingly the *foot soldiers* who actually turn [national] brainstorms into public reality"[11] (recall a similar implication in chapter 5, regarding increased centralization in intergovernmental relations). Such expertise is not confined to the national government, but wherever it is found its significance has become unmistakable—and related much more to the expanding *role* of government than simply to numbers of people on a government payroll. We shall deal further with the rise of professionals in the public service later in this chapter.

EVOLUTION OF PUBLIC PERSONNEL ADMINISTRATION

The evolution of public personnel administration, from 1789 to the present, did not occur in a social or political vacuum. Rather, development of the personnel function and of specific practices was related to other changes in public administration and society. We shall discuss six major phases in the evolution of personnel administration, focusing mainly on the national government. The categorization of time periods is that of public administration scholar Frederick Mosher.[12]

Government by "Gentlemen," 1789–1829

The period 1789–1829 was characterized by limited political participation; consequently, those in government service came almost exclusively from the participating segments of society (wealthier, white, male, landowners). Government positions were filled on a basis that blended patronage and merit appointment. That is, political loyalty to the chief executive was a major consideration, just as in modern patronage arrangements. But in addition, "proper" social standing and advanced education—being a "member of the establishment"[13]—were also necessary. In this forty-year period, most government personnel were hired through a "patronage of the elite" system. Both the Federalists and the Democratic-Republicans supported this arrangement, and throughout most of the 1820s, "tests of loyalty, regional considerations, preference for veterans, and consultation with Congress remained factors in public service staffing."[14]

There is evidence, also, that "[k]inship as well as class helped to assure the elite character of the early civil service."[15] As political scientist Michael Nelson has noted:

> Forty percent of [President John] Adams' high-level appointees were relatives of other high-level appointees in his or Washington's administration, and though Jefferson made a point of selecting Republicans, so were 34 percent of his, including 22 percent who shared common kinship with earlier Federalist appointees. Some subsecretarial American civil servants, like their British counterparts, asserted not only a property right to their offices, but a *right of inheritance* as well.[16]

Thus *nepotism* (family favoritism or ties) also played a role in this first phase of government personnel management, though (like patronage) it was limited to the "gentry" of American society.

Government by the "Common Man," 1829–1883

Political ferment intensified during the 1820s, focusing on greatly expanding the right to participate in processes of government. In this period eleven new states were admitted to the Union—nine in the West—and political parties were being built up in all parts of the country. The traditions of the frontier, where equality was a strong norm and no established aristocracy ruled the political scene, permeated the rest of society. In many states and localities, egalitarianism and an interest in strengthening party organizations merged in the form of extending the right to vote to the "common man." Partisan patronage—blunt, straightforward, without apology—was born in many western state and local governments, and was used deliberately to build up loyal party followings. In the late 1820s this approach spread to the national government.[17]

The individual most commonly associated with this broad movement for democratization was Andrew Jackson. In 1828 Jackson ran for president and won handily, ushering in an era in which "establishment" credentials were not only unnecessary but also an affront to "ordinary citizens," who looked upon the aristocracy in government as hostile to their political interests. This early version of populist politics—supporting the "little people" or, simply, "the people" against those with wealth, title, education, and political power—was to be echoed in numerous political movements in subsequent years, in every instance demonstrating the link between strong executive leadership and some form of political representativeness.

Jacksonian democracy and later populist movements shared a belief that common folk were capable of discharging the responsibilities of public office. President Jackson inaugurated a full-scale spoils system of personnel appointment, following the principle "to the victors belong the spoils of victory." Government jobs were offered to those with the "right" political loyalties, without major emphasis on job-related competence, since "everybody was competent to perform public service." Jackson is remembered as the father of the patronage system, though Thomas Jefferson was the first president to view partisan loyalty as an important criterion in the selection of public servants.[18] Moreover, Jackson insisted on some competence in government employees and was not nearly as abusive in his patronage tactics as were some later presidents (notably James Buchanan and Abraham Lincoln).[19]

A rising tide of political protest against the spoils system began to make itself felt during the 1860s and 1870s. In the late 1870s, civil service reform associations were formed in thirteen states, and in 1881 they banded together as the National Civil Service Reform League. Personnel expert O. Glenn Stahl suggests that four developments were crucial in this period: (1) the persistence of a group of intellectual idealists, led by George William Curtis, who kept up a drumbeat of reform agitation during the 1870s; (2) the formation of the National Civil Service Reform League; (3) the preparation of a report on the British civil service by Dorman B. Eaton, at the request of President Rutherford Hayes; and (4) the assassination in 1881 of President James Garfield by a frustrated officer-seeker who also was mentally ill.[20] Also, as noted earlier, fear of the growing political power of ethnic immigrants was a motivating force behind a reform that served to limit ethnics' access to political influence.

Garfield's assassination was the catalyst for definitive action, and in 1883 Congress passed the Civil Service (Pendleton) Act. This act created a bipartisan commission, responsible to the president, that was to administer open competitive examinations for civil service positions. In principle, the new system was to afford an equal chance for all to compete for government employment, but practical, job-related skill was required to actually obtain a position. That was a far cry from the partisan favoritism of the preceding half-century. It also held out some hope of ending massive turnover of personnel at each change of presidential administration, the exalting of inexperience, and day-to-day partiality in the routine business of government. Finally, in making politically neutral competence a major criterion for government service, the act deemphasized both strong executive leadership and representativeness.

Government by the "Good," 1883–1906

The period immediately following passage of the Pendleton Act was one of intensive change in public personnel administration. The most direct effect was creation of the Civil Service Commission to oversee the new system under rules and regulations it established. In a broader sense, the period 1883–1906 was one of consolidation, when the successful drive for merit reform had to be translated into workable day-to-day arrangements. The moral fervor of the civil-service reformers left an imprint in several respects. One was the fact that efficiency in government referred less to any systematic managerial concerns than it did to ending corruption in hiring practices. (Other dimensions of efficiency as a management objective emerged only after 1906.)[21] Government efficiency came to be viewed as the opposite of government corruption, and the dichotomy between politics (corruption) and administration (efficient, nonpoliticized processes) took root. As discussed in chapter 2, this distinction has continued to influence perceptions and assumptions concerning American public administration.

Another emphasis of this period was a self-conscious egalitarianism in the new system. There was an attempt to avoid creation of an administrative class in the civil service, and to keep the service open to anyone who could pass the competitive entrance examinations. This meant that no provision was made for those with better education to automatically achieve higher placement in the public service. Not until the 1930s was any major effort made to upgrade the level of education in the bureaucracy, or to ensure that educational preparation counted for something in obtaining national government employment.[22]

Finally, the Civil Service Commission took up the task of insulating the new personnel system against political pressures from Congress and the White House. This meant that the commission itself had to be substantially independent of both the chief executive and the legislature.[23] Initially the commission focused on screening applicants and little else, but as time went on it became active in a wider range of personnel policy making. The presidency of Theodore Roosevelt marked a confirmation of the power and prestige of the commission, and it continued to increase its role in directing personnel policies for the entire executive branch.[24]

At state and local levels, similar stirrings were evident, but the pace of reform was predictably much more uneven. New York and Massachusetts passed civil service legislation in 1883 and 1884, respectively. During the first decade of this century, four more states—Wisconsin, Illinois, Colorado, and New Jersey—followed suit. And between 1910 and 1920, Ohio, California, Connecticut, and Maryland did the same. The other states did not act for at least another fifteen years, though most now have some kind of civil service system in effect (some systems, admittedly, quite a bit more thoroughgoing than others). At the local level a great deal of controversy surrounded efforts to do away with urban political machines (see chapter 3, regarding the politics of organization), but many municipal governments were successfully reformed. In county governments and most other rural entities, civil service reform has come much later, if at all.[25]

Government by the "Efficient," 1906–1937

The major focus of public personnel administration from 1906 to 1937 was maintenance of the merit system of political neutrality, as well as pursuit of efficiency in the management of government programs. The doctrine of separation between politics and administration was in full bloom—and indeed was strengthened—and scientific management exerted increasing influence on both business and public administration. It has been suggested that efficiency was the major conceptual emphasis within a "package" that included goodness, merit, morality, neutrality, and science—a "somewhat inconsistent but soothing amalgam of beliefs."[26]

The Civil Service Commission and agency personnel administrators concentrated on classifying government positions in a rational relationship to one another, and on writing job descriptions and analyses of responsibilities for each position. This made possible extension of merit coverage to a larger number of positions, the percentage of those covered rising from about 45 percent in 1900 to some 80 percent by 1930.[27]

The emphasis on efficiency and neutrality permitted further expansion of seemingly nonpoliticized administrative machinery, which was fully in keeping with prevailing values in both government and society. It also made it possible for Franklin Roosevelt to inherit a government bureaucracy that focused on good, effective management. This was not unimportant, as Roosevelt began increasingly to involve bureaucracy in planning and managing new programs, leading to basic changes in the role of government in American society.

Government by "Administrators," 1937–1955

By 1937, government generally and public administration in particular were seen as spearheading efforts to overcome the effects of the Great Depression. This was a new view of the public service—one of an activist administrative apparatus that was able to respond to Roosevelt's vigorous policy leadership. The enlarged policy-making role of public administrators was directly related to the political initiatives of the Roosevelt administration.

That fact, however, necessitated some change in prevailing thinking about the politics-administration dichotomy. Some began to feel that under a strong president (whom they liked and supported), *political* representativeness in government personnel might not be such a bad thing after all. Further, the possibility that politics and administration might mix to some extent without "polluting" the administrative process gained greater acceptance. Some allowance was made, in principle, for overlap between politics and administration without completely letting go of the idea that administration should be separated from the political process.

Two major reports to the president marked the beginning and end, respectively, of this period. The first was the so-called Brownlow Report, named after the chairman of Roosevelt's Committee on Administrative Management. The Brownlow Report called on the president to assume greater responsibility and authority for directing executive branch activities, and for the centralization and consolidation of responsibility throughout the executive establishment. It also advocated extension of merit protection and favored administrators with broad, general skills as opposed to narrow, overly specialized bureaucrats. One important consequence of the report was an executive order issued by Roosevelt mandating professional personnel administrators for every agency. Another result was that the president began to pay ongoing attention to matters such as directing the bureaucracy, clarifying lines of authority, and defining relationships among the different parts of the executive structure. Yet another consequence, which took longer to be fully recognized, was the growing need to decentralize management of many personnel responsibilities from the Civil Service Commission to agency personnel officers.[28]

The second of these reports was from the second Hoover Commission to President Eisenhower in 1955. Formally known as the Commission on Organization of the Executive Branch of the Government and chaired by former President Herbert Hoover, it followed up on studies conducted by the first Hoover Commission, which had reported to President Truman in 1949. The second Hoover Commission was appointed partly because, after twenty years out of power, the Republicans had captured the White House in 1952 and found themselves facing a bureaucracy founded on principles of political neutrality but populated by many Democrats drawn into national government service during the Roosevelt and Truman presidencies. However, the most notable contributions of the commission were only indirectly of value to President Eisenhower as he wrestled with political problems posed by the bureaucracy.

A general section of the commission's report dealt for the first time with relations between political appointees and career public servants. Among the specific recommendations was the creation of a "Senior Civil Service," comprised of about 3,000 upper-level career executives serving in administrative positions for which their particular skills and competencies were suited, and from which they could transfer into similar positions in other agencies.[29] Until the Senior Executive Service was established in 1978, these elements were never incorporated into general personnel practices in the national government.

The period of government by administrators, in sum, saw the elevation of public personnel administration to a place alongside other managerial tasks of traditional public administration. Accompanying this development was concern for the manner in which expanding governmental responsibilities were discharged, and, in the early 1950s, a growing interest in the individual skills of bureaucratic employees.

Government by "Professionals," 1955 to the Present

The year 1955 saw the establishment of the Federal Service Entrance Examination (FSEE), designed to accomplish several objectives. One was to provide a single point of entry into the U.S. civil service, through a common examination that could be used as a broad basis for personnel decisions. A companion objective was to make it possible for public servants to transfer from one agency to another. As long as each agency had had its own entry and placement tests, it was extremely difficult for a career bureaucrat to be mobile within the public service. Creation of a common entry examination, after which individual agencies could test further for particular skills, increased prospects for mobility. Finally, the FSEE allowed the Civil Service Commission to engage in more systematic recruiting, especially on college and university campuses. Recruitment, in fact, became a conscious activity of the national bureaucracy for the first time in 1955, and until the late 1970s it was still a prominent concern.

The major development since 1955 has been the rise of widespread professionalism in the public service and a partial shift to a career emphasis that differs in significant ways from the traditional civil service emphasis. It is not surprising that demand for professionally trained employees has risen in the government bureaucracy, since it has just about everywhere else. But this development has posed some problems for personnel administration.

For one thing, it has meant that rules and regulations sufficient to cover government employees in the past are no longer flexible enough. As one example, separate salary schedules have had to be established in selected personnel grades for professionals in printing management, engineering and architecture, medicine and nursing, metallurgy, and veterinary medicine, among others. Another salary issue concerns the fact that although total size of the bureaucracy has stabilized or slightly declined in recent years, the cost (mainly in salaries) of running it has risen dramatically, due both to inflation and to a larger proportion of higher-level administrators (with higher salaries) in the civil service. Also, diversity of skills and training among government employees makes it difficult to implement personnel procedures such as job classification and evaluation.

Another effect of professionalism has been the establishment of ties with institutions of higher education that can provide training of needed professionals. Increasingly, universities and colleges have provided applicants for government positions, individuals with both bachelor's and graduate degrees in academic specialties demanded by government agencies. These ties grew stronger as recruitment became more systematic.

Perhaps the most important impact of professionalism on the public service, however, is a largely conceptual one. The most common emphasis since 1883 has been on developing a system of administrative positions that function in a coherent relationship to one another, and on developing in turn necessary procedures for filling those positions on the basis of job-related competence (merit). The emphasis has been on the *job*, the position, and formal responsibilities associated with it. With the rise of professionalization in the public service, however, a second emphasis has developed—an emphasis on the *people* filling government posts and on their *career* needs within their professions. The rise of the latter, which is in basic conflict with the former as a basis of personnel management, has created new stresses in personnel systems.

For example, personnel (and other) administrators must plan for agency needs at the same time that a growing proportion of their employees are pursuing career interests that may take little account of the agency. For another, professional methods and standards may be the employee's chief concern rather than performing a job in accord with *agency* objectives and needs. There is also the strong possibility that loyalty to the ethics of a profession (such as medicine or law) may supersede loyalty to the agency as the principal standard by which professional employees judge their own work and their contributions to the organization.[30] Individual loyalties to widely varying professional standards can create tensions within an agency, and it can be very difficult to deal with these effectively. In sum, contemporary personnel administration must take account of the needs of both public agencies and their professional employees.

Politically, the power of the various professions has become a force to be reckoned with in the administrative process. One important study in the late 1970s identified five major avenues to political power.[31] These are: (1) election or appointment to high office (dominated by lawyers); (2) effective control by an individual profession—if not a near monopoly—of important managerial positions in an agency (for example, educators in the Office of Education, engineers in public works agencies, or Foreign Service officers in the State Department); (3) a professional *presence* in an agency, but without professional *domination* (all agencies have legal counsel, budgeters, planners, and personnel specialists); (4) an ability to generate pressure on decision makers from fellow or allied professionals outside the governmental structure; and (5) an ability to operate through the system of intergovernmental relations, by collaborating with fellow professionals in other units of government (that is, through the "guilds" or "vertical functional autocracies'' described in chapter 5). In some cases, a profession can additionally exercise a direct voice in public policy making, with adverse consequences for popular control and accountability. Licensing of insurance agents and realtors at the state level and regulatory processes at the national level are two areas where professional influence is strong—some say, too strong. Professions such as law, medicine, and civil engineering have been described by different observers as enjoying excessive influence in formulating and implementing public policy. The lack of public accountability of such professional associations is central to critiques of their role.[32]

Professionalism, then, is a new feature of bureaucracy that has implications for the general conduct of public affairs and for particular aspects of personnel administration. One indication of its impact was the establishment of the Professional and Administrative Career Examination (PACE) in 1974, to replace the FSEE. More than the title of the examination was changed. The content was geared to the professional training of prospective employees, though without sacrificing interest in a general background. Similar developments have taken place, varying in extent, in state and local governments that have strong merit systems.

Merit and Patronage in Perspective

The merit-versus-patronage debate arouses deep passions in many Americans. The devotion of so many people to what they see as interconnected values of efficiency, economy, political neutrality, and governmental integrity fosters a strong preference for merit system practices, often accompanied by contempt for patronage. Both have a rich history in American public personnel administration, yet in the past century merit has clearly held favor among middle- and upper-class Americans (the chief beneficiaries of such a system).

The distinctions between merit and patronage systems can be boiled down to a difference in defining job qualifications. Those who favor merit are fond of saying that ''you don't have to be qualified'' to get a patronage job, but that is not really true—the qualifications are political rather than job-related, but they are job requirements just the same. Put simply, merit judges what you know, while patronage is more interested in whom you know, and how you can help politically. Each system has some clear advantages to recommend it.

The most obvious advantage of a merit system is its ability to bring into the public service individuals who are considered competent (by management's standards) to perform the tasks required in a given position. Doing a job well is a strong value in both private and public sectors, and it is the root of the value system favoring merit. There is also some value in having a reasonable degree of continuity and stability in the public service instead of the dramatic (and traumatic) turnovers in personnel experienced at the beginning of every new administration between 1829 and 1881.[33]

On the other side of the coin, a patronage system also affords some advantages. The most important one (as noted earlier) is that the chief executive can command much more effectively the loyalties of bureaucratic subordinates. Every local, state, and national "boss" has had that ability, and the effect in each case has been to buttress chief executive leadership (see chapter 4). It is undoubtedly true that this approach yields a vastly different kind of bureaucracy, and very likely a different set of social, economic, and political priorities in public policies. But to the extent that we value strong leadership, we may favor patronage.

The tensions between merit and patronage are rooted in a deeper philosophical and political conflict affecting personnel management. The merit concept is built around the use of *achievement-oriented* criteria—that is, making personnel judgments based on the individual's demonstrated, job-related competence. By contrast, in patronage systems (and in some other approaches to personnel decision making) judgments are based on *ascriptive* criteria—that is, on attributes or characteristics of the individual other than his or her skills and knowledge. Examples of approaches using ascriptive criteria include patronage (where personnel decisions are based at least in part on the individual's party or other organizational loyalties), affirmative action (where one's race or sex is given strong consideration), veterans' preference (military service), and nepotism. Though all such approaches seem to conflict with merit principles, each is said to have certain advantages—not only for the individuals affected, but also for the general personnel system and perhaps society at large.[34] (We will discuss affirmative action and veterans' preference later in this chapter.)

Are merit and patronage, then, permanent and inevitable opposites? Perhaps surprisingly, the answer is no. In practice, neither merit selection nor patronage exists in a pure form. Some political influence is not unknown in merit systems, though it is ordinarily quite subtle. In some states and cities, the appearance of a merit system may mask an effectively functioning patronage arrangement. Knowing someone is still useful to the candidate for a merit position. By the same token, patronage practices have been affected by governments' having to hire individuals with needed technical skills. The era of the political hack, if not gone forever, has been significantly transformed by the changing needs of a technological, complex society. In sum, there is overlap in practice between the two.

FORMAL ARRANGEMENTS OF PERSONNEL SYSTEMS

All civil service systems are not created equal, but the national government arrangements will serve as an illustrative model for discussion of the structure of most merit personnel systems. Many state arrangements, among the nearly forty states that have merit systems, closely resemble the national government format, though with some variations.

About 93 percent of all national executive branch employees are presently covered by some merit system, most under the system administered by the Office of Personnel Management (OPM), which replaced the Civil Service Commission in 1979. The proportion of national executive employees working within competitive merit systems has risen steadily, if gradually. It stood at about 10 percent in 1884 (one year after passage of the Pendleton Act), 45 percent in 1900, almost 80 percent in 1930, and 85 percent in 1950, exceeding 90 percent for the first time during the 1970s.[35]

Partly due to prodding from the national government, state governments have gradually extended (or first established) merit systems in their executive branches. For example, Congress has required states to organize merit systems in single state agencies designated as grant-in-aid recipients; the tremendous proliferation of grants has thus had the spinoff effect of strengthening merit principles in state government. The Intergovernmental Personnel Act of 1970 greatly reinforced that requirement; most states now have many merit features built into their personnel arrangements. Local governments have been similarly affected, but to a lesser extent.

The system of classifying positions is central to any personnel structuring. In the national government, jobs are classified according to eighteen *grades*, or levels, which make up the General Schedule (GS). GS-1 through -4 are lower-level positions, of the secretarial-clerical-janitorial type. Grades GS-5 through -11 cover lower-middle management posts, but are divided into two subschedules: GS-6, -8, and -10 are for the most part technical, skilled crafts, and senior clerical positions, while GS-5, -7, -9, and -11 are professional career grades. The latter four grades are the most common entry-level grades for college graduates. Grades GS-12 through -15 are upper-level positions, reflecting career advancement and acceptable job competence. GS-16 through -18 are the so-called ''supergrades,'' filled by senior civil servants who serve as bureau chiefs, staff directors, and so on. Their superiors are the political appointees who head most executive branch agencies. Promotion from one grade to the next is not automatic and, at the outset of one's career, retention in the service itself is not assured. A probation period of six to eighteen months must be served before full merit protection is attained, and not all employees are put under merit. In many instances promotion comes after one year in the service (for example, from GS-9 to -11), and in some agencies failure to achieve promotion in that time is tantamount to an invitation to leave.

In keeping with the recent emphasis on general preparation and skills, it is not difficult for an employee in the public service to transfer from one agency to another—or even from one merit system to another. OPM has reciprocal agreements with the Tennessee Valley Authority and Panama Canal Zone, for example, which permit employees to transfer to the other systems, and vice versa, with no loss of pension benefits or grade level. This interagency mobility has advantages not only for employees but also for agencies looking for varied combinations of skill and experience.

In some state merit systems it is possible to move up the ladder very rapidly. In Illinois, for example, competitive examinations for higher-level jobs—open only to those already holding state positions—are given with some frequency. A capable individual who has landed a first job can take the examinations every time they are administered and, if successful, can achieve significant career advancement in a relatively short time. It is not unknown for an employee to move from an entry-level post to a staff director's job within four years. That is unusual, but advancement through the ranks—on the basis of on-the-job performance, competitive examinations, time in grade, and so on—is far from an impossible dream for many state government employees.

FORMAL TASKS OF PERSONNEL ADMINISTRATION

The formal tasks of personnel administration have traditionally included position classification, recruitment, examination, selection, and compensation. More recently, as management of complex organizations has itself become more complex, administrators (including personnel administrators) have had to become better grounded in manpower planning,[36] counseling, motivating employees, labor relations, interpersonal skills, social and behavioral psychology, and dealing with legal constraints.

Position Classification

The major purpose of position classification, referred to previously, is to facilitate performance of other personnel functions across a wide range of agencies within the same general personnel system. Many positions in different agencies have similar duties, so it makes sense to group into one classification jobs with essentially the same responsibilities. Otherwise, recruitment and examination would be far more complex. Both of these tasks (discussed in more detail shortly) have more flexibility and greater value if potential employees can be evaluated in terms of their suitability for the general duties and responsibilities of a GS-11 or GS-13. Pay scales, as another example, can only be set up if positions are grouped so that it is possible to award "equal pay for equal work," which has been an underlying rationale of position classification since passage of the Pendleton Act (though that principle has been implemented only partially).

A written description of responsibilities involved in a position is the basis for its classification. Analysis of those functions is the basis for distinguishing it from other jobs. But there are obstacles to effective classification. While description of duties is relatively easy, the exact responsibilities of a position—supervisory tasks, evaluation of the work of subordinates, and expectations for initiative, innovation, or suggestions—can be elusive. How challenging the duties and responsibilities are is another ambiguous aspect of position descriptions. In an effort to counteract these problems, some weighting of the various features of the job—frequency of supervision, difficulty and complexity of each task, and so on—has been tried, so that classifications reflect as accurately as possible the true nature of each position. But the obstacles are not easily overcome, and many classification systems consequently (perhaps inevitably) contain some ''soft spots'' that require continuing attention.

The following aspects of classification deserve some mention.[37] First, while each agency is responsible for classifying, according to existing schedules, the positions in that agency, there is a legitimate interest in maintaining some consistency in classifications from one agency to the next. Consequently, most states and localities as well as the national government provide for reviews and audits by a central personnel office with authority to change, if necessary, agency classifications that are out of line. Second, there is concern that overly narrow specialization in many job descriptions has hampered efforts to attract into the public service qualified individuals who lack *exactly* the right combination of skills for a given position. In this respect, position classification may be said to interfere with the merit principle itself, in that job-related competence is defined too narrowly. Also, because of the diversity among public service professionals, it is more difficult to identify and classify meaningful parallels, for purposes of rationalizing the overall personnel structure. Third, there is always the possibility that, without adequate monitoring, an existing classification system will become outdated due to rapidly changing job requirements. Fourth, it has been contended that as task-oriented groups become more common, position classification geared to hierarchical organization will itself become obsolete. That is a problem that bears watching, but because most government organizations still are arranged hierarchically, position classification is likely to remain both appropriate and useful.

Recruitment, Examination, and Selection

Attracting, testing, and choosing those who join the public service have been systematic activities of personnel administration for a relatively limited period of time. Concerns and issues involved in these areas overlap one another to some extent, but deserve separate discussion.

Recruitment was something of a problem for far longer than it was recognized as such. During the early decades of this century, a combination of low pay and low prestige—not unrelated—made working for the government distinctly unattractive. The prestige problem was a matter of public values and attitudes toward government generally; even among those who favored strong administrative capabilities, "politics" was seen as unsavory and something to be tolerated rather than actively joined. While remnants of that attitude persist, the prestige of government service has increased significantly over the past few decades. Increased compensation has been both cause and effect of the change in prestige. It has thus become less difficult to arouse the interest of skilled and competent individuals in government service. But quite an effort had to be made.

The most important developments were the establishment of systematic ties to recruiting services on college campuses—in search of the professionally trained student as well as the liberal arts graduate—and to professional associations. At the same time, a host of requirements (filing fees, residency, and the like) that had acted to constrict access to the public service were dropped, and open competitive examinations were adopted. In a word, the recruitment process was democratized.

In recent years the recruitment picture has changed somewhat, in a number of respects. In general, the necessity to go out and "beat the bushes" for prospective employees has been greatly reduced. At times in the 1970s, the number of people who took the PACE test was twenty to thirty times the number of those hired into the bureaucracy.[38] On the other hand, the demand for qualified employees still exceeds supply in selected occupational areas (engineers, scientists, occasionally secretaries and clerks) and in different parts of the country. Thus, some need persists for the government to recruit employees actively.

The *examination* process is a complex one, if for no other reason than that a wide variety of positions stand to be filled by individuals whose first screening is a broad-gauged systemwide examination. Thus, an examination must be broad enough to test adequately for skills that will be used in widely varying agencies, yet still precise enough to be meaningful in testing specific skills and competencies. Many national agencies, as noted earlier, supplement general examinations with more specialized tests, interviews, written work submitted by the applicant, and so on. In state and local government, similar sorts of examinations are often used, but not as much attention has been paid to problems of testing as part of the personnel process.

Most government entrance examinations are written, though it is becoming more common to incorporate both written and oral portions. Also, most tests attempt to measure both aptitude and achievement (not unlike standardized college and graduate school entrance exams). As alternative methods of measuring competence, it is common practice to give some weight to education and experience, and in some instances enough of one or both can substitute for taking the initial examination. In the great majority of cases, a combination of written and oral examinations, personal interviews, education and experience, and written statements is used as the basis for evaluating prospective employees.

A central concern of the examination process is the *validity* of examinations, that is, how well they actually test what they are designed to test. In the face of changing job requirements, maintaining test validity must be an ongoing concern. Another consideration is whether tests should measure specific work skills or such factors as imagination, creativity, managerial talent, and the capacity to learn and grow on the job. Clearly, for some positions work skills deserve major emphasis, while for others the second set of abilities should also be considered. And of growing concern in recent years is the matter of bias in testing—specifically, whether examinations have exhibited an unintentional cultural bias that unfairly discriminated against members of minority groups. In 1979 the PACE test became the focus of a

---

SAMPLE TEST QUESTIONS DEALING WITH ADMINISTRATION FROM NEW YORK CITY POLICE EXAMINATIONS*

1. "Records of attendance, case load, and individual performance are ordinarily compiled for a police department by a records unit." A plan is suggested whereby all patrol sergeants would regularly review summaries of these detailed records, insofar as they concern the men under them. The adoption of such a plan would be
(A) inadvisable; the attention of the patrol sergeant would be unduly diverted away from the important function of patrol supervision.
(B) advisable; the information provided by summaries of detailed records would conclusively indicate to the patrol sergeant the subordinates who should be given specific patrol assignments.
(C) inadvisable; the original records should be reviewed in detail by the patrol sergeant if he is to derive any value from a record review procedure.
(D) advisable; the patrol sergeant would then have information that would supplement his personal knowledge of his subordinates.

2. In planning the distribution of the patrol force of a police department, the one of the following factors that should be considered first is the
(A) availability of supervisory personnel for each of the predetermined tours of police duty.
(B) hourly need for police services throughout the 24 hours of the day.
(C) determination of the types of patrol to be utilized for the most effective police effort.
(D) division of the total area into posts determined by their relative need for police service.

3. There are some who maintain that the efficiency of a police department is determined solely by its numerical strength. This viewpoint oversimplifies a highly complex problem mainly because
(A) enlargement of the patrol force involves a disproportionate increase in specialized units and increased need for supervision.
(B) supervisory standards tend to decline in an enlarged department.
(C) the selection and training of the force, and the quality of supervision, must also be considered.
(D) the efficiency of the department is not related to its numerical strength.

Source: Modern Promotion Courses publications, New York City.
*(Correct answers: 1-D, 2-B, 3-C)

lawsuit brought by a group of blacks and Hispanics against OPM, alleging that it was culturally biased and that it tested for general knowledge not required for the 118 job categories for which it was used. The claim of bias was based on the fact that between 1974 (when PACE was instituted) and 1979, 42 percent of white applicants passed the exam, while the corresponding percentages for Hispanics and blacks were 13 and 5, respectively. The case, however, never came to trial. Carter administration officials negotiated with the plaintiffs over plans to phase out the exam, replacing it with up to 118 separate tests designed to measure specific skills for each position. Shortly before President Carter left office, the Justice Department filed its plan in U.S. district court in Washington as a consent decree to settle the suit. Acting under the consent decree, the Reagan administration abolished the PACE examination in August of 1982.

Subsequently, OPM established a new system (known as "Schedule B hiring authority") to serve as an interim replacement for PACE, pending development of alternative competitive examining procedures. However, that "interim" lasted well into 1985.[39] Some viewed this (noncompetitive) hiring method as a threat to the competitive merit system. Others criticized the fact that agency use of Schedule B meant there was no central point in the national government to which individuals could apply for jobs. On the other side of the coin, the proportion of blacks and Hispanics hired for professional and administrative positions rose considerably between late 1982 and mid-1984. On balance, however, there was growing concern early in President Reagan's second term that the Schedule B arrangements constituted a violation by OPM of the consent decree, and were "depriving agencies of the tools necessary to hire needed staff."[40]

Selection processes vary widely from government to government, and here as elsewhere the national government was the first to develop systematic procedures. There clearly is no overall pattern, since merit systems are not identical, and patronage still operates in many state and local governments. But national government practice (until PACE was abolished) suggests what is possible—and some idea of the limitations.

The normal procedure was as follows. After qualifying through examination, education, or experience, an applicant received a merit rating (GS-7 or GS-9, for example). Applicants' names also were placed on a register, meaning that they were officially under consideration for appropriate positions as these became available throughout the bureaucracy. At that point it was up to each agency to notify OPM as positions opened up. OPM then forwarded to the agency names of those it found qualified for the particular position, and the agency took it from there.

In this procedure there were two general "rules of thumb" helping shape the final decision. The first was called the *rule of three*, referring to OPM's practice of sending three names at a time to agencies with one position to fill; those individuals were, literally, finalists in the competition. The other rule of thumb—veterans' preference—helped determine whose names were included in that vital set of three, because it affected total points assigned to each applicant. All veterans who achieved the minimum passing score of 70 on the PACE test got a five-point bonus (with the exception, after 1979, of nondisabled military retirees at or above the rank of major or lieutenant commander); all disabled veterans received a ten-point bonus, as did Vietnam veterans; and those disabled in Vietnam received a fifteen-point bonus. In some instances, survivors of veterans killed in action received these bonuses as well. In many states and localities, disabled veterans still receive an absolute preference, going well beyond even the generous bonus arrangements of the national government. Veterans' preference reflects the political strength of veterans' groups, as well as the generally high regard in which America's veterans have been held (though Vietnam veterans did not enjoy the same stature in the 1970s as did those of earlier conflicts).[41]

It should be noted that veterans' preference—a decidedly ascriptive personnel criterion—has had significant impact on the composition of the national government's workforce. Defenders of the merit system are hard pressed to support this kind of noncompetitive generosity, even toward veterans. Some states employ veterans' preference as a criterion for promotion as well as entry, and nearly two-thirds of those in senior grades of the national bureaucracy are veterans. Alan K. Campbell, OPM director under President Carter and a key architect of civil service reform in the late 1970s, argues that veterans' preference ''has damaged the quality of the senior civil service, to say nothing of discriminating against women in the [national] government.''[42] (There is considerable irony here in the fact that two quite different ascriptive criteria—veterans' preference and affirmative action—*clash with each other* as well as with the abstract concept of merit.) Despite President Carter's efforts to limit this practice, veterans' preference remains largely unchanged, even with the demise of PACE. (Other Reagan-era developments affecting recruitment, selection, and the like will be treated later in this chapter.)

Compensation

Deciding how much to pay employees is one of the more delicate and occasionally controversial tasks confronting any government personnel system. In one sense the task is made easier by the fact that legislatures almost always must approve pay scales and other rules of compensation, but hard decisions about what to propose remain a central responsibility of personnel administration.

There are several key considerations in determining a reasonable level of compensation. One is the necessity to pay employees enough to fulfill their minimum economic needs. Closely related is the question of compensation in proportion to the work being done in terms of its importance, quality, and quantity. These can be highly subjective measures, permitting considerable disagreement about what is appropriate. A third consideration is comparability of pay scales. This has two dimensions: (1) ensuring that wage and salaries for a given classification bear a reasonable pay relationship to others in terms of complexity, responsibility, and skill, and (2) maintaining rates of compensation for government employees that are not dramatically different from wages and salaries paid for similar kinds of work in the private sector.

An issue within the comparability question concerns variations throughout the nation, and even within many states, in wage and salary levels paid in business and industry, which makes it difficult to align government salaries with them on a truly comparable basis. In the mid-1970s another factor entered into this equation: cost-of-living variations and how these affected compensation. There appears to be a trend emerging—sometimes formalized, sometimes not—to tie government wage and salary levels to changes in the cost of living. As a practical matter, that avoids some tough questions, but the harm it does to the expectation that more skilled individuals will be better paid is obvious.

In recent times government compensation policies have been questioned from several vantage points. First they came under fire for being too low; critics included scholarly observers, some legislators, some citizens, and many government employees. At the national level a concerted effort was made in the 1950s and, especially, the early 1960s to improve the situation. In 1962 President John Kennedy signed the Federal Salary Reform Act, which established the principle of pay comparability to private-sector jobs for all national government positions across the country. And in the Pay Comparability Act of 1970, Congress delegated to the president authority to set the salaries of all General Schedule and Foreign Service employees, subject to congressional disapproval. During the late 1960s and early 1970s, salaries rose rapidly, though more so in the middle and lower grades than in the upper grades.

Table 10-3 indicates salaries paid for GS-1 through -18 positions as of January 1985; the pay steps within each grade show the range of compensation possible without requiring promotion to the next higher grade. Note that pay steps of one grade tend to overlap steps of the grades immediately above and below; for example, the top pay step at GS-14 is higher than the bottom step at the GS-15 level. That is deliberate, to allow an employee to win some recognition for competent job performance without having to wait for promotion, while promotion still can carry with it a financial award as well—for example, from step 9 at GS-12 to step 4 at GS-13. Until the advent of "merit pay" for those in grades GS-13 through -15 (to be discussed later in this chapter), increases from one salary step to the next were granted to virtually all employees at one- to three-year intervals, according to a set formula. While in theory poor job performance could cause a civil servant to be denied an increase, some evidence suggests that this happened in practice infrequently.[43]

Table 10-3
U.S. GENERAL SCHEDULE SALARIES

Grade					Pay Step					
	1	2	3	4	5	6	7	8	9	10
GS-1	9,339	9,650	9,961	10,271	10,582	10,764	11,071	11,380	11,393	11,686
GS-2	10,501	10,750	11,097	11,393	11,521	11,860	12,199	12,538	12,877	13,216
GS-3	11,458	11,840	12,222	12,604	12,986	13,368	13,750	14,132	14,514	14,896
GS-4	12,862	13,291	13,720	14,149	14,578	15,007	15,436	15,865	16,294	16,723
GS-5	14,390	14,870	15,350	15,830	16,310	16,790	17,270	17,750	18,230	18,710
GS-6	16,040	16,575	17,110	17,645	18,180	18,715	19,250	19,785	20,320	20,855
GS-7	17,824	18,418	19,012	19,606	20,200	20,794	21,388	21,982	22,576	23,170
GS-8	19,740	20,398	21,056	21,714	22,372	23,030	23,688	24,346	25,004	25,662
GS-9	21,804	22,531	23,258	23,985	24,712	25,439	26,166	26,893	27,620	28,347
GS-10	24,011	24,811	25,611	26,411	27,211	28,011	28,811	29,611	30,411	31,211
GS-11	26,381	27,260	28,139	29,018	29,897	30,776	31,655	32,534	33,413	34,292
GS-12	31,619	32,673	33,727	34,781	35,835	36,889	37,943	38,997	40,051	41,105
GS-13	37,599	38,852	40,105	41,358	42,611	43,864	45,117	46,370	47,623	48,876
GS-14	44,430	45,911	47,392	48,873	50,354	51,835	53,316	54,797	56,278	57,759
GS-15	52,262	54,004	55,746	57,488	59,230	60,972	62,714	64,456	66,198	67,940
GS-16	61,296	63,339	65,382	67,425	69,468*	71,511*	73,554*	75,597*	77,640*	
GS-17	71,804*	74,197*	76,590*	78,983*	81,376*					
GS-18	84,157*									

*The rate of basic pay for employees at these grades and pay steps is limited to $68,700, as of January 1, 1985.

Source: U.S. Office of Personnel Management, Washington, D.C. These salaries were in effect as of January 1985.

As a result of actions taken to raise the salaries of national government employees, the pendulum now has swung the other way. There is some concern among the general public that government employees are being paid *too* well! Certainly the pace of increase has been lively, and as noted earlier, the growing presence of skilled professionals has had the effect of pulling the general salary scale higher. So has inflation, for that matter. But existing concern stems in part from an implicit assumption that salaries were adequate before increases were granted, and that to have salaries rise so rapidly cannot be justified. In contrast, if we assume salaries and wages were lagging badly behind the private sector—for equivalent positions and responsibilities—then recent pay hikes really represent a needed realignment. Most studies have found that public-sector salaries did in fact lag behind, but there remains some unease about the rate of increase, as well as about salary levels themselves. The Gallup poll referred to earlier found that 64 percent of those surveyed believed government employees were paid more than their counterparts in nongovernmental jobs, and 77 percent believed fringe benefits available to government workers (such as health insurance and vacations) were better than those in similar jobs in the private sector.[44]

In spite of presidential and congressional action in behalf of salary comparability with the private sector, it is far from clear that true comparability exists; one recent study suggests a very "mixed bag" with wide variations among different grades and types of jobs.[45] One generalization with few exceptions is that the salaries of some 7,000 high-level career executives lag far behind those of their counterparts in private business and industry. This is especially true in view of a "pay cap" that exists on salaries paid to those in grades GS-15 through -18 (see the note at the bottom of Table 10-3). The highest salary payable to senior career executives since the pay cap was put in place is just under $70,000; private-sector executives holding positions of similar responsibility (directing organizations with 100,000 employees, and the like) regularly earn two and three times that figure.[46] The same is true of those holding Cabinet and subcabinet-rank positions. When William Simon became treasury secretary under Gerald Ford, leaving a senior position with a Wall Street brokerage firm, he took a pay cut of about 80 percent—from $200,000 to a Cabinet member's salary of $42,000 (that figure is now higher, but still far from comparable to private-sector executive salaries).

A second generalization—one with more exceptions—applies at the other end of the pay-grade structure: lower-level civil servants are paid more than *their* private-sector counterparts. The differences are not great, overall, especially for positions such as middle-level secretaries at the GS-5 level; most secretaries earn about what is paid to business secretaries doing similar work. However, for some occupations (for example, research chemists) employment in private industry is far more lucrative.[47] One's status in the lower pay grades vis-à-vis private business may hinge on the type of job held.

Three other generalizations should be noted. One is that, overall, fringe benefits "are generally better than those in the private sector"[48] (thus confirming public opinion on that point). A second is that since the reforms of the late 1970s, pay for top-level executives in the new Senior Executive Service may be augmented by performance bonuses of as much as $20,000, altering to some degree the relative positions of these individuals. However, controversy over payment of these bonuses broke out soon after they were authorized; we will consider that issue later in this chapter. Finally, despite some exceptions, it appears that those in the GS-9 through -15 range are paid salaries at least comparable to those in the private sector for the same types of work, and some are better paid.

What of state and local government compensation? Generally, national government employees are paid substantially better than their state and local counterparts. Within that overall comparison, there are other variations. One is the proportion of state and local government employees working in education (see Table 10-2); another is the greater impact of public employee unions and collective bargaining on wages and salaries (see chapter 11). In making interstate or interlocal comparisons, other factors that help explain variations in level of compensation include the degree of urbanization and industrialization in the government jurisdiction and the extent to which a bureaucracy has become professionalized.

CURRENT DEVELOPMENTS IN PERSONNEL ADMINISTRATION

Over the years there has clearly been a great deal of ferment and change in the processes of fulfilling government's need for qualified people ("qualified" by whatever criteria). More recently, public personnel administration has become even more susceptible to both internal and external pressures for change, and for adaptation to changing values and conditions (for example, the phasing out of the PACE test). In addition, the Carter administration's efforts to reform important aspects of the civil service system have had consequences which merit discussion. Furthermore, since 1981 various Reagan administration actions have had both direct and indirect personnel impacts. Five developments illustrate the scope and potential significance of recent change in personnel management. They are: (1) impacts on the civil service of budget cuts enacted during Ronald Reagan's first term in office, (2) implementation of the Civil Service Reform Act (CSRA) of 1978, (3) affirmative action efforts in hiring and promoting women and members of minority groups, (4) changing guidelines governing patronage and other partisan activity, and (5) the emerging "comparable worth" issue, related to both compensation and affirmative action concerns.

Budget Cutting and the Civil Service

Like most other areas of government activity, the civil service has felt keenly the effects of Reagan administration initiatives to reduce government spending. Ronald Reagan's first formal act as president—literally minutes after he was inaugurated in 1981—was to impose a freeze on government hiring. Though hiring resumed shortly thereafter, it has gone on at a much slower rate ever since. Limited entry into the civil service thus has been the rule for most of this decade. Closely related is the imposition of so-called "RIFs" (reductions in force) on most domestic agencies. The number of *positions* allocated to each agency has been reduced, resulting in a net decline in civil service employment of some 12,000 between 1981 and 1985 (with more expected). Much of this decline has occurred in senior career positions; we will examine that in more detail, shortly. A third element is "bumping" of employees to lower ranks in the career service, as part of efforts both to reduce costs and to strengthen agency command structures. Yet another development is increased turnover rates among those remaining in the civil service. As uncertainties increased, individuals often tried to anticipate changes in their agencies by voluntarily seeking other posts. Finally, pay freezes for many civil servants have contributed to each of the phenomena just mentioned, as well as undercutting employee morale. While the rate of change in these respects has slowed somewhat, the immediate effects on government personnel are obvious. Moreover, the potential long-range impacts on the civil service are significant, if the net effect is to lessen the attractiveness of government employment, damage the management capacities of executive agencies, and reduce the effectiveness and productivity of government programs.

The Civil Service Reform Act of 1978

In the course of administering the civil service system throughout this century, both advantages and disadvantages of the 1883 law became clearer. Numerous choices had been made in its implementation that had affected merit personnel management. Each time presidential and other commissions had examined the national bureaucracy, personnel problems were on their agendas, but prior to 1978 little in the way of comprehensive change had been brought about. When Jimmy Carter became president, a new effort was begun to alter merit system practices.

The principal targets of the Carter reforms were numerous; each had evolved over long periods of time, and solving them posed political as well as managerial challenges. Certainly one of the most important was the evolution of the merit system from a protection against blatant political manipulation to a system that provided what many called excessive job security for employees (competent or not), made possible virtually automatic salary increases (deserved or not), and made it very difficult for responsible managers to dismiss unproductive employees (warranted or not). Former OPM Director Campbell has labeled this a "protected employment system,"[49] and suggested that a principal aim of these reform efforts was to alter it significantly. The system was a major source of public dissatisfaction with "the bureaucracy," generally—the perception of unresponsive, insensitive public servants frustrating rather than facilitating the public will. More to the point for a management-conscious president, existing arrangements made it difficult at best for public managers to direct operations of their agencies effectively. And there was some interest on the part of the Carter administration in increasing the political responsiveness of top career civil servants.

Other concerns addressed by the 1978 legislation included (1) the fact that no statute or executive order ever had spelled out the *merit principles* that comprised the foundation of the merit system; (2) what, if any, personnel practices were *prohibited* (for example, management retaliation against "whistle-blowers"—those disclosing waste, fraud, abuses, or other mismanagement); (3) the status of veterans' preference; (4) the informal—and often haphazard—manner in which employee performance was evaluated; and (5) the lack of a statutory basis for the conduct of labor relations (specifically, collective bargaining) with national government employees.

One final, rather subtle problem had developed regarding the roles—many said, conflicting roles—of the old Civil Service Commission. On the one hand, the Commission functioned as an adviser to the president and to agency managers, albeit in an independent capacity partially free from presidential control. On the other hand, it was also responsible for protecting rights and interests of employees, with many of the latter claiming it had supported management positions in the event of conflict, in too many cases. Simultaneously, the president lacked the sort of direct control many felt necessary for initiating and effectively implementing basic personnel policies.[50] Thus, some momentum had developed for overhauling the central instrument of executive branch personnel management.

The Civil Service Reform Act (CSRA), enacted in October 1978 and effective January 1, 1979, did the following:[51]

1. Created the Office of Personnel Management and the Merit Systems Protection Board, replacing the Civil Service Commission;
2. Delegated personnel management authority to agencies, notably regarding performance appraisal;
3. Streamlined the process used to discharge employees;
4. Strengthened procedures to protect whistle-blowers;
5. Established a comprehensive statutory framework for conducting labor-management relations;

PROVISIONS OF THE CIVIL SERVICE REFORM ACT OF 1978

Merit System Principles	Prohibited Personnel Practices
Personnel practices and actions in the federal government require:	*Officials and employees who are authorized to take personnel actions are prohibited from:*

- Recruitment from all segments of society, and selection and advancement on the basis of ability, knowledge, and skills, under fair and open competition.

- Fair and equitable treatment in all personnel management matters, without regard to politics, race, color, religion, national origin, sex, marital status, age, or handicapping condition, and with proper regard for individual privacy and constitutional rights.

- Equal pay for work of equal value, considering both national and local rates paid by private employers, with incentives and recognition for excellent performance.

- Discriminating against any employee or applicant.
- Soliciting or considering any recommendation on a person who requests or is being considered for a personnel action unless the material is an evaluation of the person's work performance, ability, aptitude, or general qualifications, or character, loyalty, and suitability.
- Using official authority to coerce political actions, to require political contributions, or to retaliate for refusal to do these things.
- Willfully deceiving or obstructing an individual as to his or her right to compete for Federal employment.
- Influencing anyone to withdraw from competition, whether to im-

---

6. Authorized a merit pay system for middle-level supervisors, based on performance rather than longevity;
7. Established a Senior Executive Service (SES) for top-level career decision makers;
8. Required that "objective, job-related, measurable performance evaluation"[52] [appraisal] be developed for members of the SES; and
9. Enacted both a set of explicit merit principles and a statement of prohibited personnel practices (see box).

Unlike the Pendleton Act of 1883, which was devoted almost solely to eliminating patronage practices, the CSRA incorporated a wide variety of objectives. That by itself would have made its implementation highly complex. In addition, however, many of the objectives were interrelated. For example, the design of the SES included the following expectations: (1) SES members (drawn primarily from the "supergrades," that is, GS-16 through -18) would be able to work more closely and harmoniously with political appointees, at the "interface [point of contact] between the political head of

- High standards of integrity, conduct, and concern for the public interest.

- Efficient and effective use of the Federal work force.

- Retention of employees who perform well, correcting the performance of those whose work is inadequate, and separation of those who cannot or will not meet required standards.

- Improved performance through effective education and training.

- Protection of employees from arbitrary action, personal favoritism, or political coercion.

- Protection of employees against reprisal for lawful disclosures of information.

prove or worsen the prospects of any applicant.

- Granting any special preferential treatment or advantage not authorized by law to a job applicant or employee.

- Appointing, employing, promoting, or advancing relatives in their agencies.

- Taking or failing to take a personnel action as a reprisal against employees who exercise their appeal rights; refuse to engage in political activity; or lawfully disclose violations of law, rule, or regulation, or mismanagement, gross waste of funds, abuse of authority, or a substantial and specific danger to public health or safety.

- Taking or failing to take any other personnel action violating a law, rule, or regulation directly related to merit system principles.

Sources: U.S. Civil Service Commission, *Introducing the Civil Service Reform Act* (Washington, D.C.: U.S. Government Printing Office, November 1978), p. 2; reprinted from N. Joseph Cayer, *Managing Human Resources: An Introduction to Public Personnel Administration* (New York: St. Martin's, 1980), p. 32.

the agency and the career people''[53] (see chapter 4); (2) the responsiveness of these senior career officials to presidential policy leadership would thus be enhanced; (3) incentives could be developed for greater productivity on the part of senior executives (especially considering that they would sacrifice substantial job security upon joining the SES); (4) financial bonuses—and greater acknowledgment of careerists' policy advisory roles[54]—would serve as those incentives; (5) job performance of senior civil servants could be appraised more systematically; and (6) based on those appraisals, decisions about awarding bonuses could be made fairly and objectively.

Similarly, for the ''merit pay'' system effective in late 1981, ''agencies were required to develop performance appraisal systems which included performance standards. For the GS-13–GS-15 grades, merit pay was to be tied to performance as measured by the appraisal process.''[55] Underlying both the SES and merit pay were several operative assumptions: ''protected employment'' would be diluted, performance of middle- and top-level managers would be better evaluated, and pay-for-performance would serve as a positive incentive to those affected. It was hoped that as a consequence of these reforms, the overall productivity and effectiveness of national government programs would be enhanced. (Stronger protections for whistle-blowers were to be another means of achieving the same end.[56])

The early promise of the CSRA has given way instead to considerable frustration, in several respects. One overriding difficulty, especially in 1981, was the dramatic change in the political and governmental environment which accompanied the transition from the Carter to the Reagan administrations. As public administration expert Lloyd Nigro described it:

> Severe budgetary cutbacks, real and potential layoffs, the PATCO [Professional Air Traffic Controllers Organization] strike, and radical changes in the policy emphases of OPM contributed to a climate of extreme uncertainty. All of these dislocations took place during the year that the performance appraisal and merit pay provisions of the [CSRA] were to have been made fully operational. It is difficult to imagine an environment less conducive to a smooth process of implementation.[57]

CSRA implementation went forward, however, in spite of these (and some other) constraints. Developments since 1981 can be categorized under the headings of *performance appraisal, pay,* and *politics.* We will examine each of these briefly.

Because responsibility for performance appraisals was decentralized from OPM to individual agencies, it is very difficult to generalize about the ways these new systems have operated. However, some observations are both possible and appropriate. First, in many cases the appraisal procedures may have been put in place too quickly, and often without sufficient consultation with affected employees. One observer has suggested that ''in a number of departments, we have tried to move too rapidly. We did not undertake the degree of pilot [test] operations . . . this massive a change required. . . .''[58] However, there also is evidence that in numerous agencies the new procedures have worked—and, in some areas, worked quite well.[59] Second, there is some belief (though not universal) that the decentralization of operating responsibility was accompanied by a failure on OPM's part to properly monitor and evaluate the new appraisal procedures once they were in operation. In testimony before congressional committees, as well as in studies conducted by the General Accounting Office (GAO), OPM is depicted as having missed an excellent opportunity to direct initial implementation of a central part of the new overall personnel process.[60] Third, to the extent that the new performance appraisal systems were to serve as the basis for personnel judgments (including salary increases and bonus awards), external constraints made it more difficult for them to do so. In particular, the credibility of the appraisal process suffered because of President Reagan's continuing emphasis on budget cuts, combined with an existing pay cap (set at just over $50,000 during the Carter years). Also (and somewhat predictably), there was concern among career executives that even where pay adjustments could be made, factors other than objective performance were the basis for some of those adjustments. Numerous studies on this sensitive subject appeared in the early 1980s; one suggested, for example, that attributes such as loyalty and commitment to the organization—rather than objectively measured performance quality—can have important impacts on superiors' perceptions of their subordinates' work.[61] With all this, however, there is evidence of increasing levels of satisfaction among senior executives as performance appraisal has become better established.[62] In sum, it appears that the new performance appraisal procedures are "playing to mixed reviews," both inside and outside the civil service.

Pay issues took several forms. One, already referred to, was the pay cap that was first put in place in 1979. Even though that limit was raised to $58,500 in 1982, and later raised further (see Table 10-3), a major consequence of the cap—which has been only partially corrected—was a compression of salary ranges (so-called "pay compression"). For the better part of a decade, the highest-salaried employees in the civil service (meaning SES members, for the most part) were unable to receive increases in compensation, due to the "lid" on what could be paid. Furthermore, those in the personnel grades immediately below them could (and did) close the gap in salary terms, leading to a situation in which "the highest-ranking members of the SES [were] earning no more than the lowest."[63]

Other pay problems centered on the bonus award system in use for SES members, and on merit pay for those in grades GS-13 through -15. The CSRA provided that up to 50 percent of SES members could be eligible for bonus awards. Congress, however, reduced that figure in 1980 to only 25 percent (in response to bonus awards made by a few agencies, awards that "approached the outer limits of the law in both numbers and size of bonuses"[64]). One immediate reaction was a significant exodus of senior executives—not only from the SES but also from government service itself. Of those entering the SES in 1979, fully 40 percent had left the public service by the spring of 1984.[65] The limit on bonuses was raised to 35 percent for fiscal year 1984, with some prospect for OPM raising it to the original statutory 50 percent in the near future. But the initial reduction's effects on morale within the SES were sharply negative, and have by no means disappeared.

Another problem that has persisted alongside the bonus ceiling is concern that the basis for the awards (that is, performance appraisal) is still not all it should be, even given the positive opinions noted earlier. Still another concern is the degree of fairness in awarding bonuses. In one study, some 60 percent of career executives interviewed said that bonuses "had been disproportionately awarded to those executives in more prominent programs or higher-level positions, and to those who worked most closely with political appointees."[66] (Nearly all those who said this attributed the phenomenon to the 20 percent limit on the number of bonuses, rather than to any deliberate attempt to sabotage the system.) On balance, however, many senior executives are dissatisfied with a bonus system that never has been made fully operational.

Merit pay, as distinct from SES performance bonuses, appears to have been founded on the concept of equal pay for equal *contribution,* rather than equal *activity,*[67] for managers and supervisors in grades GS-13 through -15. Here again improved performance appraisal has been the foundation for merit pay decisions—and, it appears, with similarly mixed results. One evaluation, conducted by the GAO, centered on the 1981 and 1982 merit pay cycles in four agencies, covering about one fourth of the total merit pay population. GAO reported to Congress that (1) factors other than employee performance have influenced the amount of merit pay employees received; (2) performance standards—while clearer and more systematic in 1982 than in 1981—still warranted management attention; (3) employee perceptions of the merit pay program were low; and (4) OPM's efforts to evaluate agency merit pay programs needed to be stepped up.[68] Another critique suggested that the new system (like performance appraisal) had not been adequately pretested. Also, there was evidence that many employees believed the appraisal system itself was inadequate as a basis for linking pay to performance, thus defeating the very purpose of the merit pay innovation.[69]

It appears, however, that merit pay's most critical problems are to be found in its organizational and political environment. It has "encountered difficulties . . . peculiar to its public sector context [, including] an inherently ambiguous performance environment, tight budgetary restraints, freedom of information about individuals' salaries, diffuse authority for implementation, a major managerial [presidential] succession, and significant changes in organizational goals."[70] Another observer cites three other constraints: "inconsistent coverage decisions, the presence of only a negative incentive for employees already salaried high in the pay range, and pay compression."[71] As a consequence, there has been another exodus from government, this one among middle-level managers (though not on the scale of the SES departures noted earlier). Rightly or wrongly, "[m]any people hold pay-for-performance at least partially responsible" for the increased incidence of voluntary separations from the civil service, among both experienced executives and younger managers with most of their careers still ahead of them.[72] With these sorts of assessments commonly being made, it appears that merit pay has fallen well short of the goals its advocates envisioned for it when CSRA was enacted.

The *politics* of civil service reform has affected virtually every aspect of the changes of the past decade, but with particularly significant impacts in certain areas. One example is the SES, designed initially as a "meeting ground" for political and career executives. The CSRA specified that some 10 percent of SES members would be "noncareer" appointments. In practice, especially since 1981, the percentage has been higher than that, and these political executives have been concentrated at the top of the hierarchy where they can exercise considerable authority over the careerists. The latter, having sacrificed job security in order to do more meaningful work and possibly earn SES bonuses, have raised objections to what they see as politically motivated decisions which, in their view, adversely affect them and the programs they manage. Compounding this situation is the exodus of so many career executives, thus increasing the relative proportion of more explicitly "political" managers in top-level positions. Furthermore, "[r]elations between career and political people have deteriorated"[73] within this atmosphere of frustration and dissatisfaction.

Another dimension of politics in recent years has been the perception of some observers that both Jimmy Carter and Ronald Reagan have been more interested in their own versions of patronage than in civil service reform—and, indeed, at the expense of such reform. According to Bernard Rosen, a former executive director of the Civil Service Commission:

> In the Reagan years . . . the administration's interest in reducing government spending led the OPM director to take the initiative in cutting the OPM staff far below the minimum required to carry out the law, and *as in the previous administration*, . . . a tolerance for patronage has outweighed the requirements for appointments based on merit.[74]

Three other political aspects of national government personnel management also should be mentioned. One is the decision made by the Reagan administration in 1982 not to develop a replacement for the PACE examination, because "the cost of developing validated competitive examinations consistent with the [consent] decree would be prohibitive. . . ."[75] It was decided, instead, "to exempt the positions formerly filled by PACE from the competitive service."[76] Some accused OPM Director Donald Devine of failing to develop a new entry-level test (or tests) in order to increase the administration's political flexibility in the highest grades of the civil service, not simply to cut costs. Administration defenders note, however, that the CSRA made it possible (and legitimate) for political leaders to seek greater policy responsiveness from career subordinates, and that to increase political flexibility in this manner was consistent with the CSRA's intent. One answer to that has been, in effect, that "achieving greater responsiveness is one thing; gutting the competitive service at the higher grades is quite another." As noted earlier, that debate is likely to continue in the near future.[77]

The second dimension concerns OPM's role in conducting evaluations of performance appraisal, merit pay, and other CSRA innovations. Two things have been noted about OPM activities since 1981: (1) it abandoned an existing productivity measurement program shortly after President Reagan assumed office,[78] and (2) in late 1982 it reorganized its evaluation unit under a politically appointed directorship for public affairs,[79] thus signaling its intention to formulate evaluation goals and instruments in something other than a fully impartial manner.

The final political dimension has a larger context, and perhaps wider-ranging consequences. It has been said with some justification that the amount and intensity of criticism aimed at public administrators has reached a level unprecedented in the last 100 years.[80] Those who find this development disturbing (and many do) freely acknowledge that government officials must be held accountable—that, as a nation, we have a legitimate interest in official actions being linked appropriately to established public purposes and policies. On the other hand, the sort of "scapegoating" of bureaucracy that has become part of our national folklore does nothing to promote accountability, and may do a great deal to undermine the morale and self-confidence of conscientious public servants. This denigration (downgrading or deriding) of civil servants often has surfaced in the public utterances of candidates for elective office—including candidates Carter and Reagan, the first time each ran for the presidency. As a consequence, it is argued, many talented and experienced officials—with a wealth of "institutional memory" and understanding of public programs—are leaving government service. Those who replace them are inevitably less experienced, less aware of past failures and successes, less familiar with their programmatic and political "territory." The net result may well be a government service less prepared to manage programs involving hundreds of billions of dollars, and to plan responsibly for policy and program needs ten and twenty years hence. Representative Patricia Schroeder (D.-Colorado), chairman of the House Subcommittee on Civil Service, has aptly summarized this point of view: "Any employer who treats its employees poorly [in several senses] is soon going to end up with poor employees. We are rapidly moving in this direction."[81]

Affirmative Action

In the public service, as elsewhere, there has been emphasis in recent years on affirmative action programs in hiring and advancement of minorities and of women. The rationale behind the affirmative action movement is that these individuals and groups have been unfairly—in some cases, arbitrarily—discriminated against in the past, and that seeking to bring them into government service is one effective way to redress old grievances. The national government has gone a long way, under provisions of legislation such as the 1964 Civil Rights Act and the 1972 Equal Employment Opportunity Act, to ensure that women and minorities are given at least strong consideration, if not outright preferential treatment, in decisions to hire government (and not a few other) employees.

The issues raised by affirmative action programs are weighty ones. First, if a merit system is viewed as one that goes strictly according to the applicant's job-related competence, affirmative action can conflict with that objective. This has been the basis of many criticisms of such programs. Those who support affirmative action point out, however, that it is entirely appropriate in light of the long-time lack of access to jobs suffered by minorities and women. They also point to such features as veterans' preference, and failure to enforce standards of competence as vigorously after appointment as before, as evidence of imperfection in existing merit practices. The essence of their contention is that denial of access through accidental or systematic exclusion of certain groups is best remedied by practicing *systematic inclusion* through affirmative action. They claim, also, that this makes the public service more truly representative of different groups in the population, and consequently more responsive to their concerns (see chapter 15).

Affirmative action is also said to be needed because of past biases in testing for employment. With some support from scholarly research,[82] it is alleged that competitive examinations have often been discriminatory, above and beyond the *necessary* discrimination (that is, distinguishing) among the various skills of those seeking employment. Advocates of this view argue that tests based on the experience and training of a white, middle-class population will almost inevitably discriminate unfairly against those whose experience and training are very different. There has been quite a bit of attention given to this problem in recent years, and pressure has been applied for further changes in methods of testing—thus the decision to phase out the PACE test as a point of entry into the national bureaucracy.

Another major area of controversy regarding affirmative action is the issue of quotas in hiring—setting aside a fixed percentage of all positions for members of certain ethnic groups and for women. Court decisions have alternately supported and rejected this practice, though rigid adherence to quota systems is increasingly under fire. Again, the conflict is between those who see systematic inclusion (which is what quotas really amount to) as a remedial device for decades of exclusion for significant numbers of American citizens, and those who prefer to staff the public service on the basis of job-related competence and other relatively objective criteria, such as education and experience.

The debate over affirmative action and quotas—indeed the whole area of what has come to be called "reverse discrimination"—is likely to continue, regardless of decisions made in legislatures or courts in the immediate future. But what difference has all this furor made? Two generalizations are possible. First, there has been an overall significant increase in the proportions of minorities and women present in the work forces of national, state, and local governments; to that extent, affirmative action employment programs would appear to be succeeding. Second, it is clear that of the minorities and women in public employment, a substantial majority still tend to occupy the less responsible positions, relative to white males, and many are found at lower grade levels of the civil service hierarchy with correspondingly lower salary or wage levels. This is a reflection, in part, of the dominance of veterans in upper-level posts.

Predictably, the picture varies at different levels of government. National government data for 1983 indicated, for example, that women held 30 percent of the positions in grades GS-9 through -12 (up from the 1974 figure of 19 percent), 10 percent of GS-13 through -15 positions (up from 5 percent), and 6 percent of GS-16 through -18 positions (up from 2 percent).[83] Also, whereas women constituted 19 percent of all full-time professionals in the national bureaucracy in 1974, that proportion had increased to 25 percent by 1983.[84] Corresponding percentage figures for racial minorities, including Hispanics, were considerably below those for women. This was true even though about 30 percent of all minorities were employed at grades GS-9 and above in the late 1970s,[85] and despite the fact that (as noted earlier) the proportion of blacks and Hispanics hired for professional and administrative positions under ''Schedule B'' authority rose considerably in the early 1980s.

States and localities present a much more varied picture, partly due to lack of equally recent data. As of 1980, there was evidence that white women, and minorities of both sexes, had made marked gains in government employment generally, but at a slower pace in state and local governments (especially for minorities) than at the national level. Also, as in the case of the national government, white males still predominate in the higher personnel grades and pay levels. Not surprisingly, there is great variation among the states and thousands of local governments, as well as among different functional areas.[86] (Note, however, that women and minorities have fared much better in the public sector, overall, than in the private sector.)

Clearly, affirmative action has not done all its proponents hoped it would; it is questionable that it *could* have tilted the balance as far as some preferred. Furthermore, the outlook for the immediate future is mixed; some developments augur well for affirmative action, and others decidedly do not.

Proponents point hopefully to numerous court decisions which have sustained various practices, or required government actions, consistent with the affirmative action principle. As one example, the U.S. Supreme Court refused in early 1985 to hear a case brought by fifteen white New York state correctional officers, who protested that they were unfairly ''bumped'' down a promotion list when the state civil service commission adjusted test results to give more minority candidates passing scores.[87] On the other hand, public administration scholar David Rosenbloom has predicted that affirmative action (at least in the national government) will become a less salient concern through the rest of the 1980s. He notes, among other things, the absence of a strong national consensus supporting affirmative action, and the rise of new personnel concerns (for example, retrenchment and productivity).[88] It is doubtful that affirmative action will be thrust aside entirely, given its statutory foundations. But continuing changes in emphasis appear likely.

Personnel and Partisanship

The desirability of linking government personnel practices to partisan politics has been a matter of controversy in this nation for nearly the whole of our political history. It is no different now, and two aspects of the subject have loomed large in recent developments in personnel administration.

One revolves around judicial determinations concerning patronage, and in particular a number of decisions in which various courts have ruled that dismissal of, or other adverse actions against, non-merit-protected employees solely on partisan grounds could be construed as a violation of constitutional rights protected by the First and Fourteenth Amendments to the U.S. Constitution. Major cases relevant to this point include *Elrod* v. *Burns* (1976), in which the U.S. Supreme Court ruled that lower-level government workers cannot be fired for partisan reasons; *Hollifield* v. *McMahan* (1977), in which a U.S. District Court judge in Tennessee applied the principle to a dismissal of a deputy sheriff after the deputy had openly and actively supported his superior's opponent in an election campaign; *Shakman* v. *The Democratic Organization of Cook County* (1979), in which another District judge in Illinois extended that ruling to include promotions and demotions; and *Branti* v. *Finkel* (1980), in which the Supreme Court held that two assistant public defenders in Rockland County, New York, could not be dismissed by their new Democratic boss solely because they were Republicans (extending the principle now to higher-level officials).[89] The Reagan administration encountered a great deal of legal uncertainty in its early months in office over what would be viewed by the courts as appropriate policy in filling top positions, because of these various decisions (especially the *Branti* case). These rulings do not apply to "confidential policy-making" jobs, but the courts have not yet determined where to draw the line between these and other posts.

The other dimension of personnel and partisanship is the issue of whether or not civil servants should be required to maintain partisan neutrality, by virtue of their *being* civil servants. This was a primary objective of merit reformers in the nineteenth century, and was embodied in the Political Activities Act of 1939 (the Hatch Act). This legislation, as amended in 1940 and 1966, prohibited any active participation in political campaigns by national government employees, state and local employees working in any nationally funded program, and employees of private organizations working with community-action programs funded by the Economic Opportunity Act.[90] But as rights of government employees became more of a concern in the 1960s and early 1970s, efforts were made to limit or overturn the Hatch Act. The reasoning behind these efforts was that provisions barring political involvement were said to infringe on rights that could be exercised by others, thus rendering government personnel second-class citizens. The right to vote was not enough, it was argued; government employees should have the right to participate in all aspects of politics.

In a series of court cases in the early 1970s, several state and local versions of the Hatch Act were challenged, some successfully. In 1972, the U.S. District Court for the District of Columbia declared the Hatch Act itself unconstitutional on grounds of vagueness and of First Amendment violations.[91] But in 1973, the Supreme Court reversed that lower court ruling on a 6 to 3 vote, upholding the act and its constitutionality. Since that time, efforts have centered on getting Congress to loosen restrictions on government employees' political activities. Jimmy Carter's election boosted the hopes of those seeking change, and he supported such legislation in the 95th Congress in early 1977, achieving House passage of a bill that would have eased existing restrictions. That effort failed in the Senate, however, and no serious prospect for passage of a similar bill has existed since that time.

Comparable Worth: The "Issue of the '80s"?

The principle of "equal pay for equal work" was firmly established by the national Equity Pay Act in 1963, requiring an end to any sex-based (or other) discrimination in compensation for individuals engaged in similar work. The issue of "comparable worth," however, goes beyond that principle. It addresses the question of how to set pay levels for individuals doing work that is *different*, but comparable in value to the employing organization, government, or society at large.

Apart from the intrinsic issues, there is a key relationship here to affirmative action. "The concern about equal pay for unlike jobs that are nonetheless comparable stems from social practices of identifying certain jobs with either males or females but not both sexes."[92] For example, most secretaries, librarians, and nurses are female; most engineers and painters—and high-level organizational managers—are male. For advocates of determining comparable worth, "the example cited most frequently is the $2,000 difference in the salaries of secretaries and the salaries of stock clerks, the former traditionally female and the latter traditionally male."[93]

The reasons advanced for such discrepancies in compensation are simultaneously the rationales for what to do about this problem—or even whether to *identify* it as a "problem." Some try to justify lower pay for "women's work" on the grounds that, until recently, women have not been the principal breadwinners; that many younger women are in the work force only until they marry and start a family; or that the forces of labor supply and demand (not sex discrimination) have worked to depress compensation levels for nurses, secretaries, telephone operators, and the like. Others argue that these and similar assumptions—however accurate or inaccurate—represent a deep-seated social perception of women as second-class laborers.[94] (Some of these arguments, on both sides, have merit; how pertinent they are may depend on one's perspective.)

A crucial aspect of the comparable worth debate is the methodology that would be used to *determine* comparability among diverse occupations. There are vastly differing perceptions of how practical a task that is. Some have argued, for example, that organizational contributions of dissimilar jobs can be ranked "in terms of the knowledge and skills required, accountability attached, and accompanying working conditions"; a suggested technique is known as "objective job evaluation."[95] Others have maintained that it would be difficult, if not impossible, to conduct such evaluations, and question seriously whether it is possible to determine with confidence the comparability of different jobs.[96] Still others have suggested that even to make the effort does considerable harm to established practices of personnel management such as position classification, and places the task of decision making regarding comparable worth in the hands of the judiciary, where (it is argued) it does not really belong.[97] Nevertheless, by the summer of 1985 some thirty states had either enacted statutes containing comparable worth language, completed studies of the possible consequences of implementing the concept, or both.[98] The situation in the national government was less clear, with President Reagan expressing strong reservations about the concept at the same time that Congress was considering whether it should order a study of the national government's civilian pay and job classification systems. In April 1985, the U.S. Civil Rights Commission, by a 5–2 vote, voiced its opposition to comparable worth—a significant development, considering past positions on equal rights issues taken by that agency. Perhaps more important, two months later the Equal Employment Opportunity Commission (EEOC) ruled that it would not act on behalf of women who allege discrimination in pay on the basis of comparable worth. The EEOC decision came with more than 260 comparable worth cases pending before the commission; women involved in those cases (and others yet to come) now must seek redress through the courts.[99] It seems certain that the debate over comparable worth will remain with us, at least in the near future.

PERSPECTIVES AND IMPLICATIONS

The U.S. civil service has existed for more than a century on a foundation of belief and practice clear in intent and quite consistent in manner of operation. Now, however, all the assumptions underlying past practice have become shaky indeed. The merit system has been modified to accommodate veterans' preference, and more recently demographic representativeness. At the same time efforts are under way to breathe new life into the meaning of "merit" by linking performance to compensation and other incentives such as promotion. The Carter administration, as we have seen, sought to achieve a significant degree of change in the merit system in this respect. The Reagan administration has undertaken other initiatives, designed for the most part to enhance presidential influence over the activities of career civil servants. In terms of the assumptions underlying personnel manage-ment, this means favoring political responsiveness over politically neutral competence, at least to some extent. The resultant uncertainties have com-pounded those associated with civil service reform in the late 1970s. (Also significant, perhaps, is OPM Director Devine's departure from his position in June of 1985.) Other dimensions of potential change include the impact of future court decisions on patronage practices and the fate of comparable worth, to name only two. State and local government personnel practices also are undergoing change, partly in direct response to initiatives from Washington (including the courts), and partly due to forces at work within their respective jurisdictions.

In short, change has been both monumental and fundamental. This kind of turmoil in a central area of public administration has an effect on quality of performance and the condition of the public service. The more essential point to consider is the *vast uncertainty* surrounding public person-nel functions, triggered by political pressures for *different sorts* of change. What public personnel administration will look like in the 1990s and be-yond is anyone's guess, as basic concepts and their meanings continue to undergo a long-term process of redefinition.

SUMMARY

Public personnel administration has evolved from a fairly routine function of government to a more controversial one. Personnel practices that have been in effect have varied a great deal, reflecting at different times the val-ues of strong executive leadership and political representativeness, on the one hand, and politically neutral competence, on the other.

Public personnel administration is the organizations, policies, and processes used to match the needs of governmental agencies and the peo-ple who staff those agencies. The *public* aspect reflects the impacts of other political institutions, the politics of interest groups and associates, political parties, and the mass media.

The size of government bureaucracies is a matter of some concern to personnel administrators, as is the diversity of skills of government em-ployees. A related problem is the apparent public unease about the growth and current size of administrative structures. The greatest increases have come in state and local governments, particularly educational employment. Other changes have also occurred, related less to sheer size than to scope of bureaucratic influence—through greater regulation, grant-in-aid activity, and expanded state and local bureaucracies.

Public personnel administration has evolved, at the national level, through a series of stages related to changing values in society about government and administration. Government by "gentlemen" reflected the powerful influence of the American quasi-aristocracy on all of politics. Government by the "common man" resulted from the movement toward a more egalitarian political system. Government by the "good" focused on elimination of corruption in hiring practices and equality of access to competitive entrance examinations. Government by the "efficient" was characterized by maintenance of the merit system and of political neutrality, and by the pursuit of management efficiency. Government by "administrators" saw the development of an activist political role for public administrators. Government by "professionals" has been a period of greater concern for recruitment, testing generalized skills of job applicants, and meeting the challenges as well as the opportunities of increased professionalism in the public service.

Merit versus patronage is an old debate that is still very much with us. Merit systems emphasize competence related to the job; patronage systems favor political connections and loyalties. Merit offers some continuity and stability in personnel; patronage permits a chief executive to select loyal subordinates. In practice, they overlap.

The formal arrangements of most merit systems are similar. In the national government over 90 percent of all employees are under a merit system of some kind. However, there is great variation in the extent of merit coverage in state and local governments.

Formal tasks of personnel administration include some traditional and other relatively new functions. Position classification is essential in order to conduct recruitment, administer a broad-gauged entrance examination, and award "equal pay for equal work."

Recruitment, examination, and selection all have undergone considerable change in recent times. Recruitment in the 1950s became both more systematic and less restricted. Consequently, greater numbers of applicants were recruited, at least until the early 1980s. Examination processes are more complex; in the national government the PACE test has been abolished, and no alternative competitive examining procedures have been developed to replace it. Achievement-oriented factors such as education and experience, and ascriptive criteria such as veterans' preference and demographic representativeness, have played a role in both examination and selection.

Compensation is designed to be proportionate to the work being done and comparable to that in the private sector for similar types of jobs. Salary and wage levels have risen rapidly in the national government; state and lo-cal government levels of compensation ordinarily are lower. Efforts to achieve true comparability with compensation levels for similar jobs in the private sector have succeeded only partially.

Current developments in public personnel administration include the effects of budget cuts, civil service reform, affirmative action, changes in patronage rules, and "comparable worth." Budget cuts, especially in the national government, have been felt in the form of limited entry, reductions-in-force (RIFs), "bumping" of employees to lower ranks, in-creased turnover, and pay freezes. The CSRA was an attempt to reform the national government merit system fundamentally by introducing perform-ance appraisal systems and financial incentives for higher-quality perform-ance and greater productivity. While the new systems established under the CSRA are operating, problems have developed in recent years that threaten the long-range success of the whole enterprise. Affirmative action programs have continued, since the early 1970s, to produce gradual in-creases in the proportions of minorities and women holding responsible government positions. White males still dominate in most instances, how-ever. Personnel and partisanship, an old issue in personnel administration, has seen some changes recently. Patronage has been challenged success-fully in a number of court cases, and further court action seems likely. Ex-panding the scope of permissible political activity for merit employees, which has been sought by some for a number of years, has also suffered setbacks lately. Finally, "comparable worth" has emerged as an issue in the 1980s.

Public personnel administration, as it has been for several decades, is a dynamic, fluid area of public administration. The outlook is for more of the same.

NOTES

1. Herbert Kaufman, "Administrative Decentralization and Political Power," *Public Administration Review*, 29 (January/February 1969), 3-15. See also chapter 2.
2. N. Joseph Cayer, *Public Personnel Administration in the United States* (New York: St. Martin's, 1975), p. 1.
3. N. Joseph Cayer, *Managing Human Resources: An Introduction to Public Personnel Administration* (New York: St. Martin's, 1980), pp. 6–11.
4. Cayer, *Public Personnel Administration in the United States*, p. 12.
5. Gallup poll, published in the Bloomington-Normal (Ill.) *Daily Pantagraph*, June 12, 1977, p. D-2.
6. See Frederick C. Mosher, "The Changing Responsibilities and Tactics of the Federal Government," *Public Administration Review*, 40 (November/December 1980), 541–48, at p. 543.
7. U.S. Bureau of the Census, *Public Employment in 1983* (Washington, D.C.: U.S. Government Printing Office, 1984), Series GE83, No. 1, p. 3.

8. Ibid.
9. This discussion draws upon Kathy Sawyer, "Federal Workforce Shifting Roles," Bloomington-Normal (Ill.) *Daily Pantagraph*, August 31, 1980, p. A-5. The account first appeared in the Washington *Post*.
10. Ibid.
11. Ibid. (emphasis added).
12. See Frederick C. Mosher, *Democracy and the Public Service*, 2nd ed. (New York: Oxford University Press, 1982), chapters 3 and 4.
13. Nicholas Henry, *Public Administration and Public Affairs*, 2nd ed. (Englewood Cliffs, N.J.: Prentice Hall, 1980), p. 240.
14. Cayer, *Managing Human Resources*, p. 20.
15. Michael Nelson, "A Short, Ironic History of American National Bureaucracy," *Journal of Politics*, 44 (August 1982), 747–78, at p. 758.
16. Ibid. (emphasis added).
17. Cayer, *Managing Human Resources*, p. 20.
18. Ibid., p. 21.
19. Ibid. Lincoln resorted to patronage to assure loyalty to the Union during the Civil War.
20. O. Glenn Stahl, *Public Personnel Administration*, 8th ed. (New York: Harper & Row, 1983), p. 37. See also Henry, *Public Administration and Public Affairs*, p. 241.
21. Henry, *Public Administration and Public Affairs*, pp. 242–43.
22. Ibid., p. 242.
23. Ibid., p. 243.
24. Cayer, *Managing Human Resources*, p. 27.
25. Stahl, *Public Personnel Administration*, p. 38.
26. Henry, *Public Administration and Public Affairs*, p. 244.
27. Stahl, *Public Personnel Administration*, p. 42.
28. Cayer, *Managing Human Resources*, p. 28.
29. Henry, *Public Administration and Public Affairs*, p. 247.
30. Cayer, *Managing Human Resources*, p. 35.
31. The following is taken from Frederick C. Mosher, "Professions in Public Service," *Public Administration Review*, 38 (March/April 1978), 144–50, at pp. 145–46.
32. See Guy Benveniste, *The Politics of Expertise*, 2nd. ed. (San Francisco: Boyd and Fraser, 1977), for a careful examination of the role and influence of experts in public policy making.
33. Cayer notes that one reason Congress acted in 1883 to pass the Pendleton Act was a fear by its Republican majority that the Democrats could win the presidency in 1884 and "clean out" the GOP-dominated bureaucracy. By passing the act when it did, Congress made it possible to extend merit protection to incumbents in the bureaucracy. Cayer, *Managing Human Resources*, p. 24.
34. It is also true, however, that managers must find ways to deal with the pressures generated by these conflicting personnel approaches. One way to address this problem is suggested in Debra W. Stewart, "Managing Competing Claims: An Ethical Framework for Human Resource Decision Making," *Public Administration Review*, 44 (January/February 1984), 14–22.
35. Stahl, *Public Personnel Administration*, p. 42.
36. See Alyce M. Kwiecinski, "Mini-Symposium on Manpower Planning," *Public Administration Review*, 44 (March/April 1984), 162–76.

37. Cayer, *Managing Human Resources*, chapter 5. See also Robert D. White, "Position Analysis and Characterization," *Review of Public Personnel Administration*, 4 (Spring 1984), 57–67.

38. Steven J. Chapman, "Inflated Pay," in "What's Wrong with the Civil Service," *The Washington Monthly*, 9 (April 1977), 60; "OPM Ends Toll-Free Service for Federal Job Information," *Public Administration Times*, 2 (March 1, 1979), 2 (published by the American Society for Public Administration; Washington, D.C.); and "PACE Examinations Scheduled for October," *Public Administration Times*, 4 (July 15, 1981), 12.

39. "OPM Delays Initiation of PACE Alternative," *Public Administration Times*, 8 (February 1, 1985), 3.

40. Ibid.; the statement quoted was made by Rep. Patricia Schroeder (D.-Colorado), chairman of the House Civil Service Subcommittee. See also *Appointments to Professional and Administrative Career Positions*, A Report to the Congress of the United States by the Comptroller General, General Accounting Office Report No. GAO/GGD-85-18 (Washington, D.C.: U.S. Government Printing Office, December 10, 1984). For discussion of related issues, see Carolyn Ban and Toni Marzotto, "Delegations of Federal Examining," *Review of Public Personnel Administration*, 5 (Fall 1984), 1–11, and Marilyn K. Quaintance, "Moving Toward Unbiased Selection," in Michael Cohen and Robert T. Golembiewski, eds., *Public Personnel Update* (New York: Marcel Dekker, 1984).

41. Another rule of thumb—geographic representativeness—was repealed by statute in February 1978, after being in effect since passage of the Pendleton Act in 1883.

42. The quote is taken from David Broder's column about Campbell not long after he became Civil Service Commission head. The column appeared under the headline "New Look in Civil Service," in the Bloomington-Normal (Ill.) *Daily Pantagraph*, May 25, 1977, p. A-4.

43. See, among others, Marjorie Boyd, "Inflated Grades," in "What's Wrong with the Civil Service," *The Washington Monthly*, 9 (April 1977), 51.

44. Gallup poll, June 12, 1977.

45. The following is taken from Joel Havemann and William J. Lanouette, "The Comparability Factor in Federal Employees' Pay," *National Journal*, 10 (September 30, 1978), 1552–55.

46. One indication of the disparities between public-sector and private-sector salaries was suggested by Alan Campbell, in "The Public Service as Institution: A Symposium," *Public Administration Review*, 42 (July/August 1982), 304–20, at p. 315.

47. Havemann and Lanouette, "The Comparability Factor in Federal Employees' Pay," p. 1552.

48. Ibid.

49. Conversation with the author, July 29, 1981.

50. Felix A. Nigro, "The Politics of Civil Service Reform," *Southern Review of Public Administration*, 3 (September 1979), 196–239, at p. 198.

51. The following overview of the CSRA is adapted from James S. Bowman, "Introduction," in James S. Bowman, ed., "Symposium on Civil Service Reform," *Review of Public Personnel Adminstration*, 2 (Summer 1982), 1–3, at p. 1; and Lawrence S. Buck, "Executive Evaluation: Assessing the Probability for Success in the Job," in Nicholas P. Lovrich, Jr., ed., "Performance Appraisal Reforms in

the Public Sector: The Promise and Pitfalls of Employee Evaluation—A Symposium," *Review of Public Personnel Administration*, 3 (Summer 1983), 63–72, at p. 63. See also Nigro, "The Politics of Civil Service Reform"; Michael Cohen, "Two Fundamental Civil Service Reforms," in Cohen and Golembiewski, eds., *Public Personnel Update*; Patricia W. Ingraham and Carolyn Ban, eds., *Legislating Bureaucratic Change: The Civil Service Reform Act of 1978* (Albany, N.Y.: State University of New York Press, 1984); *The Senior Executive Service*, Hearings before the Subcommittee on Civil Service, Committee on Post Office and Civil Service, U.S. House of Representatives, 98th Congress, 2nd Session (Washington, D.C.: U.S. Government Printing Office, 1984); U.S. Office of Personnel Management, *Civil Service Reform: A Report on the First Year* (Washington, D.C.: OPM, January 1980); and *Civil Service Reform—Where It Stands Today*, A Report to the Congress of the United States by the Comptroller General, General Accounting Office Report No. FPCD-80-38 (Washington, D.C.: U.S. Government Printing Office, May 13, 1980). For a comprehensive treatment of current civil service law, see Ellen M. Bussey, ed., *Federal Civil Service Law and Procedures: A Basic Guide* (Washington, D.C.: BNA Books, 1984).

52. Buck, "Executive Evaluation," p. 63.

53. Testimony of Rep. Patricia Schroeder, *Hearings on The Senior Executive Service*, p. 134.

54. Testimony of Alan K. Campbell, *Hearings on The Senior Executive Service*, p. 314.

55. Joyce D. Ross, "Commitment and Loyalty as a Determinant of Performance Ratings," *Review of Public Personnel Administration*, 3 (Summer 1983), 105–16, at p. 105.

56. Whether the protections for whistle-blowers have, in fact, operated as projected is open to question. See, among others, James S. Bowman, "Whistle Blowing: Literature and Resource Materials," *Public Administration Review*, 43 (May/June 1983), 271–76; "Federal Whistle Blower's Transfer Order Probed," an Associated Press wire service story appearing in the Bloomington-Normal (Ill.) *Daily Pantagraph*, March 18, 1983, p. A-3; "Whistleblower Protection Program Questioned," *Congressional Quarterly Weekly Report*, 42 (November 3, 1984), 2872–73; and "Schroeder Says 'Whistleblower' Office Failed," *Congressional Quarterly Weekly Report*, 43 (June 22, 1985), 1226.

57. Lloyd G. Nigro, "CSRA Performance Appraisals and Merit Pay: Growing Uncertainty in the Federal Work Force," *Public Administration Review*, 42 (July/August 1982), 371–75, at p. 371.

58. Testimony of Dwight A. Ink, *Hearings on the Senior Executive Service*, February 28, 1984, p. 91.

59. Ibid.

60. See, for example, *Evaluations Called For to Monitor and Assess Executive Appraisal Systems*, A Report to the Congress of the United States by the Comptroller General, General Accounting Office Report No. FPCD-81-55 (Washington, D.C.: U.S. Government Printing Office, August 3, 1981); and testimony of Hugh H. Heclo, *Hearings on the Senior Executive Service*, April 12, 1984, pp. 336–37.

61. Ross, "Commitment and Loyalty as a Determinant of Performance Ratings." See also Craig Eric Schneier and Richard W. Beatty, "Performance Appraisal and the Law: Methods for Meeting Legal Requirements in Assessing Behavior at Work," in Cohen and Golembiewski, eds., *Public Personnel Update*; Lovrich, ed., "Performance Appraisal Reforms in the Public Sector: The Promise and Pit-

falls of Employee Evaluation—A Symposium,'' in *Review of Public Personnel Administration*, 3 (Summer 1983), 1–132; Ronald W. Clement and Eileen K. Aranda, ''Performance Appraisal in the Public Sector: Truth or Consequences?'' *Review of Public Personnel Administration*, 5 (Fall 1984), 34–42; Nicholas P. Lovrich, Jr., Ronald H. Hopkins, Paul L. Shaffer, and Donald A. Yale, ''Participative Performance Appraisal Effects Upon Job Satisfaction, Agency Climate, and Work Values: Results of a Quasi-Experimental Study in Six State Agencies,'' *Review of Public Personnel Administration*, 1 (Summer 1981), 51–73; Roger B. Parks, ''Linking Objective and Subjective Measures of Performance,'' *Public Administration Review*, 44 (March/April 1984), 118–27; and Les Canges, ''The Factor/Anchored Performance Appraisal System: Implementing and Evaluating a Performance Appraisal System to Support Pay-for-Performance in the State of Colorado,'' paper delivered at the annual conference of the American Society for Public Administration; Denver, Colorado; April 8–11, 1984.
62. Cited in *Hearings on The Senior Executive Service*, p. 159.
63. William J. Lanouette, ''SES—From Civil Service Showpiece to Incipient Failure in Two Years,'' *National Journal*, 13 (July 18, 1981), 1296–99, at p. 1296.
64. Bernard Rosen, ''Uncertainty in the Senior Executive Service,'' *Public Administration Review*, 41 (March/April 1981), 203–7, at p. 206.
65. Testimony of Hugh H. Heclo, *Hearings on The Senior Executive Service*, p. 338. Numerous witnesses referred to this exodus in the course of these hearings in late 1983 and early 1984.
66. Cited in *Hearings on The Senior Executive Service*, p. 159.
67. Stahl, *Public Personnel Administration*, p. 322.
68. *A 2-Year Appraisal of Merit Pay in Three Agencies*, A Report to the Congress of the United States by the Comptroller General, General Accounting Office Report No. GAO/GGD-84-1 (Washington, D.C.: U.S. Government Printing Office, March 26, 1984).
69. See Jone L. Pearce and James L. Perry, ''Federal Merit Pay: A Longitudinal Analysis,'' *Public Adminstration Review*, 43 (July/August 1983), 315–25.
70. Ibid., p. 324.
71. Buddy Robert Silverman, ''The Merit Pay System: Prognosis,'' *Review of Public Personnel Administration*, 2 (Summer 1982), 29–34, at p. 31.
72. Daniel E. O'Toole and John R. Churchill, ''Implementing Pay-For-Performance: Initial Experiences,'' *Review of Public Personnel Administration*, 2 (Summer 1982), 13–28, at p. 26.
73. Testimony of Rep. Patricia Schroeder, *Hearings on The Senior Executive Service*, p. 373. One possible remedy for this deterioration is discussed in Paul Lorentzen, ''Stress in Political-Career Executive Relations,'' *Public Administration Review*, 45 (May/June 1985), 411–14.
74. Bernard Rosen, ''Effective Continuity of U.S. Government Operations in Jeopardy,'' *Public Administration Review*, 43 (September/October 1983), 383–92, at p. 390 (emphasis added).
75. Cited in *Hearings on The Senior Executive Service*, p. 242.
76. Ibid.
77. A comprehensive compilation of statements and articles by OPM Director Devine can be found in *Public Administration in the Reagan Era: Instructional Materials for Use in OPM Executive and Management Development Programs*, Publication Number P-91 (Washington, D.C.: U.S. Office of Personnel Management, Feb-

ruary 1985). For another perspective, see James P. Pfiffner, "Political Public Administration," *Public Administration Review*, 45 (March/April 1985), 352–56.

78. Testimony of Alan K. Campbell, *Hearings on The Senior Executive Service*, p. 318.
79. Testimony of Hugh H. Heclo, *Hearings on The Senior Executive Service*, p. 337.
80. Rosen, "Effective Continuity of U.S. Government Operations in Jeopardy," especially pp. 383–86. Numerous references were made to this phenomenon in the Senior Executive Service Hearings as well. See also Richard E. Schmidt and Mark A. Abramson, "Politics and Performance: What Does It Mean for Civil Servants?" *Public Administration Review*, 43 (March/April 1983), 155–60.
81. Testimony of Rep. Patricia Schroeder, *Hearings on The Senior Executive Service*, p. 373. For discussion of a related set of issues, see Charles H. Levine, ed., *The Unfinished Agenda of Civil Service Reform* (Washington, D.C.: Brookings, 1985).
82. See, among others, Ollie A. Jensen, "Cultural Bias in Selection," *Public Personnel Review*, 27 (April 1966), 125–30.
83. *Distribution of Male and Female Employees in Four Federal Classification Systems*, A Report to the Congress of the United States by the Comptroller General, General Accounting Office Report No. GAO/GGD-85-20 (Washington, D.C.: U.S. Government Printing Office, November 27, 1984), Table 1.
84. Ibid., Table 5.
85. "Minorities, Women Gain in White-Collar Jobs," *Public Administration Times*, 3 (July 15, 1980), 12.
86. See, among others, N. Joseph Cayer and Lee Sigelman, "Minorities and Women in State and Local Government: 1973–1975," *Public Administration Review*, 40 (September/October 1980), 443–50; Frank J. Thompson, "Deregulation at the EEOC: Prospects and Implications," *Review of Public Personnel Administration*, 4 (Summer 1984), 41–56, at p. 52; and Nelson C. Dometrius and Lee Sigelman, "Assessing Progress Toward Affirmative Action Goals in State and Local Government: A New Benchmark," *Public Administration Review*, 44 (May/June 1984), 241–46, especially p. 244. The Thompson article, and that by David Rosenbloom cited in note 88, appear in Jack Rabin, ed., "The Future of Affirmative Action and Equal Employment Opportunity: A Symposium," *Review of Public Personnel Administration*, 4 (Summer 1984), 1–82. See also Stahl, *Public Personnel Administration*, pp. 71–87; Dennis L. Dresang, *Public Personnel Management and Public Policy* (Boston: Little, Brown, 1984), chapter 5; Steven W. Hays and T. Zane Reeves, *Personnel Management in the Public Sector* (Boston: Allyn and Bacon, 1984), chapter 11; Edward J. Clynch and Carol A. Gaudin, "Sex in the Shipyards: An Assessment of Affirmative Action Policy," *Public Administration Review*, 42 (March/April 1982), 114–21; Rita B. Bocher, "Does Tradition Affect Affirmative Action Results? How Pennsylvania Achieved Changes at the Middle Management Level," *Public Administration Review*, 42 (September/October 1982), 475–78; and Hindy Lauer Schachter, "Retroactive Seniority and Agency Retrenchment," *Public Administration Review*, 43 (January/February 1983), 77–81.
87. "Reverse Discrimination Claim Rejected," a Los Angeles *Times* wire service story, appearing in the Bloomington-Normal (Ill.) *Daily Pantagraph*, January 8, 1985, p. A-1. The case was *Bushey* v. *New York State Civil Service Commission*, 84-336.
88. See David H. Rosenbloom, "The Declining Salience of Affirmative Action in Federal Personnel Management," *Review of Public Personnel Administration*, 4

(Summer 1984), 31–40. Rosenbloom argues, however, that progress toward a socially representative public work force still can be maintained, even if his prediction proves correct.

89. *Elrod* v. *Burns,* 427 U.S. 347 (1976); *Hollifield* v. *McMahan,* 438 F. Supp. 591 (1977); *Shakman* v. *The Democratic Organization of Cook County,* 481 F. Supp. 1315 (1979); and *Branti* v. *Finkel,* 100 S. Ct. 1287 (1980). For a penetrating critique of the *Elrod* and *Branti* decisions, see Kenneth John Meier, "Ode to Patronage: A Critical Analysis of Two Recent Supreme Court Decisions," *Public Administration Review,* 41 (September/October 1981), 558–63.

90. This description is taken from Philip L. Martin, "The Hatch Act in Court: Some Recent Developments," *Public Administration Review,* 33 (September/October 1973), 443–47, at p. 443.

91. *National Association of Letter Carriers, AFL-CIO* v. *United States Civil Service Commission,* 346 F. Supp. 578 (1972).

92. Dresang, *Public Personnel Management and Public Policy,* p. 270.

93. Ibid., p. 271.

94. Ibid.

95. Elaine Johansen, "Managing the Revolution: The Case for Comparable Worth," *Review of Public Personnel Administration,* 4 (Spring 1984), 14–27, at p. 15. See also by Johansen, "Comparable Worth: Surveying the Controversy," *The Bureaucrat,* 13 (Spring 1984), 8–11, and "Comparable Worth: The Character of a Controversy," *Public Administration Review,* 45 (September/October 1985), 631–35. See also Lois Friss, "Equal Pay for Comparable Work: Stimulus for Future Civil Service Reform," *Review of Public Personnel Administration,* 2 (Summer 1982), 37–48; and Mary Helen Doherty and Ann Harriman, "Comparable Worth: The Equal Employment Issue of the 1980s," *Review of Public Personnel Administration,* 1 (Summer 1981), 11–31.

96. Geoffrey Cowley, "Another Terrible Idea," *The Bureaucrat,* 13 (Spring 1984), 16–19. In the same issue, see O. Glenn Stahl, "Neo-Job-Evaluation and Old Obstacles," pp. 12–14.

97. Stahl, *Public Personnel Administration,* pp. 323–24.

98. "States Lead the Way in Pay Equality," an Associated Press wire service story appearing in the Memphis (Tenn.) *Commercial-Appeal,* August 14, 1984, p. C-6; *Public Administration Times,* 8 (July 1, 1985), 3.

99. See "Reagan Says Comparable Pay Program Might Pose Intrusion," an Associated Press wire service story appearing in the Bloomington-Normal (Ill.) *Daily Pantagraph,* October 20, 1984, p. A-6; *Public Administration Times,* 8 (March 15, 1985), 1; and *Public Administration Times,* 8 (July 1, 1985), 1.

SUGGESTED READINGS

Cayer, N. Joseph. *Managing Human Resources: An Introduction to Public Personnel Administration.* New York: St. Martin's, 1980.

_____. *Public Personnel Administration in the United States,* 2nd ed. New York: St. Martin's, 1986.

Dresang, Dennis L. *Public Personnel Management and Public Policy.* Boston: Little, Brown, 1984.

Hays, Steven W., and T. Zane Reeves. *Personnel Management in the Public Sector*. Boston: Allyn and Bacon, 1984.

Hurley, Charlotte. "Civil Service Reform: An Annotated Bibliography." *Review of Public Personnel Administration*, 2 (Summer 1982), 59–90.

Krislov, Samuel, and David H. Rosenbloom. *Representative Bureaucracy and the American Political System*. New York: Praeger, 1981.

Lee, Robert D., Jr. *Public Personnel Systems*, 3rd ed. Baltimore: University Park Press, 1982.

Levitan, Sar A., and Alexandra B. Noden. *Working for the Sovereign*. Baltimore: The Johns Hopkins University Press, 1983.

Matzer, John, Jr., ed. *Creative Personnel Practices: New Ideas for Local Government*. Washington, D.C.: International City Management Association, 1984.

Mosher, Frederick C. *Democracy and the Public Service*, 2nd ed. New York: Oxford University Press, 1982.

Nigro, Felix A., and Lloyd G. Nigro. *The New Public Personnel Administration*, 2nd ed. Itasca, Ill.: Peacock, 1981.

Patten, Thomas H., Jr., ed. *Classics of Personnel Management*. Oak Park, Ill.: Moore Publishing, 1979.

Rosenbloom, David H., ed. *Centenary Issues of the Pendleton Act of 1883: The Problematic Legacy of Civil Service Reform*. New York: Marcel Dekker, 1983.

Shafritz, Jay M., Albert C. Hyde, and David H. Rosenbloom. *Personnel Management in Government: Politics and Process*, 3rd ed. New York: Marcel Dekker, 1986.

Stahl, O. Glenn. *Public Personnel Administration*, 8th ed. New York: Harper & Row, 1983.

Thompson, Frank J., ed. *Classics of Public Personnel Policy*. Oak Park, Ill.: Moore Publishing, 1979.

11

Collective Bargaining in the Public Sector

A local teachers' association authorizes its negotiating team to call for a strike vote as bargaining with the school board threatens to bog down—with the first day of school fast approaching! Firemen go on strike because agreement cannot be reached on whether fire captains and lieutenants should be considered as part of the bargaining unit (labor) or as supervisory personnel (management). After years of discontent with Federal Aviation Administration policies toward air traffic controllers, the controllers' union goes on strike over salaries and number of hours in the work week—and the Reagan administration responds by firing over 11,000 controllers from their jobs. Police in an eastern city stage a "sick-in" (the "blue flu"), with nearly half of the normal force staying home on grounds of illness. A mayor proclaims he will "stand up" to union demands for higher salaries; he submits the question to a public referendum, and the voters side with the mayor—by a wide margin!

These incidents (all of them real cases), and others like them, suggest the emergence of a dimension of public personnel administration very different from much of our past experience. Especially since the late 1950s, collective bargaining procedures—modeled largely after those in the private sector—have replaced traditional management-oriented (and controlled) personnel practices in many jurisdictions, at all levels of government. As a consequence, there have been frequent and significant shifts in effective decision-making authority on personnel matters, changes in the distribution of political and policy influence, and, on occasion, very visible implications for the delivery of even the most essential public services.

In this chapter we shall examine (1) the general nature and dynamics of public-sector collective bargaining; (2) the history and recent resurgence of public employee labor organizations; (3) the sequence of steps involved in the actual process of collective bargaining between employers and em-

354

ployees; (4) resolving labor-management disputes, through arbitration, mediation, or the strike; and (5) the impacts and likely future of collective bargaining in the public sector.

GOVERNMENT LABOR-MANAGEMENT RELATIONS: AN OVERVIEW

The term *labor-management relations*—the framework for collective bargaining—suggests something quite specific about the kinds of interactions that take place between managers and their employees. At the very least, it implies that employees have consciously chosen to organize themselves for the purpose of dealing with their superiors concerning terms and conditions of employment. Beyond that, in both public and private sectors, what is suggested is *greater sharing* of control over what, at one time, were strictly management's prerogatives in managing the workplace—that is, a basic reordering of the power to determine distribution of responsibility on the job, levels of compensation for work performed, procedures for airing and resolving grievances, conditions in the workplace, and the like. Viewed another way, labor-management relations represent a form of organizational participation—permitting individuals and groups other than formal leaders to have a meaningful voice in directing the organization. Many government employees (for example, police and fire personnel) have had influence in dealing with their employers in the past. But this newer form of participation is normally governed rather strictly by contractual provisions arrived at through a joint process, and ratified by both management and labor. Thus, an essential element of labor-management relations is the phenomenon of *structured relationships* between *formally organized* participants, in a *shared* management process.

This description could apply equally to industrial and governmental labor-management relations. However, it would be a mistake (here as elsewhere in public administration) to overlook significant differences that exist between the two settings.[1] For example, top public managers are chosen through elections and political appointments, both of which labor groups and the general public influence; such is not the case in private management. Another difference is the near impossibility of separating public-sector bargaining from the political process. Thus, the term "multilateral" bargaining (many-sided) is increasingly used in the public sector, rather than "bilateral" (two-sided), reflecting the involvement of many others besides management and labor bargaining teams. A third difference is the obvious contrast in types of products in public and private sectors—there are different markets for each, their purposes differ, and (most important to some observers) most public organizations have had a virtual monopoly over the rendering of certain essential public services—such as police, fire,

Figure 11-1   Dimensions of Bargaining

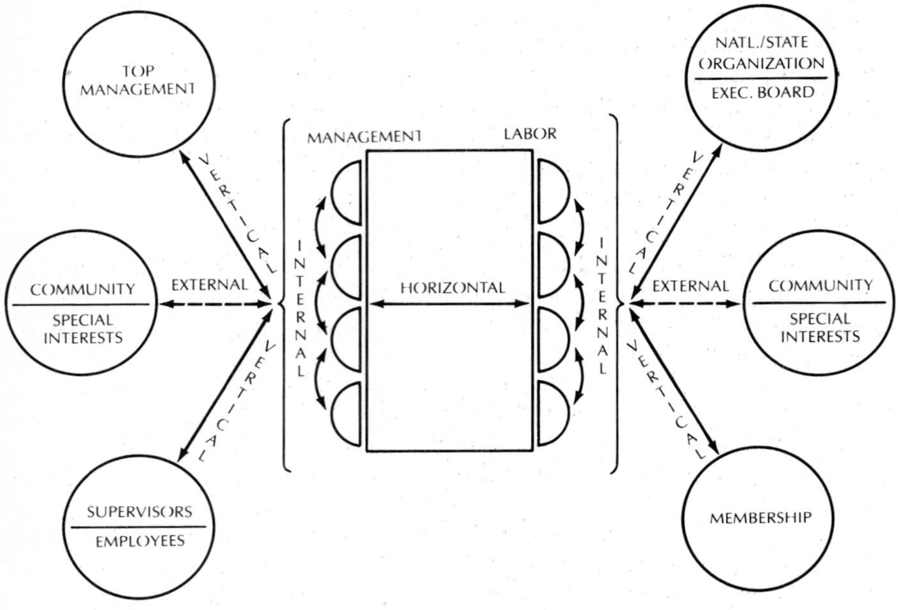

Source: The author is indebted to Professor Irving O. Dawson for this figure.

and sanitation—making the nonmonetary costs to public health and safety very high in the event of a strike or work slowdown.

A fourth difference is the degree to which the public can come to be involved in management's choices of general policy options and specific bargaining proposals in the collective bargaining process. Members of a local school board would be wise to heed strong public sentiments—about teachers' salary levels, school being held, children receiving a good education—when dealing with the teachers' association. While private managers must be mindful of economic impacts of their choices in dealing with labor, they are immune from public reprisals in the form of being thrown out of office. Also, both management and labor must be attentive to preferences of their respective organized constituency groups (see Figure 11-1). Still another difference is the fact that public managers, unlike their private counterparts, rarely have the last word on a labor-management agreement; legislative controls, the possibility of appeals to the courts, state government restrictions on many local governments, and so on, highlight the precarious position in which many public managers often find themselves. One final, and crucial, difference is the tremendous variety of *legal* frameworks for public sector labor relations that exists in the fifty states and the thousands of separate local governments (and the national government). This is in stark contrast to the single national framework for the private sector; we shall treat this aspect more fully, later in the chapter. In short, politics—in its many forms—pervades labor-management relations in the public sector in ways not found in private industry.

A caution may be in order about important distinctions among some of the catchwords most commonly encountered in dealing with this subject. First, not all employee organizations are formally labor unions. Other historically prominent types of organizations include various employee and professional *associations* (for example, of nurses and social workers). Early objectives of such groups included bettering the status of their members and improving the well-being of the respective professions.[2] These organizations have been drawn increasingly into the arena of collective bargaining, as a result of pressures from rival organizations formed, many times, explicitly for the purpose of bargaining. For example, the National Education Association (NEA), representing some 1.8 million teachers, has become significantly more militant in response to the growing success of the American Federation of Teachers (AFT), a self-conscious labor union committed to the collective bargaining process.[3]

A second caveat is simply that collective bargaining, as a process, is of recent vintage as a significant element of public employer-employee relations. In fact, only since the 1960s has collective bargaining played an important role in public personnel administration.

A third cautionary note is that neither collective bargaining nor labor unionization is necessarily synonymous with public employee strikes. Although strikes are by far the most widely reported, visible, and controversial of all the varied aspects of public-sector labor-management relations, that should not be permitted to obscure the fact that *most* labor-management interactions—including *most* collective bargaining processes and outcomes—*do not result* in strikes by public employees. The strike issue is one component of the total topic; while feelings often run high on that issue, one should take care to consider other aspects of labor relations as they deserve to be considered—that is, separate from the strike question.

Finally, it should be noted that neither management nor labor is all-powerful in decision making about management of the public workplace. Especially in recent years, the interest of ordinary citizens has grown considerably in the contents and procedures of labor-management relations. If nothing else, the taxpayer still has to foot the bill (however indirectly) for costs incurred in reaching agreements. Consequently, it is no longer the case (if it ever really was) that formal bargaining and other forms of decision making in this area can take place without some accounting having to be made to the ultimate board of directors, that is, the people. This is a central dimension of *multilateralism* in public-sector bargaining, and it has taken many forms. Two examples from the education area are instructive. In California, the state "sunshine" bargaining law requires that proposals be publicly disclosed before school boards may begin negotiations with teachers.

And in 1976, Rochester (New York) adopted a "parent involvement policy," which among other things invites parent participation in collective bargaining by: (1) having parents work with the school board as it prepares its bargaining position before the opening of negotiations, and (2) appointing one carefully selected parent to serve on the board's bargaining team.[4] Thus, the larger reality of accountability to the general public is inescapable. And in ways decidedly different from private-sector bargaining, both parties to labor-management agreements must be mindful of the impacts on the citizenry, and of possible public backlash against particular provisions or the whole system of bargaining. In this era of declining public confidence, as well as tighter government budgets, such concerns merit a great deal of attention from both union officials and public managers—and they are increasingly receiving that attention.

HISTORICAL DEVELOPMENT OF PUBLIC EMPLOYEE ORGANIZATIONS

Since the mid-1800s, various types of public employee organizations have been in existence, but none of them engaged at first in collective bargaining. One of the earliest examples of unionization was craftsmen in naval installations, dating back to the early 1800s.[5] Also at the national government level, the National Association of Letter Carriers was formed (in the late 1800s) as an affiliate of the fledgling American Federation of Labor (AFL).[6] Teacher associations date from the 1850s; police fraternal associations originated in the 1880s; and the International Association of Fire Fighters (IAFF) was formed in the 1880s, serving at the outset as "local social clubs and firemen's benefit societies."[7] Even in this early period, and in the absence of a formal bargaining process, there were confrontations, leading to some labor gains: work stoppages at U.S. Navy Yard installations in the 1830s (which produced a shorter work day at the order of President Martin Van Buren in 1840);[8] police strikes in Cincinnati in 1918 and Boston in 1919 (the latter led in the short run to the firing of 1,200 striking policemen, though it became a rallying point for emerging militancy among police associations); and passage by Congress, in 1912, of the Lloyd-La Follette Act, which granted national government employees the right to join labor organizations and to petition Congress concerning conditions of employment without fear of reprisal.[9]

Two national government employee unions—the National Federation of Federal Employees (NFFE) and the American Federation of Government Employees (AFGE)—were founded in 1917 and 1932, respectively, and the American Federation of State, County, and Municipal Employees (AFSCME) was established in 1936. A number of other unions also have been formed within specific national government departments or professions, such as the National Treasury Employees Union and the National Association of Letter Carriers.[10]

Taken together, these unions and others like them came to constitute a potentially formidable base for labor activity in the public sector. Still, until the early 1960s, few of these developments led to actual establishment of collective bargaining machinery. Exceptions include a 1954 executive order issued by New York City's Mayor Robert Wagner granting municipal employees the right to organize, with collective bargaining machinery operating by 1958; the decision by the state of Wisconsin in 1959 to authorize collective bargaining for local government employees;[11] and the practice in some major northeastern cities of negotiating conditions of employment (in the absence of legal authorization) since before World War II (Philadelphia has negotiated labor agreements with provisions for union security and exclusive recognition since 1939[12]).

The real turning point for public-sector labor unions, one which signaled the rapid rise of collective bargaining on a large scale, came in the early 1960s, when President John F. Kennedy convened a Task Force on Employee-Managment Relations in the Federal Service, chaired by Labor Secretary Arthur Goldberg. After a careful study of labor-managment practices in the private sector, in public jurisdictions, and in the national government itself (as well as practices in selected countries overseas), the Task Force made its report to the president. On the basis of that report, Kennedy issued Executive Order (EO) 10988 in 1962. It extended to national government employees the right to organize and engage in collective bargaining, providing, among other things, for withholding of union dues and for advisory arbitration of employee grievances, and prohibiting union shops (where all employees are compelled to be union members). While this order legally altered the policy of only the national government on bargaining with its own employees, "it also stimulated state and local governments to reexamine and change many of their policies."[13] Thus, while the national government was not the first to establish comprehensive new labor relations policies, Kennedy's action (which redeemed a 1960 presidential campaign pledge) served as a catalyst for change, with nationwide repercussions at all government levels.

Recent National Government Experience

In the national government, following Kennedy's executive order, there began a period of intensive growth in membership in most unions spurred on by deliberate efforts by various union organizers to increase membership.[14] Table 11–1 presents data indicating numbers and percentages of national government employees who belonged to labor organizations representing *exclusive bargaining units* (those represented in negotiations by only one labor group, chosen by majority vote), or who were covered by formal labor-management agreements, during the period 1963–1983.

Table 11-1
NATIONAL GOVERNMENT EMPLOYEES IN EXCLUSIVE UNITS AND
COVERED BY AGREEMENT, 1963–1983

| | | | Employees in Exlusive Units | | | | Employees Covered by Agreement | |
| | Total Employees | | Wage System Employees | | General Schedule Employees | | | |
Year[1]	Total	Per-cent	Number	Per-cent	Number	Per-cent	Number	Per-cent
1963	180,000							
1964	230,543	12					110,573	6
1965	319,724	16					241,850	12
1966	434,890[2]	21	226,150	40	179,293	15	291,532	14
1967	629,915	29	338,660	54	291,255	21	423,052	20
1968	797,511	40	400,669	67	396,842	28	556,962	28
1969	842,823	42	426,111	72	416,712	29	559,415	28
1970	916,381	48	429,136	81	487,245	35	601,505	31
1971	1,038,288	53	437,586	84	600,702	42	707,067	36
1972	1,082,587	55	427,089	83	655,498	46	753,247	39
1973	1,086,361	56	404,955	84	681,406	47	837,410	43
1974	1,142,419	57	406,000	82	736,419	48	984,553	49
1975	1,200,336	59	410,716	84	789,620	51	1,083,017	53
1976	1,190,478	58	384,820	83	806,658	51	1,059,663	52
1977	1,197,910	58	376,229	81	821,681	52	1,059,635	51
1978	1,228,136	60	382,154	85	845,982	53	1,120,326	55
1979	1,245,988	61	376,707	81	869,281	55	1,148,822	56
1980	1,249,999	61	375,141	86	874,858	54	1,167,265	57
1981	1,234,256	61	384,890	88	849,366	54	1,152,509	57
1983	1,234,831	61	378,320	88	856,511	54	1,140,001	56

[1]1963–1966 statistics are based on figures as of mid-year; 1967–1981 figures are as of November; no statistics were issued in 1982; 1983 figures are as of January 31,1983.

[2]Wage system and general schedule do not equal total due to the unavailability of information on the status of some employees.

Source: U.S. Office of Personnel Management, Office of Labor-Management Relations, *Union Recognition in the Federal Government,* OALMR 83-1, December 1983, p. 30. The author is indebted to Professor Irving O. Dawson for suggesting this data source, and to Alan V. Stevens of the Census Bureau for furnishing the data. The figures quoted are for executive branch employees excluding the Postal Service, FBI, CIA, NSA, TVA, and foreign nationals employed outside the United States.

As the data indicate, the total number of employees in exclusive units increased nearly sixfold between 1963 and 1971 (from 180,000 to just over 1 million), with the rate of increase slowing somewhat after that date. Also, both the number and the percentage of all employees covered by formal agreements increased significantly, from some 110,000 in 1964 to over 1.1 million in 1983—a tenfold jump. As of 1983, nearly 1.24 million national government civilian employees were represented by non-postal labor unions (over 60 percent of all such employees), and an additional half million postal employees also had union representation. After that time, however, the percentage of non-postal union members in the national government began a slight downturn, and future trends are unclear. Also, it should be noted that with regard to these and any other figures dealing with union size, the number of union *members* is not the same as the number of employees having union *representation*. The latter is almost always considerably higher than the former, since those who do not pay union dues can also be represented in collective bargaining, and are governed by any contractual agreements reached.

Growth in union membership and representation was not the only important development in the national government. Three additional executive orders—two issued by Richard Nixon and one by Gerald Ford—further clarified and elaborated on "rules of the game" first laid down in EO 10988, in response to pressures for change from both labor and management. Executive Order 11491 (October 1969), amended further by EO 11616 (August 1971), made these changes (among others) in the provisions of President Kennedy's order.[15]

First, three new agencies were created in order to centralize decision making that had previously been in the hands of individual executive branch agencies. These were the Federal Labor Relations Council (to administer EO 11491), the Federal Service Impasses Panel (to aid in resolving negotiating impasses), and a new Assistant Secretary of Labor for Labor-Management Relations (who exercised responsibility for making decisions concerning, among other things, bargaining units, representation, and unfair labor practices).[16]

Second, the Federal Mediation and Conciliation Service (already in existence) was given a role in mediating negotiation disputes.

Third, a requirement for reporting and disclosure procedures similar to those demanded of unions in private employment was imposed for the first time.

In February 1975, Gerald Ford issued EO 11838, further amending the previous orders. The major issues dealt with by this order were: (1) consolidating existing bargaining units; (2) definition of a supervisor (the layer of management closest to the actual work unit); (3) limitations on the right of individual agencies, through their respective regulations, to restrict the scope of negotiations—that is, what issues are to be subjects of collective bargaining; (4) expansion of grievance and arbitration procedures; (5) placing time limits on agency heads for approval of contracts; and (6) settlement of negotiability disputes arising from unfair labor practices.

A further significant step was taken with passage of Jimmy Carter's Civil Service Reform Act of 1978 (see chapter 10). One of the most important consequences of the Act was to place in statutory form (in Title VII) many terms of the various executive orders, so that "presidents no longer have the authority to regulate the process on their own."[17] Title VII represents a comprehensive, rather than incremental, statement of labor-management regulations. Some specifics in the Act that pertain to collective bargaining included creation of an independent Federal Labor Relations Authority, with powers greater than those of the old Federal Labor Relations Council (including a general counsel authorized to bring unfair labor charges); negotiated grievance procedures were brought into the scope of bargaining; labor unions were extended free automatic dues checkoff, if authorized by the employee; any agencies that issue governmentwide regulations were required to consult with unions before taking any action that would make a substantial change in employment conditions; and judicial review of some Federal Labor Relations Authority final orders was permitted.[18] The net effect of these changes in the past twenty-five years has been to put in place a complex and varied set of regulations governing a wide range of labor-management relations in the national government service. The days of unilateral personnel management, without the participation of—and accommodation to—government employees represented by their unions, are long gone.

Recent State and Local Government Experience

At state and local levels, the labor relations picture is quite different from that in the national government, in several key respects. For one thing, the total *number* of public employees belonging to labor unions, or covered by

Table 11-2
ORGANIZED FULL-TIME EMPLOYEES, BY LEVEL AND TYPE OF GOVERNMENT, 1982

Level and Type of Government	Organized Full-time Employees	
	Number	Percent Organized (of All Full-time Employees)
Total	4,645,060	45.7%
State governments	1,065,981	37.4
Local governments	3,579,079	48.9
Counties	536,847	35.1
Municipalities	1,053,069	52.7
Townships	138,225	62.4
Special districts	141,666	36.4
School districts	1,709,272	53.8

Source: U.S. Bureau of the Census, *1982 Census of Governments, Vol. 3, No. 3, Labor-Management Relations in State and Local Governments,* U.S. Government Printing Office, Washington, D.C., 1985. Percentage figures shown indicate proportion of full-time employees in each category who are organized. All figures are as of October 1982.

Table 11-3
ORGANIZED FULL-TIME EMPLOYEES, BY LEVEL OF GOVERNMENT AND FUNCTION, 1982

Function	State and Local Governments	State Governments	Local Governments
Total	45.7%	37.4%	48.9%
For selected functions:			
Education	51.6	26.9	57.3
Instructional staff	61.1	30.2	64.3
Other	34.9	25.3	40.0
Highways	44.2	53.2	36.0
Public welfare	43.8	46.3	41.7
Hospitals	30.0	43.2	16.2
Police protection	51.2	46.1	51.9
Local fire protection	66.5	—	66.5
Sanitation other than sewerage	43.8	—	43.8
All other functions	38.7	37.9	39.1

Source: U.S. Bureau of the Census, *1982 Census of Governments, Vol. 3, No. 3, Labor-Management Relations in State and Local Governments*, U.S. Government Printing Office, Washington, D.C., 1985. Percentage figures shown indicate proportion of full-time employees in each category who are organized. All figures are as of October 1982. For the data in Tables 11-2 and 11-3, the author is indebted to Alan V. Stevens; Chief, Employment Branch; Governments Division; U.S. Bureau of the Census; Washington, D.C.

bargaining agreements, far exceeds that at the national level; in *percentage* terms, however, state-local unionization covers just under half of all full-time employees (compared to some 60 percent in the national government). Since the early 1960s a tremendous increase has occurred in state-local labor organization membership in the public sector. About 1.6 million public employees belonged to labor organizations in 1962, by one estimate; by 1980, the number had risen to just over 5 million, before falling to 4.6 million in 1982. Of that total, some 1 million were state employees. The remaining 3,580,000 worked for municipalities, counties, townships, school districts, and other special districts, representing just under one-half of all full-time local government employees (down, however, from 56 percent in 1974).[19]

Tables 11-2 and 11-3 present more detailed data for the year 1982, indicating in addition to the figures shown that school districts alone accounted for 48 percent of all organized—that is, unionized—local government employees, and 37 percent of all organized employees in state and local governments combined. Also, school districts and municipalities together accounted for over three-fourths of organized local employees, and almost 60 percent of those organized in both state and local governments. The functions in state government most heavily unionized were highways, public welfare, and police protection, each with about one-half of all employees organized; at the local level, fire protection and teaching in the schools stood out above the rest.

The largest state-local employee organization (with some 1.8 million members) is the NEA—perhaps significantly, traditionally the less militant of the teachers' organizations.[20] Other organizations with sizeable, powerful, and stable or growing memberships include AFSCME, AFT, and IAFF.[21] These last three experienced especially rapid growth in the 1960s and 1970s; AFSCME membership grew from about 235,000 to over 1 million, while AFT swelled its ranks from 100,000 to well over 600,000.

A second important difference between the state-local and national settings is the far greater complexity of state and local laws and regulations governing collective bargaining. As political scientist N. Joseph Cayer has noted, "There is no common legal framework under which state and local government labor relations are governed. . . . Labor relations take place under policies made through common law doctrines, judicial decisions, executive orders, and statutes and ordinances."[22] Political scientist Richard Kearney has described the overall situation this way:

> These policies exhibit considerable divergence. State legislation, for instance, ranges from a single comprehensive statute providing coverage for all public employees in Iowa, to coverage of only firefighters in Wyoming, to the total prohibition of collective bargaining in North Carolina. In other states, public employees bargain under the authority of an attorney general's opinion (North Dakota), an executive order (Illinois state employees [until 1984]), or civil service regulations (New Mexico state employees). . . . [A]t least one group of public workers is covered under labor legislation permitting negotiations in forty states, and all but Arkansas, Arizona, and Mississippi have passed laws regulating some aspect of employer-employee relations. . . . Twenty-six states currently provide bargaining coverage for all major employee groups, either through a single comprehensive public employee relations policy or separate policies for different functions. Fourteen states regulate employer-employee negotiations in one to four occupational categories, whereas ten states [all but one in the South and Rocky Mountain regions] do not have public policies permitting bargaining for any group of employees.[23]

Labor relations experts Marvin Levine and Eugene Hagburg have stated, in sum, that "the labor relations situation for public employees is different in every city, county, and state, and the *general* status of public sector labor relations is still undefined."[24] Kearney notes, however, the recent trend toward extending comprehensive coverage to all state and local government workers.[25]

A third difference between the national government and state-local government is the extent to which public employees have resorted to the strike as an instrument of labor-management relations—even in government jurisdictions (the overwhelming majority) that forbid employees from going out on strike! The strike is prohibited entirely at the national government level, and only in the past twenty years has there been any moderating of state resistance to permitting it. Since the 1960s, nine states have provided for a limited right to strike (Alaska, Hawaii, Minnesota, Montana, Oregon, Pennsylvania, Rhode Island, Vermont, and Wisconsin).[26] For a strike to fall within permissible limits, it must not endanger public health, safety, or welfare; it can occur only after the parties have exhausted mediation and fact-finding efforts, in good faith; unions must file notice of intent to strike; and the dispute must not have been ruled upon by an arbitrator.[27] Nevertheless, in the face of legal limitations and outright prohibitions, there have been literally hundreds of strikes since the 1960s. While strikes against the national government draw wide attention (e.g., the postal strike at the beginning of the 1970s and the air traffic controllers' strike of 1981), the vast majority of such actions occurs at state and, especially, local levels—where publicity is more concentrated geographically, yet the impacts may be felt even more keenly by the affected public.

Thus, labor-management relations loom larger in state and local personnel management than in the national government—in quantitative terms, in complexity, and with regard to use of the strike. States and larger localities increasingly have looked to full-time labor relations specialists for guidance and expertise. In some government jurisdictions, such specialists are given major responsibility for conducting collective bargaining with employee representatives. With or without the assistance of these experts, however, public managers have had to become increasingly sensitive to, and skillful in dealing with, the needs and preferences—and formal demands—of their respective labor forces. In particular, they have had to learn the art of collective bargaining as a central element of personnel management.

THE COLLECTIVE BARGAINING PROCESS

The process of collective bargaining is comprised of a number of distinct steps and decision points, which are usually specified in some detail in government jurisdictions operating under comprehensive bargaining legislation. In such jurisdictions, the law specifies relevant organizational and administrative arrangements for implementing and enforcing the collective bargaining statute. In cases where there is no comprehensive statutory authority, many of the same procedural steps are also found, but they are lacking both the detail and the implementation mechanisms characteristic of more far-reaching legislation.[28]

Whatever the steps in the actual bargaining process, it is standard for bargaining to be supervised by an agency with specific oversight responsibility. Here, as in other aspects of collective bargaining, there is considerable variety in the specific form such supervision takes. In the national government, under terms of the 1978 Civil Service Reform Act, it is the Federal Labor Relations Authority (FLRA) that oversees the process of determining the appropriateness of bargaining units to be represented, supervising elections held for the purpose of choosing employee bargaining agents, and coordinating overall agency labor-management activities.[29] (These responsibilities assigned to the FLRA represent a reallocation of functions substantially differing from those made in Executive Order 11491, discussed earlier. Another change was to assign to a general counsel responsibility for investigating unfair labor practices. The role of the Federal Services Impasses Panel, however, was left largely unchanged.)

In state and local governments, a number of different arrangements are possible for supervising the bargaining process. In some states (such as Maine, New York, and Hawaii), an agency is created for the sole purpose of supervising collective bargaining as well as all other aspects of public employee labor relations; in some other states, responsibility is assigned to personnel departments, departments of labor, or personnel boards (as in Alaska, Massachusetts, Montana, and Wisconsin). Another variation involves supervision by a state board of the overall process, but with delegation to individual departments of specific responsibility for bargaining in their respective areas; examples might include a state department of education or a local board of education.[30]

The bargaining sequence consists of the following:

1. Labor organizing efforts, followed by the union seeking recognition as the bargaining agent;
2. Selection of the bargaining team, by both employees and management;
3. Defining the *scope* of bargaining, that is, just what issues will be subject to negotiation and what will *not* be, within the limits set by statute or executive order;
4. Putting forward proposals—and counterproposals;
5. Reaching agreement at the negotiating table (this assumes that agreement can be reached);
6. Submitting any agreement reached to a ratification vote of both employees and management;
7. In the event agreement cannot be reached, attempting to resolve impasses through impasse procedures (mediation, fact finding, arbitration, or referendum);
8. Dealing with the possibility—or reality—of a strike;
9. Once a contract is signed, collaborating in the implementation of its provisions (contract administration).

This is, in reality, a *cycle* rather than a literal sequence. Except for the very first contractual arrangement between management and labor, these steps are repeated periodically, with considerable incentive for both sides to prepare carefully—during the last "step" of the cycle, namely, contract implementation—for the next round of bargaining by keeping a complete record of "all problems, disputes, grievances, and interpretations" en-countered in administering the previous agreement.[31] After the process has become well established, the first two steps are normally omitted, unless there arises strong sentiment among employees for a change in the organi-zation representing them, or unless it is deemed desirable by one or both sides to change the composition of their respective bargaining teams.

Preliminary Steps

Assuming, however, a bargaining process that is just starting up, the first step calls for an effort by one or more labor organizations to seek recogni-tion from management as the bargaining representative of the labor force, or any part thereof. This may or may not be *exclusive* recognition, but if it is, the implications are important—for the employee, the union, and manage-ment. Under exclusivity, the union represents *all* employees, whether they voted for the union or not (and whether or not they formally join the un-ion). Management no longer can deal unilaterally with employees—it must consult with the union, and should management make separate deals with individuals, it would be guilty of an unfair labor practice.[32] There are ad-vantages, however, for both sides if a single voice speaks for employees during bargaining, the most important being the predictability and stability stemming from consistent, unified positions being taken. The recognition step usually involves a supervised election, in which employees choose among competing labor organizations seeking to represent them (such competition does not always occur, of course). The designated labor group then formally requests management recognition as bargaining agent.

Second, both management and employees must select their respec-tive bargaining teams. Employees have ordinarily had little difficulty in constituting their bargaining committees, drawing mostly from the mem-bers of the employee organization's executive board; almost always, this body enters into negotiations with a list of demands already formally ap-proved by the full membership.[33] Until recent years, however, management was often confronted with the necessity of overcoming splintered authority at the bargaining table. In many municipal governments, for example, re-sponsibility for personnel issues was shared (not always equally), among the local chief executive, the city council's finance committee, a department head, the budget director, the city controller, the city attorney, and possibly others.[34] As management suffered, however, for its lack of cohesion—and for the lack of expertise in negotiating that frequently accompanied this dif-fusion of responsibility—efforts were increasingly made to remedy such sit-uations. At the very least, one qualified individual is ordinarily agreed upon as chief spokesman for the management team; the larger the local government jurisdiction, the more likely that that individual is a labor rela-tions specialist. In the absence of such a specialist, officials such as those mentioned above, plus personnel or labor relations managers, might well be a part of the management team.[35] Some municipalities call upon elected officials—the mayor and members of the city council—to conduct labor negotiations. This arrangement, however, is widely viewed as unsatisfactory, due in part to the negotiators' lack of expertise in collective bargaining, and in part to the possibility—even the likelihood—that elected-official negotiators will lack familiarity with labor conditions, management negotiating positions, and consequences of bargaining in other government jurisdictions. Even in some smaller cities, responsible public officials sometimes contract with private professional labor relations firms to conduct negotiations on behalf of the city government. It has been said that this yields considerable benefit to the city by avoiding the pitfalls noted above.[36] All in all, many combinations of officials are possible in the composition of management's bargaining team; also, *"how formally organized* such a team is depends upon the jurisdiction."[37]

The Scope of Bargaining

The third step in the bargaining process is determining the scope of bargaining—what is and is not included on the list of negotiable issues. The most basic determining factor in this regard is the existence or absence of specific legislation pertaining to the scope of bargaining—statutory law that spells out what employee representatives may or may not bring to the bargaining table as appropriate subjects. Generally speaking, management prefers to limit the scope of bargaining, while employee bargainers—particularly those in labor unions—"want to expand the scope of bargaining as much as they can."[38] Thus, any legislation on the subject amounts to a clarification of *management's* rights, since without that, labor groups can make the scope of bargaining itself part of the list of negotiable issues!

Traditionally, at least in the private sector, bargaining centers on the issues of wages, hours, and working conditions as set out in the Taft-Hartley Act of 1947 (the basic law governing private-sector labor relations).[39] The majority of public employee bargaining statutes follow such precedents, though with considerable variation as to what else is negotiable. In the national government (perhaps alone among jurisdictions with formalized collective bargaining rules), pay, fringe benefits, and the work week are generally *excluded* from bargaining, while in state and local government even these "basics" are on occasion defined somewhat differently for purposes of negotiation. Generally speaking, however, most state and local governments have moved, at least partially, in the direction of using "total compensation"—the cost of *all* pay and benefits—as the basis for negotiation on these items.

The fact that compensation may not be negotiated in the national government, however, does not mean that the scope of bargaining is never an issue there. For example, in the summer of 1980 the FLRA ruled that performance standards for national government employees are not negotiable under terms of the 1978 Civil Service Reform Act.[40] In effect, the ruling was an extension of Executive Order 11491, under which work standards themselves were not negotiable, but the *procedures for establishing* those standards were subjects for negotiation. Consequently, while agency management has primary responsibility for setting standards of performance, it is unlikely that the standards established will become frozen into labor contracts, beyond the reach of employee negotiators.

During the past decade, the scope of bargaining in many government jurisdictions has been broadened (by *management*, in this case) to include the issues of "pay for performance" (that is, "merit pay" and the like) and wage "give-backs." These have emerged as bargaining issues due in large measure to the rising importance of budget constraints and fiscal retrenchment, and to the need for greater government productivity (see chapters 12 and 13). Public employees have been confronted with these issues at the bargaining table and have had to grapple with them, or else face an increased possibility of layoffs. These and similar issues are almost certain to become more prominent, in this era of more limited fiscal resources.

As in the private sector, there are three types of bargaining subjects, defined by statute.[41] *Mandatory* subjects are those that, by definition, must be negotiated; examples could include the whole area of wages (encompassing merit increases, incentive pay, holiday and vacation pay, and Christmas bonuses, among others), employment conditions (e.g., pension plans, insurance programs, terminations, and layoffs), changes in hours, rest and lunch periods, and changes in seniority. These, clearly, are basic to the interests of employees and their bargaining representatives. *Permissive* subjects, which management may negotiate but is not compelled to, might include training programs or counseling services,[42] location of facilities, services to be provided, and composition of the supervisory work force. *Illegal* or *prohibited* subjects—items outside the permissible scope of bargaining—might include provisions that promote arbitrary discrimination on the basis of race, sex, and the like, or that result in favored treatment for union members over nonmembers.

Among states, there is predictable variety in provisions governing the scope of bargaining. Most, as noted previously, permit bargaining on wages and fringe benefits (some, such as Nevada, make it mandatory to bargain on pay and other issues[43]). California, for one, opens virtually all personnel matters to the bargaining process, and in that state, the same applies for the municipal governments of Los Angeles and San Francisco. Some states, such as Hawaii, Maine, and Pennsylvania, "exclude issues such as merit systems policies, personnel direction, or items subject to managerial discretion. . . ."[44] In other places, mainly at the local level, the scope of bargaining may be restricted somewhat by civil service regulations and the "legal restraints of sovereignty,"[45] in addition to statutory provisions.

There is another factor, or set of factors, affecting what may be negotiated. Political scientist Alan Bent and public administrationist T. Zane Reeves have noted that union leaders, in particular, believe that "the application of political power in the course of negotiations is an acceptable strategy, and one that has become widely employed in public sector labor relations. For all practical purposes, it has become clear that the *relative power of the negotiating parties* will determine the scope of bargaining."[46] Bent and Reeves further describe just what this implies:

> Power, in public sector labor relations, is the ability of one side to apply the most telling pressure influencing the outcome of the negotiation in its favor. This may be done by mobilizing effective political support through lobbying of key institutions or key officials, or somehow gaining the support of the public. Another manifestation of power is the capability to, at least, inconvenience the public, and, at most, potentially or actually endanger their health, safety, and welfare, by deprivation of public services. . . . Finally, the power capability of a union is also the product of the will of the membership, i.e., how strongly the members feel on an issue.[47]

(To this last point, it might be added that the will of management in defining both scope and content of bargaining is also relevant, as a function of the political pressure management can bring to bear.)

As a consequence, it might be said that under circumstances where one side (if not both) seeks to shift the locus of decision making to the political arena, the actual bargaining process "becomes a mere facade, and the real confrontation over issues takes place at other levels and institutions of government. Put another way, collective bargaining becomes a sideshow, while the main event is played in the political environment."[48] Examples of this phenomenon would certainly include the interplay of forces in New York City's labor relations/collective bargaining (where agreements reached on pension plans, especially, are likely to prove costly to future generations, but with little direct *political* cost to those who negotiated the issue); and the unsuccessful efforts by employee organizations in New Orleans and Atlanta in the late 1970s to influence management by direct appeals to the general public, and to the business community, more specifically.[49] It goes almost without saying that this dimension of bargaining is a major difference between the public and private sectors.

Reaching and Ratifying an Agreement

Once the scope of bargaining (at least in the formal sense) *is* agreed upon, however, the negotiating process can go forward in a predictable sequence—although what each subsequent step produces in the way of agreement or disagreement is by no means foreordained. Normally, the first move is up to the employee representatives, who may present proposals on the items they wish to consider.[50] After agreement on procedural ground rules for the negotiations, management then gives its responses to the first proposals, and further reciprocal reactions and counterproposals constitute the focus of ensuing bargaining. In this series of interactions, of course, the behavior of the two sides may vary considerably, depending on the degree of mutual cordiality or hostility that exists prior to actual bargaining, the intensity with which the negotiators support their respective positions, the gaps that separate the two sides on each issue (and the cumulative distance between them), the bargaining and consultation that goes on among members of the *same* team, and how strong the incentives are either to reconcile their divergent positions or to wear down the opposition.

The combination of these factors will largely shape the dynamics of actual negotiations, and the likely outcomes. Taking a hard line is one possible tactic, reflecting intensity of feeling, confidence in ultimately prevailing, a need to simply appear aggressive, and the like. Concentrating on a few key provisions and readily conceding on other points may be an effective alternative approach. Another possibility is to combine the two approaches by taking one stance publicly (probably the former) while bargaining privately in more of a give-and-take atmosphere, so as to reach an agreement that can be defended to the negotiators' constituencies without its appearing to be the product of weakness. In many cases, the particular bargaining strategy chosen depends on how far apart the parties are, to start, and just how crucial the issues are to each side.

In the great majority of cases, agreement is reached at the negotiating table, without the need for impasse procedures (described below) or for a strike. Ratification of any agreement, however, must be secured both from the employee organization's members and from those to whom management must account (usually the legislative body). If either rejects the tentative pact, further negotiations are necessary; much of the time, however, ratification is achieved. Cayer notes that at the state and national levels, specific legislative approval is not necessary, except in those states where salaries and fringe benefits have been negotiated. In such instances, the legislature must appropriate the necessary funds, thus indirectly giving an agreement its stamp of approval.[51]

Impasse Procedures

If negotiations do not lead to agreement at the bargaining table, the resulting impasse can and must be dealt with expeditiously. Impasses can develop both early and late in the bargaining process—for example, over union representation itself, composition of the bargaining unit, or grievance resolution stemming from implementation of an existing agreement. A number of formal *impasse procedures* can be called into play, including: (1) mediation, (2) fact finding, (3) arbitration, and (4) referendum; all involve outside parties (we will deal with strikes in a separate section later).[52]

Mediation is the most common form of impasse procedure and appears to be effective in resolving most impasses. A neutral, third-party individual, often highly skilled and trained in labor negotiations, is called upon to promote a compromise between the two sides. The presence of a mediator in local education impasses, for example, is a phenomenon familiar to many Americans in recent years. Mediators are not empowered to impose solutions; rather, their role is to assist in identifying key points of disagreement and to work toward improving the atmosphere between the two sides so that they can hammer out an acceptable compromise.

A variation of mediation is *fact finding*, often utilized when the former has failed to produce an agreement. The key difference between the two devices is that fact finding involves a formal investigation and issuance of a formal report by the fact finder (or fact-finding panel). That report, stating the facts of the situation as viewed by the neutral investigator, is designed to generate pressure on the parties to settle their differences. Some jurisdictions (for example, the states of New York and Wisconsin) require that fact-finding reports be made public, in hopes of activating public opinion in support of reaching a resolution.

Should neither mediation nor fact finding lead to a contract settlement, some form of *arbitration* becomes the only immediate alternative to a strike. Again, a neutral third party is called in, but in this case the role and purpose are different. A labor arbitrator, by law or mutual consent, has authority to impose a settlement if the parties to negotiation have failed to reach one any other way.[53] Arbitration, however, has four possible forms. *Advisory* arbitration involves recommending a solution; it is still up to the two sides to accept it, and the arbitrator's role is most limited under this form. *Binding/compulsory* arbitration, on the other hand, involves the two parties' giving their consent—in advance—to acceptance of the arbitrator's decision, whatever that may turn out to be. In a minority of cases, *final-offer* arbitration is used, where each side makes one last proposal, and the arbitrator is empowered to select one of them; again, the understanding is that both sides agree to abide by that decision. Final-offer arbitration can apply to a "package" or can be used on an issue-by-issue basis. The underlying rationale for final-offer arbitration is that both sides will put forward their most reasonable proposals, for fear that the arbitrator might select a less acceptable one suggested by the other side (this often has the effect of narrowing the differences). The evidence is mixed, however, on the actual effects of this mechanism, with various studies in disagreement on whether more or less equitable settlements emerge from final-offer arbitration.

The fourth variety of arbitration is *mediation-arbitration* (med-arb), which permits a neutral third party to act as a mediator at first, and subsequently—if mediation fails—as an arbitrator. The rationale for this hybrid device is that, with arbitration as an alternative, mediation efforts will be taken more seriously by both sides. If experience in the state of Wisconsin is any indication, that rationale is well founded. From January 1, 1978, to September 28, 1979, the Wisconsin Employment Relations Commission was involved with nearly 750 requests for either mediation or med-arb; of these, only 93 required a mediation-arbitration award. Thus, in nearly 90 percent of the cases, agreements were reached without having to go through all the steps of med-arb. In addition, the number of municipal strikes sharply declined after med-arb procedures were instituted.[54]

The last formal impasse procedure is *referendum*, under which either side may take contested questions to the public. While not widely used (Colorado is one of the few states to do so), its potential is intriguing, particularly as the prospect of direct popular approval/disapproval influences the behavior of the bargainers. Some believe that in an era of disgruntled taxpayers, both sides in a bargaining process—but especially employees— might feel compelled to moderate demands that may prove costly, incurring the wrath of the people. The evidence is limited, to date, but there is reason to believe that as in the case of final-offer arbitration, "the referendum approach could bring pressure to get the decision [an agreement] made early in the bargaining process so as to avoid potentially harsher agreements imposed from outside."[55]

An *informal* impasse procedure has been tried in Massachusetts, where animosity between municipal managers and their police and fire employees reached a crest in 1977. Effective in January 1978, a Joint Labor-Management Committee for Municipal Police and Fire was empowered to oversee police and firefighter negotiations, and to act as a clearinghouse mechanism for facilitating voluntary settlement of disputes. Emphasizing informality rather than structured procedures, the Committee is credited with greatly reducing the number of cases going to final-offer arbitration. From January 1978 to November 1979, only five cases went that far; between fiscal year 1975 and fiscal year 1977, ninety-seven disputes had to be resolved that way. The Committee's creation was an outgrowth of the realization, on both sides, that the formal procedures in existence were ineffective; more to the point, perhaps, was recognition of the fact that the will to settle disputes was also lacking.[56] Perhaps a crucial lesson in the Massachusetts experience is that if the will is present, on both sides, to achieve labor-management peace, the particular methods of doing so are less important than commonly supposed. On the other hand, if such will is absent, the best forms in the world will not do the job.

Contract Implementation

Once an agreement is reached, and ratified by both sides, the last step in the cycle begins—namely, contract administration or implementation. Management is generally conceded to have the bulk of the responsibility for contract administration, but employees obviously have a vested interest in the particular ways that contractual provisions are carried out. In a sense, this is both the last step of one cycle and the first step of the next, for the experience under a contract during the period it is in force will become part of the basis for the next round of negotiations, when the contract expires.

In the meantime, a number of individuals and offices play key parts in contract administration. One, found in nearly all government jurisdictions, is the person (or office) in charge of the overall labor relations program; though a part of management, the responsibility rests here for coordinating implementation and for ensuring that others in management ranks fully understand the terms and provisions of the agreement. A second key actor is the first-line supervisor—the individual who interacts with workers on a daily basis, and whose interpretations of contractual provisions have the most immediate impact. Finally, the employee designated as spokesman on contract matters is the shop steward, through whom complaints are registered (and efforts made to resolve problems), and who has responsibility for monitoring contract administration on behalf of employees.

One other feature of implementing the agreement should be mentioned. In the event that a complaint cannot be resolved at the level of the first-line supervisor, and appeals to higher managers do not produce a satisfactory resolution, the procedure of grievance impasse resolution is invoked. This is analogous to arbitration procedures as a means of resolving bargaining impasses, with an expectation that all parties are bound by the outcome. Should there be no such clause in the basic bargaining agreement, other personnel or civil service rules govern the methods for resolving complaints arising during contract administration.

Related Dimensions of Collective Bargaining

An important aspect of the environment of collective bargaining is the existence, in most jurisdictions, of a code of unfair practices. While not a formal part of actual bargaining, or even of the scope of negotiations, such codes do play a part by restricting certain kinds of behavior by both sides that would have the effect of poisoning the atmosphere of negotiations if they did occur. Included among prohibited behaviors are such things as dismissing employees for union organizing, physical intimidation or attempted bribery to influence the outcome of union representation elections, discriminating arbitrarily against employees for nonmembership in a union, and of course, refusing to enter into collective bargaining where it is provided for. Any activity that is thought to violate codes of unfair practices can become grounds for initiating grievance proceedings, under terms of most labor-management agreements.

Another dimension of bargaining that has emerged only in recent years is so-called *productivity bargaining*. Following the example of the private sector, public managers have attempted, with some success, to negotiate contract provisions whereby employee wage increases are linked to various cost-cutting efforts—including increasing productivity on the job—as an alternative to layoffs. In large cities such as New York and Washington, D.C., contracts with very specific clauses were signed during the 1970s under which labor unions agreed to help cut labor costs and increase output; in the case of the former, this was part of the mid-1970s fiscal crisis and efforts by all levels of government to prevent New York City from going into bankruptcy.[57] In a period of growing fiscal stress for many American municipalities, productivity bargaining would seem to be one device likely to see increasing future use.

Two other aspects of bargaining deserve mention. First, the public sector has contributed an innovation to the bargaining scene through use of computers to assist in ''costing out'' the demands of employee organizations. As a tool to aid management in assessing comprehensively what various packages would cost, computer-assisted negotiations also can help give a better overall picture of the position classification structure and the larger personnel management function. Second, in the public sector (unlike the private) there is a particular pressure of timing surrounding collective bargaining. It is necessary to conduct—and conclude—bargaining talks so that necessary funding to cover the costs of the agreement can be requested from the legislature in the normal course of the appropriations process. All the chief executive can promise, in effect, is to ask the legislature for funding; yet in reality, while the legislature is not bound to honor such requests, its members know that much more serious labor-management problems would result if money to pay for contractual provisions were withheld for any but the most pressing of fiscal reasons. The point is, however, that even where legislators willingly provide funds, the timetable of negotiations must be coordinated with budget timetables as well.

In one form or another, these are the major steps and considerations involved in the collective bargaining process. But one further area remains to be explored—the controversial phenomenon of public employee strikes, as an instrument to be used in the event all other efforts to reach agreement have failed. Because work stoppages or slowdowns have become widespread, and because there are numerous arguments supporting and opposing the right to strike (even though they are illegal almost everywhere), the subject clearly warrants more extended treatment.

PUBLIC EMPLOYEE STRIKES

The phenomenon of the strike is most evident in state and local government; in fact, only postal workers and members of the Professional Air Traffic Controllers Organization (PATCO) have actively defied the prohibition on strikes by employees of the national government. Strike activity increased dramatically during the 1960s, but several things should be mentioned in connection with that increase. First, strikes were far from unknown, particularly against local government, in earlier years; figures from the U.S. Bureau of Labor Statistics indicate that in fiscal years (FY)

1942–1958, there were 490 work stoppages in state and local government (all but 6 against localities). The largest number in any one year was 61, in FY 1946 (this, in fact, was the highest annual total for any year up to 1966, when the recent surge in strike activity first appeared). Second, the increase was concentrated in the period 1966–1969; the number of strikes in each of those four years was 142, 181, 251, and 411, respectively. Third, with the exception of fiscal 1975, the number of strikes annually from 1969 to 1977 was approximately 300 to 400, indicating that the labor relations situation had stabilized somewhat in states and localities. In FY 1978–1980, however, the number of strikes surged again (to 481, 593, and 536, respectively),[58] before beginning another decline in the early and mid-1980s.

Data for one year in the mid-1970s may suggest more general trends and patterns in public employee strikes.[59] Nearly one-half of all work stoppages in state and local government occurred in school districts; in this period, education was followed in order by highways and sanitation as the government functions most affected by strikes. They suggest that strikes were most likely during renegotiation of an existing contract and were caused in most cases by disputes over compensation or hours-of-work issues. While complete data are lacking for other years, there is good reason to believe that, at least in many jurisdictions, these patterns are also evident.

One problem in accurately conveying the extent of strike activity in the public sector is that it is sometimes difficult to say just whether a strike occurred. Particularly since strikes are prohibited almost everywhere, a "job action" of some kind—of which strikes are only one variety—may take another form (see box). One hears of the "blue flu" afflicting substantial numbers of police officers—all the same day, with some attendant publicity beforehand; or of teacher "sick-ins," or sanitation worker "slowdowns." What constitutes an actual strike against government employers, in short, may not be as easy to say as one might think. Thus, a count of the number of strikes—as distinct from other kinds of job actions—must be received a bit skeptically. The count would be far higher if *all* types of job actions were surveyed, though that too would pose some difficulties.

The fact that strikes are almost universally illegal obviously has not prevented them from occurring. It also has done little to dampen the argument over whether public employees *should* be permitted to strike (indeed, the continued prohibition has probably served only to intensify that debate). Over the years, opponents and proponents of the right to strike have had ample opportunity to develop and present their arguments, and it is possible to summarize briefly the major themes of each side.[60]

Opponents have made the following arguments:

1. Permitting public employees to strike amounts to legitimizing rebellion against established, sovereign government authority—a violation of sovereignty (this argument is heard much less often, currently);

A STRIKE BY ANY OTHER NAME . . .

Firefighters have called in sick with the "red rash," police with the virulent "blue flu," and teachers with "chalk-dust fever."

On August 19, 1977, thousands of Pennsylvania state workers called in with severe cases of "budgetitis," in protest over receiving no paychecks for four weeks because of the state legislature's failure to enact a new budget.

In Knoxville (Tenn.), police officers threatened to engage in a "pray-in" by attending evangelist Billy Graham's Crusade each night until the city council took action on a pay proposal put forward by the Fraternal Order of Police (FOP). The local FOP president stated, tongue-in-cheek: "I cannot advocate work stoppages, strikes, or sick call-ins, but I am a firm believer in prayer."

Source: Adapted from Richard C. Kearney, *Labor Relations in the Public Sector* (New York: Marcel Dekker, 1984), pp. 207-8.

---

2. Government services are inelastic, that is, there are few available substitutes for at least some public services, and consequently, public employees have considerable leverage in bargaining for their objectives by threatening to strike, or actually going on strike;

3. Many public services are essential, and suspension of them through work stoppages threatens public safety, health, and the like (e.g., police and fire protection, and sanitation);

4. Since strikes in the public sector are essentially political strategies rather than economic ones, they give an unfair added advantage to public employee organizations over other groups, in the traditional competition for budget allocations by chief executives and legislatures;

5. Public employees work for a "model employer" by serving in government and are already privileged as a group by civil service protection, so that job insecurity is far less than in the private sector;

6. Strikes push taxes up and aggravate inflation;

7. If strikes are authorized for some categories of public employees but not for others, there will be continuing controversy over which employees should and should not be permitted to strike.

Advocates of the right to strike counter with the following major arguments:

1. The sovereignty doctrine is outmoded, especially since government engages in extensive "contracting out" of public services to private firms, and no one argues that a strike of laborers under government contract undermines sovereignty in that instance;

2. Strikes occur in vital industries in the private sector without crippling society; similar strikes in government may indeed be inconvenient, but not as serious as opponents make them seem;

3. Strikes occur now, in great number, in the face of prohibitions common to all but a handful of government jurisdictions; the prudent course is to legalize, legitimize, and regularize the processes surrounding the right to strike, so that the problem (assuming it *is* a problem) can be dealt with through well-structured channels;

4. The strike would serve the purpose of legitimizing and channeling labor-management conflict; this would enhance group identity and conflict resolution;

5. Employees' bargaining position is weakened if they lack the ultimate ability to withdraw their services;

6. There is a great deal of inconsistency in the fact that private-sector employees performing many of the same functions as public employees— for example, transit, health care, and teaching—have the right to strike, but public employees do not;

7. There is inconclusive evidence about whether legalizing the strike actually leads to more strikes, thus tending to reinforce the earlier argument that strikes occur regardless of their being permitted or prohibited—so why continue to prohibit them?

What one makes of these conflicting arguments is a highly subjective matter, of course. It is clear, however, that there has been movement toward dealing more forthrightly with strikes, and with public employee organizations in general, as a result of pressure from public-sector labor groups. *How public management* responds to labor may ultimately prove to be the most important variable in defining the course of labor relations.

COPING WITH STRIKES: RECENT TRENDS IN LAW AND MANAGEMENT

When public employee strikes first stimulated any sort of public policy response from government decision makers (in the mid-1940s), the response was primarily in the form of punitive antistrike legislation. In 1946 and 1947, nine states passed such laws, with penalties including firing, ineligibility for reemployment for twelve months, fines, imprisonment, and misdemeanor penalties. New York's Condon-Wadlin Act (1947) ''required that rehired workers be placed on probation for five years and receive no pay increases for three years.''[61] When it became apparent that imprisoning individual strikers was both impractical and ineffective, later legislation provided for imprisonment of union leaders only (where jail terms were still used), and for fines—sometimes quite heavy—levied against labor organizations authorizing a strike. (It should be noted that imprisonment was most common as a punishment for contempt of court, that is, for disobeying a back-to-work order issued in the form of a court injunction.) Fines have been known to range as high as $650,000, though most are much lower.

More recently, the behavior of public managers has become much more central in the process of dealing with strikes, both in preparing for such an eventuality and in reacting to a strike situation. Preparations for a strike are virtually a necessity in many jurisdictions, if only to assure continuation of a public service affected by a walkout. Specific preparatory steps include agreements for intergovernmental mutual assistance, intergovernmental cooperation in training and information distribution regarding the bargaining process, multiemployer bargaining, and conscientious contingency planning by an individual government. Of these, multiemployer bargaining has the widest potential impact. While considerably more complicated than bargaining between a single jurisdiction and one or more unions, it has the advantages of reducing "whipsawing" (using one settlement as the rationale for demands elsewhere), making it more difficult to employ wage/fringe benefit/working condition comparisons as a basis for labor demands, avoiding duplication of bargaining costs, and expanding opportunities for acquiring greater expertise at the bargaining table. Multiemployer bargaining may not be workable in all instances—due to a lack of common working conditions, difficulties in applying common contract language to diverse departments, and the like—but it has been used widely enough to hold some promise for other jurisdictions.[62]

Another aspect of management behavior relevant to strikes is the fact that more and more public managers are deciding to stand up to union demands, bolstered by increasing taxpayer discontent with government performance, generally, and with heavier tax burdens, specifically. Since the mid-1970s, examples of public manager resistance to labor demands have become more numerous. In Kansas City, Missouri, a firefighters' strike that lasted only four days led to negotiations over major union demands that went on for nearly a year, with city officials showing as much determination and staying power as did the firefighters.[63] In another case, in 1976, a Massachusetts state judge fined a striking state employee union $250,000 per day; not surprisingly, the union did not remain off the job for very much longer.[64] The next year, Atlanta (Georgia) Mayor Maynard Jackson fired 900 striking sanitation workers; striking workers were also dismissed from their jobs as a strike-breaking action in San Antonio in 1978.[65] Also in 1978, the nation's longest firefighters' strike—lasting fifty-six days, in Normal, Illinois—saw strike leaders jailed for contempt of court for forty-two days (though ultimately the union's key demand regarding composition of the bargaining unit was largely acceded to by the city).

One of the most dramatic episodes came in 1979, when police in New Orleans went on strike during Mardi Gras—the city's busiest tourist season. The rationale for doing so was obvious: to bring maximum pressure to bear on city officials, since business and other community interests presumably would not stand for any interference with the flood of tourist dollars, thus hastening a settlement. However, the plan misfired—the city "dug in" by curtailing much of the Mardi Gras festivities, and the police union lost both credibility and support. The net result: management held out until the police accepted essentially what management had offered originally.[66]

Other bitter strikes occurred in 1979 and 1980 in cities as diverse as New Orleans, New York, and Kansas City (again), Toledo, Nashville, and Chicago (that city's first firefighters' strike). Though the settlements varied in substance, these and other stoppages were characterized by a new vigor on the part of management in meeting the unions head on. Journalist Neal R. Peirce, an expert observer of state and local government, observed in mid-1980 that these confrontations "point up the contentious, difficult labor relations atmosphere predicted to last through most of the 1980s. . . . Cities have little choice. They must hang tough in dealing with unions. They must be willing to face up to strikes; experience shows laws banning them are ineffectual. They must maintain management prerogatives. . . ."[67] Such a view, of course, is not universally held, but it is gaining wider appeal.

Seldom has management hung so tough, or met a union head on with greater force, than in the national government's response to the air traffic controllers' strike in 1981. After negotiations between PATCO and the Department of Transportation deadlocked over compensation and length of the work week, union president Robert Poli led the controllers off the job. President Reagan and Transportation Secretary Drew Lewis answered by first warning the striking controllers that they faced loss of their jobs—and then by firing over 11,000 who did not return to their posts! The administration's view was straightforward and to the point: these individuals had violated the law that prohibited strikes by national government employees, as well as their oath of office. Therefore, by striking, they had left their jobs, and the administration had every right to begin recruitment and training of new controllers to replace them. The response did not end there—later in the summer of 1981, the FLRA decertified PATCO as the labor representative of the controllers. (In July 1982, the union filed for bankruptcy.[68]) Such a series of steps had rarely (if ever) been taken against striking public employees, even though numerous other strikes also were illegal, strictly speaking. Whether the Reagan administration's actions come to serve as a precedent in other strike situations remains to be seen.

An intriguing approach to strike management was utilized by the government of Grand Rapids, Michigan, during a 1980 walkout by members of AFSCME Local 1061, affecting primarily operations at the water and sewer plants, and garbage collection (but, significantly, not police, firefighters, or bus drivers).[69] Having experienced a walkout in 1974, city officials began careful preparation for another possible strike, and they chose a simple yet highly effective course of action: individuals in supervisory ranks throughout city departments were given one day of "cross-training" per year, that is, put in charge of responsibilities in departments or offices other than their own. For example, city planners were trained to operate water pumps or man booths at the parking ramps; the parks director worked as a grave digger. Cross-training offers yet another choice for public managers who, in Peirce's words, "must be willing to face up to strikes. . . ."

All our attention, thus far, has been directed to coping with strikes once they occur. But if it is true that "an ounce (or gram) of prevention is worth a pound (kilogram) of cure," then we must ask if there are any ways to anticipate the likelihood of a strike (other than simply by being prepared). A 1978 study suggests some of the sources of impasses, treating them as *predictive* factors. These are: (1) economic, political, or legal environments; (2) structural and organizational context of bargaining; (3) interpersonal relationships between the parties; (4) personal characteristics of the negotiators; and (5) history of previous rounds of bargaining. Interestingly, the economic environment did not serve to distinguish between those situations in which an impasse was reached and those in which settlements were reached earlier in the process. Economic *disputes* were, however, more drawn out and harder to settle, short of an impasse procedure. More important as a predictor of impasses was the profile of political and organizational factors. So, also, were the existence of interpersonal hostilities between the parties, the use of hired professional or highly experienced negotiators, and a history of previous impasses. In short, any attempt to ascertain the probability of impasses in public-sector negotiations should take into consideration these multiple sources or factors; the more of them present in a given situation, the greater the likelihood of a protracted impasse, and very possibly a strike.[70]

COLLECTIVE BARGAINING: IMPACTS AND IMPLICATIONS

Amid much speculation about the consequences—positive and negative— of collective bargaining, a number of efforts have been made to assess its impacts, particularly in local government and politics. One useful source on this subject is a review of existing empirical research, by public administrationists David T. Methé and James L. Perry.[71] They make several important observations about these research studies.[72] First, a majority of the studies focused on the uniformed services (police, fire, and transit), while little or no research has been done on recreation, libraries, or social services. Second, the data bases for most of the studies are drawn from the 1960s and early 1970s—the height of the surge in unionization and the spread of collective bargaining. Thus, some caution should be exercised in interpreting conclusions based on these data, as the turmoil of the period may itself have been an influence on the relationships between bargaining and local services. Third, more attention was paid to wages/salaries than to any other single factor in these studies, regarding bargaining's effects. This phenomenon was very pronounced in the early years of the period covered, but—perhaps significantly—other factors came into increasing prominence as later studies were conducted. That is to say, researchers developed a wider scope in examining elements of local government service delivery—for example, productivity and service effectiveness—upon which collective bargaining may have had an impact.

The major findings of the twenty studies reviewed by Methé and Perry can be summarized as follows.[73] First, some occupational groups—for example, firefighters and transit operators—have achieved significant gains in wages and fringe benefits because of collective bargaining; others, however, have achieved only marginal changes, or none at all. Second, collective bargaining has had variable influences—both positive and negative—on productivity and work management; little in the way of a common pattern can be said to exist. Third, collective bargaining has had the effect of driving municipal expenditures and fiscal effort upward—though here, too, variations exist in degree. Fourth, limited evidence indicates that collective bargaining has had no impact on effectiveness of local services. Additional research appears to be badly needed in several areas, notably the impacts of bargaining on effectiveness of local service delivery. It also seems likely, judging from other comments on the research, that future directions in local collective bargaining may well include shifts in emphasis from basic compensation to hours of work, fringe benefits, work rules, and—perhaps most important—productivity.[74]

Labor relations experts Raymond Horton, David Lewin, and James W. Kuhn have suggested that it is difficult, at best, to formulate reliable generalizations; their view is supported by some of Methé and Perry's findings, among others. Horton, Lewin, and Kuhn note that ''the impacts of public sector labor relations decisions on governmental management reflect sharp differences that exist among and even within governments with respect to structural, political, organizational, and union variables.''[75] They suggest that five ''impact areas'' of collective bargaining exhibit considerable variation and warrant particular analytical concern in the future. These are: (1) compensation, (2) service provision and delivery (referring to impacts on work rules and procedures, personnel schedules, and job assignments), (3) traditional ''merit''-oriented personnel administration, (4) formal governmental structure, and (5) informal politics.

In each of these areas, Horton, Lewin, and Kuhn question findings that suggest that collective bargaining has common impacts. Rather, *diversity* is the norm, with no clear-cut pattern evident for which at least one significant alternative pattern cannot also be found. This undoubtedly reflects the variety of legal frameworks for collective bargaining, discussed earlier in this chapter; but those frameworks themselves may reflect a deeper diversity among government jurisdictions. In sum, no *one* set of impacts can be identified; no one set can be predicted for different jurisdictions, even those with many similarities in their history, structure, and socioeconomic makeup.

Implications of Collective Bargaining

It is clear from this discussion of public-sector collective bargaining, and of unionism generally, that the past quarter-century has seen unparalleled— and undoubtedly permanent—changes in many aspects of personnel management. Equally obvious are what Joseph Cayer describes as the "clear implications for financial management, budgeting, personnel, and planning, and for the roles of employees and managers in the system."[76] Let us look briefly at each of these.

First, with regard to fiscal implications, two elements stand out: (1) higher personnel costs are associated with collective bargaining (though *how much* higher is not always predictable), and (2) agreements negotiated between labor and management tend to reduce somewhat the flexibility of those responsible for drawing up and approving government budgets, by creating wage/salary and fringe benefit figures that could be changed only with great difficulty by budget makers after a contract is ratified by the negotiating parties. Another, more general dimension of the fiscal issue is the fact that labor organizations in comparable jurisdictions (e.g., suburban communities within the same metropolitan area) often seek comparability in pay and the like, thus adding pressure to the budgetary process in any one jurisdiction. (One response to this problem is the growing phenomenon of multiemployer bargaining, referred to earlier.) And, to the extent that planning and budgeting are to be coordinated functions, they are under greater constraint due to the need to permit negotiators to decide issues that may have long-term consequences.

Second, the personnel function itself—besides having become a largely shared responsibility—is likely to become a subject of future collective bargaining. Since the scope of bargaining can change in successive negotiation cycles, aspects of personnel management that have not been bargainable (e.g., merit system principles, and work rules and regulations) could well become so. Thus, depending on how much of an effort labor organizations make to bargain on such issues, and on management's ability to counter such attempts effectively, the personnel function could well undergo further—and even more fundamental—change. Part of this evolution lies in what many see as the basic philosophical conflict between collective bargaining and merit principles—though that is not a universally held position.[77] It is even argued that the personnel function of the future will largely center on labor relations and position classification—that the personnel function may very well be one of labor relations, primarily.[78]

As for management in the public sector, collective bargaining offers both disadvantages and advantages—the former more readily noted by some observers than the latter. Assuming that management's prerogative to "run the operation" on its own is entirely legitimate, one might then say that having to share the power to do so is a disadvantage. An accompanying problem (assuming the same thing) is the probable difficulty management encounters in developing a consistent personnel policy among diverse groups of employees in the same agency.

On the other hand, a number of distinct advantages have also been suggested. One is that bargaining requires all those interested in effective public management to deal with the management function in all its dimensions, not just whether enough money is available, or whether enough authority has been delegated, or whether city council will support top-level managers in this or that conflict. A second advantage lies in the fact that having to be prepared for bargaining forces managers—and *their* superiors—to carefully identify managerial weaknesses, in general, and negotiate on training needs, in particular, and to remedy them; otherwise the unions might well hold the upper hand in the bargaining process. (This is complicated where supervisory and managerial unions exist—a phenomenon unique to the public sector.) Where management has previously labored under the burden of its own structural or procedural shortcomings, it can be said that collective bargaining has served the interests of governmental effectiveness by forcing attention to be paid to those shortcomings.

Finally, the implications for employees are numerous. An obvious one is the opportunity to participate more meaningfully in organizational affairs and decision making. Another is the likelihood that management will no longer be able to make decisions in an arbitrary fashion; it would have to submit to grievance procedures, if a watchful labor group wished to pursue a claim of arbitrariness—a very different (and improved) situation for employees. Less obviously, it has been suggested that employees have more readily developed a consciousness and group solidarity as a result of bargaining; this has been especially true for those employed in positions (such as sanitation and garbage collection) considered least desirable, and often filled by racial and other ethnic minority workers. One other implication for employees also has some impact on the organization as a whole: consistent with various concepts of democratic administration, employees are likely to have greater commitment to their organization as a result of having a larger voice in how it is managed. That, perhaps, can be said to benefit both management and labor in the long run—not to mention the citizenry at large.

A LOOK TO THE FUTURE

In the immediate future, it seems all but certain that collective bargaining will continue to be a centrally important process in public personnel administration. The gains made during the 1960s and 1970s will continue at perhaps a slower pace, but this may represent a period of consolidation as much as a stiffening of resistance to public-sector labor organizations. Still, management's ability to confront squarely the challenges of collective bargaining appears to have increased, thus in all likelihood bringing a measure of equilibrium to the collective bargaining arena that may have been lacking in some government jurisdictions.

For public-sector unions, the immediate future may hold promise of less-than-ideal developments, from their perspective.[79] For one, collective bargaining may prove to be something other than the answer to all their problems, and unions may continue to resort to interest group tactics such as lobbying, which have met with success in the past. For another, competition for members may only become more complicated than it already is; conflicts between the likes of the NEA and the AFT may be joined by the activities of private-sector unions (such as the Teamsters) organizing public employees. Finally, in the second half of the 1980s—at least in state and local government—job security, not wages or working conditions, may become the main issue for unions as they attempt to hold and add members. Such developments may cause changes in union behavior, and in labor-management relations more generally. As collective bargaining continues to move past its early stages of development, and public-sector organizations continue adjusting to new political and economic realities, the 1980s—and beyond—promise to be lively times.[80]

SUMMARY

Public-sector collective bargaining has emerged in the past thirty years as a major force in public personnel administration at all levels of government. Within a framework of "labor-management relations," what has evolved is a pattern of unified employee organizations created to share control with management over terms and conditions of employment. While similar to—and patterned after—collective bargaining in the private sector, bargaining in governmental arenas differs in a number of important respects. Various types of employee organizations—most prominently, public employee unions—have become involved in collective bargaining.

The existence of public employee organizations dates back to the mid-1800s, though collective bargaining was virtually unknown until the 1930s and did not become a major factor in governmental labor relations until the 1960s. The catalyst for change was action by President John Kennedy in 1962, in the form of an executive order permitting national government employees to organize and to bargain collectively with agency employers. In the national government, since then, union membership has increased significantly; further executive orders clarified and expanded bargaining procedures; and the Civil Service Reform Act of 1978 codified in statutory form many of the provisions already in force. State and local experience, though much more varied, has included major union gains in membership, extension of collective bargaining rights in both state and local governments, and greater frequency of public employee strikes. Unlike the situation in the national government, public-sector labor relations in states and localities still lack common legal (and political) definition, though a trend has emerged toward comprehensive coverage of all state and local employees. At all levels of government, however, public managers have had to master new skills in meeting the challenge of collective bargaining.

The *process* of collective bargaining entails a sequence of steps that are generally followed in most jurisdictions; events at each stage, however, are far from automatic or predictable. The steps are: (1) labor organizing, and seeking recognition as bargaining agent; (2) selecting the bargaining team (employees and management); (3) defining the scope of bargaining; (4) making proposals and counterproposals; (5) reaching agreement at the bargaining table; (6) achieving ratification of an agreement; (7) resolving impasses in cases where no agreement is reached (through mediation, fact finding, arbitration, or referendum); (8) dealing with employee strikes; and (9) implementing the contract once final resolution of disagreements is worked out. Since contracts are in force for specified periods, these steps constitute a cycle, and are repeated over time. Usually associated with collective bargaining processes are, among other things, codes of unfair practices and "productivity bargaining."

Public employee strikes became much more numerous in the 1960s and 1970s, though they were not unknown previously. Most work stoppages have occurred in state and local governments; education, highway maintenance, and sanitation are the government functions most often affected. Strikes have occurred in spite of their being almost universally banned, though strong arguments have been made both for and against their being made legal. Opponents of the right to strike cite the inelasticity of government services, the politics of strikes, civil service protections, and fiscal implications of strike settlements as justification for their position. Advocates of the right to strike respond that sovereignty is outmoded, that strikes occur against private industries providing vital services without crippling society, that legalizing strikes would facilitate their resolution, that employees' bargaining positions are weakened without strike rights, and that legal prohibitions have not prevented strikes in any case. Legal or not, strikes—and management's responses to them—are a reality in contemporary government labor relations.

Methods of coping with the threat or the reality of a public employee strike have evolved through legal restrictions and penalties and through improved managerial response. Laws providing for imprisonment or fines of strikers and union leaders are now complemented by specific management strategies designed to prevent and resolve work stoppages. Intergovernmental assistance, multiemployer bargaining, resistance to union demands, and even dismissal of striking employees have all become part of management's array of weapons against strikes. Experience in cities such as Kansas City, New Orleans, and Atlanta—and the national government—demonstrates the emerging assertiveness of public managers, and the not infrequent willingness of the voters to back them strongly. It is useful, as well, to be able to anticipate the likelihood of a walkout; one study suggests that impasses or strikes are more likely where interpersonal hostilities exist, political and organizational arrangements are inadequate, and impasses have occurred previously.

There are several types of impacts of collective bargaining in the public sector; most studies on this subject have focused on effects on wages and salaries of employees represented in bargaining. Other consequences, only recently receiving more attention by researchers, include the degree of effectiveness in service delivery, and levels of worker productivity. Much of the conventional wisdom regarding bargaining's effects still is in the realm of mythology rather than established fact; more empirical research on bargaining impacts remains to be done. It is clear, however, that bargaining impacts are diverse.

General implications of collective bargaining include somewhat higher personnel costs, though how much higher is not clear, with accompanying constraints on budgetary decision making; reshaping of the overall personnel function (and, many believe, continuing conflict between merit principles and collective bargaining) in response to rising labor organization power, possibly to the point of making traditional management prerogatives part of the scope of bargaining; the need for public managers to be trained to participate effectively in negotiations with labor representatives, and more generally to develop better management practices; and expanded employee rights, solidarity, consciousness, and organizational participation.

Public-sector collective bargaining is likely to continue to operate, though with modifications brought about by changing managerial, fiscal, and political environments.

NOTES

1. This discussion is drawn from N. Joseph Cayer, *Managing Human Resources: An Introduction to Public Personnel Administration* (New York: St. Martin's, 1980), pp. 176–77; Lee C. Shaw and R. Theodore Clark, Jr., "The Practical Differences Between Public and Private Sector Collective Bargaining," *UCLA Law Review*, 19 (1972), 867–86; and Harry H. Wellington and Ralph K. Winter, Jr., "The Limits of Collective Bargaining in Public Employment," in Wellington and Winter, *The Unions and the Cities* (Washington, D.C.: Brookings, 1971), pp. 12–32. See also Louis V. Imundo, Jr., "Some Comparisons Between Public Sector and Private Sector Collective Bargaining," *Labor Law Journal*, 24 (December 1973), 810–17; and Clyde W. Summers, "Public Employee Bargaining: A Political Perspective," *The Yale Law Journal*, 83 (1974), 1156–200.
2. Cayer, *Managing Human Resources*, pp. 181–82.

3. Ibid., p. 182. See also Richard C. Kearney, *Labor Relations in the Public Sector* (New York: Marcel Dekker, 1984), pp. 14 and 30.

4. My thanks to an anonymous reviewer for this information.

5. Cayer, *Managing Human Resources*, p. 171.

6. Ibid., p. 172.

7. Ibid.

8. J. D. Williams, *Public Administration: The People's Business* (Boston: Little, Brown, 1980), p. 411.

9. Cayer, *Managing Human Resources*, p. 173.

10. Alan Edward Bent and T. Zane Reeves, *Collective Bargaining in the Public Sector* (Menlo Park, Calif.: Benjamin/Cummings Publishing, 1978), pp. 17–20; Kearney, *Labor Relations in the Public Sector*, pp. 7–8 and 19–20. See also M. J. Fox, Jr., and Marvin Judah, "National Treasury Employees Union: Description of a Federal Employee Union," in Harry Kershen, ed., *Collective Bargaining by Government Workers: The Public Employee* (Farmingdale, N.Y.: Baywood Publishing, 1983), pp. 131–42.

11. Cayer, *Managing Human Resources*, p. 173.

12. Marvin J. Levine and Eugene C. Hagburg, *Public Sector Labor Relations* (St. Paul: West Publishing, 1979), p. 67.

13. Cayer, *Managing Human Resources*, p. 174.

14. The period through the mid-1970s is treated fully in Murray B. Nesbitt, *Labor Relations in the Federal Government Service* (Washington, D.C.: Bureau of National Affairs, 1976). See also Kearney, *Labor Relations in the Public Sector*, pp. 16–20.

15. This discussion of Executive Orders 11491, 11616, and 11838 is taken from Levine and Hagburg, *Public Sector Labor Relations*, pp. 23–24. See also Kearney, *Labor Relations in the Public Sector*, pp. 43–49.

16. Bent and Reeves, *Collective Bargaining in the Public Sector*, p. 219.

17. Cayer, *Managing Human Resources*, p. 172.

18. *Congressional Quarterly Weekly Report*, 36 (October 14, 1978), 2,950.

19. U.S. Bureau of the Census, *1982 Census of Governments, Vol. 3, No. 3, Labor-Management Relations in State and Local Governments*, U.S. Government Printing Office, Washington, D.C., 1985; and Levine and Hagburg, *Public Sector Labor Relations*, p. 75.

20. Bent and Reeves, *Collective Bargaining in the Public Sector*, p. 21.

21. Ibid., pp. 18–21; Kearney, *Labor Relations in the Public Sector*, pp. 28–34.

22. Cayer, *Managing Human Resources*, p. 174.

23. Kearney, *Labor Relations in the Public Sector*, pp. 53–55.

24. Levine and Hagburg, *Public Sector Labor Relations*, p. 65 (emphasis added).

25. Kearney, *Labor Relations in the Public Sector*, p. 55.

26. Ibid., pp. 220–21.

27. Levine and Hagburg, *Public Sector Labor Relations*, p. 86.

28. The following discussion relies on Levine and Hagburg, *Public Sector Labor Relations*, pp. 78–85 and 93–95; Cayer, *Managing Human Resources*, pp. 178–89; Bent and Reeves, *Collective Bargaining in the Public Sector*, chapter 2; and Kearney, *Labor Relations in the Public Sector*, chapter 3.

29. Cayer, *Managing Human Resources*, p. 178.

30. Ibid., pp. 178–79.

31. Levine and Hagburg, *Public Sector Labor Relations*, p. 79.

32. Felix A. Nigro and Lloyd G. Nigro, *The New Public Personnel Administration*, 2nd ed. (Itasca, Ill.: Peacock, 1981), p. 177.
33. J. Joseph Loewenberg, "Labor Relations for Policemen and Firefighters," *Monthly Labor Review*, May 1968, pp. 36–40; cited in Levine and Hagburg, *Public Sector Labor Relations*, p. 80.
34. Levine and Hagburg, *Public Sector Labor Relations*, p. 80.
35. Ibid.
36. Ibid.
37. Cayer, *Managing Human Resources*, p. 178 (emphasis added).
38. Bent and Reeves, *Collective Bargaining in the Public Sector*, p. 60.
39. Levine and Hagburg, *Public Sector Labor Relations*, pp. 81–82.
40. See Chester Newland, "FLRA Limits Union Role in Performance Standards," *Public Administration Times*, 3 (August 15, 1980), 1 (published by the American Society for Public Administration, Washington, D.C.).
41. Levine and Hagburg, *Public Sector Labor Relations*, p. 80.
42. Cayer, *Managing Human Resources*, p. 183.
43. Ibid.
44. Ibid.
45. Bent and Reeves, *Collective Bargaining in the Public Sector*, p. 60.
46. Ibid. (emphasis added).
47. Ibid., pp. 62–63.
48. Ibid., p. 61.
49. Cayer, *Managing Human Resources*, pp. 177 and 183. For a more detailed examination of the situation in New York, see Raymond D. Horton, *Municipal Labor Relations in New York City: Lessons from the Lindsay-Wagner Years* (New York: Praeger, 1973).
50. This summary is taken from Cayer, *Managing Human Resources*, pp. 183–89.
51. Ibid., p. 184.
52. Ibid., pp. 184–85.
53. An important study of New York state arbitrators' perceptions, attitudes, and practices pertaining to the arbitrator's role and function is Gerald M. Pops, *Emergence of the Public Sector Arbitrator* (Lexington, Mass.: D. C. Heath, 1976).
54. See Midwest Center for Public Sector Labor Relations, *Impasse Resolution in the Public Sector: New Directions—A Practitioner's Guide* (Bloomington, Ind.: School of Public and Environmental Affairs, Indiana University, 1980), pp. 7–13. See also David C. Haman, Arthur P. Brief, and Richard Pegnetter, "Studies in Mediation and the Training of Public Sector Mediators," and George T. Sulzner, "The Impact of Grievance and Arbitration Processes on Federal Personnel Policies and Practices: The View from Twenty Bargaining Units," in Kershen, ed., *Collective Bargaining by Government Workers*, pp. 250–64 and 157–71, respectively; and Kerry D. Steadman, "The Future of Mediation, Factfinding, and Arbitration in the Public Sector," paper delivered at the annual conference of the American Society for Public Administration; Denver, Colorado; April 8–11, 1984. For discussion of a related issue, see Susan A. MacManus, "State-Mandated Collective Bargaining and Compulsory Binding Arbitration: The Fiscal Effect on Municipal Governments," *Public Administration Quarterly*, 7 (Winter 1984), 411–28.
55. Cayer, *Managing Human Resources*, p. 185. See also Kearney, *Labor Relations in the Public Sector*, pp. 71–73.

56. Midwest Center for Public Sector Labor Relations, *Impasse Resolution in the Public Sector*, pp. 2–6. This general approach is treated more fully in Jonathan Brock, *Bargaining Beyond Impasse: Joint Resolution of Public Sector Labor Disputes* (Dover, Mass.: Auburn House, 1982).

57. Levine and Hagburg, *Public Sector Labor Relations*, pp. 82–83.

58. These data are taken from the *1981 Annual Report* of the U.S. Bureau of Labor Statistics, cited by Kearney, *Labor Relations in the Public Sector*, p. 209.

59. Levine and Hagburg, *Public Sector Labor Relations*, p. 89.

60. This overview of the strike debate is drawn from Levine and Hagburg, *Public Sector Labor Relations*, pp. 85–88; and Bent and Reeves, *Collective Bargaining in the Public Sector*, pp. 222–31.

61. B. V. H. Schneider, "Public-Sector Labor Legislation—An Evolutionary Analysis," in Benjamin Aaron, Joseph R. Grodin, and James L. Stern, eds., *Public–Sector Bargaining* (Washington, D.C.: Bureau of National Affairs, 1979), pp. 191–223, at p. 195.

62. Some evidence exists suggesting that there is resistance to multiemployer bargaining, despite its alleged advantages. See Peter Feuille, Hervey Juris, Ralph Jones, and Michael Jay Jedel, "Multiemployer Negotiations Among Local Governments," in David Lewin, Peter Feuille, and Thomas A. Kochan, eds., *Public Sector Labor Relations: Analysis and Readings* (Glen Ridge, N.J.: Thomas Horton & Daughters, 1977), pp. 131–38.

63. A first-person account of this episode, by Mayor Charles Wheeler of Kansas City, appears in "Two Mayors and Municipal Employee Unions," in A. Lawrence Chickering, ed., *Public Employee Unions: A Study of the Crisis in Public Sector Labor Relations* (San Francisco: Institute for Contemporary Studies, 1976), pp. 77–89.

64. Cayer, *Managing Human Resources*, p. 188.

65. Ibid., p. 180.

66. Ibid.

67. Neal R. Peirce, writing in the Bloomington-Normal (Ill.) *Daily Pantagraph*, June 15, 1980, p. A-5.

68. For a more detailed account of the PATCO strike, see Kearney, *Labor Relations in the Public Sector*, pp. 234–36, and Sar A. Levitan and Alexandra B. Noden, *Working for the Sovereign* (Baltimore: The Johns Hopkins University Press, 1983), pp. 99–102.

69. This account is taken from the Associated Press report that appeared in the Bloomington-Normal (Ill.) *Daily Pantagraph*, September 11, 1980, p. A-9.

70. The study cited is that of Thomas A. Kochan and Jean Baderschneider, "Dependence on Impasse Procedures: Police and Firefighters in New York State," *Industrial and Labor Relations*, 31 (July 1978), 431; discussed by Thomas A. Kochan, "Dynamics of Dispute Resolution in the Public Sector," in Aaron, Grodin, and Stern, eds., *Public-Sector Bargaining*, pp. 150–90, at pp. 163–64.

71. David T. Methé and James L. Perry, "The Impacts of Collective Bargaining on Local Government Services: A Review of Research," *Public Administration Review*, 40 (July/August 1980), 359–71.

72. Ibid., pp. 360 and 366.

73. Ibid., p. 368.

74. Ibid., p. 369.

75. Raymond Horton, David Lewin, and James W. Kuhn, "Some Impacts of Collective Bargaining on Local Government: A Diversity Thesis," *Administration and Society*, 7 (February 1976), 497–516, at p. 498.
76. Cayer, *Managing Human Resources*, p. 189. These comments draw upon Cayer, pp. 189–91.
77. For a critique of the view that merit and collective bargaining necessarily are in conflict, see David Lewin and Raymond D. Horton, "The Impact of Collective Bargaining on the Merit System in Government," *The Arbitration Journal*, 30 (September 1975), 199–211.
78. My thanks to an anonymous reviewer for this observation.
79. My thanks to an anonymous reviewer for suggesting these possibilities.
80. See Benjamin Aaron, "Future of Collective Bargaining in the Public Sector," in Aaron, Grodin, and Stern, eds., *Public Sector Bargaining*, pp. 292–315, and Kearney, *Labor Relations in the Public Sector*, chapter 9, especially pp. 326–28.

SUGGESTED READINGS

Aaron, Benjamin, Joseph R. Grodin, and James L. Stern, eds. *Public-Sector Bargaining*. Washington, D.C.: Bureau of National Affairs, 1979.

Bent, Alan Edward, and T. Zane Reeves. *Collective Bargaining in the Public Sector*. Menlo Park, Calif.: Benjamin/Cummings Publishing, 1978.

Cayer, N. Joseph. *Managing Human Resources: An Introduction to Public Personnel Administration*. New York: St. Martin's, 1980, chapter 10.

Kearney, Richard C. *Labor Relations in the Public Sector*. New York: Marcel Dekker, 1984.

Levine, Marvin J., and Eugene C. Hagburg. *Public Sector Labor Relations*. St. Paul: West Publishing, 1979.

Levitan, Sar A., and Alexandra B. Noden. *Working for the Sovereign*. Baltimore: The Johns Hopkins University Press, 1983, chapters 2, 3, and 4.

Lieberman, Myron. *Public-Sector Bargaining: A Policy Reappraisal*. Lexington, Mass.: Lexington Books, 1980.

Nigro, Felix A., and Lloyd G. Nigro. *The New Public Personnel Administration*, 2nd ed. Itasca, Ill.: Peacock, 1981, chapters 6 and 7.

Paterson, Lee T., and Reginald T. Murphy. *The Public Administrator's Grievance Arbitration Handbook*. White Plains, N.Y.: Longman, 1983.

Perry, James L., ed. "The 'Old Testament': A Litany of Beliefs About Public Sector Labor Relations—A Symposium." *Review of Public Personnel Administration*, 5 (Spring 1985), 1–77.

Rabin, Jack, Thomas Vocino, W. Bartley Hildreth, and Gerald J. Miller, eds. *Handbook on Public Personnel Administration and Labor Relations*. New York: Marcel Dekker, 1983.

12

Government Budgeting

THE mayor of a financially beleaguered city orders layoffs of some white-collar workers, police and fire personnel, and sanitation workers in a last-ditch effort to balance the budget. The governor of a midwestern state receives a report from the state comptroller that the state's cash accounts are getting dangerously low, due to declining tax revenues and rising unemployment compensation and welfare costs. The president of the United States, intent on gaining greater control over the bureaucracy and on reducing bureaucratic activity, seeks substantial spending cuts—and wins congressional approval. Department heads and bureau chiefs, at all levels of government, feverishly search for ways to cut back on projected spending levels—a step made necessary by a general fiscal ''crunch'' and political demands for more efficient program management. Legislators seek to satisfy their clientele groups by approving program spending, but they must cast a wary eye on a public growing restless with ''big government.''

In all of these examples, government budgets and budget processes are at the core of both political and managerial controversies. Budgeting in the public sector is a process central to politics, particularly to administrative politics and the operation of government agencies and programs. It is the major formal mechanism through which necessary resources are obtained, distributed, spent, and monitored. Competition for a share of the fiscal ''pie'' has always been keen, but never more so than in this era when the pie is shrinking. The size and shape of individual budgets, and the processes involved in proposing and approving them, are all changing rapidly, with unpredictable consequences for a wide variety of political interests—and government programs.

A number of fiscal and other purposes can be served through budgeting, some or all of them simultaneously. At its simplest, a budget can be a device for counting and recording income and expenditures. It may not even be appropriate to label such a document as a budget; perhaps ''ledger'' is better. Budgeting, however, does include this purpose. Another function of budgeting is to generate a statement of financial intent, constructed on the basis of anticipated income and "outgo." A closely related function is to indicate programmatic intent, showing both preferences and (more important) priorities in deciding what to do with available funds. This suggests still another function of budgets, intentional or not: they reflect the political priorities of those who formulated them. Mention also should be made of the fact that in recent decades, the role of the budget in the national government's efforts to manage the economy has increased substantially. That is, many budget decisions are made and evaluated in terms of how they affect general economic growth, as well as specific economic interests and concerns.

One other purpose bears mention: controlling the bureaucracy and shaping agency programs. Legislators who cherish control of the purse strings often use that control to influence agency behavior. Ronald Reagan, from the very start of his presidency, used a comprehensive assault on the national government budget as the key to his attempt to reshape the national bureaucracy and the programs it operates. Reagan has demonstrated convincingly that the most direct way (if not always the easiest, politically) to control an agency is to cut—or increase—its budget. Thus, chief executives who seek to direct bureaucratic operations have a strong and continuing interest in budgets and budget making.

A government budget may be read as something of an index to relative distribution of power in the political and economic system in which the budget was enacted,[1] by examining both how it was made up and what resources were distributed to different participants within that system. This is true whether we are speaking of university decisions to allocate a certain amount for academic scholarships or more faculty, or of national government appropriations for the Pentagon's latest weapons systems. Budgets represent decisions to spend money in certain ways, in preference to others, and such decisions do not just happen. They are made through a political process in which power is crucial to success.

Since the outcomes of budgetary decision making are so important to all participants and beneficiaries, the formal nature of the decision process has long been central to budgetary politics. Throughout much of our history, decisions about public spending could best be characterized as *incremental*, following the model described in chapter 8. Changes in spending levels from one year (or biennium) to the next—and in the policies such spending supported—tended to be gradual rather than drastic. Much of the status quo was simply assumed to be beyond questioning; "how much more shall be allocated?" was a common theme, and a key focus of budget processes.

In recent decades, however, the incremental decision model has had *decreasing* applicability in explaining how budgets are proposed and enacted. In the 1960s, efforts were mounted (though with limited success) to make budgeting more "rational"—to reduce the influence of "politics as usual" and to strengthen the role of long-range planning, in hopes of increasing programmatic effectiveness. The 1970s saw another sort of change: the emergence of legislative formulae as the basis for allocating funds in some programs, with spending increasing *automatically* as the number of those eligible for a particular government benefit rose. (Such programs have become known as "entitlements.") A continuing issue during this period has been the question of *which political interests* are best served by a given budgetary device. Incrementalism has not disappeared as a consequence of these changes, but budgetary decision making is far more complex and unpredictable than in the past. We will discuss the impacts and implications of these developments, later in the chapter.

Budgetary decisions and decision processes also have been heavily influenced by their environments.[2] In recent years, government budget makers have been confronted by the twin challenges of worldwide recession and inflation, growing pressures on revenue sources, and citizen resistance to increased public spending. Government budgets have been subjected to more intense scrutiny, as decision makers have been forced by prevailing public sentiment to cut back on rates of growth in spending— indeed on *existing* expenditure levels, in some instances. (Note that the incremental model does not apply very readily to decisions concerning budget *reductions*.[3]) California's Proposition 13 in 1978 and Proposition 2½ in Massachusetts two years later were just two of many citizen initiatives undertaken in recent years to slow the pace of taxing and spending by government. (Not all these proposals were adopted by the voters, and some that won approval already have been repealed.) Ronald Reagan's election in 1980, as already noted, signaled the beginning of similar efforts to cut back domestic spending, and to reduce the role of the national government— efforts that continue currently. Budgets and budget making have been sharply affected by all this; both the processes and the outcomes of budgetary decisions will continue to change in the immediate future. This is especially significant because of the extensive impacts government expenditures have on large segments of society.

GOVERNMENT BUDGETS AND FISCAL POLICY

Economist Jesse Burkhead has noted the potential importance of government budgets as instruments for managing national economies, pointing out that a budget's impact will depend on the relative importance of the public sector in the total economic picture and on "prevailing attitudes toward the role and responsibility of government."[4] The budget can be regarded as a "tool of *fiscal policy*, that is, as an instrument for consciously influencing the economic life of a nation."[5] Different governments regard this potential budgetary role quite differently. Similarly, the extent to which national budgets in other countries are treated as tools of fiscal policy varies widely. As Burkhead (and we) use the term, fiscal policy refers to government actions aimed at development and stabilization of the private economy—taxation and tax policy, expenditures, and management of the national debt. Related to fiscal policy—and, ideally, fully coordinated with it—are monetary and credit controls. We shall briefly examine these tools and relate them to the budget process, relying largely on Burkhead's analysis.

Fiscal Policy Tools

Traditionally, *taxation* was viewed simply as a means of raising government revenue and very little more. For the past forty to fifty years, however, taxation and tax policy have also been used to influence the volume of spending by private citizens and organizations. Raising taxes has at times been a weapon against inflationary spending, since it reduces the amount of disposable personal income; conversely, reducing taxes has been viewed as one means of boosting consumer spending. Such policy was relatively clear-cut until the recent wave of worldwide inflation-recession, which seemed to violate the economic principle that *either* inflation *or* recession could cause problems for a national economy, but not both at once. Reducing taxes, for example, to "spend our way out of recession" works very nicely, assuming that such spending will not trigger an inflationary spiral. But if any significant increase in spending is inflationary, then the old rules do not work any more. The uncertain condition of the economy has raised new questions about how to use tax policy as an instrument of economic management.

As with tax policy, there has been a fundamental change in attitude toward *government expenditures*. The traditional view was that as government spent money, the sums expended were a replacement for private-sector spending, representing a "last resort" action when the private sector could not carry on whatever activities the money paid for. Now, however, the government's spending practices are seen as an essential part of total spending for goods and services, and as having major impact on private-sector expenditures. That is not surprising, considering, for example, that the national government budget called for well over $900 billion in expenditures for fiscal 1986.

Another example, governmental decisions to close or not to close several large military installations in 1975 and 1976—the Boston Navy Yard and the Frankford Arsenal in Philadelphia, among them—carried with them crucial economic implications. When the installations were opened, there had been an infusion of new dollars into the local (and state) economies. A *multiplier*, or "ripple effect,"[6] prevailed—sales and rentals of housing were brisk; retail and wholesale business was up; there was a sharp rise in demand for goods and services of all kinds. This had the effect of increasing tax revenues in all taxing jurisdictions (both state and local), and in general strengthening the localities' financial bases because of new jobs created and increased population. The outcry from local politicians and civic leaders, state officials, and members of Congress from the affected areas was ample testimony that they understood what the impact would be if the installations were closed—that is, a negative ripple effect. On a much larger scale, efforts by the Reagan administration to cut national government domestic spending sparked a similar political reaction in the early and mid-1980s, tempered to some extent by public perceptions that spending had indeed become excessive.

Political influence over such decisions can be valuable to a local community. One classic illustration is Charleston, South Carolina, which benefited hugely from defense spending while its U.S. Representative, Democrat L. Mendel Rivers, chaired the House Armed Services Committee. Another example is the NASA Space Center in Houston (rather distant from Florida's Cape Canaveral), which was placed in the Texas city during the time that Representative Olin Teague of Texas was chairman of two House subcommittees—Manned Spaceflight and NASA Oversight—and Representative Albert Thomas (from Houston) chaired the Independent Agencies subcommittee of the House Appropriations Committee, which had jurisdiction over NASA appropriations. No mere coincidence there![7]

A third fiscal policy tool is *management of the national debt*. Sale of government bonds and other obligations took on fiscal policy overtones for the first time during World War II, when the sale of war bonds was touted as another means of holding down consumer spending for scarce goods and services. In selling bonds, "a government changes the composition of privately held assets—converts private assets from money to bonds."[8] This has an impact, though indirect, on the amount and composition of private holdings and on income and spending rates.

Furthermore, in recent years government borrowing and public debt have become major political issues. When President Reagan took office in 1981, the national debt was about $985 billion, rising in fiscal 1986 to nearly $2 *trillion*—an imposing figure, though some say it should be of less concern because most of the government's creditors are U.S. citizens, banks, and businesses. More important than the size of the debt itself (at least in the short run) is the annual cost of interest that must be paid. In fiscal 1984 net interest alone amounted to *$111 billion*—an increase of $36 billion just since fiscal 1980—and approached the $150 billion mark in fiscal 1986.[9] In light of such figures, continued efforts by political leaders to reduce government spending and balance the national government budget are not surprising.

In state and local government, debt management is somewhat more complex, if only because many state constitutions require both state and local governments to operate with balanced budgets. Nevertheless, most states and localities have extensive bonded indebtedness (meaning that they issue interest-bearing bonds to raise funds for specific purposes). They must manage the debts they owe to holders of those bonds over the bonds' lifetime—paying interest on schedule and at the rate stipulated, and redeeming the bonds at agreed-upon times.[10] The difficulties experienced by larger, older cities (such as New York and Cleveland in the 1970s, and Detroit in the early 1980s) in meeting their financial obligations suggest that, at least at the local level, problems of debt management may become more severe in the near future. This is especially true in light of reductions in intergovernmental aid (see chapter 5).

Another fiscal policy tool of some importance is *tax spending*—the practice of giving "tax breaks" for certain kinds of spending by individuals and corporate enterprises. For example, the national government permits income tax deductions for interest expenditures by individuals—on home mortgages and installment purchases, to mention two of the most common. Businesses receive substantial tax breaks if they invest in purchases of new equipment; the oil industry, in particular, benefited from exemptions related to drilling for new oil, in 1981 tax legislation. In maintaining such tax incentives, the government must balance revenues lost against probable gains in private-sector expenditures, and the tax benefits realized by all levels of government as a result of increased private-sector activity. A significant component of President Reagan's 1985 tax reform bill was a proposal to eliminate most such tax breaks, though some of those most strongly supported, politically, may well be retained.[11]

Monetary and Credit Controls

Monetary controls are ordinarily exercised in four forms by national and state governments. First, the Board of Governors of the Federal Reserve System regulates the supply of money released into circulation. Restricting the money supply has been used to restrain inflation; increasing the supply, to stimulate economic activity. This function of "the Fed" is carried on outside the direct control of the president; he appoints its members but does not have command authority over their decisions. Thus, chairman Paul Volcker (a believer in high interest rates as a device for "damping down" inflation) could operate virtually independently of President Carter, even though the two disagreed strongly over that particular monetary policy. Second, interest rates charged by lending institutions are subject to regulation by the states, and, as we have seen in recent times, the prime lending rates that banks make available to their prime borrowers have a lot to do with business investment, home construction, and financing of home mortgages. Third, government loan programs make a crucial difference in a wide range of activities—disaster loans for flooding victims, and VA or FHA loans for buying or building a house. Loans are controlled in part by the budgetary process, in the form of initial appropriations and of yearly expenses to continue operation of loan programs. Fourth, loan *guarantees* have become increasingly important—for New York City, the Chrysler corporation, and college students, among many others.

Economic Coordination

Underlying all government activity to influence the private economy is public acceptance, in principle, of that activity. The national government's role in this respect gained wide—though far from universal—acceptance during the Great Depression years and after, marked particularly by passage of the Employment Act of 1946 to combat the postwar recession. This act made promoting maximum employment, production, and purchasing power an ongoing governmental commitment. In addition, the act established the president's Council of Economic Advisors (CEA), discussed in chapter 1. These steps were important both in themselves and as indicators of likely governmental responses to subsequent economic crises.

Central economic coordination has come to mean a dominant role for the president, both in determining the existence of crisis conditions and in directing governmental responses. Perhaps the most significant step in this respect during the last twenty years was enactment of the Economic Stabilization Act of 1970, the statutory basis for Richard Nixon's move in August 1971 to impose a ninety-day freeze on prices, rents, wages, and salaries. This intricate and comprehensive program marked "a watershed in economic policy, placing the [national] government in *direct control of the economy*, as distinguished from the more indirect methods utilized in fiscal and monetary policy."[12] Though the president's authority under that specific act lapsed later in the 1970s, a precedent has been set for future chief executives to use. Office of Management and Budget (OMB) Director David Stockman, among others, urged President Reagan to declare an economic emergency upon taking office in 1981, which would have allowed the president to exercise a wide range of emergency powers—granted under other legislation—in coordinating economic activity.

Even with all of these at the president's disposal, however, there is still some question whether presidential coordination can be truly effective. One observer has suggested that though we expect the president to influence the economy significantly, "he lacks the tools to manage its performance in all but the most indirect and crude fashion."[13] Still, the president's role in this area has greatly expanded in the last forty years.

In sum, we now have not only a "mixed economy" in which the public and private sectors overlap considerably, but also a mixed set of economic controls available to the national government with vast potential for influencing decisively virtually every kind of economic activity.

The Reagan presidency has given rise to three important issues concerning the relationship between governmental activity and the national economy. One is the role of government spending as an economic stimulus.

Since the 1930s, prevailing economic doctrines assumed that government played an important role in periods of economic downturn, because of its ability to spark demand for goods and services produced in the private economy. Moreover, since the late 1960s, stimulating private-sector activity has been a consistent (and deliberate) budgetary objective, regardless of economic cycles, and has come to be a generally accepted part of the national government's overall economic role. Reagan administration actions clearly have led to a reassessment of this aspect of government budgeting, in view of the president's determination to limit government spending (some say, without regard to the adverse economic consequences of doing so).

A second issue is the economic impact of continuing budget deficits, with some (including the president) arguing that if left unchecked, deficits will hamper economic recovery and perhaps trigger new cycles of inflation and recession. A related concern is that the government's need to borrow money from private lenders will have the effect of crowding others seeking credit out of the market. (There is less disagreement about the second proposition than about the first.)

The third issue concerns the consequences of the economy's performance for government budgets. As unemployment increases, government spending must also rise (for unemployment compensation and the like), at the same time that revenues from sales and income tax receipts usually decrease. Those patterns always have been true. More important now, however, is that instead of the 3 or 4 percent unemployment which existed thirty years ago (constituting what most economists regarded as "full employment"), contemporary unemployment levels have held fairly steady at 7 to 10 percent. Furthermore, there is reason to believe that these levels are the new norm—that because of more people entering the work force (for example, working women), and because of basic changes in the kinds of jobs available (more white-collar and professional positions, with fewer industrial jobs), we face higher levels of "structural" unemployment that will be far more difficult to deal with. In turn, due both to larger government payments for unemployment compensation (and perhaps welfare) and to less tax revenue, reducing budget deficits will be more difficult. Regardless of how this problem is addressed, it seems clear that the "rules of the game" in coping with budget deficits are changing, in the context of overall economic policy.

Links to Government Budgeting

All government instruments to influence the national economy as well as state and local economies are connected to budgeting directly or indirectly. Debt management as well as monetary and credit controls have only incidental relationship to the budgetary process—the former in that debates over budget allocations may hinge in part on whether adequate revenues are available to finance proposed programs without increasing the debt, the latter in that appropriations are needed to pay expenses of ongoing loan programs. Of much more direct consequence to budgeting are tax policy, expenditures, and economic coordination.

Tax policy obviously influences how much revenue is available for government programs. Tax decisions, however, are normally made outside the direct focus of budget making and involve a different set of participants both on Capitol Hill—the House Ways and Means Committee and the Senate Finance Committee, primarily—and in the executive branch. Tax policy, while significant, lacked any direct relation to the national government's budget until the mid-1970s.

Expenditure policy *is* budget making when all is said and done. The effects of spending decisions on the national economy can be very dramatic—as in the case of government installations—or hardly visible. But large or small individually, their cumulative consequences act to shape or reshape economic activity in significant ways. A case can be made for the position that the national government budget is as important for its effects on the nation's economy as for how it affects the operations of government agencies funded through direct budgetary allocations.

Finally, economic coordination in the broad sense is tied closely to budget making, since the budget is a major instrument of government— especially presidential—economic policies. The budget is related to economic coordination not only because it reflects chosen courses of action in existing fiscal policy but also because it can be a major battleground in determining the shape of that policy, and consequently economic activity in both public and private sectors. This is why the budgetary process is so heavily laden with political conflict: control over the content of budgets means the ability to allocate resources to some and not others. The president has other means at his disposal to use in economic coordination, but the budget remains an instrument of the highest importance.

FOUNDATIONS OF MODERN GOVERNMENT BUDGETING

Prior to the Civil War, budgeting was rather informal and routine at all levels of government. The national budget was fairly small, amounting to some $63 million in 1860, though it rose sharply during the Civil War and never returned to that modest level.[14] The budgetary process was fragmented, with little systematic direction. Beginning with the presidency of Thomas Jefferson, agencies seeking funds had dealt mainly on their own with congressional committees having jurisdiction over their respective operations. The president had no authority to amend agency requests and no institutional means of influencing their formulation. Congress made its appropriations very detailed, both to control executive discretion to transfer funds from one appropriation account to another and to keep spending within appropriations limits.[15]

Starting with the Civil War, some important long-term changes began to affect numerous government practices, and the framework of a truly national economy slowly took shape. The war itself was a watershed in national-state relations, as well as in development of the presidency as a predominant force in national politics. During the 1870s and later, three general patterns of governmental behavior became more prominent, with implications for the rise of the modern budgetary process.

The first of these was growth of the national government's authority to monitor and regulate the expanding industrial economy, and to exercise the war power and related prerogatives in foreign affairs (especially by the president). At the same time, the tax power was used to a greater degree than ever before. The regulatory power, given institutional form for the first time with creation of the Interstate Commerce Commission (ICC) in 1887, represented a governmental response to the industrial revolution and to the emergence of powerful private economic interests. The war power was exercised most visibly in the Civil War and in the Spanish-American War, and U.S. diplomatic involvement was on the rise as well. The tax power was expanded by a constitutional amendment in 1913 permitting a graduated income tax.

The second pattern—government involvement in the private economy—meant more than simply regulating the flow of commerce. Starting in 1864, when the National Banking Act created a single, unified banking system as another step toward a national economy, the government's role in monetary and financial affairs became more regularized. Equally important, the way was paved for further expansion of governmental activity, which in this century has come to include not only increasing regulation of private economic enterprise but also participation in planning and managing various public enterprises affecting, more or less directly, the course of the national economy. Since 1933 and the New Deal, fiscal policy has been the predominant instrument of the national government in influencing the economy, one that presidents of both parties have not hesitated to use when it has suited their economic and political purposes. That being the case, it is not hard to see how budgetary processes and their substantive outcomes have grown in importance, since their consequences now reach far beyond the government itself.

The third pattern was growth in presidential strength and influence, beginning in the last half of the nineteenth century and continuing to the present. The first enthusiastically activist president was Theodore Roosevelt. Others after him, notably Woodrow Wilson and Franklin Roosevelt, made even more dramatic and significant changes in the presidential role. Truman, Kennedy, Johnson, and Nixon all actively supported expansion of presidential prerogatives, albeit for widely varying purposes; and Dwight Eisenhower—though not associated with an activist view of the office—presided over a fairly rapid expansion of the role of the executive branch generally, and he did little to roll back changes made before he took office. Action by Congress delegating discretionary authority to the president was a recurring feature of these years. Gerald Ford and Jimmy Carter exercised presidential prerogatives a bit more cautiously, in view of the public's reaction to Watergate, but the office itself remains very strong. Ronald Reagan, intent on reversing expansion of government's overall role, has capitalized on the powers of the presidency in his quest to reduce that role—a major change for a "strong" president.

Taken together, these three patterns had several important consequences in the development of modern budgetary practice. First, they raised the stakes of budgetary decision making by increasing the scope and economic impact of such decisions, and the political interests affected as a result. Second, they created both the possibility and the necessity of more effectively coordinating scattered spending activities of the national government—possibility, because of growing capabilities of the presidential office; necessity, because expenditures were rising and some centralization of control seemed appropriate. Third, they prompted the first stirrings of budgetary reform in the early 1900s. Primary among these was the concept of the *executive budget,* with the chief executive placed in charge of developing and coordinating budget proposals for the entire executive branch prior to their presentation to the legislature.

BUDGET CONCEPTS IN THE EXECUTIVE BRANCH

The growing importance of the executive budget has been a hallmark of American national politics in this century. As the national government budget became an instrument of economic policy, it became steadily more important to have a central budget mechanism that could respond to changing economic conditions and needs. Various efforts at reforming the executive budget have been made. Budget reform, in fact, has been a recurrent theme, at first stressing control of expenditures, then performance measures aimed at improving management. Prior to 1960 these two emphases dominated the reform movement.

Line-Item Budgeting

The first actions for budget reform were taken at the local level as part of a larger movement for general local government reform, including the drive to establish the city-manager form of government.[16] By the mid-1920s, most major American cities had adopted some form of budgeting system, in most cases strengthening the chief executive's budgetary role. At the state level, a strong movement for reform was under way between 1910 and 1920, centering on making "the executive accountable by first giving him authority over the executive branch."[17] By 1920, budget reform had occurred to some extent in forty-four of the (then) forty-eight states, and by 1929 all the states had central budget offices.

Action was also being taken at the national level throughout this same period, triggered by President William Howard Taft's Commission on Economy and Efficiency, which was established in 1909 and made its final report to the president three years later. That report recommended that a budgetary process be instituted under direction of the president, a proposal greeted by considerable skepticism from those who feared any such grant of authority to the chief executive. One who felt that way was Woodrow Wilson, who as president vetoed legislation in 1920 that would have set up a Bureau of the Budget in the executive branch and a General Accounting Office as an arm of Congress. One year later, President Warren Harding signed virtually identical legislation into law, and a formalized executive budget system was instituted. The 1921 act vested in the president "sole authority to consolidate agency budget requests and to present to Congress an overall recommendation."[18]

The central purpose in all these developments was *control* of expenditures, with emphasis on accounting for all money spent in public programs. This was the first modern budget concept to gain currency, and it remained the predominant approach to budgeting through the 1930s. In this period budgets were constructed on a *line-item*, or *object-of-expenditure*, basis, indicating very specifically items or services purchased and their costs. "The hallmark of control was the detailed itemization of expenses, by means of which central supervision was maintained over purchasing and hiring practices, and agency spending was closely monitored."[19] The focus was on *how much* each agency acquired and spent, with an eye to completeness and honesty in fiscal accounting.

Performance Budgeting

The next broad phase of reform involved a conceptual change and further structural adjustment. Beginning with the New Deal, when management of national programs became centrally important, the line-item budget was partially replaced by *performance budgeting*. Performance budgeting differed from the previous control orientation in several ways. First, it was directed toward promoting effective management. Second, it dealt not only with the quantity of resources each agency acquired but also with *what was done* with those resources. Third, it called for "redesign of expenditure accounts, the development of work and cost measures, and adjustments in the roles of central budgeters and in their relationships with agencies."[20]

Performance budgeting demanded a greater degree of centralized coordination and control. In that connection, the Bureau of the Budget (BOB) was transferred from the Treasury Department, where it had been lodged by the Budgeting and Accounting Act of 1921, to the newly established Executive Office of the President (EOP) in 1939. (EOP was itself a product of the movement for consolidation of executive control over administrative activities.) Ironically, under performance budgeting procedures, control and planning functions were dispersed to agency heads rather than being retained in BOB. Alleged agency failures to maintain control and to plan adequately for future activities later led to proposals for centralization of these functions within BOB.

During the performance budgeting era, which spanned approximately twenty years (1939–1960), there were a number of noteworthy developments contributing to more systematic executive budget making. The major one was World War II, during which both presidential powers and the scope of the national budget expanded markedly. In 1940 the total budget was just over $9 billion; only five years later it was nearly $98.5 billion, or roughly eleven times as large. As happened following the Civil War, the budget total dropped sharply after its wartime peak, but it remained substantially higher than prewar levels.[21] A second step was enactment of the Employment Act of 1946, discussed previously, which signaled governmental intent to utilize fiscal policy and economic planning to an unprecedented degree. A third development at about the same time was the first Hoover Commission's report to President Truman in 1949 on improving government management practices. The report made clear that performance budgeting was more coherent and illuminating than line-item budgeting, indicating more clearly what agencies were actually doing. The report also recommended expansion of BOB's role in budget and management coordination, again emphasizing growing presidential influence in both aspects of administrative operations.

In 1950 Congress passed the Budget and Accounting Procedures Act, which mandated performance budgeting for the entire national government. Aiming at developing work-load and unit-cost measures of activities, it appeared to do much more than simply control and record aggregate expenditures. But as it turned out, though performance budgeting was very good at measuring *efficiency* of government programs, it did little or nothing to measure *effectiveness*. "The efficiency of a school district, for instance, might be measured in terms of the cost per student, but the effectiveness might be measured by whether graduates can read and write, are accepted into universities, or obtain and retain well-paying jobs."[22] The difference is between assessing programs in terms of their operations as such, and assessing them in terms of end-products, the results and impacts, of program activities. Nowhere was this difficulty more pronounced than in the Defense Department, where, for example, data on training soldiers expressed in per-unit cost told little about whether the "right" things were being taught or the "right" number of soldiers were in training.[23] Little wonder, then, that the next movement for executive budget reform was first tested out in the Pentagon budget—a mechanism emphasizing planning and its links to budgetary decisions, known as planning-programming-budgeting (PPB).

PPB: Rise and Fall of "Rationality"

Planning-programming-budgeting (PPB) was an instrument of budgeting designed to alter processes, outcomes, and impacts of government budgeting in significant ways.[24] As the label implies, it was aimed at improving the planning process in advance of program development and before budgetary allocations were made. It was designed also to allow budget decisions to be made on the basis of previously formulated plans.

Second, PPB was intended to make programs, not agencies, the central focus of budget making. Incremental budgeting focused on programs to a degree, but there was little demand for choosing one and only one program of a particular type. By budgeting incrementally it was possible for two or more similar programs to be approved by Congress. PPB was seen as a device for reducing duplicative and overlapping programs, but it was necessary to study programs more or less in isolation from their agency "homes" in order to select the optimum one.

Third, PPB was designed to make it possible to relate budget decisions to broad national goals. In the words of one observer, "the determination of public objectives and programs became the key budget function."[25] Put another way, PPB represented an effort to incorporate *rationality* in budgetary decision making, in place of existing (and well-entrenched) incrementalism. The language and logic of systems theory, systems analysis, and budgetary rationality were employed as part of the effort to introduce PPB into national (and some state and local) budget processes.

Fourth, PPB was designed to facilitate assessments not only of agency resources and activities (as under line-item and performance budgeting), but also of actual external effects of those activities. To accomplish that, it was necessary to design new information systems and, more important, to obtain new and objective information that would demonstrate on a firm factual basis which programs were most likely to achieve their objectives. Part of this effort was directed toward identifying possible alternatives to existing programs that might be more effective. Systematically evaluating programs, and budgeting for them, in terms of their actual consequences had been suggested on occasion previously,[26] but it had never been tried.

Finally, PPB contained a distinct economics emphasis. Implementation depended on the presence in the bureaucracy and in BOB (and later, OMB) of individuals skilled in economic analysis—specifically, cost-benefit analysis of national programs. Furthermore, in assessing consequences of budget decisions, advocates of PPB called for examination of their economic impacts on society.

One other aspect of PPB should also be noted. Though there is informed opinion to the contrary,[27] it seems apparent that to make PPB work for the entire executive branch would require centralized control over composition of executive budget proposals, as well as over planning, determination, and evaluation of goals. This, in fact, was one of the arguments made in support of PPB: that it would bring some coherence, consistency, and rationality into a budget picture said to be notably lacking in those characteristics. But depending on one's point of view, increased centralization could be an argument against PPB as well—and that argument was used during the early hectic days of the 1960s.

Shortly after John Kennedy's inauguration and Robert McNamara's appointment as defense secretary, PPB was established in the Defense Department. In that setting, unlike most of the rest of the executive branch, it was not a major break with past practice; efforts to install performance budgeting, to make more informed choices, and to evaluate military operations more systematically had gone on for close to twenty years at that point. Yet these efforts had not been successful. By attempting to link planning and budgeting staffs as well as functions, and by promoting use of a five-year defense plan, McNamara sought to organize all defense activities on a multiyear basis within a mission context, permitting incremental decision making but tying such decisions to clearly defined long-range program goals.[28]

Lyndon Johnson ordered in August 1965 that PPB be applied to all civilian agencies. It was assumed—perhaps wrongly—that what worked in the Defense Department could be adapted for use elsewhere. The agencies were to submit to BOB, with their budget requests, a multiyear Program and Financial Plan (PFP); they were to request changes subsequently in the PFP through detailed Program Memoranda; and they were to support their documents with Special Analytic Studies—all of which were aimed at the same objectives of consistency and rationality.

Expectations ran high for PPB in its early stages. Some thought it would reform budgeting in the national government so as to bring about greater rationality, less "politics," better and more informed decisions, and so on. But for a variety of reasons, PPB failed to gain a permanent place in national budget making. That may be because expectations were inflated, or because PPB was flawed, or because those who were to implement it were not sufficiently knowledgeable, experienced in planning and analysis, or motivated to make it work (and some actively resisted it). Most likely, all these explanations have some validity.

There was one other major source of resistance to PPB for much of this period: Congress, especially the Appropriations Committees. Members of Congress, who in some instances had spent years building up their contacts, understanding, and knowledge of agency budgets, were not favorably disposed toward a new budgeting system that in their view threatened to disrupt their channels of both information and influence. Even at its peak, budgets were not sent to Congress solely in the PPB arrangement. Agencies and OMB were told to submit budgets in the old agency format as well as the new program format, and to indicate where an individual expenditure proposal fit into each. More important, Congress did not change its appropriations practices to accommodate PPB. Many legislators regarded McNamara and others at the Pentagon—the modern pioneers of PPB—as "whiz kids," a label not meant to be complimentary. Also, Congress objected to the implication that it was up to the executive branch, by whatever method, to determine what the nation's programmatic goals were and what programs were satisfactorily directed toward achieving those goals. Finally, a Congress in which "political rationality" and political consequences of spending were at least as important as economic, cost-effectiveness criteria; where simplifying complex budget choices was a way of life; and where consensus and compromise were preferred to direct conflict over choices, was not a Congress likely to be very receptive to a budget system stressing economic "rationality."[29]

The reaction to PPB from different groups and coalitions in national politics varied according to its perceived impact on their success in securing budgetary resources. To the extent that PPB strengthened objective assessment of budgetary requests without as much regard for political strength or weakness in the budgetary process, it posed something of a threat to those groups that were already strong. Conversely, it held out some hope for agencies and their constituencies that had previously lacked the strength to win some of their budget battles. One assessment of PPB's failure to be sustained in the national budget process suggests that "however ineffective, PPB was *too* effective for the groups presently dominating the budgetary process."[30] It is a mark of their political strength that these groups (primarily dominant subsystems) succeeded in sharply limiting the impact—and the duration—of PPB.

Budget expert Allen Schick wrote in 1973 that PPB had not worked, and that in fact OMB had signaled its demise by lifting requirements for submission of PFPs, Program Memoranda, and Special Analytic Studies.[31] Schick did not say that PPB had had no impact on national budgeting, but did say that it had not achieved its primary goal—"to recast [national] budgeting from a repetitive process for financing permanent bureaucracies into an instrument for deciding the purposes and programs of government."[32] Schick's assessment should not be taken to mean that PPB or its residual effects have totally disappeared, however. One observer has noted that much of the PPB "package" may have been dismantled, but some components live on and in some cases are thriving: (1) a basic focus on information, (2) concern with the impact of programs, (3) emphasis on goal definition, and (4) a planning perspective. Furthermore, it was also suggested that the emphasis on rationality characteristic of PPB may be a healthy counterweight to "less ordered techniques such as confrontation and participation" in policy making, and that government is strengthened by the interaction of both kinds of processes. Summing up, PPB "is alive and well, though it has new names and wardrobes."[33] Implementation of

PPB has gone forward in several states and a number of local governments, many of which tried it in the wake of the national government experience.

PPB, then, made quite a splash at the start of the 1960s, but its actual impacts at all three levels of government were a great deal more modest than some early claims for it. With the coming of the 1970s, different sorts of concerns began to emerge that caused attention to shift away from PPB and toward different issues in the budgetary process.

Zero-Base Budgeting (ZBB)

Activities of government, in virtually every respect, came under increasing pressure in the 1970s for a combination of reasons. Clearly, one reason was growing public restlessness about particular policy directions, such as the war in Vietnam, civil rights enforcement, and some regulatory activities of the national government. A second reason was the tightening fiscal crunch in which many governments found themselves, necessitating a more careful choosing among competing interests of what would be funded and what would not be. Third, there developed a general feeling, reflected in opinion polls, that the public was not getting its money's worth from more costly government programs, and that a harder look needed to be taken at what was working and what wasn't.

Problems of financing activities and evaluating their effectiveness are not confined to government; business and industry also have had to confront these issues. It is no accident that zero-base budgeting developed in industry during the same period when some in government—notably state government—were installing elements of it there. *Zero-base budgeting* (ZBB) got its start at Texas Instruments, Inc., under the guidance of Peter Pyhrr, who later helped implement it in Georgia during the administration of Governor Jimmy Carter (1971–1975). It is from this base that ZBB was launched in about a dozen other states, numerous industries, some local governments, and in the national government.[34]

ZBB involved three basic procedural elements within each administrative entity. The first was identification of "decision units," the lowest-level entities in a bureaucracy for which budgets are prepared—staffs, branches, programs, functions, even individual appropriations items. Second was analysis of these decision units and formulation of "decision packages" by an identifiable manager with authority to establish priorities and to prepare budgets for all activities within the administrative entity. The analysis began with administrators providing estimates of agency output at various funding levels (for example, 80, 90, 100, and 110 percent of current amounts), and assessing cost-effectiveness and efficiency of the unit, then proceeded to formulation by each administrator of decision packages. The third procedural element was ranking of decision packages in an order from highest to lowest priority. Higher-level agency officials next established priorities among all packages from all units, with the probable available funding in mind. The high-priority packages that could be funded within the probable total dollar allocation were then included in the agency budget request, and the others were dropped.[35]

An important aspect of the whole process was that each manager prepared several different decision packages pertaining to the same set of activities, so as to allow those conducting higher-level reviews to select from alternative sets of proposals for essentially the same program or function. Packages received higher priority as their cost declined, again assuming the same activity or set of activities.[36]

ZBB, in practice, has not had the effect of literally projecting budgetary allocations at zero before analysis of activities is begun, or of reallocating funds on a large scale from some policy areas to others.[37] While ideally it calls for reexamining every item in the budget periodically—every one, two, or five years, for example—realistically this would not be workable; "it demands too much budgetary upheaval without equipping budget makers with the tools to redirect budgetary outcomes."[38] An experiment during fiscal 1962 in the U.S. Department of Agriculture attempted just this kind of examination "from the ground up," but after considerable effort, little change could be discerned in the budget that was actually submitted to BOB and to Congress.[39]

In practice, according to Allen Schick, zero-base budgeting was "*more a form of marginal analysis* than a requirement that the budget be built up from scratch each year. It [was] a device for shifting some budget attention from increments above [additions to] the base to decrements below [subtractions from] the base."[40] This suggests that ZBB, though regarded by some as a rational-comprehensive budgetary tool, was essentially a form of *incremental* budgeting.[41] While others may reasonably differ, based on particular applications of ZBB, the general evidence seems to support this conclusion.

At this point we can review and compare the major concepts of the last sixty years in executive budgeting. Table 12-1 presents key conceptual differences among line-item budgeting, performance budgeting, PPB, and ZBB. It is significant that the wider the scope of a budget device (see Table 12-1), the less its chances of full implementation. It is almost certain, however, that the search will go on for further tools that will enhance executive budget control.

THE PROCESS OF BUDGET MAKING

The role of the executive branch, including central budget agencies and the multitude of operating agencies, is far from the whole story of budget making. In American governments, the essential "power of the purse" is uni-

Table 12-1
SOME DIFFERENCES AMONG BUDGETARY CONCEPTS

Feature	Line-Item	Performance	PPB	ZBB
Basic orientation	Control	Management	Planning	Decision making
Scope	Inputs	Inputs and outputs	Inputs, outputs, effects, and alternatives	Inputs, outputs, effects, and alternatives
Personnel skills	Accounting	Management	Economics and planning	Management and planning
Critical information	Objects of expenditure	Activities of agency	Purposes of agency	Purpose of program or agency
Policy-making style	Incremental	Incremental	Systemic	Marginal analysis
Planning responsibility	Largely absent	Dispersed	Central	Decentralized
Role of the budget agency	Fiscal propriety	Efficiency	Policy	Policy prioritization

Source: Adapted from Nicholas Henry, *Public Administration and Public Affairs*, 2nd ed. (Englewood Cliffs, N.J.: Prentice-Hall, 1980), p. 226.

versally vested in the legislative branch; this extends to the authority to levy taxes, determine spending levels, actually appropriate funds, monitor expenditure activities of executive agencies, and establish a wide variety of formulas by which more or less "automatic" spending decisions are mandated, year after year. The rise of the executive budget has sparked frequent, often intense conflict between the two branches of government over definition of spending purposes and control of expenditures. As the budget has grown in importance as a tool of policy formulation, legislative-executive conflict has widened to include that dimension as well. Consequently, the role of legislatures has begun to undergo change in recent years, serving only to complicate further the intricate interactions that take place in budgetary decision making.

We will examine the essentials of budget making, focusing primary attention on the national government, without overlooking state and local variations. One problem here is that less is known, from systematic study, about state and local budgeting, though research into that area has increased. Of particular importance, by itself and as a model adaptable elsewhere, is reform of the congressional budget process, begun in 1974.

Essentials of the Process

Nowhere does the fragmented nature of American political decision making have more of an impact on the complexity of the process than in budget making.[42] In addition to institutional conflict between president and Congress, the House and Senate often treat legislation, including money bills, differently. Committees within the two chambers guard *their* respective jurisdictions and are sensitive to any perceived "invasion of their turf." In addition, revenue and spending bills are handled by different committees on both sides of Capitol Hill. Tax bills are handled by the House Ways and Means Committee and the Senate Finance Committee (all tax bills must originate in the former); appropriations bills, by the respective appropriations committees. Only since the reforms of the mid-1970s, when Congress created independent (and potentially powerful) budget committees in each chamber, have institutional mechanisms of any sort existed on Capitol Hill for monitoring the relationship over time between revenues and expenditures. In sum, budget making in the national government (as in many states and localities) is characterized by both institutional and political fragmentation, opening the way for influence to be exerted at multiple points during the process—a system that virtually requires compromise as the ultimate basis for most budgetary decisions.

Most governments budget on an annual (twelve-month) or biennial (two-year) basis, though not all funds approved in a given year for expenditure are actually spent in that year. The budget covers a *fiscal* year rather than the calendar year that runs from January 1 to December 31; presently the national government fiscal year runs from October 1 to September 30. (In state and local governments, the fiscal year begins most commonly on July 1.) Each stage of budget making is predominantly under auspices of either the executive or legislative branch, though few functions in budgeting are *exclusively* the responsibility of either one.

Time frames of government budgets involve several elements worth noting. One is that even though a government as a whole may budget on an annual basis, individual agencies within that government may be permitted an alternative arrangement, such as a three-year budget. Another, more important, element is the distinction between budget *obligations* (also referred to as "budget authority") and actual *outlays* of funds. Obligations against the budget are comprised of orders placed, contracts awarded, services rendered, or other commitments made by government agencies during a given period, which will require expenditure of funds (outlays) during the same or some future period. The outlays themselves are expenditures within a given fiscal year, regardless of when the funds were obligated.[43] The significance of this distinction is that they imply *two separate budgets*, each with its own political and fiscal life. As much as one-third (sometimes more) of annual budget expenditures may support obligations from previous fiscal years. Budget planning and revenue requirements, among other things, are affected by this.

Government budgets progress in their annual or biennial cycle through five broad stages. In sequence, they are (1) *preparation*, which is almost wholly internal to the executive branch; (2) *authorization*, principally a function of the legislature; (3) *appropriations*, a legislative function; (4) *execution* (implementation), mainly—but by no means entirely—an executive function; and (5) *audit*, carried out by both legislative and executive entities, but ordinarily independently of one another. We will examine each stage in some detail, considering not only the essential procedures of each but also important concepts employed at different times. We will focus on the national government for illustrative purposes, though some similarities in the mechanics can be found in many state and local governments.

THE BUDGET: MASTERING THE LANGUAGE

The budget is the president's financial plan for the national government. It accounts for how government funds have been raised and spent, and it proposes financial policies for the coming *fiscal year* and beyond.

The budget discusses *receipts* (amounts the government expects to raise in taxes and other fees); *budget authority* (amounts that agencies are allowed to obligate or lend); and *outlays* (amounts actually paid out by the government in cash or checks during the year). Examples of outlays are funds spent to buy equipment or property, to meet the government's liability under a contract, or to pay employees' salaries.

The budget earmarks funds to cover two general kinds of spending. *Mandatory* spending covers *entitlement* programs (such as food stamps, Social Security, and agricultural subsidies) that may be used by anyone who meets eligibility criteria. Mandatory spending may not be limited in the annual appropriations process. *Discretionary* spending is set annually in the appropriations process.

The budget has a twofold purpose: to establish governmental priorities among programs, and to chart U.S. *fiscal policy*, which is the coordinated use of taxes and expenditures to affect the economy.

Congress adopts its version of the budget in the form of *budget resolutions*. The first budget resolution, which is supposed to be adopted by May 15 of each year, sets Congress's overall goals for taxes and spending, broken down among major budget categories, or *functions* (the president's budget is similarly divided by function). The second budget resolution, to be adopted by September 15, sets binding budget figures. An important step in congressional budgeting is the *reconciliation* procedure, when Congress enacts spending reductions and revenue increases (or both) in order to bring existing law into line with spending targets adopted in the spring budget resolution. Subsequently, if Congress is unable to pass a budget, or to approve major appropriations bills for executive branch agencies, it may adopt *continuing resolutions*, which authorize expenditures at the same levels as in the previous fiscal year, until formal action is completed on the budget or appropriations.

An *authorization* is an act of Congress that establishes government programs, defines their scope, and sets a ceiling for how much can be spent on them. Authorizations do not actually spend the money. In the case of authority to enter contractual obligations, however, Congress authorizes the administration to make firm commitments for which funds later must be provided. Congress also occasionally includes mandatory spending requirements in an authorization, in order to ensure program spending at a certain level.

An *appropriation* provides money for programs within the limits established in authorizations. An appropriation may be for a single year, a specified period of years, or an indefinite time, according to the restrictions Congress wishes to place on spending for particular purposes.

Appropriations generally take the form of *budget authority*, which can differ from actual outlays. That is because, in practice, funds actually spent or obligated during a fiscal year may be drawn partly from budget authority conferred in that year, and partly from budget authority conferred in previous years.

Source: Adapted, with revisions, from *Congressional Quarterly Weekly Report*, 43 (February 9, 1985), 220.

OMB and Budget Preparation

Preparation of the budget begins when OMB, having made some preliminary economic studies and fiscal projections, sends out a "call for estimates" to all executive agencies. This occurs some fifteen to nineteen months before the fiscal year begins—in late spring of the previous calendar year. The call for estimates is a request for agencies to assemble and forward to OMB their projections as to funding they will need for ongoing and new programs in that fiscal year. This requires heads of agencies and of their subordinate units to develop program and fiscal data that make it possible to formulate an estimate of overall agency needs. It is at this stage of the process that the budget concept being used—line-item, performance, PPB, or ZBB—has the greatest impact on the shape of budget proposals. This information is sent on to OMB together with supporting memoranda and analytic studies, especially with regard to proposals for new or expanded programs.

OMB next calls on individuals bearing the title of "budget examiner," about 600 in all, each one of whom is assigned on a continuing basis to an agency or agencies for the purpose of becoming thoroughly acquainted with agency activities and expenditure needs. The examiners are, in effect, OMB's field workers, holding hearings with agency representatives on programmatic, management, and budget questions.[44] The agency's representatives normally include unit heads and agency budget officers, though others may be included. While budget examiners work *with* agencies, they most definitely work *for* OMB; their job is to probe and question every major expenditure proposal that agency leaders have felt important enough to include in a budget estimate.

When this process is completed, the examiners make their recommendations to OMB. In the meantime, the director of OMB and the president work out general budget policy, major program issues, budgetary ceilings, and other fiscal projections, ultimately developing ceilings for each agency. The examiners' recommendations are incorporated into reviews of each agency's estimates, and are often the basis for revision ordered by OMB. After a process that usually takes four to six months, original estimates are generally trimmed somewhat, and all agency requests are assembled into a single budget document running to several hundred pages. This becomes the president's budget message, which is submitted to Capitol Hill shortly after the first of the (calendar) year (see Figure 12-1).

Part of the politics of budget making centers on interactions between each agency and the central budget office (OMB, a state Bureau of the Budget, a city finance office). Since the central budget entity speaks and acts for the chief executive, while operating agencies usually have markedly different priorities, a certain amount of tension between their *budget* priorities is inevitable. Considerable evidence exists to suggest that deliberate strategies must be followed by agencies seeking to increase their allocations, and that the preparation stage is an important opportunity for them to press their case. Agency assertiveness—a strategy calling for an agency to ''come in as high as you can justify'' when submitting initial estimates—appears to carry with it a greater probability of success in increasing the ultimate amounts appropriated by the legislative branch.[45]

Authorizations and Appropriations

The *authorization* stage involves determination of maximum spending levels for each program approved by the legislative branch. This can occur during, or apart from, the formal budget process, and is the responsibility of standing committees in each chamber, such as the Senate Committee on Banking, Housing, and Urban Affairs, and the House Committee on Foreign Affairs. The committees make recommendations to the full chambers for the agencies under their respective jurisdictions. After chamber approval a bill is normally considered by a conference committee, which irons out differences in amounts authorized by each chamber. Assuming that agreement is reached (which is almost always the case), the authorization bills are forwarded to the chief executive for approval.

As noted earlier, authorizations may be enacted for expenditures in the same or subsequent years, making this step highly significant in terms of specific authorization provisions. Furthermore, depending on legislative politics, individual programs or agencies may be granted *standing* authorizations for funding—that is, open-ended authority for fiscal support subject only to yearly appropriations, without need for reauthorization prior to appropriations action. That status signifies considerable influence in the legislature enjoyed by the agency or program so favored; it also weakens to some degree the control a chief executive can exercise over such an agency's fiscal and political fortunes.

One other point should be made about the authorization process. The majority of states, and almost all local governments, draw up their budgets *without* incorporating an authorization stage into their procedures. Thus, as a formal step in determining expenditures, authorization has its greatest role and influence in Congress. This is a reflection of the less formalized budget procedures present in many states and localities, as well as the more extensive division of power (between standing committees and the appropriations committees) in Congress.

The *appropriations* stage is one of the most crucial to budget making. Appropriations, as distinguished from authorizations, grant the money to spend or the power to incur financial obligations, and the appropriations committees in the two houses (of Congress and most state legislatures) play the major role in this phase of the budgetary process.[46] According to existing rules of procedure, no appropriation may be voted until after an authorization has been approved for a particular program. But it has been known to happen otherwise. Reporter John Hart of "NBC-TV News" reported in late June of 1977 that the House had appropriated funds for development of the controversial neutron bomb—a weapon said to kill by radiation without destroying neighboring populations or property—before any formal authorization had been made. It was a bomb, some said, that nobody knew we had, and the appropriation had been "buried" in a $10.4-billion water, power, and energy research appropriation bill.[47] This can work the other way as well. That is, legislation authorizing a certain level of spending for an agency can include language *mandating* (ordering) the agency to spend this or that amount of money for specified purposes. As an example, a military authorization bill for weapons systems development may contain a provision directing the Pentagon to spend $125 million on research for medium-range missiles. When that happens, it virtually forces the House and Senate Appropriations Committees to approve that funding, since the agency would be violating the law if it did not spend the money as directed. This practice, known as "back-door financing," is not surprisingly a source of considerable irritation to appropriations committee members. More important, back-door financing eliminates discretionary decisionmaking control from the appropriations stage and forces anyone wishing to challenge such expenditures to seek to amend the authorization. That is often difficult to do, politically; as a result, back-door financing has the effect of reducing control over the general level of expenditures.

In the national government, the House of Representatives is the first stop for all money bills, and the House Appropriations Committee (HAC) has wielded tremendous influence over spending legislation for quite a few years. Political scientist Richard Fenno, in appraising both chambers' committees on appropriations, has said that the House committee, rather than its Senate counterpart, "dominates appropriations politics in Congress."[48]

Figure 12-1 Formulation of Executive Budget

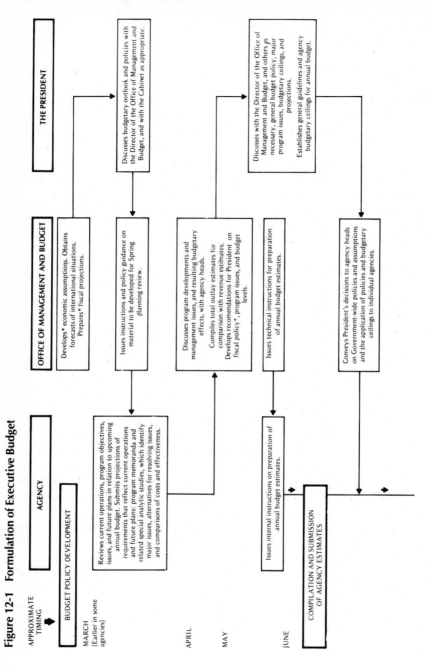

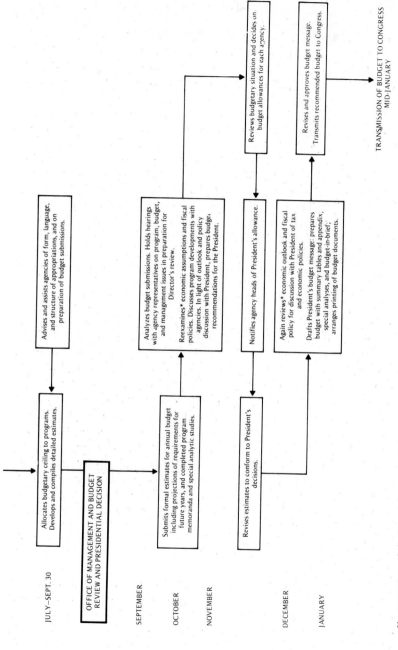

JULY–SEPT. 30

Allocates budgetary ceiling to programs. Develops and compiles detailed estimates.

Advises and assists agencies of form, language, and structure of appropriations, and on preparation of budget submissions.

OFFICE OF MANAGEMENT AND BUDGET REVIEW AND PRESIDENTIAL DECISION

SEPTEMBER

OCTOBER

Submits formal estimates for annual budget including projections of requirements for future years, and completed program memoranda and special analytic studies.

Analyzes budget submissions. Holds hearings with agency representatives on program, budget, and management issues in preparation for Director's review.

Reexamines* economic assumptions and fiscal policies. Discusses program developments with agencies. In light of outlook and policy discussion with President, prepares budget recommendations for the President.

NOVEMBER

Reviews budgetary situation and decides on budget allowances for each agency.

DECEMBER

Revises estimates to conform to President's decisions.

Notifies agency heads of President's allowance.

Again reviews* economic outlook and fiscal policy for discussion with President of tax and economic policies.

JANUARY

Drafts President's budget message: prepares budget with summary tables and appendix, special analyses, and budget-in-brief; arranges printing of budget documents.

Revises and approves budget message. Transmits recommended budget to Congress.

TRANSMISSION OF BUDGET TO CONGRESS MID-JANUARY

*In cooperation with the Treasury Department and Council of Economic Advisers.

Source: Executive Office of the President/Office of Management and Budget, January 1977.

The HAC, numbering fifty-five members, is the largest committee on Capitol Hill, containing more than one-eighth of the total House membership of 435. Perhaps more important, it contains one-fourth of the number needed to pass legislation in that chamber (218, assuming everyone votes). For many years, the HAC was very influential partly because its members exhibited a high degree of unity in appropriations voting on the House floor (though in the 1960s and 1970s that changed considerably).

Traditionally, the Senate and its appropriations committee have occupied a somewhat lesser role compared to that of the House and HAC, respectively. However, in recent years one of the changes in congressional budgetary behavior has been a more frequent assertion of Senate prerogatives in appropriations decision making; thus, the differences in influence have been narrowed somewhat. The Senate's role in budget cutting during the first half of 1981 was especially significant. Its Republican majority represented very reliable support for President Reagan's economic program, permitting the president to concentrate—successfully—on the House in his initial quest to make deep cuts in national government domestic spending.

One other feature of recent congressional behavior, with major implications for authorization and appropriation processes, is the dramatic growth of so-called "entitlement" programs, referred to earlier. Entitlement legislation places no limit on the total amount of budget authority for a program; eligibility standards are defined by law, and the level of outlays is determined solely by the number of eligible persons who apply for authorized benefits.[49] Thus, for example, Medicaid, Social Security, and veterans' benefits programs come under the heading of entitlements. Furthermore, many entitlements are *indexed* to the rate of inflation, with benefits rising as the cost of living goes up. The net effect of entitlements, and of indexing, has been to reduce still further the year-to-year control Congress might exercise over the rate of growth—and the substantive purposes—of national government spending. Between 40 and 50 percent of current annual spending is in the form of entitlements. President Reagan made some of these programs prime targets of his budget cutting when he took office in 1981, and that pattern continued into his second term.

The budgetary process described here is, as indicated previously, highly fragmented. As Aaron Wildavsky has assessed it, it is also specialized, conducted with an eye to past budget allocations for the same program or agency, and approached (at least in the House Appropriations Committee) with a primary concern for making "marginal, monetary adjustments to existing programs so that the question of the ultimate desirability of most programs arises only once in a while."[50] An important feature is the pattern of regarding the previous year's allocation (in nonentitlement programs) as the base for each appropriations process. Many decisions have revolved around what increase over the base amount should be allocated (note the significance of even attempting a procedure of zero-base budgeting). Thus, budget formation as viewed from both the executive branch and Congress has involved a vast series of rather narrow decisions, focusing on individual programs within individual agencies and only occasionally being reviewed in its totality—and then usually on the expenditure side only. Prior to the mid-1970s, the closest thing to a comprehensive budget review came during OMB's assembling of executive budget proposals before they were sent to the Capitol. But once that was done, OMB officials had no further part in defending the requests—agencies were on their own—and specialized consideration of specialized requests was nearly universal.

President versus Congress: Conflict over Authorizations, Appropriations, and Fiscal Control

As a consequence of the fragmentation in national budget making, the ability of any one institutional actor in the process to restrain effectively the growth of national government spending grew progressively more limited in the 1960s and early 1970s. The impacts of back-door spending and entitlement programs included political obstacles that had to be cleared in order to address the fundamental issue of whether such programs should be continued. Such questions obviously engaged political interests at a very sensitive level. But the more crucial point is that unless a coalition of forces was willing even to raise the issue, thus confronting the collective wrath of those benefiting from the particular expenditure, it was not possible to stem the rise in expenditure levels. This was the situation facing Richard Nixon in his first term (1969–1973).

A central theme of the Nixon presidency was a general moderating of certain government practices and policies, most notably government's expanding role in economic regulation and social programs. Fiscally conservative and regarded as moderate-to-conservative on social questions, Nixon not surprisingly tried to reduce spending—or at least the rate of increase in government expenditures—with emphasis on trimming programs established and/or expanded during the years of Lyndon Johnson's Great Society. Trying to limit or undo some of the Johnson legacy brought Nixon into inevitable conflict with Democrats in Congress and across the country, and with many in the bureaucracy.

Nowhere was the battle between president and Congress joined more vigorously or more significantly than in the fight over Nixon's efforts to restrain spending by impounding (withholding) funds after they had been authorized and appropriated. Impoundment is something of a "super item veto," not subject to a congressional override, as is the case with the formal veto power (see chapter 4). Nixon was not the first president to impound funds. Indeed, the practice of establishing reserves or administratively withholding spending authority from some programs dated back at least a century. "What made the situation critical in the early 1970s (beyond the general political climate) was the number and magnitude of the funds impounded on the orders of the chief executive, especially funds for those programs that had grown out of the Great Society of the Johnson years."[51] The Nixon administration impounded increasing amounts of appropriated funding in this period, culminating in a total of about $15 billion in 1973.

Members of Congress, and others, complained about this practice in speeches and press releases. Some were moved to file suit against the president, claiming that impoundment was not authorized by the Constitution and that, while precedents existed, these were not constitutionally sanctioned. In twenty-two separate court tests in 1973, for example, Nixon won one and lost twenty-one.[52] The most dramatic of these involved funding for construction of a stretch of interstate highway in Missouri; seventeen of eighteen U.S. Senate committee chairmen joined in the suit as "friends of the court"—a rare display of unity among those individuals. But Congress, growing increasingly impatient with lengthy court proceedings, took action early in 1974 to halt impoundment through statutory provision.

The Congressional Budget and Impoundment Control Act of 1974 abolished an earlier limited authorization for a president to withhold funds. It also sharply limited permissible grounds for deferring spending of appropriated funds, required positive action by both House and Senate to sustain an impoundment beyond a period of forty-five days, required monthly reports from either the president or comptroller-general (head of the General Accounting Office) on any deferred spending, and made it possible for the comptroller-general to go to court for an order to spend impounded funds if a president failed to comply with any of the preceding.[53] These provisions seemingly restored a considerable measure of congressional control over appropriations and expenditures. While Gerald Ford also engaged in some impounding, it was much less than that done by Richard Nixon. In the wake of Watergate, Ford had much higher political standing in Congress—and Congress had much lower tolerance for such actions. With other developments in Congress's budgetary role, impoundment has moved off center stage as a key question in legislative-executive relations.

Congress's New Budgetary Role

In the confrontation between President Nixon and Congress over impoundment, another crucial issue was also dealt with. That was whether Congress had the institutional capacity to monitor its own actions approving expenditures, and to put a brake on rising spending totals. Some observers believe the 1974 law was at least as important for the new congressional budgetary procedures it instituted as for the restrictions it established on presidential authority to impound funds.

The procedures previously followed, described earlier, left Congress open to the kinds of criticisms Richard Nixon had found effective in justifying greater presidential impoundment authority to control spending: fragmented consideration of and action on the budget, failure to consider financial implications of future expenditure obligations, willingness to enact supplemental appropriations (funds to cover expenses beyond original estimates), and so on.[54] In addition, two other factors had contributed to growing difficulties in maintaining control over expenditures.

First, very often a subsystem alliance—a program manager, an interested subcommittee chairman, and outside interest groups—united "to thwart the will of the President and of the Congress as a whole"[55] through its capacity to effectively control financing and administering of particular programs. Second, two of the most important operating norms of the House Appropriations Committee—guardianship of the Treasury and reciprocity among members[56]—were in noticeable decline during the 1960s and 1970s. In the past, Congress had cut requests the president made on behalf of the spending agencies, but it gradually came to cut less, and less regularly, than it once had. Appropriations subcommittees, well known for assuming that "there is no budget that can't be cut," were becoming more likely merely to hold the line at the level requested by the president than to assume that cuts would or should be made. Reciprocity, also, was waning; that is, there was less willingness to defer to the judgments of specialized subcommittees. Also, subcommittee and committee spending recommendations were being overturned on the floor of the House and Senate much more frequently—usually in the direction of higher, not lower, amounts.

The combined effect of these changes was considerably higher appropriation levels in legislation passed by Congress. More important, there was growing realization by observers in and out of Congress that little meaningful legislative control existed over the *totality* of the budget, with few having any idea what "whole" was the end-product of the "parts." The 1974 budget act attempted to deal with these problems. The new procedures mandated by the act can be analyzed in five segments.[57]

First, each chamber established a Budget Committee—currently with thirty members in the House, twenty-two in the Senate—which would consider annual budgets in their entirety, not broken up for consideration. Committee membership, particularly in the House, overlapped with membership on the Appropriations and Ways and Means Committees (five from each of those committees serve on the House Budget Committee), thus ensuring some integration of effort among those three key entities.

Second, the act established the Congressional Budget Office (CBO), with a professional staff and a director appointed jointly by the speaker of the House and the president pro tem of the Senate for a four-year term. CBO was to assist the Budget Committees and Congress as a whole in analyzing and projecting from budgetary proposals. It was to serve both as a provider of "hard, practical economic and fiscal data from which to draft spending legislation," as the House wanted, and as something of a "think tank" with a more philosophical approach to spending and an interest in examining national priorities, thus satisfying the Senate.[58] Whether CBO has succeeded, or could have, in both endeavors is not clear. Some critics in

Congress thought CBO should have been organized and functioning more rapidly and effectively than they say it was.[59]

Third, the act established a procedure whereby Congress would enact at least two concurrent budget resolutions each year, one in the spring and the other in the fall, for purposes of setting maximum spending levels during the appropriations process. The spring resolution (which must be approved by May 15) sets targets for spending, revenue, public debt, and the annual surplus or deficit, while the fall resolution (with a September 15 deadline) sets the final figures for each. Congress may enact more than two resolutions, but revenue and expenditures must be in accord with whatever the last resolution provides.

Fourth, a new timetable was put into effect, with the fiscal year beginning on October 1 instead of July 1. Table 12-2 outlines this new congressional budgetary timetable, and Figure 12-2 illustrates the major steps in the new budget process.

Table 12-2
CONGRESSIONAL BUDGETARY TIMETABLE*

Action Required	Final Date**	Explanation
President submits current services budget	Nov. 10	The "current services budget" indicates what would be necessary to maintain existing programs at current levels
Joint Economic Committee submits economic evaluation	Dec. 31	
President submits his budget	15th day after Congress meets	
Standing Committees, Joint Economic Committee, and Joint Committee on Internal Revenue Taxation submit reports to Budget Committees	Mar. 15	These reports recommend authorization levels
Congressional Budget Office submits report on fiscal policy and national budget priorities to Budget Committees	Apr. 1	(April 1 proved too late to be useful; CBO submits this report in February)
Budget Committees report first concurrent resolution to their Houses	Apr. 15	
Standing Committees report bills and resolutions authorizing new budget authority to full chambers	May 15	

Table 12-2 (continued)
CONGRESSIONAL BUDGETARY TIMETABLE*

Action Required	Final Date**	Explanation
Congress completes all action on first concurrent resolution	May 15	This sets spending, revenue, and other budget *targets*
Congress completes action on all bills and resolutions providing new budget and new spending authority	7th day after Labor Day	
Congress completes all action on second required concurrent resolution	Sept. 15	This sets spending, revenue, and other budget *ceilings*
Congress completes action on reconciliation bill or resolution, or both, implementing second required concurrent resolution	Sept. 25	Final spending recommendations must be reconciled with budget ceiling adopted in second concurrent resolution
Fiscal Year begins (beginning in 1976)	Oct. 1	

*In accordance with the Congressional Budget and Impoundment Control Act of 1974 (Public Law 93–344).

**In some years, Congress has been unable to meet these deadlines.

Source: Adapted from James J. Finley, "The 1974 Congressional Initiative in Budget Making," *Public Administration Review,* 35 (May/June 1975), 272; Allen Schick, *Congress and Money* (Washington, D.C.: The Urban Institute, 1980), p. 4; and Walter J. Oleszek, *Congressional Procedures and the Policy Process,* 2nd ed. (Washington, D.C.: CQ Press, 1984), p. 58.

Fifth, the act banned most *new* back-door spending programs, thus extending congressional control over the budget even further. However, because many such programs existed before 1974, back-door spending has not been eliminated; on the contrary, program costs have increased.

Has the new budget procedure worked? Has it done what it was supposed to do? Compared to an earlier congressional attempt in the late 1940s to establish a legislative budget and a spending ceiling—an attempt that proved to be unwieldy and woefully understaffed—this effort got off to a rousing start, but has since lost some of that early momentum.

A major factor in the early success of the new procedures was development by CBO of "objective, open, and timely cost analysis data on congressional legislation," thus contributing to a minimization of the "'budget numbers game' among the administration, agencies, lobbyists, and [Capitol] Hill staff that formerly accompanied legislative bargaining."[60] There has been some disagreement about CBO's data, but it certainly is an improvement over the fluid situation of the past, where whom to believe in forecasting or analysis was itself a big concern.

Another important factor was effective monitoring by both budget committees and CBO of Congress's revenue and spending actions. Also,

Figure 12-2 Major Steps in the Budget Process

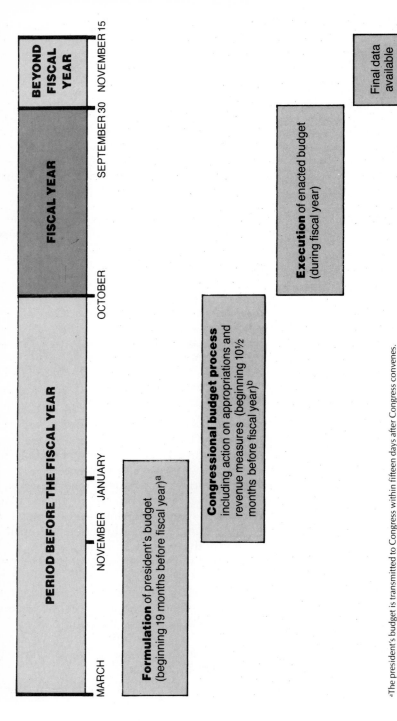

aThe president's budget is transmitted to Congress within fifteen days after Congress convenes.
bIf appropriation action is not completed by September 30, Congress enacts temporary appropriation (i.e., continuing resolution).

Source: Executive Office of the President/Office of Management and Budget, January 1977.

the budget committees, through their initial responsibility for projecting total revenues, the annual deficit, and the level of the national debt, could monitor broad-gauge effects of individual committee and floor actions and duly inform the members. They were even successful at one point in defeating a tax proposal favored by Senator Russell Long, then chairman of the Senate Finance Committee, because it would have fallen far short of the revenue target set by the two budget committees.

Other factors included the severe recession of 1974–1975, which coincided with the backlash (in Congress and in the country) against presidential excesses and the resulting opportunity for Congress to assert itself; general public concern over growth of government spending; partisan jockeying during an election year; provisions of the Budget Act itself that provided for adequate staff assistance, enforcement mechanisms for various deadlines in the new budget cycle, and structural coordination among key committees; the determined leadership of Budget Committee chairmen Brock Adams in the House and Edmund Muskie in the Senate; and a great deal of plain hard work by Budget Committee members in both chambers.[61]

The budget process has encountered rougher going since the late 1970s, however. Many observers believe that after a few good years, the usual patterns of diffused influence in Congress gradually have reasserted themselves; members have paid less attention to the need for restraint, more to their geographic and interest-group constituencies. Allen Schick has suggested, however, that the process—and the Budget Committees overseeing it—"should expect to experience periodic ups and downs in their legislative fortunes. They [the committees] will have good years and bad years; they will not be listened to every year."[62] Evaluations of the process have, on occasion, resembled a press-and-public roller coaster, swinging from almost euphoric triumph to despair that Congress could ever get control of itself and its spending habits.[63] Since the process challenges established practices in one of Congress's most essential functions—allocation of resources—it should come as no surprise that those practices were resistant to change. Also, political conditions prevailing in both House and Senate have become increasingly unstable. Partisan and liberal-conservative rifts in the House, especially, have combined with intensifying pressures on most members of Congress for attentiveness to specific interests.[64] This is largely due to President Reagan's vigorous pursuit of deep cuts in domestic spending, particularly in 1981 but also in subsequent years.[65]

Other emerging difficulties in the congressional budget process include an increasing tendency for Congress to ignore—or simply not be able to carry out—a number of the most important functions in the process. One is meeting the chronological deadlines for enacting the first and second budget resolutions; beginning in the late 1970s, Congress has missed one or both deadlines as often as not. There are several reasons for this. For one, members of Congress need to make judgments about the condition of the economy as part of their budget deliberations, and they seek as much information as possible before doing so. As we saw in chapter 8, obtaining necessary information can require considerable time. Another reason is that many legislators often try to postpone the tough political choices involved in budgetary decision making until the last possible moment—a tendency often criticized, but entirely understandable. A second recurring problem has been inaccurate projections of spending and revenue targets for a given fiscal year (an indication of the difficulty in making such projections eighteen months in advance). A third phenomenon of the 1980s, reflecting both mechanical and inherently political problems, is the fact that several fiscal years have begun *without a budget* enacted into law, or at least without passage of major appropriations bills. When that happens, Congress simply authorizes agency expenditures at the same levels as in the previous fiscal year, until action is completed on the budget or on relevant appropriations legislation (this has been called, not too kindly, "government by 'continuing resolution' "[66]).

These emerging problems are part of a general evolution in the congressional budget process, which has been characterized by important (though mostly informal) changes in the ways the process actually operates, compared to its original design.[67] For one thing, the scope of the process now includes national government credit activities (such as loan guarantees for corporations and for college students). Congress now includes in its budget resolutions *advisory* targets on the "total size of . . . lending and loan-guarantee programs."[68] A second (and more significant) change is that the *first* resolution, not the second, has become the "major vehicle for congressional budgeting."[69] Twice in the early 1980s, Congress "adopted an automatic triggering device allowing the first budget resolution to substitute for the second resolution if Congress did not approve the second resolution by October 1."[70] Among other things, this means that the most intensive budgetary negotiations among the principals concerned are now concentrated in a short time period early in each calendar year (that is, prior to adoption of the first resolution).

A third change, which has contributed to the increased importance of the first concurrent resolution, is that since 1980 the reconciliation procedure has been associated with the first resolution (contrary to the formal design of the process!). *Reconciliation* involves making adjustments in existing law, to achieve conformity with current budget plans (the annual spending targets adopted in the first resolution). Those adjustments can be spending cuts, revenue boosts, or a combination of the two. The key step, following committee recommendations, is House and Senate action on an omnibus (all-encompassing) reconciliation bill. Originally that was to be done in the fall, following adoption of the second resolution. However, "[t]he first budget resolution has become the place where the important decisions are made, and reconciling the parts with the whole"[71] now occurs at that point in the process. This development has made budgetary politics prior to the first resolution even more intense, since the stakes can be even higher.

A vivid illustration of how the role of reconciliation has changed came in 1981, when President Reagan

> persuaded Congress to employ reconciliation to achieve massive cuts in domestic programs (totaling about $130 billion over three years). Never before had reconciliation been employed on such a grand scale. The entire . . . process was put on a "fast track. . . ." [R]econciliation forced numerous House and Senate committees to make unwanted cuts in programs, *including entitlements*, under their jurisdiction.[72]

The political shrewdness of this tactic has been described this way:

> By aggregating cuts and forcing a vote on them in total (the reconciliation procedure), President Reagan and the Republican legislative leadership simultaneously made large reductions attractive (because they amounted to something) and politically feasible (because mere billion-dollar cuts were harder to spot and because there were so many, Congressmen could, so to speak, "hide" amongst them).[73]

Thus, not surprisingly, the budget process has been adapted to forces both internal and external to the Congress, as budgetary pressures have mounted steadily.

An overall assessment of the new budget process is difficult to make, especially because there was and is considerable disagreement on Capitol Hill (and elsewhere) about what it was supposed to accomplish. Detractors point to the problems noted earlier; they suggest in addition that the process "is too complex and consumes too much of Congress's attention and energy,"[74] and that it is responsible for increased jurisdictional jealousies among congressional committees.[75]

Even with these tendencies, the process can be said to have accomplished a number of significant things.[76] First, in addition to limiting backdoor spending authority, both budget committees have tried to discourage the spread of entitlements into new program areas. The Budget Act contains provisions that potentially impede the enactment of entitlements, and the committees have utilized these together with publicity about the costs involved. Perhaps due to a changing fiscal outlook in Congress as well as to these efforts, there has been a definite slowing in the spread of new entitlements since fiscal 1977. In this regard, the budget and appropriations committees have been working partners.

Second, the process—in spite of some evidence to the contrary— appears to have put down fairly firm roots. Even in the years when the budget resolutions were enacted late, Congress attended to their enactment *before* going on to other business—including, significantly, appropriations.

"The budget process has become a regular, accepted feature of the congressional landscape. Its routines have been fixed in the House and Senate calendars and in the minds of members. The annual cycle of committee and floor work is oriented to the budget schedule."[77] That is no small achievement, even when there are political strains and conflicts in the process itself.

Third, members of Congress are much better informed about budgetary implications of both their own decisions and administration policies, and about the relationship between the economy and the budget. More to the point, this has resulted from Congress having its *own* information sources (CBO and the budget committees), so that members "are much less dependent on the White House and OMB for financial data and advice."[78]

Fourth, there is greater coherence in the way Congress deals with the national government budget, particularly in its being able to relate spending decisions to projected revenues and debt levels. One distinct benefit, in the minds of many members, is that "we would be looking at even greater deficits and greater problems, had we not moved in the Congress to instill some discipline within our own institution."[79]

Finally, the process has enhanced management of budgetary conflict, principally because the Budget Act "assured that conflict would be in the open."[80] The budget committees, acting on behalf of the budget process, cannot help but "step on others' toes" in the battles for government dollars. Yet though these clashes occur frequently, there has been a growing appreciation by many in Congress that the Budget Act was passed with the *expectation* of conflict and was designed to organize Congress to cope with it more effectively. Now, with resource scarcity a pervasive phenomenon and pressures for spending restraint coming from the White House, Congress is in a better position to assess its own priorities *as an institution*. Whether it continues to do so remains to be seen.[81]

Execution and Auditing of the Budget

Budget *execution* is the process of spending money appropriated by Congress and approved by the president. Money is apportioned from the Treasury, covering three-month periods beginning October 1, January 1, April 1, and July 1. Spending of funds is monitored by an agency's leadership, OMB, standing committees of Congress with jurisdiction over the agencies, and (periodically) the General Accounting Office (GAO), the auditing and investigative arm of Congress.

Administrative discretion in spending funds is considerable. Agency personnel, in the course of program operations, may transfer funds from one account to another, reprogram funds for use in different (though related) ways under established budget authority, and defer spending from one fiscal quarter to the next in order to build up some cash reserves. Administrative conduct is influenced in these respects, and others, by legislative committees with jurisdiction over the given agency; committee review and clearance is frequently obtained prior to many such spending decisions. Similarly, the president may seek to defer spending of funds as a means of influencing agency or program directions. Congress or the president may also seek to rescind (cancel) budget authority for funds previously approved for a given fiscal year. Since 1974, any deferral of spending must be reported to Congress by the president in a special message; proposed recisions must also be transmitted by the president in the same manner. Deferrals take effect unless either House passes a resolution of disapproval; for a recision to take effect, however, both chambers of Congress must approve it within forty-five days of the president's special message.[82]

One other procedural element should be noted, a consequence of the quarterly apportionment arrangement mentioned above. Most agencies will try not to spend all their quarterly allotment in that quarter, in order to maintain something in reserve—for emergencies, unforeseen expenses, or simply because costs are higher during some parts of the year than others. For example, the National Park Service's expenses in the spring and summer are far greater than during the dead of winter. In the last quarter of the fiscal year, however, this reserve buildup can lead to a strange phenomenon. Agencies do not want to turn money back to the Treasury at the end of the year; thus, in the last few weeks they will attempt to spend all but a small portion of their quarterly allotment plus any reserve accumulated through the first three quarters. The reason for reluctance to return money to the Treasury is that agencies fear being told the next time that they go before an appropriations subcommittee, "Well, you didn't need all we gave you last year, so we'll just reduce your appropriation accordingly this year." Whether that *would* happen in every instance is not clear, but the fear is strong enough to produce behavior that is a bit surprising; one might think that agencies would be proud of demonstrating their concern for the taxpayer's dollar. But it is not to be, most times.[83]

The *audit* stage really involves several functions divided among different auditors and carried out during different time periods. Informal audits are ongoing within agencies—they have to be, to generate fiscal data necessary to demonstrate proper spending of funds and programmatic efficiency. Formal audits are under the direction, at various times, of agency auditors (or of private auditing firms with which agencies contract), of OMB, and of the GAO. In some states an auditor general or auditor of accounts is responsible, full-time, for maintaining a check on agency expenditures. Also, legislative oversight amounts to an ongoing informal legislative audit, though for somewhat different purposes—programmatic as well as expenditure control.

In recent decades the focus and purpose of audits have shifted—in some cases, dramatically. While the original purpose of auditing was to ensure financial accuracy and propriety, changes came about as budgeting (and management, generally) became more systematic. A *managerial* focus developed during the same period that program efficiency was emphasized. And just in the past decade, *performance* audits have become more common, stressing (as with PPB) program effectiveness and overall agency performance. Unlike PPB, performance auditing has taken firm root in many agencies and is increasingly used by central budget offices in the executive branch to enhance budgetary control by the chief executive.

In summarizing the five stages, we should note that at any given time, an agency head or budget officer can be giving attention to as many as four fiscal years. By way of illustration, in the late spring of 1985 (during the third quarter of fiscal 1985, for the national government), audits of fiscal 1984 were nearing conclusion, expenditures in fiscal 1985 were well under way, budget submissions for fiscal 1986 already had occurred, and preliminary preparation of estimates for fiscal 1987 had begun. With the expansion of the number of actors in the budget process, its complexity has greatly increased. But another factor may now have even more impact: the growing need to budget in an era of resource scarcity, and to confront the hard choices made necessary by "fiscal retrenchment." We will examine this growing phenomenon briefly.

BUDGETING AND RESOURCE SCARCITY

Resources have always been *relatively* scarce, in the sense that there is rarely, if ever, enough to go around to satisfy all the pressures on the public treasury. What is new, since the mid-1970s, is the advent of *absolute* scarcity—of declining rates of growth, of absolute shrinkage of tax bases (not only in larger, older central cities where that problem has been evident for years), of rising inflation coupled with recession that has put governments in a new fiscal squeeze. Getting the most out of the resources we have has become a recurring theme, with renewed emphasis on both economy and efficiency, as we adjust to new, harsher realities.[84]

Among the most difficult problems has been the need to reopen seemingly settled questions concerning ongoing public needs. That is, rather than being able to deal with spending and policy priorities "on the margins" of the governmental agenda, it is becoming necessary to *continuously* assess the demand for, and appropriateness of, particular programs. The level of political tension has risen as various interests in the governmental process see all too clearly the possibility of having to defend repeatedly their claims for government support. As long as the total fiscal "pie" was expanding, which was the case for many years, competition for a share of it could be brisk without getting to be cutthroat. Now, however, as the total pie becomes stable in size, or actually declines—while costs rise rapidly— the competition greatly intensifies.[85] How much it intensifies depends on the extent of government commitment to costly existing programs, increases in costs, employee demands for wage increases, the condition of the existing fiscal base, political pressures from taxpayers for easing the tax burden, and the like. Thus, hard-pressed central cities such as New York, St. Louis, and Cleveland face a much heavier crunch than expanding states and cities of the West and Southwest, or the national government. But the differences may be more of degree than of substance; government jurisdictions presently in a more favorable position are nonetheless well advised to prepare for the fiscal pendulum to swing the other way in their cases, as well.

Under these circumstances, controllability of spending becomes a matter of premier importance. The controllability issue raises questions about government's ability—and the people's resolve—truly to control the purse strings. States, unlike the national government, often have *constitutionally* mandated expenditures, with specific earmarking of revenues for designated purposes (such as road construction and maintenance, or operating game preserves), leaving the legislature without discretion to change them. Even though the national Constitution does not impose similar constraints upon Congress, it appears that the trends toward back-door spending and entitlements (including formula grants to state and local governments) produce almost the same effect. And ironically, the decade of the 1970s—when fiscal constraints on government were growing significantly— also saw a major rise in the proportion of the national budget accounted for by "uncontrollable" expenditures (uncontrollable under existing law). "Uncontrollables" represent better than three-fourths of national spending; Schick has even suggested that *in practice*, some 95 percent of the budget is in fact uncontrollable.[86] The welter of entitlements, formula grants, and the like makes efforts to control spending *solely through budget devices* seem futile. Controllability of the budget must come through nonbudgetary mechanisms (strictly speaking), and the will to use them.

Sunset Laws

One such device is a *sunset law*, which would require that all government programs be renewed periodically through legislative action at the authorization stage, or else cease to exist. Presumably, if agencies and programs were subjected to periodic review and were forced continually to justify their activities—perhaps their very existence—they would be prevented from falling into patterns of complacency and routine behavior that have been said to make them less accountable to the legislature and, in turn, to the public.

As described by an early proponent, sunset laws should operate according to the following essential guidelines.[87] In addition to provision for termination of programs and agencies unless affirmatively reestablished by law, sunset laws should mandate periodic evaluations—for example, every five, seven, or nine years—to institutionalize the program evaluation process. The sunset mechanism should be phased in gradually, with recognition of the need to learn both why and how to use it. Programs and agencies in the same policy area should be reviewed simultaneously, to facilitate coordination, consolidation, and responsible trimming of existing entities. Preliminary evaluation work should be done by agencies such as OMB, CBO, and GAO (and their state-level counterparts), but their staff capacities for evaluation should be strengthened.

In addition, sunset proposals should establish general criteria for evaulation, to make the process meaningful. Evaluation information should be presented to top decision makers in a form that aids their understanding of actual program or agency performance. Significantly, substantial reorganization of legislative committees, including adoption of a system of rotation of committee members, is deemed necessary for purposes of more meaningful legislative oversight, according to this formulation. Such reorganization, it is felt, would sharply reduce subsystem influences and limit the impact of self-serving evaluations. Sunset mechanisms should contain safeguards against arbitrary terminations and should provide for displaced agency personnel and any remaining financial obligations. Finally, public participation should be incorporated as part of the sunset process, in the form of access to evaluation information, and public hearings held only after due notice is given as to time and place.

The political appeal of sunset laws grew very rapidly in the second half of the 1960s; by the end of the decade over half of the states had adopted some form of sunset legislation.[88] At the national level, however, efforts to enact a sunset law have thus far been more limited. That should serve as an indicator of the political dynamics likely to characterize sunset in practice: intense agency or program advocacy, in a new form, at or near a scheduled expiration date, by staunch supporters.

RONALD REAGAN AND GOVERNMENT BUDGETS

It would be difficult to overstate the impacts on budget making (at all levels of government) of Ronald Reagan's presidency. Historically, "strong" presidents have been associated with expansions of national government activity, especially in domestic policy making (for example, Franklin Roosevelt and Lyndon Johnson). For the first time, however, an occupant of the Oval Office has sought to exercise decisive, sustained presidential leadership in the quest for a *smaller-scale* national government—for reduced domestic spending and fewer public programs, less extensive regulation of private economic activity (see chapter 14), and the like. The Reagan presidency unquestionably will be remembered as an historic turning point in our governmental evolution; many of his initiatives promise to have long-term consequences, for better or for worse. In a more immediate sense, however, particular assumptions made—and concrete steps advocated—by Ronald Reagan were significant in shaping government budgets and budget making. That is because key political and economic assumptions underlying Reagan administration budgetary policies differed profoundly from those followed by many previous presidents, of both parties.

Led by OMB Director David Stockman, the Reagan administration began trying, early in 1981, to change what it saw as a pattern of "constituency-based" budget decisions, in the interest of creating (and sustaining) a "fiscal revolution" in the national government.[89] Viewing previous budgets as no more than an accumulation of claims on the national treasury made by allegedly greedy "special interests," the administration did not hesitate to propose reductions in some strongly supported domestic programs. Also important were the administration's commitments to tax reduction and to balancing the budget. These were viewed (according to "supply-side" economic theory) as essential to sparking new, noninflationary expansion of private economic activity, which it was thought would result in sustained economic growth and continued reductions in budget deficits. The president persuaded Congress to enact an across-the-board, three-year tax cut with considerable benefit to more affluent taxpayers (a continuing source of controversy). Central to all of this, however, was a determination to reduce government (especially domestic) spending, and it was to this that Stockman and President Reagan devoted considerable energy and attention throughout the president's first term and well into the second.

Whether the view of constituency greed held by the president and Stockman was accurate, and whether "supply-side" economics was truly a new doctrine or simply traditional "trickle-down" economics (a controversial view holding that economic policies benefiting the more affluent are justified, because the benefits spread throughout the economy), seems not to have mattered in the first year of efforts to create a new political climate—a "new agenda" in Washington. There were major policy and budgetary successes in that first year (for example, Congress's voting to cut spending by $130 billion), tarnished only slightly by Stockman's frank admission late in 1981 that there were few, if any, major differences between "supply-side" and "trickle-down" economics.[90]

The "mix," or composition, of the annual budget has been altered considerably since 1981. Defense spending was increased substantially, with additional long-term (and high-cost) commitments such as the MX missile likely to be pursued.[91] However, in virtually all other functional areas of discretionary domestic spending, budget reduction has been the order of the day. Among the more controversial patterns of budget cutting have been efforts to limit health-care payments, reduce social services program funding, freeze pay and reduce pensions for government civilian employees, and cut back levels of national government aid to state and local governments.[92] Adding to the controversy were claims that these expenditure areas were being made to bear a disproportionate share of budget reductions, on the grounds that *total* nondefense discretionary spending amounted to only $81 billion in fiscal 1985, out of an overall budget total of $960 billion.[93]

President Reagan also advanced proposals dealing with the nation's continuing ability to control government spending. He actively supported a constitutional amendment which would require the national government to maintain a balanced budget (though he was more ambivalent about calls for a new constitutional convention addressed—on the surface, at least—to the same objective). Mr. Reagan also advocated a constitutional amendment or legislation that would enable the president to exercise a "line-item" veto over appropriations (see chapter 4)—a proposal which attracted support from some Democrats as well as quite a few Republicans. Thus, Ronald Reagan not only altered numerous policy directions in important and enduring respects, but also attempted to revise the terms of the debate over national government spending.

Clearly the nature of budgeting has changed in the past thirty years; equally clearly, that change has not occurred in a social or political vacuum. As Allen Schick has observed: "The budget cannot make order out of chaos, it cannot bring concord where there is unlimited strife. Where there is [political] instability . . ., [b]udget issues become symbols of larger, unresolvable political conflicts."[94] That view is consistent with the position taken at the outset of this chapter, namely, that government budgets reflect political preferences and priorities of those who make them—and, by implication, of the citizenry at large. Where those preferences and priorities are very much in turmoil, as they have been in recent decades, it is not surprising that the politics of government budgeting is similarly turbulent.

Despite the deep budget cuts made by the Reagan administration,[95] public attitudes about fiscal restraint and its policy consequences still have not crystallized entirely. It appears likely that we face continuing political and fiscal uncertainty, as we grope for a new national consensus regarding the proper role of public spending.

SUMMARY

The budgetary process is central to resource allocation in the political system. The nature of budget decision making has long been an issue of considerable importance, with political influence, policy control, and "rationality" key variables. The scope of government spending, and the impacts on society accompanying that spending, have dramatically expanded in recent decades, though some modification of existing trends began during the 1970s.

Budgets can be tools used by government to influence the course of private-sector economic activity. The chief instruments related to budgeting include taxing and spending patterns, management of debt, monetary and credit controls, and economic coordination. Such uses of the budget are of relatively recent vintage, having developed fully only in the last fifty years. Accompanying these changes has been a marked increase in both the role of the national government and the influence of the president in budget and policy formulation. Other concerns, principally budget deficits, have emerged more recently. The *executive budget* has been central to all of this.

Budget formulation in the executive branch has been characterized at different times by various orientations and emphases. Line-item budgeting stressed control of, and accountability for, expenditures. Performance budgeting emphasized managerial coordination and control, focusing on program efficiency. PPB was designed to forge links between planning and budgeting processes, to make it possible to measure program effectiveness, and to introduce a greater degree of decisional "rationality" to the process. However, PPB largely failed to accomplish its purposes. ZBB provided for ranking "packages" of services, assessing impacts of various levels of services, and establishing orders of priority for funding within given revenue constraints.

The process of budget making is highly fragmented in many American governments and includes choices as to annual or multiyear budgeting, and current and future obligations. Budget preparation focuses on agencies and a central budget office (the latter usually serving the chief executive), in assembling executive budget proposals to the legislature. Authorizations are legislative determinations, first, of programs themselves, and second, of maximum spending levels. Appropriations allocate actual funding or obligations, and normally must follow—and be governed by—authorizations. However, a recent tendency has emerged toward "back-door spending" authority and semipermanent "entitlement" programs that remain in force unless deliberate action is taken to change their provisions. This has simultaneously weakened controls over spending and contributed to rapidly rising expenditures, at least in the national government budget.

The 1970s saw a concerted effort in the national government to begin to apply restraints to the rise in spending. First President Nixon engaged in the practice of impoundment, on a wider scale than most previous presidents; subsequently, Congress legislated a congressional budget process that is still not fully developed. Conflicts between specific program advocates and those supporting the larger process of congressional budget making have been numerous, but perhaps inevitable. Though the process is never likely to run entirely smoothly, it has enhanced Congress's ability to manage budget conflict, and to build better information capability.

Execution and audit of the budget, at one time fairly routine functions, are now more complex. Auditing, in particular, has become more systematic. At any one time, responsible officials may deal with budgets for as many as four years, and perhaps more.

Budgeting in an era of resource scarcity is a new, harsh reality. Rising costs of government have combined with stabilizing, or shrinking, resource bases to create a serious fiscal squeeze for many governments. Among the consequences are raising the stakes of budgetary decisions, increasing demands for controllability of expenditures, and calls for devices such as sunset laws. Ronald Reagan's presidency has produced major changes in government budgeting, many with long-term financial and policy implications. A consensus on appropriate government fiscal directions is still to emerge.

NOTES

1. Jesse Burkhead, *Government Budgeting* (New York: Wiley, 1956), p. 59.
2. See, among others, Jeffrey D. Straussman, "A Typology of Budgetary Environments: Notes on the Prospects for Reform," *Administration & Society*, 11 (August 1979), 216–26.
3. An excellent treatment of the changing relationship between budgetary incrementalism and the surrounding environment of fiscal retrenchment can be found in Allen Schick, "Incremental Budgeting in a Decremental Age," *Policy Sciences*, 16 (September 1983), 1–25. See also Lance T. LeLoup, "The Myth of Incrementalism: Analytical Choices in Budgetary Theory," *Polity*, 10 (Summer 1978), 488–509.
4. Burkhead, *Government Budgeting*, p. 59.
5. Ibid., p. 60 (emphasis added). See also Howard E. Shuman, *Politics and the Budget: The Struggle Between the President and the Congress* (Englewood Cliffs, N.J.: Prentice-Hall, 1984), chapter 5.
6. See David J. Ott and Attiat F. Ott, *Federal Budget Policy*, rev. ed. (Washington, D.C.: Brookings, 1969), pp. 72–75.
7. See Aaron Wildavsky, *The Politics of the Budgetary Process*, 4th ed. (Boston: Little, Brown, 1984), p. 50.
8. Burkhead, *Government Budgeting*, p. 63.
9. See *Congressional Quarterly Weekly Report*, 43 (February 9, 1985), 261, and *Congressional Quarterly Weekly Report*, 43 (August 31, 1985), 1,698. The rapid increase in annual interest payments may well offset gains that otherwise might have been realized in reducing the national government deficit. See, for example, "Interest Payments Swallowing Gains on Deficit," a Washington *Post* news story reprinted in the Bloomington-Normal (Ill.) *Daily Pantagraph*, July 22, 1984, p. A–1. For a broad-gauged examination of the challenges posed by continuing budget deficits, see *Fighting Federal Deficits: The Time for Hard Choices* (New York: Committee for Economic Development, September 1984).
10. See J. Richard Aronson and Eli Schwartz, eds., *Management Policies in Local Government Finance* (Washington, D.C.: International City Management Association, 1975), chapter 12, "Debt Management."
11. For an in-depth examination of tax spending, see Stanley S. Surrey and Paul R. McDaniel, *Tax Expenditures* (Cambridge, Mass.: Harvard University Press, 1985).
12. Robert D. Lee, Jr., and Ronald W. Johnson, *Public Budgeting Systems*, 3rd ed. (Baltimore: University Park Press, 1983), p. 337 (emphasis added).

13. See Robert J. Samuelson, "An Economic Minefield," *National Journal*, 12 (November 22, 1980), 1969–72, at p. 1969.
14. Lee and Johnson, *Public Budgeting Systems*, p. 33.
15. Charles L. Schultze, *The Politics and Economics of Public Spending* (Washington, D.C.: Brookings, 1968), p. 8. Schultze notes (pp. 7–8) that when Alexander Hamilton was George Washington's treasury secretary, he had established a central executive budget that gave broad discretion to the executive and "contained the potential for development of a centrally planned budget and a deliberate allocation of resources among competing agencies." Jefferson, however, ended that practice, opposing Hamilton's preferences for a strong central government and a strong executive within it.
16. Lee and Johnson, *Public Budgeting Systems*, p. 7. This description of early reform efforts relies on their treatment found on pp. 7–9.
17. Ibid., p. 7. State governments have continued to be active in budgetary reforms of various types. See, among others, Stanley B. Botner, "The Use of Budgeting/Management Tools by State Governments," *Public Administration Review*, 45 (September/October 1985), 616–20.
18. Linda L. Smith, "The Congressional Budget Process: Why It Worked This Time," *The Bureaucrat*, 6 (Spring 1977), 88–111, at p. 89.
19. Allen Schick, *Budget Innovation in the States* (Washington, D.C.: Brookings, 1971), p. 6.
20. Ibid., p. 7.
21. Lee and Johnson, *Public Budgeting Systems*, p. 33.
22. Ibid., p. 72.
23. Ibid., p. 77.
24. The literature on PPB is quite extensive. Among the most useful sources are Charles J. Hitch and Roland N. McKean, *The Economics of Defense in the Nuclear Age* (Cambridge: Harvard University Press, 1967); David Novick, ed., *Program Budgeting: Program Analysis and the Federal Budget*, 2nd ed. (New York: Holt, Rinehart and Winston, 1969); Schultze, *The Politics and Economics of Public Spending*; Dwight Waldo, ed., "Planning-Programming-Budgeting System: A Symposium," *Public Administration Review*, 26 (December 1966), 243–310; and, "Planning-Programming-Budgeting System Re-examined: Development, Analysis, and Criticism: A Symposium," *Public Administration Review*, 29 (March/April 1969), 111–202. Critical appraisals of PPB can be found in Leonard Merewitz and Stephen H. Sosnick, *The Budget's New Clothes: A Critique of Planning-Programming-Budgeting and Benefit-Cost Analysis* (Chicago: Markham, 1971), and Wildavsky, *The Politics of the Budgetary Process*, chapter 6.
25. Schick, *Budget Innovation in the States*, p. 7. See also his "The Road to PPB: The Stages of Budget Reform," *Public Administration Review*, 26 (December 1966), 243–58.
26. See, for example, Wylie Kilpatrick, "Classification and Measurement of Public Expenditures," *Annals of the American Academy of Political and Social Science*, 183 (January 1936), 19–26.
27. See, for example, William M. Capron, "The Impact of Analysis on Bargaining in Government," in James W. Davis, Jr., ed., *Politics, Programs, and Budgets: A Reader in Government Budgeting* (Englewood Cliffs, N.J.: Prentice-Hall, 1969), pp. 253–67.
28. The following discussion relies on Lee and Johnson, *Public Budgeting Systems*, pp. 89–99.

29. Some in and out of Congress, however, felt PPB might make available much better information with which Congress could judge performance of executive branch agencies, thus working to the advantage of the legislative oversight function.
30. Stanley B. Botner, "PPB Under Nixon," *Public Administration Review*, 32 (May/June 1972), 255.
31. Allen Schick, "A Death in the Bureaucracy: The Demise of Federal PPB," *Public Administration Review*, 33 (March/April 1973), 146–56.
32. Ibid., p. 146.
33. John A. Worthley, "PPB: Dead or Alive?" *Public Administration Review*, 34 (July/August 1974), 392–94. The passage quoted appears on p. 393. Worthley notes that the notion of PPB as a counterweight to confrontation was first suggested by Frederick C. Mosher.
34. This discussion of ZBB relies on the following sources: *Congressional Quarterly Weekly Report*, 35 (March 12, 1977), 441–43; Thomas D. Lynch, "A Context for Zero-Base Budgeting," *The Bureaucrat*, 6 (Spring 1977), 3–11; Peter A. Pyhrr, "The Zero-Base Approach to Government Budgeting," *Public Administration Review*, 37 (January/February 1977), 1–8; Allen Schick, "Zero-Base Budgeting and Sunset: Redundancy or Symbiosis?" *The Bureaucrat*, 6 (Spring 1977), 12–32; Graeme M. Taylor, "Introduction to Zero-Base Budgeting," *The Bureaucrat*, 6 (Spring 1977), 33–55; Perry Moore, "Zero-Base Budgeting in American Cities," *Public Administration Review*, 40 (May/June 1980), 253–58; John A. Worthley and William G. Ludwin, eds., *Zero-Base Budgeting in State and Local Government: Current Experiences and Cases* (New York: Praeger, 1979); Allen Schick, "The Road from ZBB," *Public Administration Review*, 38 (March/April 1978), 177–80; and Frank D. Draper and Bernard T. Pitsvada, "ZBB—Looking Back After Ten Years," *Public Administration Review*, 41 (January/February 1981), 76–83.
35. Taylor, "Introduction to Zero-Base Budgeting," pp. 36–37.
36. Schick, "Zero-Base Budgeting and Sunset," p. 14.
37. Ibid., p. 18.
38. Ibid., p. 13.
39. Lee and Johnson, *Public Budgeting Systems*, p. 73.
40. Schick, "Zero-Base Budgeting and Sunset," p. 16 (emphasis added).
41. Draper and Pitsvada, "ZBB—Looking Back After Ten Years," p. 78. For a fuller treatment of ZBB see, also by Draper and Pitsvada, *Zero-Base Budgeting for Public Programs* (Lanham, Md.: University Press of America, 1979).
42. This discussion relies extensively on Lee and Johnson, *Public Budgeting Systems*, chapter 9, and Wildavsky, *The Politics of the Budgetary Process*.
43. Wildavsky, *The Politics of the Budgetary Process*, pp. 288–89; and Lance T. LeLoup, *Budgetary Politics*, 2nd ed. (Brunswick, Ohio: King's Court, 1980), p. 284.
44. See Figure 12–1. See also Shelley Lynne Tomkin, "OMB Budget Examiners' Influence," *The Bureaucrat*, 12 (Fall 1983), 43–47.
45. See Lance T. LeLoup and William B. Moreland, "Agency Strategies and Executive Review: The Hidden Politics of Budgeting," *Public Administration Review*, 38 (May/June 1978), 232–39.
46. Lee and Johnson, *Public Budgeting Systems*, pp. 187–88. In addition to the formal responsibilities discharged during the authorization and appropriations stages, there are opportunities for Congress to attempt to assert greater general control over executive agencies. One example is the practice of adding "limitation

amendments" to appropriations bills, and of enacting temporary authorizations. See Allen Schick, "Politics through Law: Congressional Limitations on
Executive Discretion," in Anthony King, ed., *Both Ends of the Avenue: The Presidency, the Executive Branch, and Congress in the 1980s* (Washington, D.C.: American Enterprise Institute for Public Policy Research, 1983), pp. 154–84, at pp.
170–75.

47. Reported on "NBC Nightly News," June 24, 1977.
48. Richard F. Fenno, Jr., *The Power of the Purse: Appropriations Politics in Congress*
    (Boston: Little, Brown, 1966), p. 503.
49. Wildavsky, *The Politics of the Budgetary Process*, p. 285.
50. Ibid., chapter 2. The passage quoted appears on p. 60.
51. Ernest C. Betts, Jr., and Richard E. Miller, "More About the Impact of the Con-
    gressional Budget and Impoundment Control Act," *The Bureaucrat*, 6 (Spring
    1977), 112–20, at p. 114.
52. St. Louis *Post-Dispatch*, August 5, 1973, p. 19A.
53. *Congressional Record*, H5180–82 (Daily Record, June 18, 1974); *Congressional Quar-
    terly Weekly Report*, 32 (June 15, 1974), 1594. For analyses of the period and
    events leading to enactment of the 1974 Budget Act, see James A. Pfiffner, *The
    President, the Budget, and Congress: Impoundment and the 1974 Budget Act* (Boulder,
    Colo.: Westview, 1979); and Shuman, *Politics and the Budget*, chapter 7.
54. See Joseph P. Harris, *Congressional Control of Administration* (Washington, D.C.:
    Brookings, 1964), pp. 115–16; Wildavsky, *The Politics of the Budgetary Process*,
    p. 291; and LeLoup, *Budgetary Politics*, p. 285.
55. Betts and Miller, "More About the Impact of the Congressional Budget and Im-
    poundment Control Act," p. 114.
56. See Richard F. Fenno, Jr., "The House Appropriations Committee as a Political
    System: The Problem of Integration," *American Political Science Review*, 56 (June
    1962), 310–24.
57. The following description is based on *Congressional Quarterly Weekly Report*, 32
    (June 15, 1974), 1590–93; *Congressional Record*, H5180–5293 (Daily Record, June
    18, 1974); *Congressional Record*, S11221–43 (Daily Record, June 21, 1974); *National
    Journal Reports*, 6 (May 18, 1974), 734–42; *National Journal Reports*, 7 (September
    28, 1974), 1445–53; Allen Schick, *Congress and Money: Budgeting, Spending, and
    Taxing* (Washington, D.C.: The Urban Institute, 1980); Richard E. Cohen, "For
    the Congressional Budget Process, 1981 Could Be the Make or Break Year," *Na-
    tional Journal*, 13 (January 10, 1981), 59–63; and Shuman, *Politics and the Budget*,
    chapter 8.
58. *Congressional Quarterly Weekly Report*, 34 (June 5, 1976), 1430.
59. Ibid., pp. 1430–32.
60. Smith, "The Congressional Budget Process: Why It Worked This Time," p. 96.
    See also Douglas H. Shumavon, "Policy Impact of the 1974 Congressional Bud-
    get Act," *Public Administration Review*, 41 (May/June 1981), 339–48.
61. Smith, "The Congressional Budget Process: Why It Worked This Time," pp.
    106–7.
62. Schick, *Congress and Money*, p. 130.
63. Ibid., pp. 565–66.
64. Ibid., p. 303.
65. These heightened tensions in Congress are a reflection, to some degree, of the
    changes in the overall context of budgetary decision making in recent years. See
    Schick, "Incremental Budgeting in a Decremental Age."

66. See Walter J. Oleszek, *Congressional Procedures and the Policy Process*, 2nd ed. (Washington, D.C.: Congressional Quarterly Press, 1984), pp. 67–68.

67. This discussion of change in the congressional budget process relies on Oleszek, *Congressional Procedures and the Policy Process*, pp. 64–66.

68. Ibid., p. 64.

69. Ibid.

70. Ibid.

71. Ibid.

72. Ibid., p. 66 (emphasis added).

73. Wildavsky, *The Politics of the Budgetary Process*, p. 255.

74. Oleszek, *Congressional Procedures and the Policy Process*, p. 67. See also "Rep. Jones: Beleaguered Budget Chairman," *Congressional Quarterly Weekly Report*, 40 (June 19, 1982), 1,447–49, at p. 1,448.

75. Oleszek, *Congressional Procedures and the Policy Process*, p. 68. An interesting manifestation of these jealousies is the impact of the budget process on the Appropriations Committees—and the reactions of members of those Committees. See, for example, Timothy B. Clark, "Appropriations Committees Losing Their Grip on Spending," *National Journal*, 10 (July 22, 1978), 1,169–74.

76. The following is taken from Schick, *Congress and Money*, pp. 397–401 and 573–79; and Oleszek, *Congressional Procedures and the Policy Process*, pp. 66–67.

77. Schick, *Congress and Money*, p. 575.

78. Oleszek, *Congressional Procedures and the Policy Process*, p. 67.

79. Ibid.

80. Schick, *Congress and Money*, p. 578.

81. See also Dennis S. Ippolito, *Congressional Spending* (Ithaca, N.Y.: Cornell University Press, 1981); Rudolph G. Penner, ed., *The Congressional Budget Process After Five Years* (Washington, D.C.: American Enterprise Institute for Public Policy Research, 1981); and Thomas Wander, F. Ted Hebert, and Gary Copeland, eds., *Congressional Budgeting: Politics, Process, and Power* (Baltimore: The Johns Hopkins University Press, 1984).

82. Wildavsky, *The Politics of the Budgetary Process*, pp. 234–35. See also Louis Fisher, *Presidential Spending Power* (Princeton, N.J.: Princeton University Press, 1975).

83. See *Spending Patterns of the Departments and Agencies of the Federal Government*, A Report to the Congress of the United States by the Comptroller General, General Accounting Office Report No. PAD-80-34 (Washington, D.C.: U.S. Government Printing Office, December 20, 1979).

84. See Jerry McCaffery, ed., "Symposium on Budgeting in an Era of Resource Scarcity," *Public Administration Review*, 38 (November/December 1978), 510–44; James M. Howell and Charles F. Stamm, *Urban Fiscal Stress: A Comparative Analysis of 66 U.S. Cities* (Lexington, Mass.: Lexington Books, 1979); L. Kenneth Hubbell, ed., *Fiscal Crisis in American Cities: The Federal Response* (Cambridge, Mass.: Ballinger, 1979); Roger L. Kemp, *Coping with Proposition 13* (Lexington, Mass.: Lexington Books, 1980); Allen Schick, "Budgetary Adaptations to Resource Scarcity," in Charles H. Levine and Irene Rubin, eds., *Fiscal Stress and Public Policy* (Beverly Hills, Calif.: Sage, 1980), pp. 113–34; Jeffrey I. Chapman, *Proposition 13 and Land Use: A Case Study of Fiscal Limits in California* (Lexington, Mass.: Lexington Books, 1981); Jerry McCaffery, ed., "Special Issue: The Impact of Resource Scarcity on Urban Public Finance," *Public Administration Review*, 41 (January 1981); James N. Danziger and Peter Smith Ring, "Fiscal Limi-

tations: A Selective Review of Recent Research,'' *Public Administration Review*, 42 (January/February 1982), 47–55; James H. Carr, ed., *Crisis and Constraint in Municipal Finance: Local Fiscal Prospects in a Period of Uncertainty* (New Brunswick, N.J.: Rutgers University, Center for Urban Policy Research, 1982); Robert W. Burchell and David Listokin, eds., *Cities Under Stress: The Fiscal Crises of Urban America* (New Brunswick, N.J.: Rutgers University, Center for Urban Policy Research, 1982); John J. Kirlin, *The Political Economy of Fiscal Limits* (Lexington, Mass.: Lexington Books, 1982); Jerome G. Rose, ed., *Tax and Expenditure Limitations: How to Implement and Live Within Them* (New Brunswick, N.J.: Rutgers University, Center for Urban Policy Research, 1982); and Selma J. Mushkin, ed., *Proposition 13 and Its Consequences for Public Management* (Lanham, Md.: University Press of America, 1984).

85. Former House Budget Committee Chairman James Jones (D.-Oklahoma) once observed: ''It's not the [congressional] budget process that's irritating people. It's that dividing scarcer resources is not as easy as dividing growing resources.'' See Oleszek, *Congressional Procedures and the Policy Process*, p. 68.

86. Schick, ''The Road from ZBB,'' p. 180.

87. The following is taken from Bruce Adams, ''Sunset: A Proposal for Accountable Government,'' *Administrative Law Review*, 28 (Summer 1976), 511–42, especially pp. 527–41. See also Charlie B. Tyer, ''Sunset and Governmental Reform,'' *Southern Review of Public Administration*, 3 (September 1979), 240–48.

88. LeLoup, *Budgetary Politics*, p. 276.

89. William Greider, ''The Education of David Stockman,'' *The Atlantic Monthly*, 248 (December 1981), 27–54, at pp. 30 and 36. Based on interviews with Stockman, this article clearly lays out key assumptions made by the Reagan administration, and by Stockman in particular, during the pivotal first year of the Reagan presidency.

90. Stockman's view of the true nature of ''supply-side'' economics is discussed in Greider, ''The Education of David Stockman,'' pp. 46–47. See also Shuman, *Politics and the Budget*, chapter 9.

91. Among other sources, see *Defense Spending and Its Relationship to the Federal Budget*, A Report to the Congress of the United States by the Comptroller General, General Accounting Office Report No. GAO/PLRD-83-80 (Washington, D.C.: U.S. Government Printing Office, June 9, 1983); and William W. Kaufmann, *The 1986 Defense Budget* (Washington, D.C.: Brookings, 1985).

92. Regarding proposed budget cuts in intergovernmental aid, see, among others, ''State and Local Officials Fear Federal Budget, Tax Changes,'' *Congressional Quarterly Weekly Report*, 43 (January 12, 1985), 71–74; ''Cities, States Say Cuts in Aid Will Create an Unfair Burden,'' *Congressional Quarterly Weekly Report*, 43 (February 16, 1985), 291–94; and chapter 5.

93. The figure of $81 billion is taken from a column by Geroge F. Will, which appeared in the Bloomington-Normal (Ill.) *Daily Pantagraph*, February 1, 1985, p. A–6. The overall budget figure of $960 billion for FY 1985 is that used in the president's fiscal 1986 budget document. See also the second source cited in footnote 92.

94. Schick, ''Incremental Budgeting in a Decremental Age,'' p. 24.

95. For fuller discussions of government budgets and their possible policy implications in an era of fiscal restraints, see, among others, Congressional Quarterly, *Budgeting for America: The Politics and Process of Federal Spending* (Washington,

D.C.: Congressional Quarterly, Inc., 1981); John L. Palmer and Isabel V. Sawhill, eds., *The Reagan Experiment: An Examination of Economic and Social Policies under the Reagan Administration* (Washington, D.C.: Urban Institute Press, 1982); Barry Bozeman and Jeffrey D. Straussman, "Shrinking Budgets and the Shrinkage of Budget Theory," and Naomi Caiden, "The Myth of the Annual Budget," *Public Administration Review*, 42 (November/December 1982), 509–15 and 516–23, respectively; Gregory B. Mills, "The Budget: A Failure of Discipline," in John L. Palmer and Isabel V. Sawhill, eds., *The Reagan Record: An Assessment of America's Changing Domestic Priorities* (Washington, D.C.: Urban Institute Press, 1984); Gregory B. Mills and John L. Palmer, eds., *Federal Budget Policy in the 1980s* (Washington, D.C.: Urban Institute Press, 1984); Naomi Caiden, "The New Rules of the Federal Budget Game," *Public Administration Review*, 44 (March/April 1984), 109–18; Bernard T. Pitsvada and Frank D. Draper, "Making Sense of the Federal Budget the Old Fashioned Way—Incrementally," *Public Administration Review*, 44 (September/October 1984), 401-7; Irene S. Rubin, *Shrinking the Federal Government: The Effect of Cutbacks on Five Federal Agencies* (White Plains, N.Y.: Longman, 1985); and Eric L. Davis, *The Changing Federal Budget* (Elmsford, N.Y.: Pergamon, forthcoming).

SUGGESTED READINGS

Golembiewski, Robert T., and Jack Rabin, eds. *Public Budgeting and Finance: Behavioral, Theoretical, and Technical Perspectives*, 3rd ed. New York: Marcel Dekker, 1983.

Lee, Robert D., Jr., and Ronald W. Johnson. *Public Budgeting Systems*, 3rd ed. Baltimore: University Park Press, 1983.

LeLoup, Lance T. *Budgetary Politics*, 2nd ed. Brunswick, Ohio: King's Court, 1980.

Levine, Charles H., ed. *Managing Fiscal Stress: The Crisis in the Public Sector*. Chatham, N.J.: Chatham House, 1980.

_____, and Irene Rubin, eds. *Fiscal Stress and Public Policy*. Beverly Hills, Calif.: Sage, 1980.

Lyden, Fremont J., and Marc Lindenberg. *Public Budgeting in Theory and Practice*. White Plains, N.Y.: Longman, 1983.

Lynch, Thomas D. *Public Budgeting in America*, 2nd ed. Englewood Cliffs, N.J.: Prentice-Hall, 1985.

Mikesell, John L. *Fiscal Administration: Analysis and Applications for the Public Sector*. Homewood, Ill.: Dorsey, 1982.

Mills, Gregory B., and John L. Palmer, eds. *Federal Budget Policy in the 1980s*. Washington, D.C.: Urban Institute Press, 1984.

Mosher, Frederick C. *A Tale of Two Agencies: A Comparative Analysis of the General Accounting Office and the Office of Management and Budget*. Baton Rouge: Louisiana State University Press, 1984.

Oleszek, Walter J. *Congressional Procedures and the Policy Process*, 2nd ed. Washington, D.C.: Congressional Quarterly Press, 1984, chapter 3.

Pechman, Joseph A. *Federal Tax Policy*, 4th ed. Washington, D.C.: Brookings, 1984.

Rabin, Jack, and Thomas D. Lynch, eds. *Handbook on Public Budgeting and Financial Management*. New York: Marcel Dekker, 1983.

Schick, Allen. *Congress and Money: Budgeting, Spending, and Taxing*. Washington, D.C.: The Urban Institute, 1980.

Wildavsky, Aaron. *Budgeting: A Comparative Theory of Budgetary Processes*. Boston: Little, Brown, 1975.

_____. *The Politics of the Budgetary Process*, 4th ed. Boston: Little, Brown, 1984.

13

Managing Public Policies and Programs: Decision Making in Action

To speak of "government policy" in areas such as agriculture, environmental quality, foreign affairs, health, transportation, or land-use planning somehow conveys an impression of well-defined purposes—carefully mapped out, the necessary resources marshaled and at the ready, with consistent support through the political process. But reality is usually very different from this conception. In a complex system such as ours, there is no *one* political majority capable of determining policy in every instance. Congressional voting coalitions are usually quite temporary, changing from one issue to the next; presidential election majorities are often fashioned out of very diverse groups in the population, each with its own policy interests, which can conflict with one another; court rulings may or may not coincide with public sentiment; administrative agencies are not permanently tied to any one political coalition. The combined impact of these institutions and of a very heterogeneous population on formulating, implementing, and evaluating public policy tends to blur rather than clarify policy objectives and content. Instead of being clear and unmistakable government commitments, many policies are "mixed bags" of programs that represent a variety of past actions and declarations, *ad hoc* responses to contemporary situations, and considerable uncertainty about future policy directions.

Yet strong expectations also exist that public programs will be well managed—that they represent the culmination of deliberate efforts to plan, design, fund, and operate sets of activities appropriately directed toward accomplishing agreed-upon objectives. There is the further expectation that managers and others will be in a position to evaluate the actual achievements of government programs. For in a real sense, programs are the

444

means through which broader policy goals are to be fulfilled, if at all. Thus, though it may be difficult to identify or rationalize all aspects of a given policy, managers must focus on discrete tasks involved in organizing and operating programs.

In these endeavors, the conceptual roles of bureaucracy in society, a particular bureau in the administrative process, and the individual within a bureau come together. Managing public programs, individually and as they affect the course of public policies, involves major concerns discussed in previous chapters—executive and managerial leadership, organization structure, motivation, decision making, personnel administration, and budgeting. All of these have a bearing on the ultimate success or failure of government problem solving. And with growing sophistication in our capacity to analyze public programs has come a greater potential for more intelligent, more "rational" conduct of government activities.

In this chapter we will examine the nature of public policies; the policy-making process, particularly as it involves administrative entities; program planning and analysis; implementation, including how and to what extent some policy directions are altered in the course of implementing individual programs; how programs are (or could be) evaluated, and what is done with those evaluations; the problem of productivity; and "cutback management." Our ultimate purpose is to understand how public policies evolve as they do, the role of administrative politics in this process, and the operational realities—including problems—of managing public programs.

THE NATURE OF PUBLIC POLICIES

What precisely is public policy? It can be defined as *the organizing framework of purposes and rationales for government programs that deal with specified societal problems.* Many people regard public policies as fairly deliberate responses to programs and needs systematically identified by some legitimate means. It is commonly assumed that governmental policies are addressed to solving—or at least coping with—major social and economic problems. However, there may be some disparity between what the average citizen believes about policy processes and outcomes, and the realities of policy making in America.

Let us consider some of the most common popular assumptions about government policy. First, many people believe that governments have clearly defined policies, well thought out in advance, on all or most major issues and problems. Second, many believe these policies are established through some kind of rational choice made by political leaders and others. Third, some think—logically enough—that everything we then do about a problem or issue follows those policies. Fourth, it is often assumed that the policies of government are clearly perceived and understood by citizens. And fifth, it is commonly assumed that government policies are widely agreed upon and supported—otherwise, how could they remain in force? As appealing or logical as these ideas might be, *every one of them is a myth*.

First, public policy is *not* clearly defined in the sense that major problems are anticipated and the machinery of government geared up to meet them before they get out of hand. That would require the kind of centralized leadership resisted by most of us. Some processes designed to foresee future developments and prepare for them, such as planning and PPB, have not accomplished all they were intended to, and "circumstances beyond our control" often prevail. Also, governments do not have policies on all issues, through either inaction or a decision *not* to have a policy. Thus policies tend to be less consistent and coherent than many might like.

Second, policies are more the product of responses to particular circumstances or problems than they are of deliberate establishment. They frequently result from decisions made at many levels, at different times, and by officials and others who see only some parts of the overall problem. Rational policy choice implies a decision-making capacity largely lacking in our noncentralized government institutions.

Third, many government activities do not follow official policy directions or support official goals. Political party platforms, pronouncements by top executives, even resolutions of Congress are often a better reflection of intent than of reality in policy making. What actually takes place may well differ from official definitions of what was supposed to take place.

Fourth, many policies are not clearly perceived or understood by the general population. We tend to pay attention to government activity likely to have a tangible impact on our lives, but otherwise it is unusual for large numbers of people to comprehend the intricacies of public policy. A good example is foreign policy. Different nationality groups are sensitive to even small changes in what this nation does or contemplates doing regarding "their" mother country, but most citizens have only a generalized awareness of our overall foreign policy. Many domestic policies are also understood only in broad outline. It is not accurate, in short, to assume that most Americans are knowledgeable in detail about individual policies.

Finally, it is not true that there is widespread, *active* support for existing public policies, although most have at least *passive* backing. Policy directions that offend basic values of large numbers of people are not likely to be sustained for very long without at least being challenged. Examples of sharp public reaction to unpopular policies include flagrant violations of Prohibition in the 1920s, opposition to the 1973 Supreme Court ruling on abortion permitting women to end their pregnancies in the first three months without government interference, and strong resistance to school busing designed to desegregate public school systems. In one sense, policies that exist without widespread challenge may be taken as a sort of barometer of public feeling about what is acceptable. Few policies survive that offend either powerful political interests or large numbers of ordinary citizens, or both. In sum, while support for what government does is not necessarily enthusiastic, public policies have to have a certain amount of *acceptability*.

A few other observations are in order. For one thing, it makes a difference which situations are defined as "problems" and thus deserving of attention in the policy process. Poverty, for example, was part of the American scene for years before it was identified as a problem of high priority by Presidents Kennedy and Johnson in the 1960s. Women's rights, consumer protection, and nuclear waste are other examples of current issue areas that required political definition as policy problems long before any action was taken. Also, policy initiative can come from many parts of the body politic—the president, Congress, interest groups, the mass media, state or local government, and so on. Perhaps the only policy maker prohibited from initiating policy changes on its own is the judiciary. While chief executives are usually in the best position to take the initiative, they have no monopoly on attempting to raise issues for public and governmental attention. Furthermore, most policy changes come about slowly, since it is far easier to resist change than to bring it about. American government tends to move in evolutionary fashion; incrementalism has been the order of the day, most of the time. Finally, many policy actions are more symbolic than real. Symbolism is not without value in politics, but it should be understood for what it is and not confused with substantive change.[1] Because most citizens lack comprehensive familiarity with policy, symbolic actions are often sufficient to satisfy calls for change without threatening the status quo. The passing of public attention from an issue often signals a slowdown in dealing with it, even where many in government would prefer to move more rapidly. Organized group support and opposition make a major difference in how substantive—or simply cosmetic—policy changes are.

Public policies, then, tend to be unsystematic, not widely understood or actively supported, and often inconsistently applied. Not all situations in society that might be defined as problem areas are in fact so defined. Sometimes an unspoken policy exists to take no action on a problem, and most changes in policy are rather slow and unfocused. The wonder is that any coherent policies exist.[2]

Types of Policies

Some variety exists in the kinds of policies pursued by government entities. These can be distinguished on the basis of their essential rationales, impacts on society, and the respective roles played by administrative agencies in each. Major types of policy include *distributive, regulatory, self-regulatory,* and *redistributive*.[3]

Distributive policies deliver large-scale services or benefits to certain individuals or groups in the population. One example is the loans and loan guarantees provided by the national government to the Chrysler Corporation in the early 1980s; others include agricultural price supports, airline subsidies, tax deductions for home mortgage payments, loans for college students, and government contracts. These involve policy subsystems (see chapter 3) on almost an *ad hoc* basis, with direct beneficiaries who do not pay direct costs. Bureaucracies are often—not always—involved in both the quest for enactment of such policies and their implementation.

Regulatory policies promote restrictions on the freedom to act of those subject to the regulations. Most prominent among such policies are those pertaining to business activities—for example, advertising practices, pollution control, natural gas pricing practices, and product safety. Other regulatory policies are also in effect, in areas such as civil rights and local government zoning ordinances. These are usually the product of conflict between competing forces—such as producers and consumers—each of which seeks to control the behavior of the other to some degree. Thus, regulatory policies involve greater tension among relevant actors; they also usually incorporate a larger direct role for bureaucracies. The regulative function of government has increased substantially in recent years, involving both independent regulatory commissions and many other entities (see chapter 14).

Self-regulatory policies represent a variation on regulation, in that such policies ''are usually sought and supported by the regulated group as a means of protecting or promoting their own interests.''[4] The leading example is licensing of professions and occupations, such as law, medicine, real estate, and driving a taxi. Normally (especially in the case of professions), a legislative body enacts a licensing law, providing for enforcement by a board dominated by the licensed group. Other bureaucracies, and most other interests, typically take little interest in this kind of policy.

Redistributive policies ''involve deliberate efforts by the government to shift the allocation of wealth, income, property, or rights among broad classes or groups'' within the population.[5] They often are the source of intense controversy in the political arena, and (significantly) that controversy usually affects policy execution as well as its initial adoption. Thus, redistributive policies such as the graduated income tax, medical care for the aged under Social Security, and the war on poverty were all subject to intense debate and conflict during legislative deliberations, and all attracted continuing attention from supporters and opponents as they were put into effect. This type of policy is most sensitive, politically, and thus most susceptible to political pressures in the course of implementation. Policies such as the income tax have lost much of their redistributive character due to changes (exemptions, tax shelters, and similar loopholes) made in the basic law—some of which were proposed by the agency responsible for its administration! In other instances, agencies with jurisdiction over redistributive policies have taken the lead in maintaining their essential character. One example is the Justice Department, in its enforcement of the 1965 Voting Rights Act, leading to a real redistribution of political power from whites to blacks in several southern states.

Bureaucratic agencies play somewhat different roles in each type of policy, as already implied; their roles also may vary within a given policy category, as is the case in redistributive policy. Subsystems play a considerable role in formation and implementation of distributive policies, though in a highly individualized manner. Depending on the kind of regulatory policy at issue, bureaus and their allies may be more or less involved; this hinges primarily on the extent to which formal regulatory responsibilities are assigned to a given agency. Self-regulation only sporadically engages the attention of agencies outside a specific profession or occupation (though some subsystem politics is involved). Redistributive policies, because of the level of controversy they generate, almost inevitably draw bureaucracies into the policy process directly—though many would prefer to remain on the sidelines. In sum, the part played by administrative entities in a given policy area or process can depend to a considerable extent on the type of policy as well as its specific issue content.

THE POLICY-MAKING PROCESS

The policy-making process involves all the demands, pressures, conflicts, negotiations and compromises, and formal and informal decisions that result in given policies being adopted and pursued through actions of government. This is a broad definition, and deliberately so, for making policy is not the exclusive province of any one branch or level of government in the federal system. Political scientist Charles O. Jones has emphasized the complexity of making public policy, focusing not only on interactions of national, state, and local governments, but also on involvement of private interests pressing government to respond to their specialized concerns.[6]

Other authors as well have noted the intricate and complex nature of policy making.[7] It is characterized by a lack of centralized direction at every level of government; it is very loosely coordinated, highly competitive, fragmented and specialized (like budgeting), and largely incremental. Thus, the policy process is not a smoothly functioning, ongoing sequence where one phase predictably follows another. It responds, rather, to pressures placed upon it at many points along the way, so that policy usually reflects the influence of diverse political forces.

Where administrative agencies have a central role in the policy process, policy making is best described as occurring in four stages.[8] The first is a legislative stage involving both Congress and the president (and often agency administrators), in which basic legislation is drawn up, considered, and approved as law. The second and third stages, primarily administrative in nature, involve writing by the agency of detailed regulations and rules governing application of the law, followed by actual implementation. The fourth is a review stage, by the courts or Congress or perhaps both, during which modifications of existing policy are possible for legal, substantive, or political reasons. As one observer has noted, "Problems and demands are constantly being defined and redefined in the policy process."[9] This suggests these stages are part of policy *cycles*, with incremental adjustments in existing policies a routine phenomenon.

The legislative stage normally centers on actions of the president and of key legislators on Capitol Hill (and on their counterparts in state and local governments). But the role of higher-level administrators (both political appointees and senior career officials) in formulating and proposing new policy options can be very important. For example, agency personnel— usually in responsible positions—might perceive a need to modify legislative authorizations, in order to smooth out implementation difficulties. They may wish to initiate a new activity to fulfill their own policy objectives. Or they may propose curtailing part of a program in order to concentrate attention, energies, and resources on matters of higher priority to them. In all such cases, their proposals must wend their way through the usual legislative process, and administrators must call upon legislative (and executive) allies to ensure a proper hearing for their ideas. The main point, however, is that administrators are regular participants at this stage of the policy cycle, not merely passive observers.

Administrative involvement in subsequent stages of the policy process can take a variety of forms.[10] These include rule making, adjudication, law enforcement, and program operations. *Rule making*, a quasi-legislative power delegated to agencies by Congress, represents authority to enact "an agency statement of general applicability and future effect that concerns the rights of private parties and has the force and effect of law."[11] Rules may serve different functions—elaborating on general statutory provisions, defining terms (such as "small business," "discriminate," or "safe speed"), indicating probable agency behavior in particular matters. Agencies well known for their rule-making decisions include the Federal Trade Commission (FTC), the Occupational Safety and Health Administration (OSHA), and the Department of Transportation; many others also enact hundreds of rules. Independent regulatory commissions, discussed in chapter 14, have made greater use of rule making in the past quarter-century.

Adjudication, unlike rule making, is a quasi-judicial function, involving application of "existing laws or rules to particular situations by case-to-case decision making."[12] The scope of such actions is much narrower than in rule making, but collectively they can have great impact on policy as a whole. Agencies that engage in adjudication include the National Labor Relations Board (NLRB), which often uses the process in settling unfair labor practices cases; the Social Security Administration, in determining eligibility for benefits; and the Internal Revenue Service (IRS). Adjudication is both an adaptation of, and a substitute for, possible formal proceedings in a court of law—particularly in the case of the NLRB and the IRS.

Law enforcement refers to securing compliance with existing statutes and rules (not necessarily referring to police functions), and more specifically to the enthusiasm an agency brings to the task of implementing legislative authorizations. By exercising administrative discretion, it is possible for an agency to influence the policy process by countless kinds of action— or inaction. Another factor is the techniques of enforcement available to an agency. For example, a Justice Department task force on voting rights of black Southerners might have wanted to file suit on behalf of blacks denied an opportunity to register in the early 1960s, but the 1957 and 1960 Civil Rights Acts did not confer that power on the Department. A plaintiff had to shoulder the legal burden—particularly the costs— if a case was to reach the courts. Not until the 1964 Civil Rights Act did the Justice Department acquire the ability to act on behalf of aggrieved citizens claiming improper denial of voting rights (Justice Department attorneys themselves sought that authority, at the legislative stage!). Even at that, another year passed before the Voting Rights Act broadened national authority to register voters directly where fewer than half of those eligible were registered.

Program operations—including loan, grant, insurance, service, or construction activities—constitute a large part of agencies' impacts on the policy process. Again, discretion is a key; out of literally thousands of small-scale decisions come large-scale policies. We will look in more detail at program implementation, and the politics involved, later in this chapter.

One further aspect of policy making worth mentioning is the extensive impact of intergovernmental relations and of intergovernmental policy development. As we discussed in chapter 5, many facets of both program funding and administration are tied closely either to intergovernmental collaboration or competition, or to parallel activities of some kind, as in the case of environmental policy. This serves to complicate both policy making and any effort to trace the roots of a particular policy direction. Legislative and administrative mechanisms at each level of government are fairly complex, affording numerous opportunities for interested parties to have some say in the policy-making process. Slight alterations in policy are possible each time influence is exerted, and their cumulative effects at the same level of government can be significant. It is not difficult to imagine what multiplying these patterns by three levels of government can do to the shape of policy. Intergovernmental dimensions, then, are an important contributing factor to the overall policy process.

In sum, the policy-making process helps account for the disjointed nature of most public policies. An absence of centralized direction and the opportunity for influence to be exerted at multiple points characterize many phases of policy making, producing policies that look—accurately—as though they were arrived at from many directions at once. It is not difficult for a chief executive, for example, to *define* a formal policy intention, but it is another matter altogether to put it into effect. On one occasion John F. Kennedy signed a bill into law, then turned to his aides and remarked: "We have made the law. Now it remains to be seen whether we can get our government to do it."[13]

From the earlier discussion regarding myths about public policy, it is clear "policy" refers both to *intentions* and to actual *results* of governmental activity. One must be careful, therefore, about the sense in which the term is used. Results, however, are normally sought and evaluated in the context of specific government programs rather than broad policies. Programs, in turn, can be further divided into projects dependent for their completion on individual performance on the job. The interrelationships among what might be called the "four *Ps*"—policy, program, project, and performance—are crucial to ultimate outcomes of government operations (see Figure 13-1).[14] From a managerial standpoint, no one of them stands in isolation from the other three; each is affected by the others.

The linkage uniting policies, programs, projects, and individual performance is an important one. Policies are put into effect only to the degree that program objectives related to them are met; programs in turn are the sum totals of supporting projects; and each project represents the labors of individuals within the responsible agencies. Discussion of public policy in a management sense must focus, then, on *programs* and *projects*, the essential building blocks of what government does. While there are some differences between the two in terms of organizing and directing them, we will emphasize a number of management concerns common to both. They are (1) planning, (2) analysis, (3) implementation, (4) evaluation, (5) productivity, and (6) "cutback" management. These are linked conceptually; to the extent that they are linked *in practice* (especially the first five), they greatly enhance program management and effectiveness.

Figure 13–1   The Four Ps in the Policy-Making Process

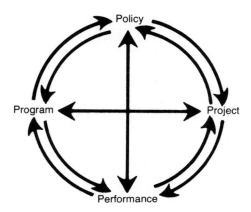

THE PLANNING PROCESS

Though broad governmental and political goals are often unclearly defined, as discussed in chapter 8, the same need not be true of individual program or project goals. Ideally, goals at this level should be clearly *operationalized*—that is, formulated in specific and tangible terms related to the more general mission or purpose of the agency. *Planning* is an essential element of the goal definition process (even though that process is carried on imperfectly, much of the time).

Planning is the "defining and choice of operational goals of the organization and the choice of methods and means to be used to achieve those goals over a specified time period."[15] All organizations function according to some type of basic plans, but program administrators must both promote planning by others in their organizations and "weav[e] various plans together into a common purpose pattern. In essence, . . . administrative planning is purposeful action to develop purposefulness."[16] The keys to planning are to be found in accurate forecasts of future need,[17] goal definition, means-ends linkages (note the heavily rationalistic flavor of these "keys"), and the kind of coordination and direction supplied by the organization's administrator.

Complicating the planning process is the fact that goals exist at different conceptual levels. Consequently, linkages among different types of goals should be forged (again, ideally). Also, the *interrelationships* among goals, plans, programs, and projects are important. For example:

> . . . one *official goal* of the United States government is the attainment of the people's welfare. . . . [An] *operational goal* is the achievement of a certain minimum income level for every American family. One *plan* for achieving this operational goal is unemployment assistance. A *program* is distributing welfare checks. A *project* is the setting up and managing of the various welfare bureaucracies in the United States.[18]

Administrators at all levels of bureaucracy must operate within this complex web of objectives and arrangements, and in particular must successfully organize activities addressed to meeting goals of the administrative unit (for example, processing welfare checks, monitoring eligibility rolls, and serving related clientele needs).

Figure 13-2 is a basic planning guide usable by public managers in determining a course of action, beginning with preliminary consideration of goals. (It will be useful to refer to Figure 13-2 throughout this discussion.) Essential steps are identifying desired outcomes, predicting what will actually take place, and assessing *probabilities* of achieving desired outcomes. Depending on the results of such deliberations, goals can be selected, and perhaps modified, by those involved. The point is, however, that in one form or another this must be done early in the life cycle of a project or program, and done periodically throughout its existence, to make any sense out of varied support activities. For example, it would be considered careless policy making to spend public funds for "improving education" without a clear idea of specific project goals—remedial reading instruction, additional equipment and materials, more counseling services, or better testing methods and devices. These are demonstrably related to the broader program goal of "improving education," which in turn may be part of an urban policy designed to "improve the quality of urban life."

The fact that these imperatives exist in an organization does not guarantee that planning will be undertaken, or that it will serve its purpose if it *is* undertaken. Other factors also may be present which can interfere with agency planning processes. These include (among others) "a threatening political environment, an unrecognized or unacknowledged intraorganizational conflict, a lack of trust or communication [among] planning participants, and conflicting perceptions of the goals, values, and norms of the organization."[19] An important task for public managers is to ensure that these potential obstacles to effective planning are recognized and dealt with in a timely way.

A useful case illustration of the links among planning, goals, and program operation concerns the Metropolitan Tulsa Transit Authority (MTTA).[20] Created in 1968 to take over operations of public transit in the Tulsa area from a private company, the Authority needed to move quickly to reverse declining ridership; perhaps more important, they faced decisions involving long-range commitments for the community. These included purchase of new buses, a maintenance system for the fleet, and developing competent operational staff. After first settling a strike among drivers and other employees, thus getting the buses back on the streets, the trustees of the MTTA turned their attention to planning for the near—and more distant—future of public transit. The Tulsa Metropolitan Area Planning Commission conducted the studies.

Several different kinds of issues confronted the planning effort—a typical situation. Basic concerns revolved around: (1) specific, short-term actions (1970–1974), their costs, and possible national government assistance; (2) the broader objectives in metropolitan Tulsa that might be served by higher levels of transit service, 1974–1990; (3) the portion of the area's transportation needs—year by year—to be met by public transit; and (4) necessary restructuring of the public transit system (including costs and outside assistance) in order to meet those needs. Policy guidelines developed by the planning commission, to guide public transit system planning, raised questions about the type of environment and communities that were desired in the Tulsa area; how the transportation system influenced, and would be influenced by, the environment and community; the "balance" between public and private transportation; and other public services. Other general concerns included demographic and land-use characteristics of the

Figure 13-2   Planning Guide for Public Managers

I. *What precisely do I want to accomplish?*
    A. First attempt to predict what will occur.
    B. Plan and implement only if
        1. Disaster appears likely (possible);
        2. Substantial improvement is likely.
    C. Identify precisely the outcome I seek.
    D. Why do I seek it?
        1. Good in itself given my values. (If so, do I wish to reconsider my values?)
        2. I believe it will lead to a further outcome which I value. (If so, can I state the causal chain so I can retest?)
        3. I believe it will lead to behavior by other governments. (If so, consider that the other government is not a unitary actor and that its bureaucracy will do only what is in their interest, in their own terms. Influence is most likely to take the form of altering incentives and power. Consider also how reliable my information is about the other government.)
    E. How likely am I to get the outcome as I desire it?
        1. Withhold judgment until working out paths to action and strategy.
        2. Consider relevant programs and standard operating procedures.
        3. Consider internal and external biases.
    F. How important is this outcome to me as compared to others?

II. *Alternative paths to action*
    A. Map out alternative routes to the desired outcome.
    B. Recognize that a change in policy may be neither necessary nor sufficient.
    C. Seek to change policy only if
        1. Necessary to remove an absolute barrier to changing action;
        2. Useful as a hunting license;
        3. Necessary given my access to those who must perform the action;
        4. Likely to lead easily to a change in action.
    D. Consider how high I need to go. (Do not involve the President unless necessary or he is likely to be sympathetic, i.e., unless he has a problem this may solve.)
    E. If seeking a change in policy, plot the action path from there to changes in actions.
    F. Consider for each path who will have the action. (Is there any path in which I will have the action?)
    G. Specify the formal actions which are necessary.
    H. What resources do I have to move action along each path with success? (Re-judge after considering tactics.) Relative advantages of each path.
    I. How will resources expended to get to one way-station outcome affect ability to get to further stations?
    J. What additional information will help? Can I get it? At what cost?

III. *Framing tactics—maneuvers and arguments—to move along a path*
    A. Identification of the participants and their interests, including those beyond the executive branch.

1. Who will inevitably be involved according to the rules of the game?
2. Who might seek to play but could be excluded?
3. Who might not seek to play but could be brought in?
4. What are the likely interests of the various participants, what face of the issue will they see, how will they define the stakes? Consider organization, personal, political, and national interests.
5. Who are natural allies, unappeasable opponents, neutrals who might be converted to support, or opponents who might be converted to neutrality?

B. How can I lead a participant to see that the outcomes I desire are in his interest as he sees it?
C. How can I change the situation to have an outcome conflicting less (or not at all) with participants' interests as they see them?
D. Do I have the resources for this purpose? If not, can I get others to use theirs?
E. What specific maneuvers should I use at what stages?
F. What arguments should I use:
1. In general?
2. On a discriminatory basis?
G. If I must get a large organization to change its behavior, I must consider the interests, standard operating procedures, and programs of that organization.
H. Should I try to bring in players outside the executive branch? If so, how?
I. How can I tell how well I am doing?

IV. *Gauging costs and benefits*
A. Reconsider all phases from time to time. Specifically:
1. How high up should one seek a decision?
2. How should the decision sought relate to the change desired, i.e., should it be a decision to change policy, to change patterns of action, or to take a single particular new step (or to stop an on-going action)?
3. By what means will the initial decision which is sought be converted into the desired action?
B. Plan of action.
1. How to move the action to the way-station and final outcome desired.
2. What maneuvers and arguments to use on or with the other participants.
3. A time sequence.
C. To what extent is this process consciously duplicated by participants seeking a change? Are some participants more likely to plan than others? To plan effectively?
D. How is the choice of way-station outcomes and route action made?

Source: Graham T. Allison and Morton H. Halperin, "Bureaucratic Politics: A Paradigm and Some Policy Implications," In *Theory and Policy in International Relations*, ed. by Raymond Tanter and Richard H. Ullman (Princeton: Princeton University Press, 1972), pp. 77–79.

area, ridership characteristics (based on a one-day survey in 1970), labor force considerations, bus routes, and maintenance practices.

From the planning effort, there emerged a series of "service standards" for the revamped public transit system. Among those adopted were routing standards (emphasizing proximity to riders and direct connections between major origins and destinations); frequency of service (thirty-minute intervals during peak periods, sixty-minute intervals at other times); dependability; special services; fare structure; availability of information (regarding schedules and routes) to riders; responsiveness to passenger communications; operating costs per bus mile; and environmental contamination (air pollution, sound, sight, and vibration).[21]

The planning effort in this case was directed toward comprehensively exploring both transportation needs and the role of public transit in the larger scheme of things in metropolitan Tulsa. The MTTA trustees, responsible as they were to the city commissioners, had to integrate a variety of transportation—and transportation-*related*—goals, both their own and those of others (riders, other city officials, and system employees, for example). The complexity of their task is apparent; but more to the point, such complexity is not at all unusual as program managers attempt to determine appropriate goals and directions for their enterprises.

However, as indicated in this case (and as noted in chapter 8), goals are not simply "there" to start with. They must be arrived at in deliberate fashion, and can reflect varying combinations of substantive and political judgments about the need to pursue them. More important in an operating sense, program and project managers ordinarily are not official goal setters (as noted in chapter 1). They may not even dominate the process, though they do usually contribute to shaping formally adopted goals. Thus, goal definition for the middle-level manager is a shared process, one in which the most influential voices are often those outside the agency. A school superintendent must heed the wishes of the school board; the trustees of the MTTA had to be sensitive to city commissioners' preferences. Yet an effort to delineate goals must be made *inside* the agency as well.[22]

ANALYSIS AND CHOICE: DECIDING WHAT ACTIONS TO TAKE

As suggested by both the MTTA experience and Figure 13-2, planning leads directly to processes of *analysis*—of examining alternative options (however systematically) and attempting to identify and compare the potential outcomes. To the extent that planning produces or represents consensus among key individuals regarding appropriate program directions, formal plans can serve as a guiding standard for subsequent analysis and choice.

If, however, significant dissent to adopted plans persists (which often happens), that dissension can complicate analysis by extending political conflict into analytic processes themselves.

Agency performance frequently depends on the quality of prior analysis regarding projected impacts of activities on the problem at hand. Politically, the old adage "good government (that is, performance) is good politics" has never been more true. For agencies with strong political backing, a solid foundation of objective program analysis adds strength to strength. For weak agencies, careful and thorough analysis of their options before selecting the most appropriate one(s) might make the difference between organizational vitality and decay. Gordon Chase, former administrator of the New York City Health Services Administration, has commented on the political importance of analysis:

> In my view, politics happens very often when there is a vacuum, when there is no real analysis. Then the resource allocation decision is usually based on who has more clout or who screams louder. . . . [I]f you don't have the analytic talent and if important decisions are up, they'll be made, but they'll be made by another process than analysis.[23]

The purpose of analysis is to facilitate the reaching of sound decisions by establishing relevant facts about a situation before attempting to change it in some way, and by determining if possible the respective consequences of different courses of action. The nature of a given problem is not always clear—for example, in education, poverty, military preparedness, or energy—and analysis can help sharpen the focus of decision makers as they consider various objectives and options. Analysis is also crucial to improving public management, as a key aid to appropriate targeting of programs. Several kinds of analysis might be used; we will review each one briefly.

Policy analysis can be defined as "the systematic investigation of alternative policy options and the assembly and integration of the evidence for and against each option."[24] While activities suggested by such a definition have long been a part of the government process, only in the past four decades has a distinct analysis function become *formally* associated with public decision making. A key emphasis is on explaining the nature of problems, and how policies addressed to those problems are put into effect. Some observers believe, however, that an equally legitimate function is to improve, in some sense, processes of policy making as well as policy content.

In its broadest sense, policy analysis makes it possible to investigate policy outcomes in interrelated fields, to examine in depth the causes of societal and other problems, and to establish cause-and-effect relationships among problems, the contexts in which they occur, and potential solutions. Most program or project managers would concentrate on analyzing those considerations most relevant to their immediate responsibilities.

Since problems vary widely in their scope and complexity, policy anal-

---

Steps in the "Standard-Form" Policy Analysis

1. Define the problem.
2. Establish the criteria for a solution.
3. Construct the alternatives.
4. Hustle the data.
5. Project the consequences of each alternative.
6. Evaluate the trade-offs.
7. Make your choice.
8. Apply the "Brooklyn cab driver test"—that is, when you have written up your preferred alternative, ask yourself whether a cab driver in Brooklyn would find your logic and solution convincing.

Source: Frank Levy, "Teaching the Standard-Form Policy Analysis," *Public Policy and Management Newsletter,* 3 (March 1981), pp. 1 and 6 (published by the Public Policy and Management Program for Case/Course Development; Cambridge, Massachusetts).

---

ysis needs to be flexible enough to permit selection of analytical approaches and techniques appropriate to the particular problem under study.[25] One proposal (among many others) for dealing with this dimension of policy analysis suggests four types of analysis suitable to four different sets of circumstances.[26] They are (1) *issue analysis,* where there is a relatively specific policy choice (for example, whether a particular group of businesses or industries should receive a tax reduction) and a highly politicized environment of decision making; (2) *program analysis,* involving both design and evaluation of a particular program (for example, a manpower-training program); (3) *multiprogram analysis,* in which decisions must be made concerning resource allocation among programs dealing with the same problem (for instance, different manpower-training programs); and (4) *strategic analysis,* where the policy problem is very large (for example, an economic development strategy for a depressed region).

At the programmatic level the process of analysis, and the analyses resulting from it, should meet most of the following criteria.[27] First, they should clearly define issues and problems being addressed, including identifying clientele groups and their future size, specifying appropriate evaluation criteria, and providing estimates of future need. Second, they should present alternatives in a form specific enough to be evaluated. Third, in considering each alternative, accurate cost estimates should be provided. These should include direct and indirect costs (employee fringe benefits as well as salaries), costs incurred by other agencies (higher jail and court costs stemming from an increased police force), documentation that demonstrates solid grounding for cost data rather than arbitrariness, and future as well as current costs. Fourth, program analyses should carefully estimate program effectiveness—by ensuring that evaluation criteria are themselves comprehensive, by using multiple measures of effectiveness, and by ensuring that data adequate to measure both present and future circumstances can be employed in assessing program results. Fifth, analyses should openly acknowledge any uncertainty in basic assumptions and program data—that is, the probability of inaccuracies and the likely consequences of error. Sixth, the time period of the program (or project) should be identified, with a clear statement of whether enough time is allowed to provide a fair comparison among alternatives. Finally, an analysis should contain recommendations based on substantive data rather than on unsubstantiated information, should discuss any anticipated difficulties in implementation, and should document all relevant assumptions.[28]

Policy analysis faces some obstacles, however. For one thing, it is not clear what kind of analysis can be done and what uses can (or should) be made of the results, where negotiation and bargaining among competing political forces are the most common means of carving out policy. Another difficulty is limitations on the applicability of various analytical techniques used, depending on the kind of problem at hand.[29] That there are any limitations at all is unfortunate, since the aim of analysis is essentially to facilitate the targeting, design, and operation of programs in the most effective and efficient ways possible. But even the most rigorous, sophisticated techniques are not always appropriate. For example, decision tools rooted in mathematics and economics are best suited to cases where problem definition is straightforward, where there is ''a convenient method of quantifying the problem (usually in terms of probability or monetary units), and where there is some function or set of functions (such as time, profit, payoff, or expected value) to be maximized or minimized.''[30] In contrast, if a problem involves questions and issues not measurable in economic or quantitative terms, these decision tools are less appropriate.

Since such tools are widely used in dealing with quantifiable problems, treatment of some of them is in order. Perhaps the broadest approach, embracing some others, is *systems analysis*. This approach is usable (in principle) for comprehensively diagnosing how *all* elements of a political, social, economic, or administrative system might affect—and be affected by—a given project or program. Managers utilizing systems analysis need to be aware of overall systemic objectives and performance (assuming these can be identified and measured), the surrounding social environment, available resources, system components (such as individual programs within a governmental system), and how the system is managed.[31] The overriding objective of systems analysis is to produce greater rationality in management decision making, and efficiency and effectiveness in actual program operations. In terms of the discussion of decision making in chapter 8, systems analysis is devoted to the *rational* approach. The comments made there about seeking comprehensiveness, coping with information needs, and maximizing return on a given investment of resources also apply here. (So, also, do the sharp *critiques* of rational decision making made by Charles

THE USES OF POLICY ANALYSIS

New York City conducts and regulates housing programs on a scale exceeded only by the national government. In the late 1960s, the city's public housing agency had half a million tenants; another 85,000 rental units had been built and were regulated under state- or city-financed middle-income housing programs. About 70 percent of all the city's rental units and nearly half of all housing units had been under rent control since 1943, a program administered by the city since 1962.

An analysis of the city's housing problems helped change policy makers' perceptions in a number of fundamental ways. It set the scene by providing *for the first time* a comprehensive presentation of all housing programs—national, state, and local—affecting the city's housing stock, pointing out not only the enormousness of total resources devoted to the city's housing "problem," but also the diversity of application of those resources and the unexpectedly powerful leverage the city's own resources could have on those from state and national sources.

The analysis proceeded to redefine the "problem." Up to that point, the city's housing problems had ordinarily been formulated in terms of how to build enough new housing from the ground up to meet the demand for housing services. After preliminary studies, however, the analysts realized that New York City was annually losing more housing units through deterioration and abandonment (38,000 units a year between 1965 and 1967) than it could possibly build. The impact of this situation on citizens and on the city treasury was significant in terms of emergency services, housing relocation costs, and tax losses, as well as in secondary effects in such areas as fire, sanitation, and crime. Working with the staff of the city's Housing and Development Administration, analysts were able to cause a major shift in priorities, from concentration on new construction as the assumed solution to the housing crisis to the problem of preservation of the existing housing stock.

The most controversial and important recommendation was reform of a sacred cow, the city's antiquated system of rent controls, which essentially reflected 1943 costs. Continuing imposition of these controls meant that rental revenues were insufficient to support adequate maintenance over the long term, leading to widespread deterioration and abandonment. Further, the controls were not designed to benefit low-income tenants, but rather made their effects felt in an arbitrary way across the income spectrum.

It was recommended that rent controls be restructured, with rent ceilings being gradually raised to levels that would permit adequate maintenance while yielding a fair return on the owner's investment. A formula for these increases was also devised, reflecting the specific characteristics of each building and apartment. In addition, rent assistance for residents unable to afford the full cost of adequate housing was proposed, again with attention to programmatic detail. Finally, an organized effort to locate and salvage properties in serious difficulty because of poor management or inadequate revenue was suggested as an alternative to punitive regulation or to tax foreclosure and city ownership by default.

Source: Adapted from Gustave H. Shubert, "Policy Analysis and Public Choice," in Robert A. Goldwin, ed., *Bureaucrats, Policy Analysts, Statesmen: Who Leads?* (Washington, D.C.: American Enterprise Institute, 1980), pp. 46–47 (footnotes omitted).

Lindblom and others. These critics entertain serious doubts about the value and efficacy of the "systems" approach to policy decision, in both theory *and* practice.[32] Their reservations should be kept in mind, even as we proceed through this discussion of the various techniques that have emerged in public policy making.)

Perhaps the greatest advantage of systems analysis is its potential for bringing some order in decision making out of the seeming disorder, confusion, and discord prevalent in the policy process at large.[33] (It was noted in chapter 12 that PPB may have had just that sort of residual effect.) A companion strength is its permitting a broader view of constraints and consequences relating to an individual program. A weakness, besides those associated with rational decision making, is the possibility that trying to achieve rationality within a single system will cause decision makers to ignore other systems that might also be relevant. An example would be an effort to analyze political factors influencing grants-in-aid to states and localities without also analyzing the nation's economy, which ultimately provides the tax base for raising revenues. A greater weakness, from a practical standpoint, is that systems analysis can generate such a staggering workload that decision makers have little chance of coping with it while still reaching a decision.

Cost-benefit analysis is a means of measuring relative gains and losses resulting from alternative policy or program options. Usually implying quantitative measures and assuming objectivity, it can assist decision makers and program managers in determining the most beneficial path of action to follow. A cost-benefit analysis seeks to identify the actions with the most desirable ratio of benefit to cost. Given adequate information, cost-benefit analysis can be useful in narrowing a range of choices to those most likely to yield desired gains for an affordable cost. An example of cost-benefit analysis might involve a decision on whether a dam should be built in an uninhabited area.[34] Both benefits (new jobs, new business, reduced flooding) and costs (construction expenses, environmental damage, foreclosed options for other uses of the land) could be calculated, as well as the ratio between them. The same technique could be used to measure alternative benefits from other uses of the same funds, and the related effects of constructing the dam (for example, on residential and tourist patterns in adjoining areas). Such an analysis might be useful both in advance of the project and as an evaluative instrument after the fact.

Operations research (OR) actually represents a collection of specific techniques. OR's greatest value is in solving problems of efficiency—such as scheduling bus stops, or processing military recruits—rather than in helping select particular alternatives. Put another way, OR "comes into play only *after* value choices have been made."[35] Where administrative problems repeat themselves, OR can be valuable.

In sum, analysis is a key managerial activity. As noted earlier, knowledge is power in administrative politics, and analysis greatly enhances a manager's ability to obtain, organize, and apply relevant information in the course of choosing desirable program options.[36]

PROGRAM IMPLEMENTATION

In speaking of implementation, we shall adopt Charles O. Jones's definition of the term, as well as his elaboration of it:

> Let us say simply that implementation is that *set of activities directed toward putting a program into effect*. Three activities, in particular, are significant: (1) *organization*—the establishment or rearrangement of resources, units, and methods for putting a program into effect; (2) *interpretation*—the translation of program language (often contained in a statute) into acceptable and feasible plans and directives; and (3) *application*—the routine provision of services, payments, or other agreed-upon program objectives or instruments.[37]

By taking legislative language and transforming it into clear administrative guidelines, by developing necessary arrangements and routines, and by actually furnishing mandated services, programs are carried out and, ultimately, policies implemented.

All that sounds rather routine. Many citizens apparently *expect* program implementation to be relatively easy under normal conditions. We therefore seek to explain programmatic failures in terms of conflict, extraordinary events, or unexpected circumstances that develop in the course of implementation. However, failure to implement programs in accord with our expectations can often be explained by looking at less dramatic factors. For example, major difficulties were encountered in putting into effect a much-heralded program of the U.S. Economic Development Administration (EDA) in Oakland, California, designed to provide permanent jobs to minorities through economic development:

> The evils that afflicted the EDA program in Oakland were of a prosaic and everyday character. Agreements had to be *maintained* after they were reached. Numerous approvals and clearances had to be obtained from a variety of participants. . . . [T]hese *perfectly ordinary circumstances present serious obstacles to implementation*. . . . If one is always looking for unusual circumstances and dramatic events, he cannot appreciate *how difficult it is to make the ordinary happen*.[38]

Thus, few things can be taken for granted in implementation, least of all that participants in a program will automatically "fall in line" in trying to make it work. Not that they harbor suspect or devious motives; it is simply a case of cooperation having to be *induced* on a routine basis rather than being *assumed*. Virtually everyone participating in program management has other responsibilities, causing some diverting of attention among even the most conscientious individuals. In sum, a concerted effort is required to manage minimal aspects of program implementation. It is no wonder, then, that so many programs (and policies) are said to be only partially implemented—contrary to legislative mandates, executive orders, and public expectations. The essential point, however, is this: failures in implementation are traceable far more often to these rather unexciting obstacles than to anything more dramatic.

Dynamics of Implementation

On occasion it is necessary to create a separate organizational unit to implement a new program or to pursue a different policy direction. This can happen in several ways. One is creation of a totally new agency, such as the national Environmental Protection Agency. Another is consolidating, upgrading, or dividing existing agencies, as in the case of splitting the Atomic Energy Commission into the Energy Research and Development Administration and the Nuclear Regulatory Commission. More often, programs are assigned to existing agencies, which must still interpret and apply the laws, and develop appropriate implementation methods.[39]

In most legislation, Congress's intentions regarding program implementation are stated very broadly, such as carrying out a program in a "reasonable" manner, or "in the public interest, convenience, and necessity."[40] Thus, the responsible agency has discretion in developing operating guidelines and substantive details. This can result in a key agency role in shaping legislated programs, and possibly *modifying* congressional intent. Political pressure on agencies responsible for implementing congressional directives is both real and constant. If it is true, as Jones suggests, that "programs often reflect an attainable consensus rather than a substantive conviction,"[41] it follows that if the *political* consensus changes in the course of implementing a law, chances are good that its implementation will also be modified to accommodate the change.

Since legislative language is so often vague, interpreting legislative intent can present pitfalls for an agency. Legislators themselves frequently cannot comprehend all the implications of their enactments. A classic illustration of that was the 1964 law creating the Office of Economic Opportunity (OEO) and undertaking a seemingly comprehensive war on poverty. Members of Congress and many others had difficulty defining precisely what the legislative mandate to OEO really was. Without clear guidance, an agency may be left to fend for itself in the political arena, and—worse— be caught up in disputes over just what the legislature meant (as happened with OEO). Not only is it difficult to make interpretations of initial legislative intent; it is also a tricky business to keep abreast of *changing* intent after passage of the original law (and in the absence of formal amendments to it). That can happen as committee memberships change, new interests surface, and the like.

Many times authorizing legislation represents the best available compromise among competing forces, as noted above. Under those circumstances it is nearly certain that conflicts avoided or diluted in the course of formulating a law will crop up in the processes of interpreting and implementing it. Such controversy is not likely to do the responsible agency any good in the political process. Thus, interpretation, while necessary, has many potential pitfalls for the administrator.[42]

Application of legislation follows from its interpretation by an agency, and usually represents a further series of accommodations. Applying a law is complicated by the likelihood that other agencies also have an interest in the policy area and may well have programs of their own, by difficulties in determining optimum methods for carrying out legislative intent, and even by continuing uncertainty about the nature of a problem or program goals. Many programs are put into operation without full appreciation of a problem's dimensions; political needs to "do something" can outweigh careful and thorough consideration of what is to be done.[43] One example of this phenomenon was the poverty program, referred to previously. Another was funding made available to local law enforcement agencies through the U.S. Law Enforcement Assistance Administration (LEAA). In the latter case, public concern about rising crime rates prompted Congress to allocate funds for more (and presumably better) crime-fighting hardware, police officer training, and so on. But in retrospect, though there have been improvements in fighting crime, it is not clear that LEAA did what it was supposed to—partly because there is less than universal agreement on just what that was, and partly because the problem of crime has many more facets to it than simply ability of the police to control it.[44] Similar obstacles hamper application of other policies and programs as well.

It is necessary, then, for agencies to determine the limits to which they can go in enforcing a policy. Usually informal understandings are reached between program managers and persons or groups outside the agency about what will and will not be done. The danger here, of course, is cooptation of the program by external forces. Depending on the balance of forces, programs may be more or less vigorously pursued; the more controversial a program, the more likely there will be resistance to it.

Support for an individual program is also affected by other programs an agency is responsible for managing, and the order of priority among them within the agency. Other factors affecting program application are the values and preferences of agency personnel concerning individual programs, as well as their own role and function. Two examples illustrate these points. The first is the response of the Economic Development Administration, particularly its Seattle regional office serving the San Francisco–Oakland area, when the head of EDA formulated a program for promoting minority hiring in Oakland. An Oakland task force was also established, bypassing normal organizational channels. Many in EDA felt more comfortable working with its traditional concern, that of *rural* economic development, and after departure from EDA of the person who had set up the

Oakland program and task force, pressure grew for greater involvement of regional office personnel. At the same time, the Oakland project was treated with far less urgency by EDA, a reflection of its standing in the eyes of most EDA employees working with it.[45]

The second example concerns the educational aid program directed toward disadvantaged students under Title I of the Elementary and Secondary Education Act of 1965 (ESEA). The U.S. Office of Education (USOE), responsible for administering Title I, had spent much of its existence providing technical help to state education agencies and local school districts, taking what one observer called "a passive role with respect to the states," with little insistence on monitoring state activities to be sure they were in compliance with national law.[46] Title I, by breaking new ground in aid to education, called on USOE to administer much larger amounts of money and to direct much of it into prevously uncharted areas, especially aid to "culturally and economically disadvantaged" school children.[47] Some of the problems said to exist under Title I are traceable to USOE's institutional inertia, stemming from unfamiliarity with, and reluctance to enter into, new policy directions staked out for it by education reformers in Congress and national educational interest groups. In sum, factors internal as well as external to an agency determine just how far, how fast, and how enthusiastically a program is implemented.

Techniques of Implementation

There are numerous program management techniques that might be used in carrying on agency activities. Traditionally, little attention was paid to this aspect of administration. It was apparently assumed that once a program was in place with adequate funding and political support, writing of operating rules and regulations and actual administering of the program followed routinely. However, specific management techniques that apply to tasks of program operation have evolved since World War II. We will examine two of the most important: Program Evaluation and Review Technique (PERT), which can include a related device known as Critical Path Method (CPM), and Management by Objectives.

PERT is founded on the belief that it is necessary to map out the *sequence* of steps in carrying out a program, or a project within a program. The steps involved normally include: (1) deciding to address a given problem; (2) choosing activities necessary to deal with all relevant aspects of the problem; and (3) drawing up estimates of the time and other resources required, including minimum, maximum, and most likely amounts.[48] These help the administrator determine what needs to be done and—more important—in what order, as well as time and other resource constraints in completing various steps in a project, or projects within a program. Ideally, a PERT chart should indicate how various activities are related to one another in terms of their respective timetables, sequence of execution, and relative resource consumption. For example, a PERT analysis of a local government construction project might indicate the following. A needs assessment would have to be conducted to determine existence of sufficient demand for the project. Suitable land would then have to be acquired; funding (public and private) assured; all permits and clearances obtained; contracts let; equipment brought in; and an adequate labor force maintained. The point of the PERT analysis is that at least some of these steps can logically be taken only *after* other steps have been completed. A clear implication of PERT is its potential for assisting program managers in their *coordinative* roles, discussed in chapters 7 and 9.

A PERT chart can also be useful in calculating not only the time, funding, personnel, and materials that will be necessary, but also how much *extra* the agency might have of each of those. For this reason PERT charts are often used to calculate probable resource requirements for alternative paths of action. Such charts enable a program manager to see which path of action represents the best choice in terms of having ''margins of safety,'' as well as to evaluate alternative paths. The path with the smallest margins of extra resources with which to complete all assigned program activities is the *critical path*, because any breakdown in program management, for whatever reason, becomes critical in determining success or failure of the program. Advance knowledge of such possibilities is clearly in the best interests of the manager, the program, and the agency. An unfortunate, but relevant, example of PERT's applicability is the ill-fated attempt in April 1980 to rescue the American hostages from Teheran, using an elaborate plan involving military helicopters, transport planes, and naval vessels hundreds of miles from the rescue site. We do not know with certainty if PERT or CPM was used in organizing the mission, but the presence of eight helicopters—when only six were deemed sufficient to make the attempt—suggests that something of the CPM idea was incorporated. That is, a significant ''cushion,'' or ''slack,'' was provided in a resource vital to the mission's success. However, due principally to a series of flukes, not two but three helicopters were disabled during the rescue effort, forcing cancellation of the mission.

Despite increasing sophistication in methods such as PERT and CPM, there remains a large component of human calculation in determining optimum paths of action. While activities are interdependent and must therefore be planned with an eye to step-by-step execution, there are no assurances that calculations will be accurate.[49] ''Best estimates'' are often the most reliable data available in projecting into the future. They can be very educated guesses, it is true, but there are risks in placing too much stock in them. Yet often that is all a program manager has to go on.

The other technique for implementing a program or policy is Management by Objectives, or MBO.[50] First outlined explicitly some thirty years ago,[51] MBO has been put into practice in national and state governments as a fairly flexible approach to defining long- and short-term agency objectives, and to keeping a "finger on the pulse" of actual program results and effectiveness. MBO is another in a succession of efforts to achieve improved governmental effectiveness and is related in some respects to performance budgeting, PPB, and other recent movements toward "better management." MBO is more effective when integrated with other management approaches than standing alone.

Public administration scholar Chester Newland has described the essentials of MBO as it unfolded within the national government in particular, but with applicability elsewhere:

1. Setting goals, objectives, and priorities in terms of results to be accomplished in a given time;
2. Developing plans for accomplishment of results;
3. Allocating resources (manpower, money, plant and equipment, and information) in terms of established goals, objectives, and priorities;
4. Involving people in implementation of plans, with emphasis on communications for responsiveness and on broad sharing in [setting] authoritative goals and objectives;
5. Tracking or monitoring of progress toward goals and objectives, with specific intermediate milestones;
6. Evaluating results in terms of effectiveness (including quality), efficiency, and economy;
7. Generating and implementing improvements in objectives and results (increasing productivity through improved technology, better utilization of people, and so on).[52]

Newland points out that no single agency utilizes all seven of these MBO elements, and the fourth—which is considered by some to be an essential element indeed—is observed least often. *"At their simplest, the elements of MBO in actual practice are these: setting objectives, tracking progress, and evaluating results."*[53]

Some important features of MBO include the possibility of making objectives explicit, recognizing the multiple-objective nature of administration, identifying conflicting objectives and dealing with them, providing opportunities for employee involvement in defining organization objectives, and providing for feedback and measurement of organizational accomplishment.[54] If, as suggested here, MBO makes it possible to pinpoint conflicting objectives before efforts begin to pursue them, it renders a significant service in organizational management. And involvement of employees in "participative management" has been regarded by some as one of MBO's most important elements; this aspect has been described as fostering employee *commitment* to organization objectives, in addition to participation in determining them.[55] (Note, by the way, the similarity between this view of necessary personal commitment and Lawrence Mohr's view of organizational goals discussed in chapter 9.) At the same time, there is evidence that MBO can have the effect of *shifting power upward* in an organization, by forcing information upward (especially "bad news" about program performance).[56] MBO thus could alter somewhat the relationship between managers and their subordinates, for two reasons: (1) because an effective MBO system makes it harder for subordinates to shield from their superiors the fact that something is awry in program activities (for which the subordinates might be responsible), and (2) because *early* information about program difficulties is very useful to agency managers if they are to succeed in correcting the problems.

As with other approaches to improving management, there are obstacles to MBO's full realization (some of which we discussed earlier in reference to goals). One observer has noted that agencies often have no *unambiguous* goals, and that it is difficult to make operational the ones they do have.[57] Another dimension is that an organization's stated objectives may not be the real ones. Furthermore, there are *"no commonly accepted standards for monitoring performance or measuring achievements of many public objectives."*[58]

If, however, objectives can be defined in operational terms, MBO can be a useful management instrument. It is capable of existing comfortably with PERT, and in the longer run with PPB, zero-base budgeting, and sunset laws. While its application in the national government already appears to have waned somewhat,[59] its residual effects seem destined to take their place alongside those of PPB and to become part of the foundation for further management developments. For one thing MBO may have value, together with ZBB, in helping decision makers choose which programs to postpone or abandon.[60] In a time of great concern about priority setting, MBO may prove to have been a harbinger of things to come.

Problems and Politics of Implementation

Despite availability of numerous techniques of implementation, problems common to many managerial situations persist. It is appropriate to treat briefly three of the most important ones.

First, management *control* is a continuing challenge. This has two dimensions—one relating to management's ability to secure subordinates' cooperation in program activities, and one concerning the agency's ability to cope with specific situations and with the surrounding environment. The more pressing of the two, from a manager's standpoint, is the former. Control of staffing, allocation of fiscal resources, designation of work assignments, and delegating discretionary authority are potentially useful devices for enhancing management control. Even these, however, do not guarantee effective direction of internal activities.

Related to management control is the challenge of developing harmonious, productive, and beneficial *working relationships* within an agency. Lessons of the "human relations" school of organization theory and of organizational humanism, and concerns about effective leadership (see chap-

---

RESISTANCE TO CHANGE: ONE EXAMPLE

Inglewood, California, has used one-man refuse trucks for more than a decade at significantly reduced cost and with fewer injuries and greater satisfaction for personnel.

Informed of the one-man trucks, the sanitation director in an eastern city using four men to a truck said he did not believe it. Having confirmed that they were in use, he opined that Inglewood's streets and contours were different from his city's. Convinced that conditions in both places were generally the same, he lamented that his constituents would never accept the lower level of service. Persuaded that the levels of service were equal, he explained that the sanitation men would not accept a faster pace and harder work conditions. Told that the Inglewood sanitation men prefer the system because they set their own pace and suffer fewer injuries caused by careless coworkers, the director prophesied that the city council would never agree to such a large cutback in manpower. Informed of Inglewood's career development plan to move sanitation men into other city departments, the director pointed out he was responsible only for sanitation.

Source: Improving Productivity in State and Local Government (New York: Committee for Economic Development, March 1976), p. 46.

---

ters 6 and 9 respectively), enter into the organizational life of both manager and employee in this regard. Of central importance are vertical (leader-follower) and horizontal (follower-follower) relationships, in all their forms. Meeting ego needs, regularizing on-the-job recognition for excellence, developing appropriate opportunities for employee independence or creativity, and facilitating communication among employees represent possible ways of creating and maintaining the kinds of relationships sought. And managers must be alert to the possibilities.

A problem associated in the public mind with bureaucracy—namely, *resistance to change*—is indeed an operating problem of some importance. Any time an organization is called on to undertake a task, the potential for change is present. Pressures for change can be real and direct, prompting employee reluctance to go along. The "conserver" in Anthony Downs's typology of bureaucrats may not be the only one within an agency to exhibit a degree of conservatism; others of every type and description may at times resist change and even the prospect of change. Overcoming such resistance is often a delicate managerial task. It is made more complicated by the fact that managers themselves may fear "upsetting the applecart" in their existing situations. Much of the time (though not always) this is due to a survival instinct, which can be difficult for outsiders to understand. Nonetheless, the problem is real. It can, for example, hamper development of new activities, adaptation of existing operations to new circumstances or challenges, and maintenance of sufficient flexibility to meet emergencies.

Whatever the causes, costs of resisting change can be substantial, and constant effort is frequently necessary to gain support for many kinds of change in administrative behavior.

In the midst of criticism concerning the failure of programs to live up to their promise, a little-noticed aspect of implementation deserves attention. That is the real possibility that agency implementation of a law may entail actually changing its purpose(s) in order to satisfy shifting political demands. If the legislative coalition that was strong enough to pass a law does not continue to support the agency in charge of implementation, it may turn out on later examination that effects of the law were different from those envisioned for it. It is not uncommon for those who failed to ''carry the day'' in the legislative struggle to recover some of their losses by applying pressure on administrative agencies, thus altering the nature of the program the majority thought it was adopting. Sometimes administrators are willing allies in this effort, sometimes not. Either way, the outcome is the same: *substantive modification* of programs (or policies).

Consider the following case history. Title I of the Elementary and Secondary Education Act of 1965 greatly increased the national government's presence in many phases of education nationwide, most of all in funding local school districts and, to a lesser extent, state education agencies.[61] Title I of ESEA ''dictated the use of massive [national] funds for the general purpose of upgrading the education of children who were culturally and economically disadvantaged,'' while leaving considerable discretion in the hands of local education agencies to develop local programs for achieving that goal.[62] ''If there was a single theme characterizing the diverse elements of the 1965 . . . Act, it was that of *reform*. . . . ESEA was the first step toward a new face for American education.''[63] The key emphasis of Title I was infusion of aid to school districts in which there were large numbers of poor children, with the idea that education could contribute to ending poverty for these students, at least in their later adult years. The national government's prevailing political focus in the mid-1960s was on combating poverty, and educational aid allocated as ''special purpose'' funding was viewed by many as essential to the antipoverty effort.

There were, however, other purposes of Title I which, though not conflicting with aid to disadvantaged students, made it more difficult to determine what its central purpose really was. These included raising achievement levels, pacifying the ghettos, building bridges to private (sectarian) schools, and providing fiscal relief to school districts.[64] Depending on which of these was to receive the greatest emphasis in Title I implementation, it would be possible to draw varying conclusions about whether or not ''the'' purpose of Title I was in fact being fulfilled.

The point to be made here, however, does not concern evaluations of Title I implementation; we shall deal with that subject shortly. Rather, it is that actual congressional intent—as distinguished from the legislation's stated purpose—may have changed during the first decade of the law's operation (1965–1975), until the only form of aid to education that could gain majority support in Congress was general purpose aid, not special purpose. As the political scene changed in the late 1960s and early 1970s, support for Title I in its original, legislated form apparently changed also. As a result, funding under Title I has come increasingly to be general purpose aid. This matches longstanding preferences of traditional bureaucrats in the Office of Education. But more significantly, Congress itself has in effect broadened Title I aid categories to include general purpose aid. What the most powerful education subsystems wanted, they got—and poverty-related education aid was not their highest priority.[65]

Redirecting implementation of a law also can occur when a new chief executive regards it as sufficiently important to do so. That happened with the national government's Surface Mining Control and Reclamation Act, passed under President Carter in 1977.[66] This statute paved the way for a major national government role in regulating surface (strip) coal mining, including reclamation of abandoned strip-mined lands. The regulatory program was to be implemented in two phases by a new Office of Surface Mining (OSM) in the Interior Department, over a three-year period. In the first phase the national government

> assumed primary responsibility for enforcing the law while the states [prepared] their own program[s] which, when judged (by OSM) to be in compliance with . . . law, would culminate in a state takeover of the . . . program. In other words, following an elaborate approval process the states would be awarded program ''primacy'' and OSM's responsibilities would shift from direct enforcement to oversight and monitoring.[67]

Also, grants were to be made available both for implementing the regulatory program and reclaiming strip-mined land.

All this was to be done in the interest of meeting ''the twin needs of environmental protection and energy production,''[68] and OSM pursued its implementation responsibilities vigorously. By January 1981 it had approved state regulatory programs for eighteen of the twenty-five coal-rich states, and was preparing its own program for a number of states with smaller coal deposits. In sum, ''implementation of the law was well along by the time the Reagan administration assumed office.''[69]

After January 1981, however, Interior Secretary James Watt led systematic efforts to redirect implementation of the surface mining law.[70] These efforts included: (1) reorganizing OSM, and speeding up the shift from direct enforcement to oversight and monitoring, (2) rewriting existing regulations, putting emphasis on greater state discretion and on the *results* (rather than detailed procedures) of mining and reclamation activities, and (3) changing OSM's enforcement style in the coal fields, emphasizing ''cooperation and persuasion rather than confrontation and coercion''[71] in dealing with coal operators. Note that throughout this process, no amendments to the original statute were even introduced into Congress. Implementation was redirected solely through efforts within the executive branch.

Political scientist Donald Menzel concludes that "a major change in the implementation of a law is most likely to occur when there are significant changes in the policy environment. In the surface mining case, the principal change . . . was the election of a new president with social and political views considerably different [from those of] his Democratic predecessor."[72] Not only were the president's *views* different. As we have seen (regarding, for example, intergovernmental relations, personnel management, and government budgeting), this president was deeply committed to *acting* on those views, in a sustained effort to bring about fundamental change across a broad spectrum of governmental practices. Redirecting implementation of this statute was but one small part of that enterprise.[73]

PROGRAM EVALUATION

In recent years evaluation of programs has become a central concern to virtually all administrative policy makers, most political executives, legislators, and the public. Whether a program is accomplishing what it was designed to do is a key question for managers; it also affects future planning of program efforts, as the policy cycle begins to repeat itself.

It is only since the early 1970s that widespread interest has developed among public managers in *systematic*, rather than intuitive, evaluation procedures. The latter have been in use for some time—by political superiors, clienteles, the mass media, and academics, among others. As used here, evaluation can be defined as "systematic measures and comparisons to provide specific information on program *results* for use in policy or management decisions."[74] This definition suggests that evaluation can be used in both policy-related and programmatic decision making. In the former, evaluation can be a useful device for identifying, documenting, and clarifying the most important objectives of a project, program, or agency; it also can be used to develop *measures* for success that can be incorporated into management processes. At the programmatic level, evaluations can help managers stay current regarding resources spent, activities under way, and actual performance compared to performance standards.[75]

It has been suggested that program evaluation can be used for three purposes: (1) to learn about a program's operations and effects, (2) to control the behavior of those responsible for program implementation, and (3) to influence the responses of those in the program's external political environment. Most agency managers fail to take full advantage of these possibilities, however—by beginning their evaluation programs too late, assigning evaluation responsibilities to staffs which lack the requisite skills, or yielding to temptations to distort or suppress unfavorable evaluation find-ings.[76] Thus, simply understanding the mechanics of conducting evalua-tions themselves is not enough. Managers also must have a sense of these kinds of potential pitfalls, and of the need to avoid them.

Evaluation Procedures

Evaluation requires certain preconditions and a series of steps. The most important preconditions are, first, an understanding of the problem toward which a government program or policy was directed, and second, clarity of goals that the program or policy was designed to achieve. It makes no sense to evaluate in a vacuum—that is, without some conception of what was supposed to be accomplished. Evaluation deliberately related to program goals has grown out of recent developments in the budgeting process, where cost-efficiency criteria had told little about what an enterprise was actually doing. Performance budgeting, too, fell short in this regard, though not by as much. For example, a study of per-capita expenditures in a government program might tell us something about political influence and governmental commitment, but not much about the *effects* of money being spent.[77] Only with increasing concern for program impact and effec-tiveness could the process of evaluation as a distinct function really come into its own. Instruments such as PERT, PPB, MBO, ZBB, and sunset laws all share a common focus: to make it possible to *judge the merits* of programs and policies in terms of what is being accomplished, relative to goals set for them.[78]

Steps to be taken in an evaluation include at least the following.[79] First, there must be *specification* of what is to be evaluated, regardless of how narrow and precise or broad and diffuse the object of evaluation is. A nationwide program to immunize children against measles and one to re-duce illiteracy among poor adults both can be specified for purposes of evaluation. The second step is *measurement* of the object of evaluation, by collecting data that demonstrate the performance and effect of the program or policy. There are several possibilities, ranging from highly systematic, empirical data and methods to casual, on-the-scene observation by an un-trained observer. The third step is *analysis*, which can vary in the rigor with which it is carried out. How each of these steps is defined and executed af-fects the final evaluation product.

In order to make a coherent and rational evaluation of program or pol-icy effectiveness, a clear cause-and-effect relationship has to be established between given actions by an agency and demonstrated impacts on a soci-etal problem. For example, FBI crime data in mid-1977 indicated that dur-ing the winter months of 1976–77, the number of crimes usually committed out-of-doors dropped dramatically—muggings, assaults, and so on. Some might have argued that this was due to beefed-up police patrols or to larger law enforcement expenditures. Yet the bitter cold weather seems to have played a bigger part than any of these. The crux of the matter, however, is that if police patrols *had* been beefed up or if expenditures *had* been up sharply, then it might have been easy—and politically profitable—to conclude that these factors, not the weather, caused the drop in crime. Simply because an intended result materializes is no guarantee that the relevant program *caused* it to occur. Certainly, there is a chance that a cause-and-effect relationship does exist, but it is useful to confirm that.

Designing a program evaluation is a complex task, with several different evaluation designs possible.[80] It is important to tailor a design to the particular program being evaluated, so that the results can be relied upon. Programs as diverse as manned space exploration, school lunches, garbage collection, and downtown redevelopment require varied evaluation schemes, appropriate to their respective objectives, modes of operation, and units of measurement. In all cases, however, the question that evaluators would ideally ask is: "What actually happened, compared to what would have happened had the program not existed and everything else been exactly the same?" Five evaluation designs are commonly used (though there are others), each of which lends itself to specific techniques.

Before versus after program comparison examines program results at some appropriate time after implementation, compared with conditions as they were just before the program got under way. It is especially useful when time and personnel available to conduct the evaluation are in short supply, and when the program is short-term and narrow in scope. One drawback is that it is difficult, using this method, to be sure that any improvements are in fact due to the program's operation (recall the example of less crime in cold weather).

Time trend projection of preprogram data versus actual postprogram data compares actual results with preprogram projections. This method can be used to measure various kinds of trends as they are affected by a program. An example might be a local newspaper recycling effort, volunteer-sponsored, which gives way to a municipal recycling program. Data can be gathered on tons of newspaper collected over a period of years prior to municipal recycling, and projections made concerning the likely increase in tonnage without the program change. Later, comparisons of actual tonnage to those projections can shed light on actual program impact.

Comparisons with jurisdictions or population segments not served by the program have the advantage of controlling for nonprogrammatic factors. That is, by comparison with other jurisdictions, or with parts of the internal population not served by the program, it is possible to determine whether any change was due to the program. An example is the state of Connecticut's strict highway speed enforcement program. One criterion for evaluating the program was its effectiveness in reducing the number of traffic fatalities per 100,000 population. Initial data indicated a decline in traffic deaths, starting at about the time the enforcement program went into effect. But could evaluators be sure that the decline was *not* due to other factors—more safe cars on the highways, more advertising stressing careful driving, poor weather, gas shortages? To answer that, Connecticut's highway death rate was compared to those in neighboring states, where no new enforcement program had gone into effect, and it was found that the fatality rate had indeed declined relative to the other states' rates. Thus it was evident that some factor unique to Connecticut—a reasonable inference being the speed enforcement program—had accounted for reducing traffic deaths.

Controlled experimentation, one of the most complex and costly methods, involves comparing preselected, similar groups of people, some served by the program and some not (or served in different ways). Most important, here, is ensuring that the two groups are as similar as possible, except for their participating (or not) in the program. The "experimental" and "control" groups (for example, individuals involved and not involved in manpower training or alcohol abuse treatment programs) would be subjected to performance measures of their relevant behaviors before and after program implementation. If trends in evaluation data were similar for both groups before program start-up, but the experimental group experienced substantially greater improvement, this would provide strong evidence that the program was responsible. This method can be used in combination with the two immediately preceding, but much greater precision is required—principally in ensuring the closest possible similarity between the two groups or populations being studied.

Comparisons of planned versus actual performance involve measuring postprogram data against targets set in prior years, whether before or during program implementation. This is a more general device, one used by many state and local governments to compare performance of a program to implied rather than explicit targets. For example, one state found that its student guaranteed loans were being used far more by middle-income families than by those with lower incomes. Not that the former were ineligible—simply that the general need for student aid was assumed to be greater among the latter (perhaps it *was*, but that apparently was not a determining factor in patterns of use). This method should ideally be used to supplement one or more of the other four techniques.

Problems and Politics of Evaluation

If the purpose of evaluation is to assess program performance and accomplishment objectively, it is evident that there are numerous difficulties involved. Some concern problems of performance measurement—the nature of evaluation data, criteria of evaluation, information quality, and the like. Others pertain to political factors that can be injected into an evaluation process, changing the nature—even the very purpose—of a program evaluation. Many times these difficulties overlap, compounding the problems that exist.

Perhaps the central problem in evaluating public programs is considerable uncertainty about the reliability of performance indicators. The available indicators of accomplishment, which have been used extensively, are widely regarded as inadequate. It has been difficult to develop measures with enough objective precision to produce meaningful evaluative results. In part, this is a matter of deficiencies in obtaining necessary information, although in recent years more sophisticated management information systems have been designed and put into operation. Improved information capability should enhance the total process of evaluation as an objective function of public administration.

Another dimension of the problem of performance indicators is the fact that the same data can often be manipulated and interpreted in different ways to produce seemingly different results. For example, educational information is quite confusing—few can be certain how well our educational systems function. Yet we have hundreds of studies of educational attainment, test scores, measures of test validity, and much more. What does it all mean? A dozen different experts might give a dozen different answers. Thus, development of improved evaluation instruments, by which to make reliable judgments about program performance, remains very much on our agenda of unfinished business.

A third factor is whether there are major disparities between the official goals of a program and those of the program's key implementers. This seems to have occurred to some extent in the case of ESEA. One of the harshest evaluations of Title I implementation (the Martin-McClure Report in 1969) accused the Office of Education of not fulfilling the mandates of Title I—specifically, of not ensuring that money intended for educating poor school children was actually being spent by state and local school officials for that purpose. The problem, according to one observer, was that the reformers and implementers were different people, and that the Office of Education staff did not regard itself as investigation-oriented and had no particular inclination to monitor state agencies in their expenditure of Title I funds.[81]

One other problem is the time frame in which programs operate, and how much time is required before a meaningful appraisal can be made of program results. Since no program works perfectly, it is natural for those in charge to seek more time than others might desire in order to correct shortcomings and produce positive results (another instance where political considerations overlap). But even in purely objective terms, required time frames of different programs vary—if Rome wasn't built in a day, neither could man land on the moon in a matter of weeks nor polio be eradicated in a month or two. Reasonable time requirements have to be taken into account—assuming that "reasonable" can be defined satisfactorily.

The politics of evaluation raises different kinds of issues, though not unrelated to those already discussed. Evaluations are used, in the most general sense, to determine *whether there is justification* for continuing a program to the same extent, in the same manner, and for the same cost. But "justification" is a tricky term, and it raises a fundamental issue in the evaluation process. On the one hand, evaluation in an ideal sense is designed to be value-free and objective. On the other hand, "justification" is a value-loaded term, since in order to "justify" something, a context of values must be present. That is, nothing is ever simply "justified"; it is only *"justified in terms of. . . ."* Thus an evaluation to determine whether a program is justified necessarily becomes bound up with different sets of values about what constitutes adequate justification. This is clearly a political question.

The usual pattern seems to be that evaluations carried out by those in charge of a program or policy are more favorable to its continuation in substantially the same form than are evaluations carried out by independent third parties, especially those who are skeptical. It is not unduly cynical to suggest that an agency will almost always be kinder in judging its own data, will adopt the time frame most likely to produce the intended program effect, and will try to ignore other variables that could produce the desired effect(s), than will others who do not have the same stake in the agency's activities.[82] Since program survival may depend on whether evaluations are positive or negative, a process which many see as value-free and therefore politically neutral is, like so many other things in public administration, weighted down with political implications. That is why internal evaluations so often point up program successes, while external evaluations tend to emphasize deficiencies and ways to improve program management.

Perhaps the mix of factors frustrating truly objective evaluations can best be summed up by the following description of Title I evaluation by the Office of Education:

> Since the beginning of the program, evaluation has been high on the list of . . . rhetorical priorities, but low on the list of actual USOE priorities. The reasons for this are many. They include fear of upsetting the [national]-state balance, recognition of [the fact] that little expertise exists at the state and local levels to evaluate a broad-scale reform program, and fear of disclosing failure. *No administrator is anxious to show that his program is not working.*[83]

There is another important dimension to the politics of evaluation, namely, how politics affects the uses made of evaluation results. Even when evaluations produce entirely objective data (which, as noted earlier, is infrequent), there is no assurance that they will become the basis of efforts to bring about significant change—whether in program goals, in the way program activities are carried on, or in ultimate performance. Concentrated and effective political support for or against a given program can render evaluations of that program virtually irrelevant, whether those evaluations are favorable or unfavorable.

Illustrating this point is the national government's housing program (particularly public housing), which consistently has fallen far short of its projected goals, according to a number of separate evaluations. A great national goal, established in 1949, was construction of 810,000 housing units for low-income families over a period of six years—and that number still has not been reached. Regardless of the many critiques of these efforts, those who favor the housing program have not generated the necessary political support for reaching its goals. The interests served by building low-income public housing (the urban poor, primarily) are severely outweighed by the influence of other interests for whom public housing is a low priority—banks, contractors, real estate brokers, and the great majority of the population that is not low-income. Since criticism of the program's alleged failures did not sway its opponents, the program has continued as merely a shadow of what it was supposed to be.[84]

Two concluding observations about evaluation are in order. First, despite the aura of value neutrality that frequently is associated with evaluation, its true significance may lie in its having caused public managers, and others, to focus "on the *fundamental value choices* that are inherent in the decision to initiate or terminate a policy, or to increase or reduce funding for a program."[85] This would indicate both how important and how difficult it is to conduct evaluations as impartially as possible. Second, it has been suggested that "evaluation is likely to lead to better program performance only if the program *design* meets three key conditions: (1) program objectives are well defined, (2) program objectives are plausible, and (3) intended use of information is well defined."[86] That is, if we are to evaluate public programs properly, those programs must have had the *capacity to be evaluated* built into them, from the outset. (This caveat brings us "full circle"—back to program planning and design as a key building block of *all* program operations and management.) As evaluation continues to grow in significance, in an era of declining resources, our sophistication in conducting and interpreting evaluations will have to keep pace.[87]

GOVERNMENT PRODUCTIVITY

Within a framework of concern for productivity in the economy generally, and for making optimum use of public resources that are not as abundant as in the past, the productivity of government programs has taken on increasing political, economic, and social significance. Links between productivity and other aspects of management have also been stressed. A brief look at key elements of productivity will indicate where scholarly observers and others have placed most emphasis.[88]

Productivity and efforts to achieve it are lineal descendants of concern for efficiency in government, yet they encompass a broader area. Productiv-

Table 13-1

SOME COMMON PROBLEMS OF LOW PRODUCTIVITY IN LOCAL GOVERNMENT AND SUGGESTIONS FOR CORRECTIVE ACTION

Problem	Possible Corrective Action	Illustrative Examples
Sufficient work not available or workloads unbalanced	Reallocate manpower	Housing complaint bureau schedules revised and temporary help employed during peak winter season.
	Change work schedules	Mechanics rescheduled to second shift when equipment is not in use.
	Reduce crew size	Collection crew size reduced from 4 to 3 men.
Lack of equipment or materials	Improve inventory control system	Inventory reorder points revised to reduce stock-out occurrences.
	Improve distribution system	Asphalt deliveries expedited to eliminate paving crew delays.
	Improve equipment maintenance	Preventive maintenance program instituted.
	Reevaluate equipment requirements	Obsolete collection trucks replaced.
Self-imposed idle time or slow work pace	Train supervisors	Road maintenance foremen trained in work scheduling, dispatching, and quality-control techniques.
	Use performance standards	"Flat rate" manual standards adopted to measure auto mechanics' performance.
	Schedule more work	Park maintenance crews mobilized and work scheduling system installed.

ity, unlike its forerunner, focuses on both efficient use of governmental resources and actual impacts of what government does—that is, on efficiency and effectiveness. It springs also from efforts to identify specific program objectives and to measure progress toward achieving them. The task is made more difficult by the fact, mentioned earlier regarding evaluation, that measures available to public managers are less precise than we might like, and are less simple than economic measures employed in the private sector. As one example, much of what government tries to do involves *preventing* various social ills—crimes, disease, destruction by fire of lives and property. How does one measure productivity of such functions? There is no easy answer. Yet it has been possible to develop some measures useful in assessing productivity of individual programs, in conjunction with other emphases in program analysis and evaluation.

The first approach deals with programs in which output is easily measurable—for example, number of tons of refuse collected per sanitation

Table 13-1 (continued)
SOME COMMON PROBLEMS OF LOW PRODUCTIVITY IN LOCAL
GOVERNMENT AND SUGGESTIONS FOR CORRECTIVE ACTION

Problem	Possible Corrective Action	Illustrative Examples
Too much time spent on nonproductive activities	Reduce excessive travel time	Permit expiration dates changed to reduce travel time of health inspectors.
	Reevaluate job description and task assignments	Building inspectors trained to handle multiple inspections.
Excessive manual effort required	Mechanize repetitive tasks	Automatic change and toll collection machines installed and toll collector staffing reduced.
Response or processing time too slow	Combine tasks or functions	Voucher processing and account posting combined to speed vendor payments.
	Automate process	Computerized birth record storage and retrieval system installed
	Improve dispatching procedures	Fire alarm patterns analyzed and equipment response policies revised.
	Revise deployment practices	Police patrol zones redefined to improve response time.
	Adopt project management techniques	Project control system installed to reduce construction cycle.

Source: So, Mr. Mayor, You Want to Improve Productivity . . . (Washington, D.C.: National Commission on Productivity and Work Quality, 1974); and Center for Productive Public Management, John Jay College, New York.

truck shift—and the goal is to reduce the unit cost while improving responsiveness. Urban problem areas such as cleaning and maintaining park facilities, patching streets, and maintenance of sanitation vehicles lend themselves to unit-cost measurement of productivity.

The second approach concerns programs or functions in which output is very hard to measure—for example, provision of police or fire protection. Here the intent is to improve deployment of resources by assessing probable needs, so as to ensure as much as possible that resources will be available when and where they are needed most. In addition to police and fire departments, this approach could be usefully employed in sanitation departments, rescue services, and civil defense offices.

But efforts to improve productivity, however measured, may encounter obstacles. Table 13-1 lists common problems at the local level, with possible ways to overcome them. Two general approaches to solving productivity problems have been used. One stresses improving organizational and processing procedures, particularly through imaginative use of computers. Government agencies extensively involved in provision of social services, with attendant record-keeping needs, may find this approach especially beneficial in increasing cost efficiency in a wide variety of programs. Data-processing improvements can make a noticeable difference in areas such as large education systems, large welfare programs, monitoring of capital construction programs, and payments to those who provide goods and services to a government or an individual agency. The other approach calls for developing new technological devices that result in more efficient use of human resources—for example, polymerized water for better and less expensive fire-fighting. Though current efforts along these lines are still relatively limited, the possibilities are impressive: improved techniques for combating air and water pollution, construction of low-cost modular housing, use of closed-circuit television for simple medical tests of government employees or prisoners, and many others.

One notable example of productivity improvement can be found in the venerable U.S. Postal Service. "Thirteen years after the old Cabinet-level Post Office Department became the independent Postal Service, the postal workers deliver 40 percent more mail—130 billion pieces in fiscal 1984—to 18 million more addresses, but with 62,000 fewer people on the payroll. And the agency, an historic money loser, . . . produced $1.5 billion in surpluses [in the period 1981–1984]."[89] Measuring productivity in the Postal Service admittedly is easier than in numerous other settings, but the record is impressive, nevertheless.

Productivity concerns will continue to be important, if for no other reason than growing awareness of the limited resources available. It is becoming more widely accepted, in government and elsewhere, that more and more we may have to "make do with what we have." The promise of productivity efforts lies in the fact that technology has not yet been fully applied to this area, and there is a growing track record of successes, which should encourage similar efforts elsewhere.[90]

"CUTBACK" MANAGEMENT

We have already noted, in the chapters on leadership and government budgeting, some implications of the era in which we now live where resources are increasingly constrained and public administration correspondingly affected. The implications of resource constraints, particularly in the fiscal realm, are obvious. Specific managerial strategies and tactics also have been devised to meet these new challenges.

Without meaning to oversimplify, the advisable tactics that can be used to achieve cutbacks are relatively easy to summarize.[91] In the context of municipal service provision (though applicable elsewhere as well), the following checklist of possible actions is representative. In *cutting back or withdrawing from service provision,* a manager might wish to begin an ongoing review of services, their output and costs, and a periodic intensive review of each service to determine continuing need. The manager may also establish a process for setting priorities (ZBB may help here); examine the possibility of staged reductions—limiting library hours or decreasing frequency of garbage collections; and investigate shifting rather than eliminating resources (such as alternative uses of public buildings). In *reducing expenditures,* a manager might consider establishing user charges and fees for services previously tax supported; joining with other jurisdictions in supporting services, utilities, resource recovery, and purchasing; and utilizing part-time employees, private suppliers of services,[92] and leasing rather than purchasing. In *broadening the jurisdiction's resource base,* a manager may seek to link locally determined fees to general increases for a particular service or to the Consumer Price Index, and upgrade cash and debt management policies. Finally, in *improving personnel management,* a manager can emphasize productivity improvements in negotiations with public employees; develop and periodically review classification and pay plans; and work closely with line managers both to establish clear goals for public employees and to help ease the psychological stress associated with *fiscal* stress. These steps are somewhat interrelated; some also echo earlier themes such as organizational communication, bargaining, leadership, performance evaluation, and productivity analysis. Depending on circumstances, such tactics may be temporary, or they could be with us indefinitely.

If, after all else fails, a program faces outright termination, other guidelines might be followed—guidelines with demonstrably ''political'' overtones.[93] Among these are: (1) maintain secrecy, so as to avoid opponents ''getting the jump'' in any fight over program termination; (2) focus attention on the program's disadvantages, even any harm it may have caused, and generate support for that view; (3) resist compromise that would permit continuation of the targeted program in a modified form; (4) recruit a newcomer to the governmental arena in a given jurisdiction to oversee the termination process; (5) avoid a legislative decision (where proponents have natural allies, in virtually all cases), but also take care to respect legislative prerogatives (by securing informal agreement from key legislators beforehand, for example); and (6) terminate what is only absolutely necessary, while emphasizing that such termination is a means to other ends, including maintenance of *some* program activities or services. This is obviously a rather messy business, but one that may command more of our attention—and political resources—in the near future.

''Cutback'' management, then, involves a complex set of activities founded on the premise of a ''no-growth'' economic base—or, at least, a no-growth governmental resource base. The administration of cutback principles can be just as delicate a matter as the politics involved (assuming they are separable). Both demand foresight and fortitude, on the part of those administering cutback policies as well as those affected and their program clienteles.

SUMMARY

Public policy making is a highly diffuse process involving a multitude of actors in and out of government. Yet program management, within policy contexts, is expected to be of good quality, leading to the achievement of program and policy goals. Managing policies and programs calls into play virtually every facet of the administrative process. Policies differ from one another in their rationales, broad impacts, and administrative components; major policy types have been described as distributive, regulatory, self-regulatory, and redistributive.

The policy-making process is complex, very loosely coordinated, highly competitive, fragmented, specialized, and largely incremental. The result is a great deal of inconsistency in the policies adopted, and sometimes outright contradictions.

Administrative policy making occurs in four stages: (1) drafting and enactment of basic legislation; (2) writing of rules and regulations governing application of the law; (3) implementation of the law; and (4) review of application and implementation, involving Congress, the courts, or both. Problems and demands are constantly defined and redefined in the policy process, suggesting a policy *cycle* that repeats these four stages more than once. Intergovernmental relations also figure prominently in the making of public policy. These and other factors in the policy process help account for the disjointed nature of most policies.

Policies, programs, projects, and performance—the ''four Ps''—are interrelated, with importance to the outcomes of government operations. Programs and projects are the building blocks of policy, and from a management standpoint require particular attention in six areas: planning, analysis, implementation, evaluation, productivity, and ''cutback'' management.

Planning is essential for meaningful program goal definition and operationalizing of goals. The planning process calls for substantive, administrative, and political skills on the part of top management; a major challenge is to develop purposefulness in agency operations.

Analysis is equally essential as a decision tool. Both informal and formal techniques abound; the latter have assumed a larger role in recent years. Among the more prominent formal analytic techniques are policy analysis, cost-benefit analysis, and operations research.

Implementation refers to those activities directed toward putting a program into effect. It is necessary for agencies to *organize, interpret,* and *apply* programmatic or policy directives contained in the authorizing legislation. Controversy over legislative intent can make interpretation a difficult task. In addition, program application often takes place through a series of compromises. Other factors affecting application include informal limits on an agency's activities, the possibility of cooptation, controversy surrounding a given program or activity, agency priorities with regard to its other responsibilities, and values and preferences of agency personnel concerning individual programs and their own general role and function.

Among the most important methods of program and policy implementation are PERT, CPM, and MBO. PERT involves mapping out the sequence of steps necessary to carry out a program or project. It also permits comparisons among different paths of action, each of which has a different "margin of safety" available in its projected resource requirements. The path with the smallest margin of extra resources is the *critical path*. Despite the sophistication of PERT and CPM, much of the calculation depends on human judgment, thus leaving its accuracy somewhat uncertain. MBO represents a fairly flexible approach to setting long-term and short-term goals while monitoring actual programmatic results and effectiveness. Among its potential benefits are helping administrators recognize conflicting objectives and deal with them, providing opportunities for employee participation in defining objectives, and providing feedback and measurement of organizational accomplishment.

A number of implementation problems confront many managers. Management control involves (1) obtaining the cooperation of subordinates, (2) developing good working relationships among followers and between leaders and followers, and (3) overcoming resistance to change. One subtle, yet crucial, aspect of implementation is the possibility that legislative purposes may be changed during the course of implementation.

Evaluation has become increasingly important in recent years, as well as more systematic. In order to conduct an evaluation, it is necessary to specify what is to be evaluated, measure the object of evaluation by collecting useful data, and analyze the data. A cause-and-effect relationship must also be established between specific program activities and apparent results.

Methods of evaluation vary widely, from institutionalized procedures and informal evaluation devices to more formalized techniques. A number of explicit evaluation designs may be, and have increasingly been, used by program evaluators. The rigor of evaluation methods and the uses made of the results will determine the value and impact of the evaluation process.

A central problem in evaluating public programs is lack of adequate indicators of performance and accomplishment. Other difficulties include defining problems, identifying specific goals, dealing with disparities between official goals and those of key implementers, and defining the time frame necessary to give the program a chance to work.

In theory, evaluation should be objective and value-free. Yet evaluations are designed fundamentally to show whether there is justification for continuing an activity, program, or policy in much the same form as before.

And "justification" is a value-loaded term, raising political questions and implications. Political factors can also affect the uses made of evaluations.

Concern for government productivity is on the rise. There are several approaches to measuring productivity, and to improving productivity levels. Under conditions of limited resources (of all kinds), productivity in government and elsewhere will continue to be important.

"Cutback" management will have its own importance, also. Various strategies and tactics have been devised for conscientious managers who need to reduce the scale of their administrative operations. Some involve fiscal actions, others focus on cutting back service provision, still others on personnel management; all can be useful. Politically, cutbacks are very sensitive matters, but ways have been suggested to handle them effectively.

NOTES

1. See Murray Edelman, *The Symbolic Uses of Politics* (Urbana, Ill.: University of Illinois Press, 1964).
2. See Charles O. Jones, *An Introduction to the Study of Public Policy*, 3rd ed. (Monterey, Calif.: Brooks/Cole, 1984), chapter 2, especially pp. 34–35.
3. This discussion is taken from James E. Anderson, *Public Policy Making*, 3rd ed. (New York: Holt, Rinehart and Winston, 1984), pp. 113–16.
4. Ibid., p. 115.
5. Ibid.
6. Jones, *An Introduction to the Study of Public Policy*, chapter 1.
7. See, among others, Richard I. Hofferbert, *The Study of Public Policy* (Indianapolis: Bobbs-Merrill, 1974); Charles O. Jones and Robert D. Thomas, eds., *Public Policy Making in a Federal System* (Beverly Hills, Calif.: Sage, 1976); Roscoe C. Martin, *The Cities and the Federal System* (New York: Atherton, 1965); Peter Woll, *Public Policy* (Cambridge, Mass.: Winthrop, 1974); and Ellen Frankel Paul and Philip A. Russo, Jr., eds., *Public Policy: Issues, Analysis, and Ideology* (Chatham, N.J.: Chatham House, 1982).
8. A. Lee Fritschler, *Smoking and Politics: Policy Making and the Federal Bureaucracy*, 3rd ed. (Englewood Cliffs, N.J.: Prentice-Hall, 1983), p. 53–54.
9. Jones, *An Introduction to the Study of Public Policy*, p. 34.
10. This description is taken from Anderson, *Public Policy Making*, pp. 97–100.
11. Ibid., p. 97.
12. Ibid., p. 98.
13. Quoted in Peter H. Rossi and Sonia R. Wright, "Evaluation Research: An Assessment of Theory, Practice, and Politics," *Evaluation Quarterly*, 1 (February 1977), 5–52, at p. 23.
14. The concept of the "four Ps" was suggested by the late Roscoe C. Martin of Syracuse University.
15. Nicholas Henry, *Public Administration and Public Affairs*, 2nd ed. (Englewood Cliffs, N.J.: Prentice-Hall, 1980), p. 212.
16. Bertram M. Gross, "Planning: Developing Purposefulness," in Frederick S. Lane, ed., *Managing State and Local Government: Cases and Readings* (New York: St. Martin's, 1980), pp. 243–50, at p. 243.

17. See, for example, William Ascher, *Forecasting: An Appraisal for Policy Makers and Planners* (Baltimore: The Johns Hopkins University Press, 1978).
18. Henry, *Public Administration and Public Affairs*, p. 212.
19. Gerald L. Barkdoll, "Concentering: A Useful Preplanning Activity," *Public Administration Review*, 43 (November/December 1983), 556–60, at p. 556.
20. The following account is taken from M. M. Hargrove, "Metropolitan Tulsa Transit Authority," in Frederick S. Lane, ed., *Managing State and Local Government: Cases and Readings* (New York: St. Martin's, 1980), pp. 250–66.
21. Ibid., pp. 257–58.
22. For more information related to planning, see, among others, Louise G. White, "Improving the Goal-Setting Process in Local Government," *Public Administration Review*, 42 (January/February 1982), 77–83; Daniel R. Jensen, "Unifying Planning and Management in Public Organizations," *Public Administration Review*, 42 (March/April 1982), 157–62; Douglas C. Eadie, "Putting a Powerful Tool to Practical Use: The Application of Strategic Planning in the Public Sector," *Public Administration Review*, 43 (September/October 1983), 447–52; and Leonard I. Ruchelman, *A Workbook in Program Design for Public Managers* (Albany, N.Y.: State University of New York Press, 1985).
23. Joseph L. Bower, "Effective Public Management: It Isn't the Same as Effective Business Management," *Harvard Business Review*, 55 (March/April 1977), 131–40, at p. 139.
24. Jacob B. Ukeles, "Policy Analysis: Myth or Reality?" in Norman Beckman, ed., "Symposium on Policy Analysis in Government: Alternatives to 'Muddling Through,'" *Public Administration Review*, 37 (May/June 1977), 223–28, at p. 223. See, in the same issue, Selma J. Mushkin, "Policy Analysis in State and Community," 245–53. See, also, Thomas R. Dye, *Understanding Public Policy*, 5th ed. (Englewood Cliffs, N.J.: Prentice-Hall, 1984), chapter 1.
25. See Laurence E. Lynn, Jr., *Designing Public Policy: A Casebook on the Role of Policy Analysis* (Santa Monica, Calif.: Goodyear, 1980); Michael Carley, *Rational Techniques in Policy Analysis* (Exeter, N.H.: Heinemann Educational Books, 1980); and Arnold J. Meltsner, *Policy Analysts in the Bureaucracy* (Berkeley, Calif.: University of California Press, 1976).
26. Ukeles, "Policy Analysis: Myth or Reality?" pp. 226–27.
27. This discussion relies on Harry P. Hatry, Louis Blair, Donald Fisk, and Wayne Kimmell, "An Illustrative Checklist for Assessing Program Analyses," in Harry P. Hatry, et al., *Program Analysis for State and Local Governments* (Washington, D.C.: The Urban Institute, 1976).
28. Another dimension of carrying out useful policy analyses—what policy *analysts* themselves can do to enhance their effectiveness—is discussed in Joseph P. Viteritti, "Policy Analysis in the Bureaucracy: An Ad Hoc Approach," *Public Administration Review*, 42 (September/October 1982), 466–74, especially p. 466.
29. This discussion relies on Barry Bozeman, *Public Management and Policy Analysis* (New York: St. Martin's, 1979), pp. 267–76.
30. Ibid., pp. 269–70.
31. Henry, *Public Administration and Public Affairs*, chapter 7, especially pp. 151–54.
32. See, for example, Ida R. Hoos, *Systems Analysis in Public Policy: A Critique*, rev. ed. (Berkeley, Calif.: University of California Press, 1983).
33. Bozeman, *Public Management and Policy Analysis*, pp. 308–9.
34. Ibid., p. 270.

35. Henry, *Public Administration and Public Affairs*, p. 158.
36. An excellent source on the general subject of policy analysis is Garry D. Brewer and Peter DeLeon, *The Foundations of Policy Analysis* (Homewood, Ill.: Dorsey, 1983).
37. Adapted from Jones, *An Introduction to the Study of Public Policy*, p. 166.
38. Jeffrey L. Pressman and Aaron Wildavsky, *Implementation*, 3rd ed. (Berkeley, Calif.: University of California Press, 1984), p. xx (emphasis added).
39. See Eugene Bardach, *The Implementation Game: What Happens After a Bill Becomes a Law* (Cambridge, Mass.: The MIT Press, 1977); Richard R. Nelson and Douglas Yates, eds., *Innovation and Implementation in Public Organizations* (Lexington, Mass.: D. C. Heath, 1978); Robert T. Nakamura and Frank Smallwood, *The Politics of Policy Implementation* (New York: St. Martin's, 1980); George C. Edwards III, *Implementing Public Policy* (Washington, D.C.: Congressional Quarterly Press, 1980); Randall B. Ripley and Grace A. Franklin, *Bureaucracy and Policy Implementation* (Homewood, Ill.: Dorsey, 1982); Walter Williams, et al, *Studying Implementation: Methodological and Administrative Issues* (Chatham, N.J.: Chatham House, 1982); and Daniel A. Mazmanian and Paul A. Sabatier, *Implementation and Public Policy* (Glenview, Ill.: Scott, Foresman, 1983).
40. Fritschler, *Smoking and Politics*, p. 53.
41. Jones, *An Introduction to the Study of Public Policy*, p. 34.
42. Ibid., pp. 178–80.
43. Ibid., p. 34.
44. A valuable case study of LEAA—but with implications for all government efforts to solve complex social problems—is Malcolm M. Feeley and Austin D. Sarat, *The Policy Dilemma: Federal Crime Policy and the Law Enforcement Assistance Administration* (Minneapolis: University of Minnesota Press, 1981).
45. Pressman and Wildavsky, *Implementation*, pp. 99–100.
46. Jerome T. Murphy, "Title I of ESEA: The Politics of Implementing Federal Education Reform," *Harvard Educational Review*, 41 (February 1971), 35–63, at pp. 41–42.
47. Stephen K. Bailey and Edith K. Mosher, *ESEA: The Office of Education Administers a Law* (Syracuse, N.Y.: Syracuse University Press, 1968), p. 3.
48. The broad outlines of this discussion are drawn from Henry, *Public Administration and Public Affairs*, Appendix A.
49. Ibid., pp. 477–78.
50. This discussion of MBO is taken from Bruce H. DeWoolfson, Jr., "Public Sector MBO and PPB: Cross Fertilization in Management Systems," *Public Administration Review*, 35 (July/August 1975), 387–94; Jong S. Jun, ed., "Symposium on Management by Objectives in the Public Sector," *Public Administration Review*, 36 (January/February 1976), 1–45; Richard Rose, "Implementation and Evaporation: The Record of MBO," *Public Administration Review*, 37 (January/February 1977), 64–71; Gary B. Brumback and Thomas S. McFee, "From MBO to MBR," *Public Administration Review*, 42 (July/August 1982), 363–71; Michael L. Moore and K. Dow Scott, "Installing Management by Objectives in a Public Agency: A Comparison of Black and White Managers, Supervisors, and Professionals," *Public Administration Review*, 43 (March/April 1983), 121–26; and James E. Swiss, "Establishing a Management System: The Interaction of Power Shifts and Personality Under Federal MBO," *Public Administration Review*, 43 (May/June 1983), 238–45.

51. Peter F. Drucker, *The Practice of Management* (New York: Harper & Row, 1954).
52. Chester A. Newland, ''Policy/Program Objectives and Federal Management: The Search for Government Effectiveness,'' in Jong S. Jun, ed., ''Symposium on Management by Objectives in the Public Sector,'' *Public Administration Review*, 36 (January/February 1976), pp. 20–27, at p. 26.
53. Ibid.
54. DeWoolfson, ''Public Sector MBO and PPB,'' pp. 388–89.
55. Peter F. Drucker, ''What Results Should You Expect? A Users' Guide to MBO,'' in Jong S. Jun, ed., ''Symposium on Management by Objectives in the Public Sector,'' *Public Administration Review*, 36 (January/February 1976), pp. 12–19, at p. 18.
56. See Swiss, ''Establishing a Management System: The Interaction of Power Shifts and Personality Under Federal MBO,'' p. 239.
57. Drucker, ''What Results Should You Expect? A Users' Guide to MBO,'' p. 13.
58. Frank P. Sherwood and William J. Page, Jr., ''MBO and Public Management,'' in Jong S. Jun, ed., ''Symposium on Management by Objectives in the Public Sector,'' *Public Administration Review*, 36 (January/February 1976), pp. 5–12, at p. 9.
59. Rose, ''Implementation and Evaporation: The Record of MBO.''
60. Drucker, ''What Results Should You Expect? A Users' Guide to MBO,'' pp. 14–16.
61. See, among others, Bailey and Mosher, *ESEA: The Office of Education Administers a Law;* Marilyn Gittell and Alan G. Hevesi, eds., *The Politics of Urban Education* (New York: Praeger, 1969); Milbrey W. McLaughlin, *Evaluation and Reform: The Elementary and Secondary Education Act of 1965/Title I* (Cambridge, Mass.: Ballinger, 1975); Philip Meranto, *The Politics of Federal Aid to Education in 1965* (Syracuse, N.Y.: Syracuse University Press, 1967); and Murphy, ''Title I of ESEA.''
62. Bailey and Mosher, *ESEA*, p. 3.
63. Murphy, ''Title I of ESEA,'' pp. 35–36 (emphasis added).
64. Ibid., p. 43.
65. Floyd R. Stoner, ''Implementation of Federal Education Policy: The Role of Local Resources,'' paper delivered at the annual meeting of the Midwest Political Science Association; Chicago, Illinois; May 1–3, 1975.
66. This discussion relies on Donald C. Menzel, ''Redirecting the Implementation of a Law: The Reagan Administration and Coal Surface Mining Regulation,'' *Public Administration Review*, 43 (September/October 1983), 411–20.
67. Ibid., p. 412.
68. Ibid.
69. Ibid.
70. Ibid., pp. 412–16.
71. Ibid., p. 415.
72. Ibid., p. 419.
73. For further information concerning implementation, see David H. Kiel, ''An OD Strategy for Policy Implementation: The Case of North Carolina State Government,'' *Public Administration Review*, 42 (July/August 1982), 375–83; Robert T. Golembiewski and Alan Kiepper, ''Lessons From a Fast-Paced Public Project: Perspectives on Doing Better the Next Time Around,'' *Public Administration Review*, 43 (November/December 1983), 547–56; and Laurence J. O'Toole, Jr., and Robert S. Montjoy, ''Interorganizational Policy Implementation: A Theoretical

Perspective,'' *Public Administration Review*, 44 (November/December 1984), 491–503.

74. Joseph S. Wholey, ''The Role of Evaluation and the Evaluator in Improving Public Programs,'' *Public Administration Review*, 36 (November/December 1976), 679–83, at p. 680 (emphasis added).

75. Ibid., p. 681.

76. Edie N. Goldenberg, ''The Three Faces of Evaluation,'' *Journal of Policy Analysis and Management*, 2 (1983), 515–25.

77. Dye, *Understanding Public Policy*, p. 346.

78. See Jones, *An Introduction to the Study of Public Policy*, chapter 9. See also Edward A. Suchman, *Evaluative Research* (New York: Russell Sage Foundation, 1967); Carol H. Weiss, *Evaluation Research* (Englewood Cliffs, N.J.: Prentice-Hall, 1972); David Nachmias, *Public Policy Evaluation: Approaches and Methods* (New York: St. Martin's, 1979); Peter Rossi, Howard E. Freeman, and Sonia R. Wright, *Evaluation: A Systematic Approach* (Beverly Hills, Calif.: Sage, 1979); Joseph S. Wholey, *Evaluation: Promise and Performance* (Washington, D.C.: The Urban Institute, 1979); Jerome T. Murphy, *Getting the Facts: A Fieldwork Guide for Evaluators and Policy Analysts* (Santa Monica, Calif.: Goodyear, 1980); Helen M. Ingram and Dean E. Mann, eds., *Why Policies Succeed or Fail* (Beverly Hills, Calif.: Sage, 1980); Harry P. Hatry, Richard E. Winnie, and Donald M. Fisk, *Practical Program Evaluation for State and Local Governments*, 2nd ed. (Washington, D.C.: The Urban Institute, 1981); and Joseph S. Wholey, *Evaluation and Effective Public Management* (Boston: Little, Brown, 1983).

79. Jones, *An Introduction to the Study of Public Policy*, p. 199.

80. This discussion of evaluation designs is taken from Hatry, Winnie, and Fisk, *Practical Program Evaluation for State and Local Governments*, chapter 3.

81. Murphy, ''Title I of ESEA,'' pp. 41–43.

82. James Q. Wilson, ''On Pettigrew and Armor,'' *The Public Interest*, 31 (Spring 1973), 132–34, cited by Dye, *Understanding Public Policy*, p. 357.

83. Murphy, ''Title I of ESEA,'' p. 43 (emphasis added). Murphy also describes USOE's political position as weak, which may have been a contributing factor.

84. Jones, *An Introduction to the Study of Public Policy*, p. 218–24. See also Charles Abrams, *The City Is the Frontier* (New York: Harper & Row, 1965); Frank W. Porell, ''The Evaluation of Federal Low-Income Housing Policy and Programs,'' in David Nachmias, ed., *The Practice of Policy Evaluation* (New York: St. Martin's, 1980), pp. 229–60; and Beverly A. Cigler and Michael L. Vasu, ''Housing and Public Policy in America,'' *Public Administration Review*, 42 (January/February 1982), 90–96.

85. Larry Polivka and Laurey T. Stryker, ''Program Evaluation and the Policy Process in State Government: An Effective Linkage,'' *Public Administration Review*, 43 (May/June 1983), 255–59, at p. 258 (emphasis added).

86. Martin A. Strosberg and Joseph S. Wholey, ''Evaluability Assessment: From Theory to Practice in the Department of Health and Human Services,'' *Public Administration Review*, 43 (January/February 1983), 66–71, at p. 66 (emphasis added). See also Ruchelman, *A Workbook in Program Design for Public Managers*.

87. Other useful sources on program and policy evaluation include Jeffrey L. Brudney and Robert E. England, ''Urban Policy Making and Subjective Service Evaluations: Are They Compatible?'' and Thomas V. Greer and Joanne G. Greer, ''Problems in Evaluating Costs and Benefits of Social Programs,'' *Public Adminis-*

tration Review, 42 (March/April 1982), 127–35 and 151–56, respectively; Barry Bozeman and Jane Massey, "Investing in Policy Evaluation: Some Guidelines for Skeptical Public Managers," *Public Administration Review*, 42 (May/June 1982), 264–70; Judith R. Brown, ed., "Mini-Symposium on Legislative Program Evaluation," *Public Administration Review*, 44 (May/June 1984), 257–67; Stuart S. Nagel, "Checklists for Evaluating Public Decisions," *Public Administration Times*, 7 (October 15, 1984), 5–6 (published by the American Society for Public Administration; Washington, D.C.); Stephen Rosenthal, "New Directions for Evaluating Intergovernmental Programs," *Public Administration Review*, 44 (November/December 1984), 469–76; "Mini-Symposium on Program Evaluation— The Human Factor," *Public Administration Review*, 44 (November/December 1984), 525–38; and Eleanor Chelimsky, ed., *Program Evaluation: Patterns and Directions* (Washington, D.C.: American Society for Public Administration, 1984).

88. This discussion relies on the useful overview in Edward K. Hamilton, "Productivity: The New York City Approach," in Chester A. Newland, ed., "Symposium on Productivity in Government," *Public Administration Review*, 32 (November/December 1972), 739–850, at pp. 784–95. See also *Improving Productivity in State and Local Government* (New York: Committee for Economic Development, March 1976); Marc Holzer, ed., *Productivity in Public Organizations* (Port Washington, N.Y.: Kennikat, 1976); Marc Holzer, "The Demand for Productivity in the Municipal Civil Service," *Public Administration Review*, 37 (September/ October 1977), 505–8; Walter L. Balk, ed., "Symposium on Productivity in Government," *Public Administration Review*, 38 (January/ February 1978), 1–50; Richard F. Keevy, "State Productivity Improvements: Building on Existing Strengths," *Public Administration Review*, 40 (September/October 1980), 451–58; John Greiner, Harry P. Hatry, et al., *Productivity and Motivation: A Review of State and Local Government Initiatives* (Washington, D.C.: The Urban Institute, 1981); and David N. Ammons and Joseph C. King, "Productivity Improvement in Local Government: Its Place Among Competing Priorities," *Public Administration Review*, 43 (March/April 1983), 113–20.

89. Roger Thompson, Editorial Research Reports, in a column appearing in the Bloomington-Normal (Ill.) *Daily Pantagraph*, December 16, 1984, p. A–15.

90. See among others Michael Weir, "Efficiency Measurement in Government," *The Bureaucrat*, 13 (Summer 1984), 38–42; and Q. Whitfield Ayres and William J. Kettinger, "Information Technology and Models of Governmental Productivity," *Public Administration Review*, 43 (November/December 1983), 561–66.

91. This discussion rests on Carol W. Lewis and Anthony T. Logalbo, "Cutback Principles and Practices: A Checklist for Managers," *Public Administration Review*, 40 (March/April 1980), 184–88, especially pp. 186–88.

92. See E. S. Savas, *Privatizing the Public Sector* (Chatham, N.J.: Chatham House, 1982).

93. Robert D. Behn, "How to Terminate a Public Policy: A Dozen Hints for the Would-be Terminator," *Policy Analysis*, 4 (Summer 1978), 393–413. See also Robert W. Poole, Jr., *Cutting Back City Hall* (New York: Universe Books, 1980); International City Management Association, *Managing With Less* (Washington, D.C.: International City Management Association, 1980); Irene S. Rubin, *Running in the Red: The Political Dynamics of Urban Fiscal Stress* (Albany, N.Y.: State University of New York Press, 1982); Terry Clark and Lorna Ferguson, *City Money: Political Processes, Fiscal Strain, and Retrenchment* (New York: Columbia

University Press, 1983); Robert P. McGowan and John M. Stevens, "Local Governments' Initiatives in a Climate of Uncertainty," *Public Administration Review*, 43 (March/April 1983), 127–36; Carol L. Ellis, "Program Termination: A Word to the Wise," *Public Administration Review*, 43 (July/August 1983), 352–57; and Patricia W. Ingraham and Charles Barrilleaux, "Motivating Government Managers for Retrenchment: Some Possible Lessons from the Senior Executive Service," *Public Administration Review*, 43 (September/October 1983), 393–402.

SUGGESTED READINGS

Bardach, Eugene. *The Implementation Game: What Happens After a Bill Becomes a Law*. Cambridge, Mass.: The MIT Press, 1977.

Bingham, Richard D., and Marcus E. Ethridge, eds. *Reaching Decisions in Public Policy and Administration: Methods and Applications*. White Plains, N.Y.: Longman, 1982.

Bresnick, David A. *Public Organizations and Policy*. Glenview, Ill.: Scott, Foresman, 1982.

Brewer, Garry D., and Peter deLeon. *The Foundation of Policy Analysis*. Homewood, Ill.: Dorsey, 1983.

Browne, Jim. *Management and Analysis of Service Operations*. New York: Elsevier, 1984.

Cochran, Clarke E., Lawrence C. Mayer, T. R. Carr, and N. Joseph Cayer. *American Public Policy: An Introduction*, 2nd ed. New York: St. Martin's, 1986.

Dye, Thomas R., and Virginia Gray, eds. *The Determinants of Public Policy*. Lexington, Mass.: Lexington Books, 1980.

Gilbert, G. Ronald, ed. *Making and Managing Policy: Formulation, Analysis, Evaluation*. New York: Marcel Dekker, 1984.

Jones, Charles O. *An Introduction to the Study of Public Policy*, 3rd ed. Monterey, Calif.: Brooks/Cole, 1984.

Levine, Charles H., ed. *Managing Fiscal Stress: The Crisis in the Public Sector*. Chatham, N.J.: Chatham House, 1980.

Mazmanian, Daniel A., and Paul A. Sabatier, eds. *Effective Policy Implementation*. Lexington, Mass.: Lexington Books, 1981.

Miser, Hugh J., and Edward S. Quade, eds. *Handbook of Systems Analysis: Overview of Uses, Procedures, Applications, and Practice*. New York: Elsevier, 1984.

Mushkin, Selma J., and Frank H. Sandifer. *Personnel Management and Productivity in City Government*. Lexington, Mass.: Lexington Books, 1979.

Nachmias, David, ed. *The Practice of Policy Evaluation*. New York: St. Martin's, 1980.

Nagel, Stuart S. *Policy Evaluation: Making Optimum Decisions*. New York: Praeger, 1982.

_____. *Public Policy: Goals, Means, and Methods*. New York: St. Martin's, 1984.

Nay, Joe N., and Peg Kay. *Government Oversight and Evaluability Assessment: It Is Always More Expensive When the Carpenter Types.* Lexington, Mass.: Lexington Books, 1982.

Nigro, Lloyd G., ed. *Decision-Making in the Public Sector.* New York: Marcel Dekker, 1984.

Palumbo, Dennis J., Stephen B. Fawcett, and Paula Wright, eds. *Evaluating and Optimizing Public Policy.* Lexington, Mass.: Lexington Books, 1981.

Palumbo, Dennis J., and Marvin A. Harder. *Implementing Public Policy.* Lexington, Mass.: Lexington Books, 1981.

Pressman, Jeffrey L., and Aaron Wildavsky. *Implementation,* 3rd ed. Berkeley, Calif.: University of California Press, 1984.

Quade, Edward S. *Analysis for Public Decisions,* 2nd ed. New York: Elsevier, 1982.

Ripley, Randall B. *Policy Analysis in Political Science.* Chicago, Ill.: Nelson-Hall, 1985.

Rosenthal, Stephen R. *Managing Government Operations.* Glenview, Ill.: Scott, Foresman, 1982.

Steiss, Alan Walter. *Management Control in Government.* Lexington, Mass.: Lexington Books, 1982.

Wholey, Joseph S. *Evaluation and Effective Public Management.* Boston: Little, Brown, 1983.

14

Government Regulation

REGULATING various aspects of our economic and social life is a longstanding part of the administrative scene at all levels of government, especially the national level. As suggested in chapter 12, much of what the national government does has an impact on individual citizens, private corporations and other business enterprises, agricultural producers and marketers, labor unions, and state and local governments. But some functions are explicitly regulative in nature, setting ground rules for many private—especially economic—activities. The first steps at the national level in this regard were taken in the late 1800s and were aimed at punishment for, then prevention of, abuses in the marketplace—prosecuting antitrust violations and price-gouging, for example. In this century, government regulation has become more far-reaching, focusing not only on preventing certain kinds of practices but also on requiring that certain operating standards and requirements be met. "Thus, before new drugs can be put on the market, they must be shown to meet the standards of *safety* in use and *efficacy* [effectiveness] for the purposes intended."[1] Other examples of operating standards include accuracy in information supplied to consumers—the "truth-in-packaging" or "truth-in-lending" requirements enacted mainly in the 1970s. Since 1960, more than a dozen new regulatory agencies in the national government have been created, with scores of new regulatory statutes. Certainly, regulatory actions touch virtually every part of our lives—our transportation (seat belts, bumper guards, freight rates), the food we eat, what can or cannot go into our beverages (for example, saccharin), medications that may be used to treat disease, chemicals used to treat clothing and furniture and paints, and the like. Some fifty-five major agencies employed about 77,500 people in fiscal 1984 (down about 13,000 from fiscal 1980), and spent approximately $7 billion for regulatory programs (though spending, too, was down from fiscal 1980 levels).[2] In addition, many of the post-1970 regulations have been of a different type from most previous ones. Economist Paul MacAvoy has noted the significant differences between what he called "traditional" regulations—emphasizing price control and service enhancement—and "new" regulations—designed to prevent harm from a process, product, or their side effects.[3] "New" regulations incorporate social as well as economic goals into the regulatory process; they have thus tended to be farther–reaching in their effect. (We will deal more fully with this distinction, later in this chapter.)

Some government actions seemingly unrelated to regulating private lives in fact do so. These include local zoning laws; housing loan programs that have an income minimum, effectively cutting off many poorer citizens from a chance to buy homes in the suburbs; school desegregation guidelines; the whole complex of equal opportunity requirements in employment, housing, and education; minimum wage laws; and tax policies at all levels of government. National and state energy policies touch many areas of our lives—auto travel, home insulation, energy conservation, and so on. Also, state and local regulation of public utilities directly affects utility rates paid by consumers.

The whole subject of government regulation in a "free enterprise" system is a bit complicated. Some contend that the most effective regulator in the marketplace is *competition* among those seeking to attract the buying public, and they argue that government regulation, by interfering with free-market mechanisms, works to the disadvantage of both consumers and producers. Advocates of government regulation, however, see greater need to monitor and guide the course of competition, believing that a completely unrestrained market will lead to monopoly practices and a lower quality of goods and services. In the twentieth century, the national government has tried increasingly to strike a balance between regulating producers and permitting, indeed encouraging, competition in the marketplace, supporting both the right of consumers to products that meet certain standards of safety and effectiveness, and the right of producers to a decent profit.

Regulatory activities are carried on by a wide variety of government entities, as suggested earlier. Though we will deal with regulation in its broader contexts, this chapter will focus on the *independent regulatory boards and commissions* of the national government, numbering about a dozen, which combine features of legislative, executive, and judicial bodies and consequently are organized somewhat differently from most other agencies. We will discuss their origins, both societal and political; analyze the formal and political setting in which they operate, and with what consequences; and discuss some of the most volatile issues concerning government regulation in the past twenty years.

THE RISE OF GOVERNMENT REGULATION

Historically, government regulatory activities have taken one of two forms: (1) putting certain limits on prices and practices of those who produce commercial goods; and (2) promoting commerce through grants or subsidies, on the theory that such payments are a public investment that will yield greater returns for the consuming public in the form of better goods and services. A prime example is airline subsidies.[4] The first of these has a longer history than the second.

Regulation of interstate commerce under Congress's direction was a constitutional power of the national government (in Article I, Section 8) right from the start. Yet for virtually all of our first century as a nation, responsibility fell to the states to carry on most of whatever regulation existed—for example, transportation tolls on and across rivers, prices farmers had to pay to grist mills and cotton gins, water rates, and railroad fares. In the period of industrialization after the Civil War, the national government gradually assumed more responsibility for both controlling and promoting commerce, though the states still played an important role in developing and testing ways of controlling prices and commercial practices. As the emerging national economy grew and flourished, however, pressure began to mount for the national government to enter more extensively into the regulatory arena. It stemmed from strong demands that abusive practices of the railroad industry, in particular, be brought under control. State regulatory agencies, some of which were quite active, lacked jurisdiction to deal with enterprises such as rail companies that crossed state lines. Beginning with the New Deal, the national government came to exercise primary responsibility for both controlling and promoting economic activity. Though the states still are primary regulators of a few industries such as insurance, and secondary regulators of industries such as banking, Washington now is the center of regulatory activity.[5]

Making government policy has been regarded as a legislative power under the Constitution.[6] Yet Congress and most state and local legislatures have found it difficult to write all the varied and detailed provisions that are necessarily part of governing a dynamic and complex society. There are two dimensions of the problem for a legislative body. First, most legislatures lack the time and technical expertise required to establish detailed rules and regulations on such complex subjects as nuclear energy, monetary policy, air safety, or exploration for and marketing of natural gas. As these and other areas of policy became important, it was increasingly necessary to create agencies able to deal with them. Second, even if legislatures had the time and skills, a large, collective decision-making body lacks the flexibility needed to adjust existing rules and regulations to changing conditions, again justifying creation of other entities to concentrate on each area. Thus, even in the nineteenth century in the national government, it was apparent that it would be necessary to delegate legislative authority to administrative agencies, with Congress monitoring their operations and adjusting their legislative charters, but doing little actual regulation. This pattern has been followed in the twentieth century as well, at all levels of government. In a very real sense, then, *regulation emerges as the outcome of legislative delegation of authority.* Thus any strengths or weaknesses of regulatory agencies and processes can be attributed in the first instance to actions of local, state, and national legislatures.

The first major institutional development in the national government was creation in 1887 of the Interstate Commerce Commission (ICC) in response to public disenchantment with the railroads, especially in the Mississippi Valley and the West. Unlike the eastern portion of the country, where numerous rail lines were engaged in vigorous competition, the nation's midsection and expanding West were served by a small number of railroads, which were thus able to engage in near-monopoly practices. Establishment of the ICC signaled a clear change from the prevailing notion of governmental action taken to punish unlawful acts after they had occurred. This was the first step to *prevent* such acts from occurring, and to do so by laying down rules which applied to a *class* of industries and actions, relieving the government of the need to proceed on the previous case-by-case basis in the courts.

Public pressure for controlling industry became stronger in the late 1800s and early 1900s, led by men such as James Weaver of the Greenback party in the 1888 presidential election, and especially William Jennings Bryan. The great "trust-buster," Theodore Roosevelt, was followed into the White House four years later by Woodrow Wilson; both men favored government measures to maintain economic competition and fair trade practices. Franklin Roosevelt opened the way for even more stringent and far-reaching regulation in the wake of the stock market crash of 1929 and other economic woes of the Great Depression. These individuals and their allies, and the policies they promoted, led to a significant increase in the scope of national government regulation.

The Sherman Antitrust Act of 1890 made it illegal to conspire to fix fares, rates, and prices, and to monopolize an industry, though enforcement mechanisms were not provided for in the original act. In 1903 the Antitrust Division of the Justice Department (not an independent regulatory agency) was created to direct enforcement of the Sherman Act. This proved difficult due both to unclear language in the law and to lack of authority delegated to the division. The result was increasing reliance on the courts to interpret legislative language and, some said, an inappropriate and perhaps excessive involvement of the courts in direct policy making. With delegation of authority to the ICC as a precedent, Congress attempted to solve the problem by creating another independent regulatory agency modeled after the ICC.[7] In 1914 the Federal Trade Commission (FTC) was established to assist in antitrust enforcement, principally by interpreting and enforcing provisions of the Clayton Act (passed the same year) which prohibited price discrimination if the purpose or effect of such discrimination was to lessen competition or to create a monopoly.[8] The FTC's involvement eased the burden on the courts, though it did not remove it entirely;

the FTC has been active continually over the years in settling antitrust questions. The FTC also was given responsibility for controlling deceptive trade practices, but until 1938 this was not its primary function.

Subsequently, other entities modeled after the ICC and FTC were also established. The Federal Power Commission (FPC) was created in 1920 to regulate interstate sale (wholesale) of electric energy, and the transportation and sale (including rates) of natural gas;[9] in 1977 the FPC was reorganized as the Federal Energy Regulatory Commission (FERC) and made part of the newly created Department of Energy. The Federal Communications Commission (FCC), established in 1934, regulates civilian radio and television communication (except for rates), as well as interstate and international communications by wire, cable, and radio (including rates). The FCC assigns frequencies and licenses operators of radio and television stations, and has become more involved in issues concerning cable television franchises and pay television. The Securities and Exchange Commission (SEC), also founded in 1934, was one means used by the government to try to prevent a repetition of the 1929 stock market crash. The SEC regulates stock exchanges and over-the-counter securities dealers, requires disclosures about securities offered for sale, and regulates certain practices of mutual funds and other financial investment concerns. The National Labor Relations Board (NLRB), established in 1935, regulates labor practices of employers and unions, and conducts elections to determine union representation when requested to do so. Finally, the Civil Aeronautics Board (CAB) was created in 1938 to regulate airline passenger fares and freight rates, to promote and subsidize air transportation, and to award passenger service routes to commercial airlines.[10] (Effective January 1, 1985, the CAB ceased to exist—the first major regulatory agency to close its doors permanently—as part of the Reagan administration's efforts toward deregulation.)

These seven agencies have been among the most prominent independent regulatory boards and commissions, but there are many others. Also, as government activity generally has increased, regulative responsibilities have come to be exercised by other types of agencies as well. It is possible to play the game of "Washington alphabet soup" with the EPA (Environmental Protection Agency), FAA (Federal Aviation Administration), FDA (Food and Drug Administration), and OSHA (Occupational Safety and Health Administration), to name only a few (see Table 14-1).

Mention should be made, also, of the complex of state regulatory agencies, many of which are patterned after those at the national level, and local regulatory activities that have an impact on certain local economic enterprises. As noted previously, states have primary responsibility for regulating insurance and are involved secondarily in regulation of banks. States also examine and license physicians, insurance agents, and real estate agents, and certify those qualified to practice law. In highly technical and professional fields, such as medicine and law, the respective professional associations have a key role in setting state standards for entry into the pro-

Table 14-1
SELECTED MAJOR U.S. REGULATORY AGENCIES*

Interstate Commerce Commission (ICC)
Founded in 1887. Regulates various aspects of routes, rates, and operations of interstate rail, trucking, bus, inland waterway, coastal shipping companies, and transportation brokers.
Budget: $51 million[a]   Personnel: 923[b]

Federal Reserve Board (FRB)
Founded in 1913. Makes and administers credit and monetary policy, and regulates commercial banks in the Federal Reserve System.
Budget: $84 million   Personnel: 1,529

Federal Trade Commission (FTC)
Founded in 1914. Regulates business competition, including some antitrust enforcement, and acts to prevent unfair and deceptive trade practices.
Budget: $64 million   Personnel: 1,168

Food and Drug Administration (FDA)
Founded in 1930. Located in HHS; conducts testing and evaluation programs—and sets standards of safety/efficacy—for foods, food additives and colorings, over-the-counter drugs, and medical devices; certifies some products for marketing; and conducts research in other areas such as radiological health, veterinary medicine, and the effects of toxic chemical substances.
Budget: $409 million   Personnel: 6,899

Federal Communications Commission (FCC)
Founded in 1934. Regulates interstate and international radio, television, cable television, telephone, telegraph, and satellite communications; licenses U.S. radio and television stations.
Budget: $92 million   Personnel: 1,868

Securities and Exchange Commission (SEC)
Founded in 1934. Regulates issuance and exchanges of stocks and securities; also regulates investment and holding companies.
Budget: $108 million   Personnel: 1,950

National Labor Relations Board (NLRB)
Founded in 1935. Conducts elections to determine labor union representation; prevents and remedies unfair labor practices.
Budget: $131 million   Personnel: 2,603

Equal Employment Opportunity Commission (EEOC)
Founded in 1964. Investigates and rules on charges of racial (and other arbitrary) discrimination by employers and unions, in all aspects of employment.
Budget: $159 million   Personnel: 2,976

Environmental Protection Agency (EPA)
Founded in 1970. Issues and enforces pollution control standards regarding air, water, solid waste, pesticides, radiation, and toxic substances.
Budget: $655 million   Personnel: 11,288

Occupational Safety and Health Administration (OSHA)
Founded in 1970. Located in Department of Labor; develops safety and health standards

Table 14-1 (continued)
SELECTED MAJOR U.S. REGULATORY AGENCIES

for private business and industry; monitors compliance and proposes penalties for noncompliance.
Budget: $213 million   Personnel: 2,210

Consumer Product Safety Commission (CPSC)
Founded in 1972. Develops and enforces uniform safety standards for consumer products and can recall hazardous products.
Budget: $34 million   Personnel: 568

Nuclear Regulatory Commission (NRC)
Founded in 1975. Issues licenses for nuclear power plant construction and operation, and monitors safety aspects of plant operations.
Budget: $429 million   Personnel: 3,491

---

*Budget figures shown represent agency budget authority; personnel figures represent "full-time equivalent" employees. The Federal Reserve Board has no budget authority; its activities are financed exclusively through assessments paid by Federal Reserve System member banks.

aApproximate fiscal year 1986 budgets; calendar year 1985 figure given for the Federal Reserve Board.

bPersonnel figures are as of January 1985; calendar year 1985 estimate given for the Federal Reserve Board.

Sources: U.S. Government Manual, 1980–81 (Washington, D.C.: Office of the Federal Register, National Archives and Records Service, General Services Administration, 1980); *U.S. Government Manual, 1984–85* (Washington, D.C.: Office of the Federal Register, National Archives and Records Service, General Services Administration, 1984); and *Budget of the United States Government, 1986—Appendix* (Washington, D.C.: U.S. Government Printing Office, 1985).

---

fession. Indeed, in some instances formal state decisions amount merely to ratifying standard-setting actions taken by a professional association (the self-regulatory category of public policy noted in chapter 13).

Other state entities also have regulative impact. As noted earlier, public utility commissions have a great deal to do with setting *intra*state retail rates for electricity and natural gas, and some also have investigative capacities. An example of the latter function was an inquiry by the New York State Public Utility Commission into operations of Consolidated Edison, which provides electricity to New York City, after a major blackout in July 1977. State commerce commissions regulate commercial activity occurring entirely within state boundaries and can have an influence on shipping rates and other shipping practices, particularly. Liquor control boards (in some states there are state-run liquor outlets), recreation departments, and environmental protection agencies are further examples of state entities that affect private economic enterprise. These all can act on their own authority and initiative without being subject to decisions made at the national level. However, in some areas of regulation state and national agencies have collaborated on standard setting, accounting systems, and the like, contributing to the patterns of specialized intergovernmental contacts discussed in chapter 5. Examples include cooperation between the ICC,

FDA, FCC, and FTC, and their respective state counterparts,[11] and in recent times, between state and national EPAs.

At the local level, regulation of business activities most often involves granting licenses for establishments such as taverns. Other kinds of local regulative activities, however, can be very significant, such as housing and building codes, zoning ordinances, and transportation planning. There has been little research on local government regulatory impacts, which may be an unfair reflection on their scope and importance.

THE "NEW" SOCIAL REGULATION

The distinction between economic ("old") and social ("new") regulation warrants further examination. That distinction has been described as follows:

> While all regulation is essentially "social" in that it affects human welfare, [there are] some very significant differences. The old-style economic regulation typically focuses on *markets, rates, and the obligation to serve.* . . . On the other hand, the new-style social regulation *affects the conditions under which goods and services are produced, and the physical characteristics of products that are manufactured.* . . . The new-style regulation also extends to far more industries and ultimately affects far more consumers than the old-style regulation, which tends to be confined to specific sectors [of the private economy]. Whereas the effects of CAB regulation [were] largely limited to air carriers (including their stockholders and employees) and air passengers, the regulations of OSHA apply to every employer engaged in a business affecting commerce.[12]

As of the early 1960s the national government had significant economic regulatory responsibilities in just four areas: antitrust, financial institutions, transportation, and communications.[13] "In each of these areas, the policy objective was to prevent or mitigate the economic damage associated with provision of goods or services, typically within a single industry. Thus, while regulatory agencies might possess broad-ranging discretionary authority to influence actions within a specific industrial sector, their standards and guidelines generally did not affect the economy as a whole."[14]

How can we account for so drastic a shift in both the substance and the processes of government regulation? One explanation is that "[b]eginning with the growing concern about cancer in the late 1950s, but rapidly accelerating because of perceived threats to ecosystems some ten years later, a series of social regulatory initiatives thrust government . . . into a host of health, environmental protection, and safety roles."[15] These initiatives were backed by the growing environmental and consumer move-

Table 14-2
SELECTED REGULATORY AGENCIES ENGAGING IN "OLD" AND "NEW" REGULATION*

"Old"

Federal Communications Commission
Federal Reserve Board
Interstate Commerce Commission
Securities and Exchange Commission

"New"

Consumer Product Safety Commission
Environmental Protection Agency
Equal Employment Opportunity Commission
Federal Trade Commission
Food and Drug Administration
National Labor Relations Board
Nuclear Regulatory Commission
Occupational Safety and Health Administration

---

*Agencies listed here are those appearing in Table 14–1, classified according to their principal responsibilities.

Source: Adapted, with revisions, from Lawrence J. White, *Reforming Regulation: Processes and Problems* (Englewood Cliffs, N.J.: Prentice-Hall, 1981), pp. 32–33 and 36–39.

ments, as well as "the activities of other specialized interest groups mobilized at least in part by *heightened awareness of risks*."[16] Thus, social regulation (unlike economic regulation) is centrally addressed to minimizing—or at least reducing—"public involuntary and occasionally even voluntary exposure to risk."[17] Congressional response to these public and scientific pressures has taken several forms: delegation of broad discretionary powers to regulatory agencies (as in the case of the Clean Air and Clean Water Acts); defining and dealing with problems in narrower terms (for example, regulation of potentially hazardous chemicals); and enlarging Congress's own "role in determining how the goals of regulation will be attained."[18] (Note, again, the importance of the role of Congress, and the significance of legislative delegation of authority as the basis for regulatory activity.) Some of these initiatives (though not all) contributed to the emergence of *intergovernmental* regulation, discussed in chapter 5.

Dealing with the problem of risk, however, has not been easy. A fundamental difficulty has been *how to determine* the degree of risk involved in use of, or exposure to, a given product or substance (such as saccharin, caffeine, or tobacco), and at what point a level of product risk becomes unacceptable (as a *general* standard). Compounding the problem are the high economic stakes involved in risk assessment, because a finding of risk has come to carry with it the very real possibility of a product being banned or otherwise restricted in the marketplace. Furthermore, the need for technical expertise—and for *agreed-upon* criteria—in defining risk was joined to the issues mentioned above. Because of the economic stakes involved, however, little agreement has been reached on risk criteria. (Failure to reach agreement has not kept government regulators from defining—and applying—such criteria, even though they often remained a focal point of impassioned debate.) Finally, with expert opinion looming ever larger in disputes over just how much risk a given product or substance entails, the spectacle of ''expert versus expert'' (in public debates, legislative testimony, agency reports, and the like) has become more frequent. Thus the stature of experts and of their knowledge became a subissue within the larger context of regulatory politics (see chapter 3). (These issues emerged in connection with regulating products which many of us voluntarily use. The question of *involuntary* exposure to products such as hazardous chemicals or toxic wastes only compounded the matter, especially with regard to the potential urgency of making new rules and regulations for risk reduction.) In sum, as even the most casual observer of recent American politics can testify, considerable tension has characterized the regulatory arena, most of it centering on the new focus—and style—of regulating private economic activity.

WHY GOVERNMENT REGULATION HAS DEVELOPED: OTHER PERSPECTIVES

The extent of regulatory activities prompts us to ask what other factors account for its development.[19] One way to explain it is a scenario of deliberate decision by bureaucrats and their political allies to expand their sphere of influence over private-sector activities. While this may have occurred in a few instances, it is not generally applicable as an explanation. More important, in political scientist Herbert Kaufman's view, is the *unintended* growth of ''red tape'' as government responds to pressures for dealing with societal problems or accomplishing broad social objectives.[20] The average citizen, confronted with nuisances (such as noise pollution) and outright menaces (such as toxic wastes), reacts by saying that ''there ought to be a law against'' the problem. If enough organized opinion exists, pressure can be brought to bear on government to enact such a law. Kaufman suggests that regulations have become more widespread in just this way, focused particularly in two directions: *demonstrating compassion* for the individual, and *assuring representativeness and fairness* in governing processes.

Motives of compassion have led, first, to rules and regulations aimed at protecting people from each other—governing relations between buyers and sellers, employers and employees, universities and students, tenants and landlords, or lenders and borrowers.[21] Government has also been asked to alleviate various kinds of human distress—through Social Security payments, aid to the handicapped and the elderly, aid to the poor, disaster relief, toxic waste cleanup, unemployment compensation, and business subsidies. In all such cases rules and regulations accompany basic legislation to make it possible to administer such programs fairly and equitably.[22] The national government, in particular, has acted to ward off major disruptions in national (and international) economic and political systems—stepping in to mediate labor-management disputes in vital industries, attempting to bring inflation under control, protecting supplies of vital natural resources, or resolving international conflicts that menace the peace.[23] It is, of course, expedient politically for leaders to respond to pleas for governmental assistance; but that only increases the proliferation of rules and regulations accompanying government action.

Regulations also stem from the impulse to increase public representativeness in decision-making processes of government as a means of maintaining popular control and equitable treatment.[24] Provisions of the Administrative Procedure Act of 1946 require procedural fairness in the operations of administrative agencies (including detailed guidelines for advance notice and public participation in many aspects of administrative decision making). A maze of rules is designed to minimize dishonesty and corruption in public affairs ("There are watchdogs who watch watchdogs watching watchdogs"[25]). Also, America's tax laws reflect a desire that citizens receive a "fair shake" from their government. Yet all such protections involve lengthy and complex elaboration in substantive and procedural rules, which add still further to the red tape present in our society.

It would seem, in short, that regulation has been fostered by a desire—and a willingness—to have government protect individuals, groups of citizens, and society at large from many ills and evils. In virtually all cases, *no intent* to create red tape existed, but it inevitably accompanied each effort. The rise of regulation might well be explained, in sum, in the words of the comic strip character Pogo the possum, who once said: "We have met the enemy, and he is us!"

STRUCTURES AND PROCEDURES OF INDEPENDENT REGULATORY AGENCIES

The national government's independent regulatory agencies have certain features in common with other administrative entities, but differ in important respects. One similarity (already noted) is that agencies operate under authority delegated by Congress, and they must therefore be aware of congressional sentiment about their operations. On occasion, Congress as a whole has been persuaded to restrict regulatory activities in some way, as happened to the FTC in the late 1970s. Business groups and others who opposed the FTC's activism in restricting advertising and various other trade

practices persuaded Congress to control the FTC's discretion more tightly—
and even managed to shut down the Commission without funds for a short
time![26] A second similarity is that there can be functional overlap among
regulatory agencies, just as with other agencies. For example, during the
controversy over cigarette smoking and public health in the mid-1960s, one
question was whether allegedly deceptive radio and television advertising
of cigarettes was properly under jurisdiction of the FTC (responsible for
controlling deceptive trade practices) or the FCC (which generally regulates
radio and television advertising).[27] A third similarity is found in the fact
that politics is as important in the regulatory process as in other aspects of
public administration—maybe more important. While the design of government regulation seems to assume some separation between regulation and
''politics,'' in truth there is considerable effort expended by interested
groups and individuals to influence regulatory activity. Close ties usually
exist between clientele groups and so-called dependent regulatory agencies
(DRAs)—charged with regulating economic activity, but housed within an
existing Cabinet department or other executive structure. Examples include
the Agricultural Marketing Service in the Department of Agriculture, the
National Highway Traffic Safety Administration (NHTSA) in Transportation, and the FDA in Health and Human Services.[28] But regardless of the
type of regulatory agency, regulatory politics is a very real phenomenon.

Differences between independent regulatory agencies and others are
significant, however. Most obvious is the nature of their work; boards and
commissions are not direct program managers. Rather, they take charge of
setting out rules and regulations governing private-sector economic activity. A second, crucial difference is in the structural design of these agencies.
This design warrants further discussion.

Regulatory Structures

The structural design is a reflection of the basic premise that these are to be
''independent'' regulatory agencies—more independent of presidential
control and influence than other administrative entities, more independent
of congressional direction in day-to-day operation (though not in their ultimate accountability to Congress), and, significantly, independent of the
businesses and industries that they are to regulate. We shall discuss later
the degree to which operating realities match this design, particularly regarding those who are regulated, but for now it is important to understand
why the formal arrangements exist as they do.

First, regulatory agencies have plural, not individual, leadership.
Since 1950, chairmen of all regulatory agencies except the ICC have been
appointed to multiyear terms by the president, subject to Senate confirmation, and given authority to choose key staff people. The chairman also pre-
sides over meetings, has greater public visibility than other members, and,
on occasion, possesses considerable influence.

Second, commissioners or board members do *not* serve "at the pleasure of the president," as do Cabinet secretaries and other political appointees, and presidential powers to remove them are sharply curtailed. Their terms of office are fixed, and are often quite long—for example, the fourteen-year terms of Federal Reserve Board members. Also, terms of office are staggered—that is, every year or every other year only one member's term expires. Consequently, no president is able to bring about drastic shifts in policy by appointing several board members at once, nor is policy within the agency likely to change abruptly because of membership turnover. Third, each commission or board has an odd number of members, ranging from five to eleven, and decisions are reached by a majority vote. Finally, there must be a nearly even partisan balance among the members— a five-member board must be 3 to 2 Republican or Democratic, a seven-member commission must be 4 to 3 one way or the other, and so on.

The combined effect of these provisions is (or at least was intended to be) a greater degree of insulation from political manipulation of these agencies than of others in the executive branch. In particular, it was deemed centrally important to prevent presidential interference with regulatory processes and to make the agencies answerable to Congress. The effectiveness of political insulation can be questioned, however. Decisions clearly favoring some interests over others are not uncommon, though most decisions have substantive as well as political roots. The larger purpose behind organizing the agencies in this manner is to protect the public interest in preference, and sometimes in opposition, to private economic interests. But where and how to draw the line between them is frequently decided through the political process rather than as a result of clearly defined boundaries.

Does regulatory structure make any real difference in the operations of regulatory agencies? Surprisingly, existing opinion on that question consists mainly of impressions and conventional wisdom rather than being based on careful research; there is very little of the latter. When comparing DRAs with independent regulatory commissions or boards (IRCs), there is no hard evidence that structure affects regulatory policy making. However, a 1980 study of twenty-three regulatory bodies (divided about equally between DRAs and IRCs) indicated that DRAs (1) have political environments much more supportive of regulation than do IRCs, (2) usually are designed to regulate *in the interests of* those regulated (which might explain the degree of support for regulation), (3) usually have other, nonregulatory functions that lead to larger work forces, larger budgets, and greater geographic decentralization, and (4) operate with more discretion and can make greater use of their rule-making powers.[29] It is perhaps significant that DRAs such as the FDA and the NHTSA generated political controversy during the 1970s, as did IRCs such as the FTC and the Consumer Product Safety Commission. Some DRAs, in other words, may be less inclined than in the past to regulate only in the interests of those regulated.

Regulatory Procedures

Procedures used by regulatory agencies fall into two broad categories: *rule making* and *adjudicatory proceedings*.[30] Agencies are empowered under the Administrative Procedure Act of 1946 to engage in *rule making*, an action quasi-legislative (in the manner of a legislature) in nature. Rule making involves issuing a formal rule that covers a general class of happenings or enterprises. It has about the same effect as a law passed by Congress or another legislature. For example, a rule issued by the ICC might limit the width of tractor-trailers on interstate highways or require lower shipping rates for products made from virgin materials than for those made from recycled material (as in the case of many paper products). Such rules apply to all individual operators, shippers, and others who come under their provisions. Rule making is characterized by its general applicability and by its uniformly affecting all within a given category.[31]

The rule-making process (see Figure 14-1) calls for agencies to issue notice of *proposed* rules, relevant to administration of any given statute, with a period of public comment lasting at least thirty days (it is often longer).[32] The notice of proposed rule making is published in the *Federal Register*—the government's official medium for disseminating information to the public concerning implementation of a statute. Written comments can be submitted by interested parties and, if deemed appropriate, oral

Figure 14-1   The Rule-making Process

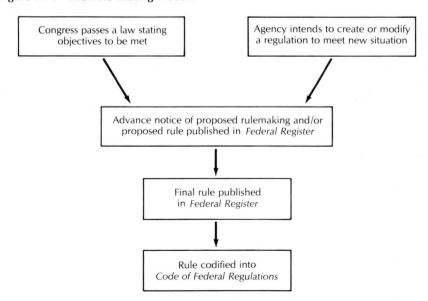

Source: The Federal Register: What It Is and How to Use It (Washington, D.C.: Office of the Federal Register, National Archives and Records Service, General Services Administration, 1980), p. 91.

presentations can also be made. While legislation can specify a deadline for publishing proposed rules and regulations, these deadlines are not always met. Considerable time can elapse between the effective date of a law and proposed rules, and again between public comment and issuance of a final rule—sometimes as long as seven years!

Several important points should be made about this process. First, it is almost always the *organized* public—clientele groups and other interest groups—that responds to opportunities for public comment; very few ''average citizens'' pay close attention to proposed rules (or anything else) in the *Federal Register*. Thus, the version of public opinion rendered in public comments is not likely to truly represent popular sentiment. Second, agencies vary in their responsiveness to public comment. The right to comment does not, by itself, confer influence over ultimate action by an agency, and more powerful groups can expect to have their views heeded more closely than those of some others. However, and perhaps most important, the fact that the general public *can* become involved in rule-making processes means that agencies must be mindful of public feeling, and must try to anticipate public reactions. In the late 1970s, seven independent regulatory agencies in the national government sponsored a program for what were called ''public intervenors''—groups funded by the agencies, with public monies, so that they could offer testimony in agency hearings that they otherwise could not afford.[33] Usually these were consumer groups and other less affluent organizations; often they voiced views on regulatory matters that provided balance to testimony by groups capable of ''paying their own way'' before the agencies. Thus the intervenor program enabled the seven agencies to obtain a fuller sampling of public feeling, while deliberating over new or revised regulations.

Adjudicatory proceedings, the second type of procedure, are quasi-judicial (courtlike), in that rulings are made on a case-by-case basis and procedural requirements resemble to some extent those observed in a court of law. In a majority of cases there is no formal proceeding prior to the decision. The agency routinely settles the question, such as FCC renewal of radio station licenses when they expire, or (in the past) CAB permission for airlines to pool their baggage facilities at a major airport.[34] In such instances an agency is likely to follow informal precedents set in earlier agency rulings involving similar circumstances, though regulatory agency precedents do not carry the same legal force as do court precedents in judicial decision making.

On some occasions, however, adjudicatory proceedings become quite formalized. This usually occurs when major interests are affected, involving thousands of people or millions of dollars, or when a case is contested, or when there is no applicable precedent.[35] Under such circumstances, the rules followed represent an adaptation of courtroom procedures and congressional hearing requirements, including rules governing attorneys, testimony, and so on.[36] Some agencies make use of a *public counsel*, who argues

the consumer's point of view at public hearings. A much more common figure in adjudicatory proceedings is the *administrative law judge*—formerly
known as hearing examiner—who acts for commissioners or board members in conducting public hearings, taking testimony, and subsequently
writing a preliminary recommendation, which is the basic factual summary
presented to the full commission or board. This procedure greatly reduces
the time it takes for an agency to reach its decision.

Administrative law judges, now numbering over 1,100, are among the
most highly specialized national employees and occupy a unique niche in
the public service; they are career employees assigned to regulatory agencies, yet they are independent of their nominal superiors and with a degree
of job security unusual even among merit employees. The nature of adjudication requires this; they are expected to avoid being arbitrary and unfair,
while exercising sufficient freedom to write recommendations on the basis
of information received and interpretation of those data.[37] Though their
recommendations do not carry final authority and can be appealed to the
full board or commission, administrative law judges enjoy considerable
prestige, and their recommendations are commonly accepted.[38]

The change of title in 1972 from hearing examiner to administrative
law judge is indicative of another change of some importance in the regulatory process. Because of the growth of government regulation and an increasing tendency to contest claims before regulatory agencies, the body of
legal doctrine known as *administrative law* has grown by leaps and bounds.
Decisions of regulatory agencies, which can be appealed to the U.S. Circuit
Court of Appeals in the District of Columbia, have mapped out what
amounts to new terrain in the law, and they have come by the hundreds.
One consequence of the growth of regulation during the 1970s is that administrative law is now the area of law with the largest number of cases re-
corded, a result of more frequent and more vigorous litigation.[39]

Apart from rule making and adjudicatory procedures, regulatory
agencies frequently attempt to resolve disputes or disagreements by encouraging informal, voluntary compliance with agency requirements. The
Federal Trade Commission, for example, employs three principal devices to
secure voluntary cooperation. The first is issuance of an *advisory opinion*, indicating clearly how the FTC would decide a particular question if it were to
come before the agency formally. Regulatory agencies, unlike courts, are
permitted to issue such opinions on questions that might, but have not yet,
come before them. The second is convening of a *Trade Practices Conference*, to
which all or most members of an industry are invited for a general airing of
their regulatory problems and, it is hoped, for promoting better understanding on all sides of the problems discussed. The third is a *consent order*,
representing an agreement voluntarily reached between the FTC and an industry before, or possibly during, an adjudicatory proceeding. (It is sometimes said that consent orders constitute a promise by an industry to stop
doing something it hasn't admitted doing in the first place![40]) Without de-

vices such as these, regulatory agencies would have an even more difficult time keeping up with their case loads than they do now.

THE POLITICS OF REGULATION

Regulatory politics is only rarely the partisan politics of Democrats and Republicans. Rather, it is the politics of *privilege*, in terms of gaining preferred access to decision makers by those with a stake in regulatory policies; and, to a lesser extent, of *patronage*, in the appointment of commissioners, board members, legal counsels, and staff personnel.[41] It also is a many-sided game played by the regulators themselves, who are sensitive to political pressures placed on their agencies and who are aware that reappointment may depend on political forces; by executives and legislators, because businesses, industries, and labor unions subject to regulation are important constituents; and by those regulated, who cannot afford not to play. One observer commented some years ago that the only ones who seemed to be excluded were consumers, though that has changed decisively; now, consumers play the game hard, and well.[42]

Regulatory politics also is characterized by issues of *distribution, quality,* and *price.* An excellent example is the burgeoning cable television industry. Communications regulators must answer a host of questions as cable television expands into more and more markets. Among the most important questions are: Who will receive cable service, to begin with? What criteria will be used in evaluating franchise applications, and how will those criteria be determined? What requirements (if any) will be imposed concerning quality of the picture provided, and the service available? How many channels will the cable system offer, and which ones? What prices will be charged, and how many price "packages" will be offered? While this is one of the most complex regulatory areas, similar issues arise in almost every other regulatory sphere.

The politics of regulation in the national government merits further discussion. A leading study of the FCC suggests that in addition to Congress there are five major institutional influences on broadcast regulatory policy: the FCC itself, the broadcasting industry, citizens' groups, the courts, and the White House.[43] It is another indication of the nature of regulatory politics, however, that the focal point of that discussion was Congress.[44] The relative political strength of these participants in broadcast regulation, their respective abilities to make Congress act, and rules Congress writes for the FCC and the courts (regarding access to judicial review of FCC decisions) all play a part in shaping broadcast policy. Regulatory policies in other areas result from similar configurations of institutions and political power.

The political setting of regulation includes many of the same features that apply to all other administrative agencies: legislative oversight by committees of Congress; appropriations concerns centering on the Appropriations Committees, OMB, and the Budget Committees; an increasing focus on potential effects of budget cuts and sunset laws; and attention to a political clientele—which for a regulatory agency is frequently *the very industry or industries it is responsible for regulating*. In addition, though the agencies are nominally bipartisan and thus seemingly removed from party struggles, the fact remains that business and corporate interests generally have their own partisan leanings. It follows that there might well be partisan undercurrents in regulatory politics, partly depending on which party holds the White House.

Furthermore, the degree of *independence* possessed by an agency may fall short of that apparently conferred upon it. For as already noted, the president, Congress, and powerful economic interests frequently interact with a regulatory agency, thereby affecting what it does. Critics of regulatory agencies have charged that they often protect the industries they are supposed to regulate more effectively than they regulate them—a charge not without some foundation. At the same time, however, another set of criticisms has begun to be heard, accusing some regulatory bodies of going too far in the exercise of their discretionary authority. Thus, regulatory agencies are increasingly "caught in a squeeze."

Independence from the President

Regulatory agencies are designed to answer to Congress's direction and to be shielded from presidential influence. Commissioners cannot be fired by the president; staggered terms inhibit presidential ability to "sweep out the old and bring in the new"; partisanship in the agencies' makeup is limited by law. At the same time, however, a president who serves two full terms—or even part of a second term, as in the case of Richard Nixon—can have a powerful impact on agency composition, and therefore policy directions. Former President Nixon, during five and one-half years in the White House, appointed or reappointed the *full* membership of eight regulatory agencies, including the FCC, CAB, FPC, and SEC, and most of the members of all other regulatory bodies.[45]

There have been other instances of presidential intervention in regulatory matters, besides simply appointing agency members. For example, in the 1950s Dwight Eisenhower's personal assistant, Sherman Adams, had to resign because of a scandal involving his having intervened on behalf of a friend, industrialist Bernard Goldfine, with the SEC and the FTC.[46] Jimmy Carter, in his 1976 presidential campaign, proposed that the chairman of the Federal Reserve Board (then Arthur Burns, a strong fiscal conservative) serve at the pleasure of the president, in order to enhance presidential control over national economic policy. In making his proposal, Carter may have been aware of the confrontation during the 1960s between another Democratic president—Lyndon Johnson—and another conservative FRB chairman—William McChesney Martin. Though nothing came of Carter's idea, it indicates some of the problems in the independent status of these agencies, especially those with real influence in areas of major policy concern to a president and to Congress (such as the FRB).

Jimmy Carter, as part of his major political themes, sought to bring regulatory bodies under tighter control and direction. In March 1978, Carter issued Executive Order 12044, designed to improve regulations in a number of ways—simplicity and clarity of the rules themselves, improved public access during rule making, and more publicity about "significant regulations under development or review." The executive order also sought more control by agency heads, some of whom were directly accountable to Carter.[47] Ronald Reagan, of course, went much further in an effort to slow regulatory growth by suspending, postponing, or cancelling numerous rules and regulations while they were still in the proposal stage. (We will discuss the Reagan regulatory initiatives later in this chapter.) Recent presidents (and Congress also, as we shall see) have moved against individual agencies, with some success, as public concern about regulation has increased.

One other aspect of presidential influence, in the realm of appointing and reappointing board or commission members, deserves mention. The most common practice is for presidents to avoid if possible any appointment that will generate controversy. The most convenient method is to allow leaders of regulated industries an informal voice in the selection process.[48] Not all presidents give equal weight to these informal recommendations, but rare indeed is the president who goes ahead with an appointment publicly and vigorously opposed by an industry.

There are two reasons for this presidential deference to industries. First, all presidents—regardless of political party—count on significant support from business and industrial leaders, and it is just common courtesy to one's supporters to "touch base" on a matter of considerable interest to them. Second, a president runs the risk of shaking business confidence and, in the long run, continued economic vitality by setting himself in perpetual opposition to the nation's business and financial communities. Consequently, most presidents take care to "keep their fences mended" with business and industry. What effect that has on a process of regulation assumed to be objective and detached is another matter, but it is the president's political needs that may account for some of the gap between promise and performance of regulatory bodies.[49]

Independence from Congress

From the standpoint of Congress as a whole, regulatory agencies have a great deal of independence. After an agency is established and the processes of regulation begun, the main contact members of Congress collectively have with it is in reviewing and voting on annual appropriations. Where Congress does exercise considerable influence, however, is through committee oversight of regulatory agencies, particularly if complaints have been received about the activities of a given agency. Because the agencies operate under delegated legislative authority, it is the prerogative of Congress to review—and possibly modify—the authority that was granted, and agencies are cautious about offending powerful interests in Congress that could trigger committee action to "rein them in." This does not happen often, but the possibility does exist.

At times Congress's interaction with, and influence over, a regulatory agency is quite direct and forceful. Two examples, both involving the FTC, illustrate this point. One concerns the controversy that raged during the 1960s and into the 1970s over health hazards said to be involved in smoking cigarettes. This involved efforts by several agencies—among them the FTC—to counter tobacco industry advertising that depicted smoking in a very favorable light. The story of this conflict highlights the problems and possibilities for a regulatory agency that takes the initiative in expanding the scope of regulation over a particular industry.[50]

There had been efforts for decades to combat the alleged evils of cigarette smoking but with a singular lack of success. Any attempt by concerned members of Congress or citizen groups to challenge the growth, marketing, advertising, or use of tobacco products was rebuffed by a tobacco subsystem. That subsystem included several bureaus in the Department of Agriculture; tobacco growers, manufacturers, and marketers; and southern members of Congress, among them the chairman of the House Agriculture Committee, which had jurisdiction over tobacco questions. (Tobacco was—and is—big business in half a dozen southern states.)

But challenges to existing tobacco policy became more frequent during the 1950s as medical research indicating that smokers were more susceptible to respiratory and other diseases than were nonsmokers began to capture public attention. During this same period, governmental attention was drawn to possible health hazards of smoking; interest grew particularly within the U.S. Public Health Service, headed by the surgeon general. Data gathered in the 1950s led to increasing certainty in the 1960s that smoking was hazardous to one's health. A new public health subsystem was created, and pressures mounted on the tobacco lobby—still, however, without notable success.

In the early 1960s the FTC got into the fray. If Congress was unwilling to legislate any limitations on the tobacco industry, the FTC through its rule-making power was both willing and able to do so. The commission was responsible for controlling deceptive trade practices, among which was deception in advertising. A plan was proposed to require disclosure by cigarette companies of *all* effects of smoking, not just those that helped sell their product. The FTC proposed rules in 1964 that said cigarettes had to be labeled as a health hazard, and that advertising had to include mention of those health hazards.[51] The FTC held hearings on the rules, but the tobacco industry's main effort to "stem the tide" was directed toward Congress, particularly the committees on Interstate and Foreign Commerce. By attempting to have Congress decide the issue, the industry was signaling its clear understanding of political realities: the tobacco subsystem was much stronger on Capitol Hill than it was in the Public Health Service (spearhead of the drive for health warnings) or the FTC. Congress's response was to pass the Cigarette Labeling and Advertising Act of 1965, which established the National Clearinghouse for Smoking and Health as part of the Public Health Service, but also suspended FTC rule-making power over cigarette advertising for four years. A bill enacted under the banner of a public health measure was, in reality, more of a victory for the tobacco lobby than it was for the public health interests. The alternative for the industry was the far more threatening FTC rules, and the implicit possibility of further FTC action in the public health controversy.[52]

The role played by Congress and its relation to the regulatory agency in the cigarette controversy is indicative of the way regulatory politics can unfold. Both the tobacco and public health lobbies knew full well where their respective interests were most likely to be favorably treated; both attempted to maneuver the decision before the particular governmental entity that would best serve their interests; and neither scored a total victory. The cigarette interests got the FTC out of the rule-making—and, therefore, the policy-making–arena for four years, during which time they hoped public attention would diminish and pressures for health warnings would ease. The public health subsystem, on the other hand, had succeeded in having a health warning placed on cigarette packages, and the National Clearinghouse for Smoking and Health afforded those interests a first-rate opportunity to coordinate nationwide research and to publicize the results.

Congress was not immune to change in public sentiment about cigarettes during the latter part of the 1960s (rarely is it totally immune to widespread public feeling), so that as the tide of public opinion began to run in favor of health considerations, congressional resistance to the FTC and the rest of the health lobby moderated noticeably. With the FTC on the sidelines, other agencies and many private research organizations continued to accumulate health data on cigarettes and to exert political pressure on the tobacco industry. By the time the moratorium on FTC rule making expired in 1969, the balance of power between the two subsystems had changed markedly. Many in and out of Congress were ready to go further in requiring disclosures about health effects of smoking, and the tobacco lobby was much less able to resist those moves.

Since 1969 a new balance of power has been struck between those who might long for the good old days of pre–health–lobby success and those who would be perfectly happy to place a far tougher warning on packages, to limit sales of cigarettes, and to ban smoking entirely in all public places. The establishment of "No Smoking" areas in many restaurants and different seating sections on airliners is clear evidence that antismoking forces continue to exercise considerable influence.

The other example of direct congressional action against a regulatory body—the FTC, again—took shape in the mid-1970s when business groups mounted a concerted campaign to limit the FTC's regulatory authority over a wide variety of business activities. In part this effort was a reaction to vigorous FTC regulation, spearheaded by its activist chairman Michael Pertschuk; in the 1970s the agency was said by many to have "been more aggressive in confronting powerful corporate interests than at any [other] time in its 65-year history."[53]

Congress itself had increased the FTC's authority to make rules affecting broad economic interest groups rather than simply individual businessmen. Yet when the FTC began to use that new authority, it generated a considerable backlash. This is not surprising, in view of the wide range of enterprises the agency sought to regulate more closely—insurance, television, advertising, used car, and funeral industries, and agricultural cooperatives.[54] The most controversial actions included alternative proposals for restricting television advertising directed at children (so-called "kid-vid" regulations), including a possible ban on advertising of high-sugar snacks, and a proposed rule requiring funeral homes to itemize their prices.

The attack on the FTC was three-pronged. First, it was proposed that Congress be given a full legislative veto over all FTC actions. Another proposal would have reduced or eliminated funding for outside organizations, such as consumer groups, which had been used to pay expenses connected with giving testimony in commission hearings. Finally, proceedings then under way, such as the proposal regarding funeral prices, would have been halted.[55] Despite intense criticism voiced during congressional debate, the net result of the moves against the FTC was a decision in 1980 to trim its authority to police "unfair and deceptive" business practices. However, it was clear that as the Reagan administration took office, and public sentiment was less favorable toward vigorous regulatory action, the FTC's troubles were far from over. Unlike Jimmy Carter, President Reagan is in sympathy with efforts both to make regulation more efficient, in the abstract, and to curtail what many in the business community see as harassment of private enterprise.[56]

With these conflicts in mind, we can ask if regulatory agencies are truly independent of Congress. The answer is "no," but a word of caution is in order. They were never designed to be *completely* independent, after all. But they can gain some measure of independence if their political support is strong enough—including that in Congress. An "essential characteristic of independent regulatory commissions is their need of political support and leadership for successful regulation in the public interest."[57] It is the exception rather than the rule to find an agency that is truly an "independent operator," since neither Congress nor industry is likely to consent willingly to such an arrangement. Agencies that try to act independently find themselves reined in by congressional committees or Congress as a whole far more often than they are turned loose. It is the nature of the game, depending on the balance of political forces at work. But a balance of *some* kind there almost always is, and agencies have to adapt to this, ensuring if possible that their support is always stronger than their opposition.[58]

The question of agency independence from the president and from Congress is one with no final answer. William Cary, onetime chairman of the Securities and Exchange Commission, once described regulatory agencies as "stepchildren whose custody is contested by both Congress and the Executive, but without very much affection from either one."[59] That sounds more like being caught in a crossfire between the White House and Capitol Hill—a situation in which regulatory agencies often find themselves. If neither the president nor Congress regularly lends support to agencies, and support is still needed, that creates a dilemma from which one escape seems most promising. They can try to reach acceptable operating understandings with the industries they regulate, in exchange for *their* support—which poses a whole new set of problems for agency independence.

Independence from Those Regulated

Among the most intense criticisms of regulatory agencies has been the charge that they are "owned," unduly influenced, or have been coopted by the industries they are supposed to regulate. The most devastating critiques probably were those of "Nader's raiders," associated with consumer advocate Ralph Nader, aimed at such venerable agencies as the ICC and (ironically) the FTC. Charges of the regulators' lack of experience, unfamiliarity with problems of particular industries, political cronyism in appointments, and lack of initiative and vigor in pursuing violators of regulatory requirements were the most common ones made. The central theme underlying such allegations was that regulatory agencies do more to protect and promote "their" industries than to regulate industry in the public interest.

In their most sweeping indictment, "Nader's raiders" characterized the entire system of government regulation as being "monopoly makers."[60] In his introduction to that work, Nader charged that "government economic regulation has frustrated competitive efficiencies and has promoted monopolistic rigidities advocated by the regulatees themselves."[61] In addition, he deplored "corporate socialism, a condition of . . . statecraft wherein public agencies control much of the private economy on behalf of a designated corporate clientele,"[62] and called the consumer the "first victim" of such an arrangement between government and corporate power. These allegations were made in connection with attempts to reform the government institutions responsible for economic regulation. While not entirely successful, they have changed the face of regulation considerably and influenced the course of the consumer movement.

However, the fact remains that those serving on regulatory agencies are not expected to isolate themselves personally from those with whom they deal. On the contrary, some interaction is considered necessary in order for those in the agency to understand fully the workings of the regulated industry. How to maintain that interaction and still keep an acceptable degree of detachment and objectivity is the central question.

Regulators have all kinds of direct social and professional involvement with individuals in the industries they regulate.[63] Frequently contact occurs in private, informal rule-making and adjudicatory proceedings, where problems can be addressed without all the trappings of a formal regulatory action. Just what comes out of such meetings in terms of protecting the public interest is not easy to determine (if the "public interest" itself can be defined), and the private nature of the conferences is one irritant to observers such as Nader and the public interest lobbying group Common Cause. A 1977 decision by the District of Columbia Court of Appeals, however, held that once a government agency asks for public comment on a proposed rule, its officials should refrain from discussing the proposal privately with interested parties. If such discussions do take place, full memoranda on what was said must be put in the public record. Many agencies had routinely written such memos about formal meetings with outsiders trying to influence the shape of a rule, but they seldom had been placed in public files. The court ruling changed that, putting industry lobbying into a fishbowl of potential public scrutiny.[64]

Also, regulatory agency members routinely attend industry conferences, where they are frequently the main speakers, and friendly conversation during the social hour is not at all out of place under such congenial circumstances. Then there are private chats in agency offices, out-of-town visits to companies by agency members, and luncheons and dinners where regulators and industry representatives are part of a larger social gathering.

Three things should be emphasized. First, these are routine occurrences, and not inconsistent with the job of regulation. Second, private industries have a legitimate economic self-interest to uphold, and there is a fear among industry executives that if they do nothing to present their case to government regulators, their competitors will. Third, out-and-out industry pressure on a regulator is rare—bribery is almost nonexistent, as are blatant attempts to intimidate or otherwise pressure regulatory officials. Direct exchanges of views, combined with the indirect pressure that can be placed on an agency through the president and Congress, usually are enough to ensure industries of a fair hearing.

The fact that regulatory agencies and their members are expected to be expert as well as detached raises yet another problem: How does one become knowledgeable about an industry without also coming to share that industry's values and outlooks? Appointees to regulatory agency positions often come from industry backgrounds, a natural training ground for acquiring relevant expertise but also a likely place to acquire perspectives favorable to industry interests. Also, a "revolving door" pattern has emerged—regulators often can expect to go to work, or go *back* to work, for a regulated industry when their terms expire. Other agency appointees have backgrounds that hardly equip them to deal with the industries—some are named as political favors, others simply because they are noncontroversial appointees (sometimes both). In either instance, the industry has an advantage; commission or board members are likely to be sympathetic to—or else largely ignorant of—the industry's problems, and consequently reluctant to intervene in industry affairs.

Sometimes an industry "maverick" is named to a regulatory agency, someone who does not share the predominant economic or social outlook of the industry, although he or she has been a part of it. Former FCC Commissioner Nicholas Johnson fits this description; during his term of office he was often openly critical both of the broadcast industry and of the FCC itself. But such appointments are exceptions to the rule; Johnson himself was frequently a dissenting minority of one in FCC decisions on everything from radio and television license renewals to public participation in making broadcasting policy. The pattern of appointing people with industry backgrounds is so well entrenched, however, it is considered news when someone is rejected by the Senate for that reason. In 1973, for example, the Senate refused to confirm an attorney for Standard Oil of California, nominated by Richard Nixon, to the Federal Power Commission; the Senate vote against him was 50–43. During Senate debate, Commerce Committee Chairman Warren Magnuson (D.-Washington) warned the president against such nominations, but it was how he phrased his warning that was particularly revealing:

> . . . the Senate is *again* asked to accept, for an independent regulatory agency with vast powers over an industry which affects vital national interest, *yet one more* nominee whose professional career has been dedicated to the furtherance of the private interests of that industry.[65]

The need for both expertise and detachment in regulatory agencies clearly presents a problem not easily solved.

Consumers, Consumerism, and Regulation

The consumer movement has had significant impact on government regulatory activity. Prior to the rise of consumerism, almost all major economic interest groups represented producers—those involved in growing, processing, shipping, and selling products in the marketplace. These groups naturally sought to shape market regulation in favor of producer needs and preferences. Consumers were largely unrepresented in any organized fashion. However, major conflicts over cigarettes and public health, and over auto safety, began to change that situation in the 1960s.

Leaders of the budding consumer movement looked to regulatory agencies and other administrative bodies to promote and protect consumer interests. They apparently placed little faith in Congress, reasoning that legislators would be far more likely to respond to producers' wishes than to contrary pressures applied by consumer groups. Rightly or wrongly, they chose to make use of administrative weapons in fighting their political battles, which of course brought them into conflict with both producers and Congress. Advocates of change, such as the Nader organizations, saw in addition a need to reform administrative regulation in order to maximize consumer gains. While not all consumer groups agreed with that view, they generally supported such efforts.

There is little question that consumerism has changed the face of government regulation, both because of new political pressures applied and because of primary reliance on regulatory agencies. "The consumer movement that began in the 1960s has given greater force to *administrative law as a tool of social change*. The procedures and the laws that agencies use for policy making are not new for the most part. What is new is their use by organized, professionally staffed consumer groups."[66] A study of consumer protection in the early 1970s noted that "the administrative process has proved to be the key element in consumer protection policy. . . ."[67] Pressure was placed on Congress, with some success, not only to respond directly to consumer demands but also to increase access to agencies and to the courts for redress of consumer grievances. Congress's record in these respects is a mixed one, but even that represents an improvement over the past, when consumer groups were much weaker and less organized, and could point to only a handful of gains over long periods of time.

The Nader phenomenon and the rise of consumerism are not unrelated. There is informed opinion that without the Nader organizations— their expertise, full-time commitment, and vigorous criticism of both corporate power and regulatory efforts—the consumer movement would not enjoy the influence it has. By awakening consciousness of consumer interests among the general public, Nader and others strengthened, perhaps created, a constituency with sufficient political power to contest the influence of long-established producer groups. Consumer pressure clearly accounted for much of the increase in government regulation during the 1970s, and for increased political conflict over regulation.

Now, however, the pendulum may be swinging the other way; there seems to be more resentment of—than sustained support for—distinctly consumer-oriented regulation. Both Congress and the president appear more sympathetic to producers than was the case only ten years ago. More important, perhaps, is the fact that public opinion is shifting as to what is appropriate government regulation. Illustrative of the interplay between regulators and public sentiment (and of the difficulties confronting conscientious regulators) is the case of the FDA. During the 1960s and 1970s, this agency acted frequently to ban various products and substances said to endanger human health, because they were either unsafe or ineffective, or both. FDA officials said more than once that the agency, under existing legislation, had no choice but to remove a product from the market when its potential disease-causing properties were demonstrated under controlled laboratory conditions. This was an especially important position, politically, in the controversy over the FDA's proposal to ban saccharin, which in a number of Canadian tests was linked to cancer, first in laboratory rats, then in human males.

The FDA's stand caused a rather powerful coalition to question the basic law requiring FDA action against carcinogens (substances linked to cancer). Key elements in that coalition were food companies, manufacturers of soft drinks (including diet soft drinks), and perhaps most important, an aroused group of citizens—for example, diabetics—who for various reasons needed or wanted sugar-free beverages available. Pressure was applied on both sides of the issue, with some arguing that suspected carcinogens should be banned as required by law, regardless of public outcry, and others arguing that it was time to update 1958 legislation requiring FDA action, to permit the FDA to examine potential benefits in relation to the cancer risk.[68] Any time an agency receives 70,000 angry letters over a single issue there is reason for it to reconsider its decision, which the FDA did. Its course of action has been affected, however, more by congressional pressure for a delay in the effective date of a saccharin ban than by either direct industry or public pressure. The latter has to be translated into congressional action to be truly effective.

The proposed saccharin ban and public reaction to it were not the only episodes where the general public has been critical of regulatory action. Another case involved Congress itself mandating an auto ignition interlock system requiring drivers to "buckle up" before they could start their cars. Public response was so intense that a bill repealing the requirement was quickly introduced and passed. Significantly, it was cosponsored in the Senate by a liberal Democrat (Eagleton of Missouri) and a Conservative-Republican (Buckley of New York).[69] As one observer put it, "Congress learned . . . that the public tolerance for forced regulation is low."[70]

Still another issue highlighting growing public frustration and disenchantment with regulation was the controversy over Laetrile as a treatment for cancer patients. Laetrile—a substance extracted from apricot pits and said by some to be effective as a cancer treatment—has not been an approved drug on the FDA lists. Yet during the late 1970s demands became more insistent that those who wanted to be treated with Laetrile should have the chance, FDA approval or not, with some arguing that this was an issue of freedom versus government control. The respective points of view have been summed up as follows:

> Freedom is the issue. The American people should be allowed to make their own decisions. They shouldn't have the bureaucrats in Washington, D.C. trying to decide for them what's good and what's bad—as long as it's safe. . . . The FDA is typical of what you get in regulatory agencies—a very protective mentality in bureaucrats who want to protect their own jobs and their own po-

sitions. It's easier for them to say "No" to a product—Laetrile or anything else—than it is to say "Yes." . . . The simple fact is that stringent drug regulation for society as a whole limits therapeutic choice by the individual physician who is better able to judge the risks and benefits for the individual patient. I think the whole argument centers on FDA's intervention on the basis of a product's efficacy. . . . I agree that no one should be allowed to defraud the public, but you don't need to rely on the FDA. . . . The real question is: Should the government be protecting you from yourself?[71]

And, on the other side of the Laetrile/FDA question:

I believe in a society that protects the consumer from the unscrupulous vendor. There was a time in America when we gave free rein to the philosophy of *caveat emptor*: let the buyer beware. We abandoned that a couple of generations ago, and now we have all kinds of consumer protections built into our society.[72]

. . . instead of freedom of choice, it could be freedom of the industry to defraud the consumer. With the tremendous number of drugs available, it is not possible for the physician and the consumer to really have the information necessary upon which to base an informed judgment in regard to the safety and effectiveness [of a drug].[73]

These statements suggest that such disputes are likely to become more heated in the immediate future.

Regulatory agencies and others in government do not appear to be slacking off in their activities, however, as the following list indicates (though not all actions were in the direction of greater regulation).

Item: In another example of the scientific community calling for social regulation, the FDA was urged by nearly 6,000 health professionals to limit the use of salt in processed foods because of its contribution to high blood pressure, strokes, and heart attacks. Consistent with its policy of careful study of possible actions such as this, the FDA delayed a decision, pending a thorough review of relevant evidence.[74]

Item: In April 1984, controversial FTC regulations went into effect requiring funeral homes to provide families with detailed price lists of all goods and services associated with funerals. A spokesman for the funeral industry predicted a slight increase in the cost of a funeral, in part because of the additional paperwork necessary.[75]

Item: The Federal Aviation Administration's special inspection of the nation's 327 airlines in the spring of 1984 disclosed that while 95 percent followed safety rules quite diligently, there were disquieting exceptions. The report suggested the need for improved FAA surveillance of the industry (especially the commuter airlines, which have proliferated rapidly since deregulation of the airlines in 1978).[76]

Item: Under strong pressure from the Secretary of Health and Human

Services and from the FDA, aspirin manufacturers agreed early in 1985 to put warning labels on aspirin products. Government pressure was prompted by research findings that children and teenagers ill with flu or chicken pox were substantially more likely to develop the often fatal Reye's Syndrome when given aspirin, compared to children who did not take the drug for the same illnesses.[77]

Item: Some two dozen state governments made serious efforts during 1985 to pass mandatory seat belt laws, following enactment of such statutes in New York, New Jersey, and Illinois. This legislative activity was prompted in part by a national Department of Transportation order requiring "automatic passenger protection devices" (in most instances, air bags) in all 1990 new car models, unless two-thirds of the nation's population is covered by mandatory seat belt laws by April 1989.[78]

Item: In March 1985, the Environmental Protection Agency (EPA) ordered gasoline refiners to remove more than 90 percent of the lead in leaded gasoline by the end of the year. The agency also said it might ban leaded gasoline altogether by 1988, in light of evidence of a "strong statistical relationship" between the amounts of lead in the air and high blood pressure. (The agency had estimated previously that 80 percent of lead in the air comes from leaded gasoline.)[79]

Whether such activity is perceived by most consumers as being in their ultimate interest appears to be at the core of current controversies surrounding government regulation. Clearly, not all consumers share the values and objectives of consumer groups, contributing to the squeeze on regulatory agencies and others, such as the Department of Transportation, that have been increasingly active in regulation. It has been well known for some time, for example, that most people do not use their auto seat belts, despite impressive statistical evidence that use of seat belts can greatly reduce risk to life and limb. General Motors at one time offered air bags as an option on its cars, but claimed buyers did not want them. Many people also resent mandatory pollution-control devices on their automobiles. Motorcyclists who opposed rules requiring them to wear safety helmets persuaded Congress in 1976 to withdraw the Department of Transportation's authority to levy sanctions against states refusing to make helmets mandatory; that authority remains suspended, despite an increase of 46 *percent* in motorcycle fatalities from 1976 to 1980.[80] The auto ignition-seat belt interlock system, referred to earlier, was defeated rather handily in Congress once the public's sentiments became evident. That could happen again—in auto safety, effectiveness of medicines, the safety of food products, and other areas.

Most of us, given the *abstract* choice between clean and polluted air, pure and impure food and drugs, and so on, would clearly select the former. But how to ensure and maintain such conditions is what the current controversies are all about. And what may be happening is simply a shift in prevailing political views about what constitutes appropriate regulation of particular products. Perhaps the best way to view such controversies is that this is a cyclical process, with the tide of public opinion ebbing and flowing on behalf of vigorous government regulation.

THE FUTURE OF GOVERNMENT REGULATION

Regulatory reform has been a recurring theme over the years, with every president since John Kennedy paying at least some public attention to the subject. Studies undertaken at presidential request, as well as other proposals, have become part of the reform literature.[81] Presidents Ford, Carter, and Reagan made regulatory reform a high-priority matter, and the issue has taken on greater urgency in and out of government.

Complicating regulatory reform, however, is the wide variety of motives, assumptions, and policy objectives that have given rise to reform efforts. More effective (and more *cost*-effective) regulation of the private sector is one potential goal. Another is enhancing regulatory agency accountability to the president; a third is increasing accountability to Congress.[82] Yet another is ending existing fragmentation in substantive areas of regulatory responsibility (for example, transportation); still another is *separating* responsibilities that can conflict, for example, *regulation* of an industry versus *promotion* of that industry's products. (Note that it would be both logically and politically difficult to pursue all of these, or even particular combinations, simultaneously.) At various times in the past twenty-five years, reform proposals have been put forward which embodied one or more of these emphases.[83]

Finally, of course, there is the policy option of pursuing *de*regulation— of reducing the national government's overall regulatory presence. Though this last goal has been most clearly identified with the Reagan administration, it was not Ronald Reagan's only regulation-related objective. Nor was he the first president to seek deregulation. Under Jimmy Carter, major steps were taken (especially in trucking, rail, and air transportation) to reduce regulatory agency activity and power.[84]

The Reagan Administration and "Regulatory Relief"

Ronald Reagan came to office committed to "regulatory relief" for American business, seeing this as "a cornerstone of [his] economic recovery program."[85] In the context of the values and objectives noted above, his program was founded on a combination of *deregulation* and *increased presidential control*, with apparent attention to more cost-effective regulation as well. Though here, as elsewhere, the president did not achieve all he sought, the impacts of his actions already are being felt, and will continue to be for some time.

The Reagan program consisted of four principal elements: (1) a review of existing rules, with intent to "defer, revise, or rescind existing and pending regulations where clear legal authority exists"; (2) a "marked slowdown" in the issuance of major new regulations; (3) relaxation of efforts to enforce existing rules; and (4) significant cuts in regulatory agency operating budgets (including personnel).[86] As noted, the president sought to establish more centralized (OMB) control over proposed new regulations, and over agency activities under existing regulations. Also, he directed that *cost-benefit analysis* be used in assessing the impacts of existing as well as proposed rules and regulations. In addition, he organized a Task Force on Regulatory Relief headed by Vice-President Bush, to examine ways to lessen the regulatory burden said to exist on many businesses. Finally, in another, less visible undertaking, top presidential aides began to explore possible ways of transferring regulatory authority from the national government to state governments, consistent with the president's intentions both to ease regulatory requirements and to shift responsibility to the states, in the spirit of "New Federalism."[87]

Wasting little time, the president—just nine days after taking office—froze 172 regulations pending when Jimmy Carter left the White House.[88] Subsequently the administration undertook efforts to rescind or modify numerous regulations. Many of these affected different aspects of the automobile industry (such as the automobile passive restraint standards of the National Highway Traffic Safety Administration [NHTSA], and various air pollution standards issued by EPA).[89]

The second element of the Reagan strategy—slowing the development of new rules—took hold very quickly. Following the initial freezing of pending regulations, both the president and vice-president moved effectively to extend that freeze. By August 1982, the administration claimed that "the flow of new rules had been reduced by one-third"—in terms of rules proposed, final rules promulgated, and number of pages in the *Federal Register* devoted to new or proposed rules.[90] "In addition, no major new areas of . . . regulation were opened up during the first two years of the administration. . . ."[91] While that has changed somewhat (for example, President Reagan's leadership in pressuring states to raise their minimum drinking ages to 21), new regulatory initiatives have been the exception, not the rule, since 1981.

The third strategic element—relaxing enforcement of existing regulations—appears to have been implemented rather broadly. Agencies as diverse as EPA, NHTSA, OSHA, and the Departments of Agriculture and the Interior conducted fewer investigations and inspections, evaluated fewer businesses for safety compliance, and issued fewer citations for violations.[92] In this respect, it is unmistakably clear that—for better or for worse—there was indeed "regulatory relief," even where the sheer number of rules and regulations did not change.

The fourth basic strategic element—budget and personnel reductions in regulatory agencies—also was pursued systematically.[93] Although a few agencies experienced increases in their budget allotments between fiscal 1982 and fiscal 1986, most saw their budgets reduced—some dramatically. For example, the Interstate Commerce Commission (ICC) was confronted with a cut of 40 percent over those four years, with its work force cut in half. The FTC's budget shrank from $78 million to $64 million, and its personnel dropped from 1,665 to 1,168 (a cut of 30 percent). The Nuclear Regulatory Commission budget was cut by about 35 percent; the Consumer Product Safety Commission's, by some 25 percent; OSHA's, by 12 percent. At the head of the list was EPA. President Reagan's fiscal 1986 budget included a request of $655 million for the agency, representing a reduction of 60 percent from the fiscal 1982 allocation of $1.6 billion. It also should be remembered that these figures are in *current* dollars; measured in constant dollars, the decline in funding is even more pronounced. If nothing else, these figures and others like them should lay to rest any doubts about the Reagan administration's seriousness of purpose in pursuing its agenda of regulatory relief.

In addition to these core elements of the Reagan strategy, efforts also went forward to consolidate presidential influence over regulatory processes (via OMB), and to establish cost-benefit analysis as a firm criterion for approving or disapproving regulatory activity. Two executive orders were central to these efforts. The first was Executive Order (EO) 12291, issued in February 1981. Under this order, agencies were obligated to: (1) apply cost-benefit analysis to all their rule making and adopt the least costly regulatory alternative (or explain why more costly options were chosen); (2) publish preliminary and final regulatory impact analyses (subject to OMB review) in the case of major rules (those costing at least $100 million annually to implement); and (3) carry out similar analyses for existing rules. OMB was placed in charge of the order's implementation.[94] The second order (EO 12498) was issued in January 1985, and "further strengthened OMB's grip on the regulatory process. The new order concentrated on controlling regulations *much earlier in their development* than the one issued in 1981."[95] Two features of these orders are worth noting: they represent a strong presidential effort to gain greater control of regulatory agencies, thereby reducing their independence from the president; and they emphasize quantifiable cost-benefit data as a (seemingly neutral) basis for regulatory policy decisions.

The use of cost-benefit analysis, however, has been challenged—successfully—on more than one occasion. So, also, has OMB's authority to review (and sidetrack) agency regulations. One instance was a Supreme Court decision just five months after issuance of EO 12291 (in June 1981), reaffirming agency powers—in this case, those of OSHA—to issue regulations based only on their *economic and technical feasibility*, rather than requiring a cost-benefit analysis. OSHA adopted health and safety standards in 1978, mandating steps to be taken by textile manufacturers to protect workers from exposure to cotton dust. The Court ruled that the cotton dust standard was feasible on both counts. It also noted that, while Congress had specifically required cost-benefit analyses in some other statutes, it had not included such language in the 1970 law creating OSHA. Another case followed the NHTSA's decision to rescind automobile passive restraint regulations. A large part of the insurance industry mounted a strong, successful court challenge to the cost-benefit determinations the agency used in reaching that decision.[96] As for OMB, numerous hearings have been held in Congress (especially the House) during the past few years, at which allegations of OMB ''intervention'' and ''interference'' with regulators (notably EPA) increasingly have been heard.[97] Clearly, the Reagan administration has remained consistent in its efforts to implement ''regulatory relief''; equally clearly, powerful forces in Congress and the nation remain committed to effective regulation (as *they* define that term), even if it means taking on a popular president and his political supporters.

As always, however, all may not be as it appears in this kind of policy debate. For one thing, it is not uncommon to find some businesses that *wish to remain regulated*—they regard regulation as advantageous to their interests. Two examples of this sentiment are various segments of the trucking industry, including the Teamsters union (even though a deregulation bill is now law), and the communications industry, particularly with reference to regulation of new video technologies.[98] Another unexpected twist is a regulatory agency wishing to ease the regulatory burden—witness the ICC, in the case of trucking, which was willing to go much further than was Congress or the industry; and the FCC, which will decide in the next few years the future course of those same video technologies, over which many broadcasters want the agency to retain a measure of control.

It is clear that continuing debate over government regulation is inevitable in the years ahead. With regulatory activity strongly supported by some as a means of ensuring fairness and equity in the marketplace—as well as good product quality—while equally strongly opposed by others on the grounds it constitutes unwarranted interference and a potential threat to individual economic and social freedoms, any conflict is bound to be intense. Regulation continues to be at a crossroads. Much more is at stake than a rule here or a regulation there—the nature of our economy and government's relation to it also are at issue.

SUMMARY

Government regulatory activity dates back to the 1800s. In this century, regulative actions have been aimed at requiring compliance with standards set by government, in a widening variety of private economic activities. Both independent regulatory agencies and other government entities have engaged in regulation. Regulation during the 1970s became broader in scope and more controversial.

Government regulation most often has been a mix of two main approaches: regulating producers and encouraging competition in the marketplace. The focal point of regulatory activity has shifted steadily over time from the states to the national government.

As problems of government became more complex in the nineteenth century, Congress and state legislatures found it necessary to delegate legislative authority for regulation to agencies created specifically for that purpose. Public pressure for controlling emerging industrial giants led to creation of several agencies during the period 1887–1938.

State and local regulation is not unimportant. In addition to regulating insurance and banking, state agencies examine and license physicians, lawyers, insurance agents, real estate agents, and so on. Professional associations are usually involved in setting state standards. State public utility commissions have influence on electricity and natural gas rates, and can act with some discretion of their own. Other examples include commerce commissions, liquor control boards, and recreation departments. Local regulation consists primarily of licensing certain businesses, and setting and enforcing various regulative codes.

Economic ("old") regulation focuses on markets, rates, and the obligation to serve. Social ("new") regulation affects the conditions under which goods and services are produced, and the physical characteristics of products that are manufactured. Social regulation also differs from economic regulation in the wider scope of its impacts. Social regulation arose out of a concern for reducing public involuntary (and voluntary) exposure to risk. However, determining risk as a basis for regulatory action has proven to be both difficult and controversial.

Government regulations have developed, in large part, as a result of decisions designed to show compassion for the individual and to maintain representativeness and fairness in governing. Compassionate motives have included protecting people from each other, alleviating distress, and preventing major systemic disruptions. Steps aimed at representativeness and fairness include requirements of procedural fairness and public participation, limitations on dishonesty and corruption, and tax laws. Much of this red tape has been unintended, yet has continued to grow.

Independent regulatory agencies are similar to other administrative entities in operating under delegated legislative authority, exhibiting functional overlap, and being affected by political considerations. They differ in the kind of work for which they are legally responsible and in structural design. Though designed to be more "insulated" politically than other agencies, there is reason to believe the insulation is thin at best.

Regulatory procedures fall into two categories: rule making and adjudicatory authority. Rule-making procedures involve proposal of rules (with notice published in the *Federal Register*), a period of public comment that includes direct testimony orally or in writing, issuance of final rules, and codification in the *Code of Federal Regulations*. The number of new or revised

rules increased substantially in the 1970s. The increase in regulatory decisions, particularly in adjudication, has meant a substantial increase in the
importance of administrative law judges (formerly, hearing examiners). The
growth of administrative law itself has been a major phenomenon of the
regulatory process. In addition, many agencies encourage voluntary compliance with agency rules and standards.

Regulatory politics is not usually partisan. Rather, it is politics of privilege and patronage, of product distribution, quality, and price. For regulators, constituency support can create an awkward and sensitive problem:
they are likely to find such support among those in the industries they regulate.

Regulatory agencies' independence from the president is far from absolute, though structural features do shield agency members from some
presidential influence. Presidential appointment power, with Senate consent, is substantial, and other forms of White House intervention are not
unknown. Proposals to make certain appointees more responsive to presidential leadership have been heard.

Independence from Congress is limited, though agencies have more
to do with individual committees than with Congress as a whole. However,
agencies occasionally become more involved with the whole Congress, and
with committees, if there is adverse public or industry reaction to proposed
agency actions. The question of agency independence seems to have an
ironic answer: agencies are independent to the extent that they have adequate political support to ensure freedom of action.

Independence from "their" industries can be a major problem for
regulatory agencies. It has also been the focal point of critical reports prepared by Ralph Nader and his associates, in which they charged widespread collaboration between regulators and those regulated.

Regulators are in frequent contact with industry leaders both professionally and socially. Industries have a legitimate self-interest to uphold,
but direct pressure is the rare exception, not the rule. Another problem is
that individuals having the kind of expertise needed in, and sought by, the
agencies often received their training and experience in the industries
themselves, and thus bring with them a not unnatural "industry slant" on
problems and needs. An alternative is to appoint someone with no expertise, which breeds another kind of problem.

Consumerism has had major impact on government regulation. Beginning with concern for health hazards of cigarette smoking and for auto
safety, the consumer movement has grown to the point that it now wields
considerable political influence. Consumer leaders have relied more on administrative regulators than on Congress for registering consumer gains,
while attempting to reshape regulation itself. The Nader phenomenon and
consumerism are not unrelated; a consumer constituency now exists, accounting for increased regulation. The fact that not everyone supports consumerism as a movement—meaning that many who are consumers oppose

the consumerists—poses political difficulties of major proportions for regulatory entities.

Regulatory reform can be addressed to a variety of objectives, which are not necessarily consistent with one another. Under Presidents Carter and Reagan, deregulation assumed greater importance. The Reagan program of "regulatory relief" involved reviews of existing rules, a slowdown in issuing major new regulations, relaxing enforcement of existing rules, and making significant reductions in regulatory agency budgets. President Reagan also sought to establish more centralized control over new and existing regulations, and mandated the use of cost-benefit analysis in assessing regulations. The president's deregulation initiatives have had considerable impact on government regulatory activity. Perhaps ironically, not all industries wish to be deregulated; not all regulators have sought to retain their authority. Debates over government regulation are likely to continue in the immediate future.

NOTES

1. James E. Anderson, *Public Policy Making*, 3rd ed. (New York: Holt, Rinehart and Winston, 1984), p. 115.
2. See the syndicated column by James J. Kilpatrick, which appeared in the Bloomington-Normal (Ill.) *Daily Pantagraph*, April 26, 1984, p. A-10; and Kenneth J. Meier, *Regulation: Politics, Bureaucracy, and Economics* (New York: St. Martin's, 1985), p. 3.
3. Paul W. MacAvoy, *The Regulated Industries and the Economy* (New York: Norton, 1979), pp. 17–24. See also William Lilley III and James C. Miller III, "The New 'Social Regulation,'" *The Public Interest*, 47 (Spring 1977), 49–61, especially pp. 52–53; Eugene Bardach and Robert Kagan, eds., *Social Regulation* (San Francisco: Institute for Contemporary Studies, 1982); James L. Regens, Thomas M. Dietz, and Robert W. Rycroft, "Risk Assessment in the Policy-Making Process: Environmental Health and Safety Protection," *Public Administration Review*, 43 (March/April 1983), 137–45, especially p. 138; and Robert E. Litan and William D. Nordhaus, *Reforming Federal Regulation* (New Haven, Conn.: Yale University Press, 1983), pp. 43–44.
4. Much of the background information on regulatory activity is derived from the treatment by Louis M. Kohlmeier, Jr., in *The Regulators: Watchdog Agencies and the Public Interest* (New York: Harper & Row, 1969), chapters 1 and 2.
5. Ibid., pp. 9–11.
6. This discussion of policy making and delegation of authority relies on A. Lee Fritschler, *Smoking and Politics: Policy Making and the Federal Bureaucracy*, 3rd ed. (Englewood Cliffs, N.J.: Prentice-Hall, 1983), chapter 4, especially pp. 52–56.
7. Ibid., pp. 57–60.
8. Ibid., pp. 59–60.
9. For a recent study of regulation in this area, see M. Elizabeth Sanders, *The Regulation of Natural Gas: Policy and Politics, 1938–1978* (Philadelphia: Temple University Press, 1981).

10. See Kohlmeier, *The Regulators*, pp. 307–9.
11. Morton Grodzins, *The American System: A New View of Government in the United States* (Chicago: Rand McNally, 1966), pp. 75–80.
12. Lilley and Miller, "The New 'Social Regulation,'" pp. 52–53 (emphasis added).
13. Regens, Dietz, and Rycroft, "Risk Assessment in the Policy-Making Process," p. 138.
14. Ibid.
15. Ibid.
16. Ibid. (emphasis added).
17. Thomas Moss and Barry Lubin, "Risk Analysis: A Legislative Perspective," in Chester R. Richmond, Phillip J. Walsh, and Emily D. Copenhaver, eds., *Health Risk Analysis* (Philadelphia: Franklin Institute Press, 1981), p. 30; cited by Regens, Dietz, and Rycroft, "Risk Assessment in the Policy-Making Process," ibid.
18. Regens, Dietz, and Rycroft, "Risk Assessment in the Policy-Making Process," ibid. See also George C. Eads and Michael Fix, *Relief or Reform? Reagan's Regulatory Dilemma* (Washington, D.C.: Urban Institute Press, 1984), chapter 5, "Social Regulation: Competing Diagnoses and Remedies."
19. This brief discussion relies on the excellent treatment by Herbert Kaufman in *Red Tape* (Washington, D.C.: Brookings, 1977), chapter 2.
20. Ibid., p. 29.
21. Ibid., pp. 30–34.
22. Ibid., pp. 34–39.
23. Ibid., pp. 39–41.
24. Ibid., pp. 42–59.
25. Ibid., p. 54.
26. See, among other sources, *Congressional Quarterly Weekly Report*, 37 (August 11, 1979), 1,647–51; *CQ Guide to Current American Government, Spring 1980* (Washington, D.C.: Congressional Quarterly, Inc., 1979), pp. 108–12; and an Associated Press story that appeared in the Bloomington-Normal (Ill.) *Daily Pantagraph*, February 2, 1981, p. A-5.
27. Fritschler, *Smoking and Politics*, p. 85.
28. See Kenneth J. Meier, "Building Bureaucratic Coalitions," in Don F. Hadwiger and William P. Browne, eds., *The New Politics of Food* (Lexington, Mass.: Lexington Books, 1978); and, also by Meier, "The Impact of Regulatory Organization Structure: IRCs or DRAs?" *Southern Review of Public Administration*, 3 (March 1980), 427–43.
29. This discussion is based on Meier, "The Impact of Regulatory Organization Structure," especially pp. 440–42. For a more detailed examination of IRCs, see David M. Welborn, *Governance of Federal Regulatory Agencies* (Knoxville, Tenn.: The University of Tennessee Press, 1977).
30. This description is derived from Kohlmeier, *The Regulators*, chapter 3, and Fritschler, *Smoking and Politics*, chapter 5. For an assessment of the political significance and implications of rule making as a policy tool, see William F. West, "The Politics of Administrative Rulemaking," *Public Administration Review*, 42 (September/October 1982), 420–26. See also Jurgen Schmandt, "Managing Comprehensive Rule Making: EPA's Plan for Integrated Environmental Management," *Public Administration Review*, 45 (March/April 1985), 309–18.

31. Fritschler, *Smoking and Politics*, pp. 67–68.
32. This description of the rule-making process is taken from *The Federal Register: What It Is and How to Use It* (Washington, D.C.: Office of the Federal Register, National Archives and Records Service, General Services Administration, 1980).
33. *Congressional Quarterly Weekly Report*, 37 (August 11, 1979), 1,647–51, at pp. 1,647 and 1,651; and *Congressional Quarterly Weekly Report*, 38 (November 1, 1980), 3,275. For analysis of other dimensions of public participation, see Robert S. Friedman, "Representation in Regulatory Decision Making: Scientific, Industrial, and Consumer Inputs to the FDA,"*Public Administration Review*, 38 (May/June 1978), 205–14; Sheldon Kamieniecki, *Public Representation in Environmental Policy Making: The Case of Water Quality Management* (Boulder, Colo.: Westview, 1980); and William T. Gormley, Jr., "Statewide Remedies for Public Underrepresentation in Regulatory Proceedings," *Public Administration Review*, 41 (July/August 1981), 454–62.
34. Kohlmeier, *The Regulators*, p. 31.
35. Ibid.
36. Fritschler, *Smoking and Politics*, pp. 68–69.
37. Ibid., pp. 94–95, and Kohlmeier, *The Regulators*, p. 32. Administrative law judges are the subject of an entire issue of *Administrative Law Review*, 25 (Winter 1973). See also Lawrence Mosher, "Here Come the Administrative Law Judges," *National Journal*, 11 (July 28, 1979), 1,247–51.
38. Kohlmeier, *The Regulators*, p. 33.
39. Like the field itself, the administrative law literature has grown quite rapidly. See, among others, Kenneth Culp Davis, *Administrative Law and Government*, 2nd ed. (St. Paul, Minn.: West Publishing, 1975); Robert S. Lorch, *Democratic Process and Administrative Law*, rev. ed. (Detroit: Wayne State University Press, 1980); Donald D. Barry and Howard R. Whitcomb, *The Legal Foundations of Public Administration* (St. Paul, Minn.: West Publishing, 1981); Kenneth F. Warren, *Administrative Law in the American Political System* (St. Paul, Minn.: West Publishing, 1982); Lief H. Carter, *Administrative Law and Politics: Cases and Comments* (Boston: Little, Brown, 1983); Phillip J. Cooper, *Public Law and Public Administration* (Palo Alto, Calif.: Mayfield, 1983); David H. Rosenbloom, *Public Administration and Law: Bench v. Bureau in the United States* (New York: Marcel Dekker, 1983); and Jerry L. Mashaw, *Due Process in the Administrative State* (New Haven, Conn.: Yale University Press, 1985). These works (with the exception of those by Davis, Carter, and Mashaw) are reviewed in Michael W. Dolan, "Administrative Law and Public Administration," *Public Administration Review*, 44 (January/February 1984), 86–89.
40. Fritschler, *Smoking and Politics*, p. 70.
41. See, for example, Seymour Scher, "Regulatory Agency Control Through Appointment: The Case of the Eisenhower Administration and the NLRB," *Journal of Politics*, 23 (November 1961), 667–88; cited by Anderson, *Public Policy Making*, p. 160.
42. Kohlmeier, *The Regulators*, pp. 34–35.
43. Erwin G. Krasnow, Lawrence D. Longley, and Herbert A. Terry, *The Politics of Broadcast Regulation*, 3rd ed. (New York: St. Martin's, 1982), chapter 2.
44. Ibid., chapter 3. For an interesting case study of regulatory politics involving

the FCC, see James L. Baughman, *Television's Guardians: The FCC and the Politics of Programming, 1958–1967* (Knoxville, Tenn.: The University of Tennessee Press, 1985).

45. As reported in the Bloomington-Normal (Ill.) *Daily Pantagraph*, September 1, 1974, p. A-5, quoting from *Congressional Quarterly Weekly Report*.
46. Kohlmeier, *The Regulators*, pp. 44–45.
47. *The Federal Register: What It Is and How to Use It*, p. 2.
48. Kohlmeier, *The Regulators*, pp. 48–50.
49. Ibid., p. 50.
50. The full story is recounted comprehensively in Fritschler, *Smoking and Politics*, from which the following account is taken. Another informative treatment of cigarette regulation is Gideon Doron, *The Smoking Paradox: Public Regulation in the Cigarette Industry* (Lanham, Md.: University Press of America, 1984).
51. Kohlmeier, *The Regulators*, p. 56.
52. Fritschler, *Smoking and Politics*, pp. 112–29.
53. *Congressional Quarterly Weekly Report*, 37 (August 11, 1979), p. 1,647.
54. Ibid. See also "The Federal Trade Commission—Business's Government Enemy No. 1," *National Journal*, 11 (October 13, 1979), 1,676–80; and "With the Cooperation of Its Friends, Sunkist Is Pulling the FTC's Teeth," *National Journal*, 12 (January 12, 1980), 49–51.
55. *Congressional Quarterly Weekly Report*, 37 (August 11, 1979),1,647.
56. Recent studies of the FTC include Robert A. Katzmann, *Regulatory Bureaucracy: The Federal Trade Commission and Antitrust Policy* (Cambridge, Mass.: The MIT Press, 1980), and Kenneth W. Clarkson and Timothy J. Muris, eds., *The Federal Trade Commission Since 1970: Economic Regulation and Consumer Welfare* (New York: Cambridge University Press, 1981).
57. The quote is taken from the *second* edition (1978) of *The Politics of Broadcast Regulation*, p. 28.
58. See Samuel P. Huntington, "The Marasmus of the ICC: The Commissions, the Railroads, and the Public Interest," *Yale Law Journal*, 61 (April 1962), 470.
59. William L. Cary, *Politics and the Regulatory Agencies* (New York: McGraw-Hill, 1967), p. 4.
60. Mark J. Green, ed., *The Monopoly Makers: Ralph Nader's Study Group Report on Regulation and Competition* (New York: Grossman, 1973).
61. Ibid., p. ix.
62. Ibid. Another study of industry–regulator relationships, with findings that contrast sharply with those of the Nader group, is Paul J. Quirk, *Industry Influences in Federal Regulatory Agencies* (Princeton, N.J.: Princeton University Press, 1981).
63. See Kohlmeier, *The Regulators*, chapter 6.
64. "The Fishbowl Approach to Agency Lobbying," *Business Week*, May 23, 1977, pp. 31–32.
65. Quoted in "Regulatory Agencies Being Studied Anew," Bloomington-Normal (Ill.) *Daily Pantagraph*, January 20, 1974, p. A-5 (reprinted from *Congressional Quarterly Weekly Report* [emphasis added]).
66. Fritschler, *Smoking and Politics*, p. 137 (emphasis added).
67. Mark V. Nadel, *The Politics of Consumer Protection* (Indianapolis: Bobbs-Merrill, 1971), p. 129; quoted by Fritschler, *Smoking and Politics*, p. 137. See also Bruce M. Owen and Ronald Breautigem, *The Regulation Game: Strategic Use of the Administrative Process* (Cambridge, Mass.: Ballinger, 1978).

68. *U.S. News and World Report*, March 28, 1977, p. 49.

69. James Buckley served one term, 1971–1977, after being elected on the Conservative party ticket in a three-way race in November 1970.

70. Linda E. Demkovich, "Saccharin's Dead, Dieters Are Blue, What Is Congress Going to Do?" *National Journal*, 9 (June 4, 1977), 856–59.

71. Interview with Representative (now Senator) Steven D. Symms (R.-Idaho), in *U.S. News and World Report*, June 13, 1977, pp. 51–52.

72. Interview with Dr. David T. Carr, Associate Director for Cancer Control, Mayo Comprehensive Cancer Center, in *U.S. News and World Report*, June 13, 1977, pp. 51–52.

73. Donald Dalrymple, assistant counsel to the House Interstate and Foreign Commerce Subcommittee on Health and the Environment, quoted in *Congressional Quarterly Weekly Report*, 35 (July 2, 1977), 1,348. See also Gerald E. Markle and James C. Petersen, eds., *Politics, Science, and Cancer: The Laetrile Phenomenon* (Boulder, Colo.: Westview, 1980).

74. An Associated Press wire service story, appearing in the Bloomington-Normal (Ill.) *Daily Pantagraph*, February 26, 1981, p. C-4.

75. A Los Angeles *Times* news service story, appearing in the Bloomington-Normal (Ill.) *Daily Pantagraph*, April 30, 1984, p. A-4.

76. A Washington *Post* news service story, appearing in the Bloomington-Normal (Ill.) *Daily Pantagraph*, December 13, 1984, p. A-11. See also *Safety Standards on Small Passenger Aircraft—with Nine or Fewer Seats—Are Significantly Less Stringent Than on Larger Aircraft*, A Report to the Congress of the United States by the Comptroller General, General Accounting Office Report No. GAO/RCED-84-2 (Washington, D.C.: U.S. Government Printing Office, January 4, 1984).

77. A Los Angeles *Times* news service story, appearing in the Bloomington-Normal (Ill.) *Daily Pantagraph*, January 12, 1985, p. A-3.

78. "Seat Belt Laws Expected in Up to 20 More States," *Public Administration Times*, 8 (March 1, 1985), 6 (published by the American Society for Public Administration; Washington, D.C.).

79. A Washington *Post* news service story, appearing in the Bloomington-Normal (Ill.) *Daily Pantagraph*, March 5, 1985, p. A-1.

80. The figure—from an NHTSA study—was cited in a United Press International wire service story appearing in the Bloomington-Normal (Ill.) *Daily Pantagraph*, August 13, 1980, p. D-3.

81. See, among others, James M. Landis, *Report on Regulatory Agencies to the President-Elect*, published as a committee print by the Subcommittee on Administrative Practice and Procedure of the Senate Committee on the Judiciary, 86th Congress, 2nd Session (Washington, D.C.: U.S. Government Printing Office, 1960); Henry J. Friendly, *The Federal Administrative Agencies: The Need for Better Definition of Standards* (Cambridge, Mass.: Harvard University Press, 1962); Roger G. Noll, *Reforming Regulation: An Evaluation of the Ash Council Proposals* (Washington, D.C.: Brookings, 1971); Paul W. MacAvoy, ed., *The Crisis of the Regulatory Commissions* (New York: Norton, 1970), and (also edited by MacAvoy) *Unsettled Questions on Regulatory Reform* (Washington, D.C.: American Enterprise Institute, 1978); and Stephen Breyer, *Regulation and Its Reform* (Cambridge, Mass.: Harvard University Press, 1982).

82. See Litan and Nordhaus, *Reforming Federal Regulation*, chapter 5, especially pp. 100–13. For an overview of presidential efforts to increase control of regulatory

agencies, see Howard Ball, *Controlling Regulatory Sprawl: Presidential Strategies from Nixon to Reagan* (Westport, Conn.: Greenwood Press, 1984).

83. See especially Landis, *Report on Regulatory Agencies to the President-Elect*; Friendly, *The Federal Administrative Agencies*; and Noll, *Reforming Regulation*. For a case study of reform in a specific context, see James R. Temples, "The Nuclear Regulatory Commission and the Politics of Regulatory Reform: Since Three Mile Island," *Public Administration Review*, 42 (July/August 1982), 355–62.

84. Regarding airline deregulation and its impacts, see, among others, *The Changing Airline Industry: A Status Report Through 1980*, A Report to the Congress of the United States by the Comptroller General, General Accounting Office Report No. CED-81-103 (Washington, D.C.: U.S. Government Printing Office, June 1, 1981); John R. Meyer, Clinton V. Oster, Jr., Benjamin Berman, Ivor Morgan, and Diana Strassman, *Airline Deregulation: The Early Experience* (Boston: Auburn House, 1981); and *The Changing Airline Industry: A Status Report Through 1982*, A Report to the Congress of the United States by the Comptroller General, General Accounting Office Report No. GAO/RCED-83-179 (Washington, D.C.: U.S. Government Printing Office, July 6, 1983). For an incisive analysis of airline, trucking, and telecommunications industry deregulation, see Martha Derthick and Paul J. Quirk, *The Politics of Deregulation* (Washington, D.C.: Brookings, 1985). Another interesting focus on deregulation is provided by Frank J. Thompson, "Deregulation by the Bureaucracy: OSHA and the Augean Quest for Error Correction," *Public Administration Review*, 42 (May/June 1982), 202–12. A comparative study of the subject, in the context of Canadian governance, is C. Lloyd Brown-John, "Rationalizing Deregulation (Some Notes from the Great White North)," paper delivered at the annual conference of the American Society for Public Administration; Denver, Colorado; April 8–11, 1984.

85. Cited in Litan and Nordhaus, *Reforming Federal Regulation*, p. 120.

86. The following treatment relies primarily on Litan and Nordhaus, *Reforming Federal Regulation*, pp. 121–31.

87. See Jerry L. Mashaw and Susan Rose-Ackerman, "Federalism and Regulation," and Michael Fix, "Transferring Regulatory Authority to the States," in George C. Eads and Michael Fix, eds., *The Reagan Regulatory Strategy: An Assessment* (Washington, D.C.: Urban Institute Press, 1984), pp. 111–45 and 153–79, respectively. For discussion of one state-level regulatory entity, see Laurence J. O'Toole, Jr., and Robert S. Montjoy, *Regulatory Decision Making: The Virginia State Corporation Commission* (Charlottesville, Va.: The University Press of Virginia, 1984).

88. Congressional Quarterly, *Regulation: Process and Politics* (Washington, D.C.: Congressional Quarterly, Inc., 1982), p. 75.

89. Litan and Nordhaus, *Reforming Federal Regulation*, pp. 122–23.

90. Ibid., p. 125. See also Congressional Quarterly, *Regulation: Process and Politics*, p. 75.

91. Litan and Nordhaus, *Reforming Federal Regulation*, p. 125.

92. Ibid., pp. 126–27.

93. This discussion relies on Litan and Nordhaus, *Reforming Federal Regulation*, pp. 127–31; Meier, *Regulation: Politics, Bureaucracy, and Economics*, p. 3; and on data drawn from *Budget of the United States Government, 1982—Appendix* (Washington, D.C.: U.S. Government Printing Office, 1981); and *Budget of the United States*

Government, 1986—Appendix (Washington, D.C.: U.S. Government Printing Office, 1985).

94. *Congressional Quarterly Weekly Report*, 39 (April 11, 1981), 627; and "Deregulation HQ: An Interview on the New Executive Order with Murray L. Weidenbaum and James C. Miller III," *Regulation*, 5 (March/April 1981), 14–23, at p. 14.
95. *Congressional Quarterly Weekly Report*, 43 (April 20, 1985), 734 (emphasis added). For discussion of cost-benefit analysis as a basis for regulatory decision making, see William F. West, "Institutionalizing Rationality in Regulatory Administration," *Public Administration Review*, 43 (July/August 1983), 326–34, at p. 329.
96. Litan and Nordhaus, *Reforming Federal Regulation*, p. 122.
97. *Congressional Quarterly Weekly Report*, 43 (April 20, 1985), 735.
98. Michael R. Gordon, "Will Reagan 'Turn Business Loose' If Business Wants to Stay Regulated?" *National Journal*, 13 (January 3, 1981), 10–13, at p. 10.

SUGGESTED READINGS

Baram, Michael S. *Alternatives to Regulation: Managing Risks to Health, Safety, and the Environment*. Lexington, Mass.: Lexington Books, 1981.

Eads, George C., and Michael Fix. *Relief or Reform? Reagan's Regulatory Dilemma*. Washington, D.C.: Urban Institute Press, 1984.

————, eds. *The Reagan Regulatory Strategy: An Assessment*. Washington, D.C.: Urban Institute Press, 1984.

Fritschler, A. Lee. *Smoking and Politics: Policy Making and the Federal Bureaucracy*, 3rd ed. Englewood Cliffs, N.J.: Prentice-Hall, 1983.

Greenwood, Ted. *Knowledge and Discretion in Government Regulation*. New York: Praeger, 1984.

Heffron, Florence, with Neil McFeeley. *The Administrative Regulatory Process*. White Plains, N.Y.: Longman, 1983.

Krasnow, Erwin G., Lawrence D. Longley, and Herbert A. Terry. *The Politics of Broadcast Regulation*, 3rd ed. New York: St. Martin's, 1982.

Levine, Adeline Gordon. *Love Canal: Science, Politics, and People*. Lexington, Mass.: Lexington Books, 1982.

Litan, Robert E., and William D. Nordhaus. *Reforming Federal Regulation*. New Haven, Conn.: Yale University Press, 1983.

Meier, Kenneth J. *Regulation: Politics, Bureaucracy, and Economics*. New York: St. Martin's, 1985.

Melnick, R. Shep. *Regulation and the Courts*. Washington, D.C.: Brookings, 1983.

Noll, Roger G., ed. *Regulatory Policy and the Social Sciences*. Berkeley, Calif.: University of California Press, 1985.

Palmer, John L., and Isabel V. Sawhill, eds. *The Reagan Experiment: An Examination of Economic and Social Policies Under the Reagan Administration*. Washington, D.C.: Urban Institute Press, 1982.

Pertschuk, Michael. *Revolt Against Regulation: The Rise and Pause of the Consumer Movement*. Berkeley, Calif.: University of California Press, 1982.

Poole, Robert W., Jr. *Instead of Regulation: Alternatives to Federal Regulatory Agencies*. Lexington, Mass.: Lexington Books, 1981.

Quirk, Paul J. *Industry Influences in Federal Regulatory Agencies*. Princeton, N.J.: Princeton University Press, 1981.

Stone, Alan. *Regulation and Its Alternatives*. Washington, D.C.: Congressional Quarterly Press, 1982.

Tolchin, Susan J., and Martin Tolchin. *Dismantling America: The Rush to Deregulate*. Boston: Houghton Mifflin, 1983.

White, Lawrence J. *Reforming Regulation: Processes and Problems*. Englewood Cliffs, N.J.: Prentice-Hall, 1981.

Wilson, James Q., ed. *The Politics of Regulation*. New York: Basic Books, 1980.

PART FIVE

Public Administration and the Future

In this concluding section we shall examine how public administration and democratic government interact, and consider the past, present, and future of public administration. The discussion of bureaucracy and democracy in chapter 15 focuses on selected current issues that pose difficult challenges for a society professing to be democratic but becoming increasingly bureaucratized. These issues include citizen participation in bureaucratic decision making; bureaucratic representativeness and accountability; and morality and ethical behavior in administrative practice, including the significance of corruption. Chapter 16 addresses the implications of, and continuing questions arising from, the totality of public administration in American government.

15

Public Administration and Democratic Government

POPULAR control of government has always been a matter of considerable importance in American politics. As we saw in chapter 2, the founding fathers emphasized those branches of government—legislative (especially) and executive—that in principle could be held directly accountable to voters through periodic elections. In this century, however, this relatively simple, clear-cut arrangement for accountability and popular control has become less workable. Many important decisions are made by officials and agencies not subject to direct electoral control and resistant to other kinds of political pressure. Thus, it is not surprising to find fresh concern about public access and influence regarding what government does.

Bureaucracy has become a focal point of discontent because of its obvious influence, its relatively obscure decision processes, and the degree to which it is insulated from direct (elective) political controls. The "tax revolt,"[1] protests against nuclear power and toxic wastes, impatience with inefficiency and red tape, and public response to regulatory actions all testify to the intensity of current feeling. More generally, they indicate a growing sense of *distance* between the people and their governing institutions. Public trust has become an issue of major proportions in recent times, and the level of trust has declined measurably.

Out of all this has come a renewed interest in democratic values, as they pertain to public impact on and control over government institutions. With the tremendous expansion of government bureaucracies, differences have become clearer between political values such as representation, participation, and accountability, and administrative values such as political neutrality and insulation, economy, efficiency, rationality, and expertise. As always when fundamentally different values clash, sparks have flown, and are still flying. But some light also has been shed on the nature of the problems we face. In this chapter we will briefly review those value conflicts, then deal more extensively with specific problems in this area.

DEMOCRATIC GOVERNMENT: NEEDS AND CONSTRAINTS

Democratic government (discussed in chapter 2) requires at least the following: (1) some mechanisms through which citizens can participate in policy making, (2) machinery for holding government accountable for its decisions, (3) an independent judiciary, and (4) regular, free elections to maintain participation and accountability.[2] The meaning and scope of these values, however, have varied over time.

Participation in the 1700s referred to voting and holding public office, and was limited by such qualifications as land or other wealth, education, social status, race, and sex. Beginning in the 1830s, eligibility for participation has been broadened, so that now virtually every citizen eighteen years of age or older can vote and otherwise become involved in politics. Lately, however, participation has taken on another, more controversial dimension—*mandatory inclusion* of various population groups in governmental decision making.

Debates over the meaning of participation are nothing new, and may indeed be inevitable. Political scientist Emmette Redford observed two decades ago that although participation is a key element of "democratic morality," a number of questions about it exist.[3] One concerns *who* should participate, with near-universal participation recommended by the believer in democracy (the "democrat"). Another question centers on the *scope* of participation—at what stages of policy making and in what ways participation is to occur. Also, a dilemma for the democrat lies in whether opportunities to participate should be afforded equally to those with high stakes in government decisions and those with little interest in specific policies. Such issues complicate the structuring of channels of participation, but a commitment to make participation possible must exist before the issues involved can be dealt with.

Accountability once meant holding officials generally responsible for their actions through direct elective mechanisms, as in the case of legislators, or through indirect machinery in which elected officials held others to account on behalf of the public. Now, however, the meaning of accountability is less clear. As discussed in chapter 3, to whom officials are *actually* accountable is a complex issue, making it difficult to determine whether they can in fact be made to answer to the general public for what they do.

Representation once referred to a general principle of legislative selection based on the number of inhabitants or amount of territory in a legislative district. But adequate representation has become a major objective of many who feel they were denied it in the past and are now seeking greater influence, particularly in administrative decision making. Closely related is *representativeness*, taken to mean that groups that have been relatively powerless should be represented in government positions in proportion to their numbers in the population (see chapter 2).

The cumulative effect of the changes in meaning has been to make it more difficult to determine whether these values are being maintained. Conceptual uncertainty about values makes it harder to deal with accusations that we are not living up to our own standards of democratic government. For example, defining representativeness a particular way might in effect include one group while excluding another from decision making, and the latter might well dispute whether representativeness in fact exists.

The larger concern, however, is for maintaining democratic norms and practices in a complex governmental system, within a complex society. Today many fear that democratic values, however defined, are endangered by government that may be moving beyond popular control. Government institutions clearly are under pressure "from the people"—left, right, and center—to stay within the public's political reach. The difficulties in maintaining democracy, however, are hardly new. Assuming that democracy implies fairly equitable access to decision makers, widespread opportunity to exert influence in the political process, and clear public preferences about public policy, the realities of American democracy have fallen short of the ideal for some time.

Access is unevenly distributed throughout the population, with the wealthy having a better chance than the poor to gain a hearing in official channels. Journalist Theodore H. White notes that the one thing most contributors seek by giving money to candidates and political parties is access to those in office after the electoral decisions are made.[4] Similarly, *influence* in the political process (partly dependent on having access in the first place) is clearly enjoyed by some more than by others. Besides money, a key factor seems to be organization, and well-organized groups have long been acknowledged as having the advantage in exercising political influence. Political scientist Theodore Lowi has suggested that the dominance of organized over unorganized interests makes it impossible to sustain a claim of comparable influence among different groups in a system where organization and political power go hand in hand.[5]

Finally, *clear public preferences* on policy questions simply do not exist in many cases. Contrary to popular belief, voters usually do not confer *policy mandates*—clear statements of policy preference—when they go to the polls. The Nixon landslide over McGovern in 1972 and Ronald Reagan's victory over Walter Mondale in 1984 were overwhelming, but many of those voting for the winners clearly did not agree with their every policy position. Narrower electoral victories, such as Jimmy Carter's defeat of Gerald Ford in 1976, may be even more ambiguous as to their policy meaning.

If policy mandates are vague, the nature of the "public interest" is even more so. While it is possible to argue that the public is the "owner" of government institutions and that those institutions should serve the owner's interest—the public interest[6]—defining what that is as a practical matter is not easy. Various contesting forces claim to be acting in and for the public interest, and each may have a legitimate case. Also, it is not clear whether the public interest is some generalized view of societal good, or the sum total of all private interests, themselves inconsistent with one another.

DEMOCRACY AND PUBLIC ADMINISTRATION

Democracy, as we have noted, requires mechanisms for both participation and accountability, ensured by an independent judiciary and free elections. Public administration, however, poses troublesome problems for any such system. It does not accord with the notion of elected public officials, since most bureaucrats are not elected, and it has emphasized expertise and knowledge over public participation. Growing societal complexity and increasing administrative responsibilities have virtually required more specialization and larger numbers of bureaucratic professionals. At the same time, disadvantaged groups and others have turned to government bureaucracy more frequently for various kinds of aid—ironically, while often voicing grievances against many of the same agencies—and to demand a greater role in making policies that affect them. The result has been a collision between the need for professionalism and technical competence, and insistent demands for citizen participation in policy making.[7] Bureaucratic accountability in such a system was to be achieved largely if not entirely through *indirect* popular influence, through the legislature and chief executive. Public administration scholar Lee Fritschler notes that it is "difficult, though far from impossible, to build both accountability and participation into the policy-making process when administrative agencies are the chief policy makers."[8]

The concerns that have come to center on bureaucracy include, besides issues of accountability and participation, the question of representativeness and the whole problem of ethics and "morality in government." In addition, the general disposition of bureaucrats and bureaucracies to operate behind a veil of secrecy, in the best tradition of Max Weber, has triggered efforts to open their activities to public scrutiny. Two such efforts are state and national freedom of information laws, and so-called "sunshine" laws, requiring that public business be conducted in open forums.

The relationship between governmental accountability and popular access to government information was recognized four decades ago. Congress, in the Administrative Procedure Act of 1946, attempted to "open up'' the bureaucracy by encouraging distribution of information to the public on a ''need to know'' basis. Under that principle, the burden rested with the inquiring citizen to demonstrate that particular information was needed from the bureaucracy; the presumption was that information could be safeguarded by the bureaucracy unless a strong case was made to the contrary. As long as popular trust of bureaucracy remained high, and no major interests felt harmed or threatened, that arrangement was satisfactory. At the same time, bureaucratic secrecy went largely unchallenged, and little information filtered out of the bureaucracy when agency personnel sought to restrict it.

By the 1960s the situation had changed. Increasing government activity bred rising citizen concern about administrative decision making, which in turn sparked calls for greater access to hard-to-get information. Congress responded, after some delay and without strong presidential leadership, by passing a Freedom of Information (FOI) Act in 1966, based on the principle that the ''timely provision of information to the American people, upon their own petition, is a requisite and proper duty of government. . . .''[9] The effect of this statute was to increase the potential for citizen access to a wide variety of government records and files.

The new policy ''significantly limited the discretion of executive branch personnel to restrict public access to government information 'in the public interest,' 'for good cause found,' or any other unqualified 'need to know' purpose. The new statute *presumed a popular right to all department and agency records* but established, as well, nine categories of exemption from this premise [most relating to defense and national security]. These exceptions were to be invoked on a limited basis. . . .''[10] Thus, the burden was shifted from those seeking information to agency personnel who might wish to restrict its release. In practice, however, administrative personnel did not enthusiastically comply with provisions of the act in the first five years of its operation; Congress itself criticized the bureaucracy for ''foot-dragging.'' Amendments adopted in 1974 were designed to ensure faithful implementation of the act, and some improvement followed. Congress acted again without leadership from the president—indeed, the amendments were passed over a presidential veto! (Lack of forceful leadership from the White House may explain some of the bureaucratic reluctance to conform to the new requirements.) And, despite the improvement noted, delay in releasing information continued to be widespread. Gradually, however, a combination of congressional oversight and educational efforts in the executive branch succeeded in bringing about greater compliance with the FOI act. One observer noted in 1979 that national government employees appeared ''less apprehensive about and less resistant to the statute.''[11] Thus, while there have been definite gains in information acquisition by private citizens,[12] those gains were achieved only after Congress demonstrated its commitment to this ideal of ''democratic morality.''[13]

(Over two-thirds of the states also have passed FOI statutes, with varying degrees of effectiveness; where they *are* effective, the experience has been similar to that in Washington.)

In mid-1981, however, the future of the national FOI Act became somewhat clouded. The Reagan administration—concerned with protecting national security, law enforcement activities, and business confidentiality—began exploring the possibility of limiting to some degree the requirements for information release contained in the act as amended. Subsequently, a pattern of decisions unfolded (mainly through administration of the FOI Act) that had the effect of reducing public access to government documents. Examples included selective granting of fee waivers (required formally for access to some documents, but in practice often waived), and delays in responding to requests for documents. However, this pattern represented apparent Reagan administration efforts to affect the FOI Act only "at the margins," rather than to undercut its core purposes. One observer commented that the administration proceeded in this fashion because top policy leaders "don't see any particular value in [the principle of] public disclosure"[14]—a far cry from outright opposition to the act's underlying assumptions. In addition, there is substantial evidence of growing agency compliance with the FOI Act.[15]

More to the point, the value of this statute increasingly is being recognized. Under FOI procedures, it was disclosed in recent years that: (1) the Energy Department decided to build a heavy-water nuclear reactor using the worst of five possible designs; (2) the Veterans' Administration spent $700,000 to renovate office space that was never used; (3) the Tennessee Valley Authority gave over $3 million to a development agency that may have been operating illegally; (4) the National Archives had tolerated certain fire and safety violations; (5) spoiled and diseased meat had been sold to the school lunch program; and (6) some defense contractors were charging lobbying and public-relations expenses to government contracts.[16] While none of these actions constituted grave threats to the nation's fundamental welfare, all demonstrated a need for substantive improvement in public management. Most important, agency accountability was greatly enhanced simply because information about agency behavior could be brought to light.

Sunshine laws, which have been passed at all levels of government and apply mainly to legislative proceedings, also have been enacted for administrative agencies. Regulatory agencies at the national level operate "in the sunshine," though required to do so by judicial rather than legislative action. In all fifty states, open meeting laws are on the books, applying to state legislative committees, state executive branches and independent agencies, and local governments.[17] As with freedom of information laws, the greatest potential beneficiaries are organized groups of citizens who seek to monitor administrative activities. City councils and local school boards have been at the center of controversies over open meetings at least as much as state or national entities. Both FOI statutes and sunshine laws have succeeded, at all levels, in opening government to greater public scrutiny, but—perhaps not surprisingly—they have fallen short of what was hoped for them by their strongest advocates. Government behavior can be changed only gradually, if experience with these devices is any guide.

There is growing insistence, also, that government and bureaucracy do more to protect individual privacy and to ensure that government records concerning affairs of private citizens are fair and accurate.[18] This is a particularly sensitive issue in view of computer information capabilities. It is perhaps ironic that the right of privacy was given constitutional protection by the U.S. Supreme Court, in the 1965 case of *Griswold v. Connecticut*, during the same period that governmental ability to intrude on that privacy increased rapidly. Prior to the 1960s, information might have been available to government, but it was costly and time consuming to have it on hand or to organize it. Computers, however, make retrieval and cross-referencing of information not only possible but very convenient. A principal concern is the extent and diversity of personal information that is now stored on computers of public and private organizations—social security data, credit ratings and transactions, drivers' license information, medical records, income figures, and so on.[19]

Both national and state governments took action during the 1970s to better safeguard an individual's right to privacy. Legislation at the national level included the Freedom of Information Act, the Fair Credit Reporting Act, the Family Educational Rights and Privacy Act, the Privacy Act of 1974, and the Fair Credit Billing Act. Congress also established the Privacy Protection Study Commission to look into intrusions on individual privacy by agencies outside the national executive branch. Over half a dozen states enacted privacy laws, and an even larger number adopted their own versions of the Fair Credit Reporting Act.[20] In short, there has been considerable government activity in this area, but concern persists that "big brother" still may have too much access to personal records.[21]

DIMENSIONS OF DEMOCRATIC ADMINISTRATION

In the remainder of this chapter we will examine in more depth selected areas in public administration that pose particular challenges for the maintenance of democratic norms and practices. We will consider each of the following: (1) citizen participation, (2) bureaucratic representativeness, (3) bureaucratic responsiveness, (4) bureaucratic accountability, (5) ethics and morality in government, and (6) administrative effectiveness as a threat to personal freedom.

Citizen Participation

The movement for greater citizen participation in government decision making was born in the 1960s out of related movements for civil rights, "black liberation," and decentralization of urban government structures. It originated in demands by nonwhites for a larger voice in determining policies and programs directly affecting them. The urban poor, at least during the 1960s, concentrated on organizing themselves and confronting those in power with demands for changes in the way things were. Their participation was formally incorporated in Model Cities and Community Action programs, and in others since then; as of the late 1970s, citizen participation requirements were included in 155 separate national grant programs (about one-third of the total), accounting for over 80 percent of grant funds.[22] Many came to demand participation not only in program implementation but also in program planning.[23] The ideology of citizen participation has developed firm roots in our political values.

The forms and practices of citizen participation are numerous (see Table 15-1).[24] In addition to attending open meetings held by administrative agencies, individuals may take part in budget and other legislative hearings, initiatives, and referenda; serve on advisory committees; respond to citizen surveys; and, in some cases, sit on governing boards of operating activities funded by government entities. Also, in the delivery of human services to citizen clienteles, individuals act as "coproducers" of the services by their deep involvement in program operations (this refers to services such as unemployment compensation, welfare, garbage collection, and education).[25] Viewing the citizen as "coproducer" is a different, but highly relevant, conception of participation that should not be overlooked.

Specific purposes of participation can include some or all of the following: (1) giving information to citizens; (2) getting information from or about citizens; (3) improving public decisions, programs, projects, and services; (4) enhancing public acceptance of governmental undertakings; (5) supplementing agency work; (6) altering political power patterns and allocations of public resources; (7) protecting individual and minority group rights and interests; and (8) delaying or avoiding difficult public policy decisions.[26] (Redistributing power and resources, and protecting minority interests, were central to the demands of urban nonwhites in the 1960s.) Though some of these are mutually incompatible, all are directed generally toward reducing citizen alienation from government.[27] The fundamental rationale for citizen participation can be summarized as follows:

> The decision makers need to know what the public wants and how the decisions they make work out in practice. For their part, citizens need to know what the officials are doing so that they can hold them responsible. The public also must know the reasons for governmental decisions if they are to retain confidence in the soundness and equity of those decisions.[28]

Table 15-1
FORMS OF CITIZEN PARTICIPATION

I. Organizational Forms

Citizen Groups
Special Interest Groups
Specific Program Clientele Groups
Official Citizen Committees

II. Individual Forms

Voting
Being a Program Client
Making Statements
Working in Public Projects
Campaigning/Lobbying
Administrative Appeals
Going to Court
Demonstrations

III. Forms of Information Dissemination

Open Government
Meetings/Speaker Bureaus
Conferences
Publications
Mass Media
Displays/Exhibits
Mail
Advertising/Notices
Hot Lines
Drop-in Centers
Correspondence
Word of Mouth

IV. Forms of Information Collection

Hearings
Workshops/Meetings/Conferences
Consultation
Government Records
Nongovernment Documents
Participant Observers
Surveys

Source: U.S. Advisory Commission on Intergovernmental Relations, *Citizen Participation in the American Federal System* (Washington, D.C.: U.S. Government Printing Office, March 1979), p. 2.

The ideology of citizen participation and debates over its place in governing are related conceptually to the continuing debate in American politics over centralization and decentralization (see chapter 7). Particularly as practiced in the federal system during the past quarter century, it represents an application of the decentralist principle, which assumes value and purpose in delegating decision-making authority to affected persons and groups. Decentralization as a mode of operation clearly permits wider participation; it gives greater assurance that the existing spectrum of opinion will receive a hearing; and it lends more legitimacy to both the process and the outcomes of decision making. Because federalism itself was designed as a bulwark against centralization, the concept of decentralization obviously has a place in operations under a federal system. Citizen participation, fostered by many national programs, has been a key mechanism used to promote decentralization of operating responsibility.

The concept of participation has been applied in different ways to varying problems. "Community control" focused on neighborhood management of schools and delivery of other essential urban services, principally in nonwhite ghetto areas of major American cities.[29] A recent adaptation of that idea, combined with other innovative efforts, involves several areas of the South Bronx in New York City. After a well-publicized visit by Jimmy Carter in October 1977, various projects were begun to reverse the pervasive decay of the South Bronx and the extreme poverty of many of its residents. Unlike 1960s-style programs involving massive national government outlays, however, these efforts have emphasized "pragmatic, incremental plans, . . . economic development, *local determination,* 'self help,' 'sweat equity,' urban agriculture, appropriate technology, public and private-sector partnerships—and low cost."[30] With the focus on extensive involvement of residents of the area, as suggested in the preceding description, there has been noticeable improvement in parts of the South Bronx. More important, perhaps, these endeavors have been watched closely as possible prototypes for future activities in combating urban blight—particularly in an era of fiscal stress and retrenchment.

In other places, neighborhood and citizen action organizations sprang up for purposes of "preserving neighborhood character," and sometimes physical structures in the neighborhood. For example, there have been concerted efforts to prevent construction of interstate highway projects that would cut through, or perhaps level, parts of established urban neighborhoods. One such case involves a continuing conflict in Memphis, Tennessee, over construction of a portion of Interstate 40 through Overton Park, one of the city's oldest park and recreation areas. The proposed stretch of road would almost certainly have an adverse impact on the inhabitants of Overton Park Zoo, not to mention residents in the surrounding neighborhood. A series of court injunctions has halted construction, though technically it still could be resumed. Another case centered on a proposal to construct a bridge between the communities of Rye and Oyster Bay, New York, across Long Island Sound. In this case a coalition of citizen action groups succeeded in defeating the proposal, which had the backing of powerful interests and individuals such as the late Governor Nelson Rockefeller, former New York Port Authority head William Ronan, and the late Robert Moses, long-time power behind the scenes in New York City.[31] Many other examples also can be cited: community groups protesting bank "redlining" (the practice attributed to some financial institutions that excludes some areas of a community from eligibility for loans); cattle ranchers, Indians, and antinuclear groups joining forces against uranium mining by energy conglomerates; and residential associations trying to attract (or repel) commercial enterprises.[32]

Citizen participation has also been incorporated into formal mechanisms for decision making. At the national level, for example, public participation in regulatory agency proceedings has been increasing since the late 1960s, though with considerable variation in agency responses and opportunities provided to citizen groups such as consumer organizations. Agencies undoubtedly have legal discretionary authority to decide just how much public participation to permit, particularly whether and how to finance participation by those with limited resources. Nonetheless, there has been considerable frustration on the part of so-called public interest groups, which have been slow to gain access to regulatory proceedings. Two observers have noted recent improvements in agency receptiveness, with more of them willing to grant direct financial aid as well as to facilitate access. Not surprisingly, most of the problems have been over funding. Agencies with consumer protection high among their priorities are most likely to offer assistance, while those in highly technological fields are most likely to resist—but even they have begun to soften their stance.[33]

At the local level, participation is now more regularized, particularly in planning. Programs in urban renewal, Model Cities, and other poverty-related areas have for some time included much greater involvement of affected citizens. As another kind of illustration, the Metropolitan Seattle Transit Planning Study was deliberately designed to include a citizen participation component.[34] Systematic efforts were made to attract "consistent voters" in King County to public meetings arranged specifically to hear citizen views. Most of those attending had been active in local organizations or on particular issues; thus, there was minimal representation of those who had not ordinarily participated in local civic affairs. Citizens and planning professionals attended the public forums, and both agreed that the citizens had had an impact on planning the rapid transit system.

The professionals and citizens were asked to assess the role played by citizen participants in the planning process. Their perceptions, as registered on a "ladder of citizen participation" (see Figure 15-1), were not identical, but both groups felt that there had been fairly significant involvement. Seventy percent of the professionals and 44 percent of the citizens indicated a consultative role, while 30 percent of the professionals and 19 percent of the citizens indicated a partnership role.[35] Analysis of the recommendations to the Metro Council indicates that the citizens did affect the proposals substantially, though far from totally.[36] For example, citizen preferences were followed on expanding bus service, the design of specific bus routes, and on emphasizing speed, low cost, and convenience over facilities such as heated shelters and food service in bus stations. However, other citizen preferences—for buses with nonpolluting engines, expansion of the existing electric trolley fleet, and financing the system through gas tax revenues—were not incorporated in the consultants' report to the council.[37]

Other evidence also exists to suggest that citizen participation has had substantive impact on governmental decision making. A 1978 survey conducted by the U.S. Advisory Commission on Intergovernmental Relations (ACIR) and the International City Management Association (ICMA) found that in important areas of local activity, citizen participation was perceived by local government officials to have been a significant component in the

Figure 15–1 The Ladder of Citizen Participation

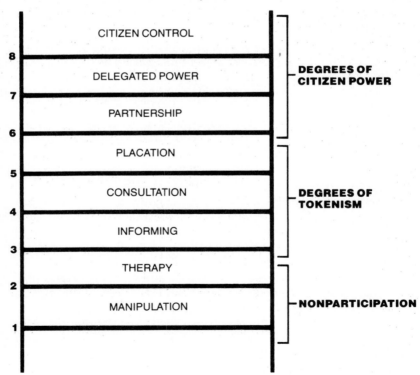

Source: Sherry R. Arnstein, ''A Ladder of Citizen Participation.'' *Journal of the American Institute of Planners,* 35(July 1969), 217.

Table 15-2
LOCAL OFFICIALS' OPINIONS ABOUT THE EFFECTS OF CITIZEN PARTICIPATION ON THE GRANT-IN-AID PROCESS AND LOCAL BUDGET DECISIONS

Question	*Percentage Yes*	
	Cities	Counties
Have grant proposals developed by local government staff been dropped because of citizen participation?	16.8%	11.8%
Have new grant proposals been developed as a result of citizen suggestions?	60.9	63.3
Has your local government transferred funding for a service or program from its general budget to a grant because of citizen participation?	19.7	26.9
Has your local government assumed the costs in its general budget for continuing a service or program funded through an expired grant because of citizen participation?	40.7	58.8
Has your local government dropped a service or program funded through a grant when the grant expired because of citizen participation?	12.2	18.6
Has citizen participation had a measurable effect on the setting of priorities within your local government's general budget?	42.9	43.8

Source: U.S. Advisory Commission on Intergovernmental Relations, *Citizen Participation in the American Federal System* (Washington, D.C.: U.S. Government Printing Office, March 1979), p. 174.

decision process (see Table 15-2). In particular, development of new grant proposals, setting local budgetary priorities, and assuming previously funded program costs after grants expired were influenced by citizen participation—or so many local officials seemed to think.

Some other dimensions of citizen participation are worth noting. For one, the matter of who is to participate, and to what extent, is not only a problem of democratic ideals as discussed earlier; it has potentially important implications strictly in an operating sense. In antipoverty programs of the mid- and late 1960s, "maximum feasible participation of the poor" was called for, but there was bitter debate over who was meant by "the poor," and how they were to be selected and incorporated into program operation.[38] Furthermore, in almost all studies of citizen participation, it has been found that:

> groups or individuals active in such programs (1) represent organized interests likely to have been previously active in agency affairs, (2) include a large component of spokesmen for other government agencies, (3) represent a *rather limited range* of potential publics affected by programs, and (4) tend toward the well-educated, affluent middle- to upper-class individuals.

Viewed in terms of the ideological program goals, programs seldom appear to . . . produce a great socioeconomic diversity among participating interests.[39]

Second, there is a distinct possibility that official groups and agencies will coopt citizen action groups. On more than one occasion, what began as a conscientious effort to build greater participation into a decision-making process ended up as more show than substance, with the newer groups occupying a place of greater visibility but little increased power. Officially sponsored citizen participation tends to be cooptation rather than representation.[40] A study of community action programs in the late 1960s indicated great variety in the relationships between neighborhood resident organizations (NROs) and city halls. Some NROs clearly were coopted; others represented neighborhood interests to which city hall was hostile; still others established a negotiation relationship that facilitated interaction as equals.[41] In sum, nothing was automatic about the manner in which participation and representation were practiced.

Third, decentralizing and localizing control over governmental programs has not been a guarantee of either increased participation at the local level[42] or more democratic operations. The late political scientist Roscoe Martin observed some years ago that government at the grass roots may indeed be *less* democratic than in a larger and more diverse political system.[43] The dangers of cooptation and of domination by a small minority of local citizens are very real, regardless of official mandates or unofficial expectations. It also has been observed that citizen participation can become a "bureaucratic ideology," to be used "against the elected officers of 'representative' government. . . ."[44] Similarly, citizen participation "can be and has been used as a means for transferring power from officials who have at least some political responsibility to the community at large to self-perpetuating local cliques or the bureaucracy."[45] All such observations clearly imply a hazard inherent in citizen participation: the potential for citizen interests to become primarily self-serving rather than representative of broader interests in the community or society.

A fourth concern is that administrative agency personnel, in their enthusiasm for satisfying immediate "citizen action" demands, may initiate responses that prove to be shortsighted when judged by more rigorous criteria over time.[46] While public administrators may wish to respond, or appear to respond, to new and powerful interests such as citizen action groups, there is danger that they may act hastily "in behalf of the public before the consequences of such action can be fully assessed by the agency or by others likely to be affected by the action."[47] Compounding this potential difficulty is a tendency for citizen groups to scorn cost-benefit analysis as an instrument of evaluation of their own proposals.[48] While cost-benefit analysis is not always an appropriate evaluative tool, it often can strengthen one's case, particularly under current conditions of fiscal stress, or at least increase a group's credibility in a political dialogue.

Fifth, if citizen participation is designed to help keep bureaucracy responsible to the general public, it has had only a mixed record of success. Citizen groups seem to have greatest impact when they have the political power to make bureaucrats listen, and when group values most nearly match those of the bureaucracy. But because of impediments on citizens' expertise, time, and access, citizen inputs are likely to have limited effect in attaining bureaucratic responsibility.[49]

Sixth, citizen participation and its impact will be affected by the degree to which contacts with those in government are characterized by confrontation as opposed to negotiation, by a sense of "we versus they" as opposed to a perceived community of interests. Tension in a political system is not uncommon, but a democratic system virtually requires that tension not be constant. Barring fundamental shifts in the locus of power in a particular decision-making system, continuous confrontation will soon reach a point of diminishing returns for those seeking access and influence.

Finally, a concept quite widespread in the area of participation is "input" from citizens, about which a cautionary note is in order. Many people seem to assume that what they should be seeking by increasing their participation is "greater input" into the mechanisms of decision making. The term is borrowed from computer science, where input makes a major difference in results. However, the concept of input carries with it an implicit acknowledgment that somebody else is "running the machine." Those who "seek input" are admitting to a *subordinate* position in the decision process. As Figure 15–1 indicates, there are other possibilities—partnership and full control, for example—for which input is an inappropriate concept. To think only in terms of input, in short, serves to limit the variety of ways that participation can occur, and to confirm the power of those already holding it.

Citizen participation, in sum, has dramatically modified the usual methods of making decisions in a host of policy areas, and has taken its place as a major feature of democratic administration. While those in positions of power often have yielded grudgingly to citizen groups, it is unlikely that the gains made will be rolled back. If anything, the near future seems to hold promise of still greater direct citizen involvement.[50]

Representation and Representativeness

Democratic government in practice has meant representative democracy rather than direct democracy, for the most part. The concept of representation may appear clear cut, but there are a number of questions to be answered and problems to be dealt with. Representativeness, a companion but not identical concept, will be discussed subsequently.

There are, first of all, several approaches to representation.[51] Should constituents' opinions and preferences be conveyed to other government officials and reflected faithfully in legislative voting, or should a representative exercise independent judgment and individual conscience in making decisions? The former, which has been labeled the "delegate" role, maximizes the public's impact on decision making but does not take advantage of the representative's potentially superior knowledge of details and of subtleties in making choices. The latter, labeled the "trustee" role, emphasizes the representative's capabilities and the public's trust that their interests will be faithfully served (thus the label of trustee). In both instances, we are depending on our representatives to somehow serve the "public interest." Unfortunately, it is rarely clear how elected officials make their decisions, and to *whose* voices they listen when they do act as delegates. Thus, in its most basic dimension, there is ambiguity concerning representation.

That ambiguity is complicated considerably when the focus shifts to the administrative context. Since bureaucracies in American politics are acknowledged to have a representative function, it follows that answers to the same sorts of questions must be found. But historically, bureaucratic agencies have served narrow clienteles with specialized interests. As noted in chapter 3, representation of those interests—and accountability to them—can be quite complete without serving the larger political system. How, then, can these administrative patterns be reconciled with democratic values that emphasize broad popular representation?

Political scientist Emmette Redford supplies some answers to this dilemma.[52] Central to Redford's argument is the following proposition: "... *the attainment of the democratic ideal in the world of administration depends much less on majority votes than on the inclusiveness of the representation of interests in the interaction process among decision makers.*"[53] Redford develops that proposition this way:

> The process can be called democratic only if the interaction process is *broadly inclusive* at two levels of decision making: first, at the level of political superstructure, where basic decisions on rules for society and roles for actors in the administrative state are made, and second, at the level of program specialization to which much of the decision making of the administrative state has been committed. The interaction process must include the participation of several types of leaders who through the diversities reflected in their participation and the influence of nonleaders upon them give representation to the manifold common and varied interests within the society.[54]

Thus the degree to which representation is *inclusive of existing interests in the society* is, in this view, a key test for how democratic administrative processes will be. Underlying this is another concern: the extent of effective *access* afforded to those not already a part of the interaction process, consistent with the norm of inclusiveness.[55] Both access and regularized interactions are crucial to democratization of administration, particularly regarding the opportunity for newer or weaker groups to gain a hearing for their interests and grievances.

Another essential difficulty in representation concerns the delegation of authority. In a fundamental sense, we delegate our authority to Congress and to state and local legislatures to make our laws, knowing as we do that representation of our every view is imperfect. Legislatures, in turn, have delegated vast amounts of authority to bureaucracies (and to chief executives), further removing decision-making power from the source of authority—that is, the people. When authority is delegated, it must be either very precisely defined and limited, which tends to be impractical and defeats the purpose of delegating, or else *discretionary*, with those who exercise it largely deciding how it should be used.

Once discretion enters the picture, which it does very early in administrative decision making, the representational quality of decisions may be diminished. This is particularly true where expertise, technical competence, and rationality are highly prized values, as they are in much of our bureaucratic structure. We come back, then, to a dilemma that troubles much of democratic administration: *the conflict between professionalism and participation/representation.* As in the Seattle transit study, citizens and professionals generally have different perspectives, particularly about what is "best for the people." Another case where this was the central issue was the Ocean Hill-Brownsville school confrontation in Brooklyn in the late 1960s, when white teachers and educational professionals clashed with black parents, students, and community organizations over what constituted "quality education" (and over who would have the power to decide that). Increasingly in recent years, "the people" have grown to resent somebody else making a judgment about what is best for them. Most of the time, that "somebody" was a professional operating within a bureaucracy. Thus, discretionary authority exercised by bureaucratic "trustees" increases the chance that the general public's feelings will not be as well represented as they might be under conditions of reduced (professional) discretion.

Another aspect of discretion should be noted. If, in the words of one observer, "good adminstration consists of making [bureaucracy] *predictably and reliably responsive*" to the wishes of the public,[56] then large areas of discretionary authority rather clearly get in the way of predictability. The only way to make bureaucracy more predictable, given our past history of delegating authority, is to tighten up dramatically on how much discretion technical experts in the bureaucracy are permitted to exercise, and that would require a fundamental reassessment of the kind of bureaucracy—and expertise—we want. Discretionary authority, in short, conflicts directly with a desire for predictability except within very broad limits.

Finally, representation by the bureaucracy is inhibited by long-time practices insulating administrative personnel from direct political pressures. Conceptually, "politics" and "representation of the public's feelings" are virtually synonymous, and to hamper political interchange is to place limits on popular representation.

Representativeness of the bureaucracy was a focal point of controversy in the 1960s and 1970s, though that is not the first time attention was paid to it. Political scientist Norton Long observed in 1952 that in terms of age, income, education, and father's occupation, the national bureaucracy was broadly representative of the population, and more so than Congress.[57] More recent studies have focused on the problem of defining representativeness, and on measuring the extent to which it exists in a number of countries, including the United States.[58]

Political scientist Samuel Krislov has argued that classical political neutrality sacrifices some of the skills and assets that bureaucrats bring with them to government employment, including social representativeness. He summed up this way:

> What is really sought is not cold-fish indifference but responsiveness to political direction, an acknowledgment of democratic political supremacy. . . .The qualities of judgment, information, and fervor that bureaucrats do bring as they aid decision makers are in fact resources of immense social advantage, not merely weaknesses men are heir to. In particular, the bureaucrats' affinity for the population has great potential advantage for social stability and increased bureaucratic responsiveness.[59]

Krislov's general point was that by incorporating the skills, viewpoints, and judgments of government bureaucrats, effectiveness *and* representative qualities of the bureaucracy will be enhanced. His is clearly an unorthodox view of bureaucratic neutrality when compared to Weber and others of traditional bent, but he provides an intellectual foundation for the position that representativeness is a value to be prized and pursued in the civil service. (In the 1960s the value of representativeness began to receive increased emphasis, with the value of administrative neutrality—as outlined by Weber and Woodrow Wilson—declining in importance.)

Whether the U.S. civil service is in fact representative of the population at large is a debatable—and frequently debated—issue. Krislov's study (covering the period 1962–1971), found a fairly close parallel between national government employees and the general public in four social characteristics: religious preference, race, age distribution, and political party identification. The greatest single disparity was in the nonwhite proportions of each grouping: 21 percent in the civil service, compared to 11 percent in the general population.[60] While that would seem to suggest the kind of demographic representativeness sought by advocates of affirmative action, Krislov's data indicated a continuing concentration of black employees in the lower personnel grades.[61]

A study by public administration expert Kenneth Meier, conducted in the early 1970s, found some representativeness in the U.S. civil service as a whole, in terms of general values and social origins.[62] He found, for example, that about the same proportions of national government employees and the general public (less than 4 percentage points apart) supported Richard Nixon in the 1972 election, identified with the Republican party, and favored military withdrawal from Vietnam. Somewhat larger differences existed (7 to 8 percentage points) on questions of increasing taxes on high-income people, legalizing marijuana, protecting rights of the accused, and the role of government in helping social minorities. Only on the issue of the United States trading with Communist nations were the two groups apart by more than nine percentage points (83 percent of government workers, but only 64 percent of the general sample, supported trade).[63]

Also of significance is Meier's finding that in terms of fathers' occupational status, the civil service is more representative of the general population than is the foreign service or politically appointed executives.[64] This is not to say, however, that it is in fact representative, only that it is more so than some other sets of government officials. Finally, Meier states unequivocally that while the civil service as a whole is fairly representative of the population at large, the upper grades—where major decision makers are concentrated—are much less representative than the lower grades.[65] This is largely consistent with the comments made above, and in chapter 10, concerning the underrepresentation of women and minorities.

Political scientists Joel Aberbach, Robert Putnam, and Bert Rockman, in a study of upper-level civil servants, legislators, and political executives in six countries, identified a number of salient characteristics of American public officials.[66] As one example, all three groupings of American officials (especially civil servants) vastly overrepresent educational attainment, with at least 90 percent of each group having a college degree; by contrast, 26 percent of the general public had completed college at the time of the study.[67] Similar patterns were found with regard to fathers' occupational status. Less than one-fourth of the general population sample had fathers in management or professional positions, but 60 to 70 percent of fathers of public servants held such positions. Nearly 40 percent of fathers in the general sample had held manual-labor jobs, whereas only 13 percent of public officials' fathers had worked at manual labor.[68] It also was found that the proportion of each grouping raised in cities over 100,000 population varied considerably—30 percent of the general public, 31 percent of legislators, 52 percent of political executives, and 60 percent of civil servants.[69] In sum, these data show that U.S. higher-level civil servants—compared to a sample of the public at large—are likely to be better educated, from a higher-status background (as measured by father's occupation), and raised in a metropolitan setting.

One other, more recent study also bears on this subject. In 1982, political scientists Stanley Rothman and S. Robert Lichter conducted interviews with 200 members of the Senior Executive Service (SES), divided about equally between a ''traditional agency'' sample (drawn from the Departments of Agriculture, Commerce, and the Treasury, and the Justice Department's Bureau of Prisons) and an ''activist agency'' sample (including, among others, EPA, the FTC, the Equal Employment Opportunity Commission, and the Department of Housing and Urban Development).[70] They succeeded in ascertaining, among other things, the senior careerists' social and personal background (see Table 15-3), presidential voting preferences

(1968 through 1980—see Table 15-4), and attitudes on selected issues (see Table 15-5). Lichter summarized the findings in 1984:

> Basically, we found that high level bureaucrats are overwhelmingly white, male, well educated, and well off. [T]hey are far more likely to classify themselves as political liberals than the general public. . . . [These SES personnel] tend to be mildly reformist, and not particularly alienated from or hostile to American institutions. So that, for example, very few of them believe that we should move toward socialism. Most of them believe that private enterprise is fair to workers. And most of them believe that less regulation of business would be good for the country. . . . On almost all of these questions, [their] views are substantially more supportive of American society than those we found among such groups as leading journalists and the heads of public interest groups. . . .[71]

Differences between "traditional" and "activist" agency personnel can be noted on numerous questions (see Table 15-5). One of the most interesting is that, despite both groups' Democratic party leanings (see Table 15-3), "traditional" SESers gave a plurality of their votes to Richard Nixon and Ronald Reagan in 1972 and 1980, respectively. Other opinion differences between traditional and activist senior careerists are noticeable on some issues, among them regulation of business, military preparedness, certain aspects of sex and morality, and affirmative action hiring practices for blacks and women.[72]

These various data suggest that national government civil servants are imperfectly representative, in demographic (and perhaps political) terms,

Table 15-3
SES SOCIAL AND PERSONAL BACKGROUNDS (percent)

Background	Traditional	Activist	Combined
White	95%	92%	94%
Male	96	90	93
From metropolitan area	40	59	50
Father a Democrat	60	55	55
Father a professional	20	28	24
Father a businessman	21	23	22
Parents above average income	31	35	33
Postgraduate degree	74	80	77
Family income $50,000 +	99	100	100
Political liberal	48	63	56
Raised in Jewish religion	13	26	20
Current religion "none"	28	36	32

Source: Stanley Rothman and S. Robert Lichter, "How Liberal Are Bureaucrats?" *Regulation*, 7 (November/December 1983), 17.

Table 15-4
SES PRESIDENTIAL VOTING PREFERENCES, 1968–1980 (percent voting for)[a]

	Traditional	*Activist*	*Combined*
1968			
Nixon	33%	23%	28%
Humphrey	67	76	72
1972			
Nixon	51	35	42
McGovern	47	65	57
1976			
Ford	35	24	28
Carter	65	76	71
1980			
Reagan	48	27	36
Carter	34	55	45
Anderson	19	18	18

[a]Percentages may not add to 100 because of rounding or votes for minor party candidates.

Source: Stanley Rothman and S. Robert Lichter, "How Liberal Are Bureaucrats?" *Regulation,* 7 (November/December 1983), 17.

of the public at large; certainly senior civil servants fit that description. Yet, given the professional nature of their work, we might expect that to be the case—at least concerning income, education, and certain issue positions. On the other hand, considering the changes already in motion regarding recruitment, promotion, and the like, greater demographic representativeness seems likely in the future.

The issue of representativeness obviously has many sides to it. One in particular that has proved controversial (see chapter 10) is the quest for representativeness of social/ethnic minorities. It was this dimension of the issue that sparked major changes in the 1970s. Ethnic minorities took the virtually unanimous position that greater ethnic representativeness was needed to enhance general understanding within the civil service of problems peculiar to minority groups. Furthermore, theirs was a call for *advocacy* of their cause, as a central activity of minority administrators. In general, the effort to increase ethnic representativeness was founded on the belief— perhaps quite valid—that government would otherwise continue to ignore minority concerns in program design and management.

Responsiveness

Responsiveness on the part of public officials to popular sentiments depends upon several factors being present in the governmental process. For one thing, it depends in a fundamental sense on the people's assumptions

Table 15-5
SES ATTITUDES ON SELECTED ISSUES (percent agreeing)

	Traditional	Activist	Combined
Economics			
Government should substantially redistribute income	49%	55%	52%
Government should guarantee jobs	33	33	33
Government should take over big corporations	3	5	4
Government should guarantee a good standard of living	41	46	43
Less regulation of business is good for U.S.	66	57	61
People with more ability should earn more	89	92	90
Social and Political Alienation			
U.S. institutions need complete overhaul	25	16	20
Structure of U.S. society causes alienation	29	26	27
U.S. legal system favors wealthy	71	80	76
In America hard work leads to financial security	72	63	67
Private enterprise is fair to workers	84	80	82
U.S. should move toward socialism	14	14	14
Foreign Policy			
We should be more forceful with the U.S.S.R.	34	27	31
CIA overthrows are sometimes necessary	57	63	60
Goal of U.S. foreign policy has been to protect business	37	49	43
U.S. military should be the strongest in the world regardless of cost	31	19	25
Disadvantaged Groups			
Women should get preference in hiring	28	40	34
Blacks should get preference in hiring	35	53	44
Blacks are denied education to advance	45	55	50
Blacks lack motivation to advance	17	13	15
Black gains come at white expense	8	6	7
Poor people are victims of circumstance	48	61	55
Sex and Morality			
Woman has right to decide on abortion	80	82	81
Homosexuals should not teach in schools	42	25	34
Homosexuality is wrong	54	40	47
Adultery is wrong	69	65	67
Energy and Environment			
Environmental problems are serious	68	76	72
We should halt nuclear energy development	5	2	3
Nuclear plants are safe	58	46	52

Source: Stanley Rothman and S. Robert Lichter, "How Liberal Are Bureaucrats?" *Regulation,* 7 (November/December 1983), 18.

about what *is* and what *should be* in the conduct of government and public policy making. It is not only a matter of what we establish, very loosely, as our governmental and societal objectives—it is also what we take for granted in our expectations about governmental activity.

Second, responsiveness requires meaningful access to the *right* decision makers, and a legitimate opportunity to be heard. Access is a key step in the policy process, and without it responsiveness cannot be assured.

Third, government and its agencies have to be *able* to respond to policy and program demands, even assuming they are willing to do so. Politically, financially, and administratively, agencies must be equipped to deliver services or otherwise satisfy public demands placed on them.

There are two major constraints on responsiveness. The first concerns public *expectations*. Ideally, public expectations should be realistic, reasonable, and manageable. Admittedly, anyone in government can hide behind excuses of unrealistic, unreasonable, or unmanageable public desires to avoid tackling hard problems that may objectively need attention. But the point here is that there may actually be conditions that for legitimate reasons are difficult to deal with—for example, environmental pollution, poverty, or nuclear waste disposal. If people assume that a problem can be solved, and it is not solved, the government may be accused (not entirely fairly) of being unresponsive to public wants. Despite our skepticism, inability to act *can* be an operating reality for a government agency—perhaps due to lack of jurisdiction, limited funds, political opposition, or merely difficulties in "making the ordinary happen" (see chapter 13).

The second constraint on responsiveness is the fact that government agencies cannot—or, at least, do not—respond equally to different societal interests. Inevitably, some groups view government as unresponsive because it does not respond to *them*. And they are often correct in that assessment. The main point, however, is that government is not simply "responsive," only "responsive *to*" interests and preferences that exist in society at large. Especially in the context of limited resources (fiscal and otherwise), government cannot be responsive to each and every interest or need, and is rarely able to satisfy fully those interests to which it does respond.

Accountability

Holding government officials to account for their actions is crucial to democratic government, even more so when substantial responsibility is entrusted to nonelected (administrative) personnel. "Governmental openness to public scrutiny is a key to accountability for official conduct,"[73] in principle. This rationale underlies freedom of information laws and sunshine laws, both of which increase the public's ability to inquire successfully into the activities of bureaucracy and other branches of government. The glare of publicity has long been known as one means of enforcing accountability, by making possible a better informed citizenry that can then act more intelligently and purposefully. Sunset laws (discussed in chapter 12) add another dimension to accountability. By requiring positive legislative action to renew agency mandates, there is a virtual guarantee that some examination of agency performance will take place. It should be emphasized, however, that merely routine reviews and near-universal renewals of agency authorizations will not serve the purposes of sunset legislation. Only careful, thorough, and demanding examinations will do.

The use of sunset laws, in particular, as an instrument of accountability is part of a widespread resurgence of legislative efforts to hold executives accountable.[74] Other institutional devices include the congressional budget procedure, involving CBO and two Budget Committees on Capitol Hill. In the best tradition of those who first shaped the political system, the public once again seems to be looking to its legislative representatives to bring about greater popular control over executive branch agencies. In both state and national government, increasing numbers of legislators seem inclined to respond positively to public pressures, and in some cases to lead public opinion as well as follow it. Further, legislative entities such as the U.S. General Accounting Office (GAO), which conduct general oversight activities, have been granted increasing authority to discipline administrative agencies. It should be noted, also, that agencies such as OMB and state bureaus of the budget ("little OMBs") are increasingly active in seeking to hold operating bureaucracies more accountable. These, too, have acquired more authority of late, to carry out that function.

Accountability is hampered by the prevalence of technical subject matter in government decision making. In many respects this limits the potential for accountability to those able to understand the nature of an issue and the implications of different proposed solutions. A case in point is the energy situation, where one thing that stands out is a need for more and better information, for decision maker and citizen alike. Few among us comprehend all the intricacies of natural gas pricing, the politics of supply here and abroad, and so on. If we, the people, cannot monitor government decisions in a knowledgeable way, how are we to ensure that those who make them can be held to account for them? There is no easy answer.[75]

Ethics, Morality, and Corruption

Public insistence in recent years on a greater degree of ethical and moral behavior in government has been principally a reaction to the traumas, untruths, and tensions of the Nixon administration, epitomized by the Watergate scandals. Yet such concerns are not new, and devising methods for ensuring ethical and moral behavior, and for reducing the incidence of corruption among government officials, is a continuing task.

As with other aspects of politics and public administration, there seems to be some feeling that it should be easy, even routine, to deal with problems of ethics and morality in the conduct of government. There are those who firmly believe there are moral and ethical absolutes that should be followed regardless of circumstance, in public affairs as well as in private life. Simply define the standards of conduct, some say, and then let the bureaucrats adhere to them in their work. But it is not that easy.

Virtually every major commentary on government ethics and morality in the literature of public administration in recent years has noted the *basic moral ambiguity* of public choices and policies.[76] Few, indeed, are the decisions in which one alternative, and one only, is clearly the most moral and ethical. How, then, can we deal meaningfully with the problem of ethics and morality without turning it simply into a matter of situation ethics, depending largely or entirely on particular issues and circumstances?

Fortunately, there are answers to that question. Some years ago, political scientist Stephen K. Bailey suggested that people need certain attitudes and moral qualities in order to behave ethically in the public service.[77] The first attitude is an *awareness* of moral ambiguity in decision making. The second is appreciation of the contextual forces at play in decision situations.[78] The third attitude is a conception of the "paradox of procedures," that is, an understanding of the need for orderly and rational procedures balanced against an understanding that procedures (red tape) can sometimes be an impediment to responsiveness and public accountability. The three moral qualities are optimism, including a willingness to take risks; courage, including the courage to avoid special favors, to make decisions that are unpopular, and to be able to decide under pressure; and charity, being fair and placing principle above personal needs for recognition, status, and power.[79]

Another aspect of ethics and morality is the question of internal (personal) versus external (legal-institutional) checks on the behavior of the individual administrator. Over the years, a debate has gone on over whether one or the other type of controls is more effective in ensuring ethical behavior, accountability, and responsibility. The classic exchange on this subject came nearly fifty years ago, between political scientists Carl Friedrich and Herman Finer.[80] Friedrich argued essentially that administrators are "responsible" if they are responsive to two "dominant factors": technical knowledge and popular (majority) sentiment. He urged reliance on these criteria for assessing responsibility, laying little if any stress on mechanisms for ensuring adherence to those standards. Finer, writing a year later, criticized the absence, in Friedrich's formulations, of any institutional safeguards for administrative responsibility. He suggested that while Friedrich defined responsibility as a "*sense* of responsibility, largely unsanctioned, except by deference or loyalty to professional standards . . . ," he (Finer) regarded it as "an arrangement of correction and punishment even up to dismissal both of politicians and officials. . . ."[81] Finer went on to warn that "sooner or later there is an abuse of power when external punitive controls are lacking."[82] Thus the central question, as framed in this exchange, is whether responsibility can be achieved by reliance on internal checks primarily, or whether it *requires* political checks and sanctions in addition to the individual administrator's own moral sense. Recent commentaries seem to be inclined toward the position that *both* types are needed. One central point made by a number of observers can be summed up as follows: "The public has to be able to rely on the self-discipline of the great majority of public servants. Otherwise the *official restraints and sanctions must be so numerous and so cumbersome* that effective public administration is impaired greatly."[83] The essential point is that while there may be some things we can—and perhaps must—do to try to ensure ethical actions in the public service, the ultimate safeguard is in the character and inclinations of bureaucrats themselves.

In addition, there are some other considerations. *Practical* ethical problems vary widely from agency to agency; they are very different, for example, at the State Department, the Department of Energy, and the Food and Drug Administration. Furthermore, there is a basic problem in "how to grasp the true meaning of ethics and morality—what it is from day to day and situation to situation—within a societal framework."[84] There is also the difficulty posed by the changing nature of public attention to ethics and morality, and different *definitions* of what is or is not acceptable behavior. And even where most of us agree on a definition, there remains the discomfiting fact that in different eras, other definitions have prevailed. In sum, though a situation ethic is not inevitable, standards of ethics and morality are not constant, universal, or applicable to all situations.

A crucial distinction in this area is between private and public morality. "John Courtney Murray, the great American Jesuit philosopher, wrote that one of the most dangerous misconceptions of the modern world is the idea that the same standards that govern individual morality should also govern national morality."[85] Behavior offensive to private morality, that is, could conceivably be moral according to standards of public morality. But what *is* "public morality"? For an answer we must look to a basic distinction between those clothed with the authority of official position and all others; a crucial difference is that *government has a monopoly on the legitimate use of force*. This means, for example, that government may use force when necessary to apprehend suspected criminals, that it may utilize the death penalty as long as it is constitutional to do so, and that it may order its soldiers to kill those of another country in wartime. We judge these acts by standards very different from those applied to private citizens, because the contexts of governmental versus individual actions are different. With power, of course, should go responsibility—some sense that there are different sorts of limits on behavior because of one's *public* obligations.

Joseph Califano, White House counselor under Lyndon Johnson and secretary of HHS under Jimmy Carter, provided a Watergate-related example in a 1973 article:

> Patrick Gray can equivocate in statements to the press, campaign while Acting FBI Director for the Republican Presidential candidate and destroy "politically dynamite" documents, but his Catholic upbringing and schooling did

not permit him to lie under oath because that involves personal morality and perhaps serious sin. The Haldeman and Ehrlichman letters of resignation pay lip service to public morality, but protest their private morality as though *that were the ultimate standard* by which their *exercise of the public trust* should be judged.[86]

And that is the point: the public trust and its exercise add a completely different dimension to what individuals do in official capacities, or in matters related to government decisions. The public trust imposes obligations on public officials over and above those arising from private moral codes.

One other example further illustrates confusion of public and private morality. The case involved the late Mayor Richard J. Daley of Chicago and two of his sons who were employed by an insurance firm in suburban Evanston. It became known that the firm had been awarded millions of dollars' worth of Chicago city government insurance contracts, without competitive bidding. When questioned by reporters about this, Daley paused and then explained that any father would do what he could to help his sons! True enough, and by Daley's strict personal moral code, entirely appropriate. But because of his public position and power, there were some, at least, who regarded this as a breach of public trust, because other insurance firms were also (corporate) citizens of Chicago, and public morality requires a government to deal equitably with all its citizens. And that, Daley clearly had not done.

Perhaps the most difficult aspect of this subject is that there is no *universal* definition of public morality, and attempts to arrive at one inevitably end up in the rough-and-tumble of the political process. An awareness that there even *is* such a thing as public morality must come before we can engage in the process of deciding what it is—and even then we might fall short.[87]

What, then, can we say of political corruption? Corruption is offensive to many traditions of private morality, yet rooting it out seems very difficult. There is one overriding truth about corruption: according to the standards many of us apply to it, *corruption is universal*, in the sense that virtually every political system has had its share of political favoritism, private arrangements between public figures, and out-and-out thievery and bribery. We find this offensive to our Western standards; but without trying to justify it, we should note that not everyone reacts the way we do. In many parts of the world, what we call corruption is part of the routine expectations of politics—and business and other enterprises, for that matter. Yet it is appropriate to combat it, if in fact corruption violates our expectations of what *our* officials should and should not do.

Corruption is a commonplace in many states and localities. Deals are made quietly, contracts awarded, jobs created, votes bartered for (and occasionally stolen), offices bandied about, power exerted, contributors rewarded, and so on, all on the basis of various forms of favoritism. The battle over municipal reform (see chapter 3) has centered on making it possible to stamp out corruption in government. Our image of corruption seems to emphasize big-city politics, but the fact is that in rural America there is the same kind of favoring friends and rewarding political loyalty as there is in the city. Patronage is rampant in some states, merely visible in others. The remarkable thing is that so much *has* been done to make the conduct of government more honest and open.[88]

One other observation is in order. Corruption, as a practical matter, is a form of *privilege,* indulged in by those in positions of power, wealth, and influence for their mutual gain. As such, corruption is inherently antidemocratic in nature, since it concentrates power and its benefits in relatively few hands. If democracy is founded in large part on a premise of equality in the political system, corruption is offensive to *that* value as well as to moral and ethical ones. Ultimately, this is another good reason for being concerned with corruption in a democratic government, one at least as relevant as moral and ethical considerations.

Administrative Effectiveness and Personal Liberty

One other topic deserves brief treatment: the possibility that as government machinery is made stronger, it acquires additional potential for diluting individual liberties. This does not necessarily occur as the product of deliberate decision in the highest councils of government. It can result simply from zealous implementation of perceived mandates by an individual agency or bureaucrat. It is even more of a possibility when strong public sentiment exists in support of particular agencies doing a job that inherently poses dangers to individual liberties.

A leading example is law enforcement agencies. In their zeal for "fighting crime," there is danger that the FBI, state law enforcement agencies, or local police may infringe on Bill of Rights protections. This is a serious concern of many people, and involves such issues as search and seizure procedures, wiretapping, the death penalty, and priorities of national security versus individual privacy, among many others. The essential point is that as the machinery of government grows stronger—whether or not it is supported by particular popular majorities—the *potential* for infringement of all sorts of individual rights grows apace. This causes operating problems for those in public administration, but all of society is ultimately involved because of the basic values at issue.

SUMMARY

Government bureaucracies pose particular difficulties for those seeking to maintain popular control over instruments of government. Their influence, coupled with the relative obscurity and political insulation of many agencies, has led to more intense pressures for greater responsiveness to, and control by, the public.

Democratic government presumes participation and accountability, with an independent judiciary and free elections as essential safeguards. The meanings of those values have changed over time, and have been significantly expanded in recent decades. Two related concepts—representation and representativeness—have taken on new meanings also, leading to definitional uncertainty. In addition, there are long-standing problems in maintaining democratic norms and practices, generally.

Public administration is particularly troublesome for a democratic system, for several reasons. Most bureaucrats are not elected. Expertise and knowledge are emphasized over participation. Specialization is valued, as is professionalism. Participation and professionalism conflict frequently, and it is difficult to incorporate both accountability and participation into policy making when administrative agencies are the chief policy makers.

Concerns about public administration and democratic government include the following. Administrative secrecy is a traditional feature of Weberian bureaucracy, though it has been weakened through the use of freedom of information laws and sunshine laws. Another recent emphasis is on the need to protect individual privacy against government invasion and against misuse of personal information. The computer and its capabilities have made this a vital issue.

Major dimensions of democratic administration include: (1) citizen participation, (2) bureaucratic representativeness, (3) responsiveness, (4) accountability, (5) ethics and morality in government, including corruption, and (6) administrative effectiveness as a threat to personal freedoms.

Citizen participation originated with efforts on the part of the urban poor (and some others) to obtain a greater voice in government decisions affecting their lives. It has now been adapted to the purposes of many other groups, white as well as nonwhite, more affluent and less affluent. Citizen participation has taken many forms: "community control" in the 1960s, preserving neighborhood character—and sometimes neighborhoods themselves—since then. It also has been incorporated into formal mechanisms for decision making. Citizen participation has had substantive impact on government decisions, but it also has its limits. Among those are: (1) some uncertainty as to its exact meaning about who is to participate, and to what extent; (2) the possibility of cooptation of citizen participants; (3) the likelihood that insufficient power, incongruent values, self-serving interests, and impediments of expertise, time, and access will hamper citizens' ability to achieve bureaucratic accountability; and (4) the conceptual implications of merely "seeking input."

Representation and representativeness in government generally and public administration specifically have recently been given more attention. Bureaucratic representation is ambiguous, though it has been suggested that "democratic morality" is best served by promoting broadly inclusive representation of interests in interactions among decision makers. Closely related is the need for access to decision makers, especially for weaker interests. Complicating representation is delegation of authority; most delegated authority is discretionary in its use. Another dimension of discretion is its diminishing bureaucratic predictability. Finally, traditional political insulation of administrative agencies somewhat limits representation.

The representativeness of government bureaucracy, a continuing concern, has been said to enhance bureaucratic effectiveness and responsiveness. A key finding of recent research is that civil servants in the upper grades are less representative than in the civil service as a whole. Representativeness of minorities, emphasized since the late 1960s, has increased in the civil service, though with what effects is not entirely clear.

Bureaucratic responsiveness depends upon popular assumptions about what *is* and *should be* in the conduct of government, meaningful access to decision makers, and agencies' ability to respond to public demands. Public expectations can affect how responsive the government is thought to be. Also, government cannot or will not respond equally to every interest or preference that exists in society.

Accountability requires government openness to public scrutiny. In this connection, freedom of information laws and sunshine laws have been enacted. Sunset laws help legislative bodies hold executive branch agencies accountable. Accountability is made more difficult by the technical subject matter in so much government activity.

Ethics and morality in government, as well as corruption, received much attention in the 1970s. For some, it is a simple matter of government officials behaving ''properly,'' by fixed and clear standards. However, ethics and morality are more likely to be achieved in the public context if bureaucrats are aware of the moral ambiguities in decision making, if they appreciate contextual forces in decision situations, and if they understand that while orderly and rational procedures are important, they should not become ends in themselves. The character of bureaucrats is a crucial factor, but legal-institutional checks are also needed to promote morality and responsibility in the public service. Practical ethical problems vary from agency to agency, situation to situation, and time to time. In addition, there are differences between private and public morality. The latter is based on the idea that special responsibilities accompany exercise of the public trust and legitimate use of force.

NOTES

1. See, among others, David O. Sears and Jack Citrin, *Tax Revolt: Something for Nothing in California*, enlarged ed. (Cambridge, Mass.: Harvard University Press, 1985).
2. A. Lee Fritschler, *Smoking and Politics: Policy Making and the Federal Bureaucracy*, 3rd ed. (Englewood Cliffs, N.J.: Prentice-Hall, 1983), p. 15.
3. Emmette S. Redford, *Democracy in the Administrative State* (New York: Oxford University Press, 1969), pp. 19–22.

4. Theodore H. White, *The Making of the President 1972* (New York: Atheneum, 1973), pp. 299–300.
5. Theodore J. Lowi, *The End of Liberalism: The Second Republic of the United States,* 2nd ed. (New York: Norton, 1979).
6. Victor A. Thompson, "Bureaucracy in a Democratic Society," in Roscoe C. Martin, ed., *Public Adminstration and Democracy* (Syracuse, N.Y.: Syracuse University Press, 1965), pp. 205–26, at p. 207.
7. William B. Eimicke, *Public Administration in a Democratic Context: Theory and Practice* (Beverly Hills, Calif.: Sage, 1974), p. 17.
8. Fritschler, *Smoking and Politics,* p. 15.
9. Harold C. Relyea, "Introduction," in Harold C. Relyea, ed., "Symposium on the Freedom of Information Act," *Public Administration Review,* 39 (July/August 1979), 310–32, at p. 310.
10. Ibid. (emphasis added).
11. Relyea, "Introduction, Symposium on the Freedom of Information Act," p. 310.
12. See Lloyd Nurick, "Access to Public Records: Strengthening Democracy," *The Bureaucrat,* 4 (April 1975), 34–44.
13. See Redford's treatment of the broader "right to know" in *Democracy in the Administrative State,* pp. 136–39. See also Itzhak Galnoor, ed., *Government Secrecy in Democracies* (New York: Harper Colophon Books, 1977); Donald C. Rowat, ed., *Administrative Secrecy in Developed Countries* (Irvington, N.Y.: Columbia University Press, 1979); and Editorial Research Reports, *The Public's Right to Know* (Washington, D.C.: Congressional Quarterly, Inc., 1980).
14. Telephone interview with a committee staff member, House information subcommittee, April 16, 1985.
15. *The Freedom of Information Reform Act,* Hearings before the Subcommittee on Information, Justice, and Agriculture, Committee on Government Operations, U.S. House of Representatives, 98th Congress, 2nd Session (Washington, D.C.: U.S. Government Printing Office, 1985), p. 696.
16. Ibid., pp. 33–34 and 693–94.
17. U.S. Advisory Commission on Intergovernmental Relations, *Citizen Participation in the American Federal System* (Washington, D.C.: U.S. Government Printing Office, March 1979), p. 289.
18. See Redford, *Democracy in the Administrative State,* pp. 149–51.
19. See Willis H. Ware and Carole W. Parsons, "Perspectives on Privacy," *The Bureaucrat,* 5 (July 1976), 141–56.
20. Ibid., pp. 144–48.
21. See also Frank G. De Balogh, "Public Administrators and 'The Privacy Thing': A Time to Speak Out," *Public Administration Review,* 32 (September/October 1972), 526–30; E. Edward Stephens, "Legal Invasions of Our Right of Privacy," *The Bureaucrat,* 4 (October 1975), 290–92; Edmund Dwyer, "The Right of Privacy versus Technological Advances," *The Bureaucrat,* 4 (October 1975), 293–98; Hugh V. O'Neill, "The Privacy Act of 1974: Introduction and Overview," *The Bureaucrat,* 5 (July 1976), 131–40; Robert P. Bedell, "The Privacy Act: The Implementation at First Glance," *The Bureaucrat,* 5 (July 1976), 157–70; and Hugh V. O'Neill and John P. Fanning, "The Challenge of Implementing and Operating under the Privacy Act in the Largest Public Sector Conglomerate—HEW," *The Bureaucrat,* 5 (July 1976), 171–88.

22. *Citizen Participation in the American Federal System*, p. 5. For a fuller treatment of participation in national programs, see Walter A. Rosenbaum, "Public Involvement as Reform and Ritual: The Development of Federal Participation Programs," in Stuart Langton, ed., *Citizen Participation in America* (Lexington, Mass.: Lexington Books, 1978), pp. 81–94.

23. Walter A. Rosenbaum, "The Paradoxes of Public Participation," *Administration and Society*, 8 (November 1976), 355–83, at pp. 362–63.

24. *Citizen Participation in the American Federal System*, pp. 2–9 and chapters 3 through 5.

25. See Gordon P. Whitaker, "Coproduction: Citizen Participation in Service Delivery," *Public Administration Review*, 40 (May/June 1980), 240–46. See also Michael R. Fitzgerald and Robert F. Durant, "Citizen Evaluations and Urban Management: Service Delivery in an Era of Protest," *Public Administration Review*, 40 (November/December 1980), 585–94; Jeffrey L. Brudney and Robert E. England, "Toward a Definition of the Coproduction Concept," *Public Administration Review*, 43 (January/February 1983), 59–65; and Charles Levine, "Citizenship and Service Delivery: The Promise of Coproduction," in H. George Frederickson and Ralph Clark Chandler, eds., "Citizenship and Public Administration: Proceedings of the National Conference on Citizenship and Public Service," *Public Administration Review*, 44 (March 1984), 178–87. A further refinement of the coproduction concept is discussed in James M. Ferris, "Coprovision: Citizen Time and Money Donations in Public Service Provision," *Public Administration Review*, 44 (July/August 1984), 324–33.

26. *Citizen Participation in the American Federal System*, chapter 3.

27. Ibid., p. 292.

28. Ibid.

29. See, among others, Alan Altshuler, *Community Control: The Black Demand for Participation in Large American Cities* (New York: Pegasus, 1970); Milton Kotler, *Neighborhood Government: The Local Foundations of Political Life* (Indianapolis: Bobbs-Merrill, 1969); and Joseph Zimmerman, *The Federated City: Community Control in Large Cities* (New York: St. Martin's, 1972).

30. Neal R. Peirce and Jerry Hagstrom, "Two Years After Carter's Visit, Islands of Hope Dot the South Bronx," *National Journal*, 11 (October 6, 1979), 1,644–48, at p. 1,644 (emphasis added).

31. For an incisive, in-depth study of the Rye-Oyster Bay Bridge controversy emphasizing the role of citizen organizations, see Thomas A. Droleskey, "The Politics of the Proposal to Construct a Bridge Crossing from Oyster Bay to Rye, New York: A Study of Group Politics and Public Policy Decision Making," unpublished Ph.D. dissertation, Graduate School of Public Affairs, State University of New York at Albany, 1977.

32. For a broad-ranging assessment of organized citizen activity, see Harry C. Boyte, *The Backyard Revolution: Understanding the New Citizen Movement* (Philadelphia: Temple University Press, 1980). The redlining and uranium mining cases are discussed at length in Boyte's work. See also Sandra Schoenberg and Patricia Rosenbaum, *Neighborhoods That Work: Sources for Viability in the Inner City* (New Brunswick, N.J.: Rutgers University Press, 1980); Richard O. Baumbach, Jr., and William E. Borah, *The Second Battle of New Orleans: A History of the Vieux Carré Riverfront-Expressway Controversy* (University, Ala.: University of Alabama Press, 1981); Jeffrey Henig, *Neighborhood Mobilization: Redevelopment and*

Response (New Brunswick, N.J.: Rutgers University Press, 1982); Si Kahn, *Organizing: A Guide for Grass Roots Leaders* (New York: McGraw-Hill, 1983); and Neil S. Mayer, *Neighborhood Organizations and Community Development: Making Revitalization Work* (Washington: The Urban Institute Press, 1984).

33. See Max D. Paglin and Edgar Shor, ''Regulatory Agency Responses to the Development of Public Participation,'' *Public Administration Review*, 37 (March/April 1977), 140–48; Joan B. Aron, ''Citizen Participation at Government Expense,'' *Public Administration Review*, 39 (September/October 1979), 477–85; and chapter 14.

34. Adepoju G. Onibokun and Martha Curry, ''An Ideology of Citizen Participation: The Metropolitan Seattle Transit Case Study,'' *Public Administration Review*, 36 (May/June 1976), 269–77.

35. Developed by Sherry Arnstein, ''A Ladder of Citizen Participation,'' *The Journal of the American Institute of Planners*, 35 (July 1969), 216–24, cited in Adepoju G. Onibokun and Martha Curry, ''An Ideology of Citizen Participation: The Metropolitan Seattle Transit Case Study,'' *Public Administration Review*, 36 (May/June 1976), 269–77, at p. 273.

36. Onibokun and Curry, ''An Ideology of Citizen Participation: The Metropolitan Seattle Transit Case Study,'' p. 273.

37. Ibid., p. 274. Another dimension of the relationship between citizenship and the role of the professional public servant is discussed in Terry Cooper, ''Citizenship and Professionalism in Public Administration,'' in H. George Frederickson and Ralph Clark Chandler, eds., ''Citizenship and Public Administration: Proceedings of the National Conference on Citizenship and Public Service,'' *Public Administration Review*, 44 (March 1984), 143–49.

38. These questions are suggested by John H. Strange, ''The Impact of Citizen Participation on Public Administration,'' *Public Administration Review, Special Issue*, 32 (September 1972), 457–70, at pp. 460–61.

39. Rosenbaum, ''The Paradoxes of Public Participation,'' p. 273 (emphasis added).

40. James A. Riedel, ''Citizen Participation: Myths and Realities,'' *Public Administration Review*, 32 (May/June 1972), 211–20, at p. 212.

41. James L. Sundquist, with the collaboration of David W. Davis, *Making Federalism Work: A Study of Program Coordination at the Community Level* (Washington, D.C.: Brookings, 1969), pp. 94–101.

42. Riedel, ''Citizen Participation: Myths and Realities,'' p. 212.

43. Roscoe C. Martin, *Grass Roots* (University, Ala.: University of Alabama Press, 1957).

44. The description is that of U.S. Senator Daniel P. Moynihan (D.-New York), in a speech delivered at Syracuse University, May 8, 1969; cited in Harold Seidman, *Politics, Position, and Power: The Dynamics of Federal Organization*, 3rd ed. (New York: Oxford University Press, 1980), p. 187.

45. Seidman, *Politics, Position, and Power*, p. 186.

46. See D. Stephen Cupps, ''Emerging Problems of Citizen Participation,'' *Public Administration Review*, 37 (September/October 1977), 478–87.

47. Ibid., p. 479.

48. Ibid., pp. 483–84.

49. Robert W. Kweit, ''Bureaucratic Decision Making: Impediments to Citizen Participation,'' paper presented at the 1977 annual meeting of the Midwest Political Science Association, Chicago, April 21–23, 1977. See also Mary Grisez Kweit

and Robert W. Kweit, *Implementing Citizen Participation in a Bureaucratic Society: A Contingency Approach* (New York: Praeger,1982).

50. For other perspectives on various aspects of citizen participation, see Karin Brown and Philip B. Coulter, "Subjective and Objective Measures of Police Service Delivery," *Public Administration Review*, 43 (January/February 1983), 50–58; Terry L. Cooper, "Citizen Participation," in Thomas D. Lynch, ed., *Organization Theory and Management* (New York: Marcel Dekker, 1983); L. A. Wilson II, "Preference Revelation and Public Policy: Making Sense of Citizen Survey Data," and Carol L. Ellis, "Program Termination: A Word to the Wise," *Public Administration Review*, 43 (July/August 1983), 335–42 and 352–57, respectively; Steven M. Neuse, "From Grass Roots to Citizen Participation: Where We've Been And Where We Are Now," *Public Administration Quarterly*, 7 (Fall 1983), 294–309; John L. Crompton, "Recreation Vouchers: A Case Study in Administrative Innovation and Citizen Participation," *Public Administration Review*, 43 (November/December 1983), 537–46; James C. Petersen, ed., *Citizen Participation in Science Policy* (Amherst, Mass.: The University of Massachusetts Press, 1984); Curtis Ventriss and Robert Pecorella, "Community Participation and Modernization: A Reexamination of Political Choices," *Public Administration Review*, 44 (May/June 1984), 224–31; Robert M. O'Brien, Michael Clarke, and Sheldon Kamieniecki, "Open and Closed Systems of Decision Making: The Case of Toxic Waste Management," *Public Administration Review*, 44 (July/August 1984), 334–40; and Curtis Ventriss, "Emerging Perspectives on Citizen Participation," *Public Administration Review*, 45 (May/June 1985), 433–40.

51. This discussion relies in part on Eimicke, *Public Administration in a Democratic Context*, pp. 33–44. See also Hanna F. Pitkin, *Representation* (New York: Atherton, 1969).

52. Redford, *Democracy in the Administrative State*, especially chapter 2.

53. Ibid., p. 44.

54. Ibid., p. 69 (emphasis added).

55. Ibid., pp. 94–95.

56. Thompson, "Bureaucracy in a Democratic Society," p. 207 (emphasis added).

57. Norton E. Long, "Bureaucracy and Constitutionalism," *American Political Science Review*, 46 (September 1952), 808–18.

58. This discussion relies principally on Samuel Krislov, *Representative Bureaucracy* (Englewood Cliffs, N.J.: Prentice-Hall, 1974); Kenneth John Meier, "Representative Bureaucracy: An Empirical Analysis," *American Political Science Review*, 69 (June 1975), 526–42; Joel D. Aberbach, Robert D. Putnam, and Bert A. Rockman, *Bureaucrats and Politicians in Western Democracies* (Cambridge, Mass.: Harvard University Press, 1981); and Stanley Rothman and S. Robert Lichter, "How Liberal Are Bureaucrats?" *Regulation*, 7 (November/December 1983), 16–22. See also Kenneth John Meier and Lloyd G. Nigro, "Representative Bureaucracy and Policy Preferences: A Study in the Attitudes of Federal Executives," *Public Administration Review*, 36 (July/August 1976), 458–69; and Samuel Krislov and David H. Rosenbloom, *Representative Bureaucracy and the American Political System* (New York: Praeger, 1981).

59. Krislov, *Representative Bureaucracy*, p. 81.

60. Ibid., p. 106.

61. Ibid., p. 113. See also David H. Rosenbloom, "Federal Equal Employment Op-

portunity: Is the Polarization Worth the Preference?'' *Southern Review of Public Administration*, 5 (Spring 1981), 63–72.

62. Meier, ''Representative Bureaucracy: An Empirical Analysis,'' p. 526.
63. Ibid., p. 541.
64. Ibid., p. 539.
65. Ibid., p. 541.
66. Aberbach, Putnam, and Rockman, *Bureaucrats and Politicians in Western Democracies*, chapter 3.
67. Ibid., pp. 47–48.
68. Ibid., pp. 53 and 55.
69. Ibid., p. 66.
70. Rothman and Lichter, ''How Liberal Are Bureaucrats?''
71. Testimony of S. Robert Lichter, *The Senior Executive Service*, Hearings before the Subcommittee on Civil Service, Committee on Post Office and Civil Service, U.S. House of Representatives, 98th Congress, 2nd Session (Washington, D.C.: U.S. Government Printing Office, 1984), p. 356 (emphasis added).
72. Support for ''representative bureaucracy'' among administrators, executives, and legislators in five state governments is treated in Dennis Daley, ''Political and Occupational Barriers to the Implementation of Affirmative Action: Administrative, Executive, and Legislative Attitudes Toward Representative Bureaucracy,'' *Review of Public Personnel Administration*, 4 (Summer 1984), 4–15. See especially Tables 1 and 2, p. 8.
73. Justice Bertram Harnett of the New York State Supreme Court, quoted in Nurick, ''Access to Public Records: Strengthening Democracy,'' p. 40.
74. Bruce Adams, ''Sunset: A Proposal for Accountable Government,'' *Administrative Law Review*, 28 (Summer 1976), 511–42.
75. Useful and insightful discussions of accountability can be found in Bernard Rosen, *Holding Government Bureaucracies Accountable* (New York: Praeger, 1982); Douglas Yates, *Bureaucratic Democracy: The Search for Democracy and Efficiency in American Government* (Cambridge, Mass.: Harvard University Press, 1982), especially chapter 6; and Richard C. Elling, ''Bureaucratic Accountability: Problems and Paradoxes; Panaceas and (Occasionally) Palliatives,'' *Public Administration Review*, 43 (January/February 1983), 82–89.
76. See, for example, Susan Wakefield, ''Ethics and the Public Service,'' *Public Administration Review*, 36 (November/December 1976), 661–66.
77. Stephen K. Bailey, ''Ethics and the Public Service,'' in Roscoe C. Martin, ed., *Public Administration and Democracy* (Syracuse, N.Y.: Syracuse University Press, 1965), pp. 283–98.
78. Ibid., p. 291.
79. Ibid., p. 293.
80. See Carl J. Friedrich, ''Public Policy and the Nature of Administrative Responsibility,'' *Public Policy*, 1 (1940), 3–24; and Herman Finer, ''Administrative Responsibility and Democratic Government,'' *Public Administration Review*, 1 (Summer 1941), 335–50.
81. Finer, ''Administrative Responsibility and Democratic Government,'' p. 335 (emphasis added).
82. Ibid., p. 337.
83. DeWitt C. Armstrong III and George A. Graham, ''Ethical Preparation for the

Public Service," *The Bureaucrat*, 4 (April 1975), 6–23, at p. 6 (emphasis added).

84. Ersa Poston and Walter D. Broadnax, "Ethics and Morality in Government: Introduction," *The Bureaucrat*, 4 (April 1975), 3–4, at p. 3.

85. Cited by Joseph A. Califano, Jr., "Richard Nixon: The Resignation Option," *The Bureaucrat*, 2 (Summer 1973), 222–31, at p. 225.

86. Ibid., p. 226 (emphasis added).

87. For further discussion of ethics in public administration, see Ivan L. Richardson and Sidney Baldwin, *Public Administration: Government in Action* (Columbus, Ohio: Charles E. Merrill, 1976), chapter 20; John Rohr, *Ethics for Bureaucrats* (New York: Marcel Dekker, 1978); Joel L. Fleishman, Lance Liebman, and Mark H. Moore, eds., *Public Duties: The Moral Obligations of Government Officials* (Cambridge, Mass.: Harvard University Press, 1981); Dennis F. Thompson, "Ethics: Presenting the Moral Issues in Politics," *Public Policy and Management Newsletter*, 3 (November 1980), 1–2 (published by the Public Policy and Management Program for Case/Course Development; Cambridge, Massachusetts); John A. Rohr, "Professional Ethics," in Thomas D. Lynch, ed., *Organization Theory and Management* (New York: Marcel Dekker, 1983); Ralph Clark Chandler, "The Problem of Moral Reasoning in American Public Administration: The Case for a Code of Ethics," *Public Administration Review*, 43 (January/February 1983), 32–39; Philip Schorr, "Learning Ethics: The Search For An Ideal Model," *Public Administration Quarterly*, 7 (Fall 1983), 323–45; Louis C. Gawthrop, *Public Sector Management, Systems, and Ethics* (Bloomington, Ind.: Indiana University Press, 1984); York Willbern, "Types and Levels of Public Morality," *Public Administration Review*, 44 (March/April 1984), 102–8; and Dennis F. Thompson, "The Possibility of Administrative Ethics," *Public Administration Review*, 45 (September/October 1985), 555–61.

88. Sources on administrative corruption include *Fraud in Government Programs: How Extensive Is It? Can It Be Controlled?*, A Report to the Congress of the United States by the Comptroller General, General Accounting Office Report No. AFMD-82-3 (Washington, D.C.: U.S. Government Printing Office, November 6, 1981); Simcha B. Werner, "New Directions in the Study of Administrative Corruption," *Public Administration Review*, 43 (March/April 1983), 146–54; and James S. Larson, "Fraud in Government Programs: A Secondary Analysis," *Public Administration Quarterly*, 7 (Fall 1983), 274–93.

SUGGESTED READINGS

Aberbach, Joel D., Robert D. Putnam, and Bert A. Rockman. *Bureaucrats and Politicians in Western Democracies*. Cambridge, Mass.: Harvard University Press, 1981.

Cooper, Terry L. "Citizen Participation," in Thomas D. Lynch, ed., *Organization Theory and Management*. New York: Marcel Dekker, 1983.

Krislov, Samuel, and David H. Rosenbloom. *Representative Bureaucracy and the American Political System*. New York: Praeger, 1981.

Kweit, Mary Grisez, and Robert W. Kweit. *Implementing Citizen Participation in a Bureaucratic Society: A Contingency Approach*. New York: Praeger, 1982.

Martin, Roscoe C. *Grass Roots*. University, Ala.: University of Alabama Press, 1957.

_____, ed. *Public Administration and Democracy*. Syracuse, N.Y.: Syracuse University Press, 1965.

Mayer, Neil S. *Neighborhood Organizations and Community Development: Making Revitalization Work*. Washington, D.C.: The Urban Institute Press, 1984.

Redford, Emmette S. *Democracy in the Administrative State*. New York: Oxford University Press, 1969.

Rohr, John A. *Ethics for Bureaucrats*. New York: Marcel Dekker, 1978.

_____. ''Professional Ethics,'' in Thomas D. Lynch, ed., *Organization Theory and Management*. New York: Marcel Dekker, 1983.

Rosen, Bernard. *Holding Government Bureaucracies Accountable*. New York: Praeger, 1982.

U.S. Advisory Commission on Intergovernmental Relations. *Citizen Participation in the American Federal System*. Washington, D.C.: U.S. Government Printing Office, March 1979.

Yates, Douglas. *Bureaucratic Democracy: The Search for Efficiency and Democracy in American Government*. Cambridge, Mass.: Harvard University Press, 1982.

16

Public Administration in a Time of Uncertainty

Our examination of public administration in the United States is now completed. From treatment of various topics in this text—values, executive leadership, intergovernmental relations, organization theory, personnel and budgeting, government regulation, and the rest—several impressions should have emerged clearly. Most important is that the current state of public administration is characterized by considerable uncertainty and change, by dramatic developments in and out of the field affecting what it presently is and does and the likely shape of its future.

Another impression is (or should have been) that while it might be desirable to maintain various features of governmental and administrative practice—such as efficiency, accountability, participation, and strong leadership—it is difficult, if not impossible, to achieve all or even most of them simultaneously. This poses hard questions for us. On which feature(s) do we place greatest value? Which are we willing to forego in order to achieve another? Who benefits and who loses from choosing one over another? In short, intricate and perplexing questions abound—questions from which there is no escape.

In this chapter we will discuss public administration in the context of continuing uncertainty. We will look first at the social and governmental environment, building on the discussion in chapter 2. Then we will consider growing ferment and change in concepts and practices of governmental administration, review evolving issues and challenges in its study and teaching, and conclude by noting several continuing features—and questions—in the field. Throughout this discussion several themes will be evident: (1) the presence of numerous paradoxes in public administration; (2) tensions existing among these paradoxes, and the challenge of dealing with them; and (3) the accelerating rate of change in administrative theory and practice.

THE SOCIAL AND GOVERNMENTAL ENVIRONMENT

For the past quarter-century social and political struggles have taken new forms in this country, imposing great pressures on our values and institutions. Rising social tension and value conflicts stem from *social and economic diversity*. Societal relations directly affect political interests and competition. If those relations are tense and competitive among a large number of groups, as they have been recently, that will be reflected in political values and procedures, including those in administration. ''[The national government] has become a microcosm of the conflicts and differences that pervade society. . . . As government becomes coextensive with society in composition and function, it experiences the disorganization . . . of society itself.''[1]

There is much more to the social and governmental environment than simply diversity, however. Recent turbulence surrounding public administration in theory and practice has resulted from a host of changes, paradoxes, and conflicts. Chief among them is *rapid social change*, not only in population growth and geographic distribution but also in economic instruments, evolving governmental roles, and technological developments. Our capacity for economic growth is seriously hampered by limits on access to needed raw materials—chiefly oil, but also metals from other countries—as well as limits resulting from depletion of our natural resources. And politically, this nation changed direction sharply in the 1980 elections, with consequences still far from certain in both the short and the long term.

Another factor is the ''knowledge explosion,'' which carries with it ''increasing potential for human intervention and control both good and bad.''[2] Growth of knowledge, science, and technology is closely linked with changes in the nature of society and in human capabilities, values, and behavior.[3] As one example, scientific explanations about origins of the universe and of life on this planet may profoundly affect traditional religious beliefs; as another example, consider the implications of unlocking the mysteries of human genetics and of death. If these were at one time the stuff of dreamers or science fiction writers, they are no longer.

Such developments have an ironic twist. We have had faith for decades that expanding our knowledge would make our world both more secure and more predictable, and that science would help us answer age-old questions with much more precision and certainty. Yet we have found just the opposite: the more we have learned, the *less* certain everything seems. Many people are disturbed by all this uncertainty, and it is possible that expanded knowledge contributes to *social instability*, with many seeking to return (in effect) to a less unnerving past. One indication of this is the phenomenon of religious revivalism, or fundamentalism, among growing numbers of Christians, Jews, and Muslims, in many countries of the world.

A further dimension of the present social and governmental environment is a focus on dealing with social problems. A direct link exists between this emphasis and public administration, since "on virtually every major problem and every major challenge and opportunity we turn to government"—controlling the weather or population growth, eliminating race or sex discrimination, guaranteeing safety and effectiveness of drugs, or rescuing a bankrupt railroad.[4] This is so in spite of the fact that many problems cannot be fully solved, only coped with;[5] thus, demands on bureaucracy to *solve* problems may be unrealistic, in some cases. Nevertheless, in terms of a balance between public and private sectors in dealing with society's problems, the public (governmental) side of the scale has received much greater weight (though now that may have begun to change). Furthermore, "as the range of public problems and programs broadens, and as knowledge relevant to each grows and deepens, it becomes less and less possible for politically elected representatives to get a handle on more than a few of the significant issues."[6] Thus, the role of expert administrators to whom responsibility for program management is delegated becomes ever larger (though it is not unlimited, by any means).

One other aspect of the immediate social and governmental environment of public administration—with enormous significance for the future conduct of government generally—is the advent of *fiscal stress*. As inflation combined with declining productivity and slower economic growth in the private sector, the revenue base of government at all levels shrank. Consequently, administrative agencies and government units, by the hundreds, are facing deep cutbacks in funding, personnel, and the levels of services they can continue to provide to the public. The general unwillingness of the taxpayer to take on additional tax burdens, as exemplified by Proposition 13, has only compounded the problem for government officials. This has obvious financial implications for budget making but also directly affects personnel management, labor relations, and the need for greater efficiency and productivity in public management.

The central difficulty, however, is the need for us to adjust our assumptions about economic growth as the foundation for continued *governmental* growth. Agencies, and their administrators and clienteles, accustomed to successive increases in operating budgets and the programmatic benefits they could provide, have been rudely jolted by new economic—and political—realities. The present environment in this respect, in short, has turned hostile toward "big government"—out of economic necessity, if not always due to direct public hostility. The long-term consequences of this change may prove to be both permanent and fundamental in their impact on government and on administrative operations in particular.

All this is occurring in the context of more fundamental value changes in society. A wide range of beliefs and institutions is under attack from new and competing ideologies. Central to change at this basic level is decline of authority; traditional sources and centers of authority—including family, religion, and law—exert diminishing influence.[7] Decline of authority suggests changing institutional patterns. The ability of government to govern may well be compromised, to say nothing of how other institutions such as churches, universities, and businesses will be affected. Current (world-wide) unrest within the Roman Catholic church illustrates the decline of authority within that system. Others are experiencing similar breakdowns.

Social and Governmental Paradoxes

Contributing still further to uncertainty in public administration is a series of paradoxical developments, some within this country alone and others worldwide in their scope. First, as noted in chapter 1, there is a blurring of distinctions between public and private sectors in this country, contrary to a widespread popular perception that they are separate and distinct. Every important program to raise income, employment, and productivity, relieve social distress, correct abuses, and protect rights has "entailed the creation of new and complex arrangements in which the distinction between public and private has become more blurred."[8] Examples are numerous: Amtrak, the Corporation for Public Broadcasting, and the Legal Services Corpora-tion, at the national level; community action agencies in the poverty pro-gram, and health systems agencies (both bridging public-private and inter-governmental boundaries); and quasi-public organizations established to work with government in public programs like Medicare, Medicaid, com-munity development, and CETA. As indicated, these "twilight zones" have grown considerably.[9]

Second, we are confronted by the legacy of a "revolution of rising ex-pectations," which still dominates politics in developing nations and some portions of our own population. At the same time, a cry has gone up from others for a lowering of our expectations. Both refer to expectations for eco-nomic development, industrialization, increased productivity, acquisition of material possessions, and a rising standard of living.[10] In this country, rising expectations and government's responses to them centered on the poor, in particular racial and ethnic minorities who have by no means given up their aspirations to the "good life." The countering trend toward lower-ing expectations reflects concern for environmental quality, finite re-sources, population stabilization rather than growth, and "quality of life" as against "standard of living."[11] Political controversies of recent years over "economy versus ecology" and over nuclear power plants illustrate this paradox.

Third, a paradox exists between continuing emphasis on industrial-ism (closely linked to economic development and rising expectations) and the emergence of what has been called the "postindustrial society."[12] Pos-tindustrialism refers to a socioeconomic order in which there is a relative decline in importance of production, land, and labor as economic forces, and a relative upsurge in importance of knowledge, new technologies, ren-dering of services (as against production of goods), and available leisure time. Implications for government and administration are immense: changes in revenue patterns, service needs, political demands, and so on. Elements of the postindustrial society have become a part of the fabric of social and economic life, and therefore of the complex forces pressing on government and administration. This paradox is complicated further by an emerging emphasis on *re*industrialization, that is, on upgrading and modernizing industry as our aging physical plant and production capacity fall behind those of other nations.

Fourth, forces of nationalism still run strong in many parts of the world, while conflicting currents of "postnationalism" have arisen and are gaining strength.[13] In some of the older nation-states, nationalism—identity with a national unit of government, patriotism, observance of duties of citizenship, pride in one's country—seems to be in decline. "Postnational" cynicism toward patriotism and political symbols such as anthems and flags, and growing alienation from government institutions, all mark this decline. Postnationalism could mean one of two things: either an awakening of feeling for "world community," for organizing political arrangements that would strengthen international bonds of cooperation and respect (such as the European Economic Community), or a trend toward emphasizing individual *group* identities within nations at the expense of established political entities. Tribalism in African nations, the Quebec separatist movement, language rivalries in Belgium, and racial separatism in the United States are examples of the latter.

A fifth paradox involves tendencies toward violence and nonviolence.[14] The former is no stranger to either world affairs or our own domestic scene. Huge stockpiles of nuclear weapons in the United States and Soviet Union, with the prospect of other countries such as Israel, Libya, and Pakistan joining the "nuclear club," create potential not only for violence but for worldwide holocaust. Nonnuclear conflicts exist between or within nations, reminding us almost constantly of how far we are from a world order characterized by the peaceful rule of law. On the other hand, there is rising sentiment for nonviolent resolution of disputes, with considerable organizational sophistication in some instances—the United Nations and its complex of organizations is the best-known example. Martin Luther King patterned his nonviolent civil rights movement after the example of Mohandas Gandhi, leader of India's independence movement against Britain in the 1940s; the antiwar movement trying to stop our involvement in Vietnam during the late 1960s and early 1970s was generally (though not entirely) nonviolent; and growing opposition to nuclear weapons (largely nonviolent) surfaced in the early 1980s. Another irony is present, however, in that "some movements for peace and brotherhood take violence as a *means*."[15]

Sixth, as noted in chapter 2, the value of limited government continues to exert a hold on our thinking in this country, yet many government programs and activities seem to conflict with it. Government regulation is a prime example. To the extent that we look to government to protect us from market abuses and related ills, we create potential for government to regulate more than economic behavior. How limited we want our government to be will continue to be an issue in politics and administration for the foreseeable future, with no clear sign now of which way it will be resolved—if in fact it *can be* resolved.

Seventh, a paradox similar to the one just noted exists in the tendencies of many people to regard government (and bureaucracy, more specifically) with hostility, at the same time that they want public agencies to satisfy their demands. A prevailing attitude appears to be one of "I want mine" from government, while not respecting or trusting government institutions very much. More generally, many have come to demand "less government" in the abstract, while still looking to government officials for protection from dangers that are all too tangible. It takes more government (and bureaucracy), not less, to protect the public against toxic wastes, nuclear wastes and accidents, or potentially unsafe modes of transportation. Another aspect of this phenomenon is the tendency of individuals to criticize the growth of bureaucracy, and to call for "corrective" measures, but somehow they always seem to be referring to programs that benefit *others*— never to the programs in which *they* are interested.[16]

Finally, multiple meanings of "representation" and "representative" pose an important paradox. Throughout our discussion we have referred to the calls for "representativeness" as meaning inclusion in decision-making processes of those whose interests are affected by decisions made, especially those previously excluded. An older, more traditional meaning of "representation" refers to "overhead democracy"—that is, majority control through political representatives, "wherein administrative officers are primarily responsible and loyal to their superiors for carrying out the directions of the elected representatives."[17] Old and new meanings of representation have collided in theory and practice during the past two decades, and no slackening of the conflict between them is in sight. Ultimately, it is a conflict between concepts stressing, respectively, *majoritarian* and *minoritarian* political representation—that is, generalized majority rule versus systematic inclusion of social, political, and economic minorities.

These paradoxes have a number of aspects in common. Where our values have changed—for example, nationalism and postnationalism—it is impossible to pinpoint just when the emphasis shifted from one to the other or, for that matter, just how far it has moved. Also, divergent tendencies present in all the paradoxes are related to one another in some instances— for example, in antipoverty programs where rising expectations, public/ private overlap, violence/nonviolence, and postnationalism come together; or in the highway program, where many people want to facilitate auto travel but worry about air pollution and, most of all, do not want highways built through their neighborhoods.

Most important, these paradoxes have certain crucial implications for public administration as a whole. Administrative machinery is "government's central instrument for dealing with general social problems" and consequently "it is located in or between" whatever paradoxes exist in the surrounding society. "It is affected by whatever forces and turbulence there are; and it attempts also to *act*, to restrain or to increase the direction or degree of change."[18] Because of public expectations that government *will* act, administrative agencies and personnel *must* do so, even when choices are unclear, consequences only dimly perceived, and political pressures arising from these paradoxes troublesome and unyielding.

In sum, the existing environment, with its turbulence and paradoxes, poses many challenges to public administration. Since the outlook is for even more societal complexity in the future, the prognosis for public administration is that it will experience continued pressures—for service delivery, adaptation to new needs and challenges, and political responsiveness to varied (and often conflicting) interests.

FERMENT AND CHANGE IN PUBLIC ADMINISTRATION: CONCEPTS AND PRACTICES

This discussion of ferment and change in "practical" public administration will cover some of the same ground explored in earlier chapters. However, it is appropriate here to reexamine the contours of change in the context of what it may portend for the future.

First, bureaucracy as Max Weber defined and described it has changed considerably in the past quarter-century. "The old Weberian description of bureaucracy, with its emphasis upon formal structure, hierarchy, routinization, and efficiency in its narrow sense, is rapidly becoming obsolete in many organizations."[19] It is especially inadequate, some say, for agencies operating within a turbulent environment, facing increasing complexity in their programs, and staffed heavily with highly professional or scientific personnel. Such organizations, in order to maintain needed flexibility, creativity, and innovativeness, must be structured around projects or problems to be solved rather than as permanent hierarchies. The latter will remain for various administrative purposes, such as record keeping and auditing, and for fixing final responsibility, but "work itself will be organized more collegially on a team basis. Generalist decisions will be reached through the pooling of the perspectives and techniques of a variety of specialists. Leadership will be increasingly stimulative and collaborative rather than directive."[20] This assessment is in keeping with the discussion of alternative forms of organization in chapter 7.

A dramatic change in Weberian *practices* as well as structures is already detectable. Among the most basic functions in Weber's model of bureaucracy were orderliness, predictability, and control,[21] each of which has been profoundly affected by contemporary turbulence in and around public administration. Another irony is evident: many people longing for bureaucratic predictability are among the harshest critics of Weberian bureaucracy, which highly values that very thing; furthermore, increased citizen participation has reduced predictability somewhat. The control function has been redefined a number of ways. Much more complex and elaborate leader-follower relations have been prescribed by the human relations school, organizational humanists, scholars of leadership such as Fred Fiedler, and advocates of ''organization development,'' who emphasize democratic leadership and employee participation. Also, the control function is disrupted by subsystem politics, discussed in chapter 3, wherein administrators develop foundations of power *outside* traditional vertical bureaucratic channels of command and responsibility.

Finally, bureaucratic secrecy, which Weber saw as a protection for bureaucrats, has been diminished considerably by efforts to increase public access to records and decision processes—what one observer calls ''watchdogging functions.''[22] Such functions have expanded significantly under prodding from the Nader organizations and groups such as Common Cause. The seemingly permanent movement away from Weberian formalism, toward much less structured and more diversified bureaucratic forms, also indicates that Weber's influence lingers, but decreasingly.

Other major changes have occurred in public administration.[23] First is a far wider range of participation and demands for new forms of it. From what is usually known as the liberal side of the political spectrum came calls for greater *internal* participation in decision making by agency employees, and *external* participation by affected clienteles. But participation has two other dimensions as well. One is *devolution* (transfer) of national government functions ''back to states and local governments,'' which is advocated by many political conservatives. The Reagan administration, through its program of block grants, has begun a major effort to shift responsibility for important social programs to state governments. The potential long-term significance of this shift is immense, politically and administratively. Both demands for greater participation and for devolution ''are responses to a feeling of powerlessness, even alienation; both manifest a distrust of bigness and distance; both represent an attempt to gain control of decisions affecting vital personal concerns.''[24]

The other dimension of participation is structural in nature, but reflects the same impulse for greater popular control over government. Regional associations of governments, economic development commissions, and community action organizations have sprung up, partly at the behest of national planners but also in response to local sentiments. Elements of both ''participation'' and ''devolution,'' as well as specific administrative and economic considerations, have played a part in developing such organizations. The point here is that various steps already have been taken to translate existing preferences for participation and devolution into organizational reality (for example, citizen action groups).

A second significant change has been development of management techniques that have contributed to more sophisticated and systematic administration. One dimension involves the growing use of quantitative methods and computers—in short, "management science." Others include project management, a package of techniques designed to move individual projects along paths set out for them, and the practice of contracting out, under which private contractors provide designated goods or services to government agencies for an agreed-upon fee. During the 1970s, hundreds of communities began contracting for services; some 2,000 (among them San Jose, Phoenix, Memphis, Boston, and Omaha) have contracted out trash removal, alone. Other services range from utility billing, voter registration, and street lighting, to ambulance services, operating prisons, maintaining golf courses, firefighting services, and street maintenance.[25] Note that contracting out is an obvious example of overlap between public and private sectors, one that promises to continue growing, due in large part to intensifying fiscal stress. (Note, also, that trends toward more participation and more systematic management methods may conflict with one another, but that has not prevented governments from pursuing both!)

A third development is public employee unionization and collective bargaining, treated in chapter 11. Underlying this development is the rise of a service-oriented economy (postindustrial), with a larger proportion of the work force engaged in public employment. Also, general social and ideological ferment has contributed to relaxation of laws and regulations restraining public-sector unionization. These developments bear directly on public personnel management, but also on government's role in economic and social affairs and on the status and nature of government itself as an employer. As noted previously, these may be changing again, only this time in different directions.

A fourth development is emphasis on evaluation and productivity, treated in chapter 13. Efforts are going forward to improve our capabilities in both of these areas, and some results are encouraging. Two problems, however, deserve mention here, in addition to those treated earlier. One is so-called "Lockheed" issues—that is, those arising from demands for government to subsidize corporate enterprises (such as Lockheed Aircraft) that have become closely government related, if and when they find themselves in financial difficulty. How one evaluates government's participation in "rescuing" such corporations is a complex question. The other problem is whether unionization and collective bargaining in the public sector will help or hinder efforts to increase productivity and improve job performance. The latter issue will hinge on whether or not union leaders and members are as concerned about these challenges as are employers.

Finally, other developments should be noted. Continuing specialization and professionalization raise the challenge of bridging gaps among specialists in different professions. Government budgets and budgeting clearly are more constrained than before. Executive reorganization promises to receive wider use in years ahead. More states permit their governors to submit "package" proposals to their legislatures, and both Presidents Carter and Reagan stressed reorganization as a policy instrument. Continuing ferment—and potentially major change—in fiscal federalism will affect state and local administration in thousands of program areas. Indeed, President Reagan proposed in 1985 to *eliminate* general revenue-sharing altogether—and Congress concurred, effective in fiscal year 1987. Also, expansion of block grants—a centerpiece of the Reagan program for reforming fiscal federalism—ran into growing political opposition from governors and mayors after the first round of grant consolidations passed Congress; thus, still more uncertainty seems likely. Finally, public administration will be affected by efforts to "debureaucratize" organizational life in the public service—by deemphasizing credentials of public servants, broadening decision making, decreasing rigidities, and increasing lateral communication within bureaucracies.

Paradoxes in Concept and Practice

Just as there are paradoxes in the environment surrounding public administration, so also in concept and practice.

First, the quest for administrative rationality—for example, PPB—is frustrated by at least three countercurrents. One is *incrementalism*, which relies on an avowedly "political" assessment of costs, benefits, and program feasibility.[26] The second is *organization development* ("OD"), noted in chapter 6 and referred to earlier in this chapter; "OD" places other values above rationality, including sensitivity to employee preferences and needs, and participative decision making. Third is the *politics of confrontation*.

In the 1960s and 1970s, the confrontation approach stressed moral imperatives in public policy, demanding that government address itself to social and economic problems that some people defined as "evil." By following a set of values measuring social phenomena according to standards of "good" and "evil," those engaging in confrontation politics crowded out alternative approaches to policy questions that attempted to deal more objectively with reality. The "confronters" defined reality according to the evils *they* perceived, and little else mattered. Such an approach threatens any enterprise in or out of government that resists being defined according to *only one* set of moral values. Public administration is a likely battleground in any future conflict over "good" and "evil" in public affairs because of its prominent role and its tradition (itself now under attack) of seeking rationality and efficiency in a presumably value-free manner.

A second broad paradox revolves around impacts of participation in administrative decision making, by divergent—and frequently conflicting—groupings of ''participants.'' These include program clienteles, public employee unions, and agency personnel seeking ''participative management'' consistent with values of organization development. All three kinds of participation offer potential opposition to the values of rationality, professionalism, leadership, and accountability.

Participation can conflict with rationality because the former is based on political inclusion of new and varied interests, while the latter presumes to identify objectively the most advantageous courses of action without regard to particular political interests or impacts on them.

Participation can conflict with professionalism because, as noted earlier, its advocates seek to have decisions framed in terms of their impacts on those affected rather than on the basis of what professionals think is ''best'' for the people (see discussion of the Seattle transit study in chapter 15). One way out of this dilemma is ''. . . some kind of political mediation by a leadership not clearly identified with either side of the debate.''[27]

However, participation also can conflict with leadership, by acting as a constraint on leaders' ability to set the direction of organizations or political systems. Participation is a potential counterweight to what leaders desire, though it also can be a source of leadership support. It comes down to a question of what views and interests are *added* to the decision-making process by expanding participation.

Finally, participation can conflict with accountability. Since the former is specifically designed to promote the latter, how can this statement be justified? The answer is this: by increasing participation in decision making, it becomes more difficult to pinpoint just who was responsible for initiating and enforcing a decision, and therefore to hold those persons to account for their actions. A skillful leader may be able to guide a participatory decision-making system along lines he or she prefers, with no one the wiser; such a technique camouflages where responsibility for a given decision really lies. Thus, though intended to promote accountability, participation has the potential for doing precisely the opposite.

Emphasis on participation reflects a strong faith in *process* leading to ''correct'' (optimum, appropriate) results. Americans have a reputation for being pragmatic people with concern for *how* things are done. Yet this discussion of participation points up an important lesson, in and out of public administration. It is that casually assuming a relationship between ''doing it the right way'' and getting the desired results can be risky. It may be necessary to examine precisely what is produced through given procedures to determine whether that is the way participants or clienteles wish to continue operating. Concern with consequences, as opposed to simply ''perfecting the machinery,'' is growing, though it is to be hoped that we will not end up ignoring means and concentrating *only* on results.

A third broad paradox involves contradictory tendencies toward centralization and decentralization. The 1960s, in particular, saw considerable centralization in and out of government, because of factors nobody could fully control. Population growth and mobility, as well as technology, produced extensive geographic interdependence in this country, and:

> interdependence forces centralization in public (as well as private) policy. The people of California have a stake in the educational standards of Mississippi, as do those of Buffalo in the waste disposal practices of Cleveland, those of New York in the economic and manpower situation in Puerto Rico, and all of us in the antipollution devices put on new cars in Detroit.[28]

Superior fiscal capacities of the national government and some state governments also have encouraged centralization because these governments can do more than others (future prospects in this regard, of course, are very unclear).

At the same time, it is clear that public opinion has increasingly demanded decentralization of administrative machinery, linked in many cases to the desire for expanded participation. How to accomplish that in the face of centralizing forces—that is, how to move in both directions at the same time—has been a key challenge. One possibility appeared in recent proposed changes in metropolitan area government. In 1970 the Committee for Economic Development (CED), a business-sponsored research organization, proposed a two-level form of government for large metropolitan areas; this would consist of a powerful metropolitan-wide unit and semiautonomous community units, existing in a federal relationship to one another.[29] Since only a few essential services—such as land-use planning, utilities, transportation, and water supply[30]—are said to require areawide coordination, this arrangement could conceivably be applied in many different places. Federation experiments in the Toronto and Miami areas[31] suggest the possibilities for practical application of this idea, though Toronto's experience more closely resembles the CED proposal than does Miami's.

Another paradox relates to a need for greater intermingling of diverse professionals, in the face of continued emphasis on professional specialization. It is not merely a matter of teams of professionals being assembled to work on specific projects. Rather, many problems in today's society have so many dimensions to them that ''crime is no longer a problem for the police alone nor health for doctors alone nor highways for engineers alone nor justice for lawyers alone.''[32] Growing professional interdependence, in short, will of necessity characterize public administration in the future much more than in the past.

Some other general comments should be made. First, those who advocate greater creativity, initiative, innovation, and experimentation in organizational life see emphasis on careerism in the public service as an impediment to those goals. This view is based on the assumption that careerism limits one's options for doing innovative work or otherwise "going out on a limb" because of real or imagined potential for harming one's career aspirations.[33] A related implication is conflict between individual talents such as creativity and initiative, and effective, coordinated organizational leadership. Obviously, that would depend on situational factors, primarily on whether tasks and leadership of an organization are conducive to allowing, perhaps encouraging, innovation by group members. There is little question, however, that often leaders regard themselves as custodians of the organization's mission, thus discouraging both member participation *and* creativity. In many cases, the pattern appears to be one of conflict between central, coordinated, directive leadership and flexible, creative, participative organizational operation.

Second, administrative discretion has become an issue and is likely to remain one for some time. While it is true that discretionary actions by professionals in public administration may not promote *representational qualities*, nevertheless discretion does not necessarily interfere with achieving *accountability*. We might legitimately try to achieve one or both, but they must be understood properly as separate and distinct features of administrative politics in order to pursue either of them sensibly.

Finally, it would appear that as a nation we are a bit uncertain about how to achieve accountability. The original design of our political system as well as later evolution of it stressed accountability to "the people" through a complex, interrelated web of institutional channels. However, current efforts seem to focus on making all of government accountable to all of the people. It is difficult to see how that can be done. Direct accountability to the people is an appealing idea, but it may also be said that if officials are accountable to everybody, they are accountable to nobody! It requires careful structuring of mechanisms of accountability to maximize the chances of attaining it. Can we, then, rely on a *single* mechanism? Probably not; that would result in an excess of power in too few hands. The next best thing would seem to be a variety of mechanisms, each acting as a channel for public control but also held to account for what *it* does. There is a label for such a complex of mechanisms: "checks and balances." We may simply need to gain better control over them—again—in order to ensure accountability to public preferences and interests.

FERMENT AND CHANGE IN PUBLIC ADMINISTRATION AS A FIELD OF STUDY

Given the wide-ranging change in concepts and practices of public administration, it is not surprising that the field of study known by the same name is subject to considerable turbulence as well. Some of these areas were dis-

FUNNY BUSINESS

cussed previously, particularly in chapter 1, but we will deal with them as interrelated factors helping to shape the future of the discipline.

First, movement away from political science—its ancestral home, so to speak—has characterized much of public administration and its academic professionals. As discussed in chapter 1, developments in both fields after World War II led to increasingly divergent emphases, with political science stressing behavioral research of a type that many in public administration found uncongenial to their work. The latter often was treated as an academic ''second class citizen,'' giving rise to pressure for separation, in the form of interdisciplinary programs in public administration and growing numbers of independent programs and departments. Yet ''postbehavioral'' changes in political science raise the possibility that the two may be closer together now than at any time in the past twenty-five years. ''A political science concerned deeply with public policy and not disdainful of the means by which policy is effectuated would be much more attractive to public administrationists than has been the political science of recent decades.''[34]

Second, schools of management and business administration have inaugurated distinct "public-sector" management portions of their course offerings, recognizing both the growing importance of education in public-sector-related fields for business graduates and the intentions of larger numbers of their students to work in the public sector upon graduation.

Third, schools, programs, and institutes of public administration proliferated in the 1960s and 1970s, with a number of distinctive features. They generally are separate from political science departments, as already implied. They tend to be graduate-level rather than undergraduate programs, building on a base of a good general education. And they clearly reflect a flexible, heterogeneous approach to the subject matter taught. Labels such as "public administration," "public policy," "public affairs," "management," and "management science" abound.

Fourth, the "New Public Administration" has had some influence in the discipline and promises to have more. This movement, based on the value of "social equity" (see chapter 6), calls for more explicit involvement by activist administrators on behalf of clienteles previously underrepresented, inadequately served, or both, by existing administrative entities. Precisely how this movement will relate to other currents in the discipline is not clear, but one effect already noticeable is modification of curricula to reflect greater social concern.

Also, organizational humanism and organization development have continued to exert an influence in public administration. The former, stressing increased self-realization and greater organizational democracy, has found some response within public administration, especially in those organizations with less structured tasks permitting greater creativity and initiative. The latter has evolved from early emphasis on hardware and systems—with no great concern for interpersonal relations—to a more widely supported focus on human components of the organization and concern for normative organizational goals (what *should* be done). OD includes, among other internal techniques, consultation, survey feedback, team building, and human relations training.[35] While both approaches have had only limited impact in the great majority of public (and private) organizations, their influence seems to be on the rise.

Furthermore, the teaching of administrative *ethics* has assumed a more prominent place in the study of public administration.[36] Bureaucrats have both the need and the opportunity to make value choices affecting the lives of others, in the course of discharging their responsibilities. Moral and ethical questions abound—occupational safety and health programs, affirmative action policies, nuclear safety, or (on an individualized level) temptations to engage in improper or outright corrupt behavior. There has been, therefore, a resurgence of interest in ethics in public administration curricula. Part of the vitality of this area lies in the growing recognition among academics of both the complexity of the subject and the diversity of possible approaches to it (see chapter 15). Attention to ethical issues, and to ethics education, is certain to continue in the immediate future.

Finally, the very nature of the academic field, and of the subject matter which comprises it, remains an unsettled question. One observer, discussing constitutional separation of powers and administrative theory, has noted the existence of three separate approaches to public administration: a "managerial" approach most closely associated with the chief executive, a "political" approach geared to legislative concerns, and a "legal" approach associated with the judiciary.[37] Another observer has described the situation this way: "Students of public administration will probably never agree on the proper blend for the elements of their discipline. What degree of prominence should be given to the study of management, politics, social psychology, economics, or law?"[38] In light of these divergent tendencies, it appears unlikely that any "*single* school of philosophy, academic discipline, or type of methodology—or combination of these—would . . . persuade public administration to march under its banner."[39] This may not be altogether a bad thing. "An untidy, swiftly changing world may be better addressed by an enterprise which contains many facets, perspectives, interests, and methodologies: one which is eclectic, experimental, open-ended."[40]

A number of other observations merit inclusion here in assessing the academic field of public administration. One of its most important functions has been professional training—in programs that offer a Master's of Public Administration or Public Affairs (MPA)—of those who go on to take positions in civil service systems at all three levels of government. Some observers are concerned about the kind of training available, stressing particularly that programs should not turn out narrowly specialized individuals who "can't see past the end of their noses." These observers advocate well-trained professionals who also have perspective on themselves and their work, and on social and political contexts in which they will find themselves working.[41] Professor Frederick Mosher has noted that universities are "equipped to open the students' minds to the broader value questions of the society and of *their professions' roles in that society*."[42] What Mosher and others fear most is continuation of an educational pattern in which professional specialists "have little systematic study beyond the high school level about the society and culture in which they will live and practice their trades."[43]

The academic discipline of public administration is likely to continue to change rapidly. If diversity and uncertainty characterize the discipline now, they will be ever more characteristic of it in the years immediately ahead. Of course, that is true of the practical side of the field as well. The interchange between the two also will prove lively and unpredictable, contributing to the general ferment.

FURTHER THOUGHTS AND OBSERVATIONS

In this closing section, the author will take the opportunity to add a few comments that seem important in the overall scheme of things in public administration. They are intended to supplement what has been said earlier in this chapter and to point out other significant areas in the field.

First, we must bear in mind the increasing importance of *managing* public programs. More to the point, those of us not engaged in managerial activities in the public sector should recognize how crucial it is that we appreciate the complexities of management (see box). It is easy enough to criticize what is done, or not done, by public administrators; we would find, however, that things look very different from the manager's perspective. Bureaucratic ways of doing things may not be entirely understandable to the outside observer, but (as noted in chapter 4) they may be justifiable in terms of bureaucracy's continuing needs and responsibilities. This is not to excuse shortcomings, or worse, in administrative behavior—it is only to suggest that we should not be too quick in passing judgment, or too harsh in our assessments, regarding bureaucratic actions. As suggested in chapter 1, public administrators may indeed be engaged in honorable work![44]

However, we also may need to pay more attention than we have recently to controlling bureaucratic waste, fraud, and mismanagement. Recently these concerns have become more of a political issue, frequently (though far from exclusively) involving defense spending. Both OMB and GAO have taken numerous steps to combat waste, fraud, and abuse. These have included investigations of allegedly lax accounting procedures; reports on government waste in areas such as Pentagon procurement contracts and spare-parts disposal practices; and—in the case of GAO—establishment of a toll-free "fraud hot line" available to government employees seeking to report incidents of possible mismanagement.[45] One potentially significant development in this area is the fact that increasing attention is being paid to financial accounting as one means of combating waste and fraud.[46] Two cautionary words are in order here. First, we should not put too much faith in sophisticated management techniques as remedies for these problems, since such techniques can be used to commit wasteful or fraudulent acts as well as to control them. We may, instead, need to rediscover and revitalize traditional practices such as financial auditing, if we are to move effectively against these challenges. Second, we should be discriminating in our judgments, in the best sense of the phrase, about bureaucrats' behavior—taking care not to condemn the many because of the actions of a relatively few. Nevertheless, our concern over such matters is entirely legitimate—indeed, crucial.[47]

In a larger sense, we should not dwell so much on problems and weaknesses of bureaucracy as a form of organization that we overlook its strengths.[48] One is bureaucracy's very orderliness, so often denounced as inflexibility; if the alternative is nepotism, capricious judgment, or chaos

THE PUBLIC MANAGER: AN OVERVIEW

Several major points should be made about the public manager's job:

1. The public manager inhabits an intensely political environment. Political processes do not abruptly stop at the door of bureaucracy; the manager's job and environment are *essentially* political, requiring a primary emphasis on the task of managing political and administrative conflict.

2. The public manager's job also contains a *variety of political dimensions*, including building support with the chief executive, dealing with related departments and interest groups, bargaining with the legislature, managing and coordinating a fragmented structure of bureaucratic subunits, and (in the national government) trying to oversee and coordinate policy subsystems extending to the operations of state and city governments.

3. The manager's primary role is to deal with competing organizational pressures and to manage political conflict. In some cases the manager will employ strategies of conflict resolution. At other times the task will be to convert the negative, adversary features of conflict into something more positive, namely, cooperation, compromise, and coalition building among both political and administrative actors. (This process of conversion is often what we have in mind when we speak of leadership.)

4. In managing this political conflict the manager faces many of the same issues that worry an advocate of pluralist democracy and, in a general way, would-be controllers of the bureaucracy. He or she has to worry about the fragmentation of bureaucratic activity, especially where it leads to strongly segmented bureaucratic structures and insulated concentrations of power. No less than the ordinary citizen, the public manager needs to "open up" the bureaucracy in order to achieve any real penetration into its operations. Finally, the public manager, along with the pluralist democrat, must worry about the balance of power among different groups: whether desirable levels of competition and bargaining exist, whether certain interests overwhelm other groups in the policy-making process, whether citizens' complaints and demands are heard and registered. In sum, the public manager, far from being the *clerk of a narrow efficiency*, faces the problems of *both* pluralist democracy and administrative efficiency.

Source: Adapted with minor changes from Douglas Yates, *Bureaucratic Democracy: The Search for Democracy and Efficiency in American Government* (Cambridge, Mass.: Harvard University Press, 1982), pp. 183–85.

(which it often was in Max Weber's time), that is a plus. Another is the system of legal guarantees against arbitrariness that governs so much of administrative activity; still another is the "commitment of bureaucracy to democratic decision making—and the processes of consultation, negotiation, and accommodation. . . ."[49] More generally, it is widely acknowledged that "[b]road and complex tasks require broad and complex organizations"[50]—a recognition of bureaucracy's appropriateness to many (though of course not all) organizational activities. Furthermore, if the rise of bureaucracy was originally tied to the increasing complexity of society, the outlook in these complex times is at least for survival of this form of organization, if not its further expansion.

There are other areas of concern. First, it is likely that there will be continued ambiguity concerning goals in politics and administration, as well as performance. Efforts to define what our goals are probably will continue, but goals also will continue to be only partially agreed upon (at best). With goals vaguely defined or even in conflict, measuring performance against common goals is, of course, impossible. Nevertheless, developing improved performance indicators within specific programs and projects will yield some benefits incrementally, in the form of improved planning and direction of those programs.

Second, the role and scope of government regulation continue to be in ferment. This has several aspects. One is the movement toward deregulation, though how fast, how far, and in how many areas of economic activity are questions still to be answered. Another aspect is the red tape sort of concern discussed in chapter 14; demands for protection and risk reduction in our daily lives account for a large part of regulatory growth. A serious issue, here, is how far we, as a nation, should *try* to go in reducing risks and assuring health and safety. Some have argued that we seemingly have decided to strive for a "no-risk" society, and that such an endeavor is not only futile but also detrimental to other functions in society (such as private-sector productivity).[51] A third aspect is the possibility of pursuing alternatives to direct regulation.[52] There is precedent for at least one alternative approach: using *government agency performance* as a basis for comparison with (a "yardstick" against which to measure) private-sector performance. A memorable case in point was (and is) the Tennessee Valley Authority, which for more than fifty years has marketed electric power in seven mid-South states at rates noticeably lower than those charged by private power companies elsewhere (this is still true, despite substantial TVA rate increases in the 1970s). Another regulation-related issue concerns the calls for use of cost-benefit analysis in evaluating proposed (and operative) regulations. The question here is whether or not such analysis is designed to be truly neutral. If so, it could add a useful dimension to processes of drafting and enforcing regulations. On the other hand, is allegedly neutral cost-benefit analysis merely symbolism for a "pro-business" program of dismantling social regulatory programs, as part of the larger effort to reduce the scope of government? A case surely could be made for the latter, but it clearly is *not neutral*. Mingling the two could be counterproductive to sensibly reforming government regulation, while maintaining regulatory effectiveness.[53]

There is one final regulatory issue. It is clear that sentiment has been growing for wholesale reduction of government regulations, of all kinds. At the same time, however, perhaps not enough attention has been paid to the consequences of that course of action.[54] There even appears to be some feeling that almost anything government does is "regulation." That perception is not accurate, of course; but in a democracy, what the citizens *believe* to be the case may be more important in some instances than the objective reality. This, then, also will influence the future course of government regulation.

Managing public personnel is another area of significant change and challenge. At least three issues are central in this regard. One is the question of maintaining the partisan and policy neutrality of the civil service, versus enhancing the political responsiveness (if not outright loyalty) to the chief executive that exists among administrative personnel. As noted in chapter 10, this has been a recurring issue in our political history, and it surfaced again in the late 1970s under President Carter. During Ronald Reagan's first term a vigorous public debate on personnel policy developed, in both philosophical and practical terms. Various actions taken by OPM, and numerous statements made by OPM Director Devine, focused considerable attention on the issue. The actions in question affected, among others, Senior Executive Service staffing, performance appraisal, pay caps, phasing out of the PACE exam, and budget reductions for personnel functions. Such actions often were rooted, at least implicitly, in a broadgauged administration effort to make it possible for President Reagan to implement his domestic policies, and in turn change the general direction of government programs. Given the magnitude of that policy agenda, both greater presidential control and greater policy responsiveness on the part of (especially) senior careerists clearly would be necessary.

On the other hand, there were many who took issue with OPM's initiatives, due to disagreement with general administration policies or with specific personnel actions, or both. They contended, among other things, that career executives in many agencies are now much less involved in the decision-making process than in the past; that open, healthy debate between career and political executives over proposed policies and program management is less frequent, and in some cases has virtually disappeared; that some career executives' responsiveness has been judged in terms of their willingness to cooperate with political executives in *not* carrying out the original legislative intent of duly enacted laws;[55] that "institutional memory, public policy insights, and program management expertise" in the civil service are in shorter supply than before, hampering effective public management;[56] and, in general, that public administrative institutions are not as healthy or vibrant as they could and should be.[57] With concern for effective executive leadership on the rise, it is not surprising to find this fundamental issue once again on the public agenda: how to keep civil service protections from interfering with presidential flexibility and effectiveness in managing the executive branch—and vice-versa.

A second basic personnel concern is related to what motivates public servants. Specifically, even though financial bonuses and "merit pay" have been established in the national civil service (with parallel systems in a growing number of states), there is some question whether monetary incentives—so crucial to recent reform initiatives—are in fact the most effective motivators of senior career executives (recall chapter 6, and the discussion of motivation in the "organizational humanism" school of organization theory). These theoretical formulations recently have been given support; from several sources has come evidence that interesting work, job satisfaction, personal and group recognition, "a sense of being valued, and the respect of one's peers *and leaders* are all much more important than bonuses."[58] To the extent that is so, it suggests that financial-incentive plans may have been misdirected. It also may help explain why these bonus plans have failed to slow the exodus of veteran senior executives from the national civil service (they could even have accelerated that trend).

Closely related to the preceding concerns (as we saw in chapter 10) is a growing morale problem, especially (but not exclusively) in the national civil service. After many years of various politicians (and the public) "taking potshots" at civil servants, these individuals now have experienced even more severe buffeting about, for example, reductions in force (RIFs) that have introduced more uncertainty into the national civil service than has existed for a century.[59] Another dimension of the morale problem springs from the belief that certain practices thought to contribute to "good management," in the abstract, now carry with them the possibility of retribution in one form or another. As one example, consider a recent "good news, bad news" finding about bureaucratic behavior in the national government. A study conducted by the Merit Systems Protection Board (MSPB) found that fewer national government employees reported instances of waste, fraud, and mismanagement in 1983 than had done so in 1980 (only 25 percent of those participating in the survey, compared to 45 percent three years earlier). But another 37 percent witnessed or knew of such incidents, and *failed to report them because of fear of reprisals*—compared to only 20 percent giving that response in the 1980 survey. This is another indication of rising tension in the working environment of the public service at the national level, since the beginning of this decade.[60] In these and other respects, there is much about which to be concerned in contemporary personnel management.

There also is growing interest in (and possibly changing perspectives on) the phenomenon of administrative discretion. The literature of public administration has begun to reflect the position that perhaps discretion should not be "hemmed in"—that perhaps we should attempt instead to legitimize the exercise of administrative discretion, with the expectation of public servants subsequently acting in the public interest (recall, in chapter 3, Woodrow Wilson's prescription for "large powers and unhampered discretion").[61] This may be more than a fleeting hope; one observer has suggested, for example, that lobbyists in Washington "make it their business to know where they are likely to receive the most favorable decisions, and *those representing business and industry have come to view Congress as being more responsive to them than [is] the bureaucracy.''*[62] Our view of administrative discretion obviously would be more favorable if it were perceived that civil servants act most frequently in the public interest. Such a view seems to be emerging, though slowly, among scholarly observers of bureaucratic behavior.

Something else to be borne in mind, as we refine our theories of organization, leadership, and management control, is that there are limits on how widely such theories can be applied. The nature of work, workers, and organizations affects applicability of theories such as organizational humanism, of leadership styles, and of methods of management control (see chapters 6, 9, and 13, respectively). These limitations must be respected to avoid problems resulting from wholesale acceptance of any theory.

Also, there is some irony in current pursuit of such administrative values as greater efficiency, rationality, and productivity—three major elements in Frederick Taylor's theory of scientific management. This is not to say we have returned to his values, with nothing else changed. However, we may find these norms more attractive due to growing constraints on our resources—financial and otherwise. It should be noted that the appeal of these values also has permeated the *study* of public administration. It has been suggested that the ''public management'' approach is characterized by ''a strong philosophical link with the scientific management tradition. . . .''[63]

Furthermore, some favorite terms and concepts we apply to public administration may require rethinking. We tend to speak of a *leader*; Fred Fiedler's research suggests we should be concerned instead with a *leader of*, defining effective leadership much more explicitly in terms of that which is led. In the same way, we may need to speak of politicians and administrators who are *accountable to*, not just accountable; *responsive to*, not simply responsive; bureaucracies *efficient at*, not merely efficient; and organizations *productive in terms of*, not just productive. We must bear in mind that these values are most important as means of achieving other, higher ends—not as ends in themselves. Yet all too often we treat them as the latter. For example, *why* is it important to be efficient? Is it *always* desirable? The norm of ''efficiency'' is not a truly neutral standard; one can only be efficient *at* something, and some values are involved almost always. Further, is efficiency (or anything else) to be pursued in all cases, even at the expense of other desired ends? These kinds of admittedly troubling considerations should give us pause, and encourage us to think clearly about our own assumptions. Clear thinking is especially necessary in turbulent times.

The *political* environment of public administration has changed dramatically, as discussed previously. But certain elements of that change deserve brief mention as we close.

First, emphasis on both effectiveness and accountability of administrative agencies has led to numerous adjustments in their relationships to other institutions in the political system. Among the areas affected by these changes are the politics of structure, bureaucratic neutrality versus nonneutrality, the significance of "overhead" control of administration (president and Congress as a whole, versus subsystems), altered budget procedures involving Congress as well as the president, ferment in intergovernmental relations, and new initiatives in public personnel administration. All of these, significantly, were controversial issue areas in the national government during the 1970s—*before* Ronald Reagan entered the White House!

The second dimension of the political environment is the Reagan presidency, and the extent of Reagan's efforts to change the direction of government as well as his success or failure. Ronald Reagan unquestionably has had two major impacts on American governance: (1) he has altered (perhaps permanently) the policy directions that will be pursued at the national level, with "ripple effects" throughout the whole fabric and structure of the political system, and (2) he has restored the presidency to a preeminent position within the political system as a whole.[64] Whether the latter will remain as it is after he leaves the White House, however, is another matter. Powerful forces (and the political system itself) act to disperse power and influence throughout the government structure; there also are risks to the president, and to the presidency, in having too much responsibility concentrated in the Oval Office.[65] There also is a certain irony in Ronald Reagan's successes, especially during his first term, when many in and out of Washington viewed his victory in ideological terms, assuming that a great conservative tide had swept Carter out and Reagan in. This is ironic because there may not have been such a tide! In 1981, no less a figure than David Stockman, Ronald Reagan's budget director, disputed the contention that Reagan's 1980 victory was ideological—even though he (Stockman) knew that many members of Congress seemed to be interpreting it that way.[66] In short, there may be more than meets the eye in any effort to assess the condition of the presidency—and of Ronald Reagan's policy leadership in that office—in the aftermath of the Reagan era. (Stockman's resignation as OMB director in the summer of 1985 may itself affect the future course of the Reagan presidency.) Despite all this, we still may have entered a momentous transition period in American politics, from the end of New Deal and Great Society politics to the beginning of other sorts of politics and policies more in tune with the Reagan philosophy and world view. The broad outlines of those policy changes already are clear; more time must pass before their impacts are felt and understood fully.

A significant legacy of the Reagan movement is ongoing effort to reduce the sheer size of the public sector—in personnel, budgets, regulatory authority, and general scope. Calls for "privatizing" the public sector have been heard,[67] and (as noted in chapter 13) various efforts already have succeeded in that direction. Numerous factors will affect whether that trend continues, though questions about it are more likely to center on the degree to which we should "privatize" rather than on whether or not we should do so at all.

Several other political dimensions also stand out. For example, as noted more than once, the courts now are involved significantly in many aspects of public administration. Most important, perhaps, are federalism and intergovernmental relations, labor relations, and government regulation; but in case after case, across the board, court decisions shape both the environment and the content of *administrative* decision. Public administration is not alone in that, but the impacts on administrative actions have been substantial.

Another aspect of uncertainty in public administration was highlighted by outgoing EPA Administrator William Ruckelshaus in late 1984. In a press interview Ruckelshaus noted that, in his view, constant attacks by environmental groups on EPA carried with them the risk of destroying the agency's ability to function. In his words:

> [T]he cumulative effect of [the attacks] is to cause the *essential trust of the society to be so eroded* it [EPA] can't function. . . . When you don't distinguish between individuals with whom you disagree, or policies with which you disagree, and the agencies themselves, . . . you risk destroying the very institutions whose success is necessary for your essential goals to be achieved.[68]

Ruckelshaus' point, though addressed to environmentalists, applies to virtually every politically active group of citizens—and to virtually any administrative agency—at all levels of government. In a turbulent and tense political atmosphere, many sincere (and often impatient) citizens might do well to consider his advice. There is another implication as well: such attacks foster an atmosphere of public cynicism and distrust, making it far more difficult for administrative agencies to *retain the capacity to respond* when we do call upon them! And we surely will continue to do so, to deal both with large-scale public problems and with individual (though still serious) crises such as the so-called Tylenol murders in Chicago in 1982, or the wildfires which devastated western-state forestlands in mid-1985.

Another point worth bearing in mind pertains to that same impatience about governmental action (or inaction), in the context of what sort of government we have. As we discussed in chapter 2, those who framed our Constitution sought generally to place limits on what government is able to do, without diluting its essential ability to govern. As one observer recently put it, the founding fathers did not want efficient or adventurous government.[69] "Overall, the government was designed to be responsive *slowly* to relatively *long-term* demands and to require the development of *relatively broad agreement* among the electorate prior to taking action."[70] In other words, for government agencies to operate *not* under pressure would require time and broad popular support—both of which often seem to be lacking in controversial policy areas such as toxic wastes or nuclear energy. Our impatience with government action seems to be directly related to the extent and the depth of policy disagreements dividing the nation. Once again, as noted earlier in this chapter, public administration is squarely in the middle of popular discontents, reflecting the disorganization (and policy differences) present in society itself.

There is one final matter to consider. For about twenty years we have been experiencing a "crisis of confidence"—indeed, a "crisis of legitimacy"[71]—regarding government and its actions. More recently, certain *new* assumptions or premises appear to be gaining currency in shaping (and perhaps reflecting) popular perceptions of government. These have been expressed as follows: (1) public programs are counterproductive to the social and economic well-being of the country; (2) the public no longer expects public programs to work, and is increasingly unwilling to spend additional funds on them; (3) public programs are better administered at the state and local level—further, many functions should be taken over by private organizations and voluntary community efforts; (4) national government program managers are becoming less important, with fewer needs; and (5) public managers already are overpaid, and any system of reward or penalties in the public sector will be abused.[72] Such thinking currently may be fashionable, but it also can be highly dysfunctional. Diminished public trust does not bode well for maintenance of either democratic processes or effective government. As conservative an individual as syndicated columnist George F. Will warned in 1981 against "indiscriminate skepticism about the competence, even the motives, of government," and against thinking that "government cannot do anything right anyway."[73] That caveat is not for conservatives only; many individuals of all political persuasions have fallen prey to this crisis of confidence.[74]

Ironically, the dark mood of mistrust is if anything *unwarranted*. Scholarly studies of public opinion, both of recent vintage and in earlier periods, have indicated that the public's voice is heard by those in government—including those in bureaucracy—if that voice is clear in what it is saying and forceful in its expression. The "voice of the people" is really many voices, saying many things—about particular policies, conduct of government generally, public ethics, and much more. Yet it has been demonstrated that when public opinion is generally united on a position, and feelings run strong on the matter, government's response is *nearly always* in the direction desired by the majority. Thus we can afford a somewhat more optimistic view of governmental responsiveness to majority preferences than many seem to hold at this point. As one knowledgeable observer has put it: "In the long run, the public almost always gets its way."[75]

What, then, is the prognosis for public administration? Without question it will continue to be a focal point of concern, with controversy encompassing every major policy area and every political interest with a stake in administrative operations. In the words of political scientist Carl Friedrich, public administration is "the core of modern government." Clearly, therefore, public administration "is and will be a focal area for change and transformation in society generally."[76] Virtually the only *certain* thing is the *uncertain* directions public administration will take.

NOTES

1. James D. Carroll, "Putting Government's House in Order," *Maxwell News and Notes*, 13 (Fall 1978), 2 (published by the Maxwell School of Citizenship and Public Affairs; Syracuse University; Syracuse, N.Y.).
2. Frederick C. Mosher, "The Public Service in the Temporary Society," *Public Administration Review*, 31 (January/February 1971), 47–62, at p. 48. The quote is originally from Paul T. David, "The Study of the Future," *Public Administration Review*, 28 (March/April 1968), 193.
3. Mosher, "The Public Service in the Temporary Society," p. 48.
4. Ibid., p. 49.
5. See Charles O. Jones, *An Introduction to the Study of Public Policy*, 3rd ed. (Monterey, Calif.: Brooks/Cole, 1984), p. 34.
6. Mosher, "The Public Service in the Temporary Society," p. 49.
7. Dwight Waldo, "Developments in Public Administration," *Annals of the American Academy of Political and Social Science*, 404 (November 1972), 217–45, at p. 245.
8. Ibid., p. 219. See also chapter 1, footnote 24.
9. Frederick C. Mosher, "The Changing Responsibilities and Tactics of the Federal Government," *Public Administration Review*, 40 (November/December 1980), 541–48, at pp. 544–45. The term "twilight zone" was suggested by political scientist Harold Seidman. See also Eileen Seidman, ed., "Public Administration/Business Administration: What's the Difference?" *The Bureaucrat*, 13 (Summer 1984), 4–32.
10. Waldo, "Developments in Public Administration," pp. 219–20.
11. Ibid.
12. Ibid., pp. 220–21.
13. Ibid., p. 221.
14. Ibid., pp. 221–22.
15. Ibid., p. 221 (emphasis added).
16. See, among others, Theodore H. White, *The Making of the President 1972* (New York: Atheneum, 1973), p. 165; and Herbert Kaufman, "Fear of Bureaucracy: A Raging Pandemic," *Public Administration Review*, 41 (January/February 1981), 1–9, at p. 3.
17. Mosher, "The Public Service in the Temporary Society," p. 51. The phrase was used originally by Emmette Redford in *Democracy in the Administrative State* (New York: Oxford University Press, 1969), p. 70.
18. Waldo, "Developments in Public Administration," p. 222.
19. Mosher, "The Public Service in the Temporary Society," p. 54.
20. Ibid.
21. David P. Snyder, "The Intolerant Society: An Assessment of Our Evolving Institutional Environment," *The Bureaucrat*, 3 (October 1974), 247–69, at p. 256.
22. Ibid.
23. The following relies on Waldo, "Developments in Public Administration," pp. 225–32.
24. Ibid., p. 226.
25. Neal R. Peirce, "Cities Find Contracting Out Efficient," *Public Administration Times*, 2 (August 1, 1979), 2 (published by the American Society for Public Administration; Washington, D.C.). The possible spread of the "privatization of corrections" has been noted in numerous media reports in recent years. See,

for example, "Private-Sector Prisons Coming," an Associated Press story appearing in the Bloomington-Normal (Ill.) *Daily Pantagraph*, December 2, 1984, p. E-4; and "Private Prison Funding Suggested in Fed Report," a Los Angeles *Times* news service story appearing in the Bloomington-Normal *Daily Pantagraph*, February 18, 1985, p. A-6. See also James C. McDavid, "The Canadian Experience with Privatizing Residential Solid Waste Collection Services," *Public Administration Review*, 45 (September/October 1985), 602-8.

26. This discussion rests on the treatment by Mosher, "The Public Service in the Temporary Society," pp. 49-52.

27. Barry D. Karl, "Louis Brownlow," *Public Administration Review*, 39 (November/December 1979), 511-16, at p. 513.

28. Mosher, "The Public Service in the Temporary Society," p. 51.

29. See *Reshaping Government in Metropolitan Areas* (New York: Committee for Economic Development, 1970).

30. See the testimony of William L. Slayton, Executive Vice-President, Urban America, Inc., in *Creative Federalism:* Hearings before the Subcommittee on Intergovernmental Relations, Committee on Government Operations, U.S. Senate, 89th Congress, 2nd Session, on the Intergovernmental Cooperation Act of 1967 and related bills, November 1966 and February 1967 (Washington, D.C.: U.S. Government Printing Office, 1967), p. 874.

31. See, for example, Edward Sofen, *The Miami Metropolitan Experiment* (Bloomington: Indiana University Press, 1963).

32. Mosher, "The Public Service in the Temporary Society," p. 52.

33. Ibid., p. 58.

34. Waldo, "Developments in Public Administration," p. 235.

35. Ibid., p. 240.

36. Discussion of problems and prospects in teaching ethics to students of public administration has become widespread. See, among others, Ann-Marie Rizzo and Thomas J. Patka, "Teaching Administrative Ethics in the Public Sector," and John C. Honey and Dennis P. Wittmer, "Teaching Ethics to Pre-Entry–Level Public Administration Students," in Guthrie S. Birkhead and James D. Carroll, eds., *Education for Public Service 1979* (Syracuse: Maxwell School of Citizenship and Public Affairs, Syracuse University, 1979), pp. 45-61 and 63-76, respectively; Joseph F. Zimmerman, "Ethics and the MPA Curriculum," in Guthrie S. Birkhead and James D. Carroll, eds., *Education for Public Service 1980* (Syracuse: Maxwell School of Citizenship and Public Affairs, Syracuse University, 1980), pp. 53-65; James S. Bowman, "Teaching Ethics in Public Administration," in Richard Heimovics and Ann-Marie Rizzo, eds., *Innovations in Teaching Public Affairs and Administration* (monograph published jointly by Florida International University, Miami, and the University of Missouri-Kansas City, 1981), pp. 79-90; and David S. Broder, "Ethics in Government?" Bloomington-Normal (Ill.) *Daily Pantagraph*, April 12, 1981, p. A-8.

37. See David H. Rosenbloom, "Public Administrative Theory and the Separation of Powers," *Public Administration Review*, 43 (May/June 1983), 219-27.

38. Michael W. Dolan, "Administrative Law and Public Administration," *Public Administration Review*, 44 (January/February 1984), 86-89, at p. 86.

39. Waldo, "Developments in Public Administration," p. 243 (emphasis added).

40. Ibid.

41. Mosher, "The Public Service in the Temporary Society," p. 56.

42. Ibid., p. 60 (emphasis added).
43. Ibid.
44. See Douglas Costle, "In Defense of the Public Service," *Public Administration Times*, 3 (May 1, 1980), 3.
45. "GAO Raps Lax Accounting," an Associated Press story appearing in the Bloomington-Normal (Ill.) *Daily Pantagraph*, September 3, 1980, p. A-6; *5-Year Summary of Results of GAO Fraud Hotline*, A Report to the Congress of the United States by the Comptroller General, General Accounting Office Report No. GAO/AFMD-84-70 (Washington, D.C.: U.S. Government Printing Office, September 25, 1984); "Tattlers' Line Saves $24 Million," an Associated Press story appearing in the Bloomington-Normal *Daily Pantagraph*, September 28, 1984, p. A-1; "Parts Disposal Policy at Pentagon Rapped," a Washington *Post* news service story appearing in the Bloomington-Normal *Daily Pantagraph*, July 10, 1984, p. A-1; "Pentagon Warned on Parts," a Washington *Post* news service story appearing in the Bloomington-Normal *Daily Pantagraph*, July 11, 1984, p. A-1; "Inspector Challenges Pentagon 'Savings,'" a Scripps-Howard news service story appearing in the Bloomington-Normal *Daily Pantagraph*, December 17, 1984, p. C-6; and "Defense Audits Miss Checks on Big Items," a Scripps-Howard news service story appearing in the Bloomington-Normal *Daily Pantagraph*, February 11, 1985, p. A-1. Ironically, GAO itself was accused of spending $13 million on a computer system that it never received. See "GAO Wasted $13 Million on Computer," an Associated Press story appearing in the Bloomington-Normal *Daily Pantagraph*, December 27, 1984, p. D-5.
46. See, for example, Leo Herbert, Larry N. Killough, and Alan Walter Steiss, *Governmental Accounting and Control* (Monterey, Calif.: Brooks/Cole, 1984).
47. See, among others, *Fraud in Government Programs: How Extensive Is It? Can It Be Controlled?*, A Report to the Congress of the United States by the Comptroller General, General Accounting Office Report No. AFMD-82-3 (Washington, D.C.: U.S. Government Printing Office, November 6, 1981); Norman Beckman and Clyde Christofferson, eds., "Waste, Fraud, and Abuse," *The Bureaucrat*, 12 (Fall 1983), 6–34; and James S. Larson, "Fraud in Government Programs: A Secondary Analysis," *Public Administration Quarterly*, 7 (Fall 1983), 274–93.
48. See Michael J. Wriston, "In Defense of Bureaucracy," *Public Administration Review*, 40 (March/April 1980), 179–83, especially p. 180; and Charles T. Goodsell, *The Case for Bureaucracy: A Public Administration Polemic*, 2nd ed. (Chatham, N.J.: Chatham House, 1985).
49. Wriston, "In Defense of Bureaucracy," p. 180.
50. Ibid.
51. See, for example, Yair Aharoni, *The No-Risk Society* (Chatham, N.J.: Chatham House, 1980).
52. A useful source on this topic is Alan Stone, *Regulation and Its Alternatives* (Washington, D.C.: Congressional Quarterly Press, 1982).
53. See Robert E. Litan and William D. Nordhaus, *Reforming Federal Regulation* (New Haven, Conn.: Yale University Press, 1983), p. 132.
54. See, among others, Susan J. Tolchin and Martin Tolchin, *Dismantling America: The Rush to Deregulate* (Boston: Houghton Mifflin, 1983).
55. Bernard Rosen, "Effective Continuity of U.S. Government Operations in Jeopardy," *Public Administration Review*, 43 (September/October 1983), 383–92, at p. 388.

56. Ibid., p. 389.
57. See, among others, the testimony of C. William Fischer, in *The Senior Executive Service*, Hearings before the Subcommittee on Civil Service, Committee on Post Office and Civil Service, U.S. House of Representatives, 98th Congress, 2nd Session (Washington, D.C.: U.S. Government Printing Office, 1984), p. 346.
58. Testimony of Charles Bingman and David T. Stanley, *Hearings on The Senior Executive Service*, pp. 272 and 286–87, respectively; the direct quotation is taken from the Bingman testimony (emphasis added). Data collected by the Merit Systems Protection Board, on the views of senior executives concerning operation of the SES in these respects, can be found in the *Hearings*, p. 436.
59. See, among others, James P. Pfiffner, "The Challenge of Federal Management in the 1980s," *Public Administration Quarterly*, 7 (Summer 1983), 162–82, at pp. 172–74.
60. The MSPB study—*Blowing the Whistle in the Federal Government: A Comparative Analysis of 1980 and 1983 Survey Findings*—is cited in *Public Administration Times*, 8 (May 1, 1985), 11. See also James P. Pfiffner, "Political Public Administration," *Public Administration Review*, 45 (March/April 1985), 352–56.
61. See H. Kenneth Hibbeln, "Confronting the Pathology of Administrative Discretion," paper delivered at the annual meeting of the American Society for Public Administration, Denver, Colorado, April 8–11, 1984; and Douglas H. Shumavon and H. Kenneth Hibbeln, eds., *Administrative Discretion and Public Policy Implementation* (New York: Praeger, 1986).
62. A. Lee Fritschler, *Smoking and Politics: Policy Making and the Federal Bureaucracy*, 3rd ed. (Englewood Cliffs, N.J.: Prentice-Hall, 1983), p. 51 (emphasis added).
63. E. Samuel Overman, "Public Management: What's New and Different?" *Public Administration Review*, 44 (May/June 1984), 275–78, at p. 278. For a useful overview of public management, see G. David Garson and E. Samuel Overman, *Public Management Research in the United States* (New York: Praeger, 1983).
64. See, among others, Fred I. Greenstein, ed., *The Reagan Presidency: An Early Assessment* (Baltimore: The Johns Hopkins University Press, 1983); and David Broder, "Reagan Impact Already Indelible in History Books," a column appearing in the Bloomington-Normal (Ill.) *Daily Pantagraph*, January 20, 1985, p. A-6.
65. According to political scientist Louis Fisher: "If it were possible, at one fell swoop, to return all administrative powers overnight to the president, the process of decentralization would begin at dawn the following day"; quoted in Ronald C. Moe, "A New Hoover Commission: A Timely Idea or Misdirected Nostalgia?" *Public Administration Review*, 42 (May/June 1982), 270–77, at p. 277. See also William Lilley III and James C. Miller III, "The New 'Social Regulation,'" *The Public Interest*, 47 (Spring 1977), 49–61, at pp. 55–56.
66. William Greider, "The Education of David Stockman," *The Atlantic Monthly*, 248 (December 1981), 27–54, at p. 43. See also Ellis Sandoz and Cecil V. Crabb, Jr., eds., *A Tide of Discontent: The 1980 Elections And Their Meaning* (Washington, D.C.: Congressional Quarterly Press, 1981).
67. See E. S. Savas, *Privatizing the Public Sector* (Chatham, N.J.: Chatham House, 1982).
68. "Environmentalists Warned to Ease Attacks on EPA," an Associated Press story appearing in the Bloomington-Normal (Ill.) *Daily Pantagraph*, December 9, 1984, p. A-7.

69. Barber Conable, "Government Is Working," *The Bureaucrat*, 13 (Fall 1984), 39–43. Conable, a Republican, served in the House of Representatives for more than twenty years, representing a district in upstate New York, and was a member of the House GOP leadership.

70. Rosenbloom, "Public Administrative Theory and the Separation of Powers," p. 225 (emphasis added).

71. See, among others, James O. Freedman, *Crisis and Legitimacy* (New York: Cambridge University Press, 1978); cited by Rosenbloom, ibid.

72. Mark A. Abramson and Sandra Baxter, "The Senior Executive Service: A Preliminary Assessment from One Department," paper presented at a 1981 symposium on civil service reform, and reprinted in the *Hearings on the Senior Executive Service*, pp. 483–513; the premises referred to appear at p. 512.

73. "GOP Finds Fed Not All Bad," Bloomington-Normal (Ill.) *Daily Pantagraph*, March 26, 1981, p. A-10.

74. Attitudes toward government and bureaucracy are discussed in Kaufman, "Fear of Bureaucracy: A Raging Pandemic"; Seymour Martin Lipset and William Schneider, *The Confidence Gap: Business, Labor, and Government in the Public Mind* (New York: Free Press, 1983); and Richard L. McDowell, "Sources and Consequences of Citizen Attitudes Toward Government," in H. George Frederickson and Ralph Clark Chandler, eds., "Citizenship and Public Administration: Proceedings of the National Conference on Citizenship and Public Service," *Public Administration Review*, 44 (March 1984), 152–56.

75. Alan D. Monroe, *Public Opinion in America* (New York: Harper & Row, 1975), p. 292.

76. Waldo, "Developments in Public Administration," p. 244. See, also by Waldo, *The Enterprise of Public Administration* (Novato, Calif.: Chandler & Sharp, 1980), and *The Administrative State*, 2nd ed. (New York: Holmes and Meier, 1984).

SUGGESTED READINGS

Aharoni, Yair. *The No-Risk Society*. Chatham, N.J.: Chatham House, 1980.

Kaufman, Herbert. "Fear of Bureaucracy: A Raging Pandemic." *Public Administration Review*, 41 (January/February 1981), 1–9.

Miewald, Robert, and Michael Steinman, eds. *Problems in Administrative Reform*. Chicago: Nelson-Hall, 1984.

Mosher, Frederick C. "The Changing Responsibilities and Tactics of the Federal Government." *Public Administration Review*, 40 (November/December 1980), 541–48.

———. "The Public Service in the Temporary Society." *Public Administration Review*, 31 (January/February 1971), 47–62.

Ostrom, Vincent. *The Intellectual Crisis in American Public Administration*, revised ed. University, Ala.: University of Alabama Press, 1974.

Snyder, David P. "The Intolerant Society: An Assessment of Our Evolving Institutional Environment." *The Bureaucrat*, 3 (October 1974), 247–69.

Waldo, Dwight. *The Administrative State*, 2nd ed. New York: Holmes and Meier, 1984.

_____. "Developments in Public Administration." *Annals of the American Academy of Political and Social Science*, 404 (November 1972), 217–45.

_____. *The Enterprise of Public Administration*. Novato, Calif.: Chandler & Sharp, 1980.

White, Orion F., Jr. "The Dialectical Organization: An Alternative to Bureaucracy." *Public Administration Review*, 29 (January/February 1969), 32–63.

Glossary

accountability a political principle according to which agencies or organizations, such as those in government, are subject to some form of external control, causing them to give a general accounting of and for their actions; an essential concept in democratic public administration.

adjudication a quasi-judicial power delegated to agencies by Congress, under which agencies apply existing laws or rules to particular situations, in case-by-case decision making; related term: *adjudicatory proceeding*.

administrative discretion the ability of individual administrators in a bureaucracy to make significant choices affecting management and operation of programs for which they are responsible; particularly evident in separation-of-powers systems; related terms: *discretionary authority, discretionary power.*

"administrative efficiency" model of administration a normative model of administrative activity, characterized by concentration of power (especially in the hands of chief executives), centralization of governmental policy making, exercise of power by experts and professional bureaucrats, separation of politics and administration, and an emphasis on technical or scientific rationality (arrived at by detached expert analysis); the principal alternative to the "pluralist democracy" model.

advisory opinion one means used by some U.S. regulatory agencies to secure voluntary compliance with agency requirements; involves issuance of a memorandum indicating how the agency (for example, the FTC) would decide an issue if it were presented formally.

affirmative action program in the context of public personnel administration, a program designed to bring into public service larger numbers of citizens who were largely excluded from public employment in previous years; applied especially to women, blacks, and minorities.

authority power defined according

607

to a legal and institutional framework, and vested in a formal structure (a nation, organization, profession, and the like); power exercised through recognized, legitimate channels.

block grant a form of grant-in-aid in which the purposes to be served by the funding are defined very broadly by the grantor, leaving considerable discretion and flexibility in the hands of the recipient; a form of national government assistance strongly favored by the Reagan administration.

budget obligations orders placed, contracts awarded, services rendered, or other commitments made by government agencies during a given fiscal period, which will require expenditure of public funds during the same or some future period.

budget outlays agency expenditures during a given fiscal period, fulfilling budget obligations incurred during the same or a previous period.

bureaucracy (1) a formal organizational arrangement characterized by division of labor, job specialization with no functional overlap, exercise of authority through a vertical hierarchy (chain of command), and a system of internal rules, regulations, and record keeping; (2) in common usage, the administrative branch of government (national, state, or local) in the U.S.; also, individual administrative agencies of those governments.

bureaucratic neutrality a feature of bureaucracy whereby it carries out directives of other institutions of government (such as the chief executive or the legislature), without acting as a political force in its own right; a traditional notion concerning bureaucratic behavior in Western governments.

capitalism a major economic doctrine that emphasizes maximum freedom for private entrepreneurs, opportunity to acquire private profits, minimal involvement of government in the private economy, and general economic growth.

categorical grant-in-aid a form of grant-in-aid with purposes narrowly defined by the grantor, leaving the recipient relatively little discretionary choice as to how the grant funding is to be used, substantively or procedurally.

Civil Service Reform Act of 1978 a landmark national government law enacted under the Carter administration, which provided among other things for a Senior Executive Service, an explicit statement of merit system principles and prohibited personnel practices, and a statutory basis for national government collective bargaining practices; the first comprehensive national government personnel legislation since the Pendleton Act of 1883.

clientelism a phenomenon whereby patterns of regularized relationships develop and are maintained in the political process, between individual government agencies and particular economic groupings, e.g. Departments of Agriculture, Labor, and Commerce, working with farm groups, labor groups, and business organizations, respectively.

closed systems organizations which, in systems theory, have very few internal variables and relationships among those variables, and little or no vulnerability to forces in the external environment.

collective bargaining a formalized process of negotiation between ''management'' and ''labor''; involves specified steps, in a specified sequence, aimed at reaching an agreement (usually stipulated in contractual form) on terms and conditions of employment, covering an agreed-upon period of time; a cycle which is repeated upon expiration of each labor-management contract or other agreement.

comparable worth a principle of compensation in personnel management, reflecting (but going beyond) the established principle of ''equal pay for equal work''; based on an assumption that it is necessary and desirable to pay comparable salaries and wages to those doing work that is different, but comparable in value to the employing organization, government, or society at large; addressed primarily to redressing compensation inequities between men and women—the latter, many argue, paid less than men performing comparable tasks.

consent order one means used by some U.S. regulatory agencies to secure voluntary compliance with agency requirements; involves a formal agreement between the agency and an industry or industries, in which the latter agree to cease a practice in return for the agency's dropping punitive actions aimed at the practice.

constant dollars dollar amounts of public and private income, expenditures, costs, etc., expressed in terms of dollar values in a given (''base'') year, and assumed to be unchanged (constant) since that year; thus, constant-dollar figures do *not* reflect changes in the price of goods and services (and in the value of the dollar) between the base year and any subsequent time period; the alternative to constant-dollar figures is *current dollars*—that is, dollar amounts which *do* reflect changes in prices of goods and services, and in the value of the dollar.

constituency any group or organization interested in the work and actions of a given official, agency, or organization, and a potential source of support for it; also, the interests (and sometimes geographic area) served by an elected or appointed public official.

contracting out a practice under which private-sector contractors provide designated goods or services to governments, or to individual agencies, for an agreed-upon fee; an example both of a ''twilight zone'' between public and private sectors, and of public-sector responses to growing fiscal stress; services contracted for include trash collection and fire protection.

co-optation a process in organizational relations whereby one group or organization acquires the ability to influence activities of another, usually for a considerable period of time; involves a surrender by a weaker entity to a stronger one of some ability to influence the former's long-term activities.

coordination the process of bringing together divided labor; efforts to achieve coordination often involve emphasis on common or compatible objectives, harmonious working relationships, and the like; linked to issues involving communication, centralization-decentralization, federalism, and leadership.

cost-benefit analysis technique designed to measure relative gains and losses resulting from alternative policy or program options; emphasizes identification of the most desirable cost-benefit ratio, in quantitative or other terms.

cost-benefit ratio the proportional relationship between expenditure of a given quantity of resources and the benefits derived therefrom; a guideline for choosing among alternatives, of greatest relevance to the rational model of decision making.

Critical Path Method (CPM) a management technique of program implementation (related to PERT) in which a manager attempts to assess the resource needs of different paths of action, and to identify the path with the smallest margin of extra resources needed to complete all assigned program activities (the "critical path").

"cutback" management a management strategy made necessary by the advent of fiscal stress; tactics can include, among others, systematic priority setting, diversifying programs, adopting user charges, improving productivity, eliminating weak programs, and decreasing services.

cybernetics a modern theory of organization that treats organizations as self-regulating; emphasizes interactions between feedback devices (both internal and external) that trigger adaptive mechanisms within the organization; a nonorganizational example of the cybernetic principle is the thermostat.

decision making a process in which choices are made to change (or leave unchanged) an existing condition, and to select a course of action most appropriate to achieving a desired objective (however formalized or informal the objective may be), while minimizing risk and uncertainty to the extent deemed possible; the process may be characterized by widely varying degrees of self-conscious "rationality," or by willingness of the decision maker to decide incrementally, without insisting on assessment of all possible alternatives, or by some combination of approaches.

economic democracy a social and political belief in equal distribution of wealth throughout a society, with few very rich or very poor; believed by some to be a key prerequisite of true political democracy.

egalitarianism a philosophical concept stressing individual equality in political, social, economic, and other relations; in the context of public personnel administration, the conceptual basis for "government by the common person."

entitlement programs programs of government financial assistance (mainly to individuals) created under legislation which defines eligibility standards, but places no limit on total budget authority; the level of outlays is determined solely by the number of eligible persons who apply for authorized benefits.

exception principle an assumption in traditional administrative thinking that chief executives do not have to be involved in administrative activities unless some problem or disruption of routine activity occurs—that is, where there is an exception to routine operations.

federalism a constitutional division of governmental power between a central or national government and regional governmental units (such as states), with each having some independent authority over its citizens.

"first-line" supervisor a worker's immediate superior on the job; the focus of research on how superiors influence workers and the work situation.

fiscal federalism the complex of financial transactions, transfers of funds, and accompanying rules and regulations (or lack thereof) which increasingly characterizes national-state, national-local, and state-local relations.

fiscal stress a condition confronting increasing numbers of governments and public agencies, resulting from a combination of economic inflation, declining productivity, slower economic growth, and taxpayer resistance to shouldering a larger tax burden; a prime cause of the need to engage in "cutback management."

formal theories of organization theories stressing formal, structural arrangements within organizations, and "correct" or "scientific" methods to be followed in order to achieve the highest degree of organizational efficiency; examples include Weber's theory of bureaucracy and Taylor's "scientific management" approach.

formula grant a type of national government grant-in-aid available to states and local governments for purposes that are ongoing and common to many government jurisdictions; distributed according to a set formula that treats all applicants uniformly, at least in principle; one type of entitlement program; examples: aid to the blind and aid to the elderly.

freedom of information law an act passed by the national and some state legislatures establishing procedures through which private citizens may gain access to a wide variety of records and files from government agencies; a principal instrument for breaking down bureaucratic secrecy in American public administration.

functional overlap a phenomenon of contemporary American bureaucracy whereby functions performed by one bureaucratic entity also may be performed by another; conflicts with Weber's notions of division of labor and specialization.

game theory a modern theory viewing organizational behavior in terms of competition among members for resources; based on distinctly mathematical assumptions, employing mathematical methods.

general revenue sharing a form of national government fiscal assistance to state governments, municipalities, counties, and townships, distributed without recipients making formal application, according to a fixed formula; use of funding is determined almost entirely by recipient governments, subject to procedural controls established by Congress; adopted in 1972 as a supplement to categorical and block grant funding; program terminated, effective fiscal year 1987.

goal articulation a process of defining and clearly expressing goals generally held by those in an organization or group; usually regarded as a function of organization or group leaders; a key step in developing support for official goals.

goal congruence agreement on fundamental goals; in the context of an organization, refers to

agreement among leaders and followers in the organization on central objectives; in practice, its absence in many instances creates internal tensions and difficulties in goal definition.

grant-in-aid a money payment furnished by a higher to a lower level of government to be used for specified purposes and subject to conditions spelled out in law or administrative regulation; the dominant form of national aid to state and local governments.

groupthink a mode of thinking that people engage in when they are deeply involved in a cohesive in-group, when members striving for unanimity override their motivation to realistically appraise alternative courses of action; facilitated by insulation of the decision group from others in the organization, and by the group's leader promoting one preferred solution or course of action.

hierarchy a characteristic of formal bureaucratic organizations; a clear vertical ''chain of command'' in which each unit is subordinate to the one above it and superior to the one below it; one of the most common features of governmental and other bureaucratic organizations.

hierarchy of needs a psychological concept formulated by Abraham Maslow which holds that workers have different kinds of needs that must be satisfied in sequence— basic survival needs, job security, social needs, ego needs, and personal fulfillment in the job.

homeostasis a concept within

open systems theory, referring to a process of spontaneous self-stabilization in the relationships among various parts and activities of a complex organization, thereby keeping it functioning in the face of disturbances in the organization's environment.

human relations theories of organization theories stressing workers' noneconomic needs and motivations on the job; sought to identify these needs and how to satisfy them; focused on working conditions and social interactions among workers.

impasse procedures in the context of labor-management relations and collective bargaining, procedures which can be called into play when collective negotiations do not lead to agreement at the bargaining table; these include mediation, fact finding, arbitration, and referendum (some in combination with one another, or following one another should one procedure fail to resolve the impasse).

impoundment in the context of the budgetary process, the practice by a chief executive of withholding final spending approval of funds appropriated by the legislature, in a bill already signed into law; may take the form of deferrals or recissions; presidential authority to impound limited by Congress since 1974.

incrementalism a model of decision making which stresses making decisions through limited successive comparisons, in contrast to the rational model; also focuses on simplifying choices rather than aspiring to complete problem analyses, on the status quo rather than abstract goals as a key point of reference, on "satisficing" rather than "maximizing," and on remedying ills rather than seeking positive goals.

individualism a philosophical belief in the worth and dignity of the individual, particularly as part of a political order; holds that government and politics should regard the well-being and aspirations of individuals as more important than those of the government.

information theory a modern theory of organization that views organizations as requiring constant input of information in order to continue functioning systematically and productively; assumes that a lack of information will lead to chaos or randomness in organizational operations.

interest group a private organization representing a portion (usually small) of the general adult population, which exists in order to pursue particular public policy objectives and seeks to influence government activity so as to achieve its objectives.

intergovernmental relations all the activities and interactions occurring between or among governmental units of all types and levels within the American federal system.

issue networks in the context of American politics (especially at the national level), open and fluid groupings of various political actors (in and out of government) attempting to influence policy; ''shared-knowledge'' groups having to do with some aspect or problem of public policy; lacking in the degree of permanence, commonality of interests, and internal cohesion characteristic of *subsystems*.

item veto a constitutional power available to approximately half of America's governors, under which they may disapprove some provisions of a bill while approving the others.

''job action'' any action taken by employees (usually unionized) as a protest against an aspect of their work or working conditions; includes, but is not limited to, strikes or work slowdowns.

jurisdiction in bureaucratic politics, the area of programmatic responsibility assigned to an agency by the legislature or chief executive; also, a term used to describe the territory within the boundaries of a government entity (as ''a local jurisdiction'').

''knowledge explosion'' a social phenomenon of the past forty years, particularly in Western industrial nations, creating new technologies and vast new areas of research and education; examples include space exploration, mass communications, nuclear technology, mass production, and energy research.

legislative intent the purposes and objectives of a legislative body, given concrete form in its enactments (though actual intent may change over time); bureaucratic behavior is assumed to follow legislative intent in implementing laws.

legislative oversight the process by which a legislative body continually supervises the work of the bureaucracy in order to insure its conformity with legislative intent.

legislative veto a provision within a law that requires the executive branch (1) to inform the legislature (or committees within it) of actions planned for implementing the law, and (2) to receive from the legislature explicit or implicit approval of those actions, within a specified time period, before carrying them out; the veto exercised by Congress for over fifty years ruled unconstitutional by the Supreme Court in June 1983.

liberal democracy a fundamental form of political arrangement, founded on the concepts of popular sovereignty and limited government.

limited government a central concept of American politics, holding that because government poses a fundamental threat to individual liberties, it must be carefully limited in its capacity to act arbitrarily; the Founders believed it was to be achieved through separation of powers, checks and balances, federalism, and judicial review.

''line'' functions substantive activities of an organization, related to programs or policies for which the organization is formally responsible, and usually having direct impact on outside clienteles; the work of an organization directed toward fulfilling its formal mission(s).

line-item budgeting the earliest approach to modern executive budget making, emphasizing control of expenditures through careful accounting for all money spent in public programs; facilitated central control of purchasing and hiring, and completeness and honesty in fiscal accounting.

"linking pins" managers within an organization who serve as coordinators among teams of experts operating as equals or near-equals, in contrast to traditional hierarchical, superior-subordinate relationships; said to be appropriate for growing numbers of organizations and work settings where diverse and complex technologies are necessary components of organizational activities.

management according to task a modern theory of organization that conceives of the internal units of an organization as structured in a manner most appropriate to their particular tasks; assumes great diversity within an organization in terms of suborganizational structures (formal, social, technological).

Management by Objectives (MBO) a management technique designed to facilitate goal- and priority-setting, development of plans, resource allocation, monitoring progress toward goals, evaluating results, and generating and implementing improvements in performance.

matrix organizations organizations constructed in a non-hierarchical fashion, with full integration of separate units of organization (line, staff, and so on); founded on premises of democratic decision making and delegated authority; individuals become members of such organizations because of their expertise in a particular project (such as NASA space exploration), and exercise authority and conduct other activities on that basis; formal rank in the organization is much less important, in this setting, than is expertise.

merit pay an approach to compensation in personnel management, founded on the concept of equal pay for equal contribution (rather than for equal activity); related to, and dependent upon, properly designed and implemented performance appraisal systems; applied to managers and supervisors in grades GS-13 through GS-15 in the national executive branch, under provisions of the Civil Service Reform Act of 1978.

mixed scanning a model of decision making that combines the rational-comprehensive model's emphasis on fundamental choices and long-term consequences with the incrementalists' emphasis on changing only what needs to be changed in the immediate situation; emphasizes short-term decisions.

modern organization theory a body of theory emphasizing empirical examination of organizational behavior, interdisciplinary research employing varied approaches, and attempts to arrive at generalizations applicable to many different kinds of organizations.

New Public Administration a movement among public administration professionals that advocates "social equity" as a central guiding principle for administrative decision making with regard to resource allocation; also concerned with how decisions are made within organizations.

Office of Management and Budget (OMB) an important entity in the Executive Office of the President that assists the president in assembling executive branch budget requests, coordinating programs, developing executive talent, and supervising program management processes in national government agencies.

Office of Personnel Management (OPM) a key administrative unit in the national government operating under presidential direction, which is responsible for managing the national government personnel system, consistent with presidential personnel policy.

open systems theory a theory of organization that views organizations not as simple, "closed" bureaucratic structures separate from their surroundings, but as highly complex, facing considerable uncertainty in their operations, and constantly interacting with their environment; assumes that organizational components will seek an "equilibrium" among the forces pressing on them and their own responses to those forces (see **homeostasis**).

organization development a theory of organization that concentrates on increasing the ability of an organization to solve internal problems of organizational behavior as one of its routine functions; concerned primarily with identification and analysis of such problems.

organizational change a theory of organization that focuses on those characteristics of an organization that promote or hinder change; assumes that demands for change originate in the external environment, and that the organization should be in the best position to respond to them.

organizational humanism a set of organization theories stressing that work held intrinsic interest for the worker, that workers sought satisfaction in their work, that they wanted to work rather than avoid it, and that they could be motivated through systems of positive incentives (such as participation in decision making).

participatory democracy a political and philosophical belief in direct involvement by affected citizens in the processes of governmental decision making; believed by some to be essential to the existence of democratic government; related term: *citizen participation*.

Pendleton Act a law, formally known as the Civil Service Act of 1883 (sponsored by Ohio Senator George Pendleton), establishing job-related competence as the primary basis for filling national government jobs; created the U.S. Civil Service Commission to oversee the new "merit" system.

performance budgeting an approach to modern executive budget making that gained curency in the 1930s, emphasizing not only resources acquired by an agency but also what it did with them; geared to promoting effective management of government programs in a time of growing programmatic complexity.

"picket-fence" federalism a term describing a new dimension of American federalism—intergovernmental administrative relationships among bureaucratic specialists, and their clientele groups, in the same substantive areas; suggests that allied bureaucrats exercise considerable power over intergovernmental programs; related term: *vertical functional autocracies.*

planning the process of defining and choosing operational goals of an organization, and choosing methods or means to be used to achieve those goals over a specified time period; an increasingly important tool of public management.

pluralism a social and political concept stressing the appropriateness of group organization, and diversity of groups and their activities, as a means of protecting broad group interests in society; assumes that groups are good and that bargaining and competition among them will benefit the public interest.

"pluralist democracy" model of administration a normative model of administrative activity, characterized by dispersion of power and a suspicion of any concentration of power; exercise of power by politicians, interest groups, and citizens; political bargaining and accommodation; and an emphasis on individuals' and political actors' own determination of interest as the basis for policy making; the principal alternative to the "administrative efficiency" model.

policy analysis the systematic investigation of alternative policy options and the assembly and integration of evidence for and against each; emphasizes explaining the nature of policy problems, and how public policies are put into effect.

policy development a general political and governmental process of formulating relatively concrete goals and directions for government activity and proposing an overall framework of programs related to them; usually but not always regarded as a chief executive's task.

policy implementation a general political and governmental process of carrying out programs in order to fulfill specified policy objectives; a responsibility chiefly of administrative agencies, under chief executive and/or legislative guidance; also, the activities directed toward putting a policy into effect.

political rationality a concept advanced by Aaron Wildavsky, suggesting that behavior of decision makers may be entirely rational when judged by criteria of political costs, benefits, and consequences, even if irrational according to economic criteria; emphasizes that political criteria for "rationality" have validity.

position classification a formal task of American public personnel administration, intended to classify together jobs in different agencies that have essentially the same types of functions and responsibilities, based on written descriptions of duties and responsibilities.

postindustrialism a social and economic phenomenon said by some to be emerging in many previously industrialized nations; characterized by a relative decline in the importance of production, labor, and durable goods, and an increase in the importance of knowledge, new technologies, the provision of services, and leisure time.

Program Evaluation and Review Technique (PERT) a management technique of program implementation in which the sequence of steps for carrying out a project or program is mapped out in advance; involves choosing necessary activities and estimating time and other resources required.

project grant a form of grant-in-aid available to states and localities, by application, for an individual project; more numerous than formula grants, with more funding available as well.

public administration (1) all processes, organizations, and individuals (the latter acting in official positions and roles) associated with carrying out laws and other rules adopted or issued by legislatures, executives, and courts; many activities are concerned also with formulation of these rules; (2) a field of academic study and professional training leading to public service careers at all levels of government.

public management a field of practice and study central to public administration, emphasizing internal operations of public agencies; focuses on managerial concerns related to control and direction, such as planning, organizational maintenance, information systems, personnel management, and performance evaluation.

public policy (1) the organizing framework of purposes and rationales for government programs that deal with specified societal problems; (2) the complex of programs enacted and implemented by government.

rational model of decision making derived from economic theories of how to make the "best" decisions; involves efforts to move toward consciously held goals in a way that requires the smallest input of scarce resources; assumes the ability to separate ends from means, rank all alternatives, gather all possible data, and objectively weigh alternatives; stresses rationality in the *process* of reaching decisions.

reconciliation process an important step in congressional budgeting, when Congress makes adjustments in existing law to achieve conformity with annual spending targets adopted in the first (spring) budget resolution; these adjustments can take the form of spending reductions, revenue increases, or both.

reductions in force (RIFs) systematic reductions in the number of personnel positions allocated to a government agency or agencies; usually the result of higher-level personnel management policy decisions related to other policy objectives (including budget considerations); a phenomenon in the national executive branch especially under the Reagan administration.

reflexive goal an organizational or individual goal related primarily to survival and maintenance; "inward-oriented" as opposed to a goal focusing on external impacts.

regulation government activity designed to monitor and guide private economic competition; specific actions (characterized as *economic regulation*) have included placing limits on producers' prices and practices, and promoting commerce through grants or subsidies; other actions emerging more recently (termed *social regulation*) have included regulating conditions under which goods and services are produced, and attempting to minimize product hazards and risks to consumers.

"revolution of rising expectations" a social phenomenon of the period since World War II, affecting many nations, in which people who have been relatively poor have sought to increase their level of prosperity both as individuals and as groups; related in part to faith in technological and social advances.

rule making a quasi-legislative power delegated to agencies by Congress; a rule issued under this authority represents an agency statement of general applicability and future effect that concerns the rights of private parties, and has the force and effect of law.

"rule of three" a procedure usually followed by the U.S. Office of Personnel Management (formerly the Civil Service Commission) in narrowing the list of people most qualified for a particular job opening in a national government agency; three names are sent to the agency, which then makes the final selection, based on test scores and other considerations.

scientific management a formal theory of organization developed by Frederick Taylor in the early 1900s; concerned with achieving efficiency in production, rational work procedures, maximum productivity, and profit; focused on management's responsibilities and on "scientifically" developed work procedures, based on "time and motion" studies.

Senior Executive Service established in the national Civil Service Reform Act of 1978; designed to foster professional growth, mobility, and versatility among senior career officials (and some "political" appointees); incorporated into national government personnel management broad emphasis on performance appraisal and merit pay concepts, as part of both the SES itself and broader merit system reform (see **Civil Service Reform Act of 1978**).

"situational" approach to leadership a method of analyzing leadership in a group or organization that emphasizes factors in the particular leadership situation, such as leader-follower interactions, group values and needs, and the work being done.

spoils system a system of hiring personnel based on political loyalty and connections; can also extend to government contracts and the like; usually takes the form of rewarding party supporters with government jobs.

"staff" functions originally defined to include all support and advisory activities of an organization, which facilitated the carrying out of "line" responsibilities and functions; more recently, redefined by some to focus on planning, research, and advisory activities (thus excluding budgeting, personnel, purchasing, and other functions once grouped under the "staff" heading).

substantive goal an organizational goal focusing on the accomplishment of tangible programmatic objectives.

subsystem in the context of American politics (especially at the national level), any political alliance uniting some members of an administrative agency, a legislative committee or subcommittee, and an interest group according to shared values and preferences in the same substantive area of policy making.

sunk cost in the context of organizational resources committed to a given decision, any cost involved in the decision that is irrecoverable; resources of the organization are lessened by that amount if it later reverses its decision.

"sunset" law a law designed to increase accountability and control over administrative agencies by requiring: (a) automatic termination of programs and agencies unless specifically reestablished by the legislature, and (b) periodic evaluations of programs and agencies prior to a termination date.

"sunshine" law an act passed by the national Congress, and by some states and localities, requiring that various legislative proceedings (especially those of committees and subcommittees) be held in public rather than behind closed doors; one device for increasing visibility and accountability.

systems analysis an analytical technique designed to permit comprehensive investigation of the impacts within a given system of changing one or more elements of that system; in the context of analyzing policies, emphasizes overall objectives, surrounding environments, available resources, and system components.

systems theory a theory of social organizations, holding that organizations—like other organisms—may behave according to inputs from their environment, outputs resulting from organizational activity, and feedback leading to further inputs; also, change in any one part of a group or organizational system affects all other parts.

"traits" approach to leadership a traditional method (now used less widely by scholars) of analyzing leadership in a group or organization; assumes that certain personality characteristics such as intelligence, ambition, tact, and diplomacy distinguish leaders from others in the group.

transitive goal an organizational goal that, if achieved, would have an impact on an organization's external environment; a goal concerned more with external than with internal consequences of organizational actions.

"twilight zones" in the context of the boundaries between public and private administration, areas of public-private overlap; these zones, or "gray areas," have expanded considerably in the past half-century; examples: Amtrak, community action agencies, and Medicare.

"whistle-blowing" the making of any disclosure of legal violations, mismanagement, a gross waste of funds, an abuse of authority, or a danger to public health or safety, whether the disclosure is made within or outside the formal chain of command.

Table 15-3, "S.E.S. Social and Personal Backgrounds," Table 15-4, "S.E.S. Presidential Voting Preferences, 1968–1980," and Table 15-5, "S.E.S. Attitudes on Selected Issues," from Stanley Rothman and S. Robert Lichter, "How Liberal Are Bureaucrats?" *Regulation*, 7 (November/December 1983), p. 17–18. © 1983 by American Enterprise Institute (AEI). Reprinted by permission.

Box, "The Public Manager: An Overview," adapted by permission from Douglas Yates, *Bureaucratic Democracy: The Search for Democracy and Efficiency in American Government*, pp. 183–85. Cambridge, Mass.: Harvard University Press, 1982.

Cartoon, "Funny Business," © 1977 Newspaper Enterprise Association, Inc. (NEA). Reprinted by permission.

Index